POETRY AND BONDAGE

Poetry and Bondage is a groundbreaking and comprehensive study of the history of poetic constraint. For millennia, poets have compared verse to bondage – chains, fetters, cells or slavery. Tracing this metaphor from Ovid through the present, Andrea Brady reveals the contributions to poetics of people who are actually in bondage. How, the book asks, does our understanding of the lyric – and the political freedoms and forms of human being it is supposed to epitomise – change, if we listen to the voices of enslaved and imprisoned poets? Bringing canonical and contemporary poets into dialogue, from Thomas Wyatt to Rob Halpern, Emily Dickinson to M. NourbeSe Philip and Phillis Wheatley to Lisa Robertson, the book also examines poetry that emerged from the plantation and the prison. This book is a major intervention in lyric studies and literary criticism, interrogating the whiteness of those disciplines and exploring the possibilities for committed poetry today.

ANDREA BRADY is Professor of Poetry in the School of English and Drama at Queen Mary University of London. Her books include *English Funerary Elegy in the Seventeenth Century* (2006), *Wildfire* (2010), *Mutability* (2012), *Cut from the Rushes* (2013), *The Strong Room* (2016) and *The Blue Split Compartments* (2021). She has held fellowships from the Leverhulme Trust and the National Humanities Center, and performed throughout Europe and in Canada, the United States, Lebanon and Chile.

POETRY AND BONDAGE

A History and Theory of Lyric Constraint

ANDREA BRADY
Queen Mary University of London

CAMBRIDGE
UNIVERSITY PRESS

Shaftesbury Road, Cambridge CB2 8EA, United Kingdom

One Liberty Plaza, 20th Floor, New York, NY 10006, USA

477 Williamstown Road, Port Melbourne, VIC 3207, Australia

314–321, 3rd Floor, Plot 3, Splendor Forum, Jasola District Centre, New Delhi – 110025, India

103 Penang Road, #05–06/07, Visioncrest Commercial, Singapore 238467

Cambridge University Press is part of Cambridge University Press & Assessment, a department of the University of Cambridge.

We share the University's mission to contribute to society through the pursuit of education, learning and research at the highest international levels of excellence.

www.cambridge.org
Information on this title: www.cambridge.org/9781108964937
DOI:10.1017/9781108990684

© Andrea Brady 2021

This publication is in copyright. Subject to statutory exception and to the provisions of relevant collective licensing agreements, no reproduction of any part may take place without the written permission of Cambridge University Press & Assessment.

First published 2021
First paperback edition 2025

A catalogue record for this publication is available from the British Library

Library of Congress Cataloging-in-Publication data
NAMES: Brady, Andrea, 1974– author.
TITLE: Poetry and bondage : a history and theory of lyric constraint / Andrea Brady.
DESCRIPTION: Cambridge : Cambridge University Press, 2022. | Includes index.
IDENTIFIERS: LCCN 2021024926 (print) | LCCN 2021024927 (ebook) | ISBN 9781108845724 (hardback) | ISBN 9781108990684 (ebook)
SUBJECTS: LCSH: Poetry – History and criticism. | Prisoners' writings – History and criticism. | Slaves' writings – History and criticism. | Metaphor in literature. | Poetics – History. | BISAC: LITERARY CRITICISM / European / English, Irish, Scottish, Welsh | LCGFT: Literary criticism.
CLASSIFICATION: LCC PN1136 .B726 2022 (print) | LCC PN1136 (ebook) | DDC 809.1–dc23
LC record available at https://lccn.loc.gov/2021024926
LC ebook record available at https://lccn.loc.gov/2021024927

ISBN 978-1-108-84572-4 Hardback
ISBN 978-1-108-96493-7 Paperback

Cambridge University Press & Assessment has no responsibility for the persistence or accuracy of URLs for external or third-party internet websites referred to in this publication and does not guarantee that any content on such websites is, or will remain, accurate or appropriate.

to Ayla, Abel, Marlow and Matt
and in memory of Sean Bonney

Contents

List of Illustrations		*pages* ix
Acknowledgements		x
	Introduction: The Fetters of Verse	1
I	**LYRIC CELLS**	29
1	The Music of Fetters: Thomas Wyatt and the Beginnings of English Carceral Lyric	31
2	The Ligature: Rob Halpern's *Common Place* and the Limits of Desire	60
3	Each in Their Separate Hell: Solitary Confinement in the Long Nineteenth Century	83
4	Hours of Lead: The Modern US Prison, Segregation and Solidarity	112
II	**THE SONGS OF SLAVERY**	149
5	Bind Me – I Still Can Sing: Emily Dickinson at the Boundaries of Lyric	151
6	The Story that Cannot Be Told: M. NourbeSe Philip's *Zong!*, from Form to Performance	180
7	The Sound Came from Everywhere and Nowhere: African American Song as Lyric Work	209
8	Singing at the Window: New Criticism and the Evolution of Lyric	246

III PLEASURES AND ORNAMENTS 281

9 A New Made Wound: Sadomasochistic Triumphs
and Missing Feet in Ovid's Elegies 283

10 The Ecstatic Lash of the Poetic Line: Swinburne, Hopkins
and the Pleasures of Bondage 311

11 Soft Architecture: Lisa Robertson and Bondage as Ornament 350

12 Silken Fetters: Phillis Wheatley and Ornament as Bondage 381

Index 414

Illustrations

4.1	'Retrospect', *San Quentin Days* (Sacramento: J. M. Anderson, 1905), p. 4 and 11	*pages* 121
4.2	'Some Day', *San Quentin Days* (Sacramento: J. M. Anderson, 1905), p. 11.	122
4.3	Folsom Prison Creative Writers' Workshop, *The Caged Collective!*, *Aldebaran Review* 28, ed. John Oliver Simon and Leslie Simon (Berkeley, CA, 1978)	124
6.1	M. NourbeSe Philip, *Zong! As told to the author by Setaey Adamu Boateng* (Middletown, CT: Wesleyan University Press, [2008] 2011), p. 111	185
6.2	M. NourbeSe Philip, *Zong! As told to the author by Setaey Adamu Boateng* (Middletown, CT: Wesleyan University Press, [2008] 2011), p. 3	187
7.1	'An African Song or Chant', transcribed by Granville Sharp 'from the information of Dr William Dickson who lived several years in the West Indies and was secretary to a Governor of Barbados', Gloucestershire County Archives, MS D3549/13/3/27, draft (a) and fair copy (b)	222
10.1	Gerard Manley Hopkins, 'Harry Ploughman', *The Poetical Works*, ed. Norman H. MacKenzie (Oxford University Press, 1990), pp. 169–70	339
12.1	'Phillis Wheatley, Negro servant to Mr John Wheatley, of Boston', by Scipio Moorhead; in *Poems on Various Subjects, Religious and Moral* (London: Archibald Bell, 1773)	388

Acknowledgements

Invisibly, writing is called upon to undo the discourse in which, however unhappy we believe ourselves to be, we who have it at our disposal remain comfortably installed.

– Maurice Blanchot

This is a book about how poets use figures of bondage to depict creative freedom or constraint, and how that figuration effaces the poetics of those who are actually in bondage. I began it in 2014 and finished it in 2020. As the readers' reports arrived, I was in 'lockdown' with my family in London. Our comfortable bourgeois life in a house with a garden was totally incommensurate with the metaphors of incarceration used by government to describe measures to slow the coronavirus pandemic. Stay home, save lives. For people in actual lockdown, in overcrowded prisons, immigrant detention centres, refugee camps, secure hospitals, or in private homes with abusers, home did not constitute refuge. Lockdown reproduced my advantages: secure employment, private property and a healthy nuclear family.

At the same time, the pandemic briefly opened a horizon on to other forms of relation based on solidarity and mutual aid. I am happy to begin with an acknowledgement of the gifts given to me in the course of the book's composition. The first, which was technically the last of these gifts, was the image for the cover by Donny Johnson. Donny is an extraordinary artist who fashions from everyday materials images of deep spiritual insight. Out of the brightly coloured commodities whose sugars are bound to the histories of slavery, candies that give us energy and pleasure and do us harm, Donny creates fields of movement, intensity and freedom. I can't think of a better image to gather together the concerns of this book. I'm grateful to Mike Dibb for putting us in touch, and for his continuing advocacy on behalf of Donny and all those who experience the torture of solitary confinement.

Acknowledgements

The ludicrous ambition of this book could only be attempted with the benefit of an extended period of leave granted by the Leverhulme Trust and by Queen Mary University of London, and a year's fellowship at the National Humanities Center in North Carolina amidst the depravities of the Trump presidency. Thanks to all the staff, especially Brooke Andrade, Sarah Harris, Joe Milillo, Tania Munz, Lynn Miller and Robert Newman, for creating conditions in which thought can flourish.

It was a joy to sit at my desk in Chapel Hill, looking out at actual deer stalking in the garden as I wrote about Wyatt's hind. As I explored my neighbourhood, I found a sign commemorating the Barbee-Hargrave Cemetery, in use from 1790 to 1915, where the graves of fifty-three enslaved labourers had been found. This sign told me that the land on which I was living had been known as the 'Chappel Tract', 640 acres belonging to the Morgan family, a large portion of which was sold to establish the University of North Carolina. It offered a powerful reminder of the displacement of enslaved persons in the making of the modern university, as well as the Indigenous people for whom it is ancestral land: the Occaneechi, Saponi and Tuscarora.

Another premise of *Poetry and Bondage* is that the perception of lyric as fundamentally individuated obscures the collective nature of poetic practice. It is a deep honour to acknowledge the many intelligences moving through this book. David Colclough was the book's first reader, and his care and encouragement helped me to finish it. I hope it makes him happy, and that he's as glad as I am to be free of its constraints. Tom Jones pressed me on certain questions about idealism and the commons at a key moment. I am very lucky to have such a fine reader as a friend. The four anonymous readers engaged with this work with tremendous generosity. Their insights helped me to reshape the book's structure, and I am deeply moved by their affirmation of what I have tried to do.

I could not have undertaken work across so many fields without drawing extensively on the expertise of outstanding colleagues who scrutinised individual chapters. These include William Andrews, Rowan Boyson, Piotr Gwiazda, Rob Halpern, Ewan Jones, Meta DuEwa Jones, Catherine Maxwell, Orlando Reade, Jeffrey Robinson, Barbara Taylor, Herbert Tucker and Kathryn Yusoff. Lisa Robertson, M. NourbeSe Philip and Rob Halpern are inspiring poets who responded to my interest in their work with generosity. Of course, the book's faults – and there must be many waiting to be discovered in it – are all manifestations of my own.

The opportunity to work through this material with colleagues at various universities was enormously beneficial to my thinking. Deepest thanks to my hosts at NYU, Yale, Virginia, Eastern Michigan, Pittsburgh, North Carolina at Chapel Hill, Chicago, and Colorado University at Boulder (USA); the Universidad Diego Portales (Chile); Lisbon and Coimbra (Portugal); Kent, Reading, King's College London, York and Cambridge (UK). For their hospitality and conversation, I am grateful to Jonathan Arac, Derek Attridge, Matthew Bevis, Julie Carr, Jennifer Cooke, Taylor Cowdery, Helen Cushman, Simon De Deo, William Ferris, Elizabeth Fowler, Paul Franz, Paul Fyfe, Starsha Gill, Rob Halpern, Njelle Hamilton, Carla Harryman, Christine Hume, Ruth Jackson, Laura McCormick Kilbride, Josh Kotin, Tim Kreiner, Dan Kubis, Angela Leighton, Luke McMullan, Brandon Menke, Molly Murray, Richard Parker, Penelope Patrix, Jèssica Pujol Duran, Peter Raleigh, Jahan Ramazani, Luke Roberts, Jocelyn Saidenberg, Roy Scranton, Caleb Smith, David Nowell Smith, Matt Smith, Cathy Wagner, Marina Warner, Richard Wolf and Jessica Wolfe. Isobel Armstrong, Catherine Bates and John Wilkinson supported crucial applications for research time without which the book would not exist. Special thanks to Susana Araujo, my host in Lisbon, where I spent a week finishing the first draft in a former prison, the overflow wing of the Aljube Resistência e Liberdade now converted into an AirBnB.

Colleagues at Queen Mary have entertained my stupid requests for years. Dominic Johnson talked with me about BDSM and shared Bob Flanagan's slave sonnets. Matt Rubery was my National Humanities Center buddy, supplier of quotes and sharer of scepticisms. Peter Howarth and I have gestated our poetry books for the same amount of time. I was lucky to participate in the Pathologies of Solitude project run by Barbara Taylor and am grateful to Clare Whitehead and all the participants. And for conspiring and commiserating with me while constructing a genuinely affable work environment, I thank all my extraordinary friends in the School of English and Drama. *La lutte continue.*

Emily Butterworth, Shane Boyle, Rowan Boyson, David Colclough, Amy De'Ath, Dom Del Re, Aline Ferrari, Tara Hutton, Sam Ladkin, Peter Manson, Molly McDonald, Tony Paraskeva, Malcolm Phillips, Robin Purves, Joad Raymond, Jana Riedel, Natasha Rulyova, Sam Solomon, Hilary Stainsby, Keston Sutherland and Hannah Westley: you are wonderful and I owe you at least a drink.

Love to the Brady clan – Suzanne, Annie, Rachel, Josh, Alexis, Cengizhan, Richard, Regina, Matt, Humaira, Kathleen, Emily, Joe, Jess, and the nieces and nephew, Isabella, Lara, Ciara, Alizeh and Zayn. Tim and Bärbl ffytche have been supportive in-laws and loving grandparents.

I am also grateful to the women whose work allowed me to give up some of my own reproductive labour in order to write this book: Leanne Smith, Anna Wielgosz, Sonali Nundoochan, Arlene Owens, Peri Graham and Mia Wotton.

As I was finishing it, I learned that a dear friend and true poet – Sean Bonney – had passed on from this world. Sean's work has been profoundly important to me since I was twenty years old. At times I imagined finishing this book with a chapter on his poetry, as the inheritor of the revolutionary and visionary traditions of Milton and Blake – an essay I began to write elsewhere. I wish he were still somewhere out there, ranting at the firmament and unravelling time in the company of Abiezer Coppe and John Coltrane. Maybe he is. Sean took very good care of the dead. Now it is up to us to take good care of him.

Finally, this book is full of thousands and thousands of words, but none of them in any combination is enough to express my love and gratitude to the people who are literally nearest to me as I write this: Matt ffytche, and our three amazing children, Ayla, Abel and Marlow. You inspire and delight and hold me together, every day. I'm sorry that I wrote this book for you instead of trying to fix the world. Now let's go and play.

INTRODUCTION

The Fetters of Verse

> *I lock you in an American sonnet that is part prison,*
> *Part panic closet, a little room in a house set aflame.*
> — Terrance Hayes

In 2018, a student asked Terrance Hayes: 'to be a poet, do you have to write in traditional poetic forms? Do you have to write in iambic pentameter?' 'If you can breakdance, that's cool,' Hayes answered. 'If you can breakdance in a straitjacket, that's even better.'[1] He returned to this image elsewhere:

> My relationship to form is that of a bird inside of a cage, moving around. Put it this way, if you were in a breakdancing competition against yourself, but said, OK, I'm going to do everything with a straitjacket on, you are automatically going to win because you are doing all the moves but now you have another barrier, and us watching you can see you being less free shows us your skill – just how free you actually are. Form allows me to get freer. I know what I'm pushing against and I need that otherwise I'm a bird out of a cage.[2]

This book will be full of caged birds and the paradoxical freedoms of constraint. But why does a straitjacket make the dancing 'even better'?

A partial answer might think through the relationship between Hayes's formalism and his own history. His mother worked as a prison guard, and he found a route to poetry at university, but for a time, 'corrections seemed like the easiest option. That or the military.'[3] He makes ample use of traditional forms like the sonnet, as well as variations of his own invention like the 'golden shovel'. In 2018, he published two books: a sequence of *American Sonnets*, and *To Float in the Space Between*, which responds to the

---

[1] Stephen Burt, 'Galaxies Inside His Head', *New York Times Magazine* (24 March 2015).
[2] Rachel Long, 'Dinner with Terrance Hayes', *The White Review* (January 2019): www.thewhitereview.org/feature/dinner-terrance-hayes/ (accessed 4 May 2021).
[3] Burt, 'Galaxies'.

work of the imprisoned writer Etheridge Knight.[4] In another poem, 'Model Prison Model', he writes: 'I feel like this is a good time / to tell you my father, mother and closest cousin / have worked decades as correctional officers.' The poem addresses the effects of mass incarceration on kin both inside and outside the cell. Nonetheless, the speaker confesses 'surprise' 'when I, a black poet, / was asked to participate in the construction' of a model prison.[5] Identifying not with the prisoner or guard but with the architect, the speaker resists biographical and racialised readings and offers up the poem itself as a 'model prison', a space that contains subjects within its formal artifice.

Hayes's formal experimentations exemplify the paradoxical freedom of constraint. That principle, and its inverse (that liberating poetry from the constraint of form is key to emancipation), are central poles around which poetry oscillates. And so this book starts with a simple claim: for centuries, poets have compared the experience of writing formally constrained verse to bondage. Bondage can be materialised as fetters, chains, shackles and chemical restraints, as well as less visible techniques of control such as coercion, terror or legal injunctions. It occurs everywhere, but certain sites are defined by it, such as the prison, the plantation and the camp. People and animals can be bound in homes, hospitals, asylums, schools, factories and workplaces, churches, public housing, ghettos, reservations, shelters, juvenile facilities, immigration detention centres, farms and abattoirs. Bondage also includes the more ambivalent example of erotic domination. It is an experience of individuals and collectives, it is sometimes voluntary and more often compulsory, and it occurs in both institutions and 'private' spaces.

A representative, though certainly not exhaustive list, of poets' use of bondage as a metaphor for verse-making would include: Samuel Daniel's urging that form does not represent a 'tyrannical bounding of the conceit', 'as if art were ordained to afflict nature, and that we could not go but in fetters', and that 'if our labours have wrought out a manumission from bondage, and we go at liberty, notwithstanding these ties, we are no longer the slaves of rhyme, but we make it a most excellent instrument to serve us' (1603); John Donne's remark that Lady Bedford 'only hath power to cast the fetters of verse upon my free meditations' (1609), and his lines – probably from the 1590s – announcing that 'Grief brought to numbers cannot be so

---

[4] Terrance Hayes, *To Float in the Space Between: A Life and Work in Conversation with the Life and Work of Etheridge Knight* (Seattle and New York: Wave Books, 2018).
[5] Terrance Hayes, 'Model Prison Model', *Rattle* 31 (Summer 2009): www.rattle.com/print/30s/i31/ (accessed 4 May 2021).

The Fetters of Verse

fierce / For he tames it, that fetters it in verse'; Margaret Cavendish's observation that 'A sad, and solemne Verse doth please the Mind, / With Chaines of Passions doth the Spirits bind' (1653); Milton's famous wish to deliver poetry from the 'modern bondage of rhyming' and restore its 'ancient liberty' in blank verse (1668); John Dryden's warning that the muse, 'When too much fettered with the rules of art, / May from her stricter bounds and limits part' (1684); Alexander Pope's similar judgement that Homer's 'measures, instead of being fetters to his sense, were always in readiness to run along with the warmth of his rapture' (1715); Samuel Johnson's description of poetic melody as that which 'shackles attention, and governs passion' (1751); Horace Walpole's letter to Voltaire, which argues that 'a great genius ... can still shine, and be himself, whatever fetters are imposed on him' (1768); William Blake's assertion that 'Poetry Fetter'd, Fetters the Human Race!' (1804); Arthur Schopenhauer's argument that 'metre and rhyme are a fetter, but also a veil which the poet cast around himself ...' (1819); William Hazlitt's opinion that 'we like metaphysics as well as Lord Byron; but not to see them making flowery speeches, nor dancing a measure in the fetters of verse' (1825); Ralph Waldo Emerson's desire to write 'such rhymes as shall not suggest a restraint but contrariwise the wildest freedom' (1839); G. H. Lewes arguing that song gives the true poet 'free movement in the absurdly called "shackles" of verse. Where ever you discern the "shackles", you may be sure the mind is a captive' (1842); Oliver Wendell Holmes depicting his Muse as 'a suppliant, captive, prostrate, bound, / She kneels imploring at the feet of sound' (1846); Coventry Patmore's 'Essay on English Metrical Law', which commends the 'shackles of artistic form' that must be learned through 'hard discipline' (1857); Herbert Spencer's comparison of the muscular excitements of poetic rhythm to a tail-wagging, jumping and wriggling dog 'chained to his kennel' (also 1857); the essay on Symbolism by Jean Moréas, which claims Verlaine 'broke his honour against the cruel fetters of verse' (1886); T. S. Eliot's essay on 'Vers Libre', which contends that 'freedom is only truly freedom when it appears against the background of an artificial limitation' (1917); D. H. Lawrence's admiration for Whitman's free verse as 'a wind that is forever in passage, and unchainable' (1919); Paul Valéry's admission that 'Whether I chain myself to the page I wish to write or to the page I wish to understand, in either case I am entering upon a phase of reduced freedom' (1937); Édouard Glissant's assertion that 'Measure ... is *choice*, by which the being puts an end to his liberty in the world and offers to share in it' (1969); John Agard's poem 'Listen Mr Oxford Don', which rejects the charge that his linguistic activity is 'mugging' or 'assault / on de Oxford dictionary': 'I ent serving no jail sentence / I slashing suffix in self-defence' (1985); Susan Howe's explanation that 'a lot of my work is about breaking free: starting free and being captured and breaking free again and being captured again' (1990); John Hollander celebrating the writer who reunites disparate sensations in metaphor 'and binds them with an indestructible chain of words', or who 'can fetter randomness and bind possibility and link design to execution in chains of its own forging which, when worked through rather than slipped off, become garlands of its own achievement' (1998); Fred Moten's declaration of interest 'in the relation between the prison cell and the sonnet' (2015); and DaMaris Hill's use of 'formal verse' as 'symbolic of the women's physical confinement' in *A Bound Woman is a Dangerous Thing* (2019).

In some of these examples, prosody constrains the poet's imagination; in others, it is the poet who imposes the chains of prosody on emotions or ideas that threaten to escape. For many of these poets, submitting voluntarily to the heteronomy of verse is perhaps the only encounter with bondage they ever have. But even that does not entail any real loss of autonomy: as Philip Sidney wrote, the poet, 'disdaining to be tied to any such subjection', is 'lifted up with the vigour of his own invention', escaping aesthetic or political law and freely ranging within the zodiac of his own wit.[6] For others, the vigour of personal invention can never be enough to escape the gravity of historical and personal bondage.

This leads me to the central question of this book. What would happen to our understanding of the history and practice of lyric if we confronted these claims about constraint with poetic witnesses to actual bondage? How does the poet's freedom and individuation look from the perspective of slavery or the prison? If as Fred Moten argues, 'freedom is in unfreedom as the trace of the resistance that constitutes constraint',[7] how can attending to actual bondage and resistance help us to track a different history of lyric poetry, one that does not map its liberation from formal constraints on to the emancipation of the individual under liberal democracy?

Poetry and Bondage examines how the *figure* of bondage is put to work by (mostly white) poets and critics in the elucidation of creative freedom. But I will also seek to understand what the bound *poet* knows, and contributes to knowledge, of freedom as concept and lived or forbidden reality. In doing so, I am drawing on numerous scholars who have argued that Enlightenment philosophies of liberty were composed not just in avoidance

---

[6] Gavin Alexander, *Sidney's 'The Defence of Poesy' and Selected Renaissance Criticism* (London: Penguin, 2008), pp. 8–9.
[7] Fred Moten, 'Taste Dissonance Flavor Escape: Preface for a Solo by Miles Davis', *Women & Performance* 17 (2007), pp. 217–46 (243).

of national complicities in the slave regimes around the world, but positively through those regimes.[8] In what follows I briefly discuss the alignment between political and formal constraint, form and body, theme and soul, and the promise that the fetters of corporeality and delusion could be unlocked through the philosophical imagination. My aim here is to establish the historical and theoretical coordinates of the close readings that follow, which will entail some fairly rapid manoeuvres over the field of lyric studies. I want not just to outline my position in relation to some dominant academic orientations, but to establish a set of claims that the rest of this book will elaborate, about the reproduction of whiteness in lyric and criticism.

The Naked Foot of Poesy

The use of the word 'fetter' to describe the confinements of verse is conventional, and suggested by the fact that a foot is a unit of prosody. The Old English word *feotor* emerges around 800, to refer to chains or shackles used on the feet of humans and animals. It is derived from the old Aryan root for 'foot'; in Latin it was the *pedica*, in Greek πέδη. The foot was regarded as one of the meanest parts of the body, farthest from the rational activity of the head. The Greek word for slave was *andrapodon*, 'man-footed creature', a coinage derived from *tetrapodon*, 'four-footed creature' – the common name for cattle.[9]

Matthew Bevis has catalogued the many associations between poetic composition and foot travel in the Romantic period, including William Hazlitt's observation that Coleridge 'liked to compose in walking over uneven ground, ... whereas Wordsworth always wrote (if he could) walking up and down a straight gravel-walk'; Byron's 'perpetual consciousness of his lameness' was also perceived in the irregularities of his metre.[10] Dorothy Wordsworth recorded that in wet weather, William went into the

---

[8] See, for example, Judith Shklar, *American Citizenship: The Quest for Inclusion* (Cambridge, MA: Harvard University Press, 1991); Orlando Patterson, *Freedom*, vol. I: *Freedom in the Making of Western Culture* (New York: Basic Books, 1991); Louis Sala-Molins, *Dark Side of the Light: Slavery and the French Enlightenment*, trans. John Conteh-Morgan (Minneapolis: University of Minnesota Press, 2006).

[9] David Brion Davis, *Inhuman Bondage: The Rise and Fall of Slavery in the New World* (Oxford University Press, 2006), p. 33.

[10] William Hazlitt, 'My First Acquaintance with Poets' (1823), in *The Complete Works of William Hazlitt*, ed. P. P. Howe, 21 vols. (London: Dent, 1930–34), 17:119, cited in Matthew Bevis, 'Byron's Feet', *Meter Matters: Verse Cultures of the Long Nineteenth Century*, ed. Jason David Hall (Athens, OH: Ohio University Press, 2011), pp. 78–104 (80, 82).

garden with an umbrella, and walked back and forth, 'fast bound within the chosen limits as if by prison walls'.[11] John Ruskin, explaining prosody to schoolchildren in 1880, described the spondee as keeping the 'perfect pace of a reasonable two-legged animal', and poetry by extension having 'correspondence with the deliberate pace of Man, and expression of his noblest animal character in erect and thoughtful motion: all the rhythmic art of poetry having thus primary regard to the great human noblesse of walking on feet.'[12] Paul Valéry offered a syllogism: walking is to dancing as prose is to poetry.[13] And then there's Frank O'Hara, track star for Mineola Prep, running away from the threatening prosodist.[14]

The foot keeps rhythm. In chapters 7 and 8, I discuss folklorists in the late nineteenth and early twentieth centuries who studied African American song traditions. One of those was Thomas Talley. In his *Negro Folk Rhymes* (1922), Talley observes that 'everyone who has listened to a well sung Negro Jubilee Song knows that it is almost impossible to hear one sung and not pat the foot'.[15] Talley understands these rhythms to be the remnants of African percussive traditions:

> When the Negroes were transported to America, and began to sing songs and to chant words in another tongue, they still sang strains calling, through inheritance, for the accompaniment of their ancestral drum. The Negro's drum having fallen from him as he entered civilization, he unwittingly called into service his foot to take its place. (234)

In the familiar account of the relation of oral to written traditions, the melancholy text substitutes for the lost conviviality of song: the hand is a prosthesis for voice.[16] In Talley's analysis, however, the foot is the vestige of a lost drum. This is a different way of thinking of the importance of the foot to poetry, not just with praise of *homo erectus* or an irritable acknowledgment of the inadequacy of Greek and Latin foot-based prosody to English rhythms, but as the instrument of a non-European heritage of lyric which is embodied, communal and adaptive to conditions of catastrophe and loss. As Talley puts it, 'the rattle of the crude drum of the Native

---

[11] Letter, May 1804, *The Letters of William and Dorothy Wordsworth: The Early Years*, ed. Chester L. Shaver (Oxford: Clarendon 1967), p. 477.
[12] John Ruskin, *Elements of English Prosody for Use in St. George's Schools* (Orpington: George Allen, 1880), pp. 4–5.
[13] Paul Valéry, *The Art of Poetry*, trans. Denise Folliot (Princeton University Press, 2014), pp. 70–1.
[14] Frank O'Hara, 'Personism: A Manifesto', *The Collected Poems*, ed. Donald Allen (Berkeley and Los Angeles: University of California Press, 1995), p. 498.
[15] Thomas Talley, *Negro Folk Rhymes: Wise and Otherwise* (New York: Macmillan, 1922), pp. 233–4.
[16] An important contribution to overcoming this simplistic teleology is Derek Attridge, *The Experience of Poetry: From Homer's Listeners to Shakespeare's Readers* (Oxford University Press, 2019).

African was loud by inheritance in the hearts of his early American descendants and its unseen ghost walks in the midst of all their poetry'.[17]

In writing this book, I have been pursuing these ghosts across the canon and outside it. I'll give my first example of such a reading. In his sonnet on the sonnet, John Keats fantasises about adorning the 'naked foot of Poesy' with more delicate rhymes:

> If by dull rhymes our English must be chain'd,
> And, like Andromeda, the Sonnet sweet
> Fetter'd, in spite of pained loveliness;
> Let us find out, if we must be constrain'd,
> Sandals more interwoven and complete
> To fit the naked foot of Poesy;
> Let us inspect the Lyre, and weigh the stress
> Of every chord, and see what may be gain'd
> By ear industrious, and attention meet:
> Misers of sound and syllable, no less
> Than Midas of his coinage, let us be
> Jealous of dead leaves in the bay wreath crown;
> So, if we may not let the Muse be free,
> She will be bound with garlands of her own.[18]

Like Andromeda, the sonnet is 'chain'd' by rhyme, a monstrous foreign technology not very suitable to the English language. But not to worry; the sonnet's 'pained loveliness' can still be (somewhat sadistically) enjoyed, once we find her a nicer pair of sandals.

Keats's argument is rather capricious: if poetry must be sacrificed, at least let the fetters be lovely and the leaves fresh – for example, with this new hybrid Petrarchan and Shakespearean sonnet. Sounds return, but in slightly unpredictable patterns, exhibiting a *sprezzatura* that beautifies the performance of necessity. But that beautification, the sonnet also argues, is achieved through jealousy, industry and greed, a miserly hoarding of rhyming capital. The lyre, inspected and weighed by a factory manager or critic, is at odds with the delicate sandals with which the poet wishes to adorn poetry's 'naked foot'. The poem's pronomial references are also confusingly 'interwoven': there is a communal 'us', whose English is bound (though it's Andromeda, and the sonnet, and the Muse, that are in chains), who are constrained and who must do the work to 'find out' better poetic means; but we are also jealous, and 'may not let the Muse be free'. Our experience of being constrained – who says we 'may

---

[17] Talley, *Negro Folk Rhythms*, p. 235.
[18] John Keats, *John Keats*, ed. Elizabeth Cook (Oxford University Press, 1990), p. 281.

not'? – motivates our constraining of the feminised and fettered figure of Poesy. She is bound because we are. Her bondage is decorated, if not relieved, by the beautification of her chains: she has been persuaded that she is bound in 'garlands of her own'. The translation of compulsory bondage into a voluntary situation will occupy me throughout this book.

Keats's sonnet has been read as an exercise in disciplinary, panoptic surveillance, foot fetishism and male sexual violence.[19] The sexual energies compressed in Andromeda's sandal might be related to a story by Strabo: as retold by Havelock Ellis, a sandal belonging to 'the courtesan Rhodope ... was carried off by an eagle and dropped in the King of Egypt's lap as he was administering justice, so that he could not rest until he had discovered to whom this delicately small sandal belonged, and finally made her his queen'. This anecdote is part of Ellis's discussion of foot fetishism, where he also notes that Roman prostitutes 'were obliged to have their feet always naked in sandals or slippers (*crepida* and *solea*), which they fastened over the instep with gilt bands. Tibullus delights to describe his mistress's little foot, compressed by the band that imprisoned it.'[20] Ovid, as we'll see in Chapter 9, fixated likewise on the naked foot of Corinna, while those tender feet appear in a rather different way in the reading of Thomas Wyatt's 'They flee from me' in Chapter 1.

But there is another frame that for me vies with psychosexual readings of this sonnet. It was written in Keats's *annus mirabilis*, 1819. As such, it is often read as an exercise in formal experimentation, which allowed him to discover the complex sound patternings he used to such great effect in his odes. That is how he presented it in a letter to his brother George.[21] The year 1819 was also that of debates leading up to the Missouri Compromise. George Keats had at that time just arrived in Louisville, Kentucky. George would become a successful entrepreneur, and – after his brother's death – an enslaver. Three enslaved people would be sold from his estate when he died.[22] Louisville is

---

[19] Grant F. Scott, 'The Muse in Chains: Keats, Dürer, and the Politics of Form', *Studies in English Literature, 1500–1900* 34.4 (Autumn 1994), pp. 771–93. A speculative reading of Keats's foot-fetish is offered by Richard Marggraf Turley, '"Strange Longings": Keats and Feet', *Studies in Romanticism* 41.1 (Spring 2002), pp. 89–106, which includes Keats's astounding fable of the pregnant woman hungry for her husband's feet.

[20] Havelock Ellis, *Studies in the Psychology of Sex* (New York: Random House, 1936), 3:25.

[21] 'I have been endeavouring to discover a better sonnet stanza than we have. The legitimate does not suit the language over-well from the pouncing rhymes – the other kind appears too elegai[a]c – and the couplet at the end of it has seldom a pleasing effect – I do not pretend to have succeeded – it will explain itself.' John Keats, *The Letters of John Keats, 1814–1821*, ed. Hyder E. Rollins, 2 vols. (Cambridge, MA: Harvard University Press, 1958), 2:108.

[22] Jonathan Clark Smith, 'George Keats: The "Money Brother" of John Keats and His Life in Louisville', *The Register of the Kentucky Historical Society* 106.1 (Winter 2008), pp. 43–68; Denise Giganti, *The Keats Brothers: The Life of John and George* (Cambridge, MA: Belknap Press of Harvard University Press, 2011), p. 399.

on the banks of the Ohio River, the frontier between slavery and freedom. Both George and John were liberals who opposed slavery in principle, though George evidently found his principles were elastic when necessary.[23] In this poem, Keats uses a classical myth to depict an enchained woman whom 'we may not let . . . be free', even if we persuade ourselves that the garlands that constrain her are 'her own': she somehow wills her own captivity. Read in the context of chattel slavery with which his brother was becoming personally acquainted, this language of inspecting, weighing, desiring and fettering a body which expediency prevents us from emancipating takes on a set of uglier meanings than a relatively simple conceit about the constraints of the sonnet.

J. S. Mill and the 'Liberal Lyric'

Another influential definition of lyric that draws on a figure of bondage can be found in John Stuart Mill's 1833 essay 'What is Poetry?' The essay reflects Mill's discovery of poetry as a space for liberated feeling after a period of intense crisis. In his autobiography, Mill describes his idiosyncratic education, directed by his formidable father John Mill, as solitary and isolated.[24] His father 'resembled most Englishmen in being ashamed of the signs of feeling, and, by the absence of demonstration, starving the feelings themselves' (53). John raised the young Mill to be 'a mere reasoning machine' (111). But in the autumn of 1826, Mill famously experienced a profound crisis of belief in his intellectual projects and was overwhelmed by despair. His recovery followed an attempt to cultivate his inner self through poetry, music and art. Reading Wordsworth's poems for the first time in the autumn of 1828 was 'a medicine for my state of mind', because 'they expressed, not mere outward beauty, but states of feeling, and of thought coloured by feeling, under the excitement of beauty' (151). Mill also visited Wordsworth in 1831 and was impressed by the poet's insights into 'real life and the active pursuits of men'.[25] That year, Mill also met Harriet Taylor, whom he would marry after the death of her husband. Their friendship opened up a point of access to feeling and to poetry that had been sealed off by his paternal education. In very moving passages written after her death,

---

[23] For a reading of how Keats mythologised Africa and enslavement, see Debbie Lee, *Slavery and the Romantic Imagination* (Philadelphia: University of Pennsylvania Press, 2002), pp. 123–41.
[24] John Stuart Mill, *Autobiography and Literary Essays*, ed. John M. Robson and Jack Stillinger (1981), vol. 1 of *The Collected Works of John Stuart Mill*, ed. John M Ronson, et al., 33 vols. (Toronto/London: University of Toronto Press and Routledge and Kegan Paul, 1963–91), pp. 37–9.
[25] *The Letters of John Stuart Mill*, ed. H. S. R. Elliot, 2 vols. (London, 1910), 1:11–12.

Mill acknowledges the enormous benefits to him of Taylor's 'meditative and poetic nature' (193) and her intellectual gifts. Through his love for Taylor, Mill's awakening sensitivities were channelled into poetry as the site of the beautiful and the sublime. Poetry taught him to feel.

It was in this context that Mill wrote his essay 'What is Poetry?', which was published in W. J. Fox's liberal *Monthly Repository* in 1833. In this essay, poetry is described as a space where 'the feeling speaks and ... impresses itself, and finds response in other hearts.' The poetic imagination is 'indebted to some dominant feeling, not ... to a dominant *thought*'.[26] And those thoughts are spoken in solitude. For Mill, 'All poetry is of the nature of soliloquy'; it is the expression of 'the poet's utter unconsciousness of a listener'.[27] While Wordsworth had famously argued that a poet is 'a man speaking to men',[28] for Mill, he is a man overheard speaking to himself: 'feeling confessing itself to itself in moments of solitude' (348). Whereas a confession is activated by the address to a listener – the interrogator, priest or God – the poet's truthful confession is guaranteed by his or her conviction that he or she is speaking in total solitude.

And yet, if the poem is written for publication, then surely the pretence of solitude is undermined at once? Isn't the poet who pretends to be alone even more of a liar than one who addresses his audience directly? Mill answers that poetry is only poetry when it can retain the authentic quality of private utterance, even when 'printed on hot-pressed paper, and sold at a bookseller's shop'. The poem is a soliloquy, and 'no trace of consciousness that any eyes are upon us must be visible in the work itself' (349).

Poetry's truthful communication of feeling is distinguished from eloquence by the absent presence of the audience. In Mill's influential formulation, 'eloquence is heard; poetry is overheard'. Eloquence is a deliberative utterance addressed to an audience. Lyric is quarantined from sociability. Anne Janowitz has argued that Mill severs the social setting from poetic intentions and renders explicit the links between the making of liberalism and the making of poetry; he is an important contributor to the tendency, from Romantic poetry forwards, to argue that 'modern lyric as poetry of inwardness and individuation is built on the ruins of the lyric of sociality'.[29]

---

[26] Alba H. Warren Jr, *English Poetic Theory 1825–1865* (Princeton University Press, 1950), p. 75.
[27] J. S. Mill, *Autobiography and Literary Essays*, p. 349.
[28] William Wordsworth, *Lyrical Ballads, and Other Poems, 1797–1800*, ed. James Butler and Karen Green (Ithaca, NY: Cornell University Press, 1992), p. 751.
[29] Anne Janowitz, *Lyric and Labour in the Romantic Tradition* (Cambridge University Press, 1998), p. 19.

But Mill's solitary poet is not imagined in an entirely abstracted setting. He is at the centre of a very social institution: the prison. Mill says that poetry 'has always seemed to us like the lament of a prisoner in a solitary cell, ourselves listening, unseen in the next'.[30] He compares the poet to a figure who was in this period at the centre of debates about prison reform and the ideal conditions for rehabilitating prisoners. Readers trained by Michel Foucault to recognise the figure of the prisoner as a self-disciplining subject under surveillance might see this theatrical scene of lyric production as a tragic one: lyric is the lament of a carceral soul abandoned to solitary confinement. Like the prisoner in Jeremy Bentham's panopticon, who would never know if the guard were watching him, this lyric poet cannot tell if he is being overheard, no matter how much he attempts to look forth into the prison structure; but if the prisoner must behave as if he is *always* being watched, the poet must behave as if he *never* is.

'What is Poetry' was published in 1833 – for context, two years after Nat Turner's Rebellion; the year that Gustave de Beaumont and Alexis de Tocqueville published their report in Paris (and in translation in the United States) on the US penitentiary system; ten years before the opening of the 'Model Prison' at Pentonville in London. Pentonville was the first British prison to be built using the 'separate system of confinement', on the model of the Eastern State Penitentiary in Philadelphia, in which prisoners spent their days and nights in absolute isolation. However, even as Pentonville was being built, the United States was abandoning the separate system, which was costly, and disastrous for the health of the imprisoned people. Inspectors at Millbank prison in London admitted in 1841 that prisoners were being injured by their conditions; numerous prisoners were removed to Bedlam suffering from 'mental derangement' as a result of extended solitary confinement.[31] This may be why Mill's comparison of poetry to 'the lament of a prisoner in a solitary cell' is deleted in the later edition of the essay (published as 'Thoughts on Poetry and Its Varieties' in 1859).

Mill's essay helped to shape Victorian poetics and New Criticism, and continues to be a touchstone in contemporary studies of the lyric. Allen Grossman, for example, mixes Hegel and Mill in his argument that poems are 'fictions of the privacy of other minds'; lyric, he writes, is 'the social form of the unknowable singularity of the liberal individual'.[32] The lyric 'I'

---

[30] Quotes from Mill's 'Thoughts on Poetry and Its Varieties' are from Mill, vol. 1, 342–65; citing *Monthly Repository* n.s. VII (Jan. 1833), pp. 60–70.
[31] Sean Grass, *The Self in the Cell: Narrating the Victorian Prisoner* (London: Routledge, 2003), p. 41.
[32] Allen Grossman with Mark Halliday, *The Sighted Singer: Two Works on Poetry for Readers and Writers* (Baltimore: Johns Hopkins University Press, 1992), p. 247.

speaks from a 'situation of psychic individuality' (240), to a you constituted by that act of address, but who can also become an I (263). This dialectical relation is, for Grossman, coextensive with class hierarchy: 'the conditions of the enjoyment of freedom by one class require the subordination of another class'; 'the possessors of freedom are at war with the new claimants' (272). These new claimants can become the subject of poetry only by casting off the fetters of an idealised history in which the power of the lyric speaker to represent him or herself is a remnant 'of the privileged speech acts of kings', while 'the chorus is still a slave collectivity' (273). Individuality is associated with regal modernity; collectivity with slave mentality and the archaic past. Grossman relates Mill's liberal fiction to class antagonisms and the historical privileges of the lyric speaker, which depend on the subjugation of a portion of the audience who will, in time, become the subject of poetry. He characterises the history of the English lyric from the Renaissance to modernity as 'the struggle of the lyric person toward self-representation as a man of the third estate': a democratisation of verse, a republic in which any commoner can be the lyric king.

Revolutionising Verse

Numerous poets and critics have, like Grossman, drawn an analogy between political and poetic freedom. Plotting 'the association of verse structure with the political ideas of its makers', Paul Fussell ascribes the predominance of prosodic orderliness in the eighteenth century to the Restoration's 'victory over barbarity, disharmony, and regularity' against 'the forces of irregularity' – wild philosophies and imaginations – that had driven the British civil wars. Later, he writes: 'a literary generation terrified by the French revolution ... saw in the rise of a more free and varied prosody a lurking and sinister Jacobinism'.[33] These arguments exemplify a long tradition of associating formalism with political conservativism, and the avant-garde's attack on inherited forms with the overthrow of hereditary capital and status. But Fussell argues against the perception that history is a record of progress towards artistic and political emancipation: 'while political history can be shown to involve a very gradual total tendency toward, say, ideals of egalitarianism or public philanthropy, metrical history exhibits no such long-term "progressive" tendency.

---

[33] Paul Fussell, *Theory of Prosody in Eighteenth-Century England* (New London: Connecticut College, 1954), pp. 1, 3, 31.

Meter has not really become "freer" over the centuries, and indeed "freedom" is not a virtue in meter: expressiveness is.'[34]

While Fussell's historicism is dubious, the point of pressure he selects – the Restoration – reflects the importance of John Milton in analogies between casting off the fetters of conventional verse forms and overthrowing tyrants. In the note on 'The Verse' that prefaces *Paradise Lost*, Milton declares his aim to recover 'ancient liberty' formally, by rebelling against the 'troublesome and modern bondage of rhyming.'[35] Blank verse is a diachronic manifestation of republicanism and messianic deliverance from the archaic wound of Adam's sin. The poem explores multiple conditions of spiritual and physical bondage: Milton's Satan, dangerously persuasive, rejects 'splendid vassalage' to a tyrannical creator, 'preferring / Hard liberty before the easy yoke / Of servile pomp' (2.252, 255–7). As always, this passage is ambivalent: Satan is rebelling against God, not a tyrant, and his rhetoric is fundamentally deceitful; but 'hard liberty' is preferable to monarchical subjugation in Milton's human politics. Similarly, in Milton's Restoration tragedy *Samson Agonistes*, Samson is 'Bound with two cords; but cords to me were threads / Touched with the flame' (ll.261–2).[36] Samson's easy triumph over the couplet of his shackles is partly attributed to the decadence of the Philistines, who are 'by their vices brought to servitude', 'to love bondage more than liberty, / Bondage with ease than strenuous liberty' (ll. 269–71). In both texts, luxuriant bondage risks turning the captive – whether falling angel or human warrior – into a 'natural' slave, and the hero's self-liberation is imagined in a verse form free of the fetters of rhyme.

William Blake was deeply inspired by Milton's poetic declaration of freedom from political tyranny, and the tyranny of rhyme, though he thought Milton had not gone far enough. Blake's prophetic poetry and prose heaves with chained figures, straining against their fetters, whether these are 'mind-forg'd' or imposed by authoritarian others. He had a traumatic encounter with the law in 1803–4, when he was accused by the soldier John Scofield of cursing the king, and tried for treason; he may also have participated in the march on Newgate prison that was part of the Gordon Riots in 1780. Then, protestors attacked the prison's gates with pickaxes and sledgehammers, climbed over walls and tore off the roofs to

---

[34] Paul Fussell, *Poetic Meter & Poetic Form*, rev. ed. (New York: McGraw Hill, 1975), p. 74.
[35] John Milton, 'The Verse', *Paradise Lost*, ed. Alastair Fowler, rev. 2nd ed. (Harlow: Pearson, 2007), pp. 54–5.
[36] John Milton, *The Complete Poetry and Essential Prose*, ed. William Kerrigan, John Rumrich, and Stephen M. Fallon (New York: Modern Library, 2007), p. 718.

allow prisoners to escape the burning building.[37] In his preface to *Jerusalem*, Blake describes his process of prosodic self-liberation:

> When this Verse was first dictated to me I consider'd a Monotonous Cadence like that used by Milton & Shakspeare & all writers of English Blank Verse, derived from the modern bondage of Rhyming; to be a necessary and indispensible part of Verse. But I soon found that in the mouth of a true Orator such monotony was not only awkward, but as much a bondage as rhyme itself. I therefore have produced a variety in every line, both of cadences & number of syllables .... Poetry Fetter'd, Fetters the Human Race![38]

We can read Blake's argument in Marxian terms: what was once revolutionary in Milton, his bursting asunder of the productive forces of rhyme, has become 'as much a bondage as rhyme itself'. Blake consequently cultivated his own idiosyncratic verse forms, from the lyrical songs through the blazing free verse of the prophetic books.

Karl Marx and Friedrich Engels repeatedly refer to history as a process of the casting-off of the 'fetters' and 'yokes' that constrained productive forces. In the *Communist Manifesto* (1848), the transition from feudalism to capitalism is represented as just such an escape: 'the feudal relations of property became no longer compatible with the already developed productive forces; they became so many fetters. They had to be burst asunder; they were burst asunder.'[39] Marxist critics have applied the metaphor to poetic constraints: forms that once provided fertile conditions for poetic production eventually prove excessively constraining and so must be burst asunder, resulting in progress towards human emancipation. Anthony Easthope, for example, characterises the emergence of blank verse as an analogue to the construction of bourgeois subjectivity and describes 'the ideological opposition between the "social" and the "individual", an opposition which envisages society as a "necessity" against and within which the individual finds his or her "freedom"'.[40] Capitalism is the setting for the emergence of a verse technology that matches the politics of liberalism, a historical process that leads inexorably to the revolutionary crisis of free verse.

---

[37] Peter Ackroyd, *Blake* (London: Sinclair-Stevenson, 1995), p. 74.
[38] William Blake, *The Complete Poetry and Prose*, ed. David V. Erdman (Berkeley and Los Angeles: University of California Press, 1965, 1981), pp. 145–6.
[39] K. Marx and F. Engels, 'Manifesto of the Communist Party,' *Marx/Engels Selected Works*, vol. 1 (Moscow: Progress Publishers, 1969), pp. 98–137.
[40] Anthony Easthope, *Poetry as Discourse* (London: Methuen, 1983), p. 68.

The twentieth-century avant-garde was particularly keen to conflate political and aesthetic freedom. As Richard Aldington wrote in the anonymous preface to the first Imagist anthology (1915): 'We do not insist upon 'free-verse' as the only method of writing poetry. We fight for it as for a principle of liberty.'[41] A full-throated overview of this form of thinking is given by Jerome Rothenberg and Pierre Joris in their *Poems for the Millennium*, whose introductions contend that 'poetry set free can free or open up the human mind'.[42] The cataclysms of the twentieth century led to a backlash against modernism, and a desire to return to 'prescriptive rhyme and meter', which they describe as a 'strange fear of "freedom"'. But the 1960s saw a resurgence of '*free* verse and *freed* words'.[43] Aesthetic freedom, in such arguments, is part of the emancipatory progress of history. The liberties of poetic expression accompany, and give birth to, the revolutionary political imagination. But whether history is a line or a circle depends on who you're asking. As Amiri Baraka attests in his short story 'Northern Iowa': 'Verse is a turn, simply. Like a wheel, it has regular changes . . . . Except what we *want* is *vers libre* – free verse. Never having been that, *free*, we want it badly. For black people, *freedom* is our aesthetic and our ideology.'[44]

While my sympathies – and the selection of poetries explored in this book – lie strongly with revolutionaries who argue for the overthrow of the ideas of the ruling class, including its poetics, there also exists a strong counter-revolutionary tradition that seeks to conserve verse forms and the political orders they are said to represent. This tendency can be found in some surprising places. In his 1786 treatise on prosody, which he contemplated while walking in the Bois de Boulogne, Thomas Jefferson describes blank verse as 'the most precious part of our poetry. The poet, unfettered by rhyme, is at liberty to prune his diction . . . . When enveloped in the pomp and majesty of his subject he sometimes even throws off the restraint of the regular pause.' Jefferson echoes Milton's note on 'The Verse' of *Paradise Lost*, and cites the opening of that poem as the case in point; but his discussion mixes revolutionary emancipation – at liberty, unfettered – with the reinstatement of pomp and majesty.[45] Jefferson's argument is

---

[41] Richard Aldington et al., *Some Imagist Poets: An Anthology* (Boston: Houghton Mifflin, 1915), p. vi.
[42] Jerome Rothenberg and Pierre Joris (eds.), *Poems for the Millennium*, vol. 1: From Fin-de-Siècle to Negritude (Berkeley and Los Angeles: University of California Press, 1995), pp. 1, 11.
[43] Jerome Rothenberg and Pierre Joris (eds.), *Poems for the Millennium*, vol. 2: From Postwar to Millennium (Berkeley and Los Angeles: University of California Press, 1998), pp. 3, 5.
[44] Amiri Baraka, *Tales of the Out & the Gone* (New York: Akashic Books, 2007), p. 133.
[45] Thomas Jefferson, 'Thoughts on English Prosody,' in *Writings*, ed. Merrill D. Peterson (New York: Library of America, 1984), pp. 593–622 (618).

surprising, given his loathing of the monarchies he had observed intimately as a minister in France. Along with the gains of a revolution against the fetters of rhyme, it acknowledges losses that must be balanced by establishing new sovereign qualities. Democracy, in poetry at least, is not entirely without its drawbacks.

A similar ambivalence can be found in the second volume of Alexis de Tocqueville's *Democracy in America* (1835; second volume published 1840). Tocqueville argues that in aristocracies, certain 'guiding principles' of literary form are agreed; 'strict canons will soon prescribe rules that may not be broken'.[46] In a democracy, however, literary rules are reinvented by each generation. Instead of the order and regularity that characterise the literature of aristocratic regimes, democracies provide the writing of 'vivid, lively emotions, sudden revelations, brilliant truths, or errors able to rouse them up and plunge them, almost by violence, into the middle of the subject', while 'formal qualities will be neglected or actually despised' (473). Eventually, democratic literature will turn 'man's imagination away from externals to concentrate on himself alone'. The autonomy of the democratic text is sentimental and isolated, refusing formal or political heteronomy, and produced through negative freedom (in Isaiah Berlin's sense of freedom from interference).

Tocqueville's argument about poetics is shaped by his suspicion that democracy would lead to the tyranny of the majority. For William Carlos Williams, free verse was a sign of anarchy and the loss of communal values. He lamented that 'Our lives also have lost all that in the past we had to measure them by, except outmoded standards that are meaningless to us. In the same way our verses, of which our poems are made, are left without any metrical construction of which you can speak.'[47] The losses of traditional social meaning and of measure in poetry are related, as part of a historical process that begins with the French Revolution and with Whitman, who – Williams argues – was

> taken up, as were the leaders of the French Revolution before him, with the abstract idea of freedom. It slopped over into all their thinking. But it was an idea lethal to all order, particularly to that order which has to do with the poem. Whitman was right in breaking our bounds but, having no valid restraints to hold him, went wild. (339)

---

[46] Alexis de Tocqueville, *Democracy in America*, trans. George Lawrence, ed. J. P. Mayer (London: Fontana, 1994), p. 472.
[47] William Carlos Williams, 'The Poem as a Field of Action,' *Selected Essays* (New York: New Directions, 1969), p. 337.

For Williams, the chaos of liberation that succeeds the bursting asunder of the fetters of metrical order is both deadly and antisocial. Late in life, the poet argues that prosodic constraints signal the continuity of aesthetic and political consensus.

For many poets (including Hayes), constraint is the *condition* of freedom and an indispensable tool of poetic invention. Michel de Certeau discusses 'the rules of meter and rhyme' as 'a body of constraints stimulating new discoveries, a set of rules within which improvisation plays'.[48] This playfulness can be seen also in the ludic experiments of the Oulipo, whose extreme constraints did produce ample new discoveries, many of which still await us, in works such as Raymond Queneau's *Cent Mille Millliards de Poèmes*. T. S. Eliot satirised poets like Aldington, and the notion that political and poetic freedom entail the overthrow of constraint: in his essay 'Reflections on Vers Libre' (1917), he argues that 'Vers libre has not even the excuse of a polemic; it is a battle-cry of freedom, and there is no freedom in art.' That free verse is not a 'genuine verse-form' is evident in the fact that 'I can define it only in negatives: (1) absence of pattern, (2) absence of rhyme, (3) absence of metre.'[49] Negative freedom is not freedom at all. Similarly, Robert Frost's famously curt dismissal of free verse from 1956 – 'I'd just as soon play tennis with the net down' – argues that form is a necessary instrument in the pursuit of new poetic ideas.[50] Like Williams, he disparaged the notion of political activism: 'Political freedom is nothing to me. I bestow it right and left. All I would keep for myself is the freedom of my material – the condition of body and mind now and then to summons aptly from the vast chaos of all I have lived through.'[51] Form, constraint, give shape and meaning to the chaos of an individual life; without them the poem cannot survive. Of course, political freedom can only be nothing to someone who has always had it.

Fettered Bodies, Free Souls

Many of these analogies between political and prosodic freedoms draw on ancient ideas about the bondage of the body and the liberation of the rational

---

[48] Michel de Certeau, *The Practice of Everyday Life*, trans. Steven Rendall (Berkeley and Los Angeles: University of California Press, 1984), p. xxii.
[49] T. S. Eliot, 'Reflections on *Vers Libre*', *To Criticize the Critic* (New York: Farrar Strauss, 1965), pp. 184–5.
[50] *Newsweek* (30 January 1956), p. 56.
[51] Robert Frost, 'The Figure a Poem Makes,' *The Collected Prose*, ed. Mark Richardson (Cambridge, MA: Belknap Press of Harvard University Press, 2007), p. 132.

mind or soul. Plato is the primary source of these arguments. His *Phaedo* and *Apology for Socrates* (the latter which Diderot translated while a prisoner in Vincennes in 1749) strongly influenced *The Consolation of Philosophy* (*Consolatio*), written by Boethius in the early sixth century. Imprisoned by Theodoric in Ticinum (modern-day Pavia), Boethius imagines being visited by Lady Philosophia, who counsels him to enjoy the freedom of his mind and be released from the fetters of the body. This prosimetric text opens with the speaker lamenting his fate in (morally dubious) elegiac distich – the metre associated with Ovidian erotic elegy, which I'll discuss in Chapter 9 – and surrounded by the Muses.[52] Philosophy arrives, banishes the sluttish Muses and begins her teaching on the nature of the universe, determinism and free will. With this *recusatio* of carnality, Boethius begins to discover the inalienable freedom of the philosophical mind.

In Chaucer's translation, Philosophy laments that the prisoner is 'constreynyd to looken on the fool erthe', physically and intellectually turning towards the ground – 'his nekke is pressed with hevy cheynes'.[53] The figure of chains recurs throughout the text, for obvious reasons, but usually to represent forms of self-constraint; the mind clouded with grief and fear is 'bownde with brydles' (I.7, p. 16). The poem builds towards a reversal of this status, revealing to the prisoner that while his body is constrained, his mind remains free. It does not, however, fantasise about a condition of total freedom from restraint. Philosophia, like nature, is providentially 'bound': 'Ther nis nothinge unbownde fram his oolde lawe ne forleetheth the werke of his propre estat' (I.5, p. 12). To sever these binds, whether they are the binds that keep the stars hovering in the air or those that sequester lust inside the sanctity of marriage, would only lead to chaos. The speaker probes Philosophy on the relation between this intrinsically determinist nature and the potential for human freedom, and she answers by expounding on how the body, and the intellect that surrenders to wickedness, are themselves prisons. The chains that preserve order and connection in the universe are generative constraints, but the prison of the self can be, must be, escaped – into mental freedom.

Platonic and Boethian arguments for the inalienable liberty of the mind, however painfully the body is constrained, have been central to prison poetry for millennia: 'Stone walls do not a prison make, / Nor Iron bars a Cage /

---

[52] Anna Crabbe, 'Literary Design in *De Consolatione*,' *Boethius: His Life, Thought and Influence*, ed. Margaret Gibson (Oxford: Basil Blackwell, 1981), pp. 237–74 (244–7).

[53] Chaucer, *Chaucer's Boece: A Critical Edition Based on Cambridge University Library, MS Il.3.21*, ed. Tim William Machan (Heidelberg: Winter, 2008), I.2, p. 5; Boethius, *The Consolation of Philosophy*, trans. P. G. Walsh (Oxford: Clarendon, 1999), p. 5.

Minds innocent and quiet take / That for an Hermitage' (Richard Lovelace); 'The form beneath its chains may pine, / The soul is mighty still' (John Greenleaf Whittier); 'there is no gate, no lock, no bolt that you can set upon the freedom of my mind' (Virginia Woolf). Gerard Manley Hopkins compared the spirit trapped in the body to a caged bird longing for escape: 'As a dare-gale skylark scanted in a dull cage, / Man's mounting spirit in his bonehouse, mean house, dwells.'[54] The bird who soars away from the earth and achieves a panoramic perspective is a common emblem of Boethian consolation, which we'll encounter again in the discussion of Phillis Wheatley's poetry. These images can also be found in the attestation of Jackie Ruzas, a writer incarcerated in New York, that 'I write because I can't fly.'[55]

The Boethian argument that prison is paradoxically liberating is also echoed in 'Two Fragments', by Shaikh Abdurraheem Muslim Dost, a prisoner in Guantánamo Bay:

> Just as the heart beats in the darkness of the body,
> So I, despite this cage, continue to beat with life.
>
> Those who have no courage or honor consider themselves free,
> But they are slaves.
>
> I am flying on the wings of thought,
> And so, even in a cage, I know a greater freedom.[56]

Transcendence of the fetters of the camp is imagined as flight, soaring aloft 'on the wings of thought' and being able therefore to achieve an unlimited perspective that distinguishes the poet from the 'slaves' who guard him. As his fellow prisoner Abdulaziz writes: 'My spirit is free in the heavens, while my body is overpowered by chains' (23). The Pentagon censored and confiscated many poems by Guantánamo detainees, advising that the 'content and format' of poetry meant it presented a 'special risk' to national security (4). The suggestion is that form conveys secret information, such as the fact that the poet lives and feels despite all efforts to erase him – the lyric is a writ of habeus corpus. We are back, in a sense, with Mill's solitary prisoner, pretending not to know anyone is listening not as a guarantee of authenticity but as a way of evading the censor and reaching beyond the barren world of the camp.

---

[54] Gerard Manley Hopkins, *The Poetical Works*, ed. Norman H. MacKenzie (Oxford University Press, 1990), p. 122.
[55] Bell Gale Chevigny, *Doing Time: 25 Years of Prison Writing* (New York: Arcade Publishing, 1999), p. ix.
[56] Marc Falkoff (ed.), *Poems from Guantánamo: The Detainees Speak* (Iowa City: University of Iowa Press, 2007), p. 36.

Lyric Whiteness

Poetry and Bondage is advertised as offering a new history and theory of the lyric. But I've so far postponed answering a fundamental question: what do I mean by lyric?

As a verse genre it is proverbially impossible to define.[57] The word lyric derives from the Greek 'lyra', of or pertaining to the lyre; thus (says the *Oxford English Dictionary*) lyric is 'characteristic of song'. The first use of the word lyric in English dates to the 1580s, when it was used to describe a melodious kind of poetry; Thomas Campion wrote in 1602 that lyric poems 'are apt to be soong to an instrument'.[58] But as Bevis observes, the word 'lyric' 'only arrived on the scene in the third century BCE, when scholars of the Alexandrian library sought to preserve poems on the page whose musical settings had been lost'.[59] Bevis points out that this loss is encoded in the *Princeton Encyclopaedia of Poetry*, whose entry for lyric in the fourth edition by Virginia Jackson describes it as 'from its inception a term used to describe a music that could no longer be heard, an idea of poetry characterised by a lost collective experience'.[60] Lyric's melancholy can be found in its apostrophe and address, its dialectic of beloved and reader, and its memory of lost songs and lost worlds – worlds of communal rhythms and social consent.

W. R. Johnson, reflecting on the lack of intact textual sources for archaic Greek lyric, remarks, 'We do not want to admit the fact of this loss, so we open the fragments and try to read ... poems that are not there.'[61] There is good reason, when reading lyric, to read what is 'not there', or who. Moten finds in Amiri Baraka 'a mode of lyricism that has been explored and cultivated precisely by folks who have both *been refused* access to that

---

[57] For attempts at definitions, or accounts of their impossibility, see Stephen Burt, 'What is this Thing Called Lyric?', *Modern Philology* 113.3 (February 2016), pp. 422–40 (425); Jahan Ramazani, *Poetry and Its Others: News, Prayer, Song, and the Dialogue of Genres* (University of Chicago Press, 2014), pp. 1–8; Nikki Skillman, 'Lyric Reading Revisited: Passion, Address, and Form in Citizen', *American Literary History* 31.3 (Fall 2019), pp. 419–57 (424–5); Marion Thain, *The Lyric Poem and Aestheticism: Forms of Modernity* (Edinburgh University Press, 2016), p. 19; Werner Wolf, 'The Lyric: Problems of Definition and a Proposal for Reconceptualisation', *Theory into Poetry: New Approaches to the Lyric*, ed. Eva Müller-Zettelmann and Margarete Rubik (Amsterdam: Rodopi, 2005), pp. 21–56.

[58] Thomas Campion, 'Observations in the Art of English Poesie' (1602), *The Works*, ed. Percival Vivian (Oxford: Clarendon, [1909] 1967), p. 309.

[59] Matthew Bevis, 'Unknowing Lyric', *Poetry* (March 2017), pp. 575–89 (579).

[60] *The Princeton Encyclopaedia of Poetry and Poetics: Fourth Edition*, ed. Roland Greene, Stephen Cushman, Clare Cavanagh, Jahan Ramazani and Paul Rouzer (Princeton University Press, 2012), p. 826.

[61] W. R. Johnson, *The Idea of Lyric: Lyric Modes in Ancient and Modern Poetry* (Berkeley and Los Angeles: University of California Press, 1982), p. 26.

normative subjectivity but who have also *refused* that normative subjectivity themselves'.[62] The lyric 'I' makes a claim to humanness, and points to a trail of losses. In following that trail, I may enact what Stephen Best has called 'melancholy historicism': a focus on what is irretrievable or lost in in the (lyric) archive, which counters that loss with an unresolvable attachment, substituting the projective identification of the feeling scholar for acceptance of 'the past's turning away as an ethical condition of my desire for it'.[63] My desire is to rethink the history of lyric by steady, historicist, but yes sometimes melancholic, reflection, which recognises that for some poets historically excluded from its use, the point is not only to deconstruct, but also to rebuild the lyric subject: as Erica Hunt put it, 'I have had to invent the person for whom poetry is possible'.[64]

Yopie Prins and Virginia Jackson have plotted the 'lyricisation' of poetry, a monopolisation by lyric from the mid-eighteenth century onwards that has made many of the other genres inaccessible to modern audiences.[65] Stephen Burt and Jonathan Culler have exposed the many historical omissions required to frame lyric as an Enlightenment invention.[66] But the power of this paradigm – the association of the lyric with selves and feelings – can lead to strange literary backformations. Paul Allen Miller argues for a much earlier invention of the lyric – to the mid-Hellenistic period – when books collecting short poems began to be written (displacing oral poetic genres), because only across such collections could a 'lyric consciousness' be gathered: one 'which projects the image of an individual and highly self-reflexive subject'.[67] The origin of the lyric, identified by Miller as a genre that 'separates the individual from his or her communal ties and responsibilities, and examines his or her most intimate thoughts and feelings' (127), is discovered by looking for a thematics of individualised subjectivity.

---

[62] Fred Moten, '"Poetry Begins with the Willingness to Subordinate Whatever the Hell it is that You Have to Say": An Interview w/Fred Moten', by Housten Donham, *Open House* (20 July 2015).
[63] Stephen Best, *None Like Us: Blackness, Belonging, Aesthetic Life* (Durham: Duke University Press, 2018), p. 20.
[64] Erica Hunt, 'Response to Race and the Poetic Avant-Garde', *Boston Review* (10 March 2015), bost onreview.net/poetry/erica-hunt-response-race-and-poetic-avant-garde (accessed 4 May 2021).
[65] Virginia Jackson, *Dickinson's Misery: A Theory of Lyric Reading* (Princeton University Press, 2005); Virginia Jackson and Yopie Prins (eds.), *The Lyric Theory Reader: A Critical Anthology* (Baltimore: Johns Hopkins University Press, 2014).
[66] Burt, 'What is this Thing', pp. 425–9; Jonathan Culler, *Theory of the Lyric* (Cambridge, MA: Harvard University Press, 2015), chapter 2 (on Prins and Jackson, see pp. 83–5).
[67] Paul Allen Miller, *Lyric Texts and Lyric Consciousness: The Birth of a Genre from Archaic Greece to Augustan Rome* (London: Routledge, 1994), pp. 1, 3, 6.

A key site for thinking through the relation of lyric to subjectivity is Hegel's *Aesthetics*. For Hegel, lyric speaks for the individual torn free from the collective; in it, the mind must 'press on to a free portrayal of itself'.[68] In this process of historical emancipation, lyric delivers 'the heart from the slavery to passion by making it see itself' and 'makes of it an object purified from all accidental moods' (1141). Lyric is the expression of freedom through the sublated particularity of individual feeling. It absorbs the object world and 'stamps' it with the poet's 'inner consciousness'; it raises the 'inner life' and the singularity of the subject to 'a universal validity' (1111). Lyric transcends the song, whose simple expression of feeling 'is renewed at every season', except 'in the case of oppressed peoples, who have been cut off from every advance and have not attained the ever newly animated joy of making poetry' (1143). The songs of oppression are simple, direct and lacking in conflict; they are unlike the lyric, in which 'the poet's own subjective freedom ... flashes out in the struggle against the topic which is trying to master it' (1142). This struggle is staged in terms that recall his dialectic of lordship and bondage. It is the metaphoric struggle of the liberal individual against the topic, not the actual struggles of the singing, oppressed peoples, that produces poetic illumination. Hegel's poetics sketch out an intimacy between lyric, individual subjectivity and freedom. The capacity to discover in one's feelings an objective universality, for the subject to 'tear itself free' from the existent worlds of prose and folk song (1127), is a consequence of historic and political development that moves away from the commons, towards an ambitiously solitary lyric 'I'. That Hegel conceives the emancipated subject of lyric as white, male and European is evident not only from his *Aesthetics*, but from his remarks about Africa's exclusion from history and the need to 'tame' the Negro, and his horror at the Haitian Revolution.[69]

Poetry and Bondage traverses a long history of lyric poetry, from Ovid through the present day, and includes laureates like Wyatt, Christopher Marlowe and Emily Dickinson, alongside those poets who are collectivised by the transmission of their work through anthologies, criticism and other institutions. While much of it dwells with historic and contemporary Black poetries, my intention is not a rebalancing of any canon so much as a fierce interrogation of the coupling of whiteness and lyric. Instead, I ask: what can readings in the history of lyric and its critics tell us about the forms

---

[68] G. W. F. Hegel, *Aesthetics: Lectures on Fine Art*, trans. T. M. Knox, 2 vols. (Oxford: Clarendon Press, 1975 [1988]), 2:1126–7, 1111.
[69] Susan Buck-Morss, 'Hegel and Haiti', *Critical Inquiry* 26.4 (Summer 2000), pp. 821–65.

whiteness takes – by which I mean not only its historical violence, but also what Cheryl Harris calls the 'common premise' whiteness shares with property: 'a right to exclude'?[70] If whiteness is a form of enclosure that bears comparison to the enclosures of the commons and the 'mastery' of human and animal life, how is that form brought to bear on the enclosures that constitute the lyric?

These questions will preoccupy me throughout this book, and as such, distinguish my project from what is known as 'new lyric studies', whose uncritical whiteness has been critiqued by a number of scholars.[71] Mark Jeffreys anticipated the lyricisation argument in a 1995 essay – 'lyric did not conquer poetry: poetry was reduced to lyric. Lyric became the dominant form of poetry only as poetry's authority was reduced to the cramped margins of culture.' As Jeffreys puts it, 'poetry was pushed into a lyric ghetto' through the dominance and privilege of the novel.[72] Whether referring to the original Jewish ghetto in early modern Venice, or the contemporary urban neighbourhoods largely populated by working class people of colour, Jeffreys implies that lyric's social function is constrained, carceral and racialised. In the cramped margins, the ghetto, poetry languishes in insignificance, dominated by the lyric.

Jeffreys's metaphor is an example of what Toni Morrison analysed as the tendency of white writers to explore their autonomy through the 'power of blackness': 'the slave population, it could be and was assumed, offered itself up as surrogate selves for meditation on problems of human freedom, its lure and its elusiveness'.[73] Using these 'conveniently bound and violently silenced black bodies' as 'playground for the imagination', white writers came to know the American self 'as not enslaved, but free; not repulsive, but desirable; not helpless, but licenced and powerful; not history-less, but historical; not damned, but innocent; not a blind accident of evolution,

---

[70] Cheryl I. Harris, 'Whiteness as Property', *Harvard Law Review* 106.8 (June 1993), pp. 1707–91 (1714).
[71] Dorothy J. Wang, *Thinking its Presence: Form, Race, and Subjectivity in Contemporary Asian American Poetry* (Stanford University Press, 2013), pp. 1–48; Sarah Dowling, *Translingual Poetics: Writing Personhood under Settler Colonialism* (Iowa City: University of Iowa Press, 2018), p. 59; Jahan Ramazani, 'Poetry and Race: An Introduction', *New Literary History* 50.4 (Autumn 2019), pp. vii–xxxvii (x); Nathan Suhr-Sytsma, 'Theories of African Poetry', *New Literary History* 50.4 (Autumn 2019), pp. 581–607 (582–3); and Kamran Javadizadeh, 'The Atlantic Ocean Breaking on Our Heads: Claudia Rankine, Robert Lowell, and the Whiteness of the Lyric Subject', *PMLA* 134.3 (2019), pp. 475–90 (476).
[72] Mark Jeffreys, 'Ideologies of Lyric: A Problem of Genre in Contemporary Anglophone Poetics', *PMLA* (March 1995), pp. 196–205 (200).
[73] Toni Morrison, *Playing in the Dark: Whiteness and the Literary Imagination* (Cambridge, MA: Harvard University Press, 1992), pp. 37–8.

but a progressive fulfilment of destiny' (52). So, too, across the history of poetics, do the people bound in prisons and chattel slavery become tropes with which privileged subjects think about creative freedom and obligation.

Alexander Weheliye asks, 'what different modalities of the human come to light if we do not take the liberal humanist figure of Man as the master-subject but focus on how humanity has been imagined and lived by those subjects excluded from this domain?'[74] In response this book questions: what lyric modalities might come to light if the liberal humanist figure of the white poet is displaced by those poetic subjects whose practices and experiences were crucial to, but also erased from, the theorisation of poetry? Who is lost when the story of the lyric is told?

Frank B. Wilderson III critiques the utility of Blackness as a 'metatheory', a lens that shows that 'Blacks are not Human subjects, but are instead structurally inert props, implements for the execution of White and non-Black fantasies and sadomasochistic pleasures', including fantasies of universal liberation and claims of a shared 'universal humanity'.[75] Morrison, Weheliye and Wilderson's thinking offers a different way of approaching the synonymity of lyric and humanness that recurs throughout literary history, and particularly in the context of the writing of bondage, in which being able to become a lyric poet is an index of the survival of the human in situations of utmost oppression. Saying 'I' in a poem lays claim to the privileges of subjectivity from which some categories of people have been historically excluded; it affirms that the particular experiences of that subject can be incubated lyrically into a universal validity; it also attests to an ongoing or emergent humanness, through the interwoven freedoms and constraints of poetic form.

This may also be why the figure of the animal reappears so frequently throughout this book. Zakiyyah Iman Jackson has theorised that discourses of liberal humanism produce a dichotomy of 'the human' and 'the animal' that is 'predicated on the abjection of blackness, which is not based on figurations of blackness as "animal-like" but rather casts black people as ontologically plastic'.[76] That plasticity will recur in lyric contexts through the invocation of half-human animals: tamed hawks or deer as

---

[74] Alexander G. Weheliye, *Habeas Viscus: Racializing Assemblages, Biopolitics, and Black Feminist Theories of the Human* (Durham: Duke University Press, 2014), p. 8.
[75] Frank B. Wilderson III, *Afropessimism* (New York: Norton, 2020), pp. 14–15.
[76] Zakiyyah Iman Jackson, *Becoming Human: Matter and Meaning in an Antiblack World* (New York University Press, 2020), p. 18.

women, tigers that resemble Haitian revolutionaries, horses made equivalent to Africans thrown overboard, imprisoned Black singers who resemble birds and who are treated like dogs, masochists who wish to draw carts and be treated like slaves, ploughmen indistinguishable from their teams, orangutans that compose odes and, only rarely, companion species.

Notes on Method

As can be intuited by my flight from Boethius to Guantánamo, or from archaic Greek poetry to Erica Hunt, this book seeks to draw out continuities of thought and practice in the *longue durée* of lyric constraint. It offers pairings of poets, often across wide historical gulfs: Thomas Wyatt and Rob Halpern; Emily Dickinson and M. NourbeSe Philip; Ovid and Marlowe and Algernon Charles Swinburne and Hopkins; Lisa Robertson and Phillis Wheatley. In each case, I'm committed to providing historicist, immanent interpretations of individual practices, while also recognising through comparative readings the long duration of structures of poetic thinking, feeling and imagining. These readings are aligned with similarly paired analyses of collectives, institutions and structures: the Romantic and the contemporary prison; African American folk song, white folklorists and the New Critics; Roman and Victorian sexualities and imperial politics. Moving between individuals and structures, the book's opening section considers the prison as a site of bondage, in early modern England, Britain and the United States in the long nineteenth century, and contemporary mass incarceration. Section 2 dwells on chattel slavery and song, as well as the institutionalisation of literary criticism. Section 3 turns to the pleasures of bondage, looking backward to the normalising of heterosexuality and soft masculinity as an alternative to Roman imperial power in Ovid's verse, and to the sexological studies of the nineteenth century and the pathologisation of sadomasochism.

My aim is not to establish a genealogy between the paired poets, implying that a trope or a tactic becomes an heritable characteristic across historical generations, or to affirm some teleological account of lyric emancipation. I am thinking in circles, not lines. These diachronic pairings instead propose a set of relationships between contemporary and historic poetics that is *figural*, in the sense elaborated by Eric Auerbach. Auerbach's famous essay on '*figura*' explores the shaping of biblical interpretation and rhetoric by the persistence of a particular trope or image, a figure. Auerbach refers to this as 'figural prophecy', a relation of textual indeterminacy and contingency in which past and future no longer fit into a linear mode of anticipation and completion. *Figura*:

> implies the interpretation of one worldly event through another; the first signifies the second, the second fulfils the first. Both remain historical events; yet both, looked at in this way, have something provisional and incomplete about them; they point to one another and both point to something in the future, something still to come, which will be the actual, real, and definitive event.[77]

As a result, history remains 'forever a figure, cloaked and needful of interpretation' (58). This event, the concealed eventuality, the to-come, is the future conditional, a space of possibility that enfolds the non-identity of past instants into one fulfilment.

The pairings of poets in this book emphasise the provisionality and contingency of any historical moment of lyric self-determination. They are intended to draw out the radical potentialities of past and present poetries, to identify how the breaking open of possibilities at specific moments also foreclosed others and to recognise how those apertures continue to give structure to our ideas about what lyric can or cannot do. I hope that the critiques of individual authors add up to a critical poetics. But they are not meant to be proscriptive. Nor does this book, long as it is, pretend to exhaust the topic of poetry as bondage, which could have led us through Milton, Blake, Walt Whitman, Oscar Wilde, Ezra Pound, Dawn Lundy Martin and numerous others. I've also not been able to grapple with other significant sites of bondage: the camp and the asylum chief among them. And if the poems I do discuss are, like this book, limited, then by acknowledging and understanding those limits, we can perhaps expand the possibilities of the lyric beyond its current constraints.

The figural method describes not just a poetics, but a politics. The histories of slavery, mass incarceration, imperial warfare or the pathologisation of sexual difference continue. My readings follow the arguments of activists and abolitionists whose demands for restorative justice and reparation make profound claims about historicity, and a relation between past and present that is contingent in senses not imagined by Auerbach.

---

[77] Eric Auerbach, *Scenes from the Drama of European Literature* (Minneapolis: University of Minnesota Press), p. 58.

Throughout this book, I foreground not an abstract or generic scholarly reading, but my own reading, limited by and situated in the particularities of my own life, and the structures I inhabit and reproduce. I am a white, cis-female, middle-class academic from a working-class family in the United States. I have a permanent job and dual citizenship in the United Kingdom, where I work at a 'Russell Group' (elite) university situated in Tower Hamlets, one of the most deprived local boroughs in England. Some 30 per cent of my students come from families whose income is less than £15,000 a year, and 60 per cent of them are people of colour, but they are taught by faculty who are almost entirely white. These facts are not intended to signal a set of virtues or their impossibility, but to explain why analysing especially the ways that whiteness has shaped the production, reading and criticism of lyric within the academy is important to me. This book reflects the many things I have learned from my students.

It is also a response to Joseph North's call for a return to criticism as a materialist and 'programmatic commitment, not just to analysing and describing the culture, but to taking action to change it'.[78] It follows lyric, which is associated with the inalienable freedoms of personhood, into the abysses where personhood has been annihilated by agents whose categories of identity I share. It recognises the urgent 'critical challenge' posed by Caleb Smith: 'to pursue, perhaps to unmake, the harrowing concept of the human on which the prison rests'.[79] It pays tribute to all I've learned from Black feminist thought, to the importance of what Christina Sharpe names 'wake work': of thinking about 'about Black flesh, Black optics, and ways of producing enfleshed work'.[80] As a white critic, I have tried to respond ethically to the call of that work by thinking about the enclosure fabricated by white thought: the hold, the cell and, sometimes, the lyric.

Poetry and Bondage is an effort to understand how dwelling in the gap or wound that separates lyric as an expression of human liberty (so free that it can even imagine itself enchained) from the lyrics actually produced in

---

[78] Joseph North, *Literary Criticism: A Concise Political History* (Cambridge, MA: Harvard University Press, 2017), p. 18.
[79] Caleb Smith, *The Prison and the American Imagination* (New Haven: Yale University Press, 2009), p. 23.
[80] Christina Sharpe, *In the Wake: On Blackness and Being* (Durham: Duke University Press, 2016), p. 21.

bondage can open up new ways of thinking about poetry: new forms of empathy, being and relating. I want to gather from the fields of poetic practice a nourishing array, to militate against enclosure and to celebrate the remedies for human suffering poems offer. I seek not the poetry of privileged re-enactment and proxy suffering that puts the prisoner to work as a figure of its own artistic limits, but waylaid voices, open commons and unspeakable imaginaries: the poetics of bondage and emancipation that can be found everywhere in the history and theory of the lyric.

PART I

Lyric Cells

CHAPTER I

The Music of Fetters
Thomas Wyatt and the Beginnings of English Carceral Lyric

> *As if the exceptional site of violence could be*
> *-come the place of sovereign love*
>
> — Rob Halpern

I'll begin this investigation of lyric relations of mastery and bondage with the poems of Sir Thomas Wyatt (1503–42). Wyatt's poetic writing includes versions of the Psalms and Boethius, humanist satire and epigrams, rondeaux and ballades, and the Petrarchan sonnets for which he is now best known. In his amorous lyrics, Wyatt represents the tensions between victims and perpetrators of erotic and political violence as oscillations between motion and fixity, human and animal figures, formal constraint and prosodic looseness, particular and inscrutable selves. Wyatt conjures spaces of minor autonomy, at home, at court, in the forest, or even in a prison cell, where the lyric subject can enjoy the freedoms of fantasy and appeal to like minds for relief from his enslavement by wrong desires. Figuring his affections as servitude, Wyatt moves fluidly between positions of domination and subordination. The speakers in his poems are free and ensnared, master and servant, hunter and prey. Their fluidity is an expression of social privilege, and depends on others who are silenced or ventriloquised: the woman, the slave and the animal.

Wyatt is often perceived to be an originator of the English Renaissance, a writer whose poems produce the effect of inwardness in rebound from eroticised oppression or oppressive eros.[1] To Wyatt is attributed the invention of literary interiority in proximity to political power. This chapter will contest some of these attributions. However, given that Wyatt's poetry is frequently situated at the threshold of the modern lyric, it can tell us something about what the modern lyric subject is supposed to be: intimate, solitary, corroded

---

[1] Michael R. G. Spiller, *The Development of the Sonnet: An Introduction* (London: Routledge, 1992), p. 84; Stephen Greenblatt, *Renaissance Self-Fashioning: From More to Shakespeare* (University of Chicago Press, 1980), pp. 154, 125.

by the sovereign who penetrates its fantasies, sadistic or masochistic, mournful for lost freedoms, split by desire; but also autonomous, creative, ironic, mobile, improvisatory, opportunistic. Wyatt had repeated, personal experience of captivity. Imprisoned three times, held in Italy by imperial forces, examined by the Inquisition, rusticated to his estate in Kent, Wyatt also saw his friends executed and members of his household threatened or arrested. His poems constantly represent the lover as a prisoner or slave, petitioning the beloved to give him his freedom. This posture of the lover as the *servus amoris* is a conventional one, and we will encounter it again later. But Wyatt reinforces the similitude between amorous service and bondage through form: the 'bridle' of the refrain, the circular rondeau, stanzaic structures and rhymes that keep the speaker in an enclosed space of diminishing returns. Caught in formal, amorous and political traps, the speaker can sometimes appear like a hunted animal, turning endlessly in search of an exit, or torn to pieces by desire and the cruelty of the mistress. This violent scattering recalls the myth of Orpheus, among whose powers was the ability to tame the wild beasts with his music. Wyatt has a much more ambivalent relationship to animals, which he sometimes dominates as a hunter, and sometimes becomes, as the prey to a mistress or his own desires. Those relations, and their implications for thinking about the early history of lyric whiteness, will come into focus with a reading of his most famous sonnet.

The Speaking Animal

Who so list to hounte I know where is an hynde;
    But as for me, helas, I may no more:
    The vayne travaill hath weried me so sore,
    I am of theim that farthest cometh behinde;
Yet may I by no meanes my weried mynde
    Drawe from the Diere: but as she fleeth afore
    Faynting I folowe; I leve of therefore,
    Sithens in a nett I seke to hold the wynde.
Who list her hount I put him owte of dowbte,
    As well as I may spend his tyme in vain:
    And graven with Diamondes in letters plain
There is written her faier neck rounde abowte:
    'Noli me tangere for Cesar's I ame,
    And wylde for to hold though I seme tame.'[2]

---

[2] Because my argument 'turns' on Wyatt's ambivalent orthography, I will be citing from the old spelling edition: Kenneth Muir and Patricia Thomson, *Collected Poems of Sir Thomas Wyatt*

In this poem, one of Wyatt's most famous, we encounter the first of the half-human animals that will appear throughout this book: the elusive hind, a female deer. She is owned, and wild; was once captured long enough to be fitted with a collar, but never held for long. She is also the site of an enunciation, an epigram inscribed on what we will remember as a collar but the poem only describes as 'written her faier neck rounde abowte'. This enunciation is in the first person, though as she is an animal the speech cannot be her own. It splits being ('I ame') from appearance ('I seme'). This split seems to be the cunning self-description of a fickle creature, but is a projection of the multiplex writer of this inscription – Wyatt as Caesar as Henry VIII or someone else entirely. (The agate stone of Wyatt's signet ring was carved in the likeness of Julius Caesar.) When the poet, or the king, makes his object say 'I am', who is really speaking?

This inscription is immensely daring: 'for Caesar's I am' recalls Christ's injunction to render to Caesar's what is Caesar's (Matthew 22:21), and *Noli me tangere* (do not touch me) is what he said to Mary Magdalene in the graveyard, after he was resurrected but not yet risen to his Father (John 20:17). Collapsed in one deer is both Christ and coin. It is proof of Christ's submission (tamed) and evasion (wild) of Caesar's dominion. The poem affirms sovereignty over things: Caesar's proprietary identification of the body of this feminised other masks her name under the brand of his own.

This dominion also draws out the speaker. He is vitiated: fainting, following, feeble, falling, an akratic subject who – as I will argue in Chapter 2 – is represented by Plato as a slave of desire. He offers knowledge – 'I know where is an hind' – and withdraws it (her location is unspecified). The speaker's previous contact with the animal asserts his success as a tracker; but now he falls behind. And yet, for all his be*hind*ness, he finds his own freedom in the forest, where he can imagine this poem. There, his wild 'mynde' can no more be 'drawe[n] from the Diere', his poetic conceit and the compulsion to hunt her, than the deer can be drawn into the open. The hind remains wild; the speaker remains feeble; this is how they might resist Caesar. In Caesar's absence, hind and speaker can engage in an erotic coupling, or a solidarity based on mutual recognition of their bondage, with only the reader as witness. This promise is hinted at by the poem, but not enacted, in part because it shows us a desirable animal who speaks to us and whose human femininity therefore appears but remains just beyond reach, across the gap that preserves desire.

(Liverpool University Press, 1969), rather than R. A. Rebholz's modernised version of Wyatt's poems (*Sir Thomas Wyatt: The Complete Poems*, New Haven: Yale University Press, 1978). Muir and Thomson, *Collected*, p. 5.

This poem lends itself to antithetical readings of Wyatt as the laureate of courtly dissimulation or free speech, of flattery or candour, of active service or Stoic retirement, of the internalisation of tyranny or the lyric discovery of autonomy.[3] Feminist critics cite it as demonstrating how the early modern women is fetishised as a 'nonhuman, nonself who, at least potentially, can belong to someone'.[4] Jonathan Crewe does not see the hind as victimised; instead, he asserts that the hind 'constitutes *herself* in the rigorously subject-forming relation of bondage' (my emphasis), making herself 'doubly invulnerable to possession' by dwelling in the forest of 'non-self-identity'.[5] This is a reading of the poem as proto-feminist: a female subject coming to both identity and voice within the liminal space of non-identity, the forest of the lyric imagination.

All of these critics perceive the poem as the performance of a profoundly ambivalent male subject in heteroerotic relation to a feminised body, which is owned. No critic, as far as I know, has called this creature a slave. This is not to say that Wyatt, or Petrarch before him, was deliberately referring to historical slavery, ancient or modern. But then, it is not Wyatt's intentions that I am tracing, but how this figure appears to us, in a poem that has circulated for centuries as a formative moment in the history of white lyric. Slavery and servitude were persistent tropes in early modern love poetry. Shortly after Wyatt's death, slavery was instituted as a remedy for poverty in England. From 1547 until its repeal in 1549, the Vagrancy Act (1 Edw. VI c. 3) condemned those who were found loitering and refusing work for more than three days to slavery; their master could 'cawse the saide Slave to worke by beating [or] cheyninge' the enslaved person's neck and legs, and lease, sell or bequeath them like 'movable goodes or Catelles'. England did not become involved in slave trading until the 1550s; in 1553, the first English expeditions to Guinea were mounted, and John Lok captured several Africans on his voyage in 1554.[6] However,

---

[3] Jon Robinson, *Court Politics, Culture and Literature in Scotland and England, 1500–1540* (Aldershot: Ashgate, 2008), p. 18.
[4] Marguerite Waller, 'The Empire's New Clothes: Refashioning the Renaissance', in *Seeking the Woman in Late Medieval and Renaissance Writings: Essays in Feminist Contextual Criticism*, ed. Sheila Fisher and Janet E. Halley (Knoxville: University of Tennessee Press, 1989), pp. 160–83 (177); Barbara L. Estrin, 'Wyatt's Unlikely Likenesses: Or, Has the Lady Read Petrarch?', in *Rethinking the Henrician Era: Essays on Early Tudor Texts and Contexts*, ed. Peter Herman (Urbana and Chicago: University of Illinois Press, 1994), pp. 219–39.
[5] Jonathan Crewe, *Trials of Authorship: Anterior Forms and Poetic Reconstruction from Wyatt to Shakespeare* (Berkeley and Los Angeles: University of California Press, 1990), p. 42.
[6] Elizabeth Donnan, *Documents Illustrative of the History of the Slave Trade to America*, 4 vols. (Washington: Carnegie Institute, 1930), 1.9; Kim Hall, *Things of Darkness: Economies of Race and Gender in Early Modern England* (Ithaca, NY: Cornell University Press, 1995), pp. 19–20.

from the 1440s, the Portuguese had brought African captives back to Iberian peninsula: 'by 1500 about a tenth of the population of Lisbon and Seville were African slaves'.[7] Roland Greene has itemised some of the many instances of Petrarchan tropes in the texts of colonial conquest, and notes that the Petrarchan sonnet that Wyatt is reworking here was imitated in Oviedo's *Quinquagenas* (1526), which compares a 'collar of gold' found in Asturias in 1496 to the mineral wealth and gold mines of Hispaniola.[8] He also locates the language of stalking by naked-footed hunters that Wyatt uses in 'They flee . . .' in contemporary descriptions of Native Americans.[9]

There is also a long tradition, well known to Wyatt, in which enslaved and free men, or animals and humans, serve as allegories for the body's necessary subjection to the soul. In the *Politics*, Aristotle famously describes the 'natural slave' as comparable to a 'wild beast':

> Therefore all men who differ from one another by as much as the soul differs from the body or man from a wild beast (and that is the state of those who work by using their bodies, and for whom that is the best they can do) – these people are slaves by nature, and it is better for them to be subject to this kind of control, as it is better for the other creatures I have mentioned. For a man who is able to belong to another person is by nature a slave. (1.5)

Here again is an image of the man created in opposition to the 'wild beast', forming a hierarchy in which the slave is a middle term that can be found between human and animal, soul and body. As Orlando Patterson puts it, 'the slave, as a socially dead person, existed in a permanent state of transition: socially dead, yet physically alive; an instrument, yet a vocal one; a two-legged beast, yet with a mind and soul; a physically separate being, yet no more than a living surrogate of the master'.[10] The hierarchy naturalises slavery rather than basing it in conquest, violence or law. But as Quentin Skinner notes, under Roman law slaves (like children) were 'not, *sui iuris*, within their own jurisdiction or right'; their 'lack of freedom derives from the fact that they are "subject to the jurisdiction of someone else" and are consequently "within the power" of another person'. Even

---

[7] Robin Blackburn, *The Making of New World Slavery: From the Baroque to the Modern, 1492–1800* (London: Verso, 2010), p. 52.
[8] Roland Greene, 'Petrarchism Among the Discourses of Imperialism', in *America in European Consciousness, 1493–1750*, ed. Karen Ordahl Kupperman (Chapel Hill: University of North Carolina Press, 1995), pp. 131, 155.
[9] Roland Greene, 'The Colonial Wyatt: Openings and Contexts', in *Rethinking the Henrician Era: Essays on Early Tudor Texts and Contexts*, ed. Peter Herman (Urbana and Chicago: University of Illinois Press, 1994), pp. 240–66 (246–8).
[10] Orlando Patterson, *Freedom*, vol. I: *Freedom in the Making of Western Culture* (New York: Basic Books, 1991), p. 238.

when acting according to their own will, that will was not free, because 'they remain at all times *in potestate domini*, within the power of their masters'.[11] The slave was defined by Varro as a 'speaking instrument', *instrumentum vocale* (R.R.1.17.1), and by Aristotle (*Politics* 1253b) as 'an animate piece of property', where property is 'a tool to live with'.[12]

However, the censored speech of the enslaved person was perceived as creating the opportunity for the development of private internal thoughts not knowable to the master – and thus the source of an anxiety that resonates with the Henrician court.[13] Steven Connor argues that the marks of the owners on the enslaved bodies of the ancient world (or later the United States) are 'uneasy': 'To make the one marked bear their [the owner's] own sign, to show forth as literally as possible their own character, is at once to reduce them to the condition of a sign, and to degrade their sign to the condition of a body'.[14] Caesar's inscription on the hind makes her into a sign of his power; but for all its opulent hardness, it also vanishes into the living materiality, the pelt of the deer: there is no collar here, just language that disappears into the body that bears it. The body of the enslaved person articulates the absolute tyranny of the state by becoming identical with its proclamations; but it also remains the inexorable, elusive, living creature who absorbs that language into itself, and turns it and tears it apart.

In the Labyrinth

Wyatt's poetry is positioned between medieval England and modern Europe, between the earliness of prosodic irregularity and the lateness of excessive control, between a proliferation that opens up to the future and an attrition that dislodges the past. His poems draw on the language of feudal relations of service and the localities of Anglo-Saxon, Chaucerian and Kentish diction; but they are also forged in the context of humanist letters, Italian lyric poetry and early modern European imperial conflict and exile.[15] They look back to values such as 'trouth' (truth and troth), but from the vantage of a modernising

---

[11] Quentin Skinner, *Liberty before Liberalism* (Cambridge University Press, 1998), pp. 40–1. See also Neil Roberts, *Freedom as Marronage* (University of Chicago Press, 2015), p. 40.
[12] William Fitzgerald, *Slavery and the Roman Literary Imagination* (Cambridge University Press, 2000), p. 6.
[13] K. McCarthy, 'Servitium Amoris: Amor Servitii', in *Slaves and Masters and the Arts of Authority in Plautine Comedy*, ed. S. R. Joshel and S. Murnaghan (Berkeley and Los Angeles: University of California Press, 1998), pp. 174–92.
[14] Steven Connor, *The Book of Skin* (Ithaca, NY: Cornell University Press, 2004), pp. 75–6.
[15] Joel B. Davis, '"Thus I restles rest in Spayne": Engaging Empire in the Poetry of Sir Thomas Wyatt and Garcilaso de la Vega', *Studies in Philology* 107.4 (Fall 2010), pp. 493–519 (498); Susan Brigden and Jonathan Woolfson, 'Thomas Wyatt in Italy', *Renaissance Quarterly* 58 (2005), pp. 464–511 (502).

society in which those values had been 'degraded' by suspicion.[16] Brian Cummings finds him caught in 'a very Tudor bind', 'between revelation and concealment, between freedom and bondage'.[17] In these readings, the most dramatically bound subject in Wyatt's poems is the lyric 'I'. But as I've begun to argue, the resources of that lyric 'I' to emancipate itself from its constraints also depend on the suppression of other real captives.

Reading Wyatt as a modern, critics tend to present the self – a secret, bland and disintegrating 'I' – in his poems as a space of retreat, reconstructed in chambers and forests and lyric poems. Anne Ferry finds him at the English beginning of what she calls lyric poetry's 'inward turn', the literary construction of the 'subjectivity effect' through spatial withdrawals into enclosed spaces such as bedchambers or cells, where the subject can resist the intrusions of state power.[18] Peter Sacks alleges that 'Wyatt pens love into its chambers', formally and 'spatially matching the temporal construction of inwardness'.[19] Michael McCanles describes him as 'an inmate of that most impregnable of prisons, that which he creates for himself in the desire to achieve the absolute freedom of his fantasy world'.[20]

But there are several problems with the narrative of Wyatt's inauguration of the solitary modern lyric, battling and internalising power through his fictions of private lyric spaces. The first lies in the modes in which Wyatt's poems circulated and were recomposed in manuscript, turned and returned by many hands. Many of Wyatt's poems are compiled in the Devonshire manuscript, where they can be read alongside amorous poems by Thomas Howard and Margaret Douglas, who were both imprisoned in the Tower.[21] Scholarship has emphasised the social and collaborative nature of this manuscript anthology, which (like the historical actuality of the prison) belies the isolation often imputed to Wyatt's poetic speakers.[22]

---

[16] Thomas M. Greene, *The Light in Troy: Imitation and Discovery in Renaissance Poetry* (New Haven: Yale University Press, 1982), pp. 254–7.

[17] Brian Cummings, *The Literary Culture of the Reformation: Grammar and Grace* (Oxford University Press, 2002), pp. 231, 225.

[18] Anne Ferry, *The 'Inward' Language: Sonnets of Wyatt, Sidney, Shakespeare and Donne* (University of Chicago Press, 1983).

[19] Peter Sacks, 'The Face of the Sonnet: Wyatt and Some Early Features of the Tradition', in *Green Thoughts, Green Shades: Essays by Contemporary Poets on the Early Modern Lyric*, ed. Jonathan F. S. Post (Berkeley and Los Angeles: University of California Press, 2002), pp. 17–40 (24).

[20] Michael McCanles, 'Love and Power in the Poetry of Sir Thomas Wyatt', *Modern Language Quarterly* 29 (1968), pp. 145–60 (150).

[21] Social Edition of the Devonshire MS (BL Add. MS 17492): en.wikibooks.org/wiki/The_Devonshire_Manuscript (accessed 4 May 2021).

[22] Jason Powell, 'Marginalia, Authorship, and Editing in the Manuscripts of Thomas Wyatt's Verse', *English Manuscript Studies 1100–1700*, vol. 15: Tudor Manuscripts 1485–1603, ed. A. S. G. Edwards (London: British Library, 2009), pp. 1–40.

Second, Renaissance prisons were also social spaces, with porous boundaries, makeshift architecture and highly contingent relations between the inmates and their jailers. Groups lodged together, often along with family members and servants who could come and go freely. Lower-class prisoners were destitute, starving, beaten and exposed to rampant disease in terribly unhygienic conditions. They were tortured by having to wear iron fetters, chains and blocks day and night, to prevent their escape or punish those who had attempted to run. (Such chains were cheaper than reconstructing walls.) But Wyatt's conditions in the Tower reflected his status as a gentleman; he could enjoy his own sparsely furnished rooms, writing materials, visitors and decent food.

Along with the prison, the court is seen by many critics as the most significant spatial enclosure in shaping Wyatt's lyrics. Both were places of punitive discipline. Wyatt's friend and the addressee of several of his poems, Sir Francis Bryan, complains in his *Dispraise of the Life of a Courtier* (1548):

> Whosoeuer leaueth the court may be bolde to say that he goeth not to dye: but may wel thinke he hath escaped from a fayre prison, from a confused life, from a daungerous sickenes, from a suspicious conuersacion, from a great sepulchre, & from a meruail without ende.[23]

Despite its dangers and resemblance to a prison, Bryan insists that court is preferable to a life of rustic *otium*; separation from power's risks and 'brackishe joyes' (Wyatt's phrase) means separation from its benefits. But he lamented: 'that worst is there is no libertie to depart hence. The yoke of the court is hard, the bondes faste tyed and the plough so tedious' (sig. L1ᵛ).

Bryan's translation goes on to use another metaphor that also appealed to Wyatt. Entering the court, 'I did cast my selfe into this perilous labyrinthe (which is to say a prison full of all snares)' (sig. N6ʳ). The courtier is lost in the labyrinth, a prison not merely by nature of its impasses but also because of the dangerous traps in which it catches its prey. The labyrinth had a powerful hold on Wyatt. He complains that:

> Alas! I tred an endles maze
> That seketh to accorde two contraries;
> And hope still and nothing hase,
> Imprisoned in libertes,
> As oon vnhard, and still that cries ...
> ('It may be good, like it who list', 17)

---

[23] Antonio de Guevara, *A Dispraise of the Life of a Courtier*, trans. Sir Francis Bryan (London, 1548), sig. D5. Cited in Peter Zagorin, 'Sir Thomas Wyatt and the Court of Henry VII: The Courtier's Ambivalence', *Journal of Medieval and Renaissance Studies* 23 (1993), pp. 113–41.

Paradoxically imprisoned by freedom or constrained by the 'liberties' that sit outside the jurisdiction of the city, hopeful and hopeless, he is lost (in the Petrarchan contraries) as in a maze. On his way back from Venice in 1527, while waiting for a change of horses and musing on the 'want of success of the King's affairs' in the papal curia, Wyatt sketched an *impresa* on the wall of his chamber, depicting 'a maze, and in it a minotaur with a triple crown on his head, both as it were falling, and a bottom [ball] of thread with certain gives [shackles] and broken chains there lying by', along with a line from the 123rd Psalm (Vulgate numbering; 124:7 in AV): *Laqueus contritus est et nos liberati sumus* ('the snare is broken, and we are delivered'). There is some debate about the meaning of this image – an anti-papal sentiment, a representation of the diplomatic maze, a recognition of the threat posed by the Emperor's German troops who were intent on sacking Rome?[24] But it also demonstrates Wyatt's preoccupation with chains and shackles, materialisations of bondage to which I'll return throughout this chapter.

Court was a labyrinth, and a prison wherein the courtier finds himself 'fettred with cheines of gold' ('In court so serue decked with freshe aray', 253). The social bondage of the court was also materially displayed. In 1514, Nicolo di Favri, attached to the Venetian Embassy in England, described Henry VIII's courtiers as wearing 'such massive gold chains that some might have served for fetters on a felon's ankles, and sufficed for his safe custody, so heavy were they, and of such an immense value'. This fashion was restrained by a 1515 sumptuary act, which decreed that 'no man under the degree of a knight were any cheyne of gold or gilte or colour [collar] of Gold or any gold about his neck'.[25] The term 'knight of the collar' was used for the convict, the executed felon and the knight. The collar was a badge of courtly service, and of slavery; of status, and its precarity. It seems that the gold chains worn by the ambassadors and bondsmen in Thomas More's *Utopia* were not entirely fictional.

Bondage loomed over the Wyatt family in more direct ways. His father was imprisoned during the reign of Richard III for his loyalty to Henry Tudor and was racked for two years, 'in irons and stoks', as Wyatt described it. Wyatt complained to his son that his own folly had brought him 'into a thousand dangers and hazardes, enmyties, hatreds,

---

[24] Greg Walker, *Writing Under Tyranny: English Literature and the Henrician Reformation* (Oxford University Press, 2005), p. 283.
[25] Venice papers II, 445, quoted in *Two Tudor Interludes: Youth and Hick Scorner* ed. Ian Lancashire (Manchester University Press, 1980), pp. 19–21.

prisonments, despites and indignations'.²⁶ He was taken hostage by mutinous imperial troops outside Bologna in 1527 and held for a large ransom. He was imprisoned in the Fleet in May 1534 following an affray in which one of the sergeants of London was killed. Again, in May 1536 he was swept up in the fall of Anne Boleyn and imprisoned in the Tower, then held for several weeks after Anne's execution.

Several of Wyatt's poems dwell on the presence of a 'thing', an alien internal object that buries itself in the subject and cannot be dislodged or even directly addressed. The most famous of these 'things' was the sight, widely surmised to be the execution of Anne Boleyn and others, which Wyatt claimed to have watched from the Bell Tower:

> The bell towre showed me suche syght
> That in my hed stekys day and nyght;
> Ther dyd I lerne out of a grate,
> Ffor all vauore, glory or myght,
> That yet *circa Regna tonat*.
> ('Who lyst his welthe and eas Retayne', 187–8)

Wyatt never specifies what this 'sight' was. Colin Burrow notes that, in contrast to Wyatt's indirection about the sight 'that in my hed stekys', very specific signifiers could at the time be seen on the bridges of London: traitors' heads on stakes.²⁷ Something like power also intrudes on the speaker, gets metaphorically inside his head. This 'thing' – a splinter of memory, or desire, or imagination – lodges in the mind, interrupting his autonomy. In another love lyric, he complains that:

> Though that with pain I do procure
> For to forgett that ons was pure
>   Within my hert shall still that thing,
>   Vnstable, vnsure, and wavering,
> Be in my mynde without recure?
> What no, perdy!
> ('What no, perdy, ye may be sure!' 34)

What is this wavering thing in the heart and mind? Though indeterminate, it sticks: and the speaker refuses to accept that he can't reason it away. The

---

²⁶ Jason Powell (ed.), 'Wyatt's First Letter to His Son Thomas' (15 April 1537), in *The Complete Works of Sir Thomas Wyatt the Elder*, vol. 1: *Prose* (Oxford University Press, 2016), pp. 63–4.
²⁷ Colin Burrow, 'The Experience of Exclusion: Literature and Politics in the Reigns of Henry VII and Henry VIII', in *The Cambridge History of Medieval English Literature*, ed. David Wallace (Cambridge University Press, 1999), pp. 793–820 (811).

internalisation of power as something that remains recognisably other but cannot be overcome is one of the poetic themes that fit Wyatt's work for modernity.

After Anne's execution, Wyatt was released to his estates in Kent with a warning from the king 'to adres hym better'.[28] It was during this period that he wrote 'Myne owne John Poynz' (88), a verse epistle modelled on a satire by the Florentine republican and exile Luigi Alamanni. Wyatt represents his rustication as voluntary: 'homeward I me drawe', fleeing the court where others 'lyve thrall', terrorised by their lord. He can at last enjoy the autonomy of his estate, recreate himself far from the court's passions and duplicity.

> This maketh me at home to hounte and to hawke
> And in fowle weder at my booke to sitt.
> In frost and snowe then with my bow to stawke,
> No man doeth marke where so I ride or goo;
> In lusty lees at libertie I walke,
> And of these newes I fele nor wele nor woo,
> Sauf that a clogg doeth hang yet at my hele:
> No force for that for it is ordered so,
> That I may lepe boeth hedge and dike full well.

The poem celebrates creative freedom within a property bounded by the land of others, or by common land. The intellectual freedom of *otium*, to 'read and rhyme' far from the business of the metropolis, is an ancient theme, and one that would also inform prison architecture from the eighteenth century onwards. But in Wyatt's satire it is multiply ambivalent: first, because his poem dwells obsessively on the court, even through apophasis; second, because as Stephen Greenblatt notes, this estate – purchased by his father from Henry VII, and 'swelled with confiscated monastic lands' – is held through the generosity of the crown; and third, because his freedom is defined by physical constraint.[29]

And this constraint turns the speaker into an animal. 'Lusty lees' (or leas) refers primarily to a lush meadow, but 'lees' was also a spelling of leash, a thong or line by which hounds or coursing-dogs were held. This double meaning is also present in the passage from Geoffrey Chaucer's poem *Troilus and Criseyde* that Wyatt is imitating here. Criseyde – contending with herself about whether she ought to love Troilus – describes herself as

---

[28] Kenneth Muir, *Life and Letters of Sir Thomas Wyatt* (Liverpool University Press, 1963), p. 35.
[29] Greenblatt, *Renaissance Self-Fashioning*, p. 29.

'Right yong, and stonde unteyd in lusty lese' (Book I, l. 752). The bridle is a key image in *Troilus*, where it is a Platonic metaphor for reason's guidance of the blind human passions; but Diomede also literally leads Criseyde away with a bridle.[30] In Wyatt's epistle, the speaker is simultaneously the exemplary gentleman landowner, free in his domain, and the fettered property of another; both the hunter and an animal, which can 'lepe' the hedges that bound his estate despite the 'clogg' that hangs at his heel.

The clog, a wooden block or log used to hobble animals (and people), is Wyatt's addition to Alamanni's satire.[31] Patricia Thomson notes an epigram recorded in a manuscript that includes the name of Wyatt and Poyns:

> qui asne est et cerff cuide bien ester
> a sallir une fosse on le puit bien cognostre.

'One who is an ass, and would well be a deer, will realise the truth on leaping the ditch.'[32] The transgression of a boundary can lead to a more modest self-perception. It can also bring the power that maintains those boundaries into the open. Thomson hears the name Anne in 'asne', but the words for deer – *cervus/cerf* – also echo the Latin for *servus* (slave), and serf; the *servus amoris* will be a key figure for thinking through the sadistic and masochistic experience of love in Ovid and Christopher Marlowe later in this book.

Wyatt was restored to royal favour from this latest fall astonishingly quickly, and resumed his ambassadorial work in 1537 with some reluctance. At the court of Charles V in Spain, he was scrutinised by the Inquisition, and members of his household held by them. Back in England his mistress Elizabeth Darrell was embroiled in the arrest of the Marquis of Exeter, and gave testimony that Wyatt had plotted to assassinate Cardinal Reginald Pole. Wyatt was recalled, to his great relief, though he was also reputedly present on the scaffold when his protector Thomas Cromwell was executed in 1540. He was in danger again: among Cromwell's papers were found documents alleging that Wyatt had conspired *with* Pole. A letter from

---

[30] John Watkins, '"Wrastling for This World": Wyatt and the Tudor Canonization of Chaucer', in *Refiguring Chaucer in the Renaissance*, ed. Theresa M. Krier (Gainesville: University Press of Florida, 1998), pp. 21–39 (31–2).

[31] Chris Stamatakis, *Sir Thomas Wyatt and the Rhetoric of Rewriting* (Oxford University Press, 2013), p. 137.

[32] Patricia Thomson, *Sir Thomas Wyatt and His Background* (London: Routledge and Kegan Paul, 1964), p. 41.

Wyatt's enemy, the Bishop of London Edmund Bonner, quoted Wyatt making indelicate (and potentially treasonous) remarks about wishing the king would be cast out of the cart's arse. Bonner was intent on incriminating the poet, but his testimony reveals that Wyatt could not forgive and forget his incarceration. Wyatt:

> dooth ofte call to his remembrance his emprisonment in the Towere, whiche semeth soo to sticke in his stomacke that he can not forget it. And his manner of speking therein is after this sorte, "Goddes bludde! was not that a prety sending of me ambassadour to th'emperour, first to put me into the Towre, and then furthewith to sende me hither? This was a waye in dede to get me credite here. By Goddes preciouse bludde, I had rather the king shuld set me in Newgate then soo doo."[33]

His imprisonment stuck in his stomach, or his mind. As a result of Bonner's testimony, Wyatt was arrested for a third time and taken in a most undignified way to the Tower of London, 'so bound and handcuffed that everyone could only suppose ill, for it is the custom in this country to take them to prison unbound, being well assured that they could not escape'.[34] His house at Allington was searched and his plate and other goods were taken for the king.

Wyatt's descriptions of prison stress its privations, and the distinction between the suffering body and the unfettered mind that has been a central trope of prison writing since Boethius. (Wyatt himself translated Boethius, who also exerted an influence on his poetry through Chaucer.)[35] One poem seems to have been written in captivity:

> Syghes ar my foode, drynke are my teares;
> Clynkinge of fetters suche musycke wolde crave;
> Stynke and close ayer away my lyf wears;
> Innocencie is all the hope I have.
> Rayne, wynde, or wether I iudge by myne eares.
> Mallice assaulted that rightiousnes should have:
> Sure I am, Brian, this wounde shall heale agayne,
> But yet, alas, the scarre shall styll remayne.
>
> (242)

The prisoner in Wyatt's poem is famished but self-sustaining: he eats his sighs and drinks his tears. He is isolated from the outside world but retains

---

[33] Powell (ed.), 'Bonners Accusations, Blois' (2 September 1538), in *Wyatt* vol. 1: *Prose*, pp. 328–9.
[34] Marillac, letter to King of France, J. Kaulek, *Correspondence Politique* (1885), pp. 261–3; Muir, *Life and Letters*, p. 176.
[35] Patricia Thomson, 'Wyatt's Boethian Ballade', *Review of English Studies* ns 15.59 (Aug. 1964), pp. 262–7.

his social connections (Wyatt addresses his friend Sir Francis Bryan). He can also displace the clinking of fetters with the 'music' of his own poetic feet. This moment leaves a scar, a sign of the reputational and physical injury caused by incarceration. The poem's continuous present represents this wound as simultaneously healed and unhealed, liable to be reopened each time the poem is read. The scar/poem as a site of a perpetually reopening wound can also be understood as an example of dehiscence in the Lacanian sense. Jacques Lacan uses this botanical and medical term to describe a 'vital dehiscence constitutive of man': the subject is split in the mirror stage, his desire for the object of the other's desire awakens, giving rise to aggressive competition, 'from which develops the triad of other people, ego, and object'.[36] The scar that marks the sealing of the subject within the symbolic, and his vulnerability to rupture, will recur throughout this book.

Muir dates this poem to 1541, on the basis that the final couplet is echoed in the speech Wyatt was then preparing for his defence following the fall of Cromwell.[37] In that statement, Wyatt affirmed his fidelity to the king, calling attention to his onerous ambassadorial service. He refers to the Treasons Act of 1534, which defined treason as to 'maliciously wish, will or desire by words or writing, or by craft imagine, invent, practise, or attempt any bodily harm' to the king. Wyatt, who did not have to prove the innocence merely of his action or words, but also his imagination, declares that he had never offended against the King 'in dede, worde, wrytinge or wysshe'; nor had he done anything secretly against his master: 'as God iudge me I am clere of thought'.[38] Nothing was stuck in his mind that might threaten his master.

Wyatt also focuses his defence on the specificity of language. When everything hangs on the interpretation of a word as the evidence of a private intention, all that's required is for one's enemy to make an emendation: 'yt is a smale thynge in alteringe of one syllable ether with penne or worde that may mayke in the conceavinge of the truthe myche matter or error. For in thys thynge "I fere," or "I truste," semethe but one smale sylbable chaynged, and yet yt makethe a great dyfferaunce'.[39] As Seth

---

[36] Jacques Lacan, 'Aggresiveness in Psychoanalysis', *Écrits*, trans. Bruce Fink (New York: W. W. Norton, 2002), pp. 82–101 (94, 92).
[37] Muir, *Life and Letters*, p. 185; 'For tho he hele the wounde yet the scharre shall remayne', *ibid.*, p. 193; Susan Brigden, '"The shadow that you know": Sir Thomas Wyatt and Sir Francis Bryan', *Historical Journal* 39.1 (March 1996), pp. 1–31 (30).
[38] Powell (ed.), 'Wyatt's Declaration', *Wyatt* vol. 1: *Prose*, p. 293.
[39] Powell (ed.), 'Wyatt's Defence', in *Wyatt* vol. 1: *Prose*, p. 308.

Lerer points out, this steadfastness is ironic given the instability of Wyatt's corpus and the regularising interventions of his editor Richard Tottel.[40] A word can be turned from truth to lie, and torn from its context, with the change of a syllable: similarly, in More's *Utopia*,

> Bona uerba inquit Petrus, mihi uisum est non ut seruias regibus, sed ut inseruias. Hoc est inquit ille, una syllaba plusquam seruias.
>
> 'Well said,' Peter replied, 'but I do not mean that you should be in servitude to any king, only in his service.'
> 'The difference is only a matter of one syllable,' Raphael replied.[41]

There is only a syllable's difference between being a servant, and subservient; between service and slavery. Wyatt's defence, or perhaps his service or the entreaties of Katherine Howard, were sufficient to ensure his release; officially he was said to have confessed. Nonetheless, the accusations reveal the lingering force of imprisonment on Wyatt's table talk, and his capacity for indiscretion.

The Knot of Service

Wyatt's tumultuous diplomatic career exposed him to domination by his own and foreign monarchs, but it also gave him opportunities to manifest the exculpatory power of eloquence. The work of an ambassador, called an 'orator' in this period, was to present both his master's wishes and himself through rhetorical performances. Cromwell instructed him:

> Your parte shalbe nowe like a good Oratour, bothe to set furthe the princely nature and inclynacion of his highness with all dexteritie, and soo to obserue Themperours answers to the said Ouerture ... as you may therby fishe oiut the botom of his stomake.[42]

His job is not only to speak, but to attend to the effects of his speech: to observe, in the attempt to draw out the secrets held within the body of a king. Wyatt was often forced by delays in communication to improvise and invent in his own person a simulacrum of the royal will. Symbolising and exercising power without possessing it, the ambassador had to speak for the monarch persuasively, but not lose himself in the performance. This

---

[40] Seth Lerer, *Courtly Letters in the Age of Henry VIII* (Cambridge University Press, 1997), p. 188.
[41] Thomas More, *Utopia*, ed. George M. Logan and Robert M. Adams (Cambridge University Press, 1989), p. 13. I'm grateful to Jessica Wolfe for referring to this passage during a discussion at UNC.
[42] Letter, 10 October 1537; quoted in Thomson, *Sir Thomas Wyatt and His Background*, p. 46.

splitting and doubling mirrors the many torn subjects we will find in Wyatt's poems, and recalls the hind who speaks for Caesar through the poet (or vice versa).

Wyatt prolongs a courtly tradition that portrays love and sex as 'my seruice and my hiere' (32), depicting political and amorous service as enslavement. As Patricia Thomson has argued, by this point in history 'the master-servant link had, in fact, lost most of its feudal strength. At most, the master represented an intermediate loyalty between servant and state.'[43] Wyatt's feudal role-playing can read like a defensive recursion to archaic models of service and protection in response to intrusive Tudor politics.[44] But the eroticisation of political service is also a way of placing the master or mistress under an obligation. In many of Wyatt's poems, the lyric subject enters voluntarily into submission, contracting a reciprocal relation with the master or mistress through the gift of his heart. I offer my 'hart and servys' to you; 'take yt to yow jentylly' and 'Reward your servant liberally' (193), he asks. Marcel Mauss analysed gift-giving as establishing relationships of reciprocity.[45] Wyatt repeatedly reminds the master or mistress of their obligations to the servant: 'And syns so muche I do desire / To be your owne assuryddly, / Ffor all my servys and my hyer / Reward your servant liberally' (99); 'Then sins that I have neuer swarfde, / Let not my paines be ondeseruid' (32): my pains are undeserved if I, the servant, am not served. The subjection of the speaker to the master or mistress in these poems involves not the total surrender of his rights, but an opportunity to articulate them. Unlike an actually enslaved person, a 'speaking instrument' whose voice must only articulate the wishes of his master, Wyatt's subject speaks for himself, performing enslavement as dissent. He makes demands; he is bitter; he expresses pain. The poem documents his irrepressible voice, even in conditions of abjection.

Wyatt's slave of love frequently protests that he cannot exercise his own free will; he must move and suffer according to the arbitrary desires of his master or mistress. In 'Myne olde dere En'mye, my forward master' (5), the speaker is ruled by a 'wicked traytour', the 'obstinate will' to love, which 'robbeth my libertie with displeasure' (6). He tries to flee, but love chases him 'Thorough desert wodes and sherp high mountaignes, / Thoroughe frowarde people and straite pressions' (7). In response, the master ridicules the speaker, who still 'stryveth with the bit, / Which may ruell him and do

---

[43] Thomson, *Sir Thomas Wyatt and His Background*, p. 52.
[44] Jonathan Kamholtz, 'Thomas Wyatt's Poetry: The Politics of Love', *Criticism* 20 (1978), p. 353.
[45] Marcel Mauss, *The Gift: Forms and Functions of Exchange in Archaic Societies*, trans. Ian Cunnison (London: Cohen & West, 1966).

him pleasure and pain' (p. 9). Submitting to the 'bit' and allowing the master to ride him wherever it pleases will save him the unnecessary pain of choosing to serve his own will. That Wyatt resented being ridden thus by his masters is apparent in his defence of his embassy in 1541:

> I, as God iudge me, lyke as I was contynually imagininge and cumpassinge what waye I myght do beste service, so restede I not day nor nyght to hunte owte for knowledge of those thynges; I trotted contynually vp and downe that hell throughe heate and stinke from councelloure to embassator, from on frende to an other.[46]

Wyatt has had to move under compulsion, 'trotting' like a beast determined to offer his 'beste service'. Surrey memorialised this constant motion in his epitaph: 'Wyatt resteth here, that quick could never rest'.

The constraints experienced by Wyatt's lyric subject are mirrored by the poems' forms, rhymes and refrains. The word 'refrain' comes from the Latin *refrēnāre*, to bridle (or leash); it is at once the repetition that prompts certain dance moves, and the restriction that holds back the poem's progress, in that each stanzaic development circles back to its first premise, even as that premise is modified by its context. Some of Wyatt's refrains reflect the inescapability of love – like 'thys paynfull fytt', a fit of diseased love and of song, a seizure and a poetic division, which 'Hath last to longe' but seemingly can never come to an end ('The knott that furst my hart dyd strayn', 184). Wyatt also plays with the rondeau, accentuating its formal entrapments with virtuosic if rather fruitless repetitions: 'Yet though thy chayne hath me enwrapt / Spite of thy hap, hap hath well hapt', goes one particularly relentless one ('In faith I wot not well what to say', 19).[47] In 'Lo, what it is to love!' (66), the circular rhyme scheme enacts the speaker's entrapment in the intrigues of love:

> Ffle alwaye from the snare,
> Lerne by me to beware
> Of suche a trayne
> Which dowbles payne,
> And endles woo and care,
> That doth retayne;
> Which to refrayne,
> Fle alwaye from the snare.

---

[46] Powell (ed.), 'Wyatt's Declaration', in *Wyatt* vol. 1: *Prose*, p. 295.
[47] John Kerrigan, 'Wyatt's Selfish Style', *Essays and Studies* n.s. 34 (1981), pp. 1–18.

This poem of amorous suffering is answered by another that refutes its 'slaunder' of love point by point, prompting a third reply that moderates between the two, affirming 'Trouth' and exposing the earlier speaker as a literary artificer: 'how you fayne / Pleasure for payne', fabricating devices of 'Suche fire and suche hete' as 'Did never make ye swete' – sweet or sweat (69). But rather than resembling anything like the stages of the dialectic, these poems – the refrains within them, and the multiplication of their responses – seem to defy development, staggering around in arid stasis.

Alongside these formal devices, Wyatt illustrates his erotic and political servitude by repeated references to chains, traps, 'bayted hookes', snares, bridles, knots, binds, bands and collars:

> The knott that furst my hart dyd strayn,
>   When that thy servant I becam,
> Doth bynde me styll for to remayn
>   Always your own, as now I am . . .
> Or yff I mynd to slyp the knoot
>   By want of fayth or stedfastnes,
> Let all my servys be fogoot,
>   And when I wold haue chefe redres,
>   Esteme me nott.
>
>   (183–4)

This 'knot' translates Petrarch's '*caro nodo*'. It is a device that *binds*, in the sense both of constraining and joining together. It rhymes with the suggestive 'not' that provides the final word for each line in the strambotto 'A lady gave me a gift which she had not', and which stands in for the female genital naught.[48] It also suggests a bridle that restrains, or a halter by which the speaker might hang himself, slipping out of service and out of life.

Several of Wyatt's poems suggest that the only escape from the knot of bondage is self-destruction. 'Yf right can have no remedie', if there is no 'lawe or libretye' that can withstand the vagaries of fortune, then only death offers a release from the vicissitudes of love ('To make an ende of all this strif', 233–4). This is a Stoic argument: that freedom is guaranteed by the possibility of suicide. My 'hand in haste' can release me from suffering, and its 'dedelye stroke' will lose the bonds that 'bounde my liberte' (234). Read in Hegelian terms, the lover as slave and the lady as master are engaged in a struggle to the death.[49] He is 'abiecte' (98), but she seems unaffected by

---

[48] Stephen Foley, *Sir Thomas Wyatt* (Boston: Twayne, 1990), pp. 50–1.
[49] G. W. F. Hegel, *The Phenomenology of Spirit*, trans. A. V. Miller (Oxford University Press, 1976), §178–96, pp. 111–19.

their relation. His fear of and proximity to death, combined with the discipline of his service to the lady, produce a recognition in the lover of his determinate being; but she remains fixed in a state of shallow defiance. The poem is the thing he works on, through which he comes to know himself. The mistress's desire for this thing – the poem – is mediated through her erotic bondsman; but she makes nothing of her own, and so is barred from self-recognition. Because she lacks both the discipline of servitude and the object to work on, this cold and superficial beloved can never achieve the kind of self-knowledge Wyatt exemplifies here:

> I am as I am and so wil I be,
> But how that I am none knoith trulie;
> Be yt evill, be yt well, be I bonde, be I fre,
> I am as I am and so will I be.
>
> (148)

Whether I am bound or free, I alone know who I truly am.

Wyatt claims that 'I am' constant, in the present and future; you 'know no more then afore ye knew' when you first met me. But that inscrutability also leaves the 'I' in this poem as a vacant mean: not rejoicing, not complaining, not mirthful or sad, just an assertion of bare subjectivity. This figure is at the heart of Wyatt's poetry, and it has led critics including John Kerrigan to attribute the anonymity of Wyatt's speakers to a 'profound distrust of the world beyond the self'.[50] As Cathy Shrank observes, Wyatt repeatedly turns Petrarchan poems in the third-person to first-person narratives, while also stripping out some of the identifying features of Petrarch's poems which provide specific and named contexts for the poems, in order to 'maintain a layer of protective opacity'.[51] It is this subjectivity without personality that may fit Wyatt out so neatly as a modern: his poetry reveals the process by which the subject comes to know himself through his encounters with loss and oppression; the lyric form allows that privileged, white male aristocratic subject to retain its autonomy through a kind of resistant indirectness that appeals to readers beneath the censorious gaze of the sovereign.

This is an explanation of the kind of 'self' that Wyatt fashions in these poems: plastic, inscrutable, but persistent. But I would also argue that a feature of Wyatt's modernity is the way the lady is instrumentalised in his poems. The servant comes to self-knowledge and frees himself from dependence on the mistress not only through his work on the lyric object,

---

[50] Kerrigan, 'Wyatt's Selfish Style', p. 14.
[51] Cathy Shrank, '"But I, that knew what harbred in that hed": Sir Thomas Wyatt and his Posthumous "Interpreters", *Proceedings of the British Academy* 154 (2008), pp. 375–401 (381, 393–5).

but because he originally possesses the social power and autonomy that she lacks. In other words, Wyatt's erotic lyrics mimic and invert a relation of political dominance, pretending to the condition of servitude and relishing the continuity of mastery. The lover emerges in his particularity through suffering, but the lady remains vague and unspecific. She is an occasion for performance that the poet makes his own. His specificity is manufactured at the cost of hers. We know little about him, but nothing about her except her effects.

While Wyatt as ambassador was called upon to speak for the king, the king could speak very well for himself. This is a crucial distinction with the lady in these poems. The hierarchy in their erotic or lyric relation inverts the actual social relation (patriarchy). Like the slave or the animal, the lady's voice and volition are suppressed; when she does speak, her question – 'how like you this?' – is a reflection of the wishes and pleasures of the male subject. Maria Menocal has traced the troubadour lyric and the courtly love paradigm back to the songs of enslaved Arabic women, taken to Provence from Arab al-Andalus by Guillaume de Montreuil. Her account is a reminder that the suppression of the female or enslaved voice in lyric history is not total.[52] But if lyric is one of the means by which a resistant, politicised subject is invented for modernity, then the erasure of these voices as an original and constitutive feature of lyric contributes to their exclusion from political recognition as subjects.

Turned and Torn

The gift of the heart in Wyatt's poems of erotic and political service is an emblem of the violent division of the self into parts in the erotic encounter that we might call *jouissance*. In 'Alas the greiff, and dedly wofull smert' (3), the speaker addresses the self as a composite of parts – service, pain, a pitiful heart, a faithful mind – and instructs them all to 'Retourn, Alas, sethens thou art not regarded'. The gifts of love are 'presented' and 'repented', given and called back. This fort-da movement contrasts with the changeful beloved, who is able freely and 'vnconstantly to raunge' (4). Finally the speaker resolves that 'Though pece mele in peces though I be torne', I shall never let anything 'again make me retorne' (6). The poem's repetitions – piecemeal pieces, turn and return, rhyme – suggest an entrapment that will

---

[52] Maria Menocal, *The Arabic Role in Medieval Literary History: A Forgotten Heritage* (Philadelphia: University of Pennsylvania Press, 1987), p. 27.

not yield to this resolution. But the fragmented pieces are gathered into the coherence of a poem, that turns, and resists being torn apart.

Wyatt's poems are obsessed with *tourning*, that which is torn and turned, in the circle of Fortune's wheel or the whirling of desire. The speakers are encircled by enemies (*Circumdederunt me inimici mei*), dwelling in a court around which thunder circles: *circa Regna tonat*. They are tossed and turned and torn. Like Orpheus scattered by the Thracian women, the speaker finds himself torn 'pece mele in peces'; suddenly, 'My hart was torne owte of hys place' ('So vnwarely was never no man cawght', 202). In another poem, the lover 'Within my bons to rankle is assind'; he resents his bonds, which 'rankle' like physical shackles. Here, the torn place is a wound, in which a weapon turns: 'In diepe wid wound the dedly strok doth torne / To curid skarre that neuer shall retorne' ('What rage is this? what furor of what kynd?', 83). Jeff Dolven describes Wyatt's style as 'self-sabotaging', betraying through its 'unanchored pronouns' and 'fragmentation of his speakers into a mix of anatomical and grammatical parts' an anxiety that 'rhetoric cannot hold him together'.[53] Love splits the subject into pieces. Poetry mobilises this fragmentary subject within the labyrinthine spaces of its formal enclosures, turning the torn self to a trope.

Reading Wyatt this way claims him for modernity. However, returning Wyatt to his medieval context would mean reversing the modern association between lyric speakers, individuality and desire. Robert Meyer-Lee describes the voice of Ricardian lyric as 'typically ... anonymous', an assumed male or female plaintive voice emptied of particularity whose anonymity signified a 'striving toward the disclosure of a *homo interior* that is individuated but undifferentiated, an *imago Dei* that is the same for all human beings'. In that context, it is sin that particularises, jeopardising our 'essential divine sameness'.[54] Desire vitiates the subject rather than creating worlds. The particularity of Wyatt's speakers does seem to confirm Meyer-Lee's proposition: they are most specific when they are enfeebled by love, or driven to sadistic fantasies of revenge. The beloved is less particular and identifiable, perhaps because she is more powerful, less injured.

Attending to the frequency of the word 'torn' in Wyatt also offers a different perspective on that famous line: 'But all is torned thorough my gentilnes' (27). Here Wyatt courts the paradox of how tenderness and

---

[53] Jeff Dolven, 'Reading Wyatt for the Style,' *Modern Philology* 105 (Aug. 2007), pp. 65–86 (84–5).
[54] Robert J. Meyer-Lee, *Poets and Power from Chaucer to Wyatt* (Cambridge University Press, 2007), pp. 29–30.

timidity might be turned back and torn apart. This tearing can be done by the turning of a word; all words can be turned, otherwise what's the point of that riddle, still puzzling the historians: 'what wourde is that that chaungeth not, / Though it be tourned and made in twain?' (36). The 'answer' is often imagined to be 'Anne, sir', or 'An, na' – no, nay. But rather than a particular woman, the poem might lead us towards an inscrutable 'I': a word that is the same coming and going. I am as I am and so will I be, however hard I am turned. But the symmetry of the 'I' should not distract us from the riddle's stipulation that to be turned is also to be torn in two. The tearing and turning memorialised in Wyatt's poems are products of repetition – indeed, the poems are themselves that repetition, formally, and thematically, reopening their wounds with each recitation. And the tropes of turning and tearing brought together in the early modern 'torn' are allied metaphorically to *verse*-making, literally a form of turning back; the turning wheel of Fortune; lathe work; and trickery.[55]

Orpheus may have tamed the wild beasts with his song; but he was paid for his service by being torn apart. The violent *sparagmos* of Wyatt's speakers also infects the images of women who are always 'turning' with the vicissitudes of love: for 'womens love is but a blast / And torneth like the wynde' ('A! Robyn', 41). Trying to catch this turning wind, the heart which 'change[s] or torne[s] as wether and wynd' ('Ys yt possyble', 195), will leave you with only a torn net. Erasmus explains in his *Adagia* that the proverb 'in a net to hold the wind' is 'used of people who toil in vain, or who chase foolishly after things they have no hope of catching, or who snatch in a futile way after futility'.[56] Behind that adage is Ecclesiastes 1:14: all is vanity, and a chasing after wind. The net also recalls Wyatt's translation of Plutarch's *The Quyete of Mynde*, where those who strive for power are criticised for foolishness and compared to those who get 'angry with fortune', and 'with vayn indevour / hunt an hart with a dragge net / and nat that they attempt to do those impossibilytes by their owne madnesse and folysshnesse'.[57] The net in which we seek to hold the wind is a figure for fugitivity, like the fruitless chase after the hind.

Wyatt describes the fool who follows his desire as fated to awake one day 'Mashed in the breers that erst was all to torne', both stuck and ripped to pieces, 'boeth sprong and spent': a sprung trap, an animal sprung from its

---

[55] Heather Dubrow, *The Challenges of Orpheus: Lyric Poetry and Early Modern England* (Baltimore: Johns Hopkins University Press, 2008), p. 22–9.
[56] Cited in Mary Thomas Crane, *Framing Authority: Sayings, Self, and Society in Sixteenth-Century England* (Princeton University Press, 1993), p. 159.
[57] Muir, *Collected Poems*, p. 452.

cover, spent or wasted, like money, bodily energy and semen ('Some tyme I fled the fyre that me brent', 44). An animal caught in a trap might also tear itself apart, trying to escape. Wyatt's poems are filled with such imagery, which draws on hunting and animal husbandry to portray love as pursuit, evasion and wounding. The cruelty of these images is filtered for modern readers not just through a cognisance of the suffering of animals bonded to us, as Donna Haraway would say, in significant otherness; but of the many times since Wyatt wrote that human beings have been hunted and torn apart by dogs and traps.[58]

The Wild to Temper

Wyatt often compares success or failure in seduction to the methods used to tame wild animals. With other animals, men 'some way, some tyme, may so contrive / By mens the wild to temper and tame'; even the lion shows some mercy to those 'that sueth mekenes' ('Processe of tyme worketh such wounder', 61). But the beloved is like a 'fiers Tigre', who gets less subdued 'the lenger I pray'. She is an animal who can prey on others, but who won't submit to his management – no matter how much I 'pray' to or on her. Sometimes the speaker himself is the prey, trapped by the beloved: 'Tanglid I was yn loves snare', like a 'birde tanglid yn lyme'; but 'ha ha ha', 'I am nowe at libretye', having escaped with 'no hurte' (227–8). Or the lover is a beast of burden, or a domesticated animal like the 'hounde that hath his keper lost' ('For want of will, in wo I playne', 246), or a hawk starved into submission: 'Refrain I must; what is the cause? / Sure as they say: so hawkes be taught' ('Suche happe as I ame happed in', 27). Wyatt's animal imagery is not only a way of representing the violence of unrequited love; it also explores the themes of liberty and constancy, embodied by animals whose wild instincts are forced to submit to serve their human masters.

In many of these poems, the tamer is singular, the animal part of a herd, just as Wyatt frames many of his poems as the expressions of individual desire addressed to a collective of readers. A poem on 'Luckes [Lux], my faire falcon', possibly written from Allington in 1540 after Cromwell's execution but before his own arrest, contrasts Wyatt's faithful hawks with friends who abandoned him in his adversity:

---

[58] Donna Haraway, *The Companion Species Manifesto: Dogs, People, and Significant Otherness* (Chicago: Prickly Paradigm Press, 2003), p. 8.

> Luckes, my faire falcon, and your fellowes all,
> How well pleasaunt yt were your libertie!
> Ye not forsake me that faire might ye befall.
> But they that somtyme lykt my companye
> Like lyse awaye from ded bodies thei crall:
> Loe what a profe in light adversytie!
> But ye, my birdes, I swear by all your belles,
> Ye be my fryndes, and so be but few elles.
>
> (241)

The falcons are proclaimed true 'friends', but they are trained through deprivation and controlled by traces. Their fidelity is sworn on their 'bells', insignia of their constraint and mechanism for their recovery if they did attempt to 'forsake' the speaker. In this way, the poem epitomises the fragile relatedness with which so many of Wyatt's poems of hunting seem to culminate. As Catherine Bates has argued, Wyatt's representation of the falcon who neither abandons his keeper nor tears him to pieces is an emblem of the 'courtesy' of man and beast, a relation not of coercion but of fleeting cooperation and mutual service.[59] Yet Wyatt's poetry is populated by many fierce animals who show no tolerance for their masters and threaten to tear them apart.

To create the wild and the domestic as categories is to decide what can be bound and what cannot. But Wyatt's poems, many of which take place in the hinterlands of managed forest that are neither completely wild nor tamed, often symbolise the irruption of the other's true self as the return of an animal to its 'kind'. This trope is also familiar from white supremacist discourses around the 'civilising' process and the tendency of Indigenous people to 'revert' to their savage natures: the plasticity, as Zakiyyah Iman Jackson puts it, of 'black(ened) flesh'.[60] It is a trope that can be found in the *Consolatio* of Boethius, which Wyatt and Chaucer both translated. In Chaucer's version, caged animals, bird and lion, may seem subdued; the Punic lion bound in 'fair[e] cheines' can be taught to take meat from her keeper's hands. But if once she tastes blood, then 'Hir corage / of tyme passeþ þat haþ ben ydel *and* rested. repaireþ / aȝein'. She remembers her nature, '*and* slaken hir nekkes from hir cheins vnbounden', tears her keepers to pieces and escapes to the woods. Likewise, the bird who is captured and 'inclosed in a streit cage': however carefully she is fed, once she sees the 'agreable shadewes of þe wodes' she will be consumed by

---

[59] Catherine Bates, *Masculinity and the Hunt: Wyatt to Spenser* (Oxford University Press, 2013), p. 51.
[60] Zakiyyah Iman Jackson, *Becoming Human: Matter and Meaning in an Antiblack World* (New York University Press, 2020), p. 19.

longing for freedom in the woodland. So all things seek again their proper course. Human or animal nature 'chaungeþ nat fro*m* hys *pro*pre kynde'.[61]

In Boethius' argument, these captive animals symbolise a constant universe in which each thing returns to its providentially assigned nature. But they also militate against notions of moral pedagogy. The animal, like Aristotle's natural slave, cannot learn; it is a prisoner of its nature. To be 'kyndely' served, in the language of 'They flee from me', is thus to be treated no better or worse than according to what we would describe as the animal's natural instinct. The 'kindness' of the human and animal species is opposed to the 'gentileness' of a politic humanity, rooted in the *gens*, the tribe. Taming wild creatures is traditionally men's work; and the suspicion that these creatures are only pretending to be tame but will revert to their true nature at the earliest opportunity, feeds into misogynist discourse around women's inclinations to infidelity and betrayal. As Othello says, comparing his wife to a hawk:

> If I do prove her haggard,
> Though that her jesses were my dear heart-strings,
> I'd whistle her off and let her down the wind
> To prey at fortune.[62]

As Sean Benson has argued, early modern comparisons between wife-taming and animal-training drew on Xenophon's *Oeconomicus*, which compared a woman to a horse that needs to be broken. But the hawk metaphor was perhaps more attractive to Wyatt because trainable hawks are usually female and are gendered as such in falconry manuals.[63] In these examples, Wyatt plays on his masculine prerogative to hunt and hawk and tame. But that prerogative also extends to the ease with which he switches identification between hunter and hunted.

These complex relations between human and animal life, wildness and tameness, predator and prey, culminate in Wyatt's best-known poem:

> They fle from me that sometyme did me seke
> With naked fote stalking in my chambre.
> I have sene theim gentill tame and meke
> That nowe are wyld and do not remembre
> That sometyme they put theimself in daunger

---

[61] Geoffrey Chaucer, *Chaucer's Translation of Boethius's 'De Consolatione Philosophiae'*, ed. Richard Morris (Oxford, 1868 [1969]), Book III, p. 68.
[62] William Shakespeare, *Othello*, ed. E. A. J. Honigmann (London: Arden, 1996), 3.3.264–7.
[63] Sean Benson, '"If I Do Prove Her Haggard": Shakespeare's Application of Hawking Tropes to Marriage', *Studies in Philology* 103.2 (Spring 2006), pp. 186–207 (188–9).

> To take bred at my hand; and nowe they raunge
> Besely seking with a continuell chaunge.
>
> Thancked be fortune, it hath ben othrewise
> Twenty tymes better; but ons in speciall
> In thyn arraye after a pleasaunt gyse
> When her lose gowne from her shoulders did fall,
> And she me caught in her armes long and small;
> Therewithall swetely did me kysse,
> And softely said 'dere hert, howe like you this?'
>
> It was no dreme: I lay brode waking.
> But all is torned thorough my gentilnes
> Into a straunge fasshion of forsaking;
> And I have leve to goo of her goodenes,
> And she also to vse new fangilnes.
> But syns that I so kyndely ame served,
> I would fain knowe what she hath deserved.
>
> (27)

Kenneth Muir and Patricia Thomson note that the opening expression follows a poem by Charles d'Orléans, another poet writing poems from prison about being imprisoned by love: 'They flee fro me they dar not onys abide'.[64] But what is it that 'With naked fote' are 'stalking in my chambre' in Wyatt's poem? Former lovers, but what else? The poem's dreamlike looseness should be a preservative against excessively strict allegorical interpretation. Nonetheless, critics have seized on its scant particulars, attempting to penetrate its gauzy ethos of power and desire. There is much debate even about what 'kind' of animal they are. Most critics think of 'them' as deer – making her gentle naming of the speaker as 'dere hert' (deer hart) a kind of punning recognition of a shared animality. Ann Berthoff, surely too pragmatically, argues that 'they' are birds, because it's hard to get deer inside a chamber;[65] as Thomas Greene observes, stalking can denote the bird's stiff steps, or the hunter's stealthy approach.[66] Richard Leighton Greene cites a fifteenth-century carol that clearly attributes to women the submissive ability to 'take bred a manus hand', to argue that no animals whatever are invoked in the poem: that it is simply an erotic image of a human woman.[67]

---

[64] R. Steele and M. Day (eds.), *The English Poems of Charles of Orleans*, Early English Text Society Original Series 215 (Oxford University Press, 1941), p. 46.
[65] Ann Berthoff, 'The Falconer's Dream of Trust: Wyatt's "They fle from me"', *Sewanee Review* 71.3 (Summer 1963), pp. 477–94 (483).
[66] Greene, *The Light in Troy*, p. 257.
[67] Richard Leighton Greene, 'Wyatt's "They fle from me" and the Busily Seeking Critics', *Bucknell Review* 12 (1964), pp. 17–30.

Wyatt's poem does not fix the animals as a particular kind; the poem is, after all, about their powers to wander and transform. At first, 'they' are tamed (taking bread at my hand); now they run away, returning to their wild nature; but they are also stalking him, turning him to the prey who is confined to a bedchamber (infidelity as the ability to range, constancy as being fixed in place). The poem shifts from a species characteristic ('they') to a particular instance ('ons in special'), before finally isolating the subject ('I lay broad waking'). 'They' become a singular 'she' who surrenders voluntarily to a momentary captivity in the lover's chamber: he can be hunter again, separating out the vulnerable individual from the herd. Whereas it is usually the poet who writes him or herself into a prison of form in order to enjoy his or her creative liberties, in this case it is the object of desire who undertakes that temporary captivity. She preserves some of her original wildness, and brings it into the chamber like the cold scent of the forest. In her embrace, the speaker becomes the 'dear heart' or hart. Once he was tracked and 'caught', now 'All is torned': turned and torn, by my gentleness, and her strangeness, tameness and wildness tumbling in memorial circles. Her turning contrasts with the stasis he must maintain in order for her to approach. But the poem's turning, the turning of tropes, allows him to range, seeking out a continual change that is not trapped in a circular form.

They stalk not with weapons or nets, but with a 'naked foot'. In Ovid's elegies, as we'll see, the naked foot is a sign of erotic intimacy. The singular 'foot' separates the animal from the herd ('ons in special'), and signals that we are moving from a general principle to a particular case; it evokes the unshoed hoof (another way the poem's animal references dissolve: deer are never shod), as well as a quietness and stealth that characterises the poem itself. But it is also an unfettered foot, free of the 'clog' that might keep it from clearing the dike and escaping, and ready to run.

Jean-Paul Sartre said that 'The Other is on principle inapprehensible; he flees me when I seek him and possesses me when I flee him.'[68] This is the paradox of courtly love, rendered as an existential condition of all relations. Desire entails motion towards an object that can never end, unless desire itself comes to an end. Augustine argued, in Hannah Arendt's paraphrase, that love is 'a kind of motion, and all motion is toward something'.[69] This is not the motion of the trotting ambassador; it is closer to the ranging of

---

[68] Jean-Paul Sartre, *Being and Nothingness*, trans. Hazel E. Barnes (London: Routledge, [1958] 1993), p. 408.
[69] Hannah Arendt, *Love and Saint Augustine*, trans. Joanna Vecchiarelli Scott and Judith Celius Stark (University of Chicago Press, 1996), p. 9.

the faithless object or free master, whose constant motion *away* from me draws me after: 'Yet may I by no meanes my weried mynde / Drawe from the Diere: but as she fleeth afore / Faynting I folowe.' And after all, perhaps it's better that way. To seize the object of desire threatens its loss, and occasions fewer poems. Anne Carson suggests as much: eros exists 'because certain boundaries do ... the boundary of flesh and self between you and me'.[70] The boundary turns space into desire. The boundary – the dike or fence around the landowner's property which the hobbled animal or enslaved person cannot leap without trapping or impaling itself – also turns space into property. In the gap between self and other, wild and tame, the motion towards the other – which is love and in which lyric can be written – is possible.

The vivid intimacy of desire that ends without ever ending is preserved in this poem, which also ends without ever ending. The poem is a space that can be endlessly revisited, so that its different kinds of ending can be experienced anew. How does the poem end? By inviting readers to make a judicial decision. The poem enacts his penalty for loving too well – the endless re-turn to the memory of pleasure that has disappeared. Maybe he gets what he deserves. But what does she deserve, now that she has released him from serving? This rhetorical question is similar to the ending of 'Like as the byrde in the cage enclosed' (243). That poem describes a choice: 'Twixte deth and prison', liberty 'By losse off liefe' or life deprived of liberty. Like the bird that escapes its cage only to find 'the hawke without', the speaker has an artificial liberty to choose the brief pain of death, or a long life of 'thraldome and doloure' in captivity. Wyatt invites the reader to act as jury to the speaker's case, and concludes by soliciting 'Your aduise, yowe louers, wyche shalbe best' (244)? Neither 'Like as the byrde' nor 'They flee' include a reply. The question is not answered by the imagined audience of readers, perhaps because what she deserves is obvious; or because it isn't. The reader can either share in the speaker's sense of injustice and participate in a collective work of imagining her punishment, or (as I do) repeatedly return to the poem's scene of gentleness turned to forsaking to ask that question again. If this feels like stalling, it is very different from the failure to progress that I kicked against in my discussion of Wyatt's refrains.

Like the hind, Wyatt was bound to speak Caesar's words. But he preserved a distinction: I am as I am and so will I be, no matter how tame I may seem. His poems hold in balance artful symmetries of power

---

[70] Anne Carson, *Eros the Bittersweet* (Champaign: Dalkey Archive, 1998), p. 30.

and weakness, flight and containment, wildness and tameness, sovereign and poetic inscription, and so provoke remarkably ambivalent readings. He complained that he was forced to trot up and down like a beast in service to the king. Retreating, inwardly or outwardly, to chambers or country estates, the heart's forest or the anonymity of a pained lyric 'I', does not obliviate the conditions of political dominance for which Wyatt was employed to speak. Rather, the poems recall that tense and tender moment in which the animal approaches, seeming tame but ready to break into wildness at the slightest trigger, as a way of dwelling with the complexities of submission and autonomy, civility and desire.

Wyatt's service to his mistresses is never far from his obligations to his king, but neither is she just a decoy; we can hear in her resistance to his love the whispers of resistance to patriarchal domination. His poems articulate the subjection of the self by constructing another, a mistress, animal or a slave, who cannot speak for herself. She is free insofar as she can no longer be touched, wild only when he attempts to hold her: it is that effort to touch that elicits who 'I am', rather than who 'I seem' to be. But there is another way of reading this injunction, *Noli me tangere*: as the most catastrophic of the prison's prohibitions, that turns the prisoner into an object not to be touched, an animal to be handled at the end of a chain. As one incarcerated person wrote to the legal theorist Colin Dayan, 'If they only touch you when you're at the end of a chain, then they can't see you as anything but a dog. Now I can't see my face in the mirror. I've lost my skin. I can't feel my mind.'[71]

---

[71] Colin Dayan, *The Law is a White Dog: How Legal Rituals Make and Unmake Persons* (Princeton University Press, 2011), p. 80.

CHAPTER 2

The Ligature
Rob Halpern's Common Place *and the Limits of Desire*

> *The body dead, the spirit had his desire;*
> *Painless was the one, the other in delight.*
>
> – *Thomas Wyatt*

I began my analysis of lyric whiteness and its adoption of voluntary, metaphoric constraints through a discussion of Thomas Wyatt's poems as key sites for the establishment of English Petrarchanism, and of the modern self-disciplining lyric subject. Wyatt's speakers retreat from political power into the spaces of intimacy, where in winter they can enjoy hunting and hawking and reading, free in their status as property owners even when subject to the tyrannical will of the king. These poems suppress the voices of their feminised, animal and enslaved objects in order to fashion a dissenting lyric subject whose privileges are hidden behind his performance of suffering. The white, male, property-owning, aristocratic subject can choose to represent himself as hunter or hunted, in pain or retired, human tamer or wild animal. And while Wyatt's poetics must be understood in his specific context, his use of the absented other to explore his subject position in relation to the sovereign are structures that some contemporary political poetry continues to inhabit.

Following the figural method I mapped in the introduction, I turn now to the poetry of the contemporary American poet Rob Halpern. Halpern lives and works between Michigan and San Francisco, and his work is in many ways shaped by New Narrative, a community of writers, artists and friends in the Bay Area whose queering of prose – as Halpern describes it – involves an 'apparent commitment to storytelling (where the narrative stakes hangs on specific bodies, often abject and marginalised, in specific communities whose boundaries often get delimited by scandal and gossip)'.[1] Halpern relates this politicised narrativisation of abjection to:

---

[1] Andy Fitch, 'Interview with Rob Halpern,' in *Sixty Morning Talks* (New York: Ugly Duckling Presse, 2014), pp. 308–316 (311): uglyducklingpresse.org/wp-content/uploads/2019/05/SixtyTalksDP.pdf (accessed 4 May 2021).

the model offered by queer art in its struggle to respond to AIDS in the late 1980s when an artwork might have had to refuse everything 'proper' about mourning, everything quiet, distant, ideal, abstract – to the point even of refusing the common sense of sympathy and compassion, whose norms often sadly serve to stabilize the status quo – in order to politicize loss under violent conditions determined to neutralise it: Throwing ashes on the White House lawn vs. Quilting panels on the Mall.[2]

This elegiac radicalism is perceptible in Halpern's book *Common Place*, published in 2015. *Common Place* is the fourth book in a tetralogy including *Rumored Place* (Krupskaya, 2004), *Disaster Suites* (Palm Press, 2009), and *Music for Porn* (Nightboat, 2012). These works concern capitalism, militarisation and ecological disaster. *Music for Porn* is most explicitly linked to *Common Place*, in that it focuses on the body of the injured soldier as a perverse erotic object.

Common Place is a collection of poetry, prose poems and essays, addressed to a Yemeni detainee captured by US forces in Kandahar in 2001 and taken to Guantánamo Bay detention camp.[3] This man's existence is known from an autopsy report that was published in the 'Guantánamo Docket' project by the *New York Times* in collaboration with *The Intercept*. He allegedly committed suicide in 2009 after multiple acts of self-harm. Although he was on suicide watch, he was apparently able to strangle himself using the waistband of his army-issued briefs as a ligature. Military staff found him in his cell, curled in a foetal position under a blanket. Significant discrepancies in the accounts by authorities at Guantánamo have been identified through FOIA requests by citizen journalists.[4]

The detainee's name is given only on page 32 of *Common Place*. I will not name him here, binding his name to this study and to Halpern's text for anyone who might still be searching for him. I think of Judith Butler's remark about the victims of torture in the Abu Ghraib photographs: 'Do we lament the lack of names? Yes and no. They are, and are not, ours to know.... Affirming this cognitive limit is a way of affirming the humanity that has escaped the visual control of the photographer.'[5] It is not necessary to give his name anyway, because I believe 'my detainee' in Halpern's text is

---

[2] Rob Halpern, 'THE WOUND & THE CAMP, or VISCERAL SOLIDARITY: Some Notes toward a Radical Queer Poetics', *Post-Crisis Poetics* (8 April 2017): postcrisispoetics.blogspot.com/2017/04/rob-halpern-wound-camp-or-visceral.html (accessed 4 May 2021).
[3] Rob Halpern, *Common Place* (Brooklyn: Ugly Duckling Presse, 2015).
[4] Jeffrey Kaye, 'New FOIA Documents Show Guantanamo Suicides Unlikely', *Medium* (12 October 2017): jeff-kaye.medium.com/new-foia-documents-show-guantanamo-suicides-unlikely-72ff098fe745 (accessed 4 May 2021).
[5] Judith Butler, *Frames of War: When is Life Grievable?* (London: Verso, 2016), p. 95.

not usefully understood as this specific person but as a member of a class whose identity has been stripped from him, first by his purgatorial incarceration in Guantánamo, and secondly as Wyatt's mistresses were, by becoming an object in verse.

Common Place is a utopian meditation whose object of desire is both the body of the detainee – imagined as living and dead – and the commons that he sometimes is, and sometimes seems to block. Its elegiac mood and radicalism are sifted through an eroticism that is sometimes obscene. The book's obscenity is the deliberate companion of its quest for intimacy, a way of making the links 'between private life and state violence' perceptible. Halpern has said, 'I'm interested in the way an intractable body – a body resistant to social apparatuses that would harness it to ends not its own – nevertheless gets caught up in processes of militarization that often escape perception.'[6] In order to make those processes perceptible to the privileged American reader (they are already perceptible to the detainee), the poems project love into the prison, understood as a space of exception. They attempt 'to arouse a sense of acute relation between my body and certain "nonsites" – the soldier's wound & the detainee's cell – where relation itself has been all but negated by a ubiquitous militarism that penetrates every segment of our lives'.[7]

Guantánamo is perhaps one of the sites where relation is maximally impeded, or indeed 'banned' (39).[8] As Gregoire Chamayou has argued, the individual placed under the ban is exiled from community, from law and from security. All solidarity with him is prohibited. He exists in a state of civil death, or as an animal: 'Society, which struck him with anathema by assimilating him to the beasts of the forest, "no longer recognised him as one of its members, not even as a man; or at least, it considered him fictively as deprived of life."'[9] But the gap between the desire for relation and its prohibition, between bare or animal life, civil death and the privileges of citizenship, is the space Halpern's poem wants to occupy: 'The more withdrawn my detainee, the more strenuously the sentence *my sensation delivery system* pushes against the social crust that bans relation

---

[6] Thom Donovan, 'Rob Halpern: on "Somatics"', *Harriet: The Poetry Foundation blog*: www.poetryfoundation.org/harriet/2011/04/rob-halpern-on-somatics/ (accessed 4 May 2021).
[7] Halpern, 'The WOUND'.
[8] Rob Halpern, 'Useless Commodities, Disposable Bodies: An Essay on Value and Waste', *Against Value in the Arts and Education*, ed. Sam Ladkin, Robert McKay and Emile Bojesen (London: Rowman and Littlefield, 2016), pp. 145–68.
[9] Grégoire Chamayou, *Manhunts: A Philosophical Theory*, trans. Steven Randall (Princeton University Press, 2010), p. 24.

here where it's most intense' (71); 'access barred, I fantasize relation where relation's been disfigured' (126).

Halpern's text raises many questions, such as – if the intention of the poem is 'to arouse a living intimacy', then who shares this intimacy: the intractable body of the detainee and the privileged body of the speaker, or that privileged body and the privileged reader?[10] Does the poem's staging of an ethical desire for relation *depend* on the inaccessibility of its object? I'll consider these questions by situating Halpern within the lyric tradition established not only by Mill's emphasis on poetry as the lament whose truth is guaranteed by the apparent absence of a listener, but also the Petrarchan imaginary of the absent beloved who sublimates the lyric subject's wrong desires and leads them towards heaven. Petrarch depicts Laura's body as 'the beautiful prison' (*la bella pregione*), both an object of desire and an obstruction that the spirit must escape in order for her spirit to go 'naked to Heaven' (*al Ciel nuda è gita*).[11] These tropes can also be found in Halpern's depiction of the corpse of the detainee, which figures as both an obstruction and an approach not to *Jannah* but to the heavenly absence of the commons.

Common Place is disturbing. The first time I heard Halpern perform it, in a flat in London, a number of people had to leave the room. The problems it causes are not accidental, and are indeed the subject of much of the book. My question is whether the disturbances the text may cause in a reader, that it causes in me, are only ones that have been deliberately plotted by the author. Are they a performance that leads back to the ethical rightness of the author, who controls and deploys them as a kind of cathartic pedagogy that also affirms his willingness to 'honestly' and 'vulnerably' 'risk the specificity of my own embodied position'?[12] Do the moral injuries the text seeks to cause crack open the foundations of the project itself? At issue is the violence of the relation not just between the speaker and the detainee, but between the reader and the text. Halpern repeatedly argues that 'there's no ethical view from nowhere that isn't bound to a specific body caught in the grid': that ethics is always grounded in relations between subjects.[13] There is 'no ethical view' from nowhere, but the ethical vantage of American subjects like Halpern and myself who

---

[10] Halpern, 'Useless Commodities', p. 154.
[11] On this image see Richard Strier, *The Unrepentant Renaissance: From Petrarch to Shakespeare to Milton* (University of Chicago Press, 2011), p. 72.
[12] Cosmo Spinosa, 'An Intense Desire for Relation at the Place of Relation's Prohibition: An Interview w/ Rob Halpern', *Open House* (15 Feb 2016), openhousepoetry.com/ (accessed 4 May 2021).
[13] Halpern, 'THE WOUND'.

are complicit in torture through the privileges of our citizenship is a specific situation, specifically debased. Knowing that, my aim is to stay with the trouble that is Halpern's book, revealing how it participates in the long history of association between erotic lyric and symbolic and actual bondage.

Autopsy's Cold Eye

Butler has argued that our response to the suffering of others depends on a field of perceptible reality. This field can be established, for example, by the embedding of reporters, or by the camera that frames the torture of detainees at Abu Ghraib; but it also includes the determination of which lives are publicly grievable, and by extension, which lives are human and which are non-human.[14] In *Common Place,* the ten-page coroner's report is the mechanism by which the detainee is made perceptible as a generic human body stripped of anything other than biologically individuating characteristics. He becomes raw matter. Halpern turns the highly conventional rhetoric of the autopsy into a field of perceptible reality through techniques of *inventio* and *dispositio.* In his 'Postscript', Halpern connects the 'common place' of his title not only to a communist horizon but also to the *topoi koinoi* of Aristotle's *Rhetoric* (157). But there is no question here of demilitarising language or syntax as a self-aggrandising revolutionary act; 'to liberate the word of the report *already autonomous* is not to emancipate its referent' (92).

Halpern's attention to the canon of classical rhetoric reflects the history of anatomy. In the Renaissance, human dissection was not only a practice of biological inquiry, but also of rhetoric and mapping.[15] Jonathan Sawday notes the importance of rhetoric as well as cartographic metaphors to Vesalian medicine: seventeenth-century anatomists 'found themselves wandering within a geographical entity. The body was a territory, an (as yet) undiscovered country, a location which demanded from its explorers skills which seemed analogous to those which were displayed by the heroic voyagers across the territorial globe.'[16] The body's depths, dimensions and shadows 'were held to be every bit as dark as the interior of the continent of the newly "found" Americas' (25). These territories could be explored but

---

[14] Butler, *Frames of War,* pp. 63–100 (esp. 78).
[15] William Harvey, *Lecture Notes on the Whole of Anatomy,* ed. Gweneth Whitteridge (Edinburgh and London: Livingston, 1961), p. 22.
[16] Jonathan Sawday, *The Body Emblazoned: Dissection and the Human Body in Renaissance Culture* (London: Routledge, 1995), pp. 23–4.

never completely known; the body was believed to retain internal '*terrae incognitae*' that could not be wholly dominated. *Common Place* restores these metaphorical readings to a modern clinical autopsy, exploring the body of the detainee as a politically territorialised space, with all the implications for domination and exploitation that the colonial metaphor retains.

The history of the autopsy is also bound to the domination of the criminal and the poor, whose bodies were rendered 'vile' by the medical profession in collusion with the judicature, in order to provide specimens for dissection.[17] Exhumation of corpses for dissection 'was not technically a crime of theft; for although dead human bodies were in fact bought and sold, in the eyes of the law a dead body did not constitute real property, and therefore could neither be owned nor stolen', Ruth Richardson argues.[18] With the passage of the 1832 Anatomy Act, the bodies of the 'unclaimed poor' could be legally appropriated for medical purposes. This act anticipated the 1834 Poor Law Amendment Act, which banned outdoor relief for the destitute and in effect confined them to workhouses. Anatomy is therefore implicated in carcerality through its use of the cadavers of convicted felons, and as a continuation of the penal regime of the workhouse. The vile bodies of the criminal and the destitute provided the experimental basis, the matter, for the postulation of universal knowledge, but they were otherwise excluded as agents in its production. One of the questions Halpern's work raises is whether a loving relation to the dissected corpse of a detainee can oppose this history.

The coroner's language is by nature absolutely specific (it describes the body in minute detail), and wholly general (it is formulaic and commonplace). It uses poetic diction that implies affective interpretation but is, in fact, generic cliché: 'glistening', 'thin and delicate', renal capsules 'strip with ease' from the underlying surfaces. Autopsy also sees the particular body as a variant on a general anatomical model. Take, for example, the detainee's skin. The coroner identifies the subject as a 'well-developed, well-nourished Caucasian male' (an obfuscation, given that he had been on sustained hunger strike). For the coroner skin is an anatomical property, not a signifier; the coroner's focal point is the body's depth rather than its surface. The detainee's body is not recognised as belonging to social categories (local, tribal and national identities), which are already sites of

---

[17] Gregoire Chamayou, *Les corps vils: Expérimenter sur les êtres humains aux XVIIIe et XIXe siècles* (Paris: La Découverte, 2008).
[18] Ruth Richardson, *Death, Dissection and the Destitute* (Harmondsworth: Penguin, 1989), p. 58.

resistance to imperialism. There is a world of difference between 'Caucasian male' as a privileged category over which no nation has an exclusive claim, and the 'Yemeni' ethnic identity that was arguably the most significant factor in the arrest and imprisonment of this individual. Autopsy's rational eye blinks at these differences. It does not document the relations, ethical and unethical, between the detainee and his jailers, which have left their marks on the body. The 'evidence of injury' which include 'dark raised legions' on the forehead, a broken rib and 'serial incisions' on the arms and legs are not a map of trauma, but items to be catalogued. For the coroner, the detainee's suffering remains a *terra incognita*.

Patiency and Shame

It is not just the detainee's textually mediated body, but also that of the speaker, that is central to the truth-claims of *Common Place*. The speaker transcribes the autopsy report by hand, submitting himself voluntarily to the constraint of the found text. He ironically compares himself to a 'scribe reproducing Torah or a monk labouring over illuminated books' (155). Transcription makes the speaker 'acutely aware of my body' (23): the embodied work of transcribing a rationalist discourse about another body is interrupted by somatic effects. The interruptions become more frequent, and the speaker becomes more distracted and aroused as the transcription proceeds. As the writing hand moves, copying and masturbating, it enacts a scribal and erotic fidelity to its object. But the virtue attributed to the labour of writing is deliberately traduced throughout the book, as it cycles through states of boredom, arousal, climax and dispersal. Transcription 'gives way to these fantasies of contact', and with them the fantasy that 'my own sentences possessed some restorative force to bring the body back' (25). Thus, two distantly separated bodies are affected by the autopsy report: one is carved up to service its production, the other inflates with its excitement; one hardens with rigor mortis, the other with desire.

In a series of prose poems entitled 'Late Nite Emissions', Halpern describes recurrent dream scenarios in which the speaker conspicuously shits, pisses or comes in public places where he is being watched. Phantasmatic performances produce 'real' spontaneous bodily emissions, cum and tears. These scenes are mirrored towards the end of the book by an account of the speaker's embarrassment in performing this text to an actual audience. In the tradition of lyric associated with Mill's solitary poet, these spontaneous emissions are proof of authenticity: the performances retain the quality of private utterance even in public. But unlike Mill's poet, who shows 'no trace of consciousness that any eyes are upon us', the speaker of *Common Place* recognises the presence of different audiences through feelings of shame.

Halpern's speaker resembles the subject of Petrarch's *Rime Sparse*, who vacillates between obsessive pleasure and a shame 'which brings all my hidden thoughts to my brow'.[19] Petrarch's shame arises from an inability to reconcile himself to Laura's mortality, and to bind himself to God alone; but he shares with Halpern a sense of the wrongness of his desire, and the necessity of its sublimation. Halpern writes of 'forcing arousal while reading this report where the wrongness of my object-choice feels unavoidable, like the limit of our knowledge as radical particularity becomes the hoax upon which the falseness of the universal hangs' (69). This wrongness could be understood as a form of *akrasia*, which for Aristotle was a condition of weakness in which reason is subjugated to *pathos*, particularly the passions of pleasure and anger.[20]

Aristotle wants to understand why people are unable to stop willing the wrong thing, even if they know it is wrong. Such behaviour was for Plato an impossibility. Aristotle cites a passage from the *Protagoras* (352b-c), where Plato summarises the general view of knowledge as subservient to other impulses:

> people think that, while a man often has knowledge in him, he is not governed by it, but by something else – now by passion, now by pleasure, now by pain, at times by love, and often by fear; their feeling about knowledge is just what they have about a slave, that it may be dragged about by any other force.[21]

Plato compares the subjection of ethical knowledge to the passions to the way a slave is ruled over by a free man. He then disputes what 'people think' (the commonplace), contending that subjection to passion or pleasure is evidence of a lack of true knowledge of the good. Aristotle, by contrast, believes that the akratic subject can have knowledge, but simply

---

[19] *Petrarch's Lyric Poems: The Rime Sparse and Other Lyrics*, trans. Robert M. Durling (Cambridge, MA: Harvard University Press, 1976), p. 430.
[20] Richard Strier, 'Bondage and the Lyric: Philosophical and Formal, Renaissance and Modern', in *The Work of Form: Poetics and Materiality in Early Modern Culture*, ed. Ben Burton and Elizabeth Scott-Baumann (Oxford University Press, 2014), pp. 73–87; Strier, *The Unrepentant Renaissance*, p. 62.
[21] Plato, *Plato in Twelve Volumes*, vol. 3, trans. W. R. M. Lamb (Cambridge, MA: Harvard University Press, 1967). Citation at Aristotle, *Ethics (The Nichomachean Ethics)*, trans. J. A. K. Thomson, rev. ed. Hugh Tredennick (London: Penguin, 1953 [1976]), book VII, p. 228.

lacks the necessary disposition to choose the good; he compares the akratic individual to 'a state which passes all the right decrees and has good laws, but makes no use of them' (VII.x, 1152a20). The slave of ethical knowledge being dragged around by passion, ethical knowledge as a broken law, and the weak and feeble desiring subject who cannot activate the good – these premises are all literalised in the figures of the detainee, prison guard and poetic speaker in *Common Place*.

Halpern's poetics are engaged in displays of weakness and passivity, or what he calls 'patency'. Halpern first coined the term in an essay on George Oppen, to describe a willing 'suspension of an agency' and a mood of 'openness: open to touch, open to penetration'. This mood, which embraces contingency, expectancy and uncertainty, holds its object 'suspended within a pathos of distance, whereby the patient fails to grasp her object within hardened structures of command that determine feeling prior to apprehension'. It is a form of eros, and recollects the mood of 'They flee from me', or the fainting follower in 'Who so list to hounte'.[22] The notion of patency is close also to Jared Sexton's advocacy of 'passivity (whether waiting or resting or languishing)' as 'a type of activity, that of our active being, that which brings forth life from the non-life with which it is commingled. Our being is active, but that doesn't mean our being is always in-action.' Sexton asks, 'What would a properly decided, freely chosen, passivity toward the social structure look like? Is there such a thing – ethically, politically – as radical passivity?'[23] The akratic speaker in *Common Place* is a way of dramatising the potential for a political and sexual passivity in the face of political tyranny. His patency is grounded in what Leo Bersani recognises as the 'equally strong appeal of powerlessness, of the loss of control'. But Bersani specifies that his notion of passivity is closer to masochistic surrender: 'I don't mean the value of gentleness, or nonaggressiveness, or even of passivity, but rather of a more radical disintegration and humiliation of the self.'[24] This is an intensification of 'patency', aligned more closely to the political gesture of throwing ashes on the White House lawn than to elegiac quilting.

Across his essays, Bersani explores the erotic shattering (*ébranlement*) of the self both as emancipatory and as reproducing existent social structures. It pertains not only to relations of interpersonal intimacy but to ontology.

---

[22] Rob Halpern, 'Becoming a Patient of History: George Oppen's Domesticity and the Relocation of Politics', *Chicago Review* 58.1 (Summer 2013), pp. 50–74 (56).
[23] Jared Sexton, 'On Black Negativity, or the Affirmation of Nothing', Interviewed by Daniel Colucciello Barber, *Society and Space* (18 September 2017), pp. 19–20.
[24] Leo Bersani, *Is the Rectum a Grave? And Other Essays* (University of Chicago Press, 2010), p. 24.

In many ways, Bersani's theorisation of the disintegration of the self, *jouissance* as powerlessness, and the pushing of form (poetic or bodily) beyond its limits, are useful descriptions of Halpern's book. But erotic shattering in these poems also revolves around an inequality. However, debased by the shamefulness of his love, the akratic speaker can never be destroyed in the way the body of his beloved object is destroyed. While the speaker succumbs to ecstatic *ébranlement*, the detainee is literally shattered (dead, his life destroyed, his body dissected); in a sense, the detainee has come to notice as an erotic object only *because* he has been destroyed, and his destruction has been catalogued in the coroner's text.

The wrongness of the speaker's arousal is offered up as an analogy for the wrongness of the wish to identify with the prisoner, and the impossibility of replacing a relation based on political domination (American subject, Yemeni object) with a fantastic one based on loving intimacy. At one point the speaker imagines being fisted by the detainee, 'his hand up my ass, gentle at the fundament, forearm engulfed by cavity, approaching the source of rhythm which, as Bob notes, is just past "the trap" of the intestines, where nothing but a filmy tissue separates one's hand from the beloved's heart' (84). The writing hand has been displaced by the detainee's hand, which penetrates the speaker, linking together waste and love, the rhythm of the pulse and the prosody of the poem. The hand is within touching distance of the speaker's heart, seat of interiority and authentic feeling. It is reaching towards the common place.

In the utopian relation of queer desire imagined in *Common Place*, the filmy (flimsy) tissue between heart and rectum is a sign of potential permeability to the gentle caress of the writerly hand. And yet, it is also one of the poem's most obdurate blockages; the whole of the body's visceral apparatus intervenes, making the perceived smallness of distance actually an impenetrable gap. This thin tissue preserves the irreducible interiority of the self and protects it from a potentially mortal grip. It is the boundary that maintains the conditions for desire. The poem represents it as a militarised barrier between poetic subjectivity and its objects: 'At once mine and not mine in the end a thin skin / Separates me like an envelope *property fence police tape* / *Cordon sanitaire* from yr banished excrescence' (105). The gap between self and other that desire cannot cross is fortified by military and police violence. The poem's political and erotic desire to make the ban in relation palpable quivers in this space of suspension. In Wyatt's motto of the leaping deer, the boundary is the line between private ownership (purchased from the sovereign) and the managed commons (a liminal space also belonging to the sovereign), where the fugitive and privileged speaker might trip and fall. It is also a ditch that shows the dear heart actually to be an ass.

The poem dwells on this barrier, between me and you, self and other, bodies and nation states. Halpern uses the detainee's incarceration as an analogue for the psychic and material blockages that prevent the free flow of libidinal energy or a truly intersubjective political life. His poems 'struggle against reason to turn the site of penetration into a scene of shameless pleasure *utopia* if only to make the obstruction to that end perceptible' (92). Halpern's work tends to 'eroticize ... the obstacle to communization, dreaming of an easy liquidation' (126), as a way of allegorising forces of revolution and counterinsurgency as libidinal blocks and flows. Like Wyatt, his poems are full of blocks, traps and clogs. These enforce distance, and impede and intensify orgasmic satisfaction: 'As the intensity of pleasure grows, I conjure pictures to block the way to climax' (128). Eventually, the poem itself becomes analogous to those blockages rather than their relief: 'I wonder whether ... the writing can only materialize the ethical bind that traps this erotic transfer of energy, arousing the affective blocks & psychic clots that keep the body emotionally remote' (92). Orgasm's relief is a paltry analogue for the coming community, and leaves the masturbatory speaker in a familiar solitude: 'as transcription gives way to the need for touch, conditions destroy its possibility and I no longer sense his presence in my lower extremities, indeed I no longer feel anything at all except this burnt desire smoldering inside some withdrawn organ that blocks the sensation it attracts' (83). Blocked and bound flows prevent us from imagining that sexuality can figure for a utopian horizon, beyond which subjects' shattered fragments could merge into an impersonal union free of the contradictions of mastery and bondage.

Bersani's criticism of the notion that sexuality offers potential redemption, and of the recuperation of queer radicalism to liberal politics, also resonates with the traumatic negativity of Halpern's book. Fantasy, Bersani insists, 'is not an act that touches or changes the world. It represents the terms in which the world inheres in the fantasizing subject, terms that can change as our position in the world changes' (148–9). Fantasy is not a form of political activism. Its limits are mourned throughout *Common Place*, even as the poem pursues 'a poetical figure that makes it possible to imagine a relation whereby touch might be the site of visceral care rather than violent pain'. But Bersani also argues that masochism is not a radical alternative to mastery, but its inversion: 'the defeat of the self belongs to the same relational system, the same relational imagination as the self's exercise of power; it is merely the transgressive version of that exercise' (110). In Chapter 10 I'll return to the ways that masochism inverts rather than destroys a relational system of mastery and bondage. In *Common Place*, the speaker's wish to eroticise the detainee's domination does not invert the sadistic torture to which the detainee was already subjected. Rather, it could be argued that it continues the practice of Guantánamo in putting the detainee to use.

Patiency, the openness of a suspended and pathetically distant object to penetration, is not just poetic fantasy, but a literal description of the detainee's condition. In response to an interviewer's inevitable question about how his poetry reflects Giorgio Agamben's notion of biopolitics, Halpern refers to patiency as centring 'the body as scene of disabused sovereignty'; it 'refers to the suspension of our proprietary relations to our and others' bodies and life processes, the recognition, and perhaps even the affirmation, of the corpus as open, disarmed, and vulnerable', and 'challenges the delusion of mastery over our own body's borders, a delusion that often converges, both semantically and materially, with a policing function'.[25] The body is a social process, an assemblage over which we have only the delusion of mastery; the feeling of owning our bodies invests us in fictions of private property and thus in privation. Yet, the imprisoned person can have little 'delusion of mastery' over her own borders or the way those boundaries – the borders of the *terra incognita* – are policed. The open, disarmed and vulnerable status of her corpus is the primary political fact of her existence.

In these ways, aligning the patiency of the poetic subject with the open, disarmed and vulnerable corpus of the detainee reveals a problem. We know from Binyam Mohamed, the British prisoner who was released from Guantánamo in 2009, that this man had acted as the prisoners' representative and addressed the camp's commanders with their concerns. This political activism within the unspeakable oppressions of the camp requires us to think of his body as part of a collective, struggling against the punitive individuation that has been one goal of prison management since the late eighteenth century. Halpern does not reflect on this detainee's political work. He also provides a sparse (just over one page, 73–4) 'Flashback' that accounts for the detainee's activities before his apprehension and transfer to Guantánamo. This life, the prisoner's agency and kinship and autonomy, are not the poem's domain. They are harder to imagine than his mutilation by captivity. In *Common Place*, the only resistance in the body of the detainee is not what the prisoner claimed for himself and his comrades during his life, but what is imputed to it, structurally, by the

---

[25] Donovan, 'Somatics', citing Giorgio Agamben, *Homo Sacer: Sovereign Power and Bare Life*, trans. Daniel Heller-Roazen (Stanford University Press, 1995).

poem's process of erotic consumption. In that sense, the detainee serves as a blank on to which the desires – for erotic relation, for political emancipation – of the privileged poetic subject can be projected.

Placeholders and Blanks

While he may wish to love the detainee back into relation, the speaker is closely related to the prison guard, whose hailing interpellates the man into his identity as prisoner. It is only momentarily, and quite late in the book, that we read that 'it's impossible to recognize myself except in the figure policing his cell' (129). The guards' addresses to the prisoner are similarly repressed in the military documentation, which describes how the detainee speaks (chatting – 'flirtatiously' – to a nurse on the night of his death, requesting a sleeping pill, asking the guard to close his bean hole cover), but not how the guards speak to him. These documents erase the asymmetry of address that is essential to the carceral situation. They imply that the jailers exercised a disciplined moderation and responsiveness to the prisoner's needs that is echoed in the disciplined and moderate language of the reports themselves.

Common Place fills the blank space where the guards' speech is redacted with its own loving apostrophe, a rhetorical figure that Jonathan Culler argues is one means by which 'post-Enlightenment poetry seeks to overcome the alienation of subject from object'. Apostrophe helps by 'constituting the object as another subject with whom the poetic subject might hope to strike up a harmonious relationship. Apostrophe would figure this reconciliation of subject and object. But one must note that it figures this reconciliation as an act of will, as something to be accomplished poetically in the act of apostrophizing.'[26] Apostrophe is a strong signal of the detachment of poetry from actual communication. Halpern's apostrophe to the detainee reveals not open address but its impossibility.

The detainee does not speak for himself. An anthology of poems from Guantánamo Bay has been published, which suggests that the camp, like most prisons, is a site of thick poetic productivity, but Halpern draws attention to his inability to access the prisoners' own writings.[27] In a section of 'Correspondences', poems addressed to specific named individuals at Guantánamo, he also acknowledges the 'total incompatibility between the

---

[26] Jonathan Culler, *The Pursuit of Signs: Semiotics, Literature, Deconstruction* (London: Routledge, 1981 [2001]), p. 158.
[27] Marc Falkoff (ed.), *Poems from Guantánamo: The Detainees Speak*, preface by Flagg Miller, afterword by Ariel Dorfman (Iowa City: University of Iowa Press, 2007); see also Butler, *Frames of War* pp. 33–62 (esp. 55–62).

idea / Of sending you this letter and the dream of the poem it / -self' (100). If the poem is a letter to the world, that world excludes the prisoners.

The ethics and aesthetics of address in the book are intrinsic also to a lyric tradition that is intent on the beloved not as an individual but as an occasion. The detainee is comparable to Petrarch's Laura, a girl glimpsed for a moment, whose absence is crucial to her utility in the poet's exploration of desire, sacrifice and transcendence. In *Common Place*, the detainee's body is multiply inaccessible, being imprisoned in Guantánamo, name and date of death withheld, and also being dead. This body is 'redacted, wasted and withdrawn to a lockdown site', its potential as signifier of transcendental subjectivity locked away and made 'unthinkable' (30). This withdrawal is the poem's ground. As in the *Rime Sparse*, the absence of the beloved is what enables the poem's meditations on ethics, eros, friendship, poetics and politics, and the speaker's complex interiority.

In Chapter 1, I argued that love – or rather desire – depends on lack, on the gap between self and other, that cannot be closed by sex. In *Common Place*, sex becomes a metaphor for the impulse to identify with the detainee. The speaker imagines that 'I can feel the thick nest of hair as my fingers touch the head of his cock, which stiffens with the touch. But none of this is true, it's my own prick getting hard as this exercise in auto-affection turns blind figures to waste' (29). Later 'I place the cord around his cock while looking sadly at my own, establishing equivalence between organs and garbage' (68); and in the act of rimming the detainee, ingesting his waste, the speaker feels 'in each of my organs the unremarkable denotation of his' (82). Waste is the surplus of process of (bodily, capitalist, military, poetic) digestion.[28] By incorporating what the common place considers valueless, the detainee's waste and the detainee *as* waste, the speaker refuses lyric valorisation. He offers his own body up patiently for an erotic and torturous penetration by feeding tube:

> He's my inner essence, the truth my body apes when every corpse in history is mine. And so, in a kind of radical mimicry *sympathetic magic* I spread my cheeks and await the tube whose insertion prefigures the future of authenticity where any hint of originality becomes criterion for kitsch. (127)

But as the poem makes clear, their positions are not fungible. One could imagine submitting patiently to sacrificial penetration. Another one could

---

[28] On the trope of waste in Halpern's poetry, see Sianne Ngai, 'Visceral Abstractions', *GLQ: A Journal of Lesbian and Gay Studies* 21.1 (2015), pp. 33–63; Christopher Schmidt, *The Poetics of Waste: Queer Excess in Stein, Ashbery, Schuyler, and Goldsmith* (Basingstoke: Palgrave Macmillan, 2014) is also relevant.

join in a collective hunger strike, refusing food and refusing to patiently submit to perpetual incarceration. One could be imaginatively passive. Another one could be strapped in a restraint chair while nasal feeding tubes were violently inserted into his body. One could engage in 'homosexual ascesis that would make us work on ourselves and invent . . . a manner of being that is still improbable'.[29] Another one could be forced by the state to live a desperate and degraded homosocial asceticism. So, what does it mean to claim patiency or passivity as a poet, lying in imagination alongside the vile body of the detainee?

Halpern opens himself up to violence and shame through an uncovering of every site of repression in this sexualised fantasy of relatedness to the body of the dead man. Here, I mean not that the desires expressed in the poem are inherently shameful, though some seem designed to elicit that judgement. Rather, the shame is the product of the speaker's incommensurability with his object, the inequality between his suffering and wishes and those of the detainee. But shame also gives way to, or is even a precondition of, ecstasy. He notices how 'Proprioceptive disorientation *looking at his limbs and feeling my own* makes it difficult for me to determine whose bruise is whose, as if his organs were inside me, the way his gestures, too, inhabit my flesh, making the phrase "my own" a stupidity, and this is an ecstasy as every body in history might as well be touching mine' (115). The intermingling of him and me becomes a figure for the commons in which the particularity of the detainee is submerged. In this utopian imaginary, the subject and the object are interchangeable, each self-identical, each preserving his singularity; but in practice the object is effaced, made to serve a political universal in which he – the dead man, the vile body and banned prisoner – cannot participate.

The detainee is also a fungible object within Halpern's tetralogy, for which he is put to work signifying the structures of American militarism and racial capitalism. In his postscript to a selection of Halpern's poems titled *Placeholder*, Sam Ladkin observes that 'inside the fantasy of the American military male that motivates *Music for Porn* we discover the repressed figure of the detainee; this is how the body of desire in one collection becomes the figure of incompletion for the next'.[30] Halpern writes that he had originally segregated the language of the Gitmo reports from the documents he used to write *Music for Porn*, out of fear that 'I'd be

---

[29] Michel Foucault, 'Friendship as a Way of Life', in *Ethics: Subjectivity and Truth*, ed. Paul Rabinow, trans. Robert Hurley and others, *The Essential Works of Michel Foucault*, vol. 1 (New York: New Press, 1994 [1997]), pp. 135–40.

[30] Rob Halpern, *[– –]: Placeholder* (London: Enitharmon, 2015), p. 140.

betraying a fundamental difference, equating the non-equitable', making the bodies 'fungible by search engine'. In writing *Common Place*, he is moved to challenge this distinction between soldier and detainee, which he experiences as a mystification: this 'haunting feeling of wrongness, as if there were an ethical imperative to preserve a radical difference between soldier and detainee to respect a mystified distinction whose breach would open my writing to violence and shame' (159–60).

Halpern decides to break down that 'radical difference' by attending to the figure of the detainee in the formal and philosophical terms established in *Music for Porn*. 'This is how my soldier becomes a Gitmo detainee' (38): through the act of transcription, a process that subverts the pain of duplication (copying texts, copying people) by introducing into it the singular and illimitable desire of the poetic subject. 'I'm aiming to preserve and nourish both young men under the double ray of tenderness and compassion, but these figures are one and the same' (79): both objects are withdrawn, and both are drowned in the speaker's 'equal and opposite excess' of need for intimate relation. In some ways, this collapsing of distinctions resembles the autopsy's smoothing of difference as a set of variations on a normative universal body; and Halpern does recognise that 'the difference between a solider and a detainee breaks down' in the passive construction that pervades anatomical discourse (29). The detainee is an especially good cipher because he is both particular (his body revealed in every detail under medical scrutiny) and general (the autopsy's formulaic language gives us no access to his inner life).

It could be argued that this fungibility of love objects is intended to mimic the translation of human singularity into an exchange value, the bounty for which the detainee could have been traded. But it alludes also to an originary loss for which these others are mere 'placeholders'. Though 'these ciphers interpenetrate' (137) each is a substitute 'for someone else', 'another body lost to me, a loss to which I've clung for years' (90), whom Halpern names as his lover James, who died in 1995. Describing how he attended to James in his illness, cleaning out the catheter inserted into his lung, Halpern writes elsewhere that 'my intimate relation to this hole is antecedent to my fantasies of other holes – a soldier's wound, for example, ... and several years later, the catheter reappeared disguised as the feeding tube of a hunger striking detainee at Guantánamo Bay, and then the ligature with which he allegedly hanged himself'.[31] This hole becomes 'my ferry, my ever-ready metaphor, a vehicle of transport'; if 'this hole can hold the whole, every singular thing in it becomes substitutable for

---

[31] Rob Halpern, *Touching Voids in Sense*, 2nd ed. (London: Veer Books, 2017), n. p.

every other thing'.³² This original hole is not only a wound but also a figure for desire and absence (abscess), a kind of blank or void that underlies the fungibility known in poetics as metaphor. Gently questioned about this loss and its influence on his poetry by his friend Bruce, Halpern writes about 'the way one death can always stand in for another, the way bodies serve as proxies, one loss arousing the memories of all its familiars'.³³ This wound becomes 'a place of absolute intimacy and absolute alienation, where immediate proximity and total mediation converge in a body I love, a body I can't save, a place where I return again and again, if only to see it return to me disfigured, deformed, transposed, and then I flee'.³⁴ The typographic placeholder 'Dear [– –] ~' offers a blank space which is held open for, and simultaneously displaces, all these beloved personal objects: 'Look how I keep slipping on the terms of contract / Substituting exchangeable names as if yrs were / Arbitrary anything to get you in my mouth ...'³⁵

The detainee is a limit-case of the absented object. He is described throughout the poem both as a two-dimensional 'blank' (surface; the page?) and a three-dimensional 'void' (depth; the body?): 'What will it take to arrive at so impossible an event, to lend positive content to the scene of that blank?' (41).³⁶ Sianne Ngai has read these voids in *Music for Porn* around which abstraction hardens or congeals as both 'the inherent emptiness of the value form', and 'a space that Halpern is careful to show as having been rendered empty, by the agency of social actors, from something in it having been actively withdrawn'.³⁷ Halpern himself invokes Alain Badiou's notion of the 'void in the situation', and refers critically to Maurice Blanchot's 'encounter with the void whose inclusion determines that reality while remaining unaccounted for within it'.³⁸ The void and the blank can be read in Lacanian terms as the lack that constitutes desire. But the word 'blank' reminds me of that elegiac passage in *Twelfth Night* where Orsino asks Viola, dressed as Cesario, about her sister:

---

³² Halpern, *Touching Voids*, n. p. ³³ Halpern, *Common Place*, p. 97.
³⁴ Halpern, *Touching Voids*, n. p. ³⁵ Halpern, *Common Place*, p. 105.
³⁶ Halpern refers to the 'blank of omission' that is his variation on Claudia Rankine's 'blink of omission': Claudia Rankine, 'The First Person in the Twenty-First Century', *After Confession: Poetry as Autobiography*, ed. Kate Sontag and David Graham (Saint Paul, MN: Graywolf), p. 132.
³⁷ Ngai, 'Visceral Abstractions', p. 52. ³⁸ Halpern, 'Useless Commodities', p. 156.

ORSINO: What is her history?
VIOLA: A blank, my lord.
She never told her love,
But let concealment, like a worm i' the bud,
Feed on her damask cheek: she pined in thought,
And with a green and yellow melancholy
She sat like patience on a monument,
Smiling at grief. (2.4.107–13)

Viola, as Cesario, speaks of an absent sister, who is herself, who was consumed by the melancholia of an impossible desire in the past, which is the new desire that began for her only a few days before, following shipwreck and the death of a beloved brother. In Freud's essay on 'Mourning and Melancholia', melancholia is a pathological state in which the patient comes to regard himself as despicable, deserving of punishment, but surprisingly lacking in shame – like the akratic subject. Freud argues cuttingly that the melancholic tells a certain truth about himself: that he is indeed worthless. The melancholic introjects the violence that he felt towards the lost loved object in order to avoid giving it up. The result is that the ambivalence that the object originally inspired intensifies into sadism against the object that has now become part of the self. This pathological introjection of the object may look like passivity, but is still a violent form of intersubjectivity.

Collars

Many of the issues I've addressed come together in the ligature: the waistband of the detainee's army-issued brief, instrument of strangulation torn from the site of banned intimacy, a provision that does not provide, a uniform that the military investigation found should have been replaced by a special 'suicide smock' issued to detainees in acute peril. The ligature is 'the defining / Thing' (138–9), because the detainee used this symbol of the mastery that had enforced itself on the most private parts of his body as the object by which to resist his bondage. The waistband becomes a version of Petrarch's *caro nodo* or dear knot, which binds the speaker to this inaccessible beloved and which he prefers to fictional liberty or salvation. The knot, Richard Streier notes, is 'Petrarch's recurrent figure for bondage of the will. But it is also his image for what makes the human condition ontologically unique.'[39] As the instrument of the detainee's death, the strangulating

---

[39] Strier, *The Unrepentant Renaissance*, p. 70.

ligature 'must be the starting point' (29). Like Wyatt's bridles and refrains, the ligature – from the Latin *ligo*, to tie or bind, and to untie; also the root of religion – marks a site of constraint and repetition. It 'plots a body displaced' (118): both the detainee's body, and the body of the poet displaced by writing. It is a means of imagining a relation that is also the impossibility of one, because it is the instrument of death. Upon waking:

> I feel for the band, and in its absence I experience the distance separating me from my detainee as the distance separating me from myself, a measure strangely commensurate with the length of this sentence. (118)

But, however hard it wishes for a lovingly reparative relation, the poem recognises that it *is* already in relation to the detainee, through the privileges of citizenship: my poetic sentences partake of the judicial sentence (or, in Guantánamo, the lack of one).

The waistband is appropriated by the speaker, becoming 'my ligature', masturbatory tool and theoretical crux: 'This cord around my balls *like my poem* belies a mannered style. It's only a question of relation between value and flesh, another false immediacy like the "thing itself," which can only be grasped as a circulation process' (125) – circulation of blood and commodities. The ligature ties the speaker to Guantánamo's detainees, materialising an attachment which 'binds / My cock it's wired to a pulley so you can conduct it / From afar' (100). The 'you' addressed here is either detainee or reader, invited to conduct (and become complicit in) the speaker's arousal. Halpern reclaims this object from the coroner's inventory, repurposes it, laying it alongside 'the metal clasp for securing a musical reed, a thing with which I conducted my earliest experiments in masturbation, before the leather cord, the plastic cuff and clamp' (66):

> A ligature identical to one el
> -astic band an intact pair
> White briefs matching those
>
> Said to have been issued to
> Decedent & retained being
> What it means to be in rel
>
> -ation to a domain of events
> Colors variations tiny anoma
> -lies receptive to my deviant
>
> Appeal made inside his body
> As if an organ were being
> Caressed by an elegant hand

> With no prior language one
> Pathological fact measures
> The space between my body
>
> And this thing most deeply
> Shared
>
> —*our happiness impossible to name.* (60)

The line breaks produce a fragmentation in which conventional denotations are lost or provisional; but they also challenge the cessation (little deaths) represented by the line endings, resurrecting and repurposing words that seem to multiply through hyphenation (ruptures) and addition (an unexpected suffix added to the root given in the previous line). In this example, 'anoma' is the sacred river of Buddhism, where Siddhārtha Gautama shed his royal clothes and began his life of ascetic wandering; this 'supreme' meaning is then submerged in the 'anomalies' which I take to represent the deviances from a medically normative body that are revealed in the autopsy. Against homogenisation, the 'ligature identical', are the 'tiny anoma/lies' that distinguish the individual. But these are only known through the coroner's language, and the 'pathological fact' of incarceration and alleged suicide (lies) that necessitated it.

Like the collar around the neck of Wyatt's hind, the ligature around the neck of the detainee is a sovereign injunction, an enunciation (property of US Army?) that displaces the speech of the enslaved object. It grasps bodies that deserve to be lovingly touched, inscribing them with the marks of ownership and dominion. In Wyatt's sonnet 'Who so list to hounte', I am wild only when you attempt to hold me: so don't touch. But it is that effort to touch that elicits who 'I am', rather than who I seem outwardly to be. In Halpern's poem, the speaker feels his body by mapping it on to the body of the detainee. This 'keeps me hard' (139): hardness, the arousal of the ferocious master as well as of the ready masculine lover, is the opposite of *akrasia*, the sore wearied pursuer who will always be outrun by the object who shows herself to him voluntarily.

Common Place's erotic strategies are deliberately shocking, and much of the book worries whether they can be justified. How can Halpern declare his desire for justice, when he superimposes his lyric subject on the privacy of the detainee's sexual intimacies and own chosen relations? What if what is at stake is not the susceptibility of this work to 'accusations of kitsch' (135) but to accusations of rape? Isn't this the possibility behind the passage of his body 'thru an Ovidian dream' (131): not its metamorphosis and sublimation but its staging of a pursuit in the interests of sexual violence? Even if many Muslim cultures are in practice deeply homosocial, the fantasied erotic relation of the male speaker to the detainee is at risk of becoming not only a cultural transgression, but also a desecration of a dead body and a continuation of the instrumentalisation and violence that began when the detainee was tracked and apprehended by the US government. More painfully, it risks being complicit with the sexualised torture of Muslim detainees across the United States' 'black sites' that Butler argues is a 'technique of modernization'. As Halpern asks in his Postscript:

> If his body has already been repressively sexualized in our militarized unconscious, is there any way to make that operation perceptible *if only to myself* except thru the sensual participation of *my* body? I don't know and I can't adequately answer these questions. I only want to wrest his body away from the use to which it's been assigned, to turn the uselessness of waste into the uselessness of pleasure. (160)

The useless pleasure of the reader or speaker depends on the use of the body of the detainee. This answer aligns the poet with the jailer, the coroner, Caesar, the sovereign who can make something out of the body of the other by making it his own.

That alignment is probably the correct one. But it also exposes the difficulty of translating pleasure into utopianism. Many readers will share the author's motives: the reimagining of the possibility of relation to those vile bodies hidden and traduced by the state. But that should not make us unwilling to recognise what it costs (what is 'wasted') to produce that reimagining of the uses to which the pleasuring body – inaccessible object, receding horizon, flaming and sputtering Bataillan sun – is put. The instrumentalisation of this body is deeply disturbing. The poem periodically confronts it, noticing the detainee curled in a foetal position 'with blanket & both feet exposed // – *to my forced production of meaning*' (58). The poem mimics the logic of capitalism in forcing this 'disposable body' to work, to create the surplus value that is its fantasy of the commons.

Trying to discover what 'can't be reduced to the biopolitical need "to take command of life in order to preserve it"', Halpern postulates love as the irreducible remainder that exceeds the management of bare life. Love becomes, in his essay 'Useless Commodities', a relation that 'belies identity, propriety, and detainment', subsuming difference in order to destroy the universal. Such love is affirmed through a 'poetical wager', 'to recover a hackneyed notion of lyric not as individual expression but as the expression of a "universal experience"'.⁴⁰ Love is the apotheosis of this critical poetics, the medium by which the dreamed-of relation can be achieved. Recovering the particularity of (the body of) the detainee from his erasure into a category of bare life through the operation of the sovereign and the philosophies that describe that operation, Halpern's poetics seeks to sublimate that particularity into what can be recognised as having universal validity: love, and the terrors of Guantánamo Bay. He aligns the detainee with a 'vanishing point of absolute uselessness, a place where I'll never quite arrive' (163). This is confusing, given the political and psychic uses to which the detainee is put – and given the long history of love as not just a coming together of equals in the open marketplace of affections, but also as a contractual relationship that entails the systematic exploitation of reproductive labour.

I find Halpern's turn to love in the labyrinth of complicity with American militarised violence and racial capitalism disturbing. It led me to write in a different way about the determination of love, and the relation of love poetry both to utopianism and catastrophe.⁴¹ For Halpern, the inaccessibility of the detainee intensifies the poetic sentence to a state of arousal that allows it to imagine a relation not confined by 'another metaphysics of capitalism'.⁴² Nonetheless, despite the intense commitment to imagining such a relation (and to drawing into the light the obstacles to its realisation), Halpern's poetics relies on tropes that pervade the carceral lyrics of Thomas Wyatt: the absence of the beloved, his or her inscrutability, the fabrication of an akratic lyric subjectivity through the projection of an indifferent other. Love makes the object of *Common Place* – the banned, destroyed body of the detainee – into a kind of sanctified materiality. Halpern's question is: 'What does it mean to love inside a system that has made love monstrous, to communize this eros'? He probes the relation of love to communism as the love of all, an affection that is held in common for the common, and an ethical injunction. Like Wyatt's, his poems pose a challenge to sovereignty through erotic relation. But lyric also knows that love, bondage and violence exist in proximity.

And maybe that's what makes Halpern's suggestion that love provides an alternative to necropolitics so troubling. Objects are not arbitrary or accidental. The poetic use of the object to communicate an inward truth reflects a political reality in which objects can be personified because people

---

⁴⁰ Halpern, 'Useless Commodities', p. 165.
⁴¹ Andrea Brady, 'The Determination of Love', *Journal of the British Academy* 5 (2018), pp. 271–308.
⁴² Halpern, 'Useless Commodities', p. 159.

can be objectified: in which art can be useless because people can be turned into utility. Here I am thinking of Fred Moten's response to Marx's passing conjecture – 'if the commodity could speak' – and the truth that its value 'is tied precisely to the impossibility of its speaking', an impossibility cut through by Aunt Hester's scream: 'where shriek turns speech turns song'.[43] But I am also thinking of the personification of objects in Monique Allewaert's study of the fetishes produced by diasporic Africans in the Black Atlantic. Objects, Allewaert argues, 'far from being wordless or mute, could be conceived as dense interiorities or constellations of force that could store, process, and actualise information and that were also crucial to the production of the collectivities, or assemblages, through which personhood was articulated'.[44] The problem with *Common Place* is that it objectifies the detainee without listening to the way that even the brute matter, the waste, of the anatomised body can speak. The detainee serves in this book as the grounds for a commons in which the broken body and the broken poem might both become obsolete. He is put to use as proof of concept, speechless instrument of critique, symbol of the emptiness of the value form. But he will always be something else: an elusive object, like the hind, that can never be captured by the sovereign inscriptions that claim him for their own.

---

[43] Fred Moten, *In the Break: The Aesthetics of the Black Radical Tradition* (Minneapolis: University of Minnesota Press, 2003), pp. 15, 22.

[44] Monique Allewaert, *Ariel's Ecology: Plantations, Personhood, and Colonialism in the American Tropics* (Minneapolis: University of Minnesota Press, 2013), p. 119.

CHAPTER 3

Each in Their Separate Hell
Solitary Confinement in the Long Nineteenth Century

> *We turn the crank, or tear the rope,*
> *Each in his separate Hell,*
> *And the silence is more awful far*
> *Than the sound of a brazen bell.*
>
> — Oscar Wilde

The relationship between lyric and bondage explored in this book has so far been grounded in individual experiences of the prison: Mill's imaginary one; Wyatt in the Tower of London; Halpern's addresses to a detainee in Guantánamo Bay. The following two chapters work towards a more collective representation of those experiences, showing how the poems produced in prisons contribute to the history and theory of the lyric. Mass incarceration in the contemporary United States is the subject of Chapter 4. Here, I offer a compressed history of prison reforms and the weaponisation of solitude in Britain and the United States from the end of the eighteenth century and through the nineteenth.

Michel Foucault's labours have familiarised most students of the humanities with the carceral production of the modern self-disciplining subject through the institutions of the school, hospital, asylum and prison (most famously Jeremy Bentham's panopticon), and through the academic disciplines that attend them. I will tell a related story, which is the emergence of solitude as a technique of discipline and a site for the production of confessional narratives that signal that the prisoner has discovered, or indeed produced, a new interiority, one of which he or she perhaps had never been aware, through the gift of intense loneliness. This ideology returns us to the quotation from Mill about the solitary prisoner, whose carceral separation from others guarantees the authenticity of his utterances. Does Mill's metaphor for lyric show the influence of prison reforms, or were prison reforms driven in part by a desire for transformation and true speech that lyric promised? This chapter will argue the former, while also thinking about the interaction between Romantic solitude and beliefs in the easeful, healthful qualities of contemplation in nature, and the idea and actuality of the Enlightenment prison. The ideology that promoted the redemptive powers of solitude led in reality not to healing but to catastrophic suffering.

Reforming Hell

The early modern British prison was a more chaotic and social space than the contemporary prison. Its boundaries were permeable: family members and servants could come and go; controls on the movement of goods and letters into and out of the prison were lax. Nonetheless, many commentators compared prison to hell.[1] Prisoners were holed up and forgotten in oubliettes and dungeons; reliant on corrupt keepers for food and other comforts, which only the well-off could pay for; exposed to numerous contagions; beaten and abused.

Reform of the nation's prisons began in earnest with the translation of Cesare Beccaria's *Dei Delitti e delle Pene* (1764) into English in 1767. Beccaria's book provoked new conceptualisations of the function and ethos of the prison. He argued that imprisonment 'ought not only to be of short duration, but attended with as little severity as possible'.[2] Referring to life imprisonment as 'perpetual slavery', he argued that it was worse than death: 'the mind, by collecting itself and uniting all its force, can, for a moment, repel assailing grief; but its most vigorous efforts are insufficient to resist perpetual wretchedness' (107–8). Punishment should be directed at preventing the criminal from committing further injuries to society, and deter others by setting a terrifying example.

Beccaria's appeals for clemency influenced some of Britain's most important prison reformers, including Jeremy Bentham, William Eden, William Blackstone and Samuel Romilly. They also provoked John Howard to leave his estate in Bedfordshire in 1773 and travel around Europe, touring institutions for the poor, learning how isolation prevented physical contagion and promoted reflection.[3] Howard's book *The State of the Prisons in England and Wales* (1777) would influence prison reform throughout the world over the course of the next century. He compiled statistics, tables of fees, architectural drawings and specific, material

---

[1] James Freize, *Every Mans Right: or, Englands Perspective Glasse* (London, 1646), p. 10.
[2] Cesare Beccaria, *An Essay on Crimes and Punishments* (London: J. Almon, 1767), p. 75.
[3] Sean Grass, *The Self in the Cell: Narrating the Victorian Prisoner* (New York: Routledge, 2003), p. 22.

evidence of the suffering in carceral institutions across Europe. Howard weighed loaves of bread and probed dungeons, defending himself against malignant air with only a few drops of vinegar; 'I entered every room, cell, and dungeon with a memorandum-book in my hand, in which I noted particulars upon the spot'.[4] While other authors used rhetoric to convey the depravity of British prisons, Howard accumulated empirical facts to depict a system of starving, idle, miserable prisoners, dressed in rags, loaded with heavy irons or dying of gaol fever, in buildings with no fresh water or sanitation. His ministrations were praised by Coleridge, who included them in his reasons for returning from his 'place of retirement' in 1795 to the political frenzy of London.[5]

Howard proposed plans for rebuilding the prison estate, hiring governors and inspectors, and maintaining an orderly and hygienic disciplinary regime. He also urged a culture change in the attitude towards imprisoned people. In another book surveying the lazarettos of Europe, he argued against use of 'gothic mode of correction, *viz.* by *rigorous severity*, which often *hardens* the heart; while many foreigners pursue the more *rational* plan of *softening* the mind in order to [encourage] its amendment'.[6] His appeals for mental amendment rather than corporal punishment influenced reformers in Pennsylvania; Benjamin Rush cites Howard in his argument against public punishment.[7] But Howard was cautious about recommending solitude as a psychic emollient, arguing that it should be broken up by periods of associated labour and communal exercise, or it would lead inmates to 'insensibility or despair'.[8]

The reform of British prisons was profoundly influenced by two American models of imprisonment: the 'separate' system, based on the Eastern State Penitentiary in Pennsylvania, and the 'silent' system, based on the Auburn State penitentiary in New York. Eastern State in Philadelphia opened in 1829 at an immense cost of $785,000 for 400 cells.[9] It was constructed as a series of blocks radiating off a central wing. Each cell had its own exercise yard. Prisoners were prevented from communicating with each other by thick stone walls. For a short period when

---

[4] John Howard, *The State of the Prisons in England and Wales* (London, 1777), p. 149.
[5] 'Reflections on Having Left a Place of Retirement' (ll. 49–50), cited in John Bugg, *Five Long Winters: The Trials of British Romanticism* (Stanford University Press, 2014), p. 47.
[6] John Howard, *An Account of the Principal Lazarettos in Europe* (London, 1791), p. 226.
[7] Benjamin Rush, *An Enquiry into the Effects of Public Punishments* (Philadelphia, 1787), p. 26.
[8] Michael Meranze, *Laboratories of Virtue: Punishment, Revolution, and Authority in Philadelphia, 1760–1835* (Chapel Hill: University of North Carolina Press, 1996), pp. 139–42.
[9] Robin Evans, *The Fabrication of Virtue: English Prison Architecture, 1750–1840* (Cambridge University Press, 1982), pp. 381, 320.

they were first admitted, prisoners would be confined in absolute isolation, without any labour to break up the monotony of time. Later they were given some work to undertake in their cells, as well as the occasional moral visitation. The solitary prisoners would be excluded from sociability, and essentially 'disappeared from the face of the earth ... . The inmate, completely cut off from the past, his future in suspension, would live only in the immediate time of his penitentiary sentence.'[10] The separate system was adopted at several British prisons, including Preston Gaol and the Brixton House of Correction. But it was Pentonville, the north London prison that opened in December 1842, which would most exactly reproduce its rigours.[11]

The separate system was an attempt to prevent physical and moral contagion by classifying prisoners with ever-increasing specificity.[12] 'Gaol fever' and other illness were rampant in prison; a parliamentary report on the Marshalsea in 1729 noted that around ten prisoners died every day from effects of want and fever.[13] Solitary confinement would contain these physical diseases, as well as the vices that overflowed from these vile bodies. After their own survey of British institutions in 1862, Henry Mayhew and John Binny regarded new prisons as sites of 'criminal quarantine'.[14] But Gustave de Beaumont and Alexis de Tocqueville argue that such classification necessarily fails: 'there are no two beings equal in regard to their morals; and every time that convicts are put together, there exists necessarily a fatal influence of some upon others'.[15] The irreducible difference between individuals makes mutual influence inevitable. 'We must therefore, impossible as it is to classify prisoners, come to a separation of all', they conclude. As reformers realised that 'there are as many types of reprobation as there are human souls', they eventually came to compartmentalise each prisoner individually: each inmate constituted his or her own category.[16]

---

[10] Thomas L. Dumm, *Democracy and Punishment: Disciplinary Origins of the United States* (Madison: University of Wisconsin Press, 1987), p. 108.
[11] Grass, *Self in the Cell*, p. 5.
[12] Randall McGowen, 'The Body and Punishment in Eighteenth Century England,' *Journal of Modern History* 59 (1987), pp. 651–79 (658–65).
[13] *Journals of the House of Commons*, 21:378,; cited in *Imprisonment in England and Wales: A Concise History*, ed. Christopher Harding, Bill Hines, Richard Ireland and Philip Rawlings (London: Croom Helm, 1985), p. 93.
[14] Henry Mayhew and John Binny, *The Criminal Prisons of London and Scenes of Prison Life* (London: Charles Griffin, 1862), p. 80.
[15] Gustave de Beaumont and Alexis de Tocqueville, *On the Penitentiary System of the US and its Application to France*, trans. Francis Lieber, introduction by Thorsten Sellin (Philadelphia, 1833; Carbondale: Southern Illinois University Press, 1964), p. 55.
[16] Evans, *Fabrication of Virtue*, p. 325.

Reformers argued that in solitude, prisoners could examine the narrative of their lives and commit themselves to change. Deprivation of social contact, conversation and intimate touch would induce reflection. Beaumont and Tocqueville expounded the advantages of solitary confinement: 'Thrown into solitude he reflects. Placed alone, in view of his crime, he learns to hate it; and if his soul be not yet surfeited with crime, and thus have lost all taste for any thing better, it is in solitude, where remorse will come to assail him.' It may be a fearful punishment; but otherwise it would hardly be a deterrent.[17] Solitude, Charles Western agreed in 1821, would 'give the culprit time for his passions to subside, and the better feelings of his nature to resume their influence [and] exhaust the animal spirits which supply him with fortitude'.[18] It helps to 'arrest the progress of corruption', and prevents 'contamination' and the shame of being exposed:

> Day after day, with no companion but his thoughts, the convict is compelled to reflect and listen to the reproofs of conscience. He is led to dwell upon past errors, and to cherish whatever better feelings he may at any time have imbibed. These circumstances are in the highest degree calculated to ameliorate the affections and reclaim the heart.[19]

Another author wrote in the *Maryland Gazette* in 1788: 'Conscience cannot long sleep in *solitude*. The worst of men, when left for a while to themselves, are made prisoners by their own reflections. These reflections are the messengers of Heaven to bring them to repentance, and a sense of their duty.'[20]

One of the most important proponents of solitary confinement was Jonas Hanway. Hanway's essay on *Solitude in Imprisonment* was published in London in 1776, in the same moment that the American Revolution made it no longer possible to sentence British convicts to transportation to the American colonies. 'Every one has a plan, and favourite system,' to solve this problem, Hanway said; 'mine is *solitude in imprisonment*, with proper profitable labour, and a spare diet, as the most humane and effectual means' of encouraging reformation (4). Solitary confinement was the 'balmy remedy' for the criminal condition: it can 'purge off' the 'foul humours of their minds' (106). Isolation would produce a spiritual awakening, driven by 'affliction', which is 'the truest friend to *repentance*:

---

[17] Beaumont and Tocqueville, *On the Penitentiary System*, p. 56.
[18] Charles Callis Western, *Remarks on Prison Discipline Delivered to the Lord Lt and the Magistrates of the County of Essex* (London, 1821), pp. 8, 13.
[19] Crawford, *Report on the Penitentiaries*, p. 11.
[20] Louis Masur, *Rites of Execution: Capital Punishment and the Transformation of American Culture* (Oxford University Press, 1991), p. 83.

solitude will create affliction, such as arises from a *consciousness of guilt*; and without this what *amendment* is to be expected?' (42). To be sure, that affliction was formidable, and solitude could be 'nauseous to the taste, or terrible to the imagination' (42). But, through reflection 'under the terrors of solitude' and labour, the prisoner 'will *open his mind*. He will feel his situation as an intermediate state between both worlds, and as a preparative for either' (103). This state of liminality between life and death, heaven and hell, induces a moral awakening that will have the lasting consequence of reforming the prisoner, preventing his recidivism and saving his soul.

In answer to the objection that '*the horror of solitary confinement [may] drive the prisoner to suicide*', Hanway drew on a tradition of the *vita contemplativa*: 'In common life retirement is found the best friend to virtue, and might often have prevented the extravagance which has ended in *suicide*' (104). Indeed, he imagines the cell as a study: 'if *books, pen, ink,* and *paper* were supplied, I should not want *company*'. Working-class prisoners, less capable of writerly reflection, should be furnished with the 'entertainment and relief of manual labour, he advised (34). Work was the remedy for despair, and would teach practical skills and moral qualities to improve the prisoner's chance of rehabilitation.

But the purported benefits of solitary confinement were discriminatory. William Crawford judged that 'the penalties of solitude ... are peculiarly irksome not to the sensitive and cultivated mind so much as to the hardened and depraved. The terrors of solitude operate most powerfully on that class in the treatment of whom severity is most desirable.'[21] Solitary confinement causes most pain to those most deserving of pain: not the 'sensitive and cultivated' members of the upper classes who are better able to profit from reflection, but the 'hardened and depraved' poor. African Americans, it was claimed, lacked the capacity for reflection that would make solitary confinement productive for white prisoners.[22] As Angela Davis has argued, the American reformed prisons 'were based on a construction of the individual that did not apply to people excluded from citizenship by virtue of their race and thus from a recognition of their communities as composed of individuals possessing rights and liberties'. They were designed to punish white wage-earning males.[23] This situation was drastically inverted over the course of the twentieth century.

---

[21] Crawford, *Report on the Penitentiaries*, p. 15.
[22] Smith, *The Prison and the American*, pp. 104–5.
[23] Angela Davis, *The Angela Y. Davis Reader*, ed. Joy James (Oxford: Blackwell, 1998), p. 97.

The Silent System

A competing regime that did not rely on separation was adopted in New York. From 1823, New York adopted the 'silent system', in which prisoners were not physically isolated but were forbidden to communicate with one another. Silence in such institutions was a means of enforcing discipline and order on the bodies and minds of prisoners. It also prevented the formation of solidarities. It was regularly noted that, under the silent regime, thirty guards were able to control the nine hundred prisoners who constructed Sing Sing. As Beaumont and Tocqueville explain, the captors are strengthened by their ability to 'communicate freely with each other, act in concert, and have all the power of association; whilst the convicts separated from each other, by silence, have, in spite of their numerical force, all the weakness of isolation' (60).

Bentham argued that 'the penitentiary act is silent', and the prison should be likewise; locked alone in his cell, the prisoner can 'render himself troublesome' only by making noise, and that can 'be subdued by *gagging*'.[24] He also imagined using music to induce co-operation among prisoners in the panopticon: 'Ablution – regeneration – solemnity – ceremony – form of prayer: – the occasion would be impressive. Grave music, if the establishment furnished it; psalmody at least, with the organ.'[25] Benjamin Rush recommended that the ideal prison should be enclosed by an iron door, whose 'grating, occasioned by opening and shutting them, [should] be increased by an echo from a neighbouring mountain, that shall extend and continue a sound that shall deeply pierce the soul'.[26] These Gothic sounds would echo in a silent institution, where guards wore felt on their shoes to prevent anyone from hearing their footsteps as they did the rounds.

Silence did not displace corporal punishment; in fact, it required strict controls on the bodies of the imprisoned. At Auburn, Austin Reed explained that 'when marching, we must keep close together, with our arms folded and our heads to the right, our heads bowed and our eyes a looking down upon the ground'.[27] Techniques such as the lockstep allowed guards to monitor prisoners' silence by forcing prisoners to move as one body, their faces all turned in the same direction. Prisoners were forced to wear the iron gag, a visor that fitted over the face and

---

[24] Jeremy Bentham, *The Panopticon Writings*, ed. Miran Božovič (London: Verso, 2010), p. 49.
[25] Jeremy Bentham, *The Works*, vol. 4 (Edinburgh: William Tait, 1843), p. 158.
[26] Rush, *Enquiry*, p. 20.
[27] Austin Reed, *The Life and Adventures of a Haunted Convict*, ed. Caleb Smith (New York: Random House, 2016), p. 144.

chained to manacles that held their hands behind the back. A prisoner died in 1833 at Eastern State after being punished for attempting to talk to another inmate by being fitted with the gag:

> An iron instrument resembling the stiff bit of a blind bridle, having an iron palet in the centre, about an inch square, and chains at each end to pass round the neck and fasten behind ... [was] placed in the prisoner's mouth, the iron palet over his tongue, the bit forced in as far as possible, the chains brought round the jaws to the back of the neck; the end of one chain was passed through the ring in the end of the other chain ... and fastened with a lock.

His hands were then 'forced into leather gloves in which were iron staples and crossed behind his back', and forced towards his head.[28] This description reveals the intense corporal violence of this supposedly spiritual disciplinary regime.

The silent system began to influence English penology after 1830. In 1834, all speech and gesture among inmates was banned at Coldbath Fields in London. But even with their use of intense violence, prison officials were powerless to prevent prisoners from communicating. 'A prison semaphor of winks, hand signs, and tapping through the pipes emerged' in these institutions, which the staff were powerless to suppress, and which left the supposedly silent prisons humming with non-verbal language.[29] Writing in 1845, Joseph Adshead observed prisoners in the tread-wheel yard at Tothill Fields prison answering questions with gestures, 'turning the hands to express unlockings or days', pointing to carvings of names and numbers on the wheel, and contriving to meet in water-closets or to speak in chapel and at night.[30] This communication was irrepressible despite 'continual punishments' (189). Mayhew and Binny also recognised that the 'silent system' was very labour-intensive and inefficient, requiring many officers to ensure that prisoners didn't communicate; the rule of silence was frequently broken through the use of 'significant *signs* among them'.[31] Moreover, the prohibition of their speech kept prisoners' minds 'perpetually on the fret', trying to devise ways to communicate secretly with others. It was 'an act of refined tyranny' to punish those who 'yield to that most powerful of human impulse – the desire of communicating' (101–2). Their critique of this system is not only that it is impossible to enforce, but that it

---

[28] Meranze, *Laboratories of Virtue*, pp. 311–12.
[29] Michael Ignatieff, *A Just Measure of Pain: The Penitentiary in the Industrial Revolution, 1750–1850* (New York: Pantheon Books, 1989), p. 178.
[30] Joseph Adshead, *Prisons and Prisoners* (London: Longmans, 1845), pp. 187–8.
[31] Mayhew and Binny, *Criminal Prisons*, p. 101.

refuses to recognise – and recruit to the use of reform – the fundamentally social, communicative nature of human beings.

Inscribing Bodies and Minds

In the silent system, the prisoner was 'required to pursue his labour with downcast eyes' and in silence, and at meals the inmates sat 'with their faces in one direction'. Those who communicated with other prisoners, even through a look, would be whipped. Making these observations, William Crawford – who had been sent by the British Home Secretary to the United States in 1834 to observe its prisons – also noted that a female prisoner, Rachael Welsh, had been held down and whipped to death.[32] Whipping seemed particularly degrading because of its association with slavery.[33] Austin Reed spent much of his youth in the juvenile House of Refuge. After a few days, 'I began to learn the winks, the motion of the fingers, the shake of the head, and in fact all of the iniquities that prevailed' (22). But he received twenty-five lashes and four weeks in solitary on bread and water for speaking to another boy (39). He was moved to sympathy when his fellow prisoner Strongman was whipped 'like a slave':

> Reader, could you told the feeling of my heart and mind as I sat there, wrapped in a fountain of tears? Could you told my sympathies as I look upon that beautiful milk white skin of Strongman's, who was to be lash and striped like a slave? ... I did not care so much about myself as I did about poor Strongman, whose skin only an hour before was clean from stripes and as white as milk. (61)

Reed fetishises his 'beautiful milk white skin', and suggests that Strongman lost the purity of his whiteness. Striped 'like a slave', his red blood and torn flesh darkened that white skin and made him wear the inmate's black-and-white stripes on the actual fabric of his body.

Reed's writings dwell on the way prison could physically mark the prisoner with indelible signs. He believed that 'the deep print of shame and misery was stamped deep into my face, ... the curse of a fugitive and a vagabond was printed deep upon my brow' (161). He feared that the 'deep print of a state prison mark' on the prisoner's brow 'will betray you wherever you go' (174). Through its inscriptions, Steven Connor argues, 'law makes the body, and more specifically its skin, bear witness. In the

---

[32] William Crawford, *Report on the Penitentiaries of the United States* (London: House of Commons, 1834), pp. 16–18.
[33] Caleb Smith, 'Editor's Introduction', Reed, *Life and Adventures*, p. xxxiv.

penal marking of the body, the law is not only done, it is seen to be done.' These marks are the 'lasting signs' of the law's action, so that long after the prisoner is released, he or she wears the signs of 'the letter of the law made actual and present in a continuing here and now'.[34] Like Wyatt, who is 'sure' that the scar of his imprisonment 'shall styll remayne', Reed fears that the moral and reputational damage as well as physical injuries of incarceration are legible inscriptions on his body.

Reflecting on 'the dark and gloomy days' when prisoners were not able to read anything other than the Bible nor 'make one single mark with a pencil', Reed associates the scarred body with other forms of inscription:

> The convict had no slate and pencil to kill time with, nor did he dare to have a knife in his possession to whittle time away. Ah, Reader, those was the dark and cruel days when young Plume was stripped stark naked and laid across the bench with his hands tied to the floor, and received such a severe punishment with the cats [cat o' nine tails] that he expired a few days after. Them was the days when the prisoner's backs was cut and lacerated with the cats till the blood came running down their backs.[35]

What is notable here, besides the outrageous cruelty and the similarity between these images of whipping and those documented in abolitionist literature, is the horrible transference from writing to whipping. The lack of writing material is remedied by the prisoner's body itself serving as a 'slate' on which the whip inscribes its disciplinary language.

Connor, exploring the early history of writing on animal skin, describes skin as the 'ideal ground or surface of writing' – letters can be incised into its surface, which is imagined as patient, suffering, passive yet impassioned by the signifying touch.[36] But the point of the extreme floggings Reed and Strongman received is 'not to mark the body of the offender so much as to destroy its capacity to bear marks', to 'annihilate the skin's power of holding, of bearing marks intact. Here, the savage and remorseless overwriting of the skin reduces it to a kind of bloody nothing, an invisibility in plain view' (80–1). These tensions between an ideal surface for the inscription of marks, and a surface so damaged it can no longer bear them, bear language, are metaphors *and* materialisations of penological history. That history is one of prisoners treated either as surfaces for moral inscription, or objects so destroyed that they can no longer be read as anything other than brute matter.

---

[34] Steven Connor, *The Book of Skin* (Ithaca: Cornell University Press, 2004), p. 74.
[35] Reed, *Life and Adventures*, p. 173.   [36] Connor, *Book of Skin*, p. 83.

Prisoners were literally inscribed with scars from penal discipline. But their minds were also considered surfaces in which redemptive narratives could be rewritten. Reverend John Clay, the chaplain at Preston jail, described solitude as a 'terrible solvent': 'a few months in the solitary cell renders a prisoner strangely impressible. The chaplain can then make the brawny navvy cry like a child; he can work on his feelings in almost any way he pleases; he can, so to speak, photograph his thoughts, wishes and opinions on the patient's mind, and fill his mouth with his own phrases and language.'[37] In the 1861 memoir based on his conversations with prisoners, Clay acts as the amanuensis for apparently illiterate prisoners, 'adopting the self-narrative "I"' on their behalf.[38] Clay's use of a recent technological metaphor for artistic reproduction is interesting; so, too, is the notion that the chaplain, having reduced the prisoner to an infant, can 'fill his mouth' with language, the inverse or even complement of the gag that imposes silence by stuffing the prisoner's mouth. As in Wyatt and Halpern's poetics, the silence of the other allows her or him to be ventriloquised, or put to work in a drama of power and resistance.

The confessional relationship between the prisoner and the chaplain has been studied in conjunction with the emergence of the novel. John Bender observes that the reformed penitentiary 'divests the criminal of narrative resources and designates a "character" to be formulated. The old prisons had allowed prisoners full access to narrative instruments: writing and publications, visits by auditors, normal reading matter . . . . The penitentiary deprives prisoners of direct communication with any audience.' The prison enforces isolation not just so that the prisoner can reflect on the past, but 'so that omniscience can restructure the inmate's identity through control of narrative resources'.[39] Bender draws out similitudes between free indirect discourse in the realist novel and the control of prisoners' reflective self-consciousness by the omniscient penal authority. However, John Bugg – discussing the writings of political prisoners in the 1790s – also shows how 'the first-person narratives of inmates are framed by the understanding that they are entering into public notice at the moment of their incarceration', making prison verse publicly visible.[40] This tension between a depersonalisation and silencing of prisoners' subjective accounts

---

[37] Walter Lowe Clay (ed.), *The Prison Chaplain: A Memoir of the Rev John Clay* (Cambridge: Macmillan, 1861), p. 386.
[38] Grass, *Self in the Cell*, p. 34.
[39] John Bender, *Imagining the Penitentiary: Fiction and the Architecture of Mind in Eighteenth-Century England* (University of Chicago Press, 1987), p. 203.
[40] Bugg, *Five Long Winters*, p. 59.

of their experiences, which is emphasised by Bender, and the self-conscious performance of an activist subjectivity, which is Bugg's focus, will also be found in writing from the contemporary prison discussed in Chapter 4.

The prison chaplain played a particularly powerful role in the remaking of prisoners' stories. Beaumont and Tocqueville describe visits at Wethersfield prison to the solitary cells from the chaplain:

> the prisoners feel pleasure when they see him enter their cell. He is the only friend who is left to them; they confide in him all their sentiments; if they have any complaint against the officers of the prison, or if they have a favour to sue for, it is he who is intrusted with their wishes .... He soon becomes initiated into all the secrets of their previous life.[41]

The logic is familiar: punishment traumatises and breaks down the inmate, leading to a strong attachment to those who show him some compassion, and a profound identification with the institution. Reed writes with great fondness and gratitude about the chaplain, whose 'sweet voice ... struck upon my ears like a band of music proceeding from the white milk throne of heaven'; even 'the tread of his very feet seemed to sound like music upon my ears'.[42] In his despair, Reed sees the chaplain as 'like a new born angel, sent from the portals of the sky to come and unlock the prisoner's door, unbind his chains, and let the prisoner free' (158). The chaplain offers sympathy and spiritual guidance; he tries 'to buoy up your down casted spirits' and delights in your attempts to do good (158).

The chaplain's task was to expose the prisoner's inner darkness, not only to the prison authorities, but to the criminal himself, like a photographer who creates a visible likeness of the self through a flash of light. John Brewster remarked, 'as human laws are unable to dive into the recesses of the heart, much less to develop its secret influences', society must find means to improve 'the mind of man' in other ways.[43] This depended on the ability to perceive the critical truth buried inside the inmate. As Foucault has shown,[44] the retreat from corporal punishment in this period entailed cunning systems for disciplining the mind instead.

---

[41] Beaumont and Tocqueville, *On the Penitentiary System*, p. 86.
[42] Reed, *Life and Adventures*, pp. 157, 159.
[43] John Brewster, *On the Prevention of Crimes, and on the Advantages of Solitary Imprisonment* (London: W. Clarke, J. Debrett, and J. Johnson, 1792), p. 4.
[44] Michel Foucault, *Discipline and Punish: The Birth of the Prison*, trans. Alan Sheridan (New York: Vintage, 1979).

Solitude as Damage

Solitude has always been regarded as dangerous, a peril that only the most robust could withstand. It exposed the individual to temptations and diabolic influence. As Barbara Taylor has argued, solitude had been critiqued 'from antiquity onward, but the rise of Enlightenment had sharpened the censure. Man, the philosophes insisted, was a naturally social animal; solitaries were misanthropes, monsters, madmen.'[45] Aristotle's often-repeated dictum from the *Politics* (1253a25-30) that, as Francis Bacon translates it, 'Whosoever is delighted in solitude, is either a wild beast or a god,' proposes that solitude can be either degenerative or exalting: that it could result in either madness, sickness and brutality, or enlightenment and transcendence.[46]

Critiques of solitary confinement began circulating in the late eighteenth century, but nonetheless, experiments with separation recurred (and failed) repeatedly throughout the nineteenth century. Before adopting the silent system at Auburn, the New York authorities first constructed a prison with eighty narrow cubicles where convicts were completely isolated. The first inmates entered the northern wing in 1821. Eighty of 'the most hardened convicts' were confined for ten months in a cell seven foot by three and a half feet. They were permitted no exercise, no change of air, no activity, and fed bread and water. 'The most disastrous consequences were naturally the result. Several persons became insane: health was impaired, and life endangered.'[47] All the prisoners were in despair; five died in the first year, one became insane, another attempted suicide. The 'trial' or experiment, 'from which so happy a result had been anticipated, was fatal to the greater part of the convicts: ... this absolute solitude, if nothing interrupt it, is beyond the strength of man; it destroys the criminal without intermission and without pity; it does not reform, it kills.'[48]

Similar results followed the introduction of solitary confinement in England. By 1841, British inspectors admitted that prisoners at Millbank were being injured by the conditions. Numerous prisoners had to be transferred to mental asylums. In its opening phase, inmates at Pentonville – who were carefully selected for their mental and physical

---

[45] Barbara Taylor, 'Rousseau and Wollstonecraft: Solitary Walkers,' in *Thinking with Rousseau: From Machiavelli to Schmitt*, ed. Helena Rosenblatt and Paul Schweigert (Cambridge University Press, 2017), pp. 211–234 (214).
[46] Sir Francis Bacon, 'Of Friendship' (1625), *The Essayes or Counsels, Civill and Morall*, ed. Michael Kiernan (Oxford: Clarendon Press, 1985), p. 80; Bacon is quoting Aristotle, *Politics*, 1253a.
[47] Crawford, *Report on the Penitentiaries*, p. 15.
[48] Beaumont and Tocqueville, *On the Penitentiary System*, p. 41.

robustness – were confined to solitary for eighteen months. Nonetheless, some had to be removed to Bedlam; fifteen cases of insanity were recorded between 1843 and 1850.[49] By the 1850s, Pentonville had abandoned the separate stalls in chapel and solitary exercise pens that enforced total isolation.[50]

Mayhew and Binny struggled to find words for the psychic effect of the pitch-black refractory cells at Pentonville, even after only a few minutes:

> The eyes not only saw, but *felt* the absolute negation of their sense in such a place. Let them strain their utmost, not one luminous chink or crack could the sight detect. Indeed, the very air seemed as impervious to vision as so much black marble, and the body seemed to be positively encompassed with the blackness, as if it were buried alive, deep down in the earth itself . . . . The continual straining of the eyeballs, and taxing of the brains, in order to get them to do their wonted duty, soon produced a sense of mental fatigue, that we could readily understand would end in conjuring up all kinds of terrible apparitions to the mind.[51]

It is hard to square these actual effects with the reformers' idea that 'agitations' would subside in conditions of total sensory deprivation. Mayhew and Binny understood that the purpose of solitary confinement was 'not only to prevent the prisoner having intercourse with his fellow-prisoners, but to compel him to hold communion with himself'. But they disparaged absolute solitary confinement as 'abandoning its victim to despair', associating it with 'the dark dungeons and oppressive cruelty of the Middle Ages' (103).

Mayhew and Binny condemned solitary confinement as a system of 'terrors' and 'intense misery' that converts men 'into mere living automata' (127) or wild animals. Instead of reforming the prisoners, it destroyed them, 'cag[ing] a man up as if he were some dangerous beast, allowing his den to be entered only by his "keeper"' (103). Working-class criminals were particularly at risk of mental injury, because their 'untutored minds are incapable of knowing the charms of intellectual culture or occupation'; they therefore 'can only fret and chafe under their terrible imprisonment, even as the tameless hyena may be seen at the beast-garden for ever fretting and chafing in its cage' (128). This is a different notion of the reversion of the captive human to its animal kind than the one we saw in Wyatt's poetics. It draws on the growing aversion to animal cruelty in the

---

[49] Grass, *Self in the Cell*, pp. 41–2.   [50] Ignatieff, *Just Measure*, p. 200.
[51] Mayhew and Binny, *Criminal Prisons*, p. 136.

late eighteenth and early nineteenth century, as well as an understanding of the importance of nature in maintaining the human spirit.[52]

In 'The Dungeon', Coleridge expresses moral outrage at the conditions in prisons.[53] The prisoner is abandoned to:

> friendless solitude, groaning and tears,
> And savage faces, at the clanking hour,
> Seen through the steam and vapours of his dungeon,
> By the lamp's dismal twilight! So he lies
> Circled with evil, till his very soul
> Unmoulds its essence, hopelessly deformed
> By sights of ever more deformity!
>
> (ll. 12–19)

Like Wyatt condemned to wear away his life in 'Stynke and close ayer', the prisoner is deformed by his environment. Coleridge contrasts the dungeon with the 'ministrations' of Mother Nature, whom he begs to 'heal' her 'wandering and distempered child':

> Thou pourest on him thy soft influences,
> Thy sunny hues, fair forms, and breathing sweets,
> Thy melodies of woods, and winds, and waters,
> Till he relent, and can no more endure
> To be a jarring and a dissonant thing
> Amid this general dance and minstrelsy;
> But, bursting into tears, wins back his way,
> His angry spirit healed and harmonised
> By the benignant touch of Love and Beauty.
>
> (ll. 22–30)

Coleridge represents the reformation of the convict – who was deformed by 'sights' of deformity, and by being seen by others through the distorting 'steam and vapours of his dungeon' – as an aural, musical process as well as a tactile one. Poetic song serves the purposes both of advocacy and therapeutic melody, gathering the 'jarring' and 'dissonant' resonance of the criminal into the 'general dance' through its own gentle regularity.

The catastrophe of solitary confinement is also evoked powerfully in George Gordon Lord Byron's 'The Prisoner of Chillon', a favourite of

---

[52] Ingrid H. Tague, *Animal Companions: Pets and Social Change in Eighteenth-Century Britain* (University Park: Pennsylvania State University Press, 2015).
[53] Samuel Taylor Coleridge, *Poetical Works*, vol. 1, in *The Collected Works*, vol. 16, ed. J. C. C. Mays (Princeton University Press, 2001), l. 5, p. 333.

Emily Dickinson.⁵⁴ The poem was based on the tale of a monk, François Bonnivard, who was imprisoned from 1530 to 1536 for having incurred the wrath of the Duke of Savoy. Byron and Shelley toured the Château de Chillon near Lac Leman (now called Lake Geneva) in late June 1816. Byron wrote an impassioned sonnet on the subject, which begins: 'Eternal Spirit of the chainless Mind! / Brightest in dungeons, Liberty! thou art,' and pays tribute to the hallowed dungeon where Bonnivard's pacing left its traces in the earth. He returned to this history in his almost four-hundred-line poem 'The Prisoner of Chillon', which acknowledges the psychic and physical harm to Bonnivard and his two brothers who were held with him in the same cell. One of the brothers is turned from human hunter to hunted animal by captivity:

> He was a hunter of the hills,
> Had followed there the deer and wolf;
> To him this dungeon was a gulf,
> And fetter'd feet the worst of ills.
>
> (ll. 103–6)

The men are 'banned, and barred' from 'the goodly earth and air'; even the sunlight is 'imprisoned'. As Bonnivard watches, his brothers decay into despair and death. Time is suspended: there is only 'silence, and a stirless breath / Which neither was of life nor death' (ll. 247–8). In this purgatorial solitude, the prisoner is neither alive nor dead, human nor stone. Byron's poem culminates in Bonnivard's physical release; but he has become so institutionalised that he will never be free again:

> At last men came to set me free;
> I asked not why, and recked not where;
> It was at length the same to me,
> Fettered or fetterless to be,
> I learned to love despair.
> And thus when they appeared at last,
> And all my bonds aside were cast,
> These heavy walls to me had grown
> A hermitage – and all my own!
>
> (ll. 370–8, p. 28)

Through a perverse 'long communion', 'my very chains and I grew friends'; his fetters make him a fettered thing, unable to escape his internal prison

---

⁵⁴ George Gordon Lord Byron, *The Works*, ed. Ernest Harley Coleridge (London: John Murray, 1901), vol. 4: *Poetry*, pp. 7–28.

even after his release. 'The Prisoner of Chillon' is an example of the moral discipline and punishment of solitary confinement gone wrong. Byron, like many of his contemporaries, feared that – unlike the caged lion or bird, which can revert to its wild nature when it is released – the captive human, removed from nature and almost all human exchange, would never again be able to cope with the world beyond his cell.

The most potent critic of the separate system was Charles Dickens. Dickens based his *American Notes* on travels in the United States in 1842, where he visited numerous 'total institutions', including workhouses, schools, asylums and prisons. His dramatic portrait of Eastern State Penitentiary begins by plainly stating that solitary confinement is 'cruel and wrong'. Though he attributes good intentions to prison wardens, he believes 'those who devised this system of Prison Discipline, and those benevolent gentlemen who carry it into execution, do not know what it is that they are doing'.[55] He argues that no one can estimate the

> torture and agony which this dreadful punishment, prolonged for years, inflicts upon the sufferers; and in guessing at it myself, and in reasoning from what I have seen written upon their faces, and what to my certain knowledge they feel within, I am only the more convinced that there is a depth of terrible endurance in it which none but the sufferers themselves can fathom. (115)

Throughout the text, Dickens's polemic draws on the imagination: unlike the wardens, who cannot empathise with the prisoners, he can hear its inaudible cries, read its 'ghastly signs and tokens' in the prisoners' faces. He attempts to put himself in the prisoner's place:

> As I walked among these solitary cells, and looked at the faces of the men within them, I tried to picture to myself the thoughts and feelings natural to their condition. I imagined the hood just taken off; and the scene of their captivity disclosed to them in all its dismal monotony. (122)

This passage demonstrates Sean Grass's point, that the success of Dickens's book relied on its ability to place 'interpretation and conjecture – narrative invention – on a level with facts as part of the account of the solitary Victorian prisoner, especially for a Victorian public accustomed to encountering the prison as a discursive rather than physical institution'.[56] Dickens's rejection of solitary confinement is based on a very literary act

---

[55] Dickens, *American Notes*, pp. 114–15. [56] Grass, *Self in the Cell*, p. 75.

of imagination and empathy, in which the convict's true suffering can be 'read' through the exercise of empathy by a specialist (literary) observer.

Wordsworth's Convicts

Many of these issues – the benefits and risks of solitude, the social and economic bases of criminality, empathy and sentiment in the representation of suffering, the irrepressibility of language and the scrutiny of one's own life through solitary reflection – are central to the Romantic poets. Wordsworth uses figures of imprisonment and slavery in his many poetic meditations on personal and political freedom, and to decry urban life and the alienating effects of socialisation: as he matures, 'Shades of the prison-house begin to close / Upon the growing Boy';[57] eventually he is 'by chains confined / Of business, care, or pleasure'.[58] In the famous opening of *The Prelude* of 1805, Wordsworth breaks his invocation to the gentle breeze with an image of bondage:

> A captive greets thee, coming from a house
> Of bondage, from yon city's walls set free,
> A prison where he hath been long immured.
> Now I am free, enfranchised and at large,
> May fix my habitation where I will.[59]

The breeze is free; the captive is loosed, and like that breeze can determine his habitation by 'will'. This freedom is articulated in the pliable constraint of blank verse, which since Milton's epochal development of it has been synonymous with a longed-for return to classical republican liberty.

Wordsworth's poems are also populated by solitary figures, recluses and speakers who wander lonely as clouds, from the 'utter solitude' of the sheepfold where Michael parted from his son, to the remote 'lonely place' where the leech gatherer sits; isolated ruined cottages and a 'brownie's cell' where 'world-wearied Men withdrew of yore'.[60] His own ideal of solitude is not enclosed but enjoyed outdoors, and often in the presence of 'My

---

[57] William Wordsworth, *Poems, in Two Volumes, and Other Poems*, ed. Jared Curtis (Ithaca, NY: Cornell University Press, 1983), ll. 66–8, p. 273.
[58] William Wordsworth, *Shorter Poems, 1807–1820*, ed. Carl H. Ketcham (Ithaca, NY: Cornell University Press, 1989), ll. 4–5, p. 53.
[59] William Wordsworth, '*The Prelude of 1805, in Thirteen Books*', *The Prelude, 1799, 1805, 1850*, ed. Jonathan Wordsworth, M. H. Abrams and Stephen Gill (London: Norton, 1979), ll. 6–10, p. 28.
[60] William Wordsworth, 'Michael', *Lyrical Ballads, and Other Poems, 1797–1800*, ed. James Butler and Karen Green (Ithaca, NY: Cornell University Press, 1992), l. 13, p. 253; 'Resolution and Independence,' *Poems, in Two Volumes,* l. 52, p. 129.

dear, dear Friend' and sister.⁶¹ Social life, particularly amidst the crowd, has its risks; Wordsworth insisted that the benefits of 'gracious, ... benign' solitude are best felt 'When from our better selves we have too long / Been parted by the hurrying world, and droop, / Sick of its business, of its pleasures tired'.⁶² But solitude is also 'Most potent when impressed upon the mind / With an appropriate human centre', Wordsworth argues:

> Or as the soul of that great Power is met
> Sometimes embodied on a public road,
> When, for the night deserted, it assumes
> A character of quiet more profound
> Than pathless wastes.⁶³

This discourse emerges after Wordsworth describes staying up all night dancing with friends; after such intense sociability, a brief moment of solitude is healthful, and magnifies the beauty of the sunrise. But what the speaker then meets on 'a public road' is not a character of quiet, but the discharged soldier. Excessively solitary, a 'ghastly' presence, the soldier is 'a man cut off / From all his kind'. As John Bugg has noted, the soldier has recently returned from service in the Caribbean, probably in San Domingue (Haiti); he wanders in illness and loneliness, 'within a climate of fear and suspicion' created by the surveillance and repression of the Gagging Acts.⁶⁴

Solitude in Wordsworth's poetry also relates to specific social conditions, including poverty, state repression and the crisis in poor relief that led to Pitt's failed attempt at reform in 1796 and the later passage of the 1834 Poor Law Amendment Act. These contexts arise in 'The Old Cumberland Beggar', one of Wordsworth's *Lyrical Ballads*. The beggar is a solitary man, who sat 'and ate his food in solitude' surrounded by 'those wild unpeopled hills'.⁶⁵ However, his solitude is interrupted, and he is supported, by companions in the villages as he 'creeps / from door to door' (ll. 79–80, p. 231), a living embodiment of the community's record of charity.⁶⁶ Absolute solitude for the Cumberland beggar would mean starvation; community makes solitude survivable. In exchange, the beggar embodies a kind of moving pedagogy, his stooped form the personification of the community's interconnectedness. He is an opportunity for charity, but

---

⁶¹ Wordsworth, *Lyrical Ballads* (1798), ll. 5–6, 117, 122, pp. 116, 119.
⁶² Wordsworth, *The Prelude* (1850), IV.353–5, p. 143.
⁶³ Wordsworth, *The Prelude* (1850), IV. 358–69, pp. 143, 145.
⁶⁴ Bugg, *Five Long Winters*, pp. 151–5. ⁶⁵ Wordsworth, *Lyrical Ballads*, ll. 14–15, p. 229.
⁶⁶ For an alternative reading of this poem, see Toby R. Benis, *Romanticism on the Road: The Marginal Gains of Wordsworth's Homeless* (New York: Macmillan and St Martin's Press, 2000), pp. 116–17.

also for reflection among 'the unlettered villagers' and bookish upper classes alike.[67] He suffers, but his vagrancy is a form of freedom too. For that reason, the poem prays that he can remain free from the workhouses:

> May never House, misnamed of industry,
> Make him a captive; for that pent-up din,
> Those life-consuming sounds that clog the air,
> Be his the natural silence of old age.
> Let him be free of mountain solitudes ...
>
> (ll. 172–6, pp. 233–4)

Wordsworth described the poem as his response to the 'war upon mendicancy in all its forms' that the 'political economists' were pursuing.[68] He saw prisons and asylums as part of emerging 'systems of segregative control' and 'state-controlled solutions to social problems'.[69] 'Pent' up like prisoners, animals or dammed streams in cities and factories, the poor are condemned to clogged air and mechanical racket, far from the 'natural silence' and freedom of the mountains.

Throughout his life, when Wordsworth represents scenes of poverty and vagrancy, he argues that the freedom to dwell in the open air, or among the community, is preferable to being interned in an institution of the state or the church.

> I know an aged Man constrained to dwell
> In a large house of public charity,
> Where he abides, as in a Prisoner's cell,
> With numbers near, alas! no company[70]

he writes in a late lyric. This old man had a robin who kept him company, when he used to beg for alms in the road; the bond between this 'solitary pair' of man and animal was 'so strong' that 'when his fate had housed him 'mid a throng / The Captive shunned all converse proffered there': in the workhouse he refused to talk with anyone else (ll. 21–4, p. 400). While prison reformers spoke of human beings turned into animals by solitary captivity, the old man's relationship to the bird reflects the importance of animal companions across prison writing, as warm and freely mobile creatures whose kindness contrasts with the cruelty of the human jailer.

---

[67] David Simpson, *Wordsworth, Commodification and Social Concern* (Cambridge University Press, 2009), p. 66.
[68] Mary Moorman, *William Wordsworth: A Biography, The Early Years, 1770–1803* (Oxford: Clarendon, 1957), p. 313.
[69] Moorman, *Wordsworth*, p. 181.   [70] William Wordsworth, *Last Poems*, ll. 1–4, p. 398.

In Wordsworth's poem, the mute animal speaks to the person abandoned by humankind.

Wordsworth is drawn to the scene of the prison or its aftermath as a site for the exploration of human and animal interdependency, the beneficial properties of nature and the destructive effects of absolute solitude. All these themes – prison reform, salutary and harmful solitude and fellowship – are gathered in 'The Convict', a poem written in 1796. The poem reflects the influence of William Godwin's *An Enquiry Concerning Political Justice* (1793), including its preference for transportation over the death penalty, corporal punishment or hard labour.[71] Godwin argued that imprisonment was only justifiable so long as the criminal was a danger to society. He viewed solitary confinement as 'uncommonly tyrannical and severe': solitude deprives man, fundamentally a social animal, of companionship and guidance; it increases 'our selfish and unsocial dispositions'; it induces the 'atmosphere of a dungeon' in the heart; and 'may be a nursery for madmen and idiots, but not for useful members of society'.[72] Wordsworth's depiction in the poem of the 'comfortless vault of disease' and 'the fetters that link him to death' refers to the gaol fever and use of chains that John Howard reported critically in *The State of the Prisons* (1777) and which featured in Godwin's book *Caleb Williams*.[73]

'The Convict' was printed in the *Morning Post* on 14 December 1797. It was republished (with several revisions) in *Lyrical Ballads* in 1798, but suppressed in the 1800 edition of that work, following criticism of Wordsworth's 'misplaced commiseration' by Charles Burney and Robert Southey.[74] The poem was included in the 1802 edition of *Lyrical Ballads* published in America. Here it is:

> The glory of evening was spread through the west;
> – On the slope of a mountain I stood,
> While the joy that precedes the calm season of rest
> Rang loud through the meadow and wood.
>
> 'And must we then part from a dwelling so fair?'   5
> In the pain of my spirit I said,

---

[71] Quentin Bailey, *Wordsworth's Vagrants: Police, Prisons, and Poetry in the 1790s* (Farnham: Ashgate, 2011), p. 4.
[72] William Godwin, *Political and Philosophical Writings*, vol. 3: *An Enquiry Concerning Political Justice*, ed. Mark Philp (London: Pickering, 1993), pp. 403–5.
[73] Howard, *State of the Prisons*, p. 2.
[74] Charles Burney, *Monthly Review* 29 (June 1799), pp. 202–10; quoted in Wordsworth, *Lyrical Ballads*, p. 161.

And with a deep sadness I turned, to repair
To the cell where the convict is laid.

The thick-ribbed walls that o'ershadow the gate
Resound; and the dungeons unfold: 10
I pause; and at length, through the glimmering grate,
That outcast of pity behold.

His black matted head on his shoulder is bent,
And deep is the sigh of his breath,
And with stedfast dejection his eyes are intent 15
On the fetters that link him to death.

Tis sorrow enough on that visage to gaze,
That body dismiss'd from his care;
Yet my fancy has pierced to his heart, and pourtrays
More terrible images there. 20

His bones are consumed, and his life-blood is dried,
With wishes the past to undo;
And his crime, through the pains that o'erwhelm him, descried,
Still blackens and grows on his view.

When from the dark synod, or blood-reeking field, 25
To his chamber the monarch is led,
All soothers of sense their soft virtue shall yield,
And quietness pillow his head.

But if grief, self-consumed, in oblivion would doze,
And conscience her tortures appease, 30
'Mid tumult and uproar this man must repose;
In the comfortless vault of disease.

When his fetters at night have so press'd on his limbs,
That the weight can no longer be born,
If, while a half-slumber his memory bedims, 35
The wretch on his pallet should turn,

While the jail-mastiff howls at the dull clanking chain,
From the roots of his hair there shall start
A thousand sharp punctures of cold-sweating pain,
And terror shall leap at his heart. 40

But now he half-raises his deep-sunken eye,
And the motion unsettles a tear;
The silence of sorrow it seems to supply,
And asks of me why I am here.

'Poor victim! no idle intruder has stood 45
'With o'erweening complacence our state to compare,
'But one, whose first wish is the wish to be good,
'Is come as a brother thy sorrows to share.

'At thy name though compassion her nature resign,
'Though in virtue's proud mouth thy report be a stain, 50
'My care, if the arm of the mighty were mine,
'Would plant thee where yet thou might'st blossom again.'[75]

In the poem's opening, we see a familiar scene of parting on a mountain-top, but not the person from whom the speaker is parted. This scene establishes a contrast and a contraction, between the calm of rest and loud ringing of joy of nature and 'the cell where the convict is laid' (l. 8). This laying introduces the convict as a passive object, laid out like a corpse, or an egg. The cell is approached through 'thick-ribbed walls': the physical metaphor suggests the institution is like a body, in which the heart (the convict?) is enfolded. These walls 'resound', echoing with a different noise from the joy that rings on the mountainside, just as Rush had recommended that the grating of an iron door should echo from a neighbouring mountain to deeply pierce the soul.

The speaker stops here, and encounters the convict first as an image. The convict's abjection is theatrical, gestural: he is still, sighing, downcast, staring implacably at his fetters 'that link him to death'. The speaker can do more, however, than only 'gaze' on a visage and a surface; like Dickens he can, through the operation of his imagination, 'pierce' to his heart, where he again encounters 'more terrible images': memorial or psychic images that are more terrible than those that can be seen, or more images that mirror the visual terror of the prison. In his state of civil death, the convict also seems actually half dead (his bones turning to ash, his blood dried up). This is attributed to the poison of his crime and his unrelieved remorse: it 'still blackens and grows on his view'. There are thus two spectacles in view. The convict is a spectacle for the speaker, the crime is a spectacle for the convict.

It is at this moment that the convict raises his eyes and looks back at the speaker. This exchange of glances, rather than any articulation, seems a challenge, or a question: why are you here? The question reflects the tradition of public visitors to prisons including Eastern State and Auburn, which was also planned for the Panopticon.[76] The speaker's reply is that he

---

[75] Wordsworth, *Lyrical Ballads*, pp. 140–2. [76] Bailey, *Wordsworth's Vagrants*, p. 6.

does not intend idly 'to compare' their states, but merely to share the convict's sorrows as a brother. They may be brothers, but they are opposites: the speaker's 'first wish is the wish to be good', while the convict is utterly corroded by his criminality. This expression of fraternity, Alan Liu argues, is part of a tendency in Wordsworth to '"familiarise" crime, to bring criminality by representation into the household', where it can be understood.[77] But what is noticeable is how the speaker's simple empathy based on brotherly identification is immediately displaced by a much more awkward identification with the sovereign: 'if the arm of the mighty were mine'. The convict's response to his visitor's benevolence is unknown. The poem ends with the speaker's wish.

As in Wyatt's and Halpern's poems, Wordsworth represses the speech of the other: unlike the speaker's statements, which are marked as quotations, the convict's question, why are you here, is indirect speech, embedded in a syntax that makes it unclear whether it is even spoken, or just something his tearful visage 'seems' to ask. Apart from this question, there is no way of accessing the convict's experience. We cannot know whether the moral conditions or feelings imputed to him by the poetic observer are in any way accurate. We do not know if his question is an expression of shame or rage or curiosity. The observer does the imagining and the reflecting *for* the convict, interpreting him as a moral specimen, and the moral inadequacies of the prison, without any input from the person who is the poem's 'subject'.

The speaker then switches from empathetic observer to judge, proposing how he would dispense justice (transportation rather than imprisonment). But the poem ends without a feeling of resolution – it seems like there is a stanza missing, one in which the speaker leaves the prison, reflects on the moral situation and its relevance to his own life, etc. Perhaps this is because the speaker has foresworn complacent comparisons of their two states, and instead committed to 'be good' and 'share' in the convict's sorrows. But he does neither. The poem halts with this suspended dialogue: the free man makes a speech, the convict does not respond. This inconclusive conclusion is characteristic of Wordsworth's poems of the 1790s, as Gary Harrison describes them, in highlighting the precarity of the speaker's own economic, social and psychic identity: 'Destabilizing the conventional relationship between spectator and spectacle, Wordsworth's itinerants leave inconclusive the spectator's own social and subjective boundaries.'[78]

---

[77] Alan Liu, *Wordsworth: A Sense of History* (Stanford University Press, 1989), pp. 228–9.
[78] Gary Harrison, *Wordsworth's Vagrant Muse: Poetry, Poverty and Power* (Detroit: Wayne State University Press, 1994), p. 77.

Wordsworth's attitude to the 'segregative institution' of the prison changed profoundly over his lifetime. His 'Sonnets upon the Punishment of Death', written in 1839–40 and published in the *London Quarterly Review* in 1841, argue that compassion that withholds the sentence of death is a dangerous incitement to crime. In response to a review of sentencing in 1837, which removed the death penalty from offences other than treason, murder and rape, Wordsworth urges 'lawgivers' to beware:

> Lest capital pains remitting till ye spare
> The murderer, ye, by sanction to that thought,
> Seemingly given, debase the general mind[79]

and undermine the whole social contract. Ironically, this argument is the exact opposite of the reforming process that resulted in the privatisation and eventual abolition of corporal punishment: the public execution was a viciously *disorderly* scene, participation in which 'debased the general mind', according to reformers including Howard and Bentham.

Sounding a bit like the Duke in *Measure for Measure*, Wordsworth asserts that severity is kindness in a judge, 'As all Authority in earth depends / On Love and Fear' (V, ll. 5–7, p. 871). He even argues that those who 'strain' Christ's mandates and commit to patience, suffering and love, 'forbid the State to inflict a pain', and risk 'Making of social order a mere dream' (VII, ll. 13–14, p. 873). In conclusion, the poems – having argued for the consistent and enduring use of the death penalty – wish that its imminence as a threat is so dreadful that it eventually need not be used: 'Strike not from Law's firm hand that awful rod, / But leave it thence to drop for lack of use: / Oh, speed the blessed hour, Almighty God!' (XIII, ll. 12–14, p. 877). That is, Wordsworth 'endorses the death penalty as a vivid source of terror that might frighten the political subject into submission' but 'cannot support it without simultaneously insisting upon its archaism and (the poet wishes) its ultimate demise'.[80]

While his *Lyrical Ballad* reflects the pleas for clemency that were issued by Beccaria, Howard and Godwin, these sonnets suggest that the death penalty is a necessary evil. In both instances, prison is a terrifying, injurious place; but where the young Wordsworth offers compassionate kinship to the convict, the older Wordsworth sees mercy in his elimination. In the

---

[79] William Wordsworth, *Sonnet Series and Itinerary Poems, 1820–1845*, ed. Geoffrey Jackson (Ithaca, NY: Cornell University Press, 2004), IV, ll. 7–9, p. 871.

[80] Mark Canuel, *The Shadow of Death: Literature, Romanticism, and the Subject of Punishment* (Princeton University Press, 2007), p. 56.

eleventh and twelfth sonnets, he argues that without the threat of death, the convict might relapse; that death is more welcome than long incarceration or transportation:

> Ah, think how one compelled for life to abide
> Locked in a dungeon needs must eat the heart
> Out of his own humanity, and part
> With every hope that mutual cares provide;
> And, should a less unnatural doom confide
> In life-long exile on a savage coast,
> Soon the relapsing penitent may boast
> Of yet more heinous guilt, with fiercer pride ...
>
> (XI, ll. 1–8, p. 875)

Mercy will leave the issue in God's hands instead. The sonnet expresses an attitude that Foucault found in nineteenth-century penal reformers: 'justice no longer takes public responsibility for the violence that is bound up with its practice. If it too strikes, if it too kills, it is not as a glorification of its strength, but as an element of itself that it is obliged to tolerate, that it finds difficult to account for.'[81]

Both the sonnets and 'The Convict' make the prisoner into a moral spectacle. When Wordsworth invites us to 'See the Condemned alone within his cell' in the 'Sonnets', he wishes that we imagine him 'a kneeling Penitent / Before the Altar', asking forgiveness and being helped by the state 'to meet the last Tribunal's voice', as if immediate judgement were better than life imprisonment (XII, ll. 1, 6–7, 12, p. 876). In putting the 'pale Convict' on display (XIII, l. 3, p. 876), Wordsworth is constructing another scene of Gothic suffering and entombment, and – like Dickens, but for contrary political effect – inviting the reader to 'think' or imagine how the incarcerated person feels about or experiences their imprisonment. The opening sonnets provoke compassion through imagery of weeping prisoners and ghastly scaffolds, only to command the reader to 'restrain compassion', if it prevents the exercise of justice (II, l. 9, p. 870).[82] Feeling is elicited, in order that the proper role of feeling (and the zones of activity from which it should be excluded) can be made clear; the reader is made to feel, then discern, like a judge. Wordsworth's argument depends on his authority as a purveyor of sympathetic poetic figures, the kind known from his earlier poems on vagrancy. And yet

---

[81] Foucault, *Discipline and Punish*, p. 9.
[82] Seraphia D. Leyda, 'Wordsworth's "Sonnets Upon the Punishment of Death"', *The Wordsworth Circle* (Winter 1983), pp. 48–53(49).

here, rather than offering a narrative of communal redemption, he hurries the condemned prisoner off to the inscrutable judgement of providence.

Wordsworth's *Sonnets* were robustly attacked by *The United States Magazine and Democratic Review*, which issued a sixteen-page rebuttal of their argument in March 1842, the first in a series of criticisms published over two years. The editor, John O'Sullivan, wrote that 'to behold him take down the sacred lyre, and attune its chords to the harsh creaking of the scaffold and the clanking of the victim's chains, seems almost a profanation and a sacrilege'.[83] O'Sullivan's critique is an ideological one, but it is pointed towards Wordsworth's musicality, his poetic diction, his sonority: Wordsworth transports 'a harp of heaven' into 'the foul and hideous harmonies of hell'. As Paul Christian Jones notes, the *Review* campaigned 'to vilify [Wordsworth] as a failed poet, a mouthpiece for an oppressive State, and an enemy of popular interest' (35). Wordsworth's support of the death penalty was particularly damaging to the campaign for its abolition, because American reviewers of *Lyrical Ballads* had held him up as the epitome of Christian benevolence and democratic equality (42).

O'Sullivan's political argument is ciphered as literary criticism. Other contributors to the *Review* also attacked Wordsworth's political position as a poetic failure: 'A poet cannot strive for despotism; / His harp lies shattered,' James Russell Lowell wrote in May 1842 (43). Both responses reflect Wordsworth's own attempt to focus his reader in the final sonnets on their form as both a means of persuasion, and a mitigation of the harshest aspects of the argument. As he explains in the 'Apology' (sonnet XIV),

> The formal World relaxes her cold chain
> For One who speaks in numbers; ampler scope
> His utterance finds; and, conscious of the gain,
> Imagination works with bolder hope
> The cause of grateful reason to sustain[.]
>
> (XIV, ll. 1–5, p. 877)

In this sequence, the formal enclosure and chain-link rhymes of the sonnet are mimetic of carceral structures, whose performance (or execution) can address the enchained mind of the social world. Speaking in 'numbers'

---

[83] Paul Christian Jones, *Against the Gallows: Antebellum American Writers and the Movement to Abolish Capital Punishment* (Iowa City: University of Iowa Press, 2011), pp. 34–5.

appeals to the 'formal' World, allowing the product of the 'imagination' to bypass the 'cold chain' of reason. But the convict's chains 'link him to death', not to other people; he is closer to the howling, chained-up dog in 'The Convict' than the human visitor.

Wordsworth suggests his sonnets have little hope of persuading anyone who is in favour of abolishing the death penalty of its merits through their argument. Their hope lies in their form, which is intended to lubricate the mind's capacity for logical judgement. But such lubrication is antithetical to the unyielding vigilance in criminal contexts that Wordsworth has been urging. Through their formality they draw out feeling and imagination; and yet the law is based not on feeling, but on rational judgement. Wordsworth had earlier warned, quoting Sir Francis Bacon, that if 'guilt escaping, passion then might plead / In angry spirits for her old free range, / And the "wild justice of revenge" prevail' (VIII, ll. 12–14, p. 873).[84]

Wordsworth's early poetry is full of empathy for the criminals, convicts and vagrants that populate it, and whose fates leave sometimes spectacular evidence of the exercise of 'justice' on the countryside. But these sympathies would yield to a more conservative view of the necessity of the ultimate judicial sanction of death. Wordsworth eventually concluded that relieving the prisoner of his life was a compassionate solution to the depravity of incarceration, as well as a necessary instrument of state power. The story of his conversion from a young radical to conservative old man pondering ecclesiastical history is well known, his 'Sonnets upon the Punishment of Death' perhaps less so. His concluding sonnet counterposes the wild justice of revenge with the cause of grateful reason, and makes a modest claim to authority – I have merely sought 'guidance' from the Lord, he writes. The poems invite all of us – 'whatso'er the way / Each takes in this high matter' – to travel together: 'all may move / Cheered with the prospect of a brighter day' (XIV, ll. 10–14, p. 877). Transported by such bland terms, it is easy to forget that what grateful reason is defending is the right to put human beings to death. The 'painful road' of national debate is less painful than the road to the gallows, and the brighter day for the reader cannot be glimpsed from the darkness of the cell.

Towards the end of his life, a poet who once regarded the spectacle of the gibbet as leaving 'dissolute men unthinking and untaught', who had once framed a poetics from the speech of ordinary people and visited the convict in the spirit of brotherly compassion, was left cold by the spectacle of the

---

[84] Francis Bacon, 'Of Revenge,' in *The Essayes or Counsels, Civill and Morall*, ed. Michael Kiernan (Oxford: Clarendon Press, 1985), p. 16.

execution. He attests that his old heart finally 'more strongly beats / Against all barriers which its labour meets / In lofty place, or humble Life's domain' (XIV, ll. 6–8, p. 877), not in the service of class struggle, but of the murder of the poor by the state. Outrage against Wordsworth's 'Sonnets' resounded most loudly in radical American publications in the mid-nineteenth century. And it is in the United States that the lessons of that earlier Romanticism – on the healthful qualities of nature and communion, solidarity and radical politics, the disasters of solitary confinement and the urgency of the imagination – have been reawakened by contemporary abolitionists seeking to overthrow the American carceral regime.

CHAPTER 4

Hours of Lead
The Modern US Prison, Segregation and Solidarity

> *Yeah smile*
> *Because when the skeletons come rising out*
> *Of your closets to haunt your poor*
> *Misguided ass*
> *I'll still be standing righteous within*
> *The valves of my own soul*
> *Even after your cages have claimed my bones.*
> — 'Derek Janson'

In this poem, a writer who has spent many years in control units in Washington state prisons proclaims an autonomy that the cage cannot break: my soul is my own, even if you possess my bones. His affirmation of the inalienable freedom of the mind in conditions of absolute oppression echoes Emily Dickinson's declaration of solitary independence: 'The Soul selects her own society.' Dickinson writes that the soul chooses one 'from an ample nation', 'Then – close the Valves of her attention – / Like Stone – .' Similarly, Janson's poem anticipates resurrection from the entombment of the cell, but not through state-enforced mechanisms of redemption. The technical image of the valve represents a different form of closure to the slamming of the cell door: it is mechanical, musical and anatomical, a regulatory device that maintains the safety and equilibrium of a system. Janson's affirmation of the valves, and values, of his own soul, tags 'you', the guard, the reader, as the one who will be haunted, while he stands in combative righteousness against the institution's administered violence.

The previous chapter argued that solitude became one of the pre-eminent carceral techniques for enforcing moral conformity at the same time that it was explored by the Romantic poets as a condition for creative self-discovery. This chapter will examine the poetics of imprisonment in the contemporary United States. It focuses on the psychic and physical suffering induced by extended periods of solitary confinement. In these conditions of torture, when the institution tries to grind the person down into bare life, lyric's promise – that it testifies to the endurance of the human individual – is particularly powerful as a form of resistance, an appeal to others, and a means of creating solidarity. Poetry is also a technique deployed by activists on both sides of the walls to make visible the obscene violence of mass incarceration. In the anthology *No Selves to Defend* edited by Mariame Kaba, for example, the biographical and judicial facts about imprisoned women are posited between a portrait (lovingly representing the woman's appearance) and a poem (interpreting those facts and contextualising them within the sexist and racist violence of the prison industrial complex; several of these poems are by the women themselves).[1]

The importance of the body of work being written in prison to a book on *Poetry and Bondage* is obvious. But there are risks in attending to these poems, too, particularly the ones that reflect experiences of extreme physical and psychic torture. Those risks include voyeurism, and collaboration with carceral regimes. As a reader, I enact what Michelle Brown calls 'penal spectatorship' – someone 'who looks in on punishment and yet is also its author'.[2] But Brown also argues it is impossible not to look in on punishment; 'penality ... is instrumental to the manner in which we produce subjectivities, modes of spectatorship, and social order', and cultural objects such as prison films are keyed to the penitentiary as a space of individual transformation, as indeed are certain traditions of the lyric.[3] Critical distance is another risk. Working in the United Kingdom, where opportunities to engage with imprisoned writers are very limited, but which also does not make use of solitary confinement with anything like the same severity and regularity as the United States, I have relied largely on books, magazines, chapbooks and other printed materials in writing this chapter, rather than direct communication with writers who are now inside. The limitations of this approach were pressed home to me by readers at Eastern Michigan University and the Women's Huron Valley correctional facility, relayed by Rob Halpern. While the mediation of these texts is part of the focus of my analysis – how does the prison anthology work for or against the institution where it is produced? – I take seriously their point that I am just 'interpreting the already interpreted'; the point, however, should be to change it.

---

[1] Mariame Kaba (ed.), *No Selves to Defend: A Legacy of Criminalizing Women of Color for Self-Defence* (2014), noselves2defend.wordpress.com/ (accessed 4 May 2021).
[2] Michelle Brown, *The Culture of Punishment: Prison, Society, and Spectacle* (New York University Press, 2009), p. 21.
[3] Brown, *Culture of Punishment*, pp. 56, 59.

Their critiques also foreground some of the central preoccupations of this book, not just about poetics, but about criticism, a professionalised and privileged form of reading whose etymology connects it to *judging*. How do I, as a non-incarcerated reader and writer, judge, or reproduce those categories of (transformed, penitent, authentic, feeling) individuality that also constitute the unit of carceral discipline? How do I choose from the enormous wealth of writing from prison, those lyrics that by virtue of being chosen then become 'exemplary' of poetry written in prison? Is there such a thing as 'the prison poem' anyway? As Dylan Rodríguez asks, 'What are the conditions of possibility for these carceral texts? What are the contexts – emphasis on the plural – of their production in U.S. prisons, jails, and detention centers? What kind(s) of political practice(s) do these texts signify, transform, and create?'[4] What happens to imprisoned people's ability to represent *themselves*, when they become the object of someone else's – my – representation?

Many poets writing in prison include in their work assertions of their desire *not* to be read as 'prison poets', but to be taken seriously as artists whose truths are not contingent on their circumstances. Nicole Fleetwood also cites numerous artists who foreground the carceral contexts of their practice, the way it shapes their materials, relationships, time and techniques. She refers to 'carceral aesthetics' as 'a range of relational art practices ... that take place across various states of un/freedom produced in the era of mass incarceration. These artworks attempt to depict the scale and reach of incarceration and simultaneously to address what one might call a provisional public, a space of engagement facilitated through and against how prisons have shaped the public sphere and relations among people differently positioned across carceral geographies.'[5] Borrowing Fleetwood's terms, in this chapter I discuss carceral poetics, writing that explicitly thematises the prison – that highlights 'the materiality, architecture, temporalities, logics, and economics of the production of prison' poetry (26).

Fleetwood's emphasis on the shaping of the public sphere and social, political and economic relations in carceral geographies draws on the work of Ruth Wilson Gilmore and others, who have made clear that the prison is not a space of exception within geographies of racial capitalist accumulation, nor is it 'possible to localize the prison as a discrete space'; it is a

---

[4] Dylan Rodríguez, *Forced Passages: Imprisoned Radical Intellectuals and the U. S. Prison Regime* (Minneapolis: University of Minnesota Press, 2006), p. 82.
[5] Nicole R. Fleetwood, *Marking Time: Art in the Age of Mass Incarceration* (Cambridge, MA: Harvard University Press, 2020), p. 25.

regime and not an institution, 'inscribed as both a localisation and a constitutive logic of the state's production of juridical, spatial, and militarised dominion'.[6] Attending to what is produced 'in prison' means attending also to who survives and who doesn't, who flourishes and who doesn't, within domestic and international regimes of racialised capitalism and state violence. It involves constituting 'prison writing' as an irrational category at the same time as working to demolish it. Anoop Mirpuri has argued that the canonisation of prison writing as a supposedly discrete genre, which – like the prison – is supposed to constitute 'a separate, bounded, and ontologically distinct space', reifies that writing, holding it apart from 'that which takes place in the so-called free world'.[7] Mirpuri calls for abolition as an interpretive practice that 'acknowledges the inescapable politics and constitutive agency of its own hermeneutic labor in making the text legible' (44).

Abolition of the conditions that produce the works studied in this chapter, and thus of the conditions that also produce this chapter, what Mirpuri calls the 'corrective-extraction complex' of academia, is the demand of those works and this chapter; but such a demand is not effective or legitimate when it is issued in a book written by an academic and published by a university press, accruing value to me and to the institutions for which I labour that is not immediately shared with the authors of these poems. Rodríguez is very clear in condemning critical engagement with contemporary prison praxis as 'a relation of appropriation and translation, structurally dominated by free world (professional and nonprofessional) intellectuals and activists' who exploit those texts for their own benefit. Rodríguez speaks of the failure of the meeting (between the imprisoned radical intellectual and the non-imprisoned activist/scholar) as a 'reifying event: the charade of "collaboration" reproduces the violent condition of its genesis, for there would have been no (alleged) collaboration absent the existence of the imprisonment regime .... In this sense, the only "good" meeting (that is, the only liberatory meeting) is the one that *foments the collapse of its condition.*'[8] Gilmore says that abolition requires 'that we change one thing, which is everything'.[9] On its way to changing everything, an abolitionist literary criticism would overturn the privileging of

---

[6] Anoop Mirpuri, 'A Correction-Extraction Complex: Prison, Literature, and Abolition as an Interpretive Practice', *Cultural Critique* 104 (Summer 2019), pp. 39–71 (47); Léopold Lambert and Ruth Wilson Gilmore, 'Making Abolition Geography in California's Central Valley with Ruth Wilson Gilmore,' *The Funambulist* 21 (Jan–Feb 2019).
[7] Mirpuri, 'Correction-Extraction', pp. 42–3.   [8] Rodríguez, *Forced Passages*, pp. 37–8; 32.
[9] Gilmore, 'Making Abolition Geography'.

the lyric subject with a different understanding of imaginative emancipation, but this is work that will not finally get done in academic books.

Criticism and the State of Carceral Exception

Fleetwood's emphasis on relationality and address are crucial for thinking about not only the making of the poems discussed in this chapter, but also their distribution. As Jimmy Santiago Baca writes in his poem 'My Dog Barks', addressing a 'professor from Flagstaff' who has invited him to participate in a conference on prison writing:

> you prefer to translate their suffering into MFA papers,
> to turn their deaths into metaphors,
> to make their real cries and real terror a tone in the text
> that people outside can philosophise about;
> it's only about writing, not what would free these men
> from their tormentors. Besides, if they weren't in prison
> you wouldn't be able to have a conference, would you?[10]

Baca's satire of the appropriation of 'prison writing' by academic critics speaks directly to, and against, me. The risks for the imprisoned poet of turning 'death into metaphor' is significantly different from that of the critic, who is a kind of parasite dependent on the free labour of the incarcerated person; Baca makes the economy of these relations and non-relations explicit, in a poetic *recusatio* which I am, again, translating into a paper.

Critics tend to read writing by imprisoned people in one of two ways: either it is sociological, valued for what it tells us about the history and function of the penal institution; or it is consecrated as 'literary', displaying qualities that are culturally valued because they can be assimilated to the history of the literary canon. While the literary approach seeks to assimilate prison writing to the values of humanist literary criticism (which it imitates but does not disturb – unlike the values of the prison industrial complex, which it does), the sociological approach condemns these texts to purposiveness, segregating them from the history and function of the lyric as such.

An example of the sociological approach can be found in Bell Chevigny's list of concrete aims that she says typify most writing from prison: 'to set the record straight, to bear witness to prison experience, to protest some facet of the criminal justice system', to fend off madness and

---

[10] Jimmy Santiago Baca, *Singing at the Gates: Selected Poems* (New York: Grove Press, 2014), p. 153.

resist institutionalisation, repression, racism and silencing, to explore emotions, or vent rage and make reparations.[11] She views these texts as *deliberative,* dedicated to specific, practical, real-life goals. Robert Ferguson follows 'captivity narratives' down a single pathway, from anxiety, to exasperation, to despair; 'Themes begin with deprivation: the loss of the natural world and outside contact, the lack of privacy, and the yearning for silence amid the endless noise of angry people in a refracting metal world', to physical annoyances, the indifference of or abuse by authority, threats of violence, fear of the unexpected, and 'how to control a helpless situation or how to hold onto identity'.[12] The narratives, he argues, are survival strategies for their writers, and seek to break the silence imposed on the captive subject through acts of address intended for outside readers.

By contrast, the literary-critical approach often looks to writing from prison as potent expressions of authenticity. Valorising the 'rawness, immediacy, and authenticity' of prison writing, critics presume that there is a 'transparent correspondence' between prison texts and their authors while erasing 'the material conditions that determine the legibility of the prison as an isolated space'.[13] Some imprisoned writers themselves ascribe to this argument: artists 'always express themselves in a soulful deep manner', and 'find atonement in their art'; 'while locked away in a cage, art allows them to free their souls', and provides a connection with 'outside patrons' who thereby recognise the incarcerated person's humanity.[14] In his introduction to *Soledad Brother*, the highly influential collection of letters by George Jackson, Jean Genet argues that a book written in prison is 'addressed chiefly perhaps to readers who are not outcasts, who have never been to jail and who will never go there'; otherwise:

> the man who writes it need only take, in order to fling them down on paper, the forbidden words, the accursed words, the words covered with blood, the unwritten words of spit and sperm – like the ultimate name of God – the dangerous words, the padlocked words, the words that do not belong to the dictionary.[15]

---

[11] Bell Gale Chevigny, '"All I Have, a Lament and a Boast": Why Prisoners Write', in *Prose and Cons: Essays on Prison Literature in the United States*, ed. D. Quentin Miller (Jefferson: McFarland, 2005), pp. 245–71 (248).
[12] Robert A. Ferguson, *Inferno: An Anatomy of American Punishment* (Cambridge, MA: Harvard University Press, 2014), p. 165.
[13] Mirpuri, 'Correction-Extraction Complex', pp. 42–3.
[14] Bobby Bostic, *Life Goes on Inside Prison* (Self-published e-book, May 2020).
[15] Jean Genet, introduction, George Jackson, *Soledad Brother: The Prison Letters of George Jackson* (Baltimore: Penguin and Jonathan Cape, 1970), p. 21.

The true writing of prison – that which is intended not for 'readers who are not outcasts' – is a writing made directly from the body, from blood, spit and sperm, the words of the outcast that don't belong to the society of the dictionary. But as Mirpuri warns, 'authenticity should be understood as the effect of an interpretive practice that secures a correction-extraction complex' (52). Like the Lomaxes going to prison to find authentic folk song, as will be discussed in Chapter 7, the critic looks to the imprisoned writer for testimony and witness: expressions of bleak subjectivity, laments without listeners in the singular language of the body.

Other critics attempt to assimilate this writing to the literary canon by recognising its artifice. Several identify topoi such as the tragic beauty of solitude; the glorification of the individual; existential anguish; dramas of fall and redemption under the aegis of Prometheus-Lucifer, recurrent biblical tropes; escape by flight, memory, dream and death; obsessive thoughts; and admiration for dissent and endurance.[16] These forms of artifice are discovered in the work of laureate writers who happened to be in prison such as St Paul, Boethius, Villon, Cervantes, Wyatt, Thomas More, Walter Ralegh, John Bunyan, the Marquis de Sade, Dostoyevsky, Oscar Wilde, Ezra Pound, etc. These writers are then privileged as the source of a universal prison poetics. Rivkah Zim attempts 'to illuminate a literary phenomenon among European dissidents and prisoners of conscience', and thereby 'to define a politics of prison writing'.[17] Ioan Davies similarly attempts to construct a 'literary philosophy of incarceration' by leaning 'heavily on a few people (some of whom were not incarcerated)', and asks: 'does prison literature convey more to us than a separate existence of which we can never be a part, or must it always be appropriated as mere metaphor?'[18] But who is this 'we'? Who is the public addressed by writing 'of which we can never be a part'? The allegation of separate existences affirms the penal regime, constructing a kind of poetic wall between writers and readers.

Davies implies that most prison writers have nothing to say 'that might be applied to non-prison situations', except as a metaphor for other, more general conditions of bondage. The metaphoricity of bondage, which has been at issue throughout this book, can also be found in a chapter on the 'literature of confinement' in the *Oxford History of the Prison* by W. B. Carnochan. He

---

[16] Victor Brombert, *The Romantic Prison: The French Tradition* (Princeton University Press, 1978), p. 9; Rivkah Zim, *The Consolations of Writing: Literary Strategies of Resistance from Boethius to Primo Levi* (Princeton University Press, 2014), p. 6.
[17] Zim, *Consolations*, p. 3.
[18] Ioan Davies, *Writers in Prison* (Oxford: Basil Blackwell, 1990), pp. 3, 8, 219.

describes actual prison as a particular case of the 'larger, metaphorical pattern that includes all manner of restraint on human action'; 'the overarching category is confinement; its subcategories are captivity of any sort and the particular experience of confinement'.[19] Carnochan wagers that 'If Western experience is conceived as having originated in a sense of confinement, the theme of imprisonment may then be thought of as one *metaphorical convenience* among others for rendering that original feeling' (my emphasis) (428).

Writing in a moment when abolition has become a mainstream political argument following the revolutionary uprisings against anti-Black police violence and mass incarceration in the wake of the murder of George Floyd, I feel it is necessary to restate that imprisonment is nothing like a metaphorical convenience, nor is it a specialised subcategory of general human experience. In 2020, 2.3 million inmates are warehoused in US prisons, roughly 40 per cent of whom are Black. The total correctional population hovers around 6.7 million: 840,000 people are on parole and 3.6 million people on probation.[20] The United States has detained one fifth of the world's prisoners.[21] Around one in five prisoners in the United States has spent time in isolation in any given year, or around 400,000 people.[22] Mass incarceration has eviscerated large proportions of communities, and disenfranchised or alienated millions long after their release.[23] As Lorna Rhodes has written, citing Avery Gordon, 'By "disappearing" large numbers of poor, mostly minority people as well as many who are seriously mentally ill, prisons exercise a kind of social magic that produces "multiple invisibilities".'[24] This blanking-out of the prison population extends to the erasure of the *writing* by these subjects themselves. I turn now to some anthologies of prison writing, as materialisations of the solidarity of imprisoned writers against the punitive individuation whose most extreme form is solitary confinement.

---

[19] W. B. Carnochan, 'The Literature of Confinement,' in *The Oxford History of the Prison: The Practice of Punishment in Western Society*, ed. Norval Morris and David J. Rothman (Oxford University Press, 1995), pp. 427–55 (427–8).

[20] Wendy Sawyer and Peter Wagner, 'Mass Incarceration 2020: The Whole Pie', *Prison Policy Initiative* (24 March 2020): www.prisonpolicy.org/reports/pie2020.html (accessed 4 May 2021).

[21] Roy Walmsley, 'World Prison Population List,' 11th ed., *World Prison Brief* (2 February 2016): www.prisonstudies.org/sites/default/files/resources/downloads/wppl_12.pdf (accessed 4 May 2021).

[22] Keramet Reiter, *23/7: Pelican Bay Prison and the Rise of Long-Term Solitary Confinement* (New Haven: Yale University Press, 2016), p. 32.

[23] Michelle Alexander, *The New Jim Crow: Mass Incarceration in the Age of Colorblindness* (New York: New Press, 2012), pp. 178–80.

[24] Lorna A. Rhodes, *Total Confinement: Madness and Reason in the Maximum Security Prison* (Berkeley and Los Angeles: University of California Press, 2004), p. 10.

Bound Together: Prison Anthologies

Prisons have always been sites of prolific textuality. As the Norfolk Prison Brothers put it, 'we be writing *everything* – love letters, hate letters, notes, songs, proposals, counterproposals, parole applications, writs – written material of every sort imaginable is constantly and voluminously produced by we who have time on our hands'. While for some writing is just a way to 'kill time', 'others take it much more seriously'.[25] Writing in these contexts can be a political and aesthetic act of resistance. Dennis Childs has argued that 'the law's gothic transmutation of living, nominally rights-bearing, human beings into "slaves of the state" has produced an unaccounted-for excess in the form of a subterranean poetics, politics, and epistemics of the living dead – an unquietly buried assemblage of black neoslave sound and theory'.[26] Writing and oral histories preserve and disseminate the political, legal, spiritual or personal knowledge that people who are imprisoned produce. *Soledad Brother* is just one example of that subterranean poetics that continues to influence activists inside and outside of the United States and its prisons.

But for this writing to circulate beyond the prison, it is particularly dependent on networks of kin and allies, political networks, formal and informal advocates including specialist presses, non-profit and charitable organisations, university programmes and so on. While some prison anthologies and magazines emerge from creative writing programmes sanctioned by prison management, others are produced by self-organised, radical groups of imprisoned writers.[27] Rodríguez elaborates on the complexities of writing 'that is both constituted and coerced by state captivity, a dynamic condition that pre-empts and punishes some forms of writing, while encouraging and even forcing others (state education, therapy, and rehabilitation programs often mandate writing exercises)' (85). In the category of 'coerced' publication, rehabilitation is often signalled through the individual's moral and aesthetic conformity to the disciplinary regime of prison, and of conventional poetics.

---

[25] Norfolk Prison Brothers, *Who Took the Weight? Black Voices from Norfolk Prison* (Boston and Toronto: Little, Brown, 1972), p. 3.
[26] Dennis Childs, *Slaves of the State: Black Incarceration from the Chain Gang to the Penitentiary* (Minneapolis: University of Minneapolis Press, 2015), p. 4.
[27] On the fraught relationships between nonincarcerated and incarcerated artists, prisons and non-profits, and academics and imprisoned students or writers, see Fleetwood, *Marking Time*, chapter 5; Rodríguez, *Forced Passages*, pp. 92–104; and Mirpuri, 'Correction-Extraction Complex', pp. 39–41.

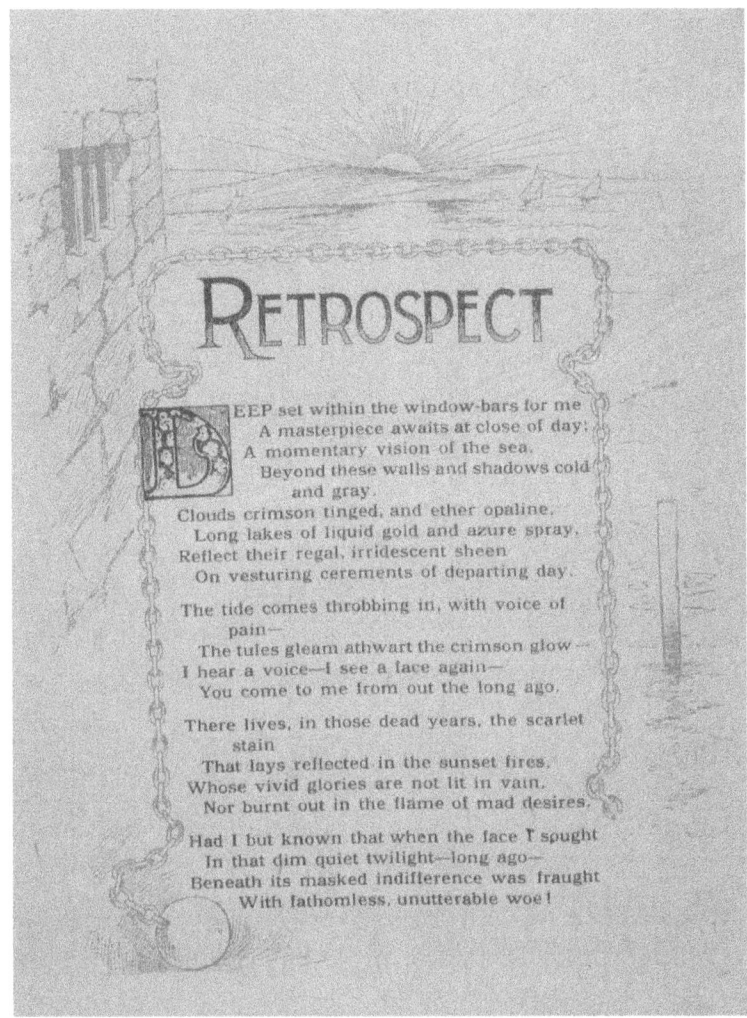

Fig. 4.1 'Retrospect', *San Quentin Days* (Sacramento: J. M. Anderson, 1905), p. 4. and 11.

An early example is *San Quentin Days*, a pamphlet of poems by an anonymous writer published in 1905 (fig. 4.1 and 4.2).[28] The poems are

---

[28] Anon., *San Quentin Days* (Sacramento: J. M. Anderson, 1905).

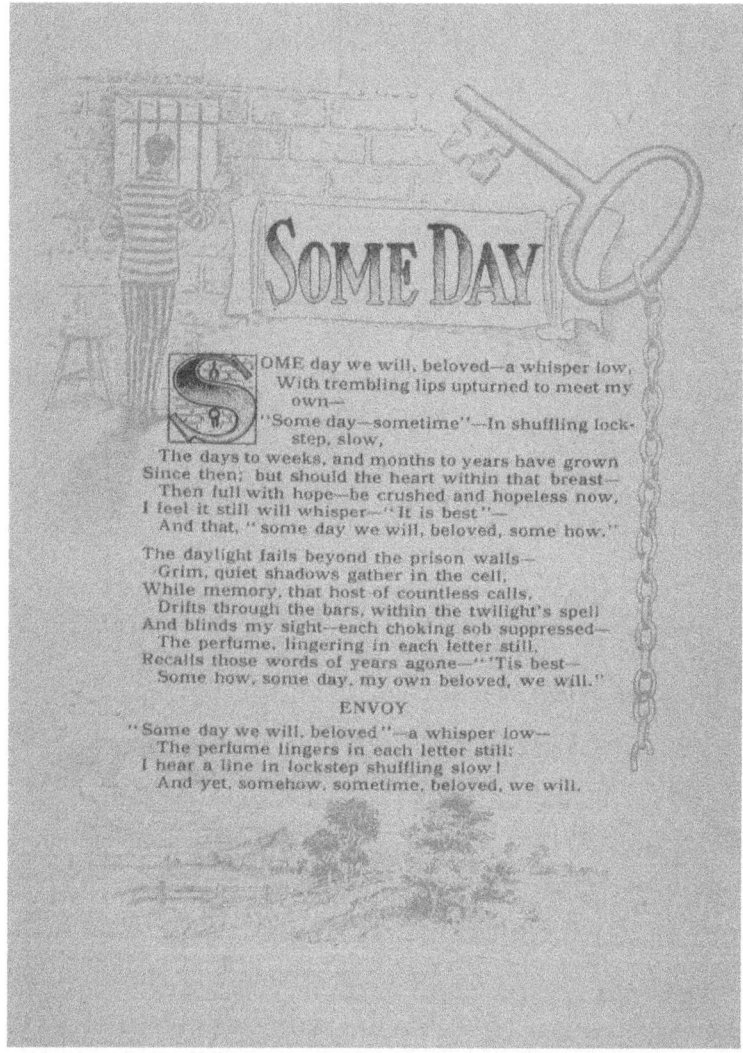

Fig. 4.2 'Some Day', *San Quentin Days* (Sacramento: J. M. Anderson, 1905), p. 11.

conventional in their verse forms and sentiments; they eulogise tender relationships, or meditate on the sunset as a prelude to regret. What is striking is the way that every poem is literally circumscribed by a carceral framework. Each page is surrounded with chains, walls and other material signifiers of the writer's penal enclosure. The *mise-en-page* makes it impossible to ignore the status of these poems as products of the prison. The inescapability of San Quentin becomes an inescapable limit to the poems themselves; freedom appears only at one exit, which leads to the idealised homestead in the distance of 'Some Day'. These texts are constrained on the page, their limits seemingly determined by the shape of intrusive icons of prison life.

A very different perspective is offered by *The Caged Collective!* (fig. 4.3), a pamphlet that represents 'The Life & Death of the Folsom Prison Creative Writers' Workshop', which was in operation for ten years before being shut down by prison authorities in 1977.[29] The gallows humour of the title suggests an ironic relation to the institution. The cover shows a table covered in writing material, with writers conferring and collaborating on documents, text and visual art. The scene is relaxed; the impression is that the people who are imprisoned are 'social equals' (22), who have taken possession of the means of production. While *San Quentin Days* is a series of poems by a single author, the Folsom model is of the workshop: an autonomous, collective endeavour by participants to uplift and educate one another. This shift from the penitent individual to the politicised collective reflects the importance of Black liberation movements, and more generally reflects Fleetwood's argument that art-making is often 'based on relationships among incarcerated people', and that both art-making and these relationships can help people to 'refuse the punitive codes, social isolation, and racial divisions that govern prison life' (57).

Those codes, isolation and divisions can also be part of the dynamics of group formation and artmaking. Eldridge Cleaver wrote about his experiences at Folsom in 1965:

> they have a writers' workshop which meets in the library under the wing of our librarian. I've never had a desire to belong to this workshop . . . Mostly, I suppose, it's because the members of the workshop are all white and all sick when it comes to color. They're not all sick, but they're not for real. They're fair-weather types, not even as lukewarm as good white liberals, and they conform to the Mississippi atmosphere prevalent here in Folsom.[30]

The *Caged Collective!* pamphlet shows how this 'white liberal' format was radicalised. Originally, as a contributor named Gordon notes, the workshop was dominated by a white chairman, whose poetry was all 'about birds n bees n honeysuckle trees'; 'this suited . . . the associated warden just fine. No

---

[29] Folsom Prison Creative Writers' Workshop, *The Caged Collective!, Aldebaran Review* 28, ed. John Oliver Simon and Leslie Simon (Berkeley, CA, 1978).
[30] Eldridge Cleaver, *Soul on Ice* (New York: McGraw Hill, 1968), p. 45.

Fig. 4.3 Folsom Prison Creative Writers' Workshop, *The Caged Collective!*, *Aldebaran Review* 28, ed. John Oliver Simon and Leslie Simon (Berkeley, CA, 1978).

politics, no anti-Americanism' (16). Then another prisoner – 'a black man and revolutionary writer' – co-opted radical writers of colour to membership, and a 'rebellious, progressive spirit' emerged (18). Their 'poetic revolution' led the prison authorities to perceive the workshop 'as a threat'. John Oliver Simon, the facilitator from outside, is interrogated by the warden ('Were we bringing radical ideas?') and finally warned: 'There's a lot of revolutionary writing coming out of that workshop, . . . and we intend to stop it' (4). Guards confiscate tapes, forbid the writers from recording their readings, censor their mail, restrict their visitation rights and prohibit them from discussing politics in the workshop (15). Key participants are framed, sent to administrative segregation or transferred to other prisons.

Simon, whose small press produced the booklet, described the writing of the Collective as 'uncensored, apocalyptic, revolutionary'. The 'outside poets' were the ones who brought that revolutionary spirit in, he claims: 'Max Schwartz bellowed "Strike! Strike!" at a poetry reading in the prison yard, and the inmates duly went on strike, which did not endear the poets to the warden. Jack Hirschman sent letters of protest to Corrections which were a visionary blend of Russian, English, utopian hyperbole and Stalinist dogma. On 27 February 1977, the authorities shut down the workshop, claiming that a tea-bag brought in by a San Francisco poet contained marijuana. Several prison poets were thrown in the hole. The Folsom Prison Creative Writers' Workshop became a cause celebre.'[31]

Consumed by 'madness' and rage after the workshop is cancelled, Steve John Burkett Sr asks: 'Now I want to know / is it the poet / they fear / or is it the poem' (29)? One participant fasted for nine months in protest (5); another shouted a poem 'at a concert in the yard which ends "Strike! Strike! Strike!" and the next day the prison population did go on strike' (5). The poets attest to the value of the workshop as a shared space of creativity and reflection, where they can develop self-determination and solidarity: 'the Workshop is the / one living thing / among the living dead / that forces me to / think,' writes Lanners L. X. (11). Pancho Aguila writes of being part of 'some new family, some new consciousness', which he can feel 'from the isolation of my cell'; 'we're writing for the many in one or one in many' (14).

These two examples gesture to the complex and sometimes antagonistic relationship between writers and prison writing programmes. In an essay entitled 'Behind the Mirror's Face' (1999), Paul St. John dramatises these in the form of a dialogue with 'Charlie', who wants to 'get our voices heard' through the production of a 'new facility mag'.[32] The speaker is sceptical. Eventually 'I find out why the warden has seen fit that a few caged birds should go to print' (59). By selecting 'two or three lifers', the warden gives the impression that 'It is time for his prisoners to be heard!' (60). But this will be 'a one-time venture, something he can show the inmate groups so

---

[31] John Oliver Simon, 'Aldebaran', from *Berkeley Daze*: www.bigbridge.org/BD-JOS-A.HTM (accessed 4 May 2021).

[32] Paul St. John, 'Behind the Mirror's Face,' in *The New Abolitionists: (Neo)Slave Narratives and Contemporary Prison Writing*, ed. Joy James (Albany: State University of New York Press, 2005), pp. 57–65 (59).

their nagging will rest' (60). The warden's token of liberality will satisfy advocacy groups, and only the most anodyne writing will be selected: writers like Charlie, whose verse is a synthesis of 'the longing of looking through iron bars at the real world, ... trademark ache/break and dove/ love rhymes': nothing as radical as '"Why the Parole Board Should Be Abolished"' (60). His poems will be censored and reshaped to fit the ideological requirements of the institution.

Meanwhile, the speaker works on his own address, to 'Mother Nature, an artist who came into the prison to "find flowers where others saw only weeds"'. He thanks this do-gooder for the opportunity 'to videotape our work for a showing at the Cultural Center', but protests: 'Please don't think that I will allow myself to be used as a consolation for a civilian audience', to make people *out there* feel better about their lives. If she really wants to heal the prisoners' hearts and minds, 'I will appreciate it very much if you'd begin with sending me some real food and vitamins', he says (61). He then addresses his fellow writers: 'A con may write fiction, but everybody will know where it comes from'; 'without the "convict point of view" there is no prison writing' (62). The imprisoned writer, like the author of *San Quentin Days*, will always be circumscribed by the institutional frame.

St. John's essay reflects the role of some writing programmes in a brief moment in US penology that ascribed to ideas of rehabilitation. In the 1950s, prison departments took up an optimistic medical model of criminality and changed their names to 'corrections'; the early 1960s was the 'treatment era'. This was a consequence of intense organising, strikes and riots by imprisoned people that began with an unprecedented series of prison rebellions in 1951–3.[33] Approximately three hundred prison riots took place from the late 1960s to the early 1980s.[34] Imprisoned activists organised unions, fought for humane treatment and ran autonomous educational, cultural and religious programmes with significant outreach beyond the walls. As a result, federal and state government and non-profit funding agencies began to back prison art and education programmes, with the aim of reasserting control, countering 'radicalisation' (especially the influence of the Black Panther Party) and lowering recidivism rates.[35] Many of these official programmes affirmed the racialised

---

[33] Lee Bernstein, *America is the Prison: Arts and Politics in Prison in the 1970s* (Chapel Hill: University of North Carolina Press, 2010), p. 14.

[34] *Ibid.*, p. 104.

[35] Lee Bernstein, 'Prison Writers and the Black Arts Movement', *New Thoughts on the Black Arts Movement*, ed. Lisa Gail Collins and Margo Natalie Crawford (New Brunswick: Rutgers University Press, 2006), pp. 297–316 (298); Bernstein, *America*, p. 78.

violence of the prison, for example, by selecting white American prisoners to participate in the best opportunities. Some imprisoned writers viewed their instructors as contributing to an attempt at 'ideological control and psychological warfare'.[36] By the 1980s, US policymakers began a backlash against even these limited programmes.[37] Construction began on supermax prisons to 'institutionalise' the lockdowns that followed the riots and actions undertaken by imprisoned activists.[38] Many forms of enrichment programming were cancelled.[39]

For the autonomously organised prison writing programmes of the 1960s and 70s, the objective was liberation, not rehabilitation. Imprisoned activists asserted that they were at the vanguard of an internationalist third-world revolution; cultural activities were a way for incarcerated people to participate in larger political and social movements.[40] From the late 1960s, prison culture was suffused by the Black Arts movement and Black nationalism, which also shaped the staffing and curriculum of writing programmes. Norfolk prison, which was built in the 1930s, had been a manifestation of the 'new penology' and its commitment to rehabilitation: it provided cooperative houses, inmate education, limited self-government and the Elma Lewis Technical Theatre Training Program. Famously, it is where Malcolm X honed his debating skills.[41] The Norfolk Prison Brothers, whose name linked their activities to the Soledad Brothers in California, published the anthology *Who Took the Weight?* in 1972. The poems in that anthology reflect the contributors' Black nationalist politics, and use free-verse forms to explore identity, ontology and race. They don't adopt the deferential attitude satirised by St John; while they refer to the prison, they explore political and philosophical questions that transcend the carceral frame. Many other anthologies from this period argue for the demolition of the prison as a site and symbol of racialised violence. Against the forms of solidarity embodied in the anthologies of this period, prison authorities designed violent mechanisms to enforce separation that in many ways continued the worst practices of the nineteenth century.

---

[36] Bernstein, 'Prison Writers', p. 300. [37] Rhodes, *Total Confinement*, p. 139.
[38] Reiter, *23/7*, p. 57.
[39] Victor Hassine, *Life Without Parole: Living in Prison Today*, ed. Robert Johnson and Thomas J. Bernard, 3rd ed. (Roxbury, [1996], 2011).
[40] Bernstein, *America*, p. 7. [41] Bernstein, 'Prison Writers', p. 300.

The Unwritable Book

> 'Of lockdown, hunger time & the blackened flower –
> Ain't nothing worth knowing.'

So, Reginald Dwayne Betts writes in his collection *Felon*, a book of poems grappling with incarceration and its aftermath, of what is and what isn't worth knowing or remembering. The poems are a way of coming to know that 'hunger time', and to leave it behind, here in a corona of sonnets called 'House of Unending'. The circularity and constrictions of the form imply the impossibility of release: 'Mornings I rise twice: once for a count / That will not come & later with the city's / Wild birds.'[42] The temporality and routines of prison impose themselves on the body in its apparent freedom, birds continuing to regulate its rhythms. Poetry is an attempt to reclaim those rhythms for the reflecting subject, to displace the surveillance count with the prosodic measure and join the wild birds, rather than the caged ones.

Time in prison is a unit of punishment; it is 'something being done to you, instead of something you do things with'. It is rigidly segmented: food, showers, counts and short sessions in the 'dog run' are all dictated by a strict schedule. But each day blends into the next.[43] Time no longer belongs to the person; she is trapped in 'someone else's time, prison time': she is 'doing time' or 'serving life', not 'my time' or 'my life'.[44] Another temporality takes hold, what Jared Sexton calls 'the slow time of captivity, the dilated time of the event horizon, the eternal time of the unconscious, the temporality of atomization'.[45] In this respect, carceral time mimics the 'temporal domination [that] is essential to slavery; its purpose is to disorient, objectify, and terrify . . . . The captive lives outside of metaphysical time, without a future, without an accessible past (natal alienation), and in a present overwhelmed with the immediacy of bodily pain, psychic torment, and routine humiliation.'[46] For people held within these distorted,

---

[42] Reginald Dwayne Betts, *Felon* (New York: W. W. Norton, 2019), pp. 81, 84.
[43] Adam Gopnik, 'The Caging of America', *New Yorker* (30 January 2012), p. 72; Lisa Guenther, *Solitary Confinement: Social Death and Its Afterlives* (Minneapolis: University of Minnesota Press, 2013), p. 195.
[44] Kimberly Drake, 'Doing Time in/as "The Monster": Abject Identity in African-American Prison Literature', in *From the Plantation to the Prison: African-American Confinement Literature*, ed. Tara T. Green (Macon: Mercer University Press, 2008), p. 146.
[45] Jared Sexton, 'The Social Life of Social Death: On Afro-Pessimism and Black Optimism,' *InTensions* 5 (Fall/Winter 2011), p. 5.
[46] Calvin Warren, 'Black Time: Slavery, Metaphysics, and the Logic of Wellness', in *The Psychic Hold of Slavery: Legacies in American Expressive Culture*, ed. Sonya Diggs Colbert, Robert J. Patterson and Aida Levy-Hussain (New Brunswick: Rutgers University Press, 2016), pp. 55–68 (60).

oppressive temporalities, the poem offers an occasion for resistance through the rediscovery and assertion of subjective time, or to mourn its inaccessibility.

In 'On Being Counted', a poem from her 1979 volume *Prison Solitary and Other Free Government Services*, Carolyn Baxter describes an environment that has become the physical corollary to her melancholy. Institutional time contrasts with her own embodied and memorial time:

> It's lights out,
> yawns, coughs, and dreams from different realities.
> [...] I smell the questioning flashlights,
> walking down the hall, closing the storage doors
> on dead lives,
>
> demanding I recite the patented number, stamped on
> my ass,
> which is presently subletting the space
> my soul used to own.
> I'm also asked where I got my map of the justice system.
> I say the judge traded it for my birth certificate.
>
> [...] The closing door joins the lock in the key
> of finality, in three years from today time.
>
> [...] I hear the radiator whispering, how stupid I was to
> trade your warmth for his.
> And I brood over you not letting me steal your hands.
> To dry up my pains.
>
> Asking do I know the words to nobody knows da
> trouble I seen.
>
> [...] So I hum, off key thoughts, that were one time, real.
> But are now like houses that have been torn down
> and families that have moved away.[47]

Jared Sexton describes captivity as 'always an unsettled condition, open to an outside about which it will not know anything and about which it cannot stop thinking, a nervous system always in pursuit of the fugitive movement it cannot afford to lose and cannot live without.'[48] Baxter's poem exhibits some of this nervous 'brooding', dwelling both on the past and the future. It articulates what Orlando Patterson termed 'natal alienation': a birth

---

[47] Carolyn Baxter, *Prison Solitary and Other Free Government Services* (New York: Greenfield Review Press, 1979), pp. 33–4.
[48] Sexton, 'Social Life', pp. 9–10.

certificate is swapped for a map of the justice system, her name for a number stamped or branded on her ass.[49] It resists that alienation and makes a claim for continued possession of 'the soul I used to own'. The poem radiates a fear that 'nobody knows the trouble I seen': that the experience of incarceration is incommunicable. But the fact that this 'trouble' is signalled by a sorrow song into which an entire history of racialised oppression has already been poured, means that somebody does know.

This tension between address and the 'unspeakable pain' of incarceration can also be found in 'I Have Seen You'. Lolita Lébron describes jail as:

> A ruin that reeks of death
> and unspeakable pain.
> It is the white bear's domain.
> Keys and blows, headcounts,
> injustices and schemes.
> Undisclosed tortures
> from an unwritable book.
> The real story of death,
> unwritten, without pages.[50]

This is an elegiac topos, the paradoxical attempt to make something living out of the dead matter of prison time. Confronting the unspeakable and unwritable book of prison experience, the poet countermands the reductive carceral discipline – acutely registered through the synecdoche of 'keys and blows, headcounts', the numbers which translate the prisoner to data – with her own lyric utterances, a different kind of numbers. Yet, the hopelessness of this regime is aggravated by the fear that these attempts at disclosure in a pageless book could never be read.

Poetry is one way that someone who has been consigned to civil death can speak, communicating her reality and overcoming her erasure from civic life. Mill's fiction of liberal individualism, in which the poet laments while pretending not to know that anyone is listening, is not a condition of freedom from interference but of terrible loneliness. Against such fictions we might counterpose the poems Raymond Umar Hall wrote while working as a Prison Observation Aid, keeping watch over people who are at risk of self-harm.[51] Hall's caring presence and his poems stand guard against the

---

[49] Orlando Patterson, *Slavery and Social Death: A Comparative Study* (Cambridge, MA: Harvard University Press, 2018).
[50] Judith A. Scheffler (ed.), *Wall Tappings: An International Anthology of Women's Prison Writings* (New York: Feminist Press at The City University of New York, 2002), p. 150.
[51] Raymond Umar Hall, *The Watch* (Hamtramck, MI: Free School Press, 2017), pp. 20, 29. I'm grateful to Rob Halpern for giving me this book.

double tragedy of being unseen, and overheard by an audience whom the speaker can only persuade of his truthfulness by pretending to ignore.

Lyric is typically constructed around a double address, to an intimate listener and to the reader. In prison contexts, lyric poems often negotiate between proximate and distant audiences, between readers who have had some experience of incarceration and those who have not. In 'New Year's Poem', Judy Clark confronts a reader who cannot understand. Clark's tears and anger cannot communicate what she is going through; 'only if you come to feel the need', for yourself,

> to enter the frightening chasm
> explore the dark, nightmare void between us
> between "free-world" and prison
> between outside and in

will you ever come to know your own 'inner world'.[52] But such voluntary self-constraint – willing entry into the chasm – is fundamentally not the same as involuntary detention. Her knowledge doesn't transmit: 'Not that you will ever know / my world inside / much less my inside world'. This is the imprisoned writer's answer to everyone, critics, loved ones, who try to imagine themselves into the experience of imprisonment. The prison cell becomes an analogue for the ineluctable psychic interior. This inscrutability of the 'inside world' is exactly what drove the nineteenth-century reformers to look for signs of penitence on the body and in narrative. Its disclosure is supposed to be the lyric poem's perpetual work. Guarding that 'void' is also a way for Clark to guarantee a remnant of autonomy and privacy, within an institution that aims to eliminate those things: even the beloved, the reader, is excluded from her hard-won knowledge.

The nineteenth century suppressed prisoners' communication with disciplinary regimens for the body and mind, architecture and punitive devices. Clark's poem communicates the way the modern prison also represses communication. As Kevin Campbell writes about his experience of solitary confinement: 'This is nothing / I will express nothing.' The 'nothing' is the walls of the cell, 'so scarred / by emotional graffiti / they appear to swirl and shift'.[53] Unrepresentability is built into the

---

[52] *Hauling Up the Morning / Izando la Mañana: Writings and Art by Political Prisoners and Prisoners of War in the U. S.*, ed. Tim Blunk and Raymond Luc Levasseur (Trenton: Red Sea Books, 1990), p. 134.
[53] Kevin Campbell, 'Express Nothing', in American Friends Service Committee's *Survivors' Manual: Surviving in Solitary: A Manual Written by and for People living in Control Units*, ed. Bonnie Kerness and Holbrook Teter (2012), p. 64.

environment. In high-security prisons, everything that might be described has been flattened or removed; the walls, beds, sinks are blank; there are no windows, or the windows are so high, covered, smeared or scratched as to make it impossible to see the landscape; blurred security mirrors or shiny cardboard prevent the person from seeing their own face for years. Brian Nelson remembers pacing for eighteen hours a day, like a caged animal: 'You know Plato's cave? That's solitary. He thinks the shadows are real. Hearing voices. Seeing things. You make up a make-believe world.'[54]

Many people who are imprisoned respond to these deprivations through forms of mental escape or what Erving Goffman calls 'removal activities',[55] withdrawing into fantasy based on 'memories of the past or imaginary dramas of life after release'.[56] Mark Medley argues that one way to resist a contemporary panopticon:

> is with autistic thinking, or total absorption in fantasy of an extended period of time. A person can just absorb themselves in creating a fantasy, can say, 'I'm building an island, and this is what my island will look like, and this is what my water source will be, and these are the kinds of plants of fruits I'll have on my island.' It's like a resting period for the mind, almost like sleep, but it can be used in a sense to resist being conditioned.[57]

Retreat into the poetic imagination is a form of rest, which as Lisa Guenther puts it, 'grants the slackening of attention which allows each of us to sustain the intensity of absorption in the world'.[58] Goffman refers in similar terms to these 'little islands of vivid, encapturing activity' that appear in the 'dead sea' of institutional time.[59]

Lyric poems can also appear like little islands: isolated, fictive creations surrounded by the sea of the page's white space. Michael Knoll describes his island in a 'Prison Letter':

> You ask what it's like here
> but there are no words for it.
> I answer difficult, painful, that men
> die hearing their own voices. That answer

---

[54] Brian Nelson, 'Weak as Motherfucker', in *Hell is a Very Small Place: Voices from Solitary Confinement*, ed. Jean Casella, James Ridgeway and Sarah Shourd (New York: New Press, 2016), p. 119.

[55] Erving Goffman, *Asylums: Essays on the Social Situations of Mental Patients and Other Inmates* (New York: Anchor, 1961), p. 69.

[56] Gresham M. Sykes, *The Society of Captives: A Study of a Maximum Security Prison* (Princeton University Press, [1958] 2007), p. 80.

[57] James, *New Abolitionists*, p. 214.   [58] Guenther, *Solitary Confinement*, p. 191.

[59] Goffman, *Asylums*, p. 69.

> isn't right though and I tell you now
> that prison is a room
> where a man waits with his nerves
> drawn tight as barbed wire, an afternoon
> that continues for months, that rises
> around his legs like water
> until the man is insane
> and thinks the afternoon is a lake:
> blue water, whitecaps, an island
> where he lies under pale sunlight, one
> red gardenia growing from his hand –
>
> But that's not right either. There are no
> flowers in these cells, no water
> and I hold nothing in my hands
> but fear, what lives
> in the absence of light, emptying
> from my body to fill the large darkness
> rising like water up my legs:
>
> It rises and there are no words for it
> though I look for them …[60]

The poem stages an act of communication: you ask; I answer. It begins by aligning the speaker with the reader, at a distance from the 'man' who waits in prison 'with his nerves / drawn tight'. Knoll portrays the slow passage of time, the erosion of sanity and the emergence of psychotic fantasy, which can also be considered an act of poetic figuration. If the man 'thinks the afternoon is a lake', it is perhaps because Knoll has proposed that the time rises 'around his legs like water'. But that comparison is rejected, and the poem comes closer to the speaking 'I', who shows himself switching on the light, dwelling with the particular fear 'in my throat': the thing that sticks in the mind, as Wyatt puts it, or blocks the organ of speech. The poem tells what it is like here, in words, while conveying the unrepresentability of that experience: there are no words, though there are these words; it is a word I have no words for. This apophasis answers the question of 'what it's like here' without answering it, with the impoverishment of language. The speaker can try to imagine lakes and flowers, but this place exhausts that imagination, and finally he has 'nothing in my hands', nothing to touch or be touched by. And that,

---

[60] Chevigny, *Doing Time*, p. 184.

as I argued at the end of my first chapter on Wyatt's appropriation of Christ's command – *Noli me tangere* – is one of the prison's worst deprivations.

Life in the Hole

Jimmy Santiago Baca learned to read and write in prison.[61] His vocation emerged when he snatched a textbook of Romantic poetry through the bars at a county jail, and began to read: 'I stumblingly repeated the author's name as I fell asleep, saying it over and over in the dark: Words-worth, Words-worth.' While awaiting trial, 'I met men, prisoners, who read aloud to each other the works of Neruda, Paz, Sabines, Nemerov, and Hemingway. Never had I felt such freedom as in that dormitory.'[62] Poetry equates to freedom; literacy and hope emerge from these collectives, not from prison writing programmes:

> the real definition of censorship
> is when they keep you locked in the *hole*
> for ninety days without light or exercise
> so you have to compose your poems in your head
> and remember them. The real definition
> of a prison writing program
> is when a prisoner has to write
> a poem in blood.
>
> (154)

Baca's dramatic image of the poem written in blood reflects the reality of censorship in prison. With remarkable ingenuity, imprisoned writers and artists overcome constraints by mixing M&Ms to make paint, and decorating the walls of their cells with artwork that makes these spaces more inhabitable.[63] A corrections officer boasted to Colin Dayan: 'they beg to send this art home to their families. Maybe they spent a month or two doing it. But we take it and hang it on this wall. Once they're in SMU, it's not their property.'[64] Justifying confiscations by the search for 'intelligence', the officer makes explicit that it is not only the bodies of the artists that become the property of the state, but also their imaginative products.

---

[61] Baca, *Singing*, pp. xii, xiv. [62] Chevigny, *Doing Time*, p. 101.
[63] Keramet Reiter, 23/7, p. 25; Fleetwood, *Marking Time*, chapter 2, on repurposed state goods and 'mushfake'; and Lisa Guenther, 'A World of Colour in the Belly of the Beast', *Solitudes Past and Present* blog: solitudes.qmul.ac.uk/ (accessed 4 May 2021).
[64] Colin Dayan, *The Law is a White Dog: How Legal Rituals Make and Unmake Persons* (Princeton University Press, 2011), p. 93.

After his conviction, Baca was confined in a 'deadlock maximum security in a subterranean dungeon' for twenty-three hours a day. There, he clings to poetry as his newfound tool of emancipation. Like Emily Dickinson assembling her fascicles, he creates a journal from cardboard and state-issue paper:

> Whole afternoons I wrote, unconscious of passing time or whether it was day or night. Sunbursts exploded from the lead tip of my pencil, words that grafted me into awareness of who I was; peeled back to a burning core of bleak terror, an embryo floating in the image of water, I cracked out of the shell wide-eyed and insane. Trees grew out of the palms of my hands, the threatening otherness of life dissolved, and I became one with the air and sky, the dirt and iron and concrete. There was no longer any distinction between the other and I. Language made bridges of fire between me and everything I saw. I entered into the blade of grass, the basketball, the con's eye and child's soul.[65]

At first, this is a euphoric, visionary state, in which the poet becomes one with language and reality, and the boundaries between I and thou, self and other dissolve. His perceptions are heightened, and he achieves a Whitmanesque identity with a blade of grass. Baca feels 'richly blessed' to be 'at the portals of a destroyed being' in the prison surrounded by:

> so many men in rags and broken souls
> who crawl up with dusty shoes from gutters
> and carry blades in their pockets
> but they are flowers that have survived their thorns
> in dry baked ground
> ... I begin to sing to them
> and my song is that they must sing[66]

As in Whitman's address to 'You felons on trial in courts', Baca's poetics are based on identification, empathetic witness and an intuitive free verse expansiveness. Baca literalises Whitman's declaration that 'I feel I am of them – I belong to those convicts and prostitutes myself, / And henceforth I will not deny them – for how can I deny myself?'[67] Baca is 'of them', in that he is writing from prison himself. This role – the poet as an Orphic leader for the broken multitude of prisoners – seems to position him at the vanguard of a prison movement: 'leading them, taking them with me' (16).

---

[65] Jimmy Santiago Baca, *A Place to Stand: The Making of a Poet* (New York: Grove Press, 2001), p. 104.
[66] Baca, *Singing*, p. 12.
[67] Walt Whitman, *Leaves of Grass: A Textual Variorum of the Printed Poems*, ed. Sculley Bradley, Harold Blodgett, Arthur Golden and William White, 3 vols. (New York University Press, 1980), 2:325.

However, Baca's flight from ordinary consciousness into the visionary state during a period of isolation leads not to Boethian freedom or solidarity with these others, but to psychosis. He snaps. He hallucinates. He is moved to death row, and then to the 'nut-run'. Months pass; he becomes lethargic, and can no longer read or write. Only when he goes outside to the exercise yard does he begin to recover, and to

> give birth to myself again in the chaos. I withdrew even deeper into the world of language, cleaving the diamonds of verbs and nouns, plunging into the brilliant light of poetry's regenerative mystery. Words gave off rings of white energy, radar signals from powers beyond me that infused me with truth.

This is a tale of death and resurrection through language. In that sense it fits with the narratives of redemption that were staged in the nineteenth-century prison, where the prisoner – who sometimes entered the prison hooded like a condemned man – passes through the liminality of suffering in order to re-enter society. But its mystical presentation also retains a manic quality, indicative of what has been called 'SHU syndrome' (pronounced 'shoe'; referring to Secure Housing Units or other supermax-level prison cells).

'Control units' are the term for prisons, or parts of prison, where super-maximum-security conditions apply, and where prisoners are held in individual cells in solitary confinement, sometimes with an hour in caged exercise yards that resemble dog kennels. In Pelican Bay State Prison in California, the 1,055 cells are 'roughly the size of a wheelchair-accessible bathroom stall', and have 'only three furniture-like components: a concrete ledge with a slim stone pad, which serves as a bed; a solid-steel sink-toilet combination fixture; and two cement cubes jutting from the wall, forming an awkward chair and desk of sorts'. There are traps in the cell doors through which food trays can be passed and which serve as cuffports.[68] People are sometimes permitted a small television or radio, ten books or magazines, and one legal pad. Clocks, and almost everything else, are forbidden. 'Finely perforated steel doors allow guards to look straight into every cell, but prisoners ... have trouble seeing out. Reaching out is impossible.'[69] The cell is 'a built environment of harsh angles and flat planes, sudden noise and echoing voices that can't quite be made out,

---

[68] Joan [Colin] Dayan, 'Held in the Body of the State: Prisons and the Law', in *History, Memory and the Law*, ed. Austin Sarat and Thomas R. Kearns (Ann Arbor: University of Michigan Press, 1999), pp. 183–247 (197).
[69] Reiter, *23/7*, pp. 10, 19.

constant surveillance, and utter dependence on others for basic physical needs'.[70] The environment produces *and* imitates the inmate's derangement. The cell starts to vibrate: as one prisoner explained, 'Things just don't stay put.'[71]

SHU syndrome is a contemporary psychological term for the traumatic effects of extended isolation in such cells. Those effects have been recognised for centuries. Charles Dickens had observed the 'fluttering' of people who are imprisoned about to be released in Pennsylvania. The warden explained:

> 'Well, it's not so much a trembling,' was the answer – 'though they do quiver – as a complete derangement of the nervous system. They can't sign their names to the book; sometimes can't even hold the pen; look about 'em without appearing to know why, or where they are; and sometimes get up and sit down again twenty times in a minute. . . . Sometimes they stagger as if they were drunk, and sometimes are forced to lean against the fence, they're so bad: – but they clear off in course of time.'[72]

Loss of motor control, panic, acute confusional state and loss of memory are all known features of SHU syndrome. People who are held for long periods in isolation descend into a 'mental fog' and suffer from stupor and insomnia. They become hypersensitive to any stimulation, and fixate on minor irritations and bodily sensations. Pre-existing mental health conditions dramatically worsen. Prisoners develop dissociative conditions, massive free-floating anxiety, vivid hallucinations and sudden, violent outbursts.[73] Other symptoms include headaches, heart palpitations, muscle pains, digestive problems, diarrhoea; paranoia, depression, despair, apathy.[74] Eyesight decays as the eyes have nothing to look at or to practice seeing over long distances. People forget how to walk. In his study of people incarcerated in the Pelican Bay SHU, Craig Haney observed self-mutilation, withdrawal, ruminations, perspiring hands, dizziness, trembling, tingling sensations, fainting and suicidal ideation.[75]

---

[70] Rhodes, *Total Confinement*, p. 112.   [71] Guenther, *Solitary Confinement*, p. 72.
[72] Charles Dickens, *American Notes* (London: Chapman and Hall, n.d. [1866?]), p. 122.
[73] Stuart Grassian, 'Psychiatric Effects of Solitary Confinement', *Washington University Journal of Law & Policy* 22 (January 2006), pp. 327–83 (370–1); Stuart Grassian, 'Psychopathological Effects of Solitary Confinement', *American Journal of Psychiatry* 140 (1983), pp. 1450–4; with N. Friedman, 'Effects of Sensory Deprivation in Psychiatric Seclusion and Solitary Confinement', *International Journal of Law and Psychiatry* 8 (1986), pp. 49–65.
[74] Peter Scharff Smith, 'The Effects of Solitary Confinement on Prison Inmates', *Crime and Justice* 34 (2006), pp. 441–528 (488–93).
[75] Craig Haney, 'Mental Health Issues in Long-Term Solitary and "Supermax" Confinement', *Crime and Delinquency* 49.1 (2003), pp. 124–56 (130).

C. F. Villa offers a devastating taxonomy of the physical and psychic effects of solitary confinement, and the violence involved in keeping people there (including the use of pepper spray to perform terrifying cell extractions):

> Indignity. That choking filament that can cut air down to quarters and turn eyes purple, puffy, and watery. Drown skin and soul in chemical agents, outrage, some post-traumatic flashing ... Optical nerves damaged from light. Wrists that snap wringing clothes. Tendons that tear when reaching for a towel. Knees that don't have a leg to stand on. Teeth caught in toothbrushes. Toenails that fall into socks – rattle like loaded dice.[76]

The damage is intense, unrelenting and endures long after the person is released back into the general prison population or the community. Research suggests that around 50 per cent of prisoner suicides take place in solitary confinement, even though these prisoners make up roughly 10 per cent of the national population.[77]

Brian Nelson was held in solitary confinement at intervals from the age of fourteen, including an icy cold steel box in Illinois, and a grey hundred-degree cement box in New Mexico. He describes 'talking to the cell *like it was a person*'; after his release, he acquired 'a hundred watches ... I have time everywhere around me.'[78] Maryam Henderson-Uloho hallucinated that a little boy was outside talking to her; his encouragement offered her consolation when she was held in solitary confinement. When she was put in 'the tank' – an isolation cell in which 'they strip you buck naked. They take all your clothes, put you in a smock, take your mattress and pillow, and give you a blanket/mattress thing and a roll of toilet paper' – she survived by making flowers out of toilet paper and leaching 'the ink out of a magazine to color my flowers' (28). Judith Vazquez's hallucinations were terrifying: it seemed like the floor had cracked open and 'I was on top of the edge of some ledge where when I looked down I saw an endless pit of fire and darkness. I saw people screaming, crying, and burning.'[79]

Many people recall that in solitary confinement they became so dissociated that they could hear screaming, and only afterwards realised it was themselves. Hall observed an inmate who 'bugged out. First, he starts kicking the window, then he kept running into the door. I went to the door to make sure everything was okay. It looked like he was trying to keep something from coming out of his mouth. He exploded. I watched this guy scream and yell,

---

[76] C. F. Villa, 'Living in the SHU', *Hell is a Very Small Place*, pp. 38–9.   [77] Reiter, 23/7, p. 164.
[78] Taylor Pendergrass and Mateo Hoke (eds.), *Six by Ten: Stories from Solitary* (Chicago: Haymarket Books, 2018), pp. 40–1.
[79] Judith Vazquez, 'On the Verge of Hell', *Hell is a Very Small Place*, p. 58.

fighting himself. You would think it was three people in the room with him.'⁸⁰ Other prisoners enter into a euphoric state of reverie, including the feeling of an 'intense of love of any living things', including the spiders, mice and roaches that infest the cell. In solitary confinement in Holloway women's prison in London, Diana Christina remembers that:

> Magic happened to me then. I felt as though all tensions were melting away in the base of my skull and, in a flash, I was completely transformed. I rose up renewed both physically and emotionally. I had a feeling of complete harmony and bliss with the whole of creation.⁸¹

By the time she is released, 'I felt like a cross between someone who had been battered senseless and someone who had been endowed with a privileged sort of wisdom' through her 'mystical experiences' in isolation (87).

Jack Henry Abbott's experiences of prison were published through the patronage of Norman Mailer in 1981, and are full of vivid descriptions of torture in units like the strip-cell – a concrete box with nothing but an open toilet drain in the centre. His symptoms begin with claustrophobia. 'The air in your cell vanishes. You are smothering. Your eyes bulge out; you clutch at your throat; you scream like a banshee. Your arms flail the air in your cell. You reel about the cell, falling.'⁸² Abbott stares at the drain, and contrasts the hermitages of Romantic solitude and poetic reflection with his own grim surroundings:

> If it were desolation you were facing as you stare off in your cell, it would probably inspire you in some small way. Poets have sung songs of scenes of desolation. But what faces you is a cesspool world of murk and slime; a subterranean world of things that squirm and slide through noxious sewage, piles of shit and vomit and piss. . . . If you are in that cell for weeks that add up to months, you do not ignore all this and live "with it"; you *enter* it and become a part of it. (29)

He may have become 'oversensitive' (37), but that hyperbolic sensitivity is not a receptive, productive one. Instead, 'my very *flesh* has been made to suffer sensations and longings I never had before' (37). He sits, 'stewing in nothingness', in a state of lethargy: 'Time descends in your cell like the lid of a coffin in which you lie and watch it as it slowly closes over you. When you neither move nor think in your cell, you are awash in pure

---

⁸⁰ Hall, *The Watch*, p. 45.
⁸¹ Diana Christina and Pat Carlen, 'Christina: In Her Own Time', *Criminal Women: Autobiographical Accounts*, ed. Pat Carlen (Cambridge: Polity, 1985), pp. 59–103 (83–4).
⁸² Jack Henry Abbott, *In the Belly of the Beast: Letters from Prison* (New York: Random House, 1981), p. 25.

nothingness. Solitary confinement in prison can alter the ontological makeup of a stone' (44).

Abbott's experiences – his suffering and the visionary truths to which they lead him – are intensified when he is moved to a blackout cell. In total darkness, he experiences florid hallucinations; he sees 'vivid bursts of brilliance, of color, like fireworks . . . . My eyes *hungered* for light, for color, the way someone's dry mouth may *hunger* for saliva. They became so sensitive if I touched them; they exploded in light, in showers of white sparks shooting as if from a fountain' (26–7).[83] After years in the hole, he discovers new perceptual capacities: 'My body communicates with the cell. We exchange temperatures and air currents, smells and leavings on the floor and walls' (46). He becomes contemplative, 'inverted'; his memory is 'arrested'. 'It travels the terrain of time in a pure way, unfettered by what is, reckless of what was, what will become of it' (46). Time is altered, no longer structured by human experience. So is space, measured by the pacing of a foot: 'You can walk, placing one foot before the other, across eternity in time' (48). He finds a kind of liberty through the reconceptualisation of time and space; the trials he has experienced set him above normal human experience. Abbott describes this cognitive state as 'genius . . . *empty* intelligence, pure intelligence', a kind of 'Supersanity'. Total solitude transformed him, as Aristotle had it, to a beast or a god.

As I've already suggested in my comparison of Baca's delusions to Whitman's blade of grass, there is a similarity between the characteristics of SHU syndrome and the states of 'divine fury' and extreme psychic susceptibility cultivated by some poets and religious mystics through asceticism, physical trials or intoxicants. In the summer of 1866, Stéphane Mallarmé undertook hard work in isolation, and was so excited by the results that he planned to spend twenty years in 'monastic refuge in myself'; 'My thought has gone to the limit and thought itself through'; 'I discovered the Idea of the Universe through sensation alone . . . in order to perpetuate the indelible idea of pure Nothingness, I had to fill my brain with the sensation of absolute Emptiness.'[84] As in Abbott's writing, Mallarmé's journeys into the 'Darkness Absolute' suggest not that poetry is a refuge or defence against dehumanisation, but that through these trials a poetry can be found which is ultra-human – a 'supersanity' that aligns the writer with a demiurge, creating Ideas out of nothing.

---

[83] On colour's symbolisation of power relations in prison, and capacity to cause stress, see Fleetwood, *Marking Time*, p. 83.

[84] Stéphane Mallarmé, *Selected Poetry and Prose*, ed. Mary Ann Caws (New York: New Directions, 1982), pp. 85–6.

A similar *techne* can be found in Bob Kaufman's 'Jail Poems', which were 'written in San Francisco City Prison Cell 3, 1959'. Kaufman, who is associated with the Beat poets, was policed, incarcerated and subjected to racialised violence throughout his life. Maria Damon says that at thirteen, 'Kaufman was hung by his thumbs in an icehouse all night by a lynch mob . . . ; in his active Beat days he was arrested thirty-five times in one-and-a-half years; in 1963 he was arrested for walking on the grass in Washington Square Park, given between fifty and one hundred shock treatments, and threatened with a lobotomy.'[85] 'Jail Poems' was originally published in the *Beatitude Anthology* (1960). They consist of a numbered series of aphoristic statements, and begin with the speaker in danger of flying apart, in a condition of extreme psychic stress:

> I am sitting in a cell with a view of evil parallels,
> Waiting thunder to splinter me into a thousand me's.
> It is not enough to be in one cage with one self;
> I want to sit opposite every prisoner in every hole.[86]

Kaufman's splintering into a 'thousand me's' – a more distressing version of the ecstatic *ébranlement* that is an effect of *jouissance* – could be read as a response to trauma, a flight out of the body through derealisation.[87] But it also allows him to overcome his attachment to normative individuality. This dispersed subject challenges the premise of individual autonomy and subjective coherence on which democratic citizenship is founded and replaces it with the captive body 'judicially . . . emptied of its presumptive political and social subjectivity'.[88] He recognises that we live 'in a universe of cells', in which 'who is not in jail?' (56). This ancient metaphysical theme has more specific political resonances for Kaufman, whose Blackness and neurodiversity made him particularly vulnerable to the police, and who regarded prison as a spectacle of 'the great American windmill, tilting at itself' (57).

Like Abbott and Mallarmé, Kaufman's poem conjures up grandiose fantasies:

> My soul demands a cave of its own, like the Jain god;
> Yet I must make it go on, hard like jazz, glowing
> In this dark plastic jungle, land of long night, chilled.
> My navel is a button to push when I want inside out.

---

[85] Maria Damon, *The Dark End of the Street: Margins in American Vanguard Poetry* (Minneapolis: University of Minnesota Press, 1993), pp. 49–50; see also Will Alexander, 'Bob Kaufman: The Footnotes Exploded', *Conjunctions* 2 (1997), pp. 210–15 (214).
[86] Bob Kaufman, *Solitudes Crowded with Loneliness* (New York: New Directions, 1965), p. 56.
[87] Damon, *Dark End*, p. 50. [88] Rodríguez, *Forced Passages*, p. 80.

> Am I not more than a mass of entrails and rough tissue?
> Must I break my bones? Drink my wine-diluted blood?
>
> [...] Let me spit breath mists of introspection, bits of me
> So that when I am gone, I shall be in the air.
>
> (57)

The soul's 'demand' is for a self-made solitude, in the asceticism known to the Jain religion as Ekatva Bhavna – more like the renunciation through which Pārśvanātha was liberated from the cycles of *saṃsāra*, than the solitude imposed by a cage. 'Jail Poems' elaborates on the trials of the flesh – broken bones, blood drunk like wine, entrails and tissue – and proposes an exit through and into the body: 'my navel is a button ....' From the cage of the jail to the cave of the Jain, the soul entombed in its body is released in an aspiration of spirit. The body overspills the outside, is re-internalised, broken and drunk up; the exhalations of the breath outlast this personal dismemberment and etherealise the speaker's personhood so that it circulates freely. This 'being in the air' is also the aspiration (literally) of Kaufman's oral poetics.

Eventually, the 'I' enters a state of total effacement:

> Someone whom I am is no one.
> Something I have done is nothing.
> Someplace I have been is nowhere.
> I am not me.
>
> (58)

Turning the anthemic statement 'I am somebody' into an equivalence between someone, I and no one, Kaufman embraces an ambivalence between affirmation and dissolution that could be either a state of enlightenment, despair or a Rimbaudian alienation (*Je est un autre*).[89] For George Fragopoulos, Kaufman's negation – and his later decade-long period of silence – shows he 'is not interested in creating a new kind of identity or subjectivity. He is, instead, attempting to utterly erase the subject position from the lyric itself.'[90] In this sense, Kaufman's 'Jail Poems' offer a powerful antithesis to the liberal tradition that seeks out prison lyric as

---

[89] On the appropriation of African American culture and erasures of Black writers in the 'white Negro' Beatnik movement, see Jeffrey Falla, 'Bob Kaufman and the (In)visible Double', *Callaloo* 25.1 (Winter 2002), pp. 183–9; H. William Rice, 'Bob Kaufman and the Limits of Jazz', *African American Review* 47.2/3 (Summer/Fall 2014), pp. 403–15; and Aldon Nielsen, '"A Hard Rain": Looking to Bob Kaufman', *Callaloo* 25.1 (Winter, 2002), pp. 134–45.

[90] George Fragopoulos, '"Singing the Silent Songs, Enchanting Songs": Bob Kaufman's Aesthetics of Silence', *Journal of Modern Literature* 40.1 (Fall 2016), pp. 147–63 (155–6).

evidence of the endurance of the human subject even in the most depraved conditions.

Kaufman describes being surrounded by 'a flock of sorrows, or unoriginal sins, a litany of obscenities'. These 'sins' are part of the hallucinatory aura of the cell, which opens up forms of self-knowledge only for the subject who is able to resist the imposition of conformity through constraint. This sounds like the awakening of the conscience that was the intended effect of solitary confinement for moralising prison reformers. But it could also be his poems, or the other people who are pathologised through their imprisonment: Kaufman acknowledges that 'The defective on the floor, mumbling / Was once a man who shouted across tables,' and may be someone else, or Kaufman himself, in one of his legendary performances at the Co-Existence Bagel Shop. And while Kaufman's poems repeatedly long for solitude, the 'Jail Poems' are crowded with the loneliness of other people. They reach towards the dissolution of the self that might be the basis of a transpersonal solidarity, but finally stop short at the 'defective', a harrowing judgement of self and other that has more in common with John Wieners's portrait of the 'Children of the Working Class' (a poem he wrote 'from incarceration, Taunton State Hospital, 1972') than of a release from the punitive categories that began with Enlightenment penology.[91]

Solidarity

Repeated legal challenges have argued that solitary confinement violates the Eighth Amendment prohibition on 'cruel and unusual punishment'. The courts have decided that it is not the practice but the intention that would make solitary unconstitutional: if it is used as a 'disciplinary cell', with the intention of punishing the inmate, it is illegal; if it serves the purpose of 'administrative segregation', in order to protect the inmate from others or himself, or to maintain order and security, it can be used indefinitely. As Colin Dayan writes: 'adapting the legal language of decorum and the vocabulary of decency, these places are renamed, engaging language in legality to the extent that the new prison plantations are recast as "state-of-the-art" facilities for the incapacitation of those now known as "strategic threat groups"'.[92]

---

[91] John Wieners, *Selected Poems: 1958–1984*, ed. Raymond Foye (Santa Barbara: Black Sparrow Press, 1998), pp. 175–6.
[92] Dayan, 'Held', p. 207.

Solitary confinement is hard separation. Its intention is to isolate people from each other. As Beaumont and Tocqueville write, when people who are imprisoned are 'isolated by the cell or by silence, they are moreover reduced to their individual strength; to curb them, therefore, does not require so much material force as if they were able to unite their efforts'.[93] Like the silent system, which could enable thirty guards to control nine hundred inmates because they lacked the solidarity that arises through communication, solitary confinement prevents unity: 'They are united, but no moral connexion exists among them. They see without knowing each other. They are in society without any intercourse . . . . Their union is strictly material, or, to speak more exactly, their bodies are together, but their souls are separated.'[94]

Solitary confinement represents the most drastic enforcement of individuality against the possibility of solidarity that can be imagined. As we have seen, the separate system was the apotheosis of the classificatory systems applied by Enlightenment penology. To control moral contagion, prisoners were classified in smaller and smaller subcategories, until eventually each individual came to constitute a category of his own. The Panopticon was also intended to create for the keeper 'a *multitude*, though not a *crowd*.' But from their own point of view, the people incarcerated in the Panopticon would have been '*solitary* and *sequestered* individuals'.[95] The interdiction of the gang is another way of interrupting the formations of solidarity.

And yet, as the repeated strikes, hunger strikes and riots in America's prisons suggest, imprisoned people create and share a sense of solidarity, and reading and writing are part of that process. Todd Lewis Ashker, one of the organisers of the 2013 hunger strike in which thousands of individuals protested against solitary confinement, details how that action originated in the Pelican Bay SHU's 'Short Corridor', where 'we soon came to recognise and respect our racial and cultural differences. We shared reading material on history, culture, sociology, politics, etc. We came to recognise that we are all in the same boat.'[96]

The prison is designed to replace the collective with the multiple: the cell must not become a commons. In 'Prison Etiquette' by Dachine Rainer and Holley Cantine (1950), prison is seen as bent 'on the conscious and systematic destruction of the Person'. The inmate is kept under direct surveillance or confined to a narrow space:

---

[93] Beaumont and Tocqueville, *On the Penitentiary System*, pp. 105–6.
[94] Beaumont and Tocqueville, *On the Penitentiary System*, p. 58.
[95] Jeremy Bentham, *The Panopticon Writings*, ed. Miran Božovič (London: Verso, 2010), p. 50.
[96] Todd Lewish Ashker, 'A Tale of Evolving Resistance', *Hell is a Very Small Place*, p. 87.

when he is locked into his cell where he is allowed freedom to think, no acts may follow from that thinking that can affect either his Prison environment or the other people who are imprisoned – unless he disobeys Prison rules in some manner. ... This abrogation of the essence of the individual destroys not only each single person, but consequently, any possibility of community – except again, when Prison rules are disobeyed. ... It is calculated to create a docile, easily controlled Prison population that is largely incapable of organising resistance.[97]

In Angela Davis's view, 'the prison is a key component of the state's coercive apparatus, the overriding function of which is to ensure social control'.[98] And yet, within this apparatus of violent separation, often against the rules, incarcerated people form friendships, solidarities, intimacies and networks of mutual aid.

This is also a use of poetry in prisons: to assert solidarities based on personal experience, political affiliations or shared identities. In 'Of Poems', Susan Rosenberg describes poetry as a 'gift for me'; a 'time for myself'. But this time and gift extends to others:

> I think of the countless numbers
> of us who put down the pen to pick up
> other tools, and how of necessity we are
> returned to the pen.
> I think of the poet who said
> 'I curse the poetry of those who do not take sides.'
> I think of the torture, the degradation, and the
> humiliation that the enemy inflicts on us all
> is to teach us, to force us to lose the memory of ourselves.
> So, in that poetry becomes a weapon that guides
> us to the future.[99]

For Rosenberg, poems are continuous with the other tools of revolution, the hammer and the gun. Being stripped of our 'memory of ourselves' is the enemy's way of inhibiting solidarity; poetry is a memorial technology that 'guides us' back to 'ourselves', who are not just the individuals picking up the pen in their separate cells but 'countless numbers' doing so together.

The lyric relation between the individual and the collective is at issue throughout this book. I want to end by thinking about what pressure these poems and other writings by imprisoned people can put on the theorisation of the lyric. At the start of her exploration of *Poetry and the Fate of the Senses*, Susan Stewart presents a scene of utter dereliction:

---

[97] James, *New Abolitionists*, p. 6.
[98] Angela Y. Davis, *If They Come in the Morning: Voices of Resistance* (New York: Third Press, 1971), p. 27.
[99] Blunk and Levasseur (eds.), *Hauling up the Morning*, p. 288.

> The darkness presses against us and yet has no boundary; without edge or end, it erases and mutes the limits of our being – not as an expansion, but rather as a contraction, of whatever the mind can hold as an image of the human. It is unbearable, this loneliness of the mind working on its own to maintain the outline, the figure, of the person. Frozen, voiceless, a prisoner without sentence, the mind in the dark has no object to reflect on and no object to limit the endless racing of its reflections. In the end, the fear of the darkness is the fear that the darkness will not end.[100]

This is a vision of a terrifying space, of a darkness that encroaches on 'our' boundaries, and which itself has no boundaries – we could argue, a paranoid vision of whiteness as the demand for enclosure, for the right 'to maintain the outline, the figure, of the person' against endless blackness. Note, however, that Stewart is not describing a black-out cell. She is comparing the poet to the creative demiurge at the beginning of time. As soon becomes clear from the bricolage of philosophy she assembles, this darkness in which 'we' are 'a prisoner without sentence' is a metaphysical one, and the answer to that existential darkness is poetry. 'Poetry is a force against effacement,' a way to 'make visible, tangible, and audible the figures of persons' (2); 'the cry of the senses coming forward beyond will is transformed into the person of volition and consequence, thus necessarily a person articulated by speaking and being spoken to' (15). There is not room in Stewart's analysis to consider if the prisoner can be a person of volition and consequence, or how the conditions under which he or she speaks or is spoken to constitute a poetics, an aesthetics and an endemic state-sponsored violence.

What would it mean for theorisations of the lyric such as Stewart's to recognise that prison, bondage, sensory deprivation and isolation are not metaphors, the concretisation of the dark night of any soul, but real conditions in which poetry is produced? What if, against the poet's voluntary submission to formal constraints imagined as a form of self-incarceration, we see and read the poem as a space to transform *involuntary* submission into self-knowledge at the limits of the solitary self? What form of lyric could be conceived beyond the threshold of abolition?

Jonathan Culler argues that poetry could be returned to cultural influence by hanging on to the coat-tails of hip-hop. 'The unexpected rise of rap,' he writes (unexpected to whom?), 'a form of heavily rhythmical language that relies on rhythm and wordplay, and its enormous persisting popularity among the youth of all social strata, suggests a hunger for

---

[100] Susan Stewart, *Poetry and the Fate of the Senses* (University of Chicago Press, 2002), p. 1.

rhythmic language that might find some satisfaction in lyric.'[101] Culler is observing that hip-hop is a Black working-class art form that appeals to middle-class white people. But there is something very sad about this surmise. Is this the best a theory of lyric can offer us now?

I don't think so. I'd turn instead to abolitionist activists, militating against mass incarceration, as the theorists who are currently making the most impassioned defences of the poetic imagination. In a discussion with other activists in 2017, Alexis Pauline Gumbs refers to abolition as a 'poetic term', 'a critical and generative term, and a movement with three main components: dismantle, change, build'.[102] adrienne maree brown argues that 'our work is to make the unimaginable feel tangible, become a longing'. Gumbs agrees:

> at the same moment indigenous people are confined to reservations by the state, our imaginations are also confined. All of us. And, I would also say that the moments in which prisons became a dominant feature of the U. S., our imaginations (for all, not just those of us disproportionately imprisoned) also became imprisoned. The way we imagine work, our relationships, the future, family everything, is locked down.

For these activists, detention and mass incarceration literally and materially repress everyone's imagination. Abolition is a politics that requires fantastic speculation, a renewal of the imagination.

Imagination is the word that recurs each time abolition is defined. Emile DeWeaver quotes brown: 'We have to imagine beyond those fears. We have to ideate – imagine and conceive – together. We must imagine new worlds that transition ideologies and norms . . . .'[103] The editorial collective at Rustbelt Abolition Radio says: 'When we speak of abolition, we are striving to articulate and enact a political imaginary and practice that aims at something far more expansive than simply dispensing with police and prisons – nothing short of a world, or worlds, that lie beyond the ecological disaster that is the present, perhaps even beyond the reach of the language currently at our disposal.'[104] This is a poetics and a politics.

Jackie Wang's *Carceral Capitalism* draws on lived experience alongside historical and economic analysis to depict the oppressive disciplinary

---

[101] Jonathan Culler, 'Why Rhythm?,' in *Critical Rhythm: The Poetics of a Literary Life Form*, ed. Ben Glaser and Jonathan Culler (New York: Fordham University Press, 2019), pp. 21–39 (37).
[102] Walidah Imarisha, Alexis Pauline Gumbs, Leah Lakshmi Piepzna-Samarasinha, adrienne maree brown and Mia Mingus, 'The Fictions and Futures of Transformative Justice: A Conversation with the Authors of *Octavia's Brood*', *New Inquiry* (20 April 2017), thenewinquiry.com/the-fictions-and-futures-of-transformative-justice (accessed 4 May 2021).
[103] Fleetwood, *Marking Time*, p. 188; describing a performance by Prison Renaissance, *Metropolis*, 2018.
[104] rustbeltradio.org/transcripts/ (accessed 4 May 2021).

functions of debt, policing and mass incarceration. As her book moves towards its conclusion, it becomes more dreamlike and poetic. Wang cites Mahmoud Darwish and Rosa Luxemburg, and imagines that:

> The poet-prisoner haunts the guard, who becomes a prisoner of his own paranoia. The profession of the poet is dreaming. The profession of the jailer is to contain. The poet is the one who makes the light. The guard is the one who takes it. *He who lives on depriving others of light drowns in the darkness of his own shadow.* Will the ones who built the nightmare also drown in it? . . . The prisoner knows the true meaning of freedom while the guard knows only how to police this freedom.[105]

This trope is reflected in a wide range of poetries from Boethius to Guantánamo Bay: that the prisoner is enlightened by his or her captivity. Poetic illumination is a kind of compensation for the prisoner's suffering. But Wang also contends that mass incarceration has led in the United States to a generalised bondage of the imagination: 'Everywhere I look I see sleepwalkers under the spell of the prison,' which places a 'stranglehold on our imaginations'. In terms not imagined as part of Hegel's theorisation of the lyric, the prison has made the repression of the imaginative inner life universal.

The prison also produces its opposite, 'the intensification of the desire for life' that 'undermines the prison's capacity to structure our mental lives'. For Wang, 'imagination is excess, is that which could never be contained by the prison, that which will always exceed it' (316). The prison challenges the capacity to imagine, not only of those who have not experienced its horrors, but also those who have become accustomed to the totality of the prison-industrial state. This is the challenge set by poets and abolitionist activists: to disrupt the grammar of violence through poetic and political works of imagination, in the closed space of the poem, and the openings around it, in the exchange between writers and readers, and across the whole of the prison archipelago.

The valorisation of imagination in abolitionist politics takes us back to Romanticism. For Coleridge imagination was that which 'dissolves, diffuses, dissipates, in order to recreate'. The dissolution of the carceral state would be an opportunity for *poiesis*: for making, not only different systems of transformative justice, but for the assemblage of human being; and with that recreation a new idea of lyric subjectivity might emerge from the shackles of liberal individualism whose invention coincided with the invention of the modern prison. Rediscovering lyric as a form that is based on collective solidarities rather than solitary subjects would be only one benefit of such a project.

---

[105] Jackie Wang, *Carceral Capitalism* (Pasadena: Semiotext(e), 2018), pp. 303–4.

PART II

The Songs of Slavery

CHAPTER 5

Bind Me – I Still Can Sing
Emily Dickinson at the Boundaries of Lyric

one song would bridge the finite in silence
— M. NourbeSe Philip

On 16 August 1870, the abolitionist and essayist Thomas Wentworth Higginson paid a visit to the Dickinson homestead in Amherst, Massachusetts.[1] Higginson had been corresponding with Emily Dickinson for eight years, but had never met her. He describes how 'I heard an extremely faint and pattering footstep like that of a child, in the hall, and in glided, almost noiselessly, a plain, shy little person, the face without a single good feature … She had a quaint and nun-like look.' Dickinson eventually relaxed into conversation, offering 'quaint aphorisms' and remarks that seemed 'the very wantonness of over-statement'. But there was an 'excess of tension, and of something abnormal' here; and Higginson's instinct told him 'that the slightest attempt at direct cross-examination would make her withdraw into her shell; I could only sit still and watch, as one does in the woods; I must name my bird without a gun, as recommended by Emerson.'[2]

Higginson is referring to Ralph Waldo Emerson's poem 'Forbearance', which embraces those who enjoy nature without attempting to possess it and encounter danger 'with a heart of trust'.[3] In comparing Dickinson to a bird that must be quietly watched, Higginson identifies her as a tentative and fickle prey, in the presence of which the hunter must lay aside his customary violence. The image also recalls Higginson's comparison of her handwriting to 'the famous fossil bird-tracks in the museum of that college

---

[1] Dickinson read Higginson's 'Letter to a Young Contributor' in *The Atlantic Monthly* sometime around April 1862, and wrote to him at the end of that month. Howard N. Meyer (ed.), *The Magnificent Activist: The Writings of Thomas Wentworth Higginson (1823–1911)* (New York: Da Capo, 2000), pp. 503–5.
[2] Meyer, *Magnificent Activist*, pp. 557–9.
[3] Ralph Waldo Emerson, *Collected Poems and Translations*, ed. Harold Bloom and Paul Kane (New York: Library of America, 1994), p. 67.

town'.⁴ Ancient, fragile, nearly illegible, Dickinson's hand is naturalised and associated with birds, and thus with lyric as song.

The relevance of Higginson's imagery to Dickinson's own language of hunting, fugitivity and escape will become apparent later in this chapter. But his account of the visit was also influential in establishing the mythos of Dickinson as the nun of Amherst: childish but sophisticated, plain but with a capacity for wantonness, bound but overflowing. Dickinson's own perception of the interview is not known, though when I read about it I often think of her remark that 'Much Madness is divinest Sense – / To a discerning Eye'; but to 'the Majority', eccentricity can appear 'dangerous': resist their control and you will find yourself 'handled with a Chain' (Fr620, 1863).⁵

Dickinson's early reception was dominated by critics who interpreted her seclusion as wilful 'self-incarceration at home' or a sign of mental illness.⁶ Later critics sought to de-pathologise her physical and formal enclosures, turning them from neurotic symptoms into an aesthetic: Dickinson sought to 'lyricis[e] space, recreating in the domestic interior the very condition of poetic address and response'.⁷ In Boethian fashion, Dickinson 'isolated her physical body but allowed her intellect and imagination to trespass all boundaries.'⁸ This process of collapsing Dickinson's (voluntary or involuntary) constraints into her lyric poems began with the posthumous editing of her work by Higginson and Mabel Loomis Todd. Todd reported that 'although our interviews were chiefly confined to conversations between the brilliantly lighted drawing-room where I sat and the dusky hall just outside where she always remained, I grew very familiar with her voice'.⁹ Todd's daughter Millicent Todd Bingham likewise referred to Dickinson as 'the invisible voice, the phantom in the enchanted corridor'.¹⁰ Virginia Jackson has demonstrated how the extraction of Dickinson's verse from the social contexts of her letters suited a theory of lyric that Dickinson was made to embody and disembody as a 'speaking voice', who 'made literal the seclusion of the lyric self in its

---

[4] Meyer, *Magnificent Activist*, p. 544.
[5] Throughout this chapter, references are given to the numbering and dates of composition in Emily Dickinson, *The Poems: Variorum Edition*, ed. R. W. Franklin (Boston: Belknap Press, 1998).
[6] Jean McClure Mudge, *Emily Dickinson and the Image of Home* (Amherst University Press, 1975), p. 6.
[7] Diane Fuss, *The Sense of an Interior: Four Writers and the Rooms that Shaped Them* (London: Routledge, 2004), p. 49.
[8] Wendy Martin (ed.), *The Cambridge Introduction to Emily Dickinson* (Cambridge University Press, 2007), p. 36.
[9] Fuss, *Sense of an Interior*, p. 45.
[10] Millicent Todd Bingham, *Ancestor's Brocades: The Literary Debut of Emily Dickinson* (New York: Harper and Brothers, 1945), p. 12.

solitary cell' from Mill's theory, while the reader is positioned as an unseen listener.[11]

The fiction of the unseen listener is also enabled by Dickinson's resistance to publication. Although she did publish a small number of poems in magazines, Dickinson's rejection of the literary marketplace and her desire to circulate her poems – the 'Royal Air' of her thought (Fr788, 1863) – only within her own coterie resembles the manuscript culture in which Wyatt participated.[12] Some critics have argued that she displays an aristocratic horror at the professionalisation of literature, and a yearning for older, more exclusive forms of patronage. 'Poverty' may justify 'so foul a thing' as publication,

> but We – would rather
> From Our Garret go
> White – unto the White Creator –
> Than invest – Our Snow –
>
> (Fr788, 1863)

In this poem, Dickinson refers to publication as 'the Auction / Of the Mind of Man' (Fr788, 1863). The withdrawal from publicity is marked throughout by whiteness: the white Creator who welcomes the pure white soul, who keeps unsullied the white page, like the white dress Dickinson wore in her seclusion, and the 'little Alban House' of the white body, enclosed with its 'windows [shut] down so close' (Fr140, 1860). Benjamin Friedlander reads the references in this poem to auctions, the 'White Creator' and the 'Disgrace of Price' in relation to abolitionist rhetoric. In his reading, the snowy page, stained by ink or desecrated by circulation, is a racialised figure of privilege. Friedlander concludes that the poem argues against slavery, but resists a militant abolitionism that has led to war.[13] The poem's privileged resistance to publicity also ignores the fact 'that being bought and sold, like starvation itself, is rarely a choice: that the poem advances such an extreme position unjustly shames all of those for whom writing was a professional necessity – who published in order to survive', as Domhnall Mitchell argues.[14]

---

[11] Virginia Jackson, *Dickinson's Misery: A Theory of Lyric Reading* (Princeton University Press, 2005), p. 132.
[12] Betsy Erkkila, 'Emily Dickinson and Class,' in *The American Literary History Reader*, ed. Gordon Hutner (Oxford University Press, 1995), pp. 310–11; Janet Gray, *Race and Time: American Women's Poetics from Antislavery to Racial Modernity* (Iowa City: University of Iowa Press, 2004), pp. 53–4.
[13] Benjamin Friedlander, 'Auctions of the Mind: Emily Dickinson and Abolition,' *Arizona Quarterly* 54.1 (Spring 1998), pp. 1–25 (11–20).
[14] Domhnall Mitchell, 'Emily Dickinson and Class', in *The Cambridge Companion to Emily Dickinson* ed. Wendy Martin (Cambridge University Press, 2002), pp. 191–214 (201).

Dickinson's lyric fugitivity became a model for lyric's resistance to closure and interpretation. The ubiquity of metaphors of bondage in her work, and the particularity of her domestic life, also makes her a key figure in the history of lyric constraint. This chapter explores the significance of the prisoner, the hunted animal and the fugitive in Dickinson's poetry. It argues that between her nervous desire for escape and formal and metaphysical interest in constraint is a third term, a broken middle that Dickinson treads with great ambivalence: chattel slavery.

The extent to which Dickinson was willing to acknowledge the violence of her political moment has been a matter of considerable critical debate. While some of her poems have been read as making coded or allegorical references to war or slavery, those poems tend to translate violence into something providential. War is as natural and inevitable as the reddening of the autumn leaves; the proprietary relationship of enslavers to enslaved people is abstracted into a metaphysical condition: 'I am afraid to own a Body – / I am afraid to own a Soul – ' (F1050, 1865).

This chapter will resist such abstractions, arguing that Dickinson's poems should be read alongside the contemporary poetics of bondage. By that, I mean not only the songs of enslaved African Americans, to which I will turn in chapters 7 and 8, but also the marked bodies of imprisoned and enslaved people. The wound of slavery appears in the gaps and chasms of her poetry, in its diction of fetters, chains, scars and hunted animals. My intention in making this argument is not to 'expose' Dickinson as a conservative, or to correct the tendency of critics to impute to her a political radicalism equalling her poetic radicalism. Rather, I want to think through Dickinson's silences about the bounds of lyric whiteness.

My Gait Spasmodic

In her edition of Dickinson's letters, Mabel Loomis Todd quotes Oliver Wendell Holmes, who

> somewhere says that rhymes 'are iron fetters: it is dragging a chain and a ball to march under their encumbrance'; and if in Emily Dickinson's work there is frequently no rhyme where rhyme should be, a subtle something, welcome and satisfying, takes its place. An orchid among every-day, sweet-smelling flowers, strangeness and irregularity seem but to enhance her fascination.[15]

---

[15] Emily Dickinson, *The Letters*, ed. Mabel Loomis Todd (Boston: Roberts Brothers, 1894; Mineola, NY: Dover, 2003), p. 374.

Todd offers a decorous apology for what Higginson called Dickinson's wantonness. The absence of constraint – which Todd describes as a gap or void (not just a slant rhyme, but no rhyme) – is filled with ornament: with the flowers whose abundance and irregularity sweeten her verse. After her death, Higginson wrote that he had tried 'to lead her in the direction of rules and traditions; but I fear it was only perfunctory, and that she interested me more in her – so to speak – unregenerate condition'.[16] He came to realise that her resistance to his rehabilitative pedagogy is what made her poetry live (though he and Todd regularised her work anyway).[17]

Dickinson mostly wrote in hymn metre, but her variations from that pattern are just as consistent as her observance of it. For some critics, hymn metre was a chosen confinement that she struggled to escape; for others it was a technique for revealing her emancipation through (religious and aesthetic) nonconformity.[18] Sometimes she is transgressive; sometimes 'hypercorrect'.[19] Christina Pugh argues that 'the instinctual pulse of the four-beat line becomes the ground against which not only hesitation, but genuine metrical undecidability is posited', particularly through Dickinson's use of the dash to interrupt the prosody and introduce irregularities of emphasis.[20] David Porter argues that 'inherent in the hymn form is an attitude of faith, humility, and inspiration, and it is against this base of orthodoxy that she so artfully refracts the personal rebellion and individual feeling, the colloquial diction and syntax, the homely image, the scandalous love of this world, and the habitual religious scepticism' that typifies her poems.[21] In choosing hymn metre, Dickinson performs her carefully graded acts of heterodoxy within the boundaries of a living social form that both she and her friends and family knew, sung and held in their memories.

Dickinson herself draws connections between prosody and authority in her response to Higginson's criticism. Combining deference and resistance, she admits that 'I thanked you for your justice – but could not drop the Bells whose jingling cooled my Tramp',[22] an image that echoes Andrew

---

[16] Meyer, *Magnificent Archivist*, p. 551.
[17] On their editorial process, see Martha Nell Smith, *Rowing in Eden: Rereading Emily Dickinson* (Austin: University of Texas Press, 1992), p. 65.
[18] Victoria N. Morgan, *Emily Dickinson and Hymn Culture: Tradition and Experience* (Farnham: Ashgate, 2010), pp. 37–8.
[19] John Shoptaw, 'Listening to Dickinson', *Representations* 86 (2004), pp. 20–52.
[20] Christina Pugh, 'Ghosts of Meter: Dickinson, After Long Silence', *Emily Dickinson Journal* 16.2 (2007), pp. 1–24 (11).
[21] David Porter, *The Art of Emily Dickinson's Early Poetry* (Cambridge, MA: Harvard University Press, 1966), p. 74.
[22] Emily Dickinson, *The Letters of Emily Dickinson*, ed. Thomas H. Johnson, 3 vols. (Cambridge, MA and London: Belknap Press of Harvard University Press, 1958), L265, 7 June 1862.

Marvell's famous rebuke of John Dryden in his poem 'On Mr Milton's *Paradise Lost*'. Dickinson then quotes Higginson back at him: 'You think my gait "spasmodic" – I am in danger – Sir – / You think me "uncontrolled" – I have no tribunal' (L265, 7 June 1862). The spasmodic gait suggests a diseased, uncontrolled way of walking, a wrong-footedness. It alludes to the so-called school of 'spasmodic' Victorian poets, who had been mocked in a review in *Blackwood's Edinburgh Magazine* by William Edmonstoune Aytoun in 1854. Aytoun says that the 'gaiety' of Alexander Smith or Tennyson is 'spasmodic', their characters 'ridiculous' and comical, 'pouring forth floods of images and conceits which afford no perception of the idea their author would convey'.[23] Like Dickinson's 'wanton' and excessive verse, these poets overflow their boundaries.

Aytoun dramatises the poets' appeal for justice in the face of his charges. The critic – 'throned in his judicial chair' and brandishing 'the glittering sword' – should

> say in his heart, Peradventure there shall be found ten lines in this book – I will not destroy it for ten's sake. But, on the other hand, there is a class to which forbearance would be misapplied and criminal. It would too much resemble our prison discipline, where Mr William Sykes, after a long course of outrages on humanity, is shut up in a palace, treated like a prodigal son, and presently converted to Christianity.[24]

Aytoun alludes to *Oliver Twist*, Biblical prodigality and Genesis 18:20–23, where Abraham attempts to bargain with God to forestall the destruction of Sodom and Gomorrah – a reference that links this scene of poetic criminality to sexual transgression. He celebrates the corrective influence of those homes in England 'where fine criticism is nightly conversation', and argues that 'with such tribunals more plentiful than county courts, a man is no longer justified in decrying fame, or appealing for justice to posterity'. He suggests deviance should be punished leniently at first – 'the pantaloons should be loosed with a paternal hand' – but if the child-poet persists, force 'should be laid on till the blood comes' (346). I'll return to the association between whipping, pedagogy and prosody in Chapter 10. What is striking about these remarks is how Aytoun's portrait of the critic mixes poetic, penal and patriarchal discipline – elements that Dickinson herself seemed to cherish and resist.

---

[23] William Edmonstoune Aytoun, 'Alexander Smith's Poems', *Blackwood's Edinburgh Magazine* 75 (March 1854), pp. 345–51 (348–9).
[24] *Ibid.*, pp. 345–6.

The language of discipline threads through Dickinson's correspondence with Higginson. He said he had decided not to 'cross-examine' Dickinson in their interview. Echoing Aytoun, she laments that she has 'no tribunal'. She confesses her need for a stern hand: 'I had no Monarch in my life, and cannot rule myself, and when I try to organize – my little Force explodes – and leaves me bare and charred – ' (L271, August 1862). When she found herself on more certain ground, Dickinson was happy to assume a regal pose; her poems regularly stake out the absolute monarchy of her imaginative domain. But her letters also offer up her lawlessness for correction, treating Higginson as a surrogate father, doctor or schoolmaster (asking for him to be her 'Preceptor', L265; thanking him for 'the surgery'; signing herself 'Your Scholar', L268). Throughout their correspondence she veers between an exaggerated submissiveness and haughtiness, ironising her feminised position by overinvesting in it. But the performance of submission is not only a proto-feminist complaint. Her masochistic and sadistic fantasies about the exercise of authority also surface in Dickinson's letters, particularly in relation to vulnerable, racialised others.

The Pleasures of Submission

Alongside a desire to submit to her 'master', as in the series of mysterious letters she wrote in the late 1850s and early 1860s, Dickinson's correspondence expresses sadistic delight in scenes of whipping, and interest in the prison as a scene of cruelty, heroism and abjection. In 1851, Dickinson wrote to her brother Austin describing a fantasy of him flogging his Irish students at the Endicott School in Boston:

> I fancy little boys of several little sizes, some of them clothed in *blue* cloth, some of them clad in *gray* – I seat them round on benches in the schoolroom of my mind – then I set them all to shaking – on peril of their lives that they move their lips or whisper – then I clothe you with authority and empower you to punish, and to enforce the law, I call you 'Rabbi – Master,' and the picture is complete! It would seem very funny, say for Susie and me to come round as Committee – we should enjoy the terrors of 50 little boys and any specimens of *discipline* in your way would be a rare treat for us. I should love to know how you managed – whether government as a *science* is laid down and executed, or whether you *cuff and thrash* as the occasion dictates – whether you use *pure law* as in the case of *commanding*, or whether you *enforce* it by means of sticks and stones as in the case of *agents* – I suppose you have authority bounded but by their lives, and from a remark in one of your earliest letters I was led to conclude that on a certain occasion you *hit the boundary line*! (L48, 20 July 1851)

The tone of arousal in this letter is unmistakeable. Dickinson imagines the boys' transgressions in order to enjoy the spectacle of Austin's disciplinary authority. Assaults on pupils are fantasised as the 'boundary line' between self-control and the wildness of anger. Her fantasy is also racialised, its subjects being the 'poor little sons of Erin' who were represented in popular discourse as dark-skinned and whom she imagines being exterminated in another letter she wrote to Austin: 'Vinnie and I say masses for poor Irish boys souls. So far as *I* am concerned I should like to have you kill some – there are so many now, there is no room for the Americans' (L43, 15 June 1851).[25] On another occasion, writing to Sue Gilbert (her future sister-in-law) who was teaching in Baltimore, she indulges a similar fantasy: 'I hope you whip them Susie – for *my* sake – whip them hard whenever they dont behave just as you want to have them!' (L56, 9 October 1851). Here Dickinson sides not with the victims, as in 'From all the Jails the Boys and Girls' (Fr 1553) which imagines the children escaping for one afternoon from the 'Prison' of school, but with the whip-hand, enjoying the spectacle of their punishment.

These are not isolated examples of Dickinson's sadistic fantasy. She cites Charles Dickens to lament the departure of her friend Jane Humphrey in 1830, suggesting first that she is the prisoner, and then that Jane should be incarcerated:

> The immortal Pickwick himself could'nt have been more amazed when he found himself soul – body and – spirit incarcerated in the pound than was I myself when they said *she* had gone – gone! Gone *how* – or *where* – or *why* – who saw her go – help – hold – bind – and keep her – put her into States-prison – into the House of Correction – bring out the long lashed whip – and put her feet in the stocks – and give her a number of stripes and make her repent her going! (L30, 23 January 1830).

In a sudden inversion, Jane's escape turns Dickinson from the astonished inmate into the warden, envisioning whipping and restraining her friend, locking her in the stocks to punish her and keep her close.

These hectic associations between erotic desire, correction, law and sadistic discipline were long established when, later in life, Dickinson began her affair with Judge Otis Lord, whose marriage proposal she rejected in 1880.[26] Dickinson's passionate love letters to Lord portray her

---

[25] See Noel Ignatiev, *How the Irish Became White* (New York: Routledge, 1995).
[26] Judith Farr, 'Emily Dickinson and Marriage', in *Reading Emily Dickinson's Letters: Critical Essays*, ed. Jane Donahue Eberwein and Cindy MacKenzie (Amherst: University of Massachusetts Press, 2009), pp. 161–88.

as a legal supplicant faced with a regal authority. She asks forgiveness for 'the trespass of my rustic Love upon your Realms of Ermine' which 'only a Sovereign could forgive – I never knelt to other' (L750, 30 April 1882). And she turns witty figures in the language of the law: 'I had never tried any case in your presence but my own' (L560, *c.* 1878); 'to beg for the Letter when it is written, is bankrupt enough ... who can punish you?' (L561, *c.* 1878); 'Will you punish me? "Involuntary Bankruptcy," how could that be Crime? Incarcerate me in yourself – rosy penalty' (L559, *c.* 1878).[27] And though she enticed Lord with a wish to be 'incarcerated' in him, Dickinson also rejected the incarceration of marriage, offering him her 'no', 'the wildest word we consign to Language'.

Virginity is represented traditionally as a closed space, which Dickinson lauds as that 'Fastness' where the spirit is contained along with 'Love that never leaped it's socket – / Trust intrenched in narrow pain – ' (Fr267, 1861). In a much-quoted letter to Sue (L93, early June 1852), she speaks with intense trepidation about the scorching heat of sexual desire once it is awakened, concluding with an apology: 'if this saucy page did not here bind and fetter me, I might have had no end'. The wanton excesses of the body are bound by the 'saucy page' – the written page, though women could transgress against sexual constraint by cross-dressing as pages to serve their lovers, too. The bond and fetter of the paper recalls the many of Dickinson's poems that are plotted within constrained spaces, the flaps of envelopes or the backs of advertisements. These bounded, domesticated workspaces could be taken as constraining her overflowing creativity. But in her letter to Sue, the paper's domination of the writer has a certain flirtatious quality; and this fetter, which Dickinson explored in her envelope poems, both sets a limit to the poems' expansion, and asks the reader's body to undertake specific gestures and motions in order to turn, unlock and open it.[28]

Imaginary Prisons

Dickinson's imagination was repeatedly drawn to bounded spaces including the cellar, the grave, a childhood 'shut ... in the Cold' (Fr658, 1863), a life that feels as if it were 'shaven, / And fitted to a frame, / And could not breathe without a key' (Fr355, 1862), or the rituals of seclusion required before she can read a letter (Fr700, 1863). Dickinson frequently cites

---

[27] See also Lyndall Gordon, *Lives Like Loaded Guns: Emily Dickinson and Her Family's Feuds* (New York: Viking, 2010), pp. 160–2.

[28] Kristen Kreider, *Poetics and Place: The Architecture of Sign, Subjects and Site* (London and New York: IB Tauris, 2014), p. 88.

Byron's 'Prisoner of Chillon',[29] and described herself as a 'Fenestrellan captive', referring to X. B. Saintine's *Picciola* (1836; English translation 1839), in which the imprisoned protagonist nurtures a plant that sprouts between two paving stones.[30] Sent to Boston for treatment on her eyes in 1864, she describes how the physician 'does not let me go, yet I work in my Prison, and make Guests for myself'. She explains that the conditions would be deadly even for her dog: 'Carlo did not come, because that he would die, in Jail' (L90, early June 1864).

The many images of incarceration in Dickinson's poems are often read as self-referential. Diane Fuss argues that her bedroom was 'more a panoptic centre than an enclosed prison cell', a space that offered her 'maximum visual control'.[31] These constraints can be easily interpreted as complaints about the limitations of her feminised position within a patriarchal household: 'I was the slightest in the House – / I took the smallest Room – ' (Fr473, 1862). The speaker attempts to be the ideal child, seen but not heard (or barely even seen). But she also translates the closet of prose or the smallest room in the house into the expansive space of the poem. Most famously, she recollected:

> They shut me up in Prose –
> As when a little Girl
> They put me in the Closet –
> Because they liked me "still" –
>
> Still! Could themself have peeped –
> And seen my Brain – go round –
> They might as wise have lodged a Bird
> For Treason – in the Pound –
>
> Himself has but to will
> And easy as a Star
> Look down opon Captivity –
> And laugh – No more have I –
>
> (Fr445, 1862)

This poem in short metre has a single long line in the second and third stanzas, which exceeds the constraints and conformity of the rest. Its speaker

---

[29] See L293, to Vinnie, 1864; L29 to Samuel Bowles, 1862; L1029, to Sue, 1886; L1042, to Higginson, spring 1886; also Jay Leyda, *The Years and Hours of Emily Dickinson*, 2 vols. (New Haven: Yale University Press, 1960), 2:91, 145; Jack L. Capps, *Emily Dickinson's Reading 1836–1886* (Cambridge, MA: Harvard University Press, 1966), p. 79; Marcy L. Tanter, *The Influence of Nineteenth-Century British Writers on Emily Dickinson* (Lewiston and Lampeter: Edwin Mellen, 2014), pp. 43–9.

[30] Alfred Habegger, *My Wars Are Laid Away in Books: The Life of Emily Dickinson* (New York: Random House, 2001), p. 224.

[31] Fuss, *Sense of an Interior*, p. 56.

is also bigger than her constraints: her wheeling brain can escape the closet of prose or her body, like a bird looking down on its cage. The bird needs merely to 'will' freedom, and he can fly away; so can I, the poem alleges, opposing its imaginative liberty to a repressive household. Martha Dickinson Bianchi claims her aunt Emily once mimed twisting an imaginary key in her door, saying, 'Matty, child, no one could ever punish a Dickinson by shutting her up alone ... It's just a turn – and freedom, Matty.'[32] The fantasy that being 'shut up alone' is not a punishment because of the Dickinsons' powers of imagination reflects a familiar trope of confinement literature, and suggests that freedom is always accessible to the creative soul: 'No Rack can torture me – '; 'Captivity is Consciousness – / So's Liberty –' (Fr649, 1863). It's just a matter of choosing.

But Dickinson's poems acknowledge that not all constraints can be escaped. There are moments of unspeakable loneliness, 'With Consciousness suspended – / And Being under Lock – ' (Fr877A, 1864). There are subjects so thoroughly shrunk by captivity that they could no longer survive if released. 'A Prison gets to be a friend – ' (Fr456, 1862), for example, shows how captivity becomes consciousness, in the manner of the Prisoner of Chillon. The imprisoned person paces her cell, applying her personal geometry to 'the narrow Round' of the room. The rhythms of institutional life displace her own. She converses with the planks of wood that line the floor, until the 'Phantasm' of captivity becomes more real than the dream of 'the Cheek of Liberty' or the hope of heavenly redemption. Elsewhere, even the promise of heaven is not enough to release the captive from her misery: Dickinson wondered 'Is Heaven then a Prison?' (Fr933, 1865), and imagined her nephew Gilbert: 'Immured in Heaven! / What a Cell!' (Fr1628, 1883). Stoicism and its doctrine of autonomy through self-destruction is no use if even Heaven is a kind of prison.

Dickinson also invokes prison as a Gothic site of romanticised suffering and heroism, a melodramatic opportunity to perform extreme love. In 'Unto like Story – Trouble has enticed me,' the speaker imagines persecution and the attempt to break the 'young will' of a brother and sister through punishment and the threat of death (Fr300, 1862). The prison also accentuates the privileges of an elite who, like the Dickinsons, can never be stripped of their imaginative liberty. On the desire to 'marry whom I may' and run away 'With no Police to follow': 'What Liberty! So Captive deem / Who tight in Dungeons are' (Fr1056, 1865); on enjoying a 'sumptuous moment':

---

[32] Martha Dickinson Bianchi, *The Life and Letters of Emily Dickinson* (New York: Biblo and Tannen, 1971), pp. 65–6.

'The difference of Day / Ask him unto the Gallows led – / With morning in the sky' (Fr1186, 1870). In these examples, prison is a fictional site the hero or heroine escapes from, even through execution; the risk of death intensifies sensation and leads towards kinds of triumph over authority.

Actual incarceration, however, involves dull repetition:

> My Wheel is in the dark.
> I cannot see a spoke –
> Yet know it's dripping feet
> Go round and round.
>
> My foot is on the tide –
> An unfrequented road
> Yet have all roads
> A 'Clearing' at the end.
>
> Some have resigned the Loom –
> Some – in the busy tomb
> Find quaint employ.
> Some with new – stately feet
> Pass royal thro' the gate,
> Flinging the problem back, at you and I.
>
> (Fr61A, 1859)

This poem does not mention prison. It considers 'the problem' of eschatology that preoccupied Dickinson: what really happens after death? Oddly, the answer seems to be held in the feet, some of which pass 'royal' through death's gate, while others are forced to labour even in the tomb. Even the dead are trapped in the class struggle. Some can 'resign' the 'Loom', a mechanism of repetitive domestic, industrial and prison labour, but also of weaving and feminised creativity. And while the 'quaint employ' in the 'busy tomb' echoes Marvell's poem 'To His Coy Mistress', the Tombs were also well-known prisons in New York. The 'wheel' may be a mill-wheel; that it is driven round by 'dripping feet' suggests a treadmill. But the poem's imagery of bondage celebrates the speaker's exceptionalism. Someone's foot is bound to the wheel, in a punitive repetition and semblance of labour stripped of the utility that might make it bearable; but *my* foot is 'on the tide' – a natural cycle of repetition, an 'unfrequented' road, which distinguishes my activities from the futile ones in which others spend their lives.

In the introduction, I argued that feet are an important and recurrent image of poetic constraint. The image of feet condemned to indistinct and punitive labour, or punished by being fixed in place, can also be found across Dickinson's poems. She describes the aftermath of pain as a stiffness or

'Hour of Lead': 'The Feet, mechanical, go round – / A Wooden way / Of Ground, or Air, or Ought – ' (Fr372, 1862). The feet are often nailed down, pierced or crucified, preventing the speaker's escape. In 'They put Us far apart' (Fr708, 1863), 'we stood opon our stapled feet' as condemned convicts on the scaffold. 'Staples' refer to the ring through the nose used to drive cattle and pigs. In Dickinson's poems they are also driven through breath, puncturing and punctuating the lungs: 'that forcing, in my breath – / As Staples – driven through – ' (Fr292, 1862). Staples, pins, screws, nails and needles fill her poems, fixing the speaker painfully in place: 'A single Screw of Flesh / Is all that pins the Soul' (Fr294, 1862): 'A Weight with Needles on the pounds – / To push, and pierce, besides – ' (Fr293, 1862); 'The Cordiality of Death – / Who drills his Welcome in – ' (Fr266, 1861). In poems like these, the thrill of erotic puncturing is combined with asphyxiation or a fear of being fixed in place, like a butterfly on a pin. Unlike Dickinson's conceits of imprisonment, which allow the speaker to proclaim the freedom of her sovereign imagination and her heroic fortitude through an escape into death or the imagination, these images of screws and staples convey a tremendous anxiety about the impossibility of flight.

The Life That Tied Too Tight Escapes

Dickinson, so the story goes, chose poetry as her mode of escape: she was able to transcend her constraints through the sovereign power of her imagination, which could expand until it 'touched the Universe', then contract to nothing but a 'Speck opon a Ball' (Fr633, 1863). Escape involves thrilling flights away from the constraints of home and sociability. It is also a necessary outlet in situations of panic:

> I never hear the word '*Escape*'
> Without a quicker blood!
> A sudden expectation!
> A flying attitude!
>
> I never hear of prisons broad
> By soldiers battered down –
> But I tug, childish, at my bars –
> Only to fail again!
>
> (Fr144, 1860)

For anyone who has experienced anxiety and the flight instinct it can trigger, Dickinson's poems commemorate the repeated adrenal charge of a body whose need for escape is most urgent when no exit can be found:

> Doom is the House without the Door –
> 'Tis entered from the Sun –
> And then the Ladder's thrown away,
> Because Escape – is done –
>
> (Fr710, 1863)

The doorless house is a space that can't be entered or exited. Diane Fuss has examined the complex imagery of doors in Dickinson's writings, as places of departure, displacement and exclusion, thresholds that cannot be crossed, stimulants to anxieties about entering rooms but also openings onto receptivity.[33] There were five exits in the back hallway of her house leading to her bedroom; Dickinson called it her 'Northwest passage'.[34] Escape is thus not only a flight that takes the speaker into the wilderness beyond the prison but also a retreat deeper into the house's privacy. It is an obsession and a boon, a 'thankful Word' to tongue in the night (Fr1364, 1875).

Fugitivity and the desire for escape permeate Dickinson's poems. 'True Poems flee – ' (Fr1491, 1879), she argues, spurning their creators and their readers' desire for captive sense. Fame 'loves what spurns him – / Look behind – He is pursuing thee – ' (Fr1445, 1877). Fleeing Fame and spurning publication, Dickinson explained to Higginson: 'If fame belonged to me, I could not escape her – if she did not, the longest day would pass me on the chase – and the approbation of my Dog, would forsake me – then – My Barefoot-Rank is better – ' (L265, 7 June 1862). Fame is the property that comes to master the owner; its possession will force the poet to abandon her modest qualities and become other to herself. To be barefoot might suggest poverty. Like the stalking creatures in Wyatt's poem, it is to be unshackled or wild. But it is also to be ill equipped for running away.

Dickinson's desire for escape is repeatedly cyphered through figures of hunted animals. Excessive constraint and harsh handling might cause a domesticated animal to flee: 'The Life that tied too tight escapes' will always look behind it, like 'The Horse that scents the living Grass' (Fr1555, 1881). Through flight the animal returns to (its own) nature, and experiences an ecstasy that cannot be contained:

> A *wounded* Deer – leaps highest –
> I've heard the Hunter tell –

---

[33] Fuss, *Sense of an Interior*, pp. 38–43.
[34] Cindy MacKenzie, '"This Is My Letter to the World": Emily Dickinson's Epistolary Poetics,' in *Reading Emily Dickinson's Letters*, pp. 11–27 (19).

> 'Tis but the extasy of *death* –
> And then the Brake is still!
>
> The *smitten* Rock that gushes!
> The *trampled* Steel that springs!
> A Cheek is always redder
> Just where the Hectic stings!
>
> (Fr181, 1860)

Ecstasy is a word Dickinson uses frequently. According to her lexicon, it is a seizure or crisis in which 'the functions of the senses are suspended by the contemplation of some extraordinary or supernatural object'.[35] As in John Donne's poem 'The Extasie', where the lovers' liquid souls flow between them while their bodies 'like sepulchral statues lay', ecstasy is a paradoxical state of both overflowing feeling and paralysis: fugitivity and bondage. Dying is the ultimate escape, a deeply sensual ecstasy imagined by Dickinson as a leap, a gush, a spring and reddened cheek, liquidities of water and blood that manifest in the blush of shame, desire or smacked skin. For Sharon Leiter, the poem alludes to orgasm followed by a post-coital stillness.[36] But the wounded deer fleeing the hunter also calls up the feminised objects that Wyatt's poems associate with sexual desire and resistance. It is an image to which Dickinson repeatedly returns.

According to Martha Dickinson Bianchi, an engraving hung on the wall of the Dickinson parlour depicting 'The Stag at Bay'.[37] Dickinson dwells on this moment of capture, in which the deer surrenders to the ecstasy of death:

> The Maimed may pause, and breathe,
> And glance securely round –
> The Deer attracts no further
> Than it resists – the Hound –
>
> (Fr844, 1864)

In the slowly unfolding first three lines, she suggests that the wounded animal can 'pause, and breathe', by contrast to the deer whose 'resistance' in line four is hardened by the dash that separates it from its pursuer, the hound. Though we assume the injured animal is at its most vulnerable, an 1858 article in *Harpers* (a magazine the Dickinsons read) by Thomas Bangs Thorpe on 'The American Deer' suggested that deer could display

---

[35] Dickinson used Noah Webster's 1844 *American Dictionary of the English Language*: see *Renovated Online Edition of Noah Webster's 1844 American Dictionary of the English Language*, ed. Cynthia Hallen (Provo: Brigham Young University, 2009): edl.byu.edu/ (accessed 4 May 2021).
[36] Sharon Leiter, *Critical Companion to Emily Dickinson* (New York: Facts on File, 2007), p. 56.
[37] Dickinson Bianchi, *Life and Letters*, p. 34.

a 'remarkable ... tenacity of life': 'We have known a deer to keep its position in front of a fleet pack of hounds for near a mile, running all the while with its fore legs broken below the knee.'[38] Anecdotes of that tenacity include deer that survive musket balls and elder stalks through the heart, unhealed contusions and calcified bullet wounds – staples and holes. Deer can also be tamed: if you see one leaping the hedges of Virginia plantations, 'you know this to be a domesticated deer, not only from its sociability, but also from the little bell it wears upon its neck to protect it from the weapon of the hunter' (612). Wyatt's collar persists. These tenacious, weeping, heart-struck deer who hide in 'some matted thicket' chosen 'with remarkable sagacity to secure seclusion' (611) are distinctly lyrical creatures, but once they surrender to the hunting dogs, they will be destroyed.

In her poems, Dickinson identifies with both prey and hunter. One of Dickinson's most important hunting poems is 'My Life had stood – a Loaded Gun – ' (Fr764, 1863). The poem speaks through the gun that accompanies the hunter as he subdues the natural environment. It keeps a steady watch on him – protecting him, but also preventing his escape. In her reading of the poem, Susan Howe refers to the New World as a place of destabilising freedom, where 'communal identity has been lost, time lost, specificity of place lost, sure belief lost, purpose lost. These wayfarers are free – too free.'[39] America is a place of loss and wandering and excessive freedom. In that place, the poet is released from the constraints of land ownership, of custom and sovereignty: 'Who owns the woods? Freedom to roam poetically means freedom to hunt' (80), as if poetic composition originates in a mastery that turns living things to prey. We've seen the association between roaming, freedom and sovereignty in Wyatt's poetry; but there it was constraint – being fixed in place – that gave form to lyric suffering. By contrast, Dickinson's fixity at home is less significant for Howe than her enjoyment of an idealised American liberty, which allows her to 'hunt after some still unmutilated musical wild of the Mind's world' (105). Her metaphysical hunting takes possession of a wilderness that Howe depicts as a kind of pristine commons or paradisiacal birthright. If 'a poem is an invocation, rebellious return to the blessedness of beginning again, wandering free in pure process of forgetting and finding' (98), Dickinson embodies for Howe an originary national liberty, meandering through this *terra nullius* and making it her own.

---

[38] Thomas Bangs Thorpe, 'The American Deer: Its Habits and Associations,' *Harpers New Monthly Magazine* (October 1858), pp. 606–21.
[39] Susan Howe, *My Emily Dickinson* (New York: New Directions, 1985), p. 70.

Howe's readings of Dickinson are beautiful and informative. But her panegyric to the founding deceptions of the American polity is problematic. It is not the white settlers of Amherst who were condemned to loss and wandering. As Betsy Erkkila has argued, Howe's Eurocentric mythopoesis displaces 'the land as the actual site of historical struggle between indigenous cultures and their European conquerors with the symbolic wilderness of white mind and white writing'.[40] Howe represents Indigenous Americans as they appear in settler literature: as restless, warlike people who pose an existential threat to white planters, rather than as victims of genocide – as hunters, not prey. Her analysis of Dickinson's imagery depends on a version of American creative liberty that erases Indigenous peoples. More relevant to 'My Life had stood' is perhaps the fact that, at a family gathering in 1883, a display of Dickinson family photographs and flags was set up, along with a rifle that was said to have been 'used in killing Indians and wolves'.[41]

There is another context in which the human was transmuted into an animal to be hunted: the Fugitive Slave Law, passed in 1850, which 'gave slave agents an open hunting license to travel the free states to re-capture "escaped property"'.[42] This is not a political situation upon which Dickinson comments directly. In 1852, she wrote casually to Austin about the family's African American stableman: 'Wells Newport has disappeared, and our horse is now under the care of Jeremiah Holden, who seems a faithful hand' (L80, 7 March 1852). The phrase seems not to convey any alarm. The Dickinson household included domestic workers of various ethnicities. Not so wealthy as to be able to avoid reproductive labour, Dickinson worked in the kitchen alongside Native American, African American and later English and Irish servants. Aífe Murray identifies numerous Dickinson servants who were people of colour, including Henry Hawkins, was an Amherst College teamster who may also have been part of the Underground Railroad.[43] Austin and Sue hired a nurse for their son Ned: Aunt Abby, a formerly enslaved woman from a large Sea Island estate. This 'gay-turbaned nurse, sauntering over the grounds with baby' was dismissed soon after she was hired.[44] In her scant references to people

---

[40] Betsy Erkkila, 'The Emily Dickinson Wars,' in *The Cambridge Companion to Emily Dickinson*, pp. 11–29 (21).
[41] Habegger, *My Wars*, p. 84.
[42] Brenda Wineapple, *White Heat: The Friendship of Emily Dickinson and Thomas Wentworth Higginson* (New York: Knopf, 2008), p. 7.
[43] Aífe Murray, *Maid as Muse: How Servants Changed Emily Dickinson's Life and Language* (Durham, NH: University of New Hampshire Press, 2009), pp. 14, 18, 22.
[44] Habegger, *My Wars*, p. 432.

of colour in her letters, Dickinson is often whimsical or even callous.[45] When an African American gardener was hired in August 1881, Dickinson writes: 'We have a new Black Man and are looking for a Philanthropist to direct him, because every time he presents himself, I run, and when the Head of the Nation shies, it confuses the Foot – ' (L721, August 1881). In her family's body politic, the white bourgeois woman represents the head, and the Black worker the foot. Murray hears echoes in Dickinson's writing of the vernaculars of these workers, such as turning mass nouns into 'count nouns' ('a hay', 'a grass', 'a Dew') (125). Dickinson also mimicked their speech in her letters, writing to Austin of a '*foundling hen* into whose young mind I seek to instil the fact "Massa is a-comin!"' (L49, 27 July 1851).

When Dickinson talks about ownership of bodies, branding and fugitivity, she usually is making a point about mortality or publication rather than the torture and exploitation of enslaved people. For example, she portrays the corpse of an (ironically named) 'Indolent Housewife' as locked in by death. Although the body has now yielded its labour power at last, Dickinson describes it as marked by torturous use:

> How many times these low feet staggered –
> Only the soldered mouth can tell –
> Try – can you stir the awful rivet –
> Try – can you lift the hasps of steel!
>
> (Fr238, 1861)

The staggering feet are contained in two staggering lines: the feminine ending in lines one and three are followed by an inverted foot in line two, and three and four begin with the heavily stressed first word 'try' as an interrupting command. Karen Sánchez-Eppler emphasises the poem's satiric commentary on the 'body's inability to express the self as a breakdown in the domestic order'.[46] And certainly, proto-feminist discourse in this period drew problematic comparisons between women's domestic labour or lack of self-determination and slavery.[47] However, as Frank Wilderson has argued, 'the female slave is a possessed, accumulated, and fungible object, which is to say that she is ontologically different than a white woman who may, as a house servant or indentured laborer, be

---

[45] Mitchell, 'Emily Dickinson and Class', p. 201.
[46] Karen Sánchez-Eppler, *Touching Liberty: Abolition, Feminism, and the Politics of the Body* (Berkeley and Los Angeles: University of California Press, 1993), p. 126.
[47] See Tricia Lootens, *The Political Poetess: Victorian Femininity, Race, and the Legacy of Separate Spheres* (Princeton University Press, 2017); Kari Winter, *Subjects of Slavery, Agents of Change: Women and Power in Gothic Novels and Slave Narratives, 1790–1865* (Athens, GA: University of Georgia Press, 1992).

a subordinated subject'.[48] This tortured body, with its staggering feet, mouth soldered shut, rivets and staples and steel hasps, is an image of bondage in death that draws directly on the iconography of chattel slavery.

Descriptions of bodies like this filled the newspapers. Charles Dickens, who was entertained by Dickinson's neighbour and friend Samuel Bowles, published some of those advertisements in his book *American Notes*, which Dickinson's father Edward added to his library in April 1844.[49] Dickinson was an avid reader of Dickens, even though she was warned off him and Harriet Beecher Stowe by her father.[50] Dickens discusses the abomination of slavery:

> 'Cash for negroes' is the heading of advertisements in great capitals down the long columns of the crowded journals. Woodcuts of a runaway negro with manacled hands, crouching beneath a bluff pursuer in top-boots, who, having caught him, grasps him by the throat, agreeably diversify the pleasant text.[51]

American Notes reproduces sample ads, describing the scars and mutilations that could identify people running from slavery, for example 'Ran away, a negro girl called Mary. Has a small scar over her eye, a good many teeth missing, the letter A is branded on her cheek and forehead' (271). Austin Reed's fear that captivity had left a legible mark on him, alongside the inscriptions on the skin of barbaric whipping, shows how Dickinson's contemporaries might read these marks: not only as texts to be read in newspapers, but also on the bodies of enslaved and freed people. Hortense Spillers describes the scars on the captive body as 'a kind of hieroglyphics of the flesh', which 'create the distance between what I would designate a cultural *vestibularity* and *culture*': 'This body whose flesh carries the female and the male to the frontiers of survival bears in person the marks of a cultural text whose inside has been turned outside.'[52] In contrast to Howe's defence of settler ideology, Spillers reminds us that Dickinson's lyrics, the privileged objects of culture as interiority, must be read alongside the vestibular cultural forms that are the bodies of imprisoned and enslaved

---

[48] Saidiya V. Hartman and Frank B. Wilderson III, 'The Position of the Unthought', *Qui Parle* 13.2 (Spring/Summer 2003), pp. 183–201 (186).
[49] Eleanor Heginbotham, '"What Are You Reading Now?": Emily Dickinson's Epistolary Book Club', in *Reading Emily Dickinson's Letters*, pp. 126–60 (133, 142); Leyda, *Years and Hours*, 1:84.
[50] Dickinson, *The Letters*, ed. Todd, pp. 101–2. See also Capps, *Emily Dickinson's Reading*, pp. 93–8; Heginbotham, 'What Are You Reading,' p. 144; and Karl Keller, *The Only Kangaroo among the Beauty: Emily Dickinson and America* (Baltimore: Johns Hopkins University Press, 1979), pp. 104–5.
[51] Charles Dickens, *American Notes* (London: Chapman and Hall, n.d. [1866?]), pp. 270–1.
[52] Hortense J. Spillers, *Black, White, and in Color: Essays on American Literature and Culture* (University of Chicago Press, 2003), p. 207.

people, in order to recognise how inside and outside mutually produce each other.

A Crumb of Blood: Dickinson's Civil War

Around the same time that she wrote 'A wounded Deer,' Dickinson had a dispute with Samuel Bowles about women's rights. She later wrote to apologise:

> I am much ashamed. I misbehaved tonight. I would like to sit in the dust.
> I fear I am your little friend no more, but Mrs Jim Crow.
> I am sorry I smiled at women.
> Indeed, I revere holy ones, like Mrs [Elizabeth] Fry or Miss [Florence] Nightingale.
> I will never be giddy again. Pray forgive me now. Respect little Bob o'Lincoln again! (L223, early August 1860)

As in her toying with sadomasochistic postures in her letters, and her fantasies of schoolchildren being beaten, Dickinson exaggerates her submission and need for correction in this apology to Bowles. Her gesture of humility is undermined by her ironic 'reverence' for the prison reformer and the famous nurse, and her naming of herself as 'Bob o'Lincoln' – a parodic Irish version of the Great Emancipator. At the same time, her rhetorical adoption of blackface – Mrs Jim Crow – as a marker of her abjection infuses that submission with a tincture of white supremacy.

Dickinson seems to have taken up her father's disdain for feminism, and some of his mixed ideas about emancipation. Edward Dickinson was described by a contemporary as 'in action a *conservative* or a pro slavery man':[53] though against slavery in principle, he also opposed infringements on states' rights to self-determination. In 1840, when Dickinson was nine, Edward represented three African American men (including Hawkins) who had rescued an eleven-year-old girl from being sold into slavery by the white family for whom she worked.[54] He was elected to the House of Representatives in 1853 for one term as a 'firm, straight Whig'.[55] There, he was 'one of the most zealous supporters of the Missouri Compromise', which enacted the Fugitive Slave Law in exchange for California becoming a free state, among other measures.[56] In July 1855, he wrote a letter urging

---

[53] 24 July 1864; Leyda, *Years and Hours*, 2:92.   [54] Wineapple, *White Heat*, p. 7.
[55] Leyda, *Years and Hours*, 1:259; Coleman Hutchinson, '"Eastern Exiles": Dickinson, Whiggery, and War,' *Emily Dickinson Journal* 13.2 (2004), pp. 1–26.
[56] Leyda, *Years and Hours*, 1:303–4.

the American people to 'resolve that by the help of the Almighty God, not another inch of our soil heretofore consecrated to freedom, shall hereafter be polluted by the advancing tread of slavery'.[57] But in 1861, he denounced the 'heretical dogma' that 'the immediate and universal emancipation of slaves' should be 'the means of putting an end to the war'; he viewed it as 'subversive of all constitutional guarantees' to states' rights.[58] He supported the Northern war effort, leading a ceremony to celebrate Amherst men going off to war, and petitioning the Massachusetts governor for permission to raise a regiment.[59] When Austin and several other white men from Amherst were drafted in May 1864, they paid Chauncey "Julius" Pierce and four African American men to take their places. Austin's proxy cost $500.[60]

The Dickinsons also lived near to the Northampton Association of Education and Industry, a utopian commune that thrived from 1842 to 1846; Sojourner Truth and Frederick Douglass were sometime members. Another member of the Association was David Mack III, whose father General David Mack Jr bought the Dickinson Homestead and who was a Yale classmate of Edward Dickinson. The association was influenced by Fourier and Transcendentalist philosophy, and had strong abolitionist commitments; African American and white members lived and worked freely there together.[61] Dickinson referred jokingly to the radical movements of the 1840s:

> Magnum bonum, "harum scarum," zounds et zounds, et war alarum, man reformam, mundum changum, all things flarum?
>
> ... But the world is sleeping in ignorance and error, sir, and we must be crowing-cocks, and singing-larks, and a rising sun to awake her; or else we'll pull society up by the roots, and plant it in a different place. We'll build Alms-houses, and transcendental State prisons, and scaffolds – we will blow out the sun, and the moon, and encourage invention. Alpha shall kiss Omega – we will ride upon the hill of glory – Hallelujah, all hail! (L34, February 1850)

Here she elides reformist goals (charitable institutions, reformed prisons) with impossible desires (to blow out the sun and moon), ridiculing revolutionary intentions as magical thinking – hocus pocus. As she wrote to a friend, 'My Country is Truth. Vinnie lives much of the time in the

---

[57] Leyda, *Years and Hours*, 1:333. [58] *Ibid.*, 2:34. [59] *Ibid.*, 2:33, 64. [60] *Ibid.*, 2:88–9.
[61] Alice Eaton McBee II, *From Utopia to Florence: The Story of a Transcendentalist Community in Northampton, Mass. 1830–1852* (Northampton: George Banta Publishing Company, 1947), pp. 32–3, 49, 62–3, 47.

State of Regret. I like Truth – it ~~sets free~~ is a free Democracy.'[62] This dwelling in the country of Truth, instead of Regret or the United States, allows her to enjoy the enfranchisement of a free conscience, shun the masses and enjoy the privileges of a middle-class white woman.

For many years, Dickinson scholarship was dominated by the assumption that she was unwilling to engage with contemporary politics.[63] In an 1847 letter to her brother Austin, she inquires coyly who the candidates for President are, and whether the Mexican war has ended. She refused to contribute to the war effort by making bandages, or giving her poems to Bowles's literary miscellany in aid of sick and wounded combatants.[64] Her letters make scant reference to the war, apart from a joking message about the capture of Jefferson Davis to her sister in 1865.[65] In October 1863, she was able to write: 'Nothing has happened but loneliness, perhaps too daily to relate.'[66]

Since the 1980s, however, critics have challenged the notion that Dickinson was oblivious to the war. Karen Dandurand revealed that three of Dickinson's poems appeared in 1864 in *Drum Beat*, a Brooklyn-based periodical sold to raise funds for the Union Army.[67] Other critics have found in the sadness and morbidity of the poems she composed during the Civil War traces of 'the commonality of sorrow and anguish' that beset wartime Amherst, or of her father's Whiggish desire for compromise.[68] She was touched personally by the deaths of Amherst boys in the war, especially Frazar Stearns (L245, 31 Dec. 1861; L255, late March 1862). But when Dickinson describes in sentimental terms the return of Stearns's body to his family, she does so without any specific reference to the cause for which he died.[69] The next year, 1863, she wrote that 'It feels a shame to be Alive – / When Men so brave – are dead – ' (Fr524), their lives offered 'in Pawn for Liberty'. But along with this survivor's guilt came a sense of the aggrandisement of the poet's calling at times of national crisis. Commenting on the publication of a new volume by Robert

---

[62] Habegger, *My Wars*, p. 360.
[63] For example, Jane Donahue Eberwein, *Dickinson: Strategies of Limitation* (Amherst: University of Massachusetts Press, 1985), p. 267.
[64] Habegger, *My Wars*, p. 401   [65] Leyda, *Years and Hours*, 2:98.   [66] *Ibid.*, 2:83.
[67] Karen Dandurand, 'New Dickinson Civil War Publications', *American Literature* 56.1 (1984), pp. 17–27.
[68] Christopher Benfey, 'Emily Dickinson and the American South', in *The Cambridge Companion to Emily Dickinson*, pp. 30–50 (47–8); Cynthia Hogue, "Lives – like Dollars": Dickinson and the Poetics of Witness', *Emily Dickinson Journal* 15.2 (2006), pp. 40–6 (41).
[69] Richard B. Sewall, *The Life of Emily Dickinson*, vol. 2 (New York: Farrar, Straus and Giroux, 1974), p. 536; Leigh-Anne Marcellin, 'Singing Off the Charnel Steps: Soldiers and Mourners in Emily Dickinson's War Poetry', *Emily Dickinson Journal* 9.2 (2000), pp. 64–74 (66).

Browning in December 1862, Dickinson observes that 'Sorrow seems more general than it did, and not the estate of a few persons, since the war began':

> I noticed that Robert Browning had made another poem, and was astonished – till I remembered that I, myself, in my smaller way, sang off charnel steps. Every day feels mightier, and what we have the power to be, more stupendous. (L298, 1864?)

Dickinson recognises that the anguish that marks out her singularity is a general condition.[70] Browning's publication also draws attention to her own singing, giving her a sense of the power of poetry in times of national conflict. This leads to the grandiose ambition to become 'stupendous', in which the occasion of that song – mass death – seems lost.

Some of Dickinson's allusions to war are direct (as in the 'Braveries, remote as this / In Yonder Maryland' celebrated in Fr518, 1863), others less so. Few of the poems that have been identified as drawing on the imagery of military conflict 'appear to be "war poems"' at first glance.[71] 'A Slash of Blue! A sweep of Gray!' (Fr233B, 1861) has been read as an ironically detached, picturesque depiction of Union soldiers clashing with Confederates, possibly after the Battle of Bull Run.[72] 'Dying – to be afraid of Thee' (Fr946B, 1865) refers to artillery, batteries and other military equipment, but transfigures war into a generalised anguish at leaving behind loved ones when we die. In 'They dropped like Flakes – ' (Fr545, 1863) and 'The name – of it – is "Autumn" – ' (Fr465, 1862), pastoral landscapes are depicted as bloodsoaked battlefields. But these poems, which may have been written following the massacres at Antietam, naturalise mass slaughter, integrating it into a providential cycle of life and death.[73] If the death of soldiers is like the turning colours of the leaves, then war is not a moral or political failure but an unavoidable aspect of human life.

Dickinson may have written oblique poems about the Civil War, but she shows no sympathy to enslaved people. Abolition is not a subject that is addressed in her poems or her letters to Higginson, or that he raises in

---

[70] Shira Wolosky, 'Emily Dickinson's War Poetry: The Problem of Theodicy', *Massachusetts Review* 25.1 (1984), pp. 22–41 (25).
[71] Martin (ed.), *The Cambridge Introduction to Emily Dickinson*, p. 36.
[72] Lawrence Berkove, '"A Slash of Blue!": An Unrecognised Emily Dickinson War Poem', *Emily Dickinson Journal* 10.1 (2001), pp. 1–8.
[73] Tyler Hoffman, 'Emily Dickinson and the Limit of War', *Emily Dickinson Journal* 3.2 (1994), pp. 1–18; David Cody, 'Blood in the Basin: The Civil War in Emily Dickinson's "The name – of it – is 'Autumn' – "', *Emily Dickinson Journal* 12.1 (2003), pp. 25–52; Michelle Kohler, 'The Ode Unfamiliar: Dickinson, Keats, and the (Battle)fields of Autumn', *Emily Dickinson Journal* 22.1 (2013), pp. 30–54, and Faith Barrett, 'Addresses to a Divided Nation: Images of War in Emily Dickinson and Walt Whitman', *Arizona Quarterly* 61.4 (Winter 2005), pp. 67–99 (89).

relation to her. Higginson was a radical abolitionist, who in 1867 'advocated the confiscation of southern lands and their distribution to the freedman'.[74] He broke down a courthouse door in Boston in 1854, in an attempt to free Anthony Burns, arrested under the Fugitive Slave Act; in 1856 he helped arm anti-slavery settlers in Kansas.[75] In 1862, when she first began corresponding with him, Higginson had accepted the position of colonel to the First South Carolina Volunteers (the first regiment of formerly enslaved men mustered into the service of the United States during the Civil War); she could have tracked their progress in the *Republican* throughout the war.[76] She must also have read Higginson's description of the regiment in an essay for *The Atlantic Monthly* in 1867. Higginson's article is the first published transcription of 'Negro Spirituals'; these were republished in his *Army Life in a Black Regiment* (1870), and I will discuss them in Chapter 8. Dickinson is known to have read everything that Higginson wrote; she quotes from *Army Life* at least twice.

In her correspondence with Higginson, Dickinson mused that 'War feels to me an oblique place', and compares her garden to the Sea Islands, and his cultivation of soldiers from freed Black men to her blackberries (L280, February 1863).[77] John Shoptaw consequently reads her poem 'The Black Berry – wears a Thorn in his side – ' (Fr548, 1863) as a tribute to the 'Brave Black Berry' of Higginson's regiment, which for him 'should lay to rest any doubts about Dickinson's allegiance to the causes of abolition and racial equality'.[78] Even if Shoptaw's interpretation is correct, Dickinson is commenting on slavery very obliquely indeed.

Higginson praised the bravery and discipline of the Black soldiers under his command, but in paternalistic terms, describing them repeatedly as 'childlike'. He writes about a distinguished sergeant: 'He makes Toussaint perfectly intelligible; and if there should ever be a black monarchy in South Carolina, he will be its king.'[79] Dickinson herself wrote several poems in which she invokes 'Domingo' (Haiti), which she uses as a token of sultry exoticism (Fr95, 1859; Fr726, 1863).[80] She poses as an experienced aesthete for Higginson: 'Your letter gave no drunkenness, because I tasted rum before. Domingo comes but

---

[74] Leyda, *Years and Hours*, 2:123.   [75] Wineapple, *White Heat*, pp. 4–5.
[76] Leyda, *Years and Hours*, 2:71, 75, 76, 81, 82, 93, 101.
[77] Erica Fretwell, 'Emily Dickinson in Domingo', *J19* 1.1 (Spring 2013), pp. 71–96 (76).
[78] John Shoptaw, 'Dickinson's Civil War Poetics: From the Enrolment Act to the Lincoln Assassination', *Emily Dickinson Journal*, 19.2 (2010), pp. 1–19 (8).
[79] Thomas Wentworth Higginson, *Army Life in a Black Regiment* (East Lansing: Michigan State University Press, 1960), p. 44.
[80] On Dickinson's Orientalist sensuality, see Vivian Pollak, 'Dickinson and the Poetics of Whiteness', *Emily Dickinson Journal* 9.2 (2000), pp. 84–95.

once; yet I have had few pleasures so deep as your opinion.'[81] Here Dickinson echoes Emerson's depiction of the poet as one 'intoxicated' by imagination, which she read in his *Essays: Second Series* in 1861.[82] As Erica Fretwell points out, she is also tying her lawless style to racialised revolution, Blackness and sweetness.[83] But this association is not predicated on a respect and admiration for Black revolutionaries of the kind expressed by Higginson. Rather, Blackness for Dickinson seems to equate with a ravenous appetite and animalistic freedom from social constraint, as well as from moral reflection.

Dickinson returns to this association of Domingo with the tongue in 'As the Starved Maelstrom laps the Navies':

> As the Tiger eased
>
> By but a Crumb of Blood, fasts Scarlet
> Till he meet a Man
> Dainty adorned with Veins and Tissues
> And partakes – his Tongue
>
> Cooled by the Morsel for a moment
> Grows a fiercer thing
> Till he esteem his Dates and Cocoa
> A Nutrition mean
>
> I, of a finer Famine
> Deem my Supper dry
> For but a Berry of Domingo
> And a Torrid Eye –
>
> (Fr1064, 1865)

The tiger, constrained to a mean diet, devours the first 'dainty' man who passes by. He is transformed into a 'fiercer thing' by his consumption of human blood, and refuses his customary food. Wild animals will always revert to their natural instincts. For Ed Folsom and Kenneth Price, this is a poem about the consequences of emancipating enslaved people: according to white supremacist logic, if you give animals a taste of 'Man', then ask them to be satisfied with a dry supper, you will leave white America at the mercy of a untameable tiger.[84] The tiger, they argue, symbolises the fear

---

[81] Meyer, *Magnificent Activist*, p. 548.
[82] Ralph Waldo Emerson, 'The Poet', in *Essays, Second Series*, in *The Collected Works of Ralph Waldo Emerson*, ed. Joseph Slater, Alfred R. Ferguson, and Jean Ferguson Carr (Cambridge, MA: Harvard University Press, 1983), 3:16.
[83] Fretwell, 'Dickinson in Domingo', p. 72.
[84] Ed Folsom and Kenneth M. Price, 'Dickinson, Slavery, and the San Domingo Moment,' *The Whitman Archive*: whitmanarchive.org/resources/teaching/dickinson/intro.html (accessed 4 May 2021).

amongst white Americans that the revolutionary overthrow of colonial rule in Haiti would inspire Black Americans to rise up against their oppressors. As such, Dickinson's poem speaks to what Zakiyyah Iman Jackson refers to as the ontological plasticity of Blackness as it delineates and mixes the categories of the human and the animal.

Folsom and Price call 'Domingo' a 'vortex word': it focuses the abstract contemplation of psychic hunger and violence so common in Dickinson's poetry through an allusion to slave revolts and the dangers of slaveholding. Noting that there were frequent references to San Domingo in monthly magazines in the years preceding the Civil War, they cite Alexis de Tocqueville's prediction of a civil war in America that would resemble the Haitian Revolution, as well as the phrase 'San Domingo hour' coined in *Uncle Tom's Cabin*, which Dickinson read (L113, 2 April 1853) and that was used frequently in the popular press. But the poem also brags that the animal's frenzy of appetite is nothing compared to the speaker's ironically delicate 'finer Famine'. She is a more refined beast. To provoke her, she needs no veins and tissues, but only a 'Berry of Domingo', a substitute for the sacramental 'Crumb of Blood'. The speaker's internalised, ravenous animal might emerge once she, too, has tasted the bloody fruit.[85]

In one of her poems sent to Helen Hunt, Dickinson describes how an untreated physical or psychic injury can lead to death:

> A not admitting of the wound
> Until it grew so wide
> That all my Life had entered it
> And there were troughs] beside –   ]was space • [was] room
>
> (Fr1188, 1870)

Dickinson may have intended the wound to signify any number of things. Its inspecificity is part of its power: as with the 'thing' that stuck in Wyatt's mind, we can speculate on what the wound is, or gather it to our own specific woundedness. We've already seen how often wounded animals, ecstatic, resistant, frightful and fugitive, leap up in her poems. A wound is also an opening of the sealed enclosure of the body: a breach in its (for Dickinson) white surface. In the history of lyric which I am narrating, bondage – in the historical form of chattel slavery – is such a wound, a repressed fact like a gaping 'trough' that unattended comes to contain the whole of national life. This is not to say that Dickinson considered slavery to be a wound, or considered slavery at all. Rather, in reading her work's

---

[85] Fretwell, 'Dickinson in Domingo', p. 80.

obsessive return to imprisoned, bound and scarred bodies as figures mostly of her ambivalent retreat from sociality, we avoid recognising how slavery constitutes an open wound in her time, a wound that prevents aesthetic or communal wholeness and infects the writing also of a privileged white woman going about her work in Massachusetts.

Cathy Caruth has said that 'Trauma is always the story of a wound that cries out, that addresses us in the attempt to tell us of a reality or truth that is not otherwise available. This truth, in its delayed appearance and in its belated address, cannot be linked only to what is known, but also to what remains unknown in our very actions and our language.'[86] This delayed and belated truth, which for whatever reason was less than fully available to Dickinson, sets a limit – is a constraint – even as it cries out from between the lines. I am reminded of another wound, in the autobiography published in 1845 by someone who lived for a time just down the road from her. Frederick Douglass describes how 'My feet have been so cracked with the frost, that the pen with which I am writing might be laid in the gashes.'[87] Against the snow of the page that Dickinson refused to invest, Douglass gives us the frost-cracked foot. He returns the abstracted reading mind to the historical writing body: his foot, scarred by the depravity of slavery, is made contiguous with his hand holding the pen; while the present can represent the wounds of the past, the past also contains the present, like a pen nestled in the gash.

Bound a Trouble

In the Chapter 6, the work of M. NourbeSe Philip will guide us through the contemplation of the wound, or what she calls the 'story that cannot be told', of chattel slavery. I'll have more to say then about Dickinson's poetics of whiteness. Before I finish here, however, I want to swerve away from these historical contexts to a much more personal reading, which reflects on constraint and overflowing, fixture and fugitivity, and the plasticity of limits and the working song, in one particular poem.

One winter while working on this book, I was suddenly struck by a series of panic attacks, followed by an overwhelming anxiety that resonated with the psychic and physical states Dickinson approaches at such hard angles in

---

[86] Cathy Caruth, *Unclaimed Experience: Trauma, Narrative, and History* (Baltimore: Johns Hopkins University Press, 1996), p. 4.
[87] Frederick Douglass, *Narrative of the Life of Frederick Douglass, An American Slave*, ed. Houston Baker (Harmondsworth: Penguin, 1986), p. 72.

her poems. I read and tried to understand her poems as I choked and shook. Suddenly, one swam up to meet me.

> Bound a Trouble – and Lives will bear it –
> Circumscription – enables Wo –
> Still to anticipate] – Were not limit –   ] conjecture
> Who were sufficient to] Misery?   ] could begin on –
>
> State it the Ages – to a cipher –
> And it will ache contented on –
> Sing, at it's pain, as any Workman –
> Notching the fall of the even Sun –
>
> (Fr240B, 1861)

In this poem, which I also read as choking and shuddering with the interferences of its dashes, Dickinson seems to be telling us that 'bounding' a trouble makes it bearable – we can sustain or carry it, because we have put limits to it. Bound or circumscribed – terms that bring book-binding and writing to mind – pain can be lived with. No one could be 'sufficient' in the face of unbounded misery; none could bear its infinite demands. To anticipate pain still to come, to conjecture a limit or a future, produces the interval or fault between the experience of pain and the subject. If we can think about a time without pain, we are still able to distinguish between pain and ourselves. As she puts it in a variant of this poem, this conjecture sets a 'Limit' on 'how deep a bleeding go!' and preserves the self from mortal exhaustion.

Dickinson represents misery, woe and trouble as bound in particular by language: by 'telling' or 'stating', and by song. Her poem teaches us to sing out through misery, like a worker whose song makes exhausting labour bearable. This assimilates the poem's own song to an exercise in containing misery that passes the time until evening (the 'even' sun). That even sun shines on, evenly, despite our misery, illuminating our work and setting its limits as day, and it would do so even if we had not made ourselves 'content' (in both senses) within the form or bodily hexis imposed on us by our labour. Work also sets a limit to suffering as well as causing it: as Dickinson, a hard domestic worker throughout her life, wrote in 1878: 'I am constantly more astonished that the body contains the spirit – except for overmastering work it could not be borne' (L284).

Dickinson's fascination with borders and circumferences was macroscopic, and often fixed on the boundary between life and death: paradise lay beyond imagination. But she suspected that home was 'a bit of Eden which not the sin of any can utterly destroy' (L75, 1851); the African American servants in her household could have told her that she was already in the promised land. Her lifeworld, and the poems she made in and from it, have contributed to a notion of lyric as a genre whose aesthetic or formal constraints are voluntary – or at least they are idiosyncratic, individual and apolitical. And that notion arises through acts of erasure. Reading her friend Higginson's articles, Dickinson could have heard the singing of a different kind of workmen: the First South Carolina Volunteers. The sorrow songs were undoubtedly a form of consolation for the miseries of slavery, but they were also forced, coerced performances of contentment. These songs do not make trouble or bondage seem bearable, so long as it is constrained. But then, neither do Dickinson's poems.

Reading 'Bound a Trouble' responsibly, in the context of Dickinson's work, I feel pressured to believe that it is advising me to discover the limits of anxiety, so that I can bear it. But another meaning overflows that first and is the one I need to choose. Pain that is bound becomes an obligation; these activities of limitation enable us to live with woe, and so enable woe itself. If binding trouble means that we can bear it, it also means we *have to* bear it. Boundaries and enclosures privatise suffering, turn it into property. Unbound trouble, which exceeds all limits and our capacities to maintain them, might crush us. But unbinding trouble might also mean we don't have to retain the resilience that allows us to ache forever.

This is the paradox of anxiety, which is fundamentally a question of form. As panic, it overspills the container, or the container seems too brittle to withstand its flow. One remedy might be to set a boundary to trouble, circumscribing it and learning to articulate it to the 'cipher' of, for example, the analyst. But excessive circumscription is likely the thing that produced the anxiety in the first place. Paradoxically, relinquishing the desire for a limit to what is experienced as dangerously unbound affect might be the route out of misery. Dickinson's poem doesn't provide a command or a reparation that teaches us the destined end of distress. Instead, it teeters in an interval of indeterminacy, and that is how it gets across the broken middle of history to reach me. It plies me with what has become my culture's pat wisdom: lean in, learn to recognise your limits and you can cope with anything. This is the managerial lesson. Will I be bound by it? Not if I can remember Dickinson's warning: that you only bear this much because you are willing to contain it. The exhausting work of being contented with that ache, day after regulated day, is performed by those who are sufficient to misery. What I want to know is: how might I become sufficient to something else?

CHAPTER 6

The Story that Cannot Be Told
M. NourbeSe Philip's Zong!, from Form to Performance

'After great pain, a formal feeling comes'
– Emily Dickinson

In August 1781 a Dutch ship, the *Zong*, sailed from west Africa for Jamaica, overloaded with a cargo of 442 enslaved Africans and a crew of seventeen men. On 18 or 19 November it sighted the island of Tobago; the journey had taken much longer than the usual eight weeks, and though only twenty casks of water remained, the *Zong* did not stop to resupply. On 27 or 28 November the crew mistook Jamaica for the Spanish island of Hispaniola, and decided to sail on. The ship's master acknowledged his mistake only once the ship was 300 miles leeward of Jamaica: 380 enslaved people were still alive. The crew agreed to begin throwing people overboard. Approximately 142 were drowned, and a further 36 died from lack of water. The *Zong* arrived in Jamaica on 22 December with 208 enslaved people on board; they were sold for an average of £36 each.[1]

After its return to Liverpool, the ship's owners attempted to recover the market value of these enslaved people against the insurance policy. A special jury at Guildhall Sessions in 1783 found that the insurers were obliged to compensate for these losses. An appeal for a new trial was entered at the Court of the King's Bench, with the underwriters arguing that 'a sufficient necessity did not exist for throwing the negroes overboard'.[2] The case became a focal point for British abolitionists.[3] Olaudah Equiano brought it to the attention of Granville Sharp, who wrote to the Admiralty demanding that the crew be tried for murder. Lord Mansfield, who in 1772 had ruled

---

[1] Andrew Lewis, 'Martin Dockray and the Zong: a Tribute in the Form of a Chronology,' *The Journal of Legal History* 28.3 (2007), pp. 357–70; James Walvin, *The Zong: A Massacre, the Law and the End of Slavery* (New Haven: Yale University Press, 2011) and Ian Baucom, *Specters of the Atlantic: Finance Capital, Slavery, and the Philosophy of History* (Durham: Duke University Press, 2005).

[2] M. NourbeSe Philip, *Zong! As told to the author by Setaey Adamu Boateng* (Middletown: Wesleyan University Press, [2008] 2011), p. 210.

[3] Anita Rupprecht, '"A Very Uncommon Case": Representations of the Zong and the British Campaign to Abolish the Slave Trade', *The Journal of Legal History* 28:3 (2007), pp. 329–46.

in the Somerset case that prohibited the forcible removal of any enslaved person from the United Kingdom, argued that murder was not at issue: the jury had decided, '(tho' it shocks one very much) the Case of Slaves was the same as if Horses had been thrown overboard'.[4] Black life and animal life are equivalent in law. Nevertheless, Lord Mansfield and the other justices agreed that there were grounds for a new trial, though no records of one have been found.

The massacre resounded in the British anti-slavery movement for many years. It influenced the passage of a statute in 1790 prohibiting the insurance of enslaved people except against specific risks, as well as a 1794 bill preventing the recovery of damages for enslaved people thrown overboard.[5] It would influence J. M. W. Turner's 1840 painting *The Slave Ship* (originally known as 'Slavers Throwing Overboard the Dead and Dying: Typhoon Coming On'), and has inspired numerous literary works, recently including Fred D'Aguiar's novel *Feeding the Ghosts* (1997), which concludes that 'the past is laid to rest when it is told', and David Dabydeen's poem 'Turner' (1995), which Dabydeen described as 'a great howl of pessimism about the inability to recover anything meaningful from the past'.[6]

This flurry of numbers and facts is my attempt to situate the critical work of this chapter, by first telling you the story of the *Zong*. But M. NourbeSe Philip has argued very forcefully that the events on the *Zong* are part of a story 'that must be told; that can only be told by not telling' (*Zong!* 194), that only the soldered mouth can tell. Her book *Zong!* takes as its source *Gregson vs. Gilbert*, the document summarising appellate arguments for a new trial and the justices' responses. *Gregson vs. Gilbert* and some contemporary accounts of the trial are all that remains of the history of the *Zong*. Philip – who was born in Tobago and emigrated to Canada, and has worked as a family and immigration lawyer – has constrained herself to this two-page, 500-word summary, recombining its words, phonemes and syllables, to produce *Zong!*. Philip enters this legal document as Halpern does the autopsy report, submitting voluntarily to its generative constraint and committing 'to lock myself into this particular and peculiar discursive landscape'. But *Gregson vs. Gilbert* is only one of

---

[4] Jane Webster, 'The *Zong* in the Context of the Eighteenth-Century Slave Trade', *The Journal of Legal History* 28.3 (2007), pp. 285–98 (295).
[5] Robert Weisbord, 'The Case of the Slave Ship "Zong",' *History Today* 19.8 (1 August 1969), pp. 561–6 (567).
[6] Stef Craps, 'Learning to Live with Ghosts: Postcolonial Haunting and Mid-Mourning in David Dabydeen's "Turner" and Fred D'Aguiar's *Feeding the Ghosts*', *Callaloo* 33.2 (Spring 2010), pp. 467–75.

the archives with which she works; the others are 'the liquid and sound archive of the Atlantic ocean and, most importantly, the genealogical and spiritual archive of the Ancestors'.[7] This chapter will explore her relations to the legal, sonic and spiritual archives, and the way the project of *Zong!* moves from textuality to embodied performance to ritual commemoration.

Zong! offers a kind of reply to Dickinson's naturalising of war and ignoring slavery. The book addresses the blanks in the archives, materialising them formally and filling them through magical procedures. Philip has argued that 'that erasure is intrinsic to colonial and imperial projects. It's an erasure that continues up to the present. The idea of mutilation and the violence it implies also resonates with ... Dickinson and the violent edges of her poetry – and perhaps the violence at the edges of her poetry.'[8] *Zong!* also cycles through some of the key tropes of lyric – the autonomy of the lyric poet, writing in isolation and enclosed within the cell of the text; the poet's ability to synthesise the particular and represent a subjectivised universal – without finding satisfaction. Philip rejects the idea that lyric is a space of limitless freedom, constructed from language's infinite plenitude; 'we believe we have the freedom to choose any words we want to work with from the universe of words, but so much of what we work with is a given' (*Zong!* 192). Constraint is a paradoxical way of overcoming that givenness and accessing a kind of liberty. She says: through the 'imposition of the limitation of the text on myself, I have been able to find a lot of freedom within those limitations. I believe that this is a lesson poetry offers us – freedom within limitation'.[9]

Zong! proffers what Erica Hunt calls an 'oppositional poetics', which recognises that although 'long treatment as an undifferentiated mass of others by the dominant class fosters collective identity and forms of resistance', people still 'get stuck with the old codes even as we try to negate them. We experience acute difference: autonomy without self-determination

---

[7] 'BACKSTORY: Rana Hamadeh's Unauthorized Use of M. NourbeSe Philip's Work, *Zong!*,' from *Set Speaks - website of M. NourbeSe Philip:* www.setspeaks.com/backstory/ (accessed 4 May 2021). On the sea as a sound archive, see Tim Armstrong, *The Logic of Slavery: Debt, Technology, and Pain in American Literature* (Cambridge University Press, 2012), pp. 142–3.

[8] Andrew David King, 'The Weight of What's Left [Out]: Six Contemporary Erasurists on their Craft,' *Kenyon Review* (6 November 2012), www.kenyonreview.org/2012/11/erasure-collaborative-interview/ (accessed 4 May 2021).

[9] Patricia Saunders, 'Trying Tongues, E-raced Identities, and the Possibilities of Be/longing: Conversations with NourbeSe Philip', *Journal of West Indian Literature* 14.1/2 (Nov 2005), pp. 202–19 (218).

and group identity without group empowerment.'[10] *Zong!* opens up the archive into a history of Afrosporic community building, its rhythms, language and survival. It explores 'autonomy without self-determination' as poetic constraint, working eventually towards 'group empowerment' as it emerges into the fullness of collective performance, and turns away from the printed letter, to lived and collective performance: to song.

Stories and Forms

Philip's description of *Zong!* as the story that cannot be told, 'a poetics of the impossible the unsayable', echoes the trope of unspeakability that can be found frequently in abolitionist literature,[11] and Theodor Adorno's dictum about the barbarism of poetry after Auschwitz.[12] But *Zong!* does not represent sentimentalised images of brutality in order to ensnare the reader with feelings of empathy that crowd out reflections on one's own ethical culpability. It rejects the descriptive verisimilitude and scenic strategies of the slave narrative.[13] Barnor Hesse describes how slave narratives in the United States were packaged and sold 'to a mesmerized white audience as voyeuristic windows on bleak but distant, abject and horrific experiences'.[14] These seemingly spontaneous stories were formatted as acts of 'neutral' memorialising: they did not open on to philosophical or aesthetic questions about the status or content of memory. As a result, Hesse argues, the memory of slavery in the United States is presented as 'the memory of its heroic and inevitable abolition': narratives of redemption, the inevitable unfolding of American justice and triumph of equity (150). Unlike these narratives, *Zong!* does not permit the reader to enjoy a sympathetic identification with the victims, or a triumphant reflection that these incidents are past.

Philip's work starts in 'the wasteland between the terror of language and the horror of silence':[15]

---

[10] Erica Hunt, 'Notes for an Oppositional Poetics', in *The Politics of Poetic Form: Poetry and Public Policy*, ed. Charles Bernstein (New York: Roof Books, 1990), pp. 197–212 (200).
[11] M. NourbeSe Philip, 'Wor(l)ds Interrupted: The Unhistory of the Kari Basin', *Jacket2*: jacket2.org/article/worlds-interrupted (accessed 4 May 2021).
[12] Theodor Adorno, 'Cultural Criticism and Society', in *Prisms* (London: Sperman, 1967), p. 34.
[13] Avery Gordon, *Ghostly Matters: Haunting and the Sociological Imagination* (Minneapolis: University of Minnesota Press 1983), p. 143.
[14] Barnor Hesse, 'Forgotten Like a Bad Dream: Atlantic Slavery and the Ethics of Postcolonial Memory', in *Relocating Postcolonialism*, ed. David Theo Goldberg and Ato Quayson (Oxford: Blackwell, 2002), pp. 143–73 (146).
[15] M. NourbeSe Philip, *Bla_k: Essays & Interviews* (Toronto: Bookthug, 2017), p. 53.

> The question is, do you – should you – turn the horror of a particular history into something beautiful, because of course it is that beauty which will make the work ultimately digestible. I confess to being disturbed by texts which attempt to deal in this way with aspects of slavery . . . . For me the more seductive the language, the more I distrust it – with a centuries-old distrust. (*Bla_k* 59)

Zong! works against the beautification of history as poetry, and against narrative closure. Seedlings of narrative can be found scattered throughout the text: 'dear ruth / this is a tale told / cold a yarn / a story dear': 'there were aster s / at tea time . . .' (*Zong!* 64). The poem ends with a European man who 'takes his own life. The African man, Wale, asks him to write a letter to his wife, Sade, who, of course, has been separated from him along with their child, Ade; he then eats the letter and jumps overboard. Then the man himself – the European – also throws himself overboard.' The voice of the white, European male that emerges from Philip's combinatorial strategies is disturbing: 'ordinarily I would never have been interested in that voice . . . . I would think, "Shut the fuck up already, we've heard enough about and from you!"' But Philip insists that the voice is a consequence of an artistic process 'of allowing the voices space to tell their own stories'.[16] This signals not only her critical relation to the narrative history of the *Zong*, but also to authorial intention as a form of reparation of the wounds of the past.

It would be possible to scour the text for other stories, but this would be misleading. Reading for the story is not what *Zong!* demands. Philip wants to resist 'my urge to make sense' (*Zong!* 193), and encourages the reader to disobey the instinct to discern patterns, narratives and rhythms from *Zong!*'s fragmented ensemble. Instead, *Zong!*'s critique palpitates as form, in the gaps, surpluses, waste products and drifting phonemes that Philip exhumes from her source text.

'This story turns tail, runs from the truth, each word a stone to turn over and over: lose, find, and lose again, to fall from my lips and sink through the deep to the ruin and rune of bone.' This statement appears on page 111; it seems to describe the reader's experience of desertion in the face of the horrific truth *Zong!* is telling. The turning over of the stones of truth might allude to the creation myth of Deucalion and Pyrrha, repopulating the world devastated by an inundation; and a work of archaeological excavation, searching the ruins of a burial site. But if the truth is a stone lost in the sea, it will sink before it can be inscribed with an epitaph.

---

[16] Patricia Saunders, 'Defending the Dead, Confronting the Archive: A Conversation with M. NourbeSe Philip', *Small Axe* 12.2 (2008), pp. 63–79 (75).

```
                       is dead this
           story turns
tail runs                                   from the truth each
              word a stone
    to turn o
           ver &                 over lose find
              & lose aga                     in to fall from
my lips &                     sink through
       the deep to the ruin               &
                                               rune
              of bone there are
```

Fig. 6.1 M. NourbeSe Philip, *Zong! As told to the author by Setaey Adamu Boateng* (Middletown, CT: Wesleyan University Press, [2008] 2011), page. 111.

But this statement does not really appear on page 111. Instead, this (fig. 6.1) does. Criticism is too fast. The mutilating transcriptions of the text I provide for the sake of space throughout this chapter are a kind of critical injustice. When I turn to the pages of *Zong!*, my learned habit, in English, of reading from left to right, top to bottom, grates against the clustering of the words, proposing a multitude of different gatherings: 'my lips & the deep to the ruin' is possible, 'to turn over & & lose aga sink through & rune' is also a way of tracing a falling line of thought, dropping to the seabed. These fragments make it difficult to stitch the poem together, and force readerly haste to yield to a feeling of slowness, indeterminacy and slippage: what belongs to or with, relates to or with the other? This slowness is part of *Zong!*'s telling, and postponing the brutality of telling, the story of Black death.

The poem's meanings emerge in relation: relation, visualised as the cluster, becomes the poem's 'organising principle'. As Philip puts it:

> each word or word cluster is in relation to each other, particularly on sequential lines, and, further, no word or word cluster can come directly below another cluster of words. Another way of looking at it is that each cluster of words is seeking the space or the silence above.[17]

The importance of relation is not merely formal; it reflects the influence of Édouard Glissant on Philip's poetics. Glissant argued that the abyss of the

---

[17] Saunders, 'Defending the Dead', p. 72.

Middle Passage 'in the end became knowledge': knowledge 'of the Whole, greater from having been at the abyss and freeing knowledge of Relation within the Whole'. Relation is rhizomatic, errant and found in the shared experience of the abyss; it is not the fruit of individualistic exploration, but a communal labour, drawn from suffering and the need to 'honour our boats'. This, Glissant adds, is 'why we stay with poetry': poetry is the opposite to the technologies of exploitation that created the African diaspora. 'Our boats are open, and we sail them for everyone.'[18] This relational ethic, which excludes neither care nor oppression, is enacted in *Zong!* as words, particles and spaces create shifting relations to each other through the energies of the writer and reader and within the shared space of performance.

Section 1, *Os* [bone], begins the work by fragmenting and recombining the phrase 'the want of water' from the legal judgement (fig. 6.2). Here, the broken, stuttering w's sound both infantile (waah) and like the last utterances of a person thirsting to death; there is at once too much water and too little, as the poem 'stutters and stops; ... floods and withholds'.[19] Adrift among phonemes, I feel lost. Sometimes the letters are so densely packed they struggle for breath and articulation; sometimes so widely spaced that they become mere particles, sounds severed from the groups that could convey meaning: g, ru, se, ev, ee. This compaction (Philip calls it 'crumped', *Zong!* 205) and dispersal slow my reading and teach me to approach the text in a non-sequential fashion. My eye starts to lose its ability to perceive the leading between lines, or kerning of letters; it is drawn to form sequences and clusters from letters that have been left behind. The gaps suggest bodies and things scattered on the sea, and the lacunae in the historical record. I am tempted to rush across these voids, to tack abandoned letters on to their amputated suffixes and make the words whole again; it is difficult, frustrating, tedious to dwell in the gaps. In the concluding section, *Ebora*, words are both overprinted and greyed out. It is as if the book is a ship loaded to a point of terrible compaction.

The poem's form forces readers to make a choice: do we work to restore some conventionally meaningful propositions from this violent *sparagmos*, or do we dwell with the torn and turned scattering of language and subjectivity that Philip has so carefully composed? Is our readerly restoration, taking the scattered words or parts of words and making them whole again, coagulating them back into sentences, a minor restitution for the violent shattering and scattering that was the slave trade? Or is it an

---

[18] Édouard Glissant, *Poetics of Relation*, trans. Betsy Wing (Ann Arbor: University of Michigan Press, 1997), pp. 8–9.
[19] Sonya Posmentier, *Cultivation and Catastrophe: The Lyric Ecology of Modern Black Literature* (Baltimore: Johns Hopkins University Press, 2017), p. 217.

Zong! #1

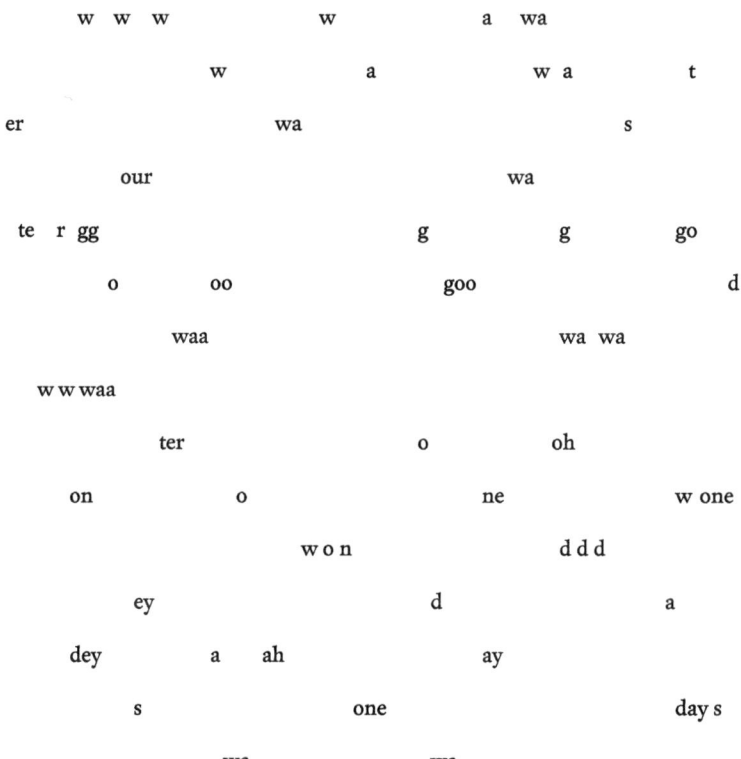

Fig. 6.2 M. NourbeSe Philip, *Zong! As told to the author by Setaey Adamu Boateng* (Middletown, CT: Wesleyan University Press, [2008] 2011), page. 3.

analogue for that murderous exploitation – our participation in the ordering, classification and redistribution of parts? Anthony Reed argues that the text's fragments 'do not give us enough to allow us to do much more than witness the unravelling of this tale'.[20] But the text confronts readers with exactly this question of what more we can do than witness: can we ravel the tale back up again? Should we?

---

[20] Anthony Reed, *Freedom Time: The Poetics and Politics of Black Experimental Writing* (Baltimore: Johns Hopkins University Press, 2014), p. 57.

Philip relates the formal difficulties of reading *Zong!* to the psychic and physical pain of encountering the history of slavery. Piecing together the poem's asyndetic fragments, readers 'become implicated in, if not contaminated by, this activity' (*Zong!* 198). She draws an analogy between the labour of reading or performing the poem, and the labour of upholding the slave trade: 'we are, none of us, innocent or absolved of our contamination'.[21] Philip describes her own relation to the legal text as mimetic of the violence of slavery:

> I am, metaphorically, at sea, having cut myself off from the comfort and predictability of my own meaning ... Like Captain Collingwood, I am now fully launched on a journey. (*Zong!* 190)

> My intent is to use the text of the legal decision as a word store; to ... lock myself into this text in the same way men, women, and children were locked in the holds of the slave ship *Zong*. (191)

> The eye trying to order what cannot be ordered, ... which is what it must have been like trying to understand what was happening on board the Zong ... The legal text parallels a certain kind of entity – a whole, a completeness which like African life is rent and torn. (192)

> This [literally cutting up the text] was most similar to the activity of the random picking of African slaves ... I mutilate the text as the fabric of African life and the lives of these men, women and children were mutilated ... I murder the text, literally cut it into pieces, castrating verbs, suffocating adjectives, murdering nouns, throwing articles, prepositions, conjunctions overboard, jettisoning adverbs ... (193)

> The poem ... is revealed only when the text is fragmented and mutilated, mirroring the fragmentation and mutilation that slavery perpetrated on Africans. (195)

Philip's contentions that her bondage by the legal judgement was 'the same' as the bondage of people in the holds, and that her authorial activity is analogous to the atrocities perpetrated by the slave traders, are startling. What can 'sameness' mean in this context?

Zong! is not a concrete poem in the fashion of Drea Brown's *Dear Girl: A Reckoning*.[22] Brown represents a 'cross section of the scooner phillis', the ship which gave Phillis Wheatley her name, as an inventory of deck, body, sugar, molasses, rum, pickled mackerel, turpentine etc., floating on a sea of indigo, waves and bodies. This vocabulary actually constitutes a shape like

---

[21] *Set Speaks*: www.setspeaks.com/about/ (accessed 4 May 2021).
[22] Drea Brown, *Dear Girl: A Reckoning* (Los Angeles: Gold Line Press, 2015), pp. 18–19. I am grateful to Meta DuEwa Jones for telling me about Brown's chapbook.

the prow of a ship on the page. Brown's poem references one of the most famous images of the slave trade: the copper engraving of the Liverpool slave ship *Brookes*, which was produced by the Abolitionist Society on the occasion of William Wilberforce's speech proposing the abolition of the slave trade in 1789.[23] That image shows the depraved compaction of Black bodies within a slice of the ship. Brown replaces the human outlines in the abolitionist text with a ship made of words: an acculturated vessel. But unlike in *Zong!*, this image does not require the reader to act. We can see and absorb it because it is already synthesised, frozen like a traumatic memory. Moreover, Brown's image is an interruption, appearing between more conventional lyric poems spoken by a fictional enslaved girl on that voyage; her poems tell the story that Philip argues cannot be told.

Philip's composition by field, and her attention to the sea and the breath, might also recall Charles Olson's mythopoesis of Gloucester. But unlike Olson's manspreading over the page space as an analogue for American imperial expansionism, *Zong!*'s unspooling is a way of inscribing the silences and gaps between words, and all the dead which they might contain. Though Philip's poetics is rooted in the mimetic possibilities of form, unlike Olson she would not subsume form as 'never more than an extension of content': form does something in *Zong!* that content alone cannot.[24] Philip does share, however, Olson's concern with the formal representation of the breath as the fundamental medium of *poiesis*. In 'Projective Verse', Olson proposes an etymology: '"Is" comes from the Aryan root, *as*, to breathe. The English "not" equals the Sanscrit *na*, which may come from the root *na*, to be lost, to perish. "Be" is from *bhu*, to grow' (242). *Zong!* reflects these etymologies, in linking being to breathing and growing, non-being to perishing. Philip describes her text as

> about co-creation, In the spaces. Left by the One. And the Other. And their relation. In the spaces allowed for breath. It is about us today breathing for those who could no longer breathe; us breathing into those who could no longer breathe; us breathing still with those whose breaths were abbreviated, cut short, becoming ga(s)ps in the unending prayer of dark water – black water. Breathing tog(a)ther.[25]

---

[23] Hugh Honour, *The Image of the Black in Western Art*, vol. 2, part 1: Slaves and Liberators (Cambridge, MA: Harvard University Press, 1989), pp. 64–5.

[24] Charles Olson, 'Projective Verse', *Collected Prose*, ed. Donald Allen and Benjamin Friedlander (Berkeley: University of California Press, 1997), pp. 239–49 (240).

[25] M. NourbeSe Philip, 'The One Murder of Rana Hamadeh or Somebody Almost Ran Off Wid Alla My Stuff', *Set Speaks*: www.setspeaks.com/about/ (accessed 16 May 2021).

For Philip, breath is relational: 'We all begin life in water / We all begin life because someone once breathed for us,' she writes elsewhere.[26] Although Philip complicates the utopian aspects of Hannah Arendt's idea of natality by thinking through the exploitation of Black women's reproductive labour – 'the enslaved mother has no choice but to breathe for the child that is forced on her body' (35) – she also finds in breath a memory of the mother's 'radical hospitality' and 'a blueprint for community and interdependency. Despite the forced couplings' (38). I'll return to the way breath animates form in the reparative work of performance in the conclusion of this chapter.

The Haunted Text

Philip's equation of bondage with textual constraint can perhaps be partially understood by thinking of this work not as a formal mimesis but as the magical language of hex and spell that constitute a ceremony of remembrance. Harryette Mullen has examined a tradition of African scriptive practices, 'whose primary means of cultural transmission have been oral and visual rather than written, and for whom graphic systems have been associated not with instrumental human communication, but with techniques of spiritual power and spirit possession'.[27] Similarly, *Zong!* gives voice to both curse (a future-oriented enunciation) and memorial (turning towards the past). In script and performance, it offers its hospitality to the spirits of the ancestors.

There is a long tradition of poetic texts writing through the Middle Passage, in which ghosts erupt as compulsive repetitions, literary tropes and figures of 'accumulated memory, knowing, belief, shared experience, and oppositional force.'[28] The hauntological texts of the Black Atlantic do not 'seek to recapture the past *for* the present'; rather, they 'demand a thorough reconceptualization *of* the present', of its nature, extent, elasticity, scope and very existence.[29] Philip regards the Zong massacre as part of a continuing history: 'today so many of us continue to live, albeit in an

---

[26] M. NourbeSe Philip, 'The Ga(s)p', in *Poetics and Precarity*, ed. Myung Mi Kim and Cristanne Miller (Albany: State University of New York Press, 2018), pp. 31–40.

[27] Harryette Romell Mullen, 'African Signs and Spirit Writing', *Callaloo* 19.3 (Summer 1996), pp. 670–89 (670–1).

[28] Lorrie N. Smith, 'Hungry Ghosts and Restless Spirits: Lyric Voices of the Middle Passage', in *Africa and Trans-Atlantic Memories: Literary and Aesthetic Manifestations of Diaspora and History*, ed. Naana Opoku-Agyemang, Paul E. Lovejoy and David V. Trotman (Trenton: Africa World Press, 2008), pp. 417–37 (421).

[29] Baucom, *Specters of the Atlantic*, p. 324.

entirely different way, either outside of the law, or literally imprisoned within it' (*Zong!* 207). The historical continuities between chattel slavery, mass incarceration and the surveillance and policing of Black life mean that *Zong!* can seem caught in between times and places: between the Ontario farmhouse where Philip was writing and the Middle Passage, between the end of slavery and its endlessness. In Fred Moten's phrasing, *Zong!* 'descends into a place from which neither return nor recovery are possible', a place that is 'a non-place, a zone of differentiated stress and distress whose particular gathering of trouble is not alleviated but redoubled by a transfer of energy from *atopos* to utopia that even all brutality and remembrance cannot still'.[30] This non-place might be experienced as a trap – a history that cannot be sublated, a zone of no return – or as an unpaid debt, a haunting of the present by the unrelieved past, which holds that present open and necessitates an ongoing exchange with the dead. But it could also be experienced as a crossing.

M. Jacqui Alexander explores African-based cosmological systems as 'the complex manifestations of the geographies of crossing and dislocation'.[31] In her quest to recover the spiritual meanings of what started as a historiographical project about 'Thisbe', an African woman accused of witchcraft in nineteenth-century Trinidad, Alexander learns to attend to the Sacred, to the invisible, that which 'constitutes its presence by a provocation of sorts, by provoking our attention' (307). This provocation works on the senses – that is, on the body – and in its presence, 'the embodiment of the Sacred dislocates clock time', holding the participant in a now crammed with the past (309). Alexander's perceptions offer spiritual companionship to the work of *Zong!*, which also begins with a desire to memorialise the past found in archival documents, and becomes a different form of embodied knowledge, ritually enacted in and through the now-time of the sacred.

Philip describes *Zong!* as 'hauntological, [. . .] a work of haunting, a wake of sorts, where the spectres of the undead make themselves present' (*Zong!* 201).[32] While it is possible to read *Zong!* through Jacques Derrida's *Specters of Marx*, which Philip cites as an important influence, the work also exceeds

---

[30] Fred Moten, 'Blackness and Poetry', *Evening Will Come* 55 (July 2015): www.thevolta.org/ewc55-fmoten-p1.html (accessed 4 May 2021).
[31] M. Jacqui Alexander, 'Pedagogies of the Sacred: Making the Invisible Tangible', *Pedagogies of Crossing: Meditations on Feminism, Sexual Politics, Memory, and the Sacred* (Durham: Duke University Press, 2005), pp. 287–332 (290).
[32] Guillermina De Ferrari, 'A Caribbean Hauntology: The Sensorial Art of Joscelyn Gardner and M. NourbeSe Philip', *Journal of Latin American Cultural Studies* (2018), pp. 1–24.

the deconstructive framing of history as hauntology (the 'spectral turn') that became popular in the late 1990s. *Zong!* is not just theory: 'I want the bones,' she says, the matter (201). As a ritual invocation of the ancestors, *Zong!* does not only remember the dead; it seeks to make them actually present, and as Katherine McKittrick argues, '*intends* to give blackness a future'.[33] Similarly, 'the "end" of the ghost dance', Gayatri Spivak suggests, is 'to make the past a future': it is 'an attempt to establish the ethical relation with history as such, ancestors real or imagined... You crave to let history haunt you as a ghost or ghosts, with the ungraspable incorporation of a ghostly body, and the uncontrollable, sporadic, and unanticipatable periodicity of haunting, in the impossible frame of the absolute chance of the gift of time, if there is any.' And while Spivak is sceptical about the ghost dance as political praxis, it is, she writes, 'the only way to go at moments of crisis; to surrender to undecidability'.[34]

As Philip inhabits the court documents, opening up the decision to undecidability and formal indeterminacy, she is herself inhabited by the dead – the byline says the book was 'told to the author by Setaey Adamu Boateng', and Philip has described herself as the amenuensis for an ancestral voice she names Abiswa. In Philip's understanding of African cosmology, 'the Ancestors, albeit no longer alive, are a living force'.[35] As she works on *Zong!*, Philip visits Ghana to talk with spiritual elders; she summons and honours the ancestors by performing magic rituals, burning incense and jangling cowrie shells. The latter were a form of 'coast money' traded for enslaved people in coastal African countries; 'the shells, so it is said, came from off-lying waters, where they fed on the cadavers of less desirable enslaved people thrown into the sea as their food. The bodies, or sometimes dismembered limbs, when pulled ashore were covered with attached cowries.'[36] The cowrie is a material remnant of a lost homeland, but also a symbol of an economy that traded in death; it creates an exoskeletal form as a kind of living monument for that which dissolves in the sea, allowing those losses to be recovered on land by those who survive.

Philip's occult procedures signal the difference between this poem and a work of documentary poetics that relies on found materials and historical

---

[33] Katherine McKittrick, 'Diachronic Loops/Deadweight Tonnage/Bad Made Measure', *Cultural Geographies* 23.1 (2016), pp. 3–18 (15).
[34] Gayatri Spivak, 'Ghostwriting', *Diacritics* 25.2 (1995), pp. 65–84 (70–1).
[35] Paul Watkins, 'We Can Never Tell the Entire Story of Slavery: In Conversation with M. NourbeSe Philip', *Toronto Review of Books* (30 April 2014).
[36] Jan Hogendorn and Marioni Johnson, *The Shell Money of the Slave Trade* (Cambridge University Press, 1986), p. 156.

research. This difference becomes clear in her essay 'Museum Could Have Avoided Culture Clash', about the Royal Ontario Museum's notorious 1989 exhibit *Into the Heart of Africa*. Philip asks an employee at the museum – an emblematic figure whom she calls 'John-from-Sussex' – 'whether I could perform *Zong!* in the presence of some of the artefacts and objects that were taken out of Africa and are now stored in the basement of the ROM'. But the request produces a crisis. She is traumatised by having to ask for 'what I should never have had to ask: permission to perform in the presence of the tangible and material legacy of the spiritual heritage of Africa'. She explains to John that

> *Zong!* is a work in which the voices of those Ancestors thrown overboard from the slave ship are allowed to surface and breathe and be heard and that it would be significant to perform that work in the presence of those objects which were stolen and brought out of Africa as the people were, and suddenly Abiswa is in the room. I feel her presence and all those who are trapped in basements of museums, on the ocean floor, in unmarked graves along the many slave routes. It was as if the spirits in the basement of the ROM had risen and come up to the modest office we were meeting in. I place my open hand over my heart as if to calm myself: I can feel something, I say to him, and he says he can feel it as well … I had re-incised the scars, opening them up as they do in traditional African cultures – oath moan mutter chant/time grieves the dimension of other … except in those cultures the opening of cicatrices is ritual, often done to beautify or to mark social status or belonging within community – these scars marked me as Other – a quantity of minus (*Bla_K* 125–6)

Philip's address to the objects invokes the spirits of the ancestors and opens a wound that is not ritualistically valued and beautifying but marks Blackness as non-being – in that Dickinsonian phrase, 'a quantity of minus'. The re-incised scar, she fears, neither beautifies nor signifies communal belonging. Instead, it is a reawakening of pain, related – as in Wyatt's injuries sustained during his imprisonment, or in the gashes on Douglass's foot – to the memorial work of writing.

Wounds like these are attended to by Jared Sexton, who describes 'this tear in the world, this tearing of the world, this torn world' as a form of dehiscence. Sexton draws out the 'helpful polyvalence' of this term, from surgical medicine – 'the opening up of a wound along the lines of incision (either because the wound was inadequately sutured or has become infected or subjected to further trauma)', botany – 'the opening up of plants along a seam at the age of maturity as a means of dissemination', and otology – 'the perforation in the inner ear labyrinth causing chronic disequilibrium or vertigo'.[37] These senses of a rupture in bodily integrity, time, fecundity and equilibrium – particularly as regulated through the ear – are all relevant to Philip's wake work. Her ritual dehiscence of the scars of slavery is profoundly destabilising, but it also brings to light the tear in the world through which the ghosts of the enslaved continue to pass.

The Law is a Ghost

Philip's hauntological procedures draw out the irrationality of the *Gregson vs. Gilbert* judgement and the occult nature of the law. As Colin Dayan describes it,

> Specters are very much part of the legal domain. Human materials are remade and persons are undone in the sanctity of the courtroom. Whether slaves, dead bodies, criminals, ghost detainees, or any one of the many spectral entities held in limbo in the no-man's-land sustained by state power, they all remain subject to the undue influences and occult revelations of law's rituals.[38]

The ascription of social death to convicts and enslaved people is a Gothic instrument in law. For Philip, the law's ability to make a person 'an object, a thing or chattel' is closer to a form of 'magic and religion', a conversion which she compares to Christian transubstantiation (*Zong!* 196). *Zong!*'s ritual procedures aim to reverse that conversion: 'the African, transformed into a thing by the law, is re-transformed, miraculously, back into human' (*Zong!* 196). The poem's incantations subvert the law's phantasmatic power, finding and restoring the human within the case and replacing relations of property with differently occulted relations of kinship. Simultaneously opening herself, in the manner of a shaman or keeper of secrets, to the irrational realm of spirit, and enclosing herself within the supposed rationality of the legal judgement, Philip is both 'censor and magician': 'As censor, I function like the law whose role is to proscribe and prescribe, deciding which aspects of the text will be removed and which remain; ... as magician, however, I conjure the infinite-(ive) of to be of the "negroes" on board the *Zong*' (*Zong!* 199).

In her 'Notanda', Philip describes the appeal of the law as a 'certain, objective, and predictable' discourse that 'would cut through the emotions like a laser to seal off vessels oozing sadness, anger, and despair' (*Zong!* 191). She had believed that poetry resembles the law in its 'concern with language'

---

[37] Jared Sexton, 'On Black Negativity, or the Affirmation of Nothing', Interviewed by Daniel Colucciello Barber, *Society and Space* (18 September 2017), p. 8.
[38] Colin Dayan, *The Law is a White Dog: How Legal Rituals Make and Unmake Persons* (Princeton University Press, 2011), p. 12.

and 'precision of expression' (*Zong!* 191). The putative rationality of the law might help suppress the affective overspill produced by thinking about the Zong, reminiscent of Wordsworth's remarks about metre as 'the co-presence of something regular, something to which the mind has been accustomed in various moods and in a less excited state'.[39] For example, a subsection of 'Sal', 'Dicta', focuses on numerical abstractions, the tallying and actuarial inventories of risk, property and losses that treat human beings as 'many / eighteen / other / three / particular' (*Zong!* 52). The momentum of these numbers, their persuasive clarity, but also their arbitrary exchangeability, is lent to the final poem in this section, which repeats: 'new case / great trial / uncommon weight', moving its empty modifiers around to show the extent to which the lawyers are speaking to and of themselves (*Zong!* 56). Philip writes in 'Notanda' that 'Dicta' are all other opinions that are extraneous to the *ratio decidendi* of case law, 'Which is what the Africans on board the Zong become – *dicta*, footnotes, related to, but not, the *ratio*' (*Zong!* 199).

Jared Sexton has described Blackness as 'a form of being that presents a problem for the thought of being itself'; a human being 'whose being human raises the question of being human at all'.[40] This problem is manifested implicitly in the reparations of lyric, as well as in the legal framing of the question of human being raised by the *Zong* case, where murdered Africans are compared to dead horses. For Ian Baucom, the *Zong* case is a paradigm of eighteenth-century finance capital and the struggles 'between an empirical and a contractual, an evidentiary and a credible epistemology' that accompanied this emergent economic system.[41] But it also poses profound questions about the *forms* in which human being can be or be thought, addressed, spoken to and with. In *Zong!*, the victims of the massacre, the 'negroes', first appear in the second poem of 'Os':

> the that fact
> the it was
> the were
> negroes
>
> (*Zong!* 5)

'Negroes' appear amidst abstractions – loss, order, fact, circumstance – and verb tenses that only gesture towards their pastness: that they *were*,

---

[39] William Wordsworth, *Lyrical Ballads, and Other Poems, 1797–1800*, ed. James Butler and Karen Green (Ithaca, NY: Cornell University Press, 1992), ll. 503–6, p. 755.
[40] Jared Sexton, 'The Social Life of Social Death: On Afro-Pessimism and Black Optimism', *InTensions* 5 (Fall/Winter 2011), pp. 6–7.
[41] Baucom, *Specters of the Atlantic*, p. 16.

indicates that they now are not, but also that they once did exist, and that this existence is only commemorated *because* their destruction came to trial: 'there is an art / to murder / with rant and curse / but the tense / is all / wrong' (*Zong!* 68).

Philip Sidney once wrote that the historian, 'with his bare *was*', can only report the facts of the past, in all its injustice; only the poet can imagine a moral order that opposes naked fact. Or, as Emily Dickinson writes: '"Was Not" – was all the statement'.[42] *Zong!* rebukes the ontological judgements made by the law through the verb *to be*. In *Zong!* #4, 'this is / not was / or / should be' resolves into 'this / should / not / be / is' (*Zong!* 7): the legal question of the existence of the 'negroes' is answered with a moral judgement. But 'is being is / or / should' (*Zong!* 37)? Bare life cannot require compassion. Compassion is a 'should': a wish, a moral contingency, not enforceable, in the face of history and the law's constative 'is'. Of one of the lost people aboard the *Zong*, Philip writes: 'her name she smiles / will be es se to be' (70). Claiming her right 'to be', this self-naming records her self-sufficient presence. Esse, the Latin verb *to be*, with its implication of present or enduring legal facts in place of absent bodies, contrasts with the devastating historical recognition of murder in the formula 'negroes / was' (*Zong!* 42). But 'suppose the law / is / not / does / not / would / not / be not': suppose the whole of the law reveals itself as 'a crime' (*Zong!* 20). What then? The 'negroes was the cause' (*Zong!* 45) of the journey and the judgement, and 'the case is / justice is / the ground is / Africa is'; but 'negroes / was' (*Zong!* 42). Simultaneously at the centre of the case and of the slave trade, these 'negroes' exercise no agency, are subjects only in the sense of being parts of speech that take a verb; but that verb, to be, is an empty copulative that connects them to no modifier that individuates them.

Lyric and Nation Language

As Philip's dissection of *Gregson vs. Gilbert* makes clear, the English language is a prison house not just in the general Nietzschean sense, but more specifically as a tool of colonial violence. This presents a problem for poets who, as Philip observes, must 'use a language whose primary purpose vis-à-vis the New World African was to destroy, exclude, deny, subjugate, or marginalize'. Philip's response is to seek out a Caribbean 'current I calling brathwaitian': 'many rivers we done cross carrying the memory

---

[42] On this poem, see Anne-Lise François, *Open Secrets: The Literature of Uncounted Experience* (Stanford University Press, 2008), pp. 136–7. I'm grateful to Jocelyn Saidenberg for recommending this book.

marronage exile hurucan and volcano'.[43] She is referring to Edward Kamau Brathwaite's idea of 'nation language'. Brathwaite argues that 'we haven't got the syllables, the syllabic intelligence, to describe the hurricane, which is our own experience, whereas we can describe the imported alien experience of the snowfall'.[44] English is an instrument of colonial domination whose vocabulary – snow, daffodils – cannot represent the Caribbean. By contrast, 'nation language', Brathwaite writes, is 'based as much on sound as it is on song. That is to say, the noise that it makes is part of the meaning' (311–12). It is an oral tradition that 'demands not only the griot but the audience to complete the community' (18). I'll return to this demand at the end of the chapter.

In an interview in 2005, Philip spoke of the 'irony' of writing from the Caribbean:

> the Caribbean was, and still is, an oral culture. I think that is one of the strands of anxiety that I feel as a writer. I utilize a form that continues to exclude so many of the people for whom I write. I mean, if I sang calypso or practised any of the more popular and performative art forms like dub or rapso, I would be more in touch with those I want to be in touch with.[45]

Zong! and Philip's poetic practice more generally seeks to reflect the full range of the Caribbean 'vocal style', which Portia Maultsby argues encompasses 'characteristics of West African traditions': 'creating a cross between speech and song, the performer dramatizes his [or her] delivering with rhythmic moans, grunts, wails, shouts, glides, bends, dips, cries, hollers, vocables (words composed of various, possibly meaningless sounds), falsetto, and melodic repetition'.[46] Philip's early work provides a taxonomy of these soundings:

> oath   moan   mutter   chant
>   time grieves the dimension of other
> babble   curse   chortle   sing
>   turns on its axis of silence
> praise-song   poem   ululation   utterance
>   one song would bridge the finite in silence
> syllable   vocable   vowel   consonant
>   one word erect the infinite in memory
>
>   (*STHT* 64)

---

[43] Philip, 'Wor(l)ds Interrupted', n. p.
[44] Edward Kamau Brathwaite, *History of the Voice: The Development of Nation Language in Anglophone Caribbean Poetry* (London and Port of Spain: New Beacon Books, 1984), pp. 8–10.
[45] Saunders, 'Trying Tongues', p. 204.
[46] Portia K. Maultsby, 'West African Influence and Retentions in U. S. Black Music: A Sociocultural Study,' *More than Dancing: Essays on African-American Music and Musicians*, ed. Irene V. Jackson (Westport: Greenwood Press, 1985), p. 49.

This is a different way of thinking of the particle poetics of *Zong!*, not only as mimetic of the violent mutilations perpetrated by the enslavers, but as a poetics of sound and movement driven through the syllable rather than the word as a whole semantic unit. Philip wants her writing to 'keep the deep structure, the movement, the kinetic energy, the tone and pitch, the slides and glissandos of the demotic within a tradition that is primarily page-bound' (*STHT* 89). To stay in 'touch' with her Caribbean and Black audiences, Philip requires a medium that involves performance, dance and song, and rhythms that are not those of traditional English prosody. Brathwaite memorably claimed that 'the hurricane does not roar in pentameters'. Philip seeks out instead the 'dactyls of calypso', 'pant pant panta meter', 'spiritual caiso mento reggae calypso rapso dub rap dance hall': a 'kinopoesis', poetry as movement.[47]

Like the English language, the lyric is for Philip 'one of the tools used to further the ends of colonialism' (*Bla_k* 58). Philip describes the anguish of trying not to 'find her voice', but to dismember it:

> I wanted to destroy the lyric voice. As a Black, female, colonised subject, what was the source of my authority, and was such authority necessary – indispensable perhaps? – to speech, public speech? To poetry? Being neither male nor white and without an observable or tangible source of authority, could I even speak? Or would I only speak a silence? (*Bla_k* 61)

Philip works within this hostile tradition to 'rewrite' history 'according to *my* dictates – *my* memories ... And if the reader stumbled, stopped and started again, if s/he choked, and gagged on the words, then it was successful' (*Bla_k* 58). She described the almost sadistic pleasure of writing one of the final sections of *Zong!*: 'there was the sense that I was really fucking with the language at its most intricate level. It was as if I was finally getting my revenge on something that had fucked me over for so long, that I felt that this broken, stumbling thing that "Ferrum" is, is my very own language. For the first time in my writing life, I felt, this is my language – the grunts, moans, utterances, pauses, sounds, and silences.'[48] The individual finds her autonomy in an individualised language, which is also a set of sounds – of physical exertion, labour, childbirth, sex, feeding, infancy and animality – and the silence of rest.

In order to find 'my language', Philip invents new methods, including the production of 'i-mages'. In an earlier work, she had argued that the African artist must 'give voice to this split i-mage of voiced silence. Ways to

---

[47] Philip, 'Wor(l)ds interrupted', n. p.   [48] Saunders, 'Defending the Dead', p. 71.

transcend that contradiction had to and still have to be developed, for that silence continues to shroud the experience, the i-mage and so the word' (*STHT* 82). In writing of 'i-mages', she uses an orthography that relates to the Rastafarian practice of privileging the 'I' in many words (*STHT* 78): "I" is often used to replace 'the subservient "me" ("I and I" is the plural of "we"), ... and has come to replace the first syllable of numerous words: "Ivine" (divine), "Ital" (vital)' etc.[49] The Rastafari 'I' refers not only to the divinity of the individual, but also to the group of which the individual is a part. As participants in the divinity of Haile Selassie, the Rastafari self 'is transformed from "my", "me" and "mine" to "I". This "I" is an individuating as well as unifying notion of identity and it is easily identified with communitarian social philosophy' such as the African concept of Ubuntu: I am I through another person.[50] As Paget Henry explains, 'membership in this I-worded spiritual community has been the basis for the primordial self that Rastafarians have been able to affirm in spite of social contempt, police violence, and other forms of socio-historical denial'.[51]

Philip's 'i-mages' are attempts to unsettle the white settler's lyric 'I', and replace it with a valued, collective, communitarian subject formed under the duress of colonisation, slavery and policing. This coinage also represents the first-person lyric speaker as *magus*, magician and wise woman. The artist produces 'i-mages that speak to the essential being of the people', and can 'alter the way a society perceives itself and, eventually, its collective consciousness. For this process to happen, however, a society needs the autonomous i-mage-maker for whom the i-mage and the language of any art form become what they should be – a well-balanced equation' (*STHT* 78). Philip mourns the destruction of African i-mage-making in the New World, and describes Caribbean identity as identified by 'a significant lack of autonomy in the creation and dissemination of i-mages' (*STHT* 79). It is the job of poets to repair that lack through their own lyric autonomy, restoring society's 'essential being' and self-perception through the fabrication of 'i-mages'.

Philip argues that the words of the poet, storyteller or singer can help society to 'accept, integrate and transcend its experiences, positive or negative' (80):

---

[49] Frank Jan van Dijk, *Jahmaica: Rastafari and Jamaican Society, 1930–1990* (Utrecht: ISOR, 1993), p. 31. Thanks to Matt Smith who shared this book with me.
[50] Lawrence Bamikole, 'Livity as a Dimension of Identity in Rastafari Thought: Implications for Development in Africana Societies', *Caribbean Quarterly* 63.4 (Dec 2017), pp. 451–66 (458). I am grateful to Njelle Hamilton, who helped me to rethink my argument on this point.
[51] Paget Henry, 'Rastafarianism and the Reality of Dread', in *Existence in Black: An Anthology of Black Existential Philosophy*, ed. Lewis R. Gordon (New York: Routledge, 1997), pp. 157–64 (161).

> The African in the Caribbean could move away from the experience of slavery in time; she could even acquire some perspective upon it, but the experience, having never been reclaimed and integrated metaphorically through the language and so within the psyche, could never be transcended. To reclaim and integrate the experience required autonomous i-mage makers and therefore a language with the emotional, linguistic, and historical resources capable of giving voice to the particular i-mages arising out of the experience. (*STHT* 81)

As she writes elsewhere, the poet is the 'medium, the membrane through which this interpenetration' of language and place occurs.[52] What is especially provocative is that Philip uses Rastafarian thought to détourne a theory of the lyric – as created by an autonomous poet, who speaks to the essential being of the people; who offers 'transcendence' for the many through the insights of the individual – which is not unlike Hegel's *Aesthetics*.

Singing *Zong!* Together

But formal devices like i-mages are not the way Philip finally found to integrate the history of slavery, nor is that history one that *Zong!* proposes can finally be sublated. Instead, Philip describes how, when a student asked her to read 'Universal Grammar', she could only answer: 'I will, if you read it with me.' This led to a profound realisation:

> In shifting the lyric voice, in at least forcing it to share the page with other voices, with other histories – moving it from centre stage and page; in clearing a space – I had allowed for other voices to be heard. A multivocal, polyvocal discourse could now be heard. It was the chorus of the unheard, the not-heard, the barely whispered. This to me was closer to the discourse of women. To the call and response of African speech. (*Bla_k* 61)

Zong!'s polyphonic structure rouses a multiplicity of voices, dissonant and harmonic, sometimes speaking singly and sometimes in concert, sometimes in the antiphonic mode of African call-and-response song. Paul Gilroy has argued that antiphony 'symbolises and anticipates (but does not guarantee) new, non-dominating social relationships. Lines between self and other are blurred and special forms of pleasure are created as a result of the meetings and conversations that are established between

---

[52] M. NourbeSe Philip, 'Earth and Sound: The Place of Poetry', in *The Word Behind Bars and the Paradox of Exile*, ed. Kofi Anyidoho (Evanston: Northwestern University Press, 1997), pp. 169–82 (176).

one fractured, incomplete, and unfininished racial self and others.'[53] The choric nature of the poem, and the relation of its fracturing to the deconstruction of lyric authority, emerges most strongly in performance, where Philip encourages the audience to read the text along with her. As Moten writes: '*Zong!* is the story of no-body and it cannot be sung alone.'[54] He adds elsewhere: 'one person can't read this poem; it has to be read symphonically'. Quoting this remark, Sonya Posmentier argues that 'perhaps it is this symphonic subjectivity that properly historicizes the ecology of the slave ship'.[55]

In 2015, Philip performed *Zong!* at a festival of poetry I organised at Queen Mary University of London. The festival was intended to celebrate the connections between the poetic histories and communities of the East End of London and diasporic communities around the world. Philip was one of the poets I was most excited to meet. She came straight from the airport to the Octagon, the grandiose hall where the readings would take place, and greeted me warmly as she set down her bags. We then both looked up, and saw beside us the foundation stone, 'laid by His Majesty Leopold II, King of the Belgians' in 1887. Leopold had taken personal control of a million square miles of the Congo two years before he presided over the opening of this library. The record of atrocities committed in his name is well known.[56] The stone has since been covered up, in response to a student campaign. But for that evening it would loom over the performances, and it continues to exist as a material reminder – like Confederate statues such as Silent Sam whose toppling provokes much bureaucratic handwringing as I write this book in Chapel Hill – of the pervasion of spaces of working, living and studying by white supremacist violence and genocide.

This stone inscription was a dehiscent scar that presided over all the performances. Philip could not heal this wound, but she dressed it. She began her reading at the back of the room, creating a space of silence and attention by ringing bells and rattling shells as she circled the audience and gradually addressed this stone, her voice speaking back to it, her ritual deconsecrating it and the space it supposedly protected.[57] Like the experience of reading *Zong!*, the pace of her performance was slow, resonating

---

[53] Paul Gilroy, *The Black Atlantic: Modernity and Double Consciousness* (London: Verso, 1993), p. 79.
[54] Moten, 'Blackness and Poetry', n. p.   [55] Posmentier, *Cultivation and Catastrophe*, p. 223.
[56] Adam Hochschild, *King Leopold's Ghost: A Story of Greed, Terror, and Heroism in Colonial Africa* (New York: Houghton Mifflin, 1999).
[57] A video of the performance can be viewed on the Archive of the Now: www.archiveofthenow.org /authors/?i=240&f=2476#2476 (accessed 4 May 2021).

with sacred intonations in that echoey hall. Philip was dressed in the white clothes not of Dickinson but of Ghanaian mourning,[58] and began speaking the words of *Zong! #15*: 'defend the dead / weight of circumstance' (25) as she moved towards the stage. She marked the reading of the names at the bottom of the page – 'Akilah Falope Ouma Weke Jubade' – by kneeling. Bending under 'the weight / in / circumstance', she also extended the '*ave* to justice' into a slow, tired groan, crossing an arm across her chest and bowing, as if before the gods or the law. Reading *Zong! #20*, she pointed as she read the opening rationalistic propositions: 'this necessity of loss / this quantity of not / perils underwriters / insurers'. But when she arrived at the 'in' that floats between the poem's opening two columns, she held it, extending the syllable into a long note that resounded as she said 'the between of day / a sea of negroes'. She then restated this theme, and again bowed and crossed her arms before singing the names. Each name found a different melody and different affect – each individual was musically individuated – before she repeated 'in the between of day'. Reading from pages 114–15 of 'Ratio', she again interpreted the text as score, repeating 'feed the sea / a sea of negroes' and '*àse*' ('may it manifest') and changing her position, from a weary seat on the edge of the stage, to standing, kneeling, as the sound of the text mounted and subsided like waves.

Though Philip performed the gaps between the words, stuttering or pausing or drawing out phonemes to represent their spacing on the page, what was striking was how speech made the poem's veiled and fragmented utterances clear: how many men on board? ship sail, ship sail, how many negroes overboard? her scent on my fingers, my hand; the scent of Africa is with me ever, on my skin my lips your scent of roses, Ruth. Repairing the aporetic text with these narratives, the performance felt like a ritual reclamation of the space, as *Zong!* reclaims the legal document, for the people exiled and wounded and murdered by slavery; but it also felt like it did not, could not do this, and that this failure was also an important part of the ethics of engaging with this performance and this history.

I describe this event not because it is paradigmatic, but because these improvisatory and site-specific performances are part of the continuous making of *Zong!*.[59] *Zong!*'s generosity as a source of improvisation is apparent in the collective, durational readings that Philip has performed with musicians and audience members, on the anniversary of the massacre,

---

[58] Phyllis Forster, 'Traditional Mourning Dress of the Akans of Ghana,' *Matatu* 41 (2013), pp. 279–291 (286).

[59] Other examples are given by Laurie R. Lambert, 'Poetics of Reparation in M. NourbeSe Philip's *Zong!*', *The Global South* 10.1 (Spring 2016), pp. 107–29 (113).

since 2011. These readings, Philip says on her website, reverse the shattering effects of the slave trade, and 'attempt an unfragmenting':

> These soundings, for that is what they are, allow for the noise and music of us collectively reading, not necessarily in unison but together; they build, even if temporarily, a community of collective sound that echoes through time. It is the sound of resistance, survival, joy and even flourishing, no matter how transitory. It is the S/Zong! that is a shout to the pastFuture and futurePast that is simultaneously Presence. Of the present. Here. Now.[60]

'Sounding' brings together the collective sound-making of the poet and other performers; the preliminary, improvisatory gathering of ideas and opinions before an action is taken; and the measuring of the depth of the sea, often with a *line*. Philip insists that *Zong!* is not just a book whose 'gatherings' are made from a 'quire' of paper, but a different kind of gathering of a choir, a commemorative moment whose temporality of performance enfolds the extended historical temporalities of death and life, the ancestors and the heirs of this present.

At such readings, the text takes all night; in the early hours before dawn, as most participants have left and those remaining drift in and out of sleep, the drum keeps the readers going through the exhaustion that is already formally inscribed in 'Ferrum'.[61] The endurance required to sustain the wake that is a complete performance of *Zong!* is physical and psychic, drawn out in conversation with the drum, an instrument that is already present in the text:

```
'captain                              their pain
                    wind
strum s                    the air
         he strums                       the oud
                              the ship
    cradles         our longing'
```

The song 'calms me', 'but then / the drums' rouse me; it makes the air 'danger ous' (81). The enslaved Africans in *Zong!* play the harp of their ribcages, emptied skulls as gourd, skin as drum, bones as flutes or drumsticks. Transforming their bodies from the instruments of capitalist labour into musical instruments, they overcome their historical silencing and unseal the grief locked in memory.

---

[60] Philip, 'About', *Set Speaks*: www.setspeaks.com/about/ (accessed 4 May 2021).
[61] Paul Watkins, 'We Can Never Tell', n. p.

In African American traditions, the drum can summon the dead, give voice to their speech and ensure they return safely to the grave.[62] The drum is also a trans-historical echo that links these traditions to their African roots: 'When you reach down for the sound, it is touched off like a drum; it releases itself and reaches as far as you wish' (*STHT* 46). It evokes contexts of collective performance, of bodies singing and moving together through their labour and into the night of its momentary relief. Its regulation during slavery also demonstrates its power as an instrument of communication and insurrection.[63] John Mowitt draws out the connections between drumming and medical tapping, patting *juba*, and violent flogging, scourging and whipping. Drumming, he notes, involves slapping the skin of the hand against an animal's skin to produce a sound that moves through the bodies of others. He describes the drum as a 'richly catachrestic instrument' that 'must be abused to be played'; 'in possessing a body, a skin, a head and a voice, the drum has long represented the expressive interiority that we call the subject, the human being insofar as it intones "I"'.[64] If in the memorial performances of *Zong!* the abuse of that body stands in for the abuses of enslaved bodies in the Middle Passage, the drum is also the instrument of what Mowitt calls a 'trans-subjective dynamism' in which the community assembles through an embodying of collective memory (76–7).

Finally, the title *Zong!* is close to song – 'And Song is what has kept the soul of the African intact' (*Zong!* 207). Song and dance can hold and express historic violence, even after the memory of ancestral languages has been lost: 'that body should speak', and limbs dance so that 'body might become tongue' (*Zong!* 72). Linguistic memory is embedded in the body, such that when the magic words are heard – 'Leg/ba', 'O/shun', 'Shan/go' – the 'heart races / blood pounds / remembers / speech' (*Zong!* 37). The repressed histories of the African diaspora are not irrecoverable, because they are still present in the body:

> Even the mere determination to remember can, at times, be a revolutionary act – like the slave who refused to forget the dance . . . . Often in contestation with history, memory has a poetics that history lacks, appearing to reside in our bodies and not solely in the mind. (*Bla_K* 66–7)

---

[62] Sterling Stuckey, *Slave Culture: Nationalist Theory and the Foundations of Black America* (Oxford University Press, 1987), pp. 19–20.
[63] Dena J. Epstein, *Sinful Tunes and Spirituals: Black Folk Music to the Civil War* (Urbana and Chicago: University of Illinois Press, 1977), pp. 59–60.
[64] John Mowitt, *Percussion: Drumming, Beating, Striking* (Durham: Duke University Press, 2002), p. 6.

Song and dance are modes of remembering the past and resisting the present. At a funeral in Ghana, Philip is told by an elder: 'We sing for death, we sing for birth. That's what we do. We sing.' Singing affirms life and helps Philip to put down the burden of the dead. 'As I say in "Notanda," *Zong!* is song – the song we have always sung, particularly when we were brought here to the land of untelling. I think that that's the gift, isn't it? – if we can get to that place of Song and Zong. It's the reward for going through the grief. It's the other side.'[65] Song is the testimony of life even at the gates of death, which releases itself and reaches as far as you wish; it is a reminder of 'another world where we could become truly embodied, with embodied addresses, so to speak. When I perform *Zong!* the distance between these two worlds becomes smaller.'[66]

Gregory Nagy has shown that in archaic Greece, *mimesis* was not imitation, but re-enactment: songs are re-composed through their performance, as the *khorós* engages in dramatic re-impersonation. Only after this dramatic context was lost, he writes, did the Aristotelian notion of mimesis as imitation begin to dominate.[67] He goes on to argue that:

> Just as every performance becomes a potential re-creation in mimesis, that is, a virtual recomposition, so also the very identity of the performer stands to be re-created, recomposed. When the performer enacts an identity formerly enacted by previous performers, he or she is re-creating his or her own identity for the moment. That is to say, a performer's identity is recomposed *in performance*. (214)

The choric nature of *Zong!* is a discovery Philip makes by passing through the liberal lyric. Having at first coveted and wished to destroy the authority of the white, male lyric poet, she then considers whether the song of destruction is the true lyric of the Black, female, colonised subject. But she arrives at an impasse: her idea that the lyric poet can offer the community a set of i-mages that bridge the traumatic past and future participates in the liberal valorisation of the individual subject. Finally, Philip finds a different way to overcome the privilege of white lyric authority through performance and ritual exchange with the ancestors, in the rhythms of dub and calypso, the liveness of performance and moving, dancing bodies that find life and meaning and value in the polyphonic chorus.

Philip names the Middle Passage as the Maafa, a Kiswahili word meaning 'terrible occurrence' or 'great disaster', 'that which is both an end and a beginning' (*Bla_k* 31). But the Maafa, or African Holocaust, is

---

[65] Saunders, 'Defending the Dead', p. 79. [66] Watkins, 'We Can Never Tell', n. p.
[67] Gregory Nagy, *Poetry as Performance* (Cambridge University Press, 1996), p. 54.

also 'the condition for the emergence of African being, just as grammar conditions the emergence of speech', as Frank B. Wilderson III puts it;[68] as such it is a sacred initiation,

> being birthed for a second time from the belly of the ship, into what we, emissaries of the Ancestors and ancestral memory, still don't fully know. Who knew what we would or could create? Other than life. Unwritten, because the palimpsest of the Maafa is the 'sea (which) is history.'[69]

For Glissant, 'this boat is a womb, a womb abyss. . . . This boat is your womb, a matrix, and yet it expels you. This boat: pregnant with as many dead as living under sentence of death.'[70] Philip also describes the Middle Passage as both womb (matrix) and abyss: the hold and the salt water are figures for the mother's belly, as well as an extrusion unto death, both literal death and the death of language, culture and human being of chattel slavery. And while *Zong!* is a work of mourning, it also looks towards that which we 'still don't fully know': the living work that follows devastation. This is the poem's tidalectical orientation towards past and future, destruction and creation, pairing 'the forceful desire for reparative return with the painful impossibility of that drive'.[71]

Philip has compared the text of *Gregson vs. Gilbert* to 'a gravestone': 'and in shattering that gravestone the voices are freed'.[72] But performance is a way of unfragmenting that shattered history. As Posmentier writes, 'there is no bleaker artistic imprisonment, no greater catastrophe than this one – the poet inside the body of enslaving discourse, replicating its murderous logic. Evoking and transforming this violence becomes the poem's curiously optimistic project.'[73] That optimism is affirmed by Philip herself, who in an interview wondered:

> What if? What if the Ancestors intended some other purpose for us to have been brought to this part of the world, entirely apart from the European lust for profit. It seems to me that just asking that question puts us in a different position and releases a tremendous amount of energy. In honoring our own dead, ... by focusing on ourselves and what the experience of slavery has meant and can't mean, even just embracing all that, somehow helps to

---

[68] Frank B. Wilderson III, 'Grammar & Ghosts: The Performative Limits of African Freedom', *Theatre Survey* 50.1 (2009), pp. 119–25 (119).
[69] Philip, 'About', *Set Speaks*, www.setspeaks.com/about/ (accessed 16 May 2021).
[70] Glissant, *Poetics of Relation*, p. 6.
[71] Aida Levy-Hussen, 'Trauma and the Historical Turn in Black Literary Discourse', in *The Psychic Hold of Slavery: Legacies in American Expressive Culture*, ed. Sonya Diggs Colbert, Robert J. Patterson and Aida Levy-Hussain (New Brunswick: Rutgers University Press, 2016), pp. 195–211 (204).
[72] Saunders, 'Defending the Dead', p. 69.   [73] Posmentier, *Cultivation and Catastrophe*, p. 219.

contain the experience so that we can benefit from the memory rather than being crushed by it.[74]

This is not a utopian overcoming of the horrific past, but a radical openness to the contingency of the present, which puts the poet in a *figural* relationship (in Auerbach's sense) not just with the wounded poetics of contemporary witness, but with the voices and memories of the dead. The incompleteness of any act of attempt at reparation holds the poem open to the future. Rather than restitution, Christina Sharpe has suggested that *Zong!* does the work of 'aspiration': 'the word for keeping and putting breath back in the body', for 'imagining and for keeping and putting breath back in the Black body in hostile weather'.[75]

I started this chapter by telling the story that Philip says cannot be told – that is to say, I laid out the numbers, the bare facts. And in telling a story, there is a temptation always to supply a happy ending. Here, that happy ending would be this: that Philip cycles through the history of lyric, from the songs and memories held in the bodies of the enslaved Africans aboard the *Zong*, through a constrained engagement with a legal text and a solitary process of composition, into a printed book, back into the body, through performance; from a collective to an individual and back again, arriving where lyric begins, with song. But I have learned enough from reading *Zong!* to be sceptical that such endings are happy, or even really endings.

Wilderson has challenged what he calls the sentimental belief that performance can 'reconcile this gap between the place of slaves and the places of all others'. He warns against being 'seduced by an overvaluation of performance art's sociopolitical effectiveness': the performance of emancipation is not emancipation; art is only an accompaniment to structural change.[76] This perspective contests the utopic reading of Black performance by Fred Moten as animated by the 'freedom drive', as 'the ongoing improvisation of a kind of lyricism of the surplus – invagination, rupture, collision, augmentation'.[77] But it is important to remember that *Zong!* refuses to subsume linguistic or historical violence as melancholy or triumphant overcoming through the rituals of contemporary performance. Saidiya Hartman has written:

> The recognition of loss is a crucial element in redressing the breach introduced by slavery. This recognition entails a remembering of the pained

---

[74] Saunders, 'Defending the Dead', pp. 69–70.
[75] Christina Sharpe, *In the Wake: On Blackness and Being* (Durham: Duke University Press, 2016), p. 113.
[76] Wilderson, 'Grammar & Ghosts,' pp. 120–1.
[77] Fred Moten, *In the Break: The Aesthetics of the Black Radical Tradition* (Minneapolis: University of Minnesota Press, 2003), pp. 12, 26.

body, not by way of a simulated wholeness but precisely through the recognition of the amputated body in its amputatedness, in the insistent recognition of the violated body as human flesh, in the cognition of its needs, and in the anticipation of its liberty. In other words, it is the ravished body that holds out the possibility of a restitution, not the invocation of an illusory wholeness or the desired return to an originary plenitude.[78]

Even as *Zong!* aspires to song, Philip cannot fantasise about a return to goodness, the phantasy of the good mother tongue, the lost African origin. Instead, there is 'only one memory. A single memory. Of loss. Loss, loss, and more loss. The challenge for me is to write from that place of loss. Of nothing, if you will. To make poetry out of silence' (*Bla_k* 60). But the poetry she makes from the silence of a summary argument, from a history of erasure, begins and ends with sound: *Zong!* is speech dragged 'through oath and through moan, through mutter, chant and babble, through babble and curse, through chortle and ululation' (*Zong!* 196). These sounds are the sounds of a body promising and uttering, complaining and enchanting, babbling and mourning: a voice at the beginnings and endings of life, singing its deathless song.

---

[78] Saidiya V. Hartman, *Scenes of Subjection: Terror, Slavery, and Self-Making in Nineteenth-Century America* (Oxford University Press, 1997), p. 74.

CHAPTER 7

The Sound Came from Everywhere and Nowhere
African American Song as Lyric Work

'Writing the collective self into history belongs to the offices of affliction.'
– Hortense Spillers

In a famous passage from his *Narrative of the Life of Frederick Douglass, an American Slave* (1845), Frederick Douglass describes the singing of the enslaved people on their way to the Great House Farm to collect their monthly allowance:

> While on their way, they would make the dense old woods, for miles around, reverberate with their wild songs, revealing at once the highest joy and the deepest sadness. They would compose and sing as they went along, consulting neither time nor tune. The thought that came up, came out – if not in the word, in the sound; – and as frequently in the one as in the other. They would sometimes sing the most pathetic sentiment in the most rapturous tone, and the most rapturous sentiment in the most pathetic tone. Into all of their songs they would manage to weave something of Great House Farm. Especially would they do this, when leaving home. They would then sing most exultingly the following words:
>
> > 'I am going away to the Great House Farm!
> > O, yea! O, yea! O!'
>
> This they would sing, as a chorus, to words which to many would seem unmeaning jargon, but which, nevertheless, were full of meaning to themselves. I have sometimes thought that the mere hearing of those songs would do more to impress some minds with the horrible character of slavery, than the reading of whole volumes of philosophy on the subject could do.[1]

---

[1] Frederick Douglass, *Narrative of the Life of Frederick Douglass, An American Slave* (1845), in *Autobiographies* (New York: Literary Classics of the United States, 1994), pp. 23–4.

Their songs celebrate this momentary escape from intolerable drudgery, but are also an expression of deep suffering that could be released in the liminal space of the woods. In the third revision, the *Life and Times of Frederick Douglass* (1881; rev. ed. 1893), Douglass also adds a verse to the song – 'My old master is a good old master' – which suggests the songs could also be used to propitiate or to 'please the pride of the Lloyds' (502).

Douglass's account proposes complex relations of theme and form, context and affect, 'meaning' and decipherability in the songs.[2] On one level, 'their' singing does not seem like something in which the young Douglass participated; the 'meaning' of these songs is known only 'to themselves', not to him, or to the (predominantly white) readers whom Douglass now addresses: 'I did not, when a slave, understand the deep meaning of those rude and apparently incoherent songs. I was myself within the circle; so that I neither saw nor heard as those without might see and hear' (24). He was in the circle of slavery, and the circle of the ring-shout. But these songs are not unmeaning 'jargon'. As Sterling Stuckey notes, their language would have reflected the mixture of English with the African languages spoken on Colonel Lloyd's farm.[3] Douglass *could* understand them: for he could also recognise the mismatch between their rapture and pathos. He remembers the words. Then Douglass implies that their 'deep meaning' is only available to those who have escaped from bondage, not to those who produce the song. But the song also has a meaningfulness that is exclusive to its performers, and to which the outside observer, whether enslaver or the reader of abolitionist literature, cannot access.[4]

Douglass calls the songs 'wild' and arrhythmic ('consulting neither time nor tune'). Associated with the liminal setting of the woods, and the bodies of enslaved people in motion rather than the mind serviced by volumes of philosophy, the songs are a ground for Douglass's modest self-critique. They are a fault line between his injured body – the foot in whose cracks a pen could nestle – and his emancipated intellect, which developed through his illegal effort to learn to read and culminated in his production of a book that he modestly suggests is less effective in revealing the true character of slavery than the unmediated song would have been. While in some ways Douglass's passage from enslavement to freedom is paralleled by his

---

[2] Paul Gilmore, 'Aesthetic Power: Electric Words and the Example of Frederick Douglass', *ATQ: 19th-Century American Literature and Culture* 16.4 (December 2002), pp. 291–311 (291).

[3] Sterling P. Stuckey, 'Afterword: Frederick Douglass and W. E. B. Du Bois On the Consciousness of the Enslaved', *The Journal of African American History* 91:4 (Fall 2006), pp. 451–8 (453).

[4] Jürgen E. Grandt, *Shaping Words to Fit the Soul: The Southern Ritual Grounds of Afro-Modernism* (Columbus: Ohio State University Press, 2009), p. 31.

journey from immersion in an oral culture to the rights and status accorded by literacy, his narrative refuses this logic of development. It does not present his distance from the singers as an unironic advance, from unmeaning to meaning, orality to literacy, absence to presence, past to future, bondage to freedom, Black singers to white readers; instead, it invites the free reader into an ambivalent hermeneutic circle whose form is determined by the (un)interpretability of song.

When Douglass was visited by the Jubilee Singers of Fisk University in the winter of 1874–5, he remarked: 'I can remember songs that I heard fifty years ago, when a slave.' Encouraged by his guests, Douglass began singing 'Run to Jesus – shun the danger – / I don't expect to stay much longer here.' He then reflected that 'It was while singing this song that the idea of escaping from slavery was first suggested to my mind … I used to sing it around the plantation continually. My master was very well pleased, for he thought I was thinking about heaven, but I was thinking all the time about that other country up North.'[5] Here, as in his discussion of the song 'O Canaan, sweet Canaan, / I am bound for the land of Canaan' in *My Bondage*, Douglass alludes to the well-known ambiguity of the spiritual, whose hopefulness could be directed to both heavenly and earthly emancipation: 'We meant to reach the *north* – and the north was our Canaan' (308).[6] It is both a reflection on his condition, and an inspiration to seek freedom.

The songs' doubling of meaning, on either side of the veil of racialised consciousness, gives them an irreconcilable quality: they are a performance intrinsic to bondage, incommunicable to those outside its conditions and places; and a 'testimony against slavery, and a prayer to God for deliverance from chains' whose most powerful meaning – Douglass insists – *would* operate on and for an absent, free readership. That testimony is communicated not by the songs themselves, but by Douglass's prosaic description of them. As Rowan Ricardo Phillips has noted, Douglass provides almost no textual space for the actual lyrics, unlike lines by Cowper, Whittier and Coleridge that ornament his prose.[7] The songs induce the anticipation of powerful testimony but that testimony cannot be heard.

---

[5] 'A Song with a History', *The New York Evangelist* (2 Sept. 1875), p. 3.
[6] Jon Cruz, *Culture on the Margins: The Black Spiritual and the Rise of American Cultural Interpretation* (Princeton University Press, 1999), p. 78.
[7] Rowan Ricardo Phillips, *When Blackness Rhymes With Blackness* (Champaign: Dalkey Archive, 2010), pp. 46, 50.

Instead, Douglass invests his autobiography with the affects of these 'wild notes'. They 'always depressed my spirit, and filled me with ineffable sadness', often bringing him to tears:

> The mere recurrence to those songs, even now, afflicts me; and while I am writing these lines, an expression of feeling has already found its way down my cheek. To those songs I trace my first glimmering conception of the dehumanizing character of slavery ... . Those songs still follow me, to deepen my hatred of slavery, and quicken my sympathies for my brethren in bonds. (24)

Anyone who wants to understand the 'soul-killing effects' of slavery need only go to Colonel Lloyd's plantation and listen to the song still being sung there. The diachronic note, heard only in memory but undoubtedly being sung somewhere as he writes, leaves a physical trace on the book: the written line imitates the line of tears traced on his cheek. It is also the trail that leads toward the future, his glimmering conception of his own humanity, and the hope for liberation of all those still in bondage.

This chapter stays with key aspects of the history and theory of the lyric, including its relation to song, representation of power and the absence or erasure of specific voices from the archive. It analyses the way whiteness went to work on African American song-making traditions in what I will sometimes call, following George Fredrickson and Bryan Wagner, the work of 'negrophile' collectors.[8] African American song-making is an important site for the production of lyric in conditions of actual bondage. These songs have been studied with great care and diligence by African American and other scholars.[9] In this and the subsequent chapter, I scrutinise the uses to which the songs were put by white collectors.

---

[8] George Fredrickson, *The Black Image in the White Mind: The Debate on Afro-American Character and Destiny, 1817–1914* (Middletown: Wesleyan University Press, [1971] 1987), p. 327.

[9] While by no means an exhaustive list, the most important scholarship for me has been LeRoi Jones (Amiri Baraka), *Blues People: A History of Negro Music in White America* (New York: Perennial [1963] 2002); John Lovell, *Black Song: The Forge and the Flame: The Story of How the Afro-American Spiritual was Hammered Out* (New York: Macmillan, 1972); Lawrence Levine, *Black Culture and Black Consciousness: Afro-American Folk Thought from Slavery to Freedom* (Oxford University Press, 1977); Dena J. Epstein, *Sinful Tunes and Spirituals: Black Folk Music to the Civil War* (Urbana and Chicago: University of Illinois Press, 1977); Eileen Southern, *The Music of Black Americans: A History*, 2nd ed. (New York: W. W. Norton, 1983); Irene V. Jackson (ed.), *More than Dancing: Essays on African-American Music and Musicians* (Westport: Greenwood Press, 1985); Sterling Stuckey, *Slave Culture: Nationalist Theory and the Foundations of Black America* (Oxford University Press, 1987); Ronald Radano, 'Denoting Difference: The Writing of the Slave Spirituals', *Critical Inquiry* 22.3 (Spring 1996), pp. 506–44; Cruz, *Culture on the Margins* (1999); Ronald M. Radano, *Lying Up a Nation: Race and Black Music* (University of Chicago Press, 2003); Shane White and Graham J. White, *The Sounds of Slavery: Discovering African American History through Songs, Sermons and Speech* (Boston: Beacon Press, 2005); Lauri Ramey, *Slave Songs and the*

Those uses, I argue, show how white literary criticism depends on an Africanist imaginary, on an idea of the lyric of Blackness, which it then represses or excludes from the theorisation of 'lyric proper'. In what follows I am less focused on the songs themselves, than on examining how they were *made to work* by white folklorists, detached from their collective performance contexts and represented as an early stage in the evolutionary history of the lyric.

Outside Over There

Douglass's account was one of the earliest polemical representations of the sorrow songs of slavery. But as those songs were collected and analysed by white observers in the late nineteenth and early twentieth century, different meanings and functions were attributed to them. Ethnographical studies of African American song began to appear in this period for three reasons. First, scholars feared that this folk tradition would wither in the aftermath of Emancipation. William Allen argued in 1867 that a 'systematic effort' to collect them was now urgent. This was because, as John Mason Brown wrote in the following year, 'the round of sacred and secular song that for many years was so familiar to every ear throughout the Southern States, is now fading from use and remembrance … . It could not be perpetuated without perpetuating slavery as it existed, and with the fall of slavery its days were numbered.'[10] Thomas Fenner likewise anticipated in 1874 that 'this people which has developed such a wonderful musical sense in its degradation will, in its maturity, produce a composer who could bring a music of the future out of this music of the past'. But he also regretted what he perceived as the shame 'freedmen' felt about this 'vestige of slavery', shame that would lead to the extinction of this musical corpus.[11] As such, the songs draw out the melancholic association between lyric and loss that I proposed in the introduction as a fundamental aspect of the genre.

In their 1925 book *The Negro and His Songs*, Howard Odum and Guy Johnson – white sociologists based at the University of North Carolina,

---

Birth of African-American Poetry (Basingstoke: Palgrave Macmillan, 2008); Bryan Wagner, *Disturbing the Peace: Black Culture and the Police Power after Slavery* (Cambridge, MA: Harvard University Press, 2009); Mellonee V. Burnim and Portia K. Maultsby (eds.), *African American Music: An Introduction*, 2nd ed. (New York: Routledge, 2015); and Clyde Woods, *Development Arrested: The Blues and Plantation Power in the Mississippi Delta* (London: Verso, 2017).

[10] John Mason Brown, 'Songs of the Slaves', *Lippincott's Magazine* 11 (December 1868), pp. 617–23 (618).

[11] Thomas P. Fenner, *Cabin and Plantation Songs as Sung by the Hampton Students* (New York: G. P. Putnam's Sons, 1901), p. iv.

who contributed to the development of what is known as the 'New South' – still assumed that these songs 'would pass away immediately with the passing of slavery'.[12] But as John Wesley Work observed:

> We sometimes hear this lamentation, 'It is too bad that the old plantation melodies are dying out.' Such laments are felt more keenly and expressed more fully by the Southern white man who was a part of the system of slaver, than by any other class.[13]

I'll return to the sentimental nostalgia of the Southern slave-owning class in the next chapter. Needless to say, the end of slavery was hardly the end of oppression. The failure of Reconstruction, Jim Crow and mass incarceration ensured that the conditions that produced these traditions would remain in place for generations.

The second reason that folklorists hastened to record the songs was that they feared that the technologies of the culture industry would render them obsolete. In 1925, Dorothy Scarborough cited her mentor, the folklorist George Lyman Kittredge, on the need to gather songs 'before the material vanishes forever, killed by the Victrola, the radio, the lure of cheap printed music'.[14] John Lomax, noting the passing of the river songs, conjectured similarly: 'soon the gangs of the black men would follow suit, as a part of the advance of the machine age'.[15] Newman Ivey White, writing in 1928, feared that the encroachment of phonographs, radios and 'Negro newspapers' was dissolving African American ethnic identity: 'the Negroes are becoming less and less a folk-group'.[16] James Weldon Johnson feared that the tradition of the Negro Spiritual was 'being destroyed not only by the changing psychology but by such modern mechanisms as the phonograph and the radio'.[17]

But technology was ambivalent. It provided an apparently 'authentic' recording of a song and undermined the possibility of authenticity; it was the cause of the tradition's vanishing, and the mechanism of its preservation. For the negrophile collectors, the unrepresentable grain of the Black

---

[12] Howard W. Odum and Guy B. Johnson, *The Negro and His Songs: A Study of Typical Negro Songs in the South* (Chapel Hill: University of North Carolina Press, 1925), p. 16.
[13] John Wesley Work, *Folk Song of the American Negro* (New York: Negro Universities Press, 1915), p. 92.
[14] Dorothy Scarborough, *On the Trail of Negro Folk-Songs* (Cambridge, MA: Harvard University Press, 1925), pp. 281–2.
[15] John A. Lomax, *Adventures of a Ballad Hunter* (Austin: University of Texas Press, 2017), p. 146.
[16] Newman Ivey White, *American Negro Folk Songs* (Cambridge, MA: Harvard University Press, 1928), p. 4.
[17] Introduction to the *Second Book of Negro Spirituals*, in James Weldon Johnson, *Writings* (New York: Literary Classics of the United States, 2004), p. 740.

voice was an echo from America's past, that could only be adequately preserved by the technology of the future. In an essay I'll discuss in the next chapter, Thomas Wentworth Higginson records some dialect from his regiment in 1862, and adds: 'This is a poor reminiscence in prose, but I wished for a phonographer in my pocket.'[18] The machines that were destroying this tradition could also be its salvation. The advent of recording equipment offered a solution to the irreproducibility of the performances and the withering of the tradition as mechanisation and industrialisation advanced. For Alan Lomax, recording heralded 'a new age of writing human history'. Textual transcriptions cannot 'write history' in the way audio and video can: we have arrived at the familiar crossroads where writing is an impoverished notation of absence, orality of the richness of presence. Lomax celebrates the ability of technology to give (in that offensive metaphor so beloved of authorities) 'a voice to the voiceless', and to 'document music, such as the complex polyphony of the blacks, which notation could not represent'.[19] Becoming 'pure voice', like the overheard solitary lamenting poet or Dickinson herself, the African American singer is a paradigmatic lyricist for the machine age.

The third reason that studies of African American folk song proliferated in this period was that it was the moment when folk culture became a subject of serious academic inquiry in the United States. Academic folklore studies were institutionalised in the 1880s and 1890s, along with the other human sciences – sociology, history and anthropology. The first meeting of the American Folklore Society was held in 1888 at Harvard, with Francis James Child presiding; Higginson was one of the founding members.[20] Harvard was an important centre of the literary approach to folklore studies (while Columbia was associated with the anthropological approach, represented by the research of Franz Boas).[21] John Lomax studied at Harvard in 1906–7 with Kittredge, a medievalist whose chair had previously been held by Child; Kittredge took up work on the tenth volume of Child's collection *Popular Ballads of England and Scotland* (1892–8). The *Journal of American Folklore* published its first issue in 1888, and proposed to collect the 'fast-vanishing remains' of the 'relics of Old English Folk-Lore, ... Lore of Negroes in the Southern States of the Union, ... Lore of

---

[18] Thomas Wentworth Higginson, *The Complete Civil War Journal and Selected Letters*, ed. ChristopherLooby (University of Chicago Press, 2000), p. 60.
[19] Alan Lomax, *The Land Where the Blues Began* (London: Minerva, 1993), p. xi.
[20] Cruz, *Culture on the Margins*, p. 116.
[21] Rosemary Lévy Zumwalt, *American Folklore Scholarship: A Dialogue of Dissent* (Bloomington and Indianapolis: Indiana University Press, 1988), pp. 14, 10.

the Indian Tribes of North America, ... Lore of French Canada, Mexico, etc.' As Ronald Judy notes, 'the beginnings of the systematic scientific study of the Negro – and significantly by Negroes – are contemporaneous with those of the research university in the United States of America'.[22] Judy contends that while 'the scientific universities were concerned with Blacks only as objects of analysis and not as thinking, cultured subjects', new Black cultural organizations emerged such as the Negro American Society (founded 1877), the Society for the Collection of Negro Folk Lore (founded 1890), the Negro Historical Society of Philadelphia (founded 1897) and the American Negro Academy (founded in 1897). These organisations' mission was 'to challenge the notions of Negro inferiority being promulgated by the new science within the university' (Judy 127–8).

From the beginning, the collection of African American folk song was a site of struggle: between a perceived obsolescence caused by the supposed end of chattel slavery, and a recognition of the continuity of practices of artmaking and domination from slavery into Jim Crow; between academics who claimed institutional authority, and so-called amateurs; between white negrophile and African American scholars; between scientistic models of ethnography and ones based on participant observation. These struggles are manifested in the work of one of the most important African American ethnographers, Zora Neale Hurston.[23] Hurston's accomplishments are manifold, and can't be easily tucked into a chapter of this kind. A student of Boas, Hurston had also worked closely with Alain Locke, and amassed a substantial collection of African American folklore through fieldwork in the American South, Jamaica and Haiti in the 1920s and 1930s. She worked alongside Alan Lomax and Mary Elizabeth Barnicle, gathering material for the Library of Congress in 1935; her efforts were often unacknowledged in publications resulting from these collaborations, and she experienced extensive racist discrimination both in the field and from colleagues.[24] Hurston was sharply critical of the Lomaxes, and of Odum and Johnson. She told Locke in 1928 that Odum and Johnson 'evidently know nothing of the how [*sic*] folk-songs grow ... he has taken several things from the phonograph records, and heaven knows there has never appeared one genuine Negro bit on there. ... White people could not be trusted to collect the lore of others,

---

[22] Ronald Judy, 'Untimely Intellectuals and the University', *boundary 2* 27.1 (2000), pp. 121–33 (122).
[23] Benigno Sanchez-Eppler, 'Telling Anthropology: Zora Neale Hurston and Gilberto Freyre Disciplined in Their Field-Home-Work', *American Literature History* 4.3 (1992), pp. 464–88.
[24] Daphne A. Brooks, '"Sister, Can You Line It Out?": Zora Neale Hurston and the Sound of Angular Black Womanhood', *Amerikastudien / American Studies* 55.4 (2010), pp. 617–27 (621).

and that the Indians were right' in maintaining a stony silence in the face of white ethnographers.[25] In a wonderfully vicious letter to Alan Lomax, she says: 'I thought that you had touched bottom in Florida and Nassau, when knowing that you knew no more about collecting folk-lore than a hog knows about a holiday, you were content to have me do it for you, but contrive to have it appear I didnt deserve any credit.' She accuses him of appropriating her work, and of blunt stupidity:

> There was you with your lies about everything that I showed you. One day you had never heard of it. Next day, you or your papa had found it in Texas. The children's cries is a case in point. You not only had heard nothing of it, I had to go to a great deal of trouble to make you understand. Hunted up some little boys and demonstrated and you were delighted. But bless me gawd a week later, you were an authority on it. You and your papa had found it in Texas. I see you tell that lie again in your book.[26]

And she told Langston Hughes: 'It makes me sick to see how these cheap white folks are grabbing our stuff and ruining it.'[27] Her letters are a powerful reminder of the way that white folklorists like the Lomaxes occluded the labour and knowledge of Black scholars and community informants.

Sonya Posmentier has offered a very compelling reading of Hurston's ethnography, describing the labourers' camps where Hurston gathered her materials as 'crucial sites of black reading and lyric reading'. She proposes that 'reading Hurston as a theorist of racial identity and a theorist of critical reading practice, and uncovering the interdisciplinarity of "close reading" unsettles the oft-supposed extradisciplinarity of blackness to literary study'.[28] Her essay opens up the relationship between ethnography and the New Critics, which I will develop in the following chapter.

Moving between close reading and context, between feeling and scientistic notions of culture, Hurston also paid careful attention to the importance of dialogue and positionality in relation to her informants, as she negotiated between rural Black communities in Florida, and academic networks based in New York and Washington. Her work exemplifies what W. E. B. Du Bois called 'double consciousness', switching between

---

[25] Carla Kaplan, *Zora Neale Hurston: A Life in Letters* (New York: Doubleday, 2002), pp. 118–21. See also Catherine A. Stewart, *Long Past Slavery: Representing Race in the Federal Writers' Project* (Chapel Hill: University of North Carolina Press, 2016), pp. 164–8.
[26] Carla Cappetti, 'Defending Hurston Against Her Legend: Two Previously Unpublished Letters', *Amerikastudien / American Studies* 55.4 (2010), pp. 602–14 (610).
[27] Kaplan, *ZNH: Life in Letters*, p. 172.
[28] Sonya Posmentier, 'Lyric Reading in the Black Ethnographic Archive', *American Literary History* 30.1 (Spring 2018), pp. 55–84 (75, 59–60).

the conventions of racist academic discourse that connote authority, and assertions of intimacy with the Black subject that promise authenticity. In the field she literally sang along with her informants until she learned the verses.[29] In the university, she spoke the language of anthropology. One of her books of folklore, *Mules and Men*, asserts that her Blackness allowed her to overcome the 'evasive' resistance of 'the Negro', but she also identified with that resistance, like the stony-faced 'Indians' who gave nothing away to white observers: 'The theory behind our tactics: "The white man is always trying to know into somebody else's business."'[30] The use of the first-person plural positions her on the side of the evasive informant, not the academic ethnographer. But the vernacular idiom that is the sign of her authenticity is also a rhetorical fiction she deploys as a writer; as Ronald Radano argues, 'for her, the vernacular was a realm for which history was already unattainable, even as it remained in the end the very basis of her literary art'.[31] Her code-switching between white Standard English and African American vernacular dramatises the different identities under which she operates.[32] Discursive shifts of this kind will play out in a number of ways throughout this chapter; I'll discuss them in relation to Paul Laurence Dunbar's poem 'A Corn Song' later.

Several of the other African American foklorists discussed in this chapter also positioned themselves within and against the Black community, struggling to be taken seriously by academic readerships by distancing themselves from that community, while also using their own Blackness to assert the authenticity of their research. John Wesley Work describes his research as 'undertaken for the love of our fathers' songs'; he 'begs' the reader 'to understand that very much of the history and description has come to me first hand from those who have been a part of them'.[33] And yet his study opens with a mythologising panegyric to the spirit of 'the African', who 'becomes less a savage, less a heathen' when studied through his music (7). Thomas Talley, who was a professor of chemistry, adopts numerous distancing strategies in his analysis of *Negro Folk Rhymes*, including scientific and naturalist metaphors, alongside disparaging remarks about the singers' capacity for reflection – a theme that prevails in the discourse of many white collectors. However, he also identifies himself as 'a Negro, [who] has spent his early years in the midst of the

---

[29] Deborah G. Plant, *Zora Neale Hurston: A Biography of the Spirit* (Westport: Prager, 2007), p. 82.
[30] Zora Neale Hurston, *Mules and Men*, in *Folklore, Memoirs, and Other Writings* (New York: Library of America, 1995), p. 10.
[31] Radano, *Lying up a Nation*, p. 48.   [32] Stewart, *Long Past Slavery*, p. 156.
[33] Work, *Folk Song*, p. 6.

Rhymes and witnessed their making', particularly 'in my early childhood'. He extrapolates from these childhood recollections backwards in history: 'Let us assume that Negro customs in Slavery days were what they were in my childhood days.'[34] Like Hurston, Talley established himself as a participant observer, but comparing slavery with his own childhood also suggests a discourse of the infantile primitive that we will encounter again.

By contrast, white ethnographers took up comfortable positions on the outside of Black communities. Some white Southerners like John Lomax laid claim to a knowledge that arose from lifelong proximity to African American people; but that knowledge tended to be paternalistic at best. Lomax described making a field recording in 1947:

> As I sat in the car and listened to the steady, monotonous beat of the guitars, accented by handclaps and the shuffle of feet – the excitement growing as time went on, the rhythm deeper and clearer – again I felt carried across to Africa, and I felt as if I were listening to the tom-toms of savage blacks. When I peered through the doors and the windows the whole house seemed to throb with the movement of the dancers. I saw the grotesque postures and heard the jumbled and indistinguishable cries of jubilant pleasure, and I realised that Alan and I were now enjoying a unique experience amid a people we really knew very little about.[35]

This is a 'unique experience' not for everyone, but for the white men; the white supremacist imagination produces an image of savagery, throbbing indistinguishable cries, pleasure and in the distance Africa, as they sit outside in the car. From their vantage point, the Black music-makers are dissolved into an indistinguishable throng, 'a people we really knew very little about'. I'll speak more about the white fantasy of the throng in the following chapter. Lomax's 'we' is not a throng. It stands not only for himself and his son Alan as collectors but also for the implicitly white readership to whom he was introducing these musical traditions.

Feeling over Meaning

For white observers such as Lomax, African American songs are overheard, naïve versions of lyric poetry as Mill describes it: 'What is poetry but the thoughts and words in which emotion spontaneously embodies itself?'[36]

---

[34] Thomas Talley, *Negro Folk Rhymes: Wise and Otherwise* (New York: Macmillan, 1922), pp. 255, 260.
[35] Lomax, *Adventures*, p. 101.
[36] John Stuart Mill, *Autobiography and Literary Essays*, ed. John M. Robson and Jack Stillinger (1981), vol. 1 of *The Collected Works of John Stuart Mill*, ed. John M Ronson, et al., 33 vols. (Toronto and London: University of Toronto Press and Routledge and Kegan Paul, 1963–91), p. 356.

Newman Ivey White, listening to 'the work songs of Negroes building a new university for the white man' in 1928, asserts that the different 'sense of logic' between the 'Negro' and the white man comes down to 'the predominance of *feeling* over *meaning*'.[37] These observers often depict the singers as either wild and barbaric, or meek and 'childlike', their songs the simple outpouring of sorrowful hearts. The Black singer is made identical with the lyric 'I', and the song is 'the spontaneous overflow of powerful feelings' that Wordsworth praises, but without any modification of thought. However, the white supremacist tendency to regard African American singers as incapable of reflection means that the songs cannot really be lyric; they cannot transcend their particular context or raise the particularity of experience to the universality that Hegel asserts is lyric's destination. Instead, these songs retain the incipience Hegel attributed to folk song – 'racial but not yet national', as Maud Cuney-Hare described them in 1936.[38]

Odum and Johnson repeatedly argued that African American music is a direct and unmediated expression of the lives and feelings of its producers. Speaking in terms that George Fredrickson has identified as 'Romantic racialism', they represent African American song as 'beautiful, childlike, simple and plaintive': unreflective, primitive, impulsive, and expressive of a simple and unmediated set of feelings that fall short of full subjectivity.[39] For them, African American song was 'not the expression of complex life, but of simple longing' (21).

For white folklorists like Odum and Johnson, African American music is simultaneously inferior to white American song and affect, and its sublime other; it is meaningless and meaningful, ordered and disordered. But if African American song seemed to resist knowledge or interpretation by white audiences, this resistance was also a radical defensive mechanism, as Hurston's remarks make clear. Saidiya Hartman has argued that the 'veiled character of slave song must be considered in relation to the dominative imposition of transparency and the degrading hyper-visibility of the enslaved, and, by the same token, such concealment should be considered as a form of resistance'.[40] The 'veil' here alludes to the famous image used by W. E. B. Du Bois, who recognised how much Black singers, through

---

[37] White, *American Negro Folk Songs*, p. 27.
[38] Maud Cuney-Hare, *Negro Musicians and Their Music* (Washington, D.C.: Associated Publishers, 1936).
[39] Odum and Johnson, *The Negro and His Songs*, p. 19; Frederickson, *The Black Image*.
[40] Saidiya V. Hartman, *Scenes of Subjection: Terror, Slavery, and Self-Making in Nineteenth-Century America* (Oxford University Press, 1997), p. 36.

fear of loss or censure, had to erase: 'Over the inner thoughts of the slaves and their relations one with another the shadow of fear ever hung, so that we get but glimpses here and there, and also with them, eloquent omissions and silences.'[41] These erasures stand in for explicit critiques of bondage, which are conveyed as allegorical content, tone and rhythm. They recall the silences of Wyatt's hind, Halpern's dead detainee, the soldered mouth of the dead housewife in Dickinson's poem, the voices of the drowned in Philip's *Zong!* and the historical imposition of silence as a disciplinary regime in the Enlightened prisons. But the songs exist: through the determination of their singers, and in part through the work of the folklorists critiqued in this chapter, we can hear the eloquence of the lyric poets of chattel slavery. The song's opacity, a word Hartman uses in the sense developed by Édouard Glissant, also troubles the distinctions 'between joy and sorrow, toil and leisure'. I will turn now to the songs' function as toil.

Work Songs, Song Work

Fig. 7.1a/b is a manuscript, held in the Gloucestershire County Archives, of a song performed by enslaved people working in a Barbados sugarcane field.[42] The path of its transmission is marked by whiteness and authority: it was 'heard' by Dr William Dickson, 'who lived several years in the West Indies', where he was Secretary to Edward Hay, the governor of Barbados in 1772–9. It was then 'taken down in Notes by G. S.', Granville Sharp, an abolitionist whose involvement in the *Zong* case I have discussed, and who will reappear in Phillis Wheatley's company in Chapter 12. There are two rough copies and one fair copy of the song in the archives; the fair copy is entitled 'A Song of the Negro slaves at Barbados' on the verso, while the second rough copy crosses out 'Negro' and replaces it with 'An African Song or Chant', foregrounding the song's diasporic origins. According to Roger Gibbs and Julie Courtney this dirge is less syncretic than other, later Barbadian songs, and its two-bar form owes much to African music.[43] Its antiphonal structure is consistent with work songs from the United States into the twentieth century: 'a single Negro (while at work with the rest of the Gang) leads the song, and the others join in Chorus at the end of every song'.

[41] W. E. B. Du Bois, *The Souls of Black Folk* (New York: Knopf, [1903] 1993), p. 203.
[42] Gloucestershire County Archives, MS D3549/13/3/27.
[43] Roger Gibbs and Julie Courtney, 'Nomination Form, International Memory of the World Register: An African Song or Chant from Barbados', *UNESCO*: en.unesco.org/memoryoftheworld/registry/223 (accessed 4 May 2021).

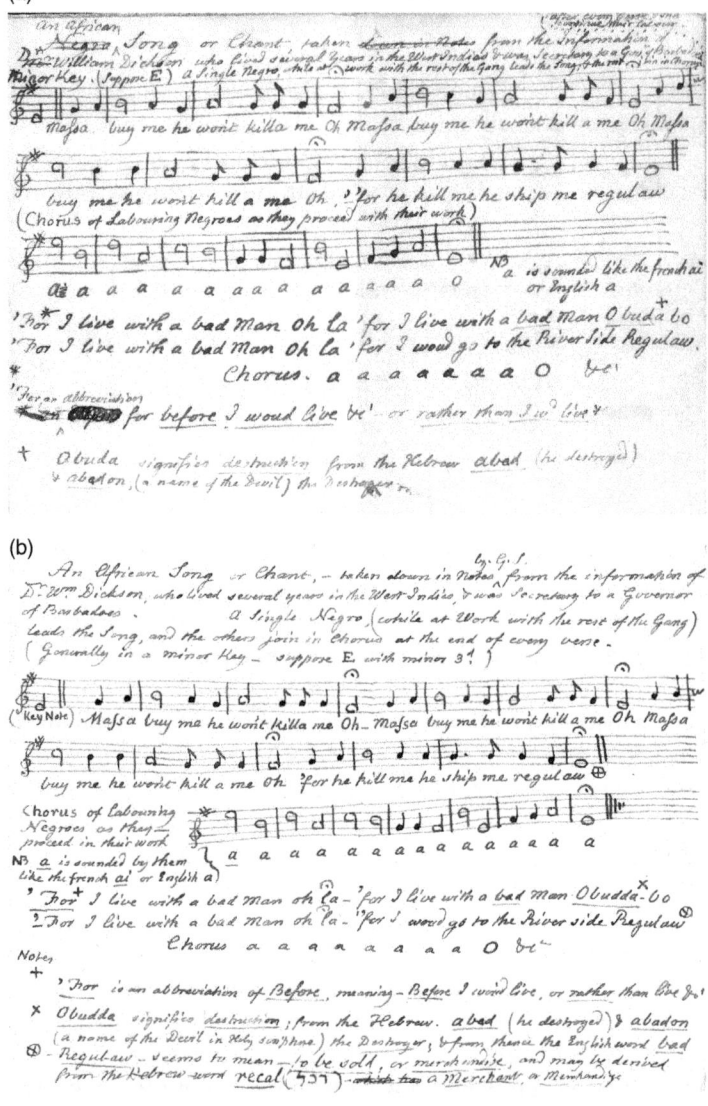

Fig. 7.1a and 7.1b 'An African Song or Chant', transcribed by Granville Sharp 'from the information of Dr William Dickson who lived several years in the West Indies and was secretary to a Governor of Barbados', Gloucestershire County Archives, MS D3549/13/3/27, draft (a) and fair copy (b).

Sharp's annotations expand on and define the contractions that keep the song's rhythm: *for* for *Before* or *rather*, 'meaning – <u>Before</u> I wou'd live, or <u>rather</u> than live die'. The note is expansive, the song contractive. But the notes don't quite know what to do with the phrase 'ship me regulaw', or with the word 'Obudda'. The latter is said to signify '<u>destruction</u>; from the Hebrew <u>abad</u> (he destroyed) & <u>abadon</u> (a name of the Devil in Holy scripture) the <u>Destroyer</u>; and from thence the English word <u>bad</u>'. It also suggests that '<u>Regulaw</u>' (not regular) 'seems to mean – <u>to be sold</u>, or <u>merchandise</u>, and may be derived from the Hebrew word <u>recal</u> – a <u>Merchant</u>, or <u>Merchandize</u>'. These conjectural etymologies set the song in a context – useful for abolitionist rhetoric – of the lamentations of the Israelites during their captivity. Similarly, he specifies that the 'a' 'is sounded by them like the French *ai* or English *a*', anchoring their tones in familiar European language sounds.

The affiliations and named identities of the white note-takers contrast with the anonymous singers identified simply as 'single Negro' and 'Gang'. Both Dickson, as secretary, and Sharp, as note-taker, are agents of written textuality; the singers are participants in the making and preservation of oral culture. Dickson was an abolitionist who wrote multiple works arguing for the end of the slave trade and the mitigation of existing slavery in the West Indies. His collection of *Letters on Slavery* (1789) details atrocities committed against enslaved people across the Caribbean. It concludes by addressing the white inhabitants of Barbados and criticising their 'barbarous doctrine': 'The present language of your law, and, I am sorry to add, of your practice, is, … "if a black man murder a white man he ought to expire by slow and barbarous tortures; but if a white man murder a black man he ought to be acquitted."'[44] Dickson knew very well that the master who bought these singers might well kill them. The song's despairing logic and fear of violence appealed directly to Dickson's abolitionist sentiments. He 'heard' the song, as if it was not being performed *for* him. But is the song a rhetorical question posed *to* Dickson, knowing he overhears? Is Dickson, as a person close to governmental authority, being asked to take notice that the master is a 'bad man'? Is Dickson himself a 'bad man', whose arguments for mitigation are nothing more than a way to 'ship me regulaw'? Dickson's overhearing, one imagines, was a cessation from his work: he must have stopped to listen to the workers as they sang; but it was also part of his work, because he overheard them in his function as secretary to the governor. The song is certainly part of the singers' work; as the notes

---

[44] William Dickson, *Letters on Slavery* (London: J. Phillips for J. Johnson, 1789), p. 169.

specify, they don't stop work to sing it: 'Chorus of labouring Negroes as they proceed in their work'.

Although this is an early example of a transcription, made by white British listeners to a song by enslaved Africans in Barbados, it shares many features with the anthologies of African American songs discussed in this chapter: the complex relation between written and oral expression, the emphasis on language as the song's chief representable element (while performance context and rhythm are unrepresentable), the under-specified social and political situations in which the listener encounters and transmits these transcriptions – hearing and overhearing, performing and performing *for*. But what I want to call attention to is the way this transcription is framed. Like the carceral symbolism of chains, keys and walls that surrounded the poems in *San Quentin Days*, Sharp's notes pin the song to its Western musical notation, in the middle of a written text that entirely surrounds the music.

Abolitionists idealised song as the testimony to a collective history of misery and endurance. It was the irruption of subjectivity and authenticity in the midst of murderous exploitation: the sound of transfiguration.[45] But as Eric Lott puts it, the spirituals and work songs were also 'command performances', 'generated out of forced labour, only to be forbidden certain musical forms of their own, from drumming to religious worship'.[46] African captives were forced to sing and dance during the Middle Passage to preserve them from sickness.[47] An eyewitness testified to the British Parliament in 1790–1 how:

> After meals they are made to jump in their irons [up on the deck]. This is called dancing by the slave-dealers. ... In his ship even those who had the flux, scurvy, and such edematous swellings in their legs as made it painful to them to move at all, were compelled to dance by the cat ... The captain ordered them to sing, and they sung songs of sorrow.[48]

They were also forced to sing in the coffle, a long chain to which enslaved people were handcuffed when they were being transported over land. Eileen Southern reprints one such song, which includes lines like: 'We are stolen and sold to Georgia, will you go along with me?,' 'See wives and

---

[45] Paul Gilroy, *The Black Atlantic: Modernity and Double Consciousness* (London: Verso, 1993), p. 37.
[46] Eric Lott, 'Songs Are Like Tattoos: A Response', *New Literary History* 46.4 (Autumn 2015), pp. 823–830 (827).
[47] Epstein, *Sinful Tunes*, Prologue.
[48] *An Abstract of the Evidence Delivered Before a Select Committee of the House of Commons in the Years 1790 and 1791* (London, 1791), pp. 33-6. Cited in David Brion Davis, *Inhuman Bondage: The Rise and Fall of Slavery in the New World* (Oxford University Press, 2006), p. 92.

husbands sold apart, / The children's screams! – it breaks my heart.'⁴⁹ This song communicates the shared grief of the singers, but it is also a compulsory performance, enforced by threat of physical violence. Similarly, the Rev John Sella Martin, who was born to an enslaved woman in 1832 in North Carolina, recalled that people chained together in the coffle were forced to 'strike up lively', or sing, so as 'to prevent among the crowd of negroes who usually gather on such occasions, any expressions of sorrow for those who are being torn from them'; but the negroes 'often turn the song thus demanded of them into a farewell dirge'.⁵⁰

As Hartman and Dennis Childs have both shown, enslaved people in the Americas were forced to perform their acquiescence in song and dance, forms of 'unproductive' work that 'were as essential to the formation of white mastery as their "productive" labour in cotton, rice, tobacco, and sugarcane fields'.⁵¹ 'I Live with a Bad Man' is such a work song. Like many of the other songs collected by white folklorists discussed in this chapter, it resembled, facilitated or even was work. When he revises his account of the sorrow songs for *My Bondage and My Freedom* (1855), Douglass emphasises this fact first:

> Slaves are generally expected to sing as well as to work. A silent slave is not liked by masters or overseers. '*Make a noise,*' '*make a noise,*' and '*bear a hand,*' are the words usually addressed to slaves when there is silence amongst them.⁵²

Enslaved people may sing unbidden, to lament their condition or enjoy a rare moment of respite and sociability; but they are also forced to sing in order to let the overseer know where they are and that they are moving on with the work.

Overseers demanded happy, sprightly rhythms instead of slow, dolorous ones because they increased outputs. As Frances Anne Kemble recalled, 'I have heard that many of the masters and overseers on these plantations prohibit melancholy tunes or words and encourage nothing but cheerful music and senseless words, deprecating the effect of sadder strains upon the slaves.'⁵³ They also attempted to regulate the pace of work by manipulating

---

⁴⁹ Southern, *Music of Black Americans*, pp. 158–9.
⁵⁰ John W. Blassingame (ed.), *Slave Testimony: Two Centuries of Letters, Speeches, Interviews, and Autobiographies* (Baton Rouge: Louisiana State University Press, 1977), p. 705.
⁵¹ Dennis Childs, *Slaves of the State: Black Incarceration from the Chain Gang to the Penitentiary* (Minneapolis: University of Minnesota Press, 2015), p. 98.
⁵² Douglass, *Autobiographies*, p. 184.
⁵³ Frances Anne Kemble, *Journal of a Residence on a Georgian Plantation in 1838–1839*, ed. John A. Scott (London: Jonathan Cape, 1961), p. 164.

the musical tempo of enslaved singers.⁵⁴ John Mason Brown, for example, said that 'Long ago, when the mowing-machine and reaper were as yet unheard of, it was not uncommon to see, in a Kentucky harvest-field, fifteen or twenty "cradlers" swinging their brawny arms in unison as they cut the ripened grain, and moving with the regulated cadence of the leader's song.'⁵⁵ Many ethnographers noted that, unlike white work gangs, African American ones often organised the timing of their own labour through music: a caller would set the pace for lifting heavy rails, striking with hoes or hammers, cutting trees and so forth, not only to expedite the work but to protect the safety of workers. As Joel Dinerstein notes, the caller 'functioned as a work-conductor, whose expertise included rhythmic steadiness, verbal dexterity, improvisation, and a management ability to focus a diverse crew of labourers on tasks requiring great collective effort'.⁵⁶ Work songs integrate the individual with the collective, and transform care, efficiency and mutual aid into rhythm.

The song traditions developed on the plantation continued to be used in penal contexts. Childs analyses the continuity between the 'musical slave' and the 'prison neoslave': like the dancing and singing 'on the decks of slave ships, auction blocks, and during plantation holiday celebrations in order to stimulate the African's "contentedness" with bondage, black postbellum prisoners have been regularly used as theatrical, musical, athletic, and filmic showpieces at Angola and other zones of neoslavery'.⁵⁷ He cites a man forced to work on a Florida chain-gang who described how 'after beating us well all week [the guard captain] and his guards would come and make us sing and dance for them' (28). Childs calls such forced performances in former plantations, now prisons, a kind of 'criminal minstrelsy' (103). It is apparent also in the performances collected by the Lomaxes. Alan Lomax recalls how: 'In 1933 forty convicts, assembled by the warden at shotgun point for a Library of Congress recording session, blasted our microphone with their roaring call for Rosie.'⁵⁸ The Lomaxes sought out the prison's quietest rooms to make their recordings; 'at one penitentiary, where the echoes interfered, we were offered the soundproof execution room, which contained as its sole piece of furniture the grim electric chain, the "hot seat," covered with a white sheet'.⁵⁹ When the Lomaxes set up

---

⁵⁴ Cruz, *Culture on the Margins*, p. 53.   ⁵⁵ Brown, 'Songs of the Slave', p. 620.
⁵⁶ Joel Dinerstein, *Swinging the Machine: Modernity, Technology, and African American Culture between the World Wars* (Amherst and Boston: University of Massachusetts Press, 2003), p. 83.
⁵⁷ Childs, *Slaves of the State*, p. 15.   ⁵⁸ Lomax, *Land Where the Blues Began*, p. 265.
⁵⁹ John A. Lomax and Alan Lomax, *Negro Folk Songs as Sung by Lead Belly* (New York: Macmillan, 1936), p. 38.

their recording studio in the armoury of State Farm, guards came in throughout the day to arm themselves as the musicians performed.[60] As he and his father contemplated the sadness of the songs they recorded, they pondered, 'Was it the forbidding iron bars, the stripes, the clank of occasional shackles, the cruel-looking black bullwhip four feet long, which in some places hung in plain sight inside the door of the main hall – was it such surroundings that made the songs seem sad?'[61]

Even in such conditions, the songs also encode forms of resistance for anyone willing to listen. At another site, the Lomaxes try to get an imprisoned man called Black Samson, 'whom we found breaking rocks in the Nashville State Penitentiary', to sing the Levee Camp Holler. Samson demurs; he has found religion and fears he will go to hell if he sings a secular song. 'At last, however, when the warden had especially urged him to sing, he stepped in front of our microphone and, much to our surprise, when he had made sure that his words were being recorded, said: "It's sho hard liens dat a poor nigger's got to sing a worl'ly song, when he's tryin' to be sancrified; but de warden's ast me, so I guess I'll have to.'[62] The warden's 'especial urging' makes this a command performance, but it is important to hear how Samson ensures there is a record of his dissent.

The coercion involved in these performances is an important part of how white folklorists such as the Lomaxes *created* the conditions they were looking to document as undisturbed sites of cultural excavation. Some of them were aware of this ethnographic dilemma. Odum and Johnson offer an anecdote about a university dean listening to an African American road gang working in front of his house. He sits on his wall, assuming the workers are oblivious to his presence: 'He marvelled that the words of the song he could not gather; nevertheless he would be persistent, he would get them.' Eventually he makes them out, and what he hears is a song about himself: 'White man settin' on wall all day long, / Wastin' his time, wastin' his time.' The parable speaks to the problems of gathering an 'authentic' folk song untroubled by the participation of the observer. Like the person overhearing the prisoner's 'solitary lament', the university dean is in a position of adjacency to the song of the road gang. But the road gang singers are not isolated individuals, and they do not affect ignorance that anyone is listening.

---

[60] Lomax, *Adventures*, p. 135.
[61] John A. Lomax and Alan Lomax, *American Ballads and Folk Songs* (New York: Macmillan, 1934), p. xxxii.
[62] Lomax and Lomax, *American Ballads*, p. 49.

A similar example can be found in the account by Charles Peabody of an archaeological excavation in Mississippi in 1901–2. Peabody overhears the singing of the African American workers employed to dig trenches. 'Busy archaeologically, we had not very much time left for folk-lore, in itself of not easy excavation, but willy-nilly our ears were beset with an abundance of ethnological material,' he writes.[63] While the collection of the archaeological material involves hard work (largely done by the Black labourers) and determination, the collection of the ethnological material is easy; it is in the air rather than the ground. Some of the songs Peabody hears are work songs that organise the rhythms of the dig; others are spirituals. But some, he acknowledges, are 'used to convey hints to us up above', such as the following:

One Saturday, a half-holiday, a sing-song came out of the trench,

Mighty long half day, Capta-i-n,

and one evening when my companion and I were playing a game of mumble-the-peg, our final occupation before closing work, our chorus shouted for us to hear,

I'm so tired I'm most dead,
Sittin' up there playing mumble-peg.

(150)

The encoding of their complaints in a song that may be overheard allows the singers a certain measure of deniability. The workers' improvisatory talents are not available for every occasion, however; Peabody complains that 'occasionally we would get them to sing to us with the guitar, but the spontaneity was lacking and the repertoire was limited'; and when the workers are 'asked to sing for my wife while she was with us on a visit, they suddenly found it too hot' (150–1). These few notes are all the residue the folkloric record provides of the singers' own experience of being compelled to perform either the labour of digging, or the labour of singing on cue.

If song was work, then it can hardly be surprising that some of the singers hoped to be compensated for their labours. The Lomaxes were perceived by their informants as being engaged in more than just an exercise in collection. John Lomax tells a story of how a letter he wrote requesting permission to record at a prison outside Columbia, South Carolina, passed along the grapevine. Eventually, it was rumoured among the prisoners that 'a man from Washington was coming to

---

[63] Charles Peabody, 'Notes on Negro Music', *The Journal of American Folklore* 16.62 (1903), pp. 148–52 (148).

investigate the prison system of South Carolina. Any prisoner who had a complaint against the food or the brutalities of the guards, or thought he should be pardoned, would be given a hearing. The New Deal was going to be extended to the convicts.' Lomax could not gain access to the prison, because – the governors said – 'these men were ready to revolt' and saw him as an agent of the state and a possible means of their deliverance.[64] He treats the incident as an unfortunate confusion; but it reveals how his informants perceived his power, and the potential rewards of performing for him. Later, in a moment which bears an uncomfortable similarity to the convict leasing system,[65] Lomax's request that a particularly talented performer known as 'Iron Head' should be released on parole to him is granted (144).

Such rumours are perhaps unsurprising, given that the Lomaxes popularised a story that Leadbelly was released from imprisonment by his singing: a literalisation of the emancipatory powers of song. Leadbelly told them that prison governor Pat Neff 'sho was crazy 'bout my singin' an dancin'. Ev'y time I'd sing a new song or cut a few steps he'd roll me a bran-new silver dollar 'cross the flo.'[66] When he left office a year later, Neff pardoned Leadbelly. The Lomaxes commented: 'With intelligence and cunning and courage he had sung his way out of a thirty-year sentence, after only six and a half years in the penitentiary' (22). Once released from prison and taken up by the Lomaxes, Leadbelly performed for them instead – as well as working as John's 'body servant', laying out his clothes, drawing

---

[64] Lomax, *Adventures*, pp. 132–4.

[65] The convict leasing system took advantage of the exception in the 13th Amendment – 'Neither slavery nor involuntary servitude, except as a punishment for crime whereof the party shall have been duly convicted, shall exist within the United States' – to continue enslaving people post-Emancipation. Under this system, convicted people were rented by landowners, many of whom were former enslavers, to perform hard labour on plantations. Many illiterate, formerly enslaved people were forced to sign contracts with their former owners, binding themselves to servitude and criminalising them if they left the plantation. Georgia was the first state to implement the convict lease system, in 1868; Alabama the last state to outlaw it, in 1928. It has been argued that leasing was actually worse than slavery for the convict, in whom the landowner had not invested his capital, so it didn't much matter if he worked the convict to death. In Alabama in 1870, prison officials reported that more than 40 percent of the convicts they leased had died. See Angela Y. Davis, 'From the Prison of Slavery to the Slavery of Prison: Frederick Douglass and the Convict Lease System', in *The Angela Y. Davis Reader*, ed. Joy James (Oxford and Malden: Blackwell, 1998), pp. 74–96; David M. Oshinsky, *"Worse Than Slavery": Parchman Farm and the Ordeal of Jim Crow Justice* (New York: Free Press, 1996); Matthew Mancini, *One Dies, Get Another: Convict Leasing in the American South, 1866–1928* (Columbia: University of South Carolina Press, 1996); Alex Lichtenstein, *Twice the Work of Free Labor: The Political Economy of Convict Labor in the New South* (London: Verso, 1996); and Pete Daniel, *The Shadow of Slavery: Peonage in the South, 1901–1969* (Champaign: University of Illinois Press, 1990).

[66] Lomax and Lomax, *Negro Folk Songs*, p. 21.

his bath, bringing him coffee and driving him around the country. John held back the profits from Leadbelly's performances, giving him a weekly allowance so Leadbelly wouldn't spend all his money on drink. Their relationship, which grew increasingly fraught, shows how the Lomaxes elided artistic performance with waged (and unwaged) labour and paternalistic control. Leadbelly's singing is part of the repertoire of services he is expected to perform for his white bosses, while they treat him like a talented child.

This extractive relation to their informants continued into the 1980s. Alan Lomax took old-timers from a Greenville bar to perform their traditional songs for the camera; they 'formed up in a ragged line with their heavy hoes, and, staggering a bit, they advanced through the shimmering mirage of heat waves toward the camera, swinging their heavy hoes with the fervor that had cultivated the gardens of Africa and the Plantations of the South'.[67] He films them re-enacting their field work on Parchman Farm – a former plantation converted into a prison. The artists are doing work for the collector. The Lomax recordings are celebrated as a monumental contribution to the history of US American folkways; they were vitally important in preserving and expanding the idea of an American national culture to include the music of people of colour and working-class artists. But these performance conditions make their recordings awkward exemplars of humanist notions about the inalienability of creative freedom and the endurance of and through art in conditions of oppression.

Dunbar's Conflicted Corn Song

Tensions between authentic, transcendent self-expression and performance under duress for white audiences can be traced through much of the poetry of Paul Laurence Dunbar. Dunbar's own aesthetic estimation of Black song varies, from the celebratory 'When Malindy Sings' to the critical poetics of 'Prometheus', where he complains 'We have no singers' like Shelley;

> We tinkle where old poets used to storm
> We lack their substance tho' we keep their form:
> We strum our banjo-strings and call them lyres.[68]

---

[67] Lomax, *Land Where the Blues Began*, p. 265.
[68] Paul Laurence Dunbar, *The Collected Poetry*, ed. Joanne M. Braxton (Charlottesville: University Press of Virginia, 1993), p. 117.

This ambivalence shows up particularly in his (often ironic) poems of nostalgia. Dunbar's 'The Voice of the Banjo' recalls the 'honey of the past', the joys and the 'care-free songs when labour's hour was o'er' (124). Song represents the relief from work and the pleasure of sharing leisure time with a community of labourers. But the poem also aligns the music of that honeyed past with 'the sweetness of the baying of the hounds'. It is hard, given the ubiquity of the hounds in chasing down enslaved or convicted fugitives, to hear that 'baying' as anything sweet.

Dunbar, born in Ohio in 1872 to parents who had been enslaved, necessarily imagined slavery differently than those who had experienced it directly. But many of his poems are infused with the strain of representing African American experience for a censorious white readership. His most famous poem, 'We Wear the Mask', confesses that though 'We sing', we also cry out to God for deliverance from our pain. 'With torn and bleeding hearts we smile,' he writes in this rondeau, which Geoffrey Jacques has argued is a version of Wyatt's 'What vayleth trouthe?'[69] We have seen that 'torn' and turned, hunted and haunted subjects are important elements in Wyatt's contestations of sovereignty. Dunbar's revision of Wyatt also draws out the contemporary contexts in which African American hearts may be 'torn and bleeding'. This tension between a purely literary referentiality, and one that accounts for anti-Black violence, can be found across Dunbar's work, particularly in its shifts between the mannered literary English of middlebrow white culture and the dialect poems for which he was most enthusiastically praised by white audiences.[70] As Fahamisha Patricia Brown notes, Dunbar was a member of the Local Colour movement, which 'gave rise to an increasing amount of regional and dialect poetry in the United States'.[71] But he regretted in 'The Poet' that the world ignored his poetry's 'deeper note' and instead 'turned to praise / A jingle in a broken tongue'.

These tensions are apparent in 'A Corn Song', a poem that Afro-British composer Samuel Coleridge-Taylor set to music in 1897.[72] Corn-shucking was

---

[69] Dunbar, *Collected Poetry*, p. 71; Geoffrey Jacques, 'A Change in the Weather: Modernist Imagination, African American Imaginary', PhD diss., City University of New York, 2004. Cited in James Smethurst, 'Paul Laurence Dunbar and Turn-into-the-20th-Century African American Dualism', *African American Review* 41.2 (Summer 2007), pp. 377–86 (380).
[70] Marcellus Blount, 'The Preacherly Text: African American Poetry and Vernacular Performance', *PMLA* 107.3 (May 1992), pp. 582–93.
[71] Fahamisha Patricia Brown, *Performing the Word: African-American Poetry as Vernacular Culture* (New Brunswick: Rutgers University Press, 1999), p. 34.
[72] Dunbar, *Collected Poetry*, p. 59; Tsitsi Jaji, 'Art Song Poetics: Performing Samuel Coleridge-Taylor's Setting of Paul L. Dunbar's "A Corn Song"', *J19* 1.1 (Spring 2013), pp. 201–6.

traditionally a time of festivity on the plantation, when white and Black labourers participated in races, wrestling and drinking, and the dance known as 'patting Juba' went on through the night.[73] In Dunbar's 'Corn Song', this festive note is absent. Instead, the poem offers sepia portraits of slavery and loneliness. 'On the wide veranda white, / In the purple failing light, / Sits the master while the sun is lowly burning' (ll. 1–3). As the enslaver sits and reflects, the enslaved singers return home with 'laboured, slow and weary' steps (l. 13), their song a literal summary of their bodily actions:

> Oh, we hoe de co'n
> Since de ehly mo'n;
> Now de sinkin' sun
> Says de day is done.
>
> (ll. 7–10)

Their song reckons the passing time through their labour: 'Sing, at it's pain, as any Workman – / Notching the fall of the even Sun,' as Dickinson wrote. Sung at sunset, the corn song mirrors the poet's description of how the sunset appears to (or for) the 'master'. Their brave, strong spirits 'Find a comforter in song' (l. 15), and the enslaver finds comfort in them. The song's 'burden, full and sweet' (l. 22) – used in the sense of a refrain, though resonating with the burden of their labour – accompanies them as they draw near to 'the cabin's restful shelter' (l. 26). Their laborious movement offers a realistic contrast to the homeward-bound speakers so often found in pastoral poems (I think, for example, of the conclusion of John Milton's 'Lycidas', but also of the ending of Du Bois's chapter on the sorrow songs, where the traveller 'girds himself, and sets his face toward the Morning, and goes his way'). Returning home is a return to a brief respite from labour, but it is also a return to the centre of their enslavement.

In 'A Corn Song', Dunbar's poetic imagination can move with ease between the spaces of the enslaver's private contemplation and the singers' communal lament. The poem works through two modes: Standard and Black vernacular English, the language of the master and that of the enslaved singers. In its structure, it recalls John Greenleaf Whittier's poem 'At Port Royal' or James Weldon Johnson's 'O Black and Unknown Bards' or even Carolyn Baxter's poem discussed in Chapter 4, all of which contain embedded sorrow songs. The poetic speaker in

---

[73] Lewis W. Paine, from *Six Years in a Georgia Prison* (1851), in *Readings in Black American Music*, ed. Eileen Southern (New York: Norton, 1971), pp. 90–1.

Dunbar's poem moves between the perspective of the enslaver, overhearing the singers, and that of the singers, watching (out for) the enslaver's mood:

> And a tear is in the eye
> Of the master sitting by,
> As he listens to the echoes low-replying,
> To the music's fading calls
> As it faints away and falls
> Into silence, deep within the cabin dying.
>
> (ll. 31–6)

Here, the song is identified by the master's tear: by its emotional affect on the listener. But the master's tears while listening to the song are very different from Douglass's.

The poem's metre consists of a heavily accented two-beat lines followed by a three-beat line whose trailing feminine ending mimic the 'dying' strain of the song. That strain, fading into silence, reflects the fading of the antebellum regime, much as in Dunbar's poem 'The Deserted Plantation', whose empty house and silent fields signal the absence of those who might have made this music, and who have abandoned the Jim Crow South: 'An' de banjo's voice is silent in de qua'ters, / D'ain't a hymn ner co'n-song ringin' in de air' (ll. 13–14, p. 67). Michael Cohen notes how the music of 'A Corn Song' is 'available to the master without any accompanying awareness of the singers', thus dislodging the song from the economy and the labour that produced it.[74] We'll encounter the claim that Southern culture was the product of the leisure of its elite, and the erasure of Black productivity and cultural work, in the next chapter. But both 'A Corn Song' and 'The Deserted Plantation' are more complicated than they appear. Alongside their sentimentality, and assimilation of a nostalgic white Southern aesthetic, the poems preserve in writing an oral tradition that testifies to Black presence. In the form of the labourer who will not emigrate in 'The Deserted Plantation', or the mobile speaker in 'A Corn Song' who can frame the nostalgia of the plantation and preserve and disseminate that song as his own through written publication, the African American singer gets the last word.

Against the Grain

Dunbar's dialect poems are the site of substantial critical vexation. Do these poems give voice to censored and repressed Black speakers, or mollify

---

[74] Michael Cohen, 'Paul Laurence Dunbar and the Genres of Dialect', *African American Review* 41:2 (Summer 2007), pp. 247–57 (253).

racist stereotypes? Are they attempts at authenticity, or a form of minstrelsy? Without wishing to enter into these debates, I would argue that they have much in common with the tensions around representing Black speech that can also be found in white ethnography. From the late eighteenth century onwards, Black speech was portrayed as resistant to transcription: 'in an ethnographic exchange, black voices did not sound like they could be indexed to their speakers'.[75] Dialect was a marker of the text's 'oral authenticity', and it enabled the songs to circulate 'as the markers of racial history, even after they were detached from their initial sites of transmission by way of print'.[76] But white collectors represented the 'easy and careless speech' of African American informants,[77] with its 'quarter tones, slides, curlecues, indefinite pitches, irregular shifting rhythms, intentional striking of notes off beat',[78] the sounds that are central to Philip's oral poetics, as fugitive from transcription.

The field holler is one example that interested folklorists very much, as 'a way of singing – free, gliding from a sustained high note down to the lowest register the singer can reach, often ending there in a grunt. It is marked by spontaneous and unpredictable changes in rhythm.'[79] John Lomax recalls hearing the holler of a singer called Enoch:

> From far off in the darkness long, lonesome, full-voiced, brooding notes pierced the stillness of a perfect night, indescribable and unforgettable. Starting on a low note, the cry reached a crescendo in such pervasive volume and intensity that it seemed to fill the black void of darkness. The sound came from everywhere and nowhere. Then the cry shaded downward, with the lower notes thrice repeated. Suddenly silence.[80]

Though it seems to come from nowhere and everywhere, the holler marks a very specific location; it is a 'solo' performed by a singular, virtuosic singer that invites a temporally and spatially extended, antiphonal call and response.[81] This practice of long-distance communication through music may be traceable to west Africa. The holler's wordless coloratura conveys information through tone in the tradition of the African talking drum.[82]

---

[75] Wagner, *Disturbing the Peace*, p. 210. Other examples are given by Tim Armstrong, *The Logic of Slavery: Debt, Technology, and Pain in American Literature* (Cambridge University Press, 2012), p. 148.
[76] Cohen, 'Paul Laurence Dunbar', p. 251.
[77] Odum and Johnson, *The Negro and His Songs*, p. 10.
[78] Lawrence Gellert, *Negro Songs of Protest* (New York: American Music League, 1936), preface.
[79] Lomax and Lomax, *Negro Folk Songs*, p. 113.   [80] Lomax, *Adventures*, p. 172.
[81] Epstein, *Sinful Tunes*, p. 182; citing Frederick Law Olmsted, *A Journey in the Seabord Slave States in the Years 1853–1854* (New York: G. P. Putnam's Sons, 1904), 2:19–20.
[82] White and White, *Sounds of Slavery*, pp. 20–5.

The range of sounds and tones produced by African American speakers, and the difficulty of their transcription, became 'the hallmark that accounted not only for slave music's tonal and rhythmic distinctiveness but also for its essential blackness, a lament turned around by later anthologists like James Weldon Johnson, who heard in this resistance an "elusive" essence that proved black songs "in their very nature" were not "susceptible to fixation" and were consequently only complete in performance', Bryan Wagner argues.[83] White folklorists were conscious of this elusiveness. They often comment on the inadequacy of their attempts to reproduce the living experience of performance: what Roland Barthes called the 'grain', which is 'the body in the voice as it sings, the hand as it writes, the limb as it performs'.[84] Whether they transcribe only the words of the songs, or invent settings for the melodies, white folklorists repeatedly emphasise that the songs cannot be adequately represented by textual marks. The songs are only fully real when they are being performed and embodied, in specific times and places. Walter Clyde Curry, a white medievalist at Vanderbilt University, described African American songs as 'rhythmical to the point of perfection':

> I myself have heard many of them chanted with and without the accompaniment of clapping hands, stamping feet, and swaying bodies. Unfortunately a large part of their liquid melody and flexibility of movement is lost through confinement in cold print; but when they are heard from a distance on quiet summer nights or clear Southern mornings, even the most fastidious ear is satisfied with the rhythmic pulse of them. That pathos of the Negro character which can never be quite adequately caught in words or transcribed in music is then augmented and intensified by the peculiar quality of the Negro voice, rich in overtones, quavering, weird, cadenced, throbbing with the sufferings of a race.[85]

The songs are not merely an oral tradition that eludes 'confinement in cold print' (the comparison of the written text to incarceration is a provocative one); it is specifically their rhythms and tones that give the songs their value, and those are things that a textual transcription is inadequate to represent. The written text will always be at 'a distance' from these scenes of performance. Their fugitive character 'can never be adequately caught'.

---

[83] Wagner, *Disturbing the Peace*, p. 211.
[84] Roland Barthes, *Image-Music-Text*, trans. Stephen Heath (New York: Hill and Wang, 1977), p. 188.
[85] Talley, *Negro Folk Rhymes*, pp. vi–vii.

The stylistic qualities of Black music – 'rhythmic complexity, gapped scales, overlapping of leader and chorus, bodily movement, extended repetition of short melodic phrases' – presented 'insoluble problems to the early collectors of slave music, who were able to do little more than notate the general outline of the melody'.[86] Some white collectors responded to these problems with apophasis, or some version of the argument that *you had to be there*. Another, emerging group of professional musicologists, folklorists and ethnographers took a 'more rationalistic, scientistic, and modern' approach.[87] They drew on efforts by comparative musicologists to develop methods and symbols to transcribe 'exotic' or non-Western music.[88] In this same period, prosodists including John Ruskin (in his *Elements of English Prosody*, 1880) and Sidney Lanier (*The Science of English Verse*, 1880) were also using musical notation to try to capture the rhythms of English poetic speech.[89]

But the new scientism was still ideological. Henry Edward Krehbiel, music critic for the *Tribune*, argues that Black music was often confined to the pentatonic, the 'oldest' scale, 'in which melody may be said to be naturally innate'. By contrast, 'the diatonic scale … as used in artistic music is a scientific evolution, and not altogether a product of nature'.[90] Black culture is natural, innate and archaic; white culture is evolved and scientific. Even the observation that 'tones are frequently employed which we have no musical characters to represent', as Thomas Fenner writes in 1874, does not lead to an admission of the inadequacy of Western musical notation.[91] Rather, it sets the songs apart, as retaining an excess that cannot be made to conform entirely to white Western musical norms.

Many of the negrophile collectors asserted that Black speech and song are hard to transcribe because they are 'natural' sounds closer to animal noises than to human voices. *Slave Songs of the United States* (1867) complains that 'the odd turns made in the throat and the curious rhythmic effect produced by single voices chiming in at different irregular intervals seem almost as impossible to place on the score as the singing of birds or the

---

[86] Epstein, *Sinful Tunes*, p. 217. [87] Cruz, *Culture on the Margins*, p. 4.
[88] Otto Abraham and Erich M. von Hornbostel, 'Vorschlage fur die Transkription exotischer Melodien', *Sammelbdnde der Internationalen Musikgesellschaft* (1909–10), pp. 1–25; 'Suggested Methods for the Transcription of Exotic Music', trans. George and Eve List, *Ethnomusicology* 38.3 (Autumn 1994), pp. 425–56. The article had a lasting influence on the field.
[89] See Yopie Prins, '"Break, Break, Break" into Song', in *Metre Matters: Verse Cultures of the Long Nineteenth Century*, ed. Jason David Hall (Athens, OH: Ohio University Press, 2011), pp. 105–34.
[90] Henry Edward Krehbiel, *Afro-American Folksongs: A Study in Racial and National Music* (New York: G. Schirmer, 1914), pp. 74, 72.
[91] Fenner, *Cabin and Plantation Songs*, p. iv.

tones of an Aeolian Harp'.⁹² As such, Black singers number amongst the 'organic Harps diversely framed' that the intellectual breeze sweeps over, from Coleridge's poem: simple and 'subject' instruments that transmit unthinkingly 'the one Life within us and abroad'. Similarly, John Lomax described song as the natural effusion of imprisoned African American men:

> He is endowed by nature with a strong sense of rhythm. His songs burst from him, when in his own environment, as naturally and as freely as those of a bird amid its native trees … . His is the real art of simplicity and naturalness. Moreover, the Negro in isolation, without books or newspapers, the radio or the telephone, sings for his own amusement, to relieve the tension of his loneliness and that of his companions in misfortune.⁹³

Lomax has thoroughly naturalised bondage, confusing his Black informants with animal life: prison is the 'native tree' in which the caged African American bird sings; and it is only natural that the Black man, whose songs burst from him naturally, and who is himself closer to nature than to reflection, performs that song. The bird is closely associated with lyric, whether it's Keats's nightingale, or Higginson's invocation of Emerson to identify Dickinson as a timid bird that must be 'named' without a gun. But in Paul Lawrence Dunbar's poem 'Sympathy' the caged bird does *not* sing 'a carol of joy or glee', the overheard expression of sentiment. Rather, the caged bird sings a 'prayer' and a 'plea' to Heaven: an eloquent expression of necessity to a specific if absent listener.⁹⁴

Like Lomax with his insistence that 'the Negro in isolation, without books or newspapers, the radio or the telephone' is the most authentic transmitter of a 'natural' folk tradition, the negrophile collectors sought out informants who did not have regular access to the technologies of the culture industry. Guy Johnson studied the folk culture of the Sea Islands in South Carolina whose unique culture Charlotte Forten (Grimké) had discussed in an 1864 article for *The Atlantic*.⁹⁵ St. Helena Island, 'being in an isolated culture area, is an excellent laboratory for the study of spirituals. Here is found little of that racial inferiority complex which for a time

---

⁹² William Francis Allen, Charles Pickard Ware and Lucy McKim Garrison (eds.), *Slave Songs of the United States* (Bedford, MA: Applewood Books, repr. 1867), p. 6.
⁹³ John A. Lomax, '"Sinful Songs" of the Southern Negro', *The Musical Quarterly* 20.2 (April 1934), pp. 177–87 (184).
⁹⁴ Many eighteenth-century writers criticised those who kept caged birds, in order to take pleasure from their singing, and compared the practice to imprisonment or slavery: see Ingrid H. Tague, *Animal Companions: Pets and Social Change in Eighteenth-Century Britain* (University Park: Pennsylvania State University Press, 2015), pp. 83–8.
⁹⁵ Charlotte Forten, 'Life on the Sea Islands', *The Atlantic* (May 1864).

threatened to destroy the spirituals in the up-country, and here there is felt comparatively little back-wash from the recent exploitation of Negro songs,' Johnson wrote.[96] The Lomaxes travelled the deep South, making recordings on the cotton plantations, and in lumber camps, farms and prisons. 'Although the spread of machine civilisation is rapidly making it hard to find folk singers, ballads are yet sung in this country.'[97] In a surprising twist on Mill's conceit of the authenticity of the lyric poet who sings his solitary lament in the isolation of a prison cell without knowing anyone is listening, Lomax argues that isolation preserves the American songs of bondage as a folk tradition: 'Because they still sing in unison with their work, because of this almost complete isolation and loneliness, because of the absence of "free-world" conventions in prison life, the Negro continues to create what we may rightly call folk-songs.'[98]

The Lomaxes were looking for the past, not the future: for 'the Negro who had had the least contact with jazz, the radio, and with the white man'.[99] In a letter to the Carnegie Foundation requesting funding, John Lomax argued that 'The Negro in the South is the target for such complex influences that it is hard to find genuine folk singing'; shame, and 'the radio with its flood of jazz, created in tearooms for the benefit of city-dwelling whites – all these things are killing the best and most genuine Negro folk songs'.[100] He proposed to go:

> where these influences are not yet dominant; where Negroes are almost entirely isolated from the whites, dependent upon the resources of their own group for amusement; where they are not only preserving a great body of traditional songs but are also creating new songs in the same idiom. (110)

That place, more often than not, was prison: the only place where the African American singer was fully 'protected' from the modernising influence of the phonograph, radio, telephone, newspaper or magazine, a place where poets and artists were forced to live a 'life of isolation', rather than voluntarily choosing one.

Just as Wordsworth turned to rural life in search of people who, 'from their rank in society and the sameness and narrow circle of their intercourse, being less under the influence of social vanity, ... convey their

---

[96] Guy Johnson, *Folk Culture on St. Helena Island, South Carolina* (Chapel Hill: University of North Carolina Press, 1930), pp. 65–6.
[97] Lomax and Lomax, *American Ballads*, pp. xxvi–xxvii.   [98] Lomax, '"Sinful Songs"', p. 184.
[99] Lomax and Lomax, *American Ballads*, p. xxx.   [100] Lomax, *Adventures*, p. 110.

feelings and notions in simple and unelaborated expressions',[101] Lomax searched the prison farm camps, where:

> the conditions were practically ideal. Here the Negro prisoners were segregated, often guarded by Negro trusties, with no social or other contacts with whites, except for occasional official relations. The convicts heard only the idioms of their own race. Many – often of greatest influence – were 'lifers' who had been confined in the penitentiary, a few as long as fifty years. They still sang the songs they had brought into confinement, and these songs had been entirely in the keeping of the black man .... Being naturally imitative, the Negro's singing, under the influence of the idiom and custom of his white neighbors, is unconsciously yet surely changed by white influence. He is apt to sing as he thinks the whites wish him to sing ... 'Learnin' Greek and Latin,' daily association with the whites, and modern education prove disastrous to the Negro's folk singing, destroying much of the quaint, innate beauty of his songs.[102]

According to Lomax, prison segregation preserves the African American heritage and idiom from the 'natural' instinct to imitate. Solitary confinement preserves the prisoner from the corroding influence of modernity – that is, from human companionship and civic participation. For him, the supposedly imitative nature of his informants is an innate tendency, not a survival strategy, or the mimicry which Homi K. Bhabha describes as the '*double* vision which in disclosing the ambivalence of colonial discourse also disrupts its authority'.[103]

Ventriloquising the Singer

In his 2016 book *Olio*, Tyehimba Jess responds to the silences and erasures in the negrophile archives. *Olio* speaks *for* such musicians as Scott Joplin, John William 'Blind' Boone, Thomas 'Blind Tom' Tom Wiggins, Sissieretta Jones and the Fisk Jubilee Singers, imagining how they felt when they were forced to perform. Jess makes use of some documentary materials, but his ventriloquisation of these artists is different from using verbatim material. It is a reparative work of imagination. For example, when 'Blind Tom Plays for Confederate Troops, 1863':

> The slave's hands dance free, unfettered, flying
> across ivory, feet stomping toward

---

[101] William Wordsworth, *Lyrical Ballads, and Other Poems, 1797–1800*, ed. James Butler and Karen Green (Ithaca, NY: Cornell University Press, 1992), p. 743.
[102] Lomax and Lomax, *American Ballads*, p. xxx.
[103] Homi K. Bhabha, *The Location of Culture* (London and New York: Routledge, [1994] 2004), p. 126.

> a crescendo that fills the forest pine,
> reminding the Rebs what they're fighting for –
> black, captive labor.[104]

This dramatic scene epitomises the dialectical nature of the sorrow song: the hands are free, the song is unfettered, but it is a product of (and incitement to maintain) 'black, captive labor'. Tom's playing is the expression of his humanity, and an inspiration to the people who keep him in bondage. 'A slaver's song at master's bidding' is a coerced performance, even if it is also a means of imagining his escape: 'Back turned to his piano, / he leans like a runner about to throw / himself to freedom through forest bramble.'

In a sequence of sonnets (in slant-rhymed couplets) that intersect the accounts of other musicians and artists, individual members of the Jubilee Singers are made to describe how they found music, or how it feels to perform it. Recalling 'Ma's singing would make our slave shack a palace' (35), one of the Jubilee Singers – Eliza Walker – says: 'When we sing, I feel / them songs getting freed up from tangled cane fields' (35). Song was transformative and elevating in captivity; now, it is the song itself that needs to be redeemed from the conditions of its production. But the poems also record an anxiety about the double nature of these songs. 'Once burst loose from human bondage, / do our songs still tow our pain like a mule?' (12). Celebrating their release from slavery in slavery's songs, the singers also keep alive the memory of pain and hard labour that was their origin; the songs are a 'heavy sack of achin / hymns, seedin' sable soul 'cross every nation' (166).

Black music in this book ranges from minstrelsy's 'Coon Songs' to the lyrics whose truth-content is a 'rambling mission / to prove how our souls are holy and human' (151). And this double nature is reflected throughout the poems' form and *mise en page*. Many are written in two columns, with different voices on either side of a divide; Jess calls this form the 'syncopated sonnet', and it can be read 'up, down, diagonally and interstitially'.[105] Form is a way of bringing the voices of these historical subjects into dialogue, and of keeping them separated (visually); but it also contributes to the intensely *written* nature of the text. Jess told an interviewer: 'Using form to distinguish the voices means that one is going to be speaking in sonnets while the other is speaking in a ghazal and the other is

---

[104] Tyehimba Jess, *Olio* (Seattle and New York: Wave Books, 2016), p. 15.
[105] Adam Fitzgerald, 'Tyehimba Jess on Excavating Popular Music Through Poetry,' *Literary Hub* (5 May 2016).

speaking in some version of golden shovel' (a form of the cento invented by Terrance Hayes).[106] But these speaking voices are strongly textural, their distinctions created through formal devices of print on the page rather than differences in timbre, rhythm, pitch or the other features of the spoken voice that tend to elude transcription.

One of these formalist representations of distinct voices is a sequence of 'syncopated sonnets' spoken by Millie and Christine McKoy, African American conjoined twins who were exhibited for money and also sang (and whose earnings allowed them eventually to buy the plantation on which they were born). In Jess's butterfly-shaped poems, the twins' separate voices are intermittently joined across the division of their subjectivities by being written continuously across the centre of the page. This formal mimesis of splitting and conjunction also represent the dialectical relationship between freedom and bondage, conditions that co-exist, define and fulfil each other, and are at once opposite and inseparable. Similarly, the 'Jubilee' poems form a corona – a suite of poems in which the last line of the preceding poem becomes the first line of the succeeding one. This circularity links the individual utterances together into a continuous chorus and symbolises the endurance of the past in the present: 'Circle round their stories to burrow through time' (222). That circling can be physically enacted, as the book's Appendix demonstrates, by removing pages from the book along prepared perforations and folding them in different forms – cylinder, rectangle, torus – to recombine the parts into new forms of syntax, new assertions (213–14). Jess commented that the form of the corona of sonnets and the 'circular structure to the book … speak to the circular, connected nature of history'.[107] The book's formal and structural circularities reflect the circle of Black death perpetuated by white supremacy, and the continuity from chattel slavery to mass incarceration.

We've seen that M. NourbeSe Philip also responds formally to absences in the legal archive, using the page space and the destruction of the word and the legal document in a mimesis of the violence of slavery. Like *Zong!*, *Olio*'s experimentation with form and *mise-en-page* seems mimetic; but the drives in the two books are very dissimilar. Where Jess uses form to bring the perspective of enslaver and enslaved musician into an uncomfortable proximity, encouraging the reader to weigh up the differences in their rhetoric or lived perspectives, Philip disperses and destabilises the subject positions that coalesce around specific identities. In his poem 'leadbelly v.

---

[106] Bob Sykora and Brooke Schifano, 'Interview: Tyehimba Jess,' *Breakwater Review* (18 January 2017).
[107] Fitzgerald, 'Tyehimba Jess.'

lomax at the modern language association conference, 1934', Jess confronts – in the form of two columns, one with Leadbelly's view, the other Lomax's – the performance expectations of the Lomaxes with (what he imagines to be) the perspectives of the performers.[108] Jess invites the reader to reorder the book, working on the page to fashion new combinations; but the material from which those combinations are made is dualistic. Philip's text is polyvocal, and the roles of enslaver, enslaved person, reader and writer drift through each other, resisting fixity or order. That drift is part of her poem's ethical demand on the reader, and reflects Philip's belief – which she shares with Jess – that the history of slavery continues.

While invoking the spirits and voices of the ancestors through occult procedures, Philip explicitly does not try to 'fill in' historic gaps in the representation or respond to the unspeakability of genocide by speaking for the enslaved. Her poetics have informed Saidiya Hartman's question: 'How can narrative embody life in words and at the same time respect what we cannot know? … How does one revisit the scene of subjection without replicating the grammar of violence?'[109] Hartman warns that 'narrative restraint, the refusal to fill in the gaps and provide closure, is a requirement of this method, as is the imperative to respect black noise – the shrieks, the moans, the nonsense, and the opacity, which are always in excess of legibility and the law' (12). In an argument that in some ways recollects Theodor Adorno's essay on 'Commitment', she suggests that the struggle with the archive must be conducted formally as well as thematically: 'the intent of this practice is not to *give voice* to the slave, but rather to imagine what cannot be verified', as a work of mourning, and a utopian praxis. Giving voice to the voiceless was, we recall, one of Alan Lomax's misguided ambitions.

Hartman's argument feels like both a description and a potential criticism of *Olio*. But Jess's book does call attention to the dialogic nature of ethnography and the ambivalence of the author's position in relation to the archive: it refers to fieldwork with African American informants conducted under the Works Progress Administration, and includes a series of interviews with acquaintances of Scott Joplin, exploring Joplin's music-making while also dramatising the complexities of dialogic research and oral history. It also compares its own process to minstrelsy. As 'Blind' Boone tells an interviewer, 'fact is that the minstrel show is only a grin or a shuffle away from any living Negro trying to tell his own true, full story and

---

[108] Tyehimba Jess, *leadbelly* (Seattle and New York: Wave Books, 2005), p. 88
[109] Saidiya Hartman, 'Venus in Two Acts', *small axe* 26 (June 2008), pp. 1–14 (2–3).

survive in the world' (88). Jess considers whether his own re-enactment of these musicians' subjectivities is not a form of minstrelsy, like Dickinson sitting in the dust and performing Mrs Jim Crow, or 'performing his art in order to accommodate the expectations and stereotypes of white folks'.[110] This, he says, is a question the Black artist must continually pose to himself: 'To what degree am I performing in the minstrel trope', against it, or escaping it?'[111]

But the book's attempt to take up historical subject positions rests on an understanding of lyric against which, as we'll hear more about in the next chapter, New Criticism militated: that the lyric 'I' reflects the experiences or subject-position of the poet. Jess describes how he was encouraged by a mentor to use the third person rather than the first in his poems. But that translation lost the poems' energy and immediacy; 'So I stayed with first person. And I think it also puts me, puts the author, in a position of trying to really empathize with the character.'[112] Empathy allows him to overcome the distinctions between his own subject position and those of the protagonists in his poems. In the case of his earlier book *leadbelly*, empathy was enabled by Jess's strong identification with the hero: 'I was ... channelling my voice through him.'[113] In *Olio*, the ability of the poet to project himself into the subjectivities of a range of historical figures determined the subject matter: if he could get inside the voice, he repeatedly tells interviewers, he was able to write the character.

Olio's empathetic identifications are also part of an African American poetics of the *persona*, which acknowledges historical subjects suppressed in the archive: '(re)building the personae of such black folk heroes allows poets to creatively imagine new, more complex narratives for them', and 'provides a unique vehicle both for signifyin' on the Archive's historical portrayal of blackness and, in complicating how past blackness is read, a concomitant means of broadening the boundaries of contemporary black identity and the corresponding racial imaginary'.[114] Howard Rambsy

---

[110] Andrew Ervin, 'Writing Double Jointed: An Interview with Tyehimba Jess', *Rain Taxi* 11.1 (2006), pp. 16–17 (16).
[111] Jessica Lanay, 'An Interview with Tyehimba Jess', *Believer* magazine (1 June 2019): believermag.com/an-interview-with-tyehimba-jess/ (accessed 6 May 2021).
[112] Lauren K. Alleyne, 'Deconstruct the History in Your Hands: An Interview with Tyehimba Jess', *Fight and Fiddle* (26 April 2019): fightandfiddle.com/2019/04/26/deconstruct-the-history-in-your-hands-an-interview-with-tyehimba-jess/ (accessed 16 May 2021).
[113] Lanay, 'An Interview'.
[114] Ryan Sharp, 'In the Shadow of the Archive: The Big Smoke and Black American Persona Poetry', *African American Review* 52.4 (2019), pp. 373–87.

argues that Jess's adoption of personae give *leadbelly* 'a striking polyvocal quality'.[115] But what I hear in these books is monody: not the 'throng' whose echo – as I'll explain in the next chapter – critics including Francis Barton Gummere heard in 'primitive' poetry, nor even the unifying voice of the spiritual or the work song that is a form of undercommons, but Jess's voice. This is not to say that they don't undertake an effort at mimesis, shifting register (for example) between different demotics when they thrust Leadbelly's internal speech up against the paternalist, Standard English of Lomax. It's just that the ventriloquisation of these historic individuals is jarring, because it seems so artificial. Does this artificiality powerfully reveal the fictive nature of all personhood? Why does it make me feel so uneasy?

Rambsy's accounts of Jess's virtuosic live performances of his poems suggests it may be that I am missing out on the importance of performance in the experience of his poems; in which case I have fallen into the same ditch as the readers of the negrophile anthologies, and not recognised that the written record is a poor shadow of the live event. Perhaps it is better, then, to consider these re-interpretations by Jess not as re-enactments – ritualised, occult resurfacings of the past in the present, as in the case of Philip's watch night readings of *Zong!* – but as dramatic, musical performances. In the music of 'Blind' Boone or 'Blind Tom' Wiggins, each man's sung 'I' becomes a collective expression of experiences shared across the group. Does song make for a less adhesive 'I' than lyric poems do?

I guess I've been sufficiently indoctrinated by New Criticism to want to avoid arguing for a crude identification between the poet and the speaker of the poem. If in order to speak like Leadbelly, a poet is required to spend many years in a convict labour camp, then I am at the same risk of fetishising authenticity that sent the Lomaxes to the prisons in the first place. But I also believe that there is finally no way – as Alan Lomax idealistically promised recording technology could do – to '*give* a voice to the voiceless'. None of the musicians in *Olio* could be construed as voiceless; Jess does not so much create a space in which they might be heard, as project his own self, or his own subjective interpretation, on to the limits of the historical archive. 'Blind Tom' Wiggins was himself known as a ventriloquist: 'he could repeat long speeches word for word, though his everyday language was limited', Tim Armstrong writes, and gave recitations 'in Greek, Latin, German, French, as well as imitations of

---

[115] Howard Rambsy, 'Catching Holy Ghosts: The Diverse Manifestations of Black Persona Poetry', *African American Review* 42:3/4 (Fall 2008), pp. 549–64 (561).

the Scotch bagpipe' and other instruments.[116] Wiggins's fame depended on his own virtuosity at mimicking musical sounds and the words of others, and here he is mimicked by Jess.

The voices in Jess's books draw attention to the disjunctions and erasures that are implicit in any act of ventriloquisation. It's not as if a twenty-first-century African American poet can give the reader insights into how Leadbelly or any of the other artists whose work was appropriated by the negrophile collectors *really felt* about their alienation and exploitation. Perhaps my critique of Jess's acts of impersonation – the inauthenticity that results – reveals the tenacity of my desire, as a white critic, to experience authenticity through the work of Black artists. I turned to Jess's books, looking for something, some witness, that could balance out this chapter, and compensate for the exclusion of African American subjects' own unmediated voice from early ethnography by white people. What I found, however, was not subjectivity – not *the real thing* – but *the subjectivity effect*. Artifice instead of truth. But wasn't that stupid of me, to go looking for a real subject? After all, isn't artifice and effect what lyric always gives? If I, a somewhat practised reader of poetry, am provoked by Jess's lyric to expect real subjectivity, and to be disappointed to find performance instead, then one of the many things *Olio* might teach me is about my formation as a white critic: that my perception of the archive of Black poetry as a record of historical suffering can sometimes stall my attention to the complexities of its forms and technique. And that puts me again on the side of the negrophile collector.

---

[116] Armstrong, *Logic of Slavery*, p. 168.

CHAPTER 8

Singing at the Window
New Criticism and the Evolution of Lyric

> The boll weevil got half the cotton
> The merchant got the rest
>
> – Traditional

Writing in 1871, the British anthropologist Edward Tylor identified vestigial cultural practices as 'survivals': remnants of outmoded beliefs and economic relations that could not be easily incorporated into contemporary culture.[1] This concept was a powerful one for the folklorists who studied African American music at the turn of the century. But it also resonated with many Black writers, for whom music was deeply connected to the endurance of the catastrophe of chattel slavery, and to the continuities between African culture and life and community in the Americas. Song is part of what Édouard Glissant calls an 'economy of survival': fugitive tactics of being and organisation employed by the unfree that include gossip, songs, whispers, laughs, euphemisms, grumblings and theatre. Musical marronage is part of an expressive repertoire of resistance that harbours moments of freedom within the absolute unfreedom of chattel slavery.[2]

This chapter continues the discussion of the last, to show how white scholars drew on evolutionary theories of poetic development in the cataloguing and celebration of this enormous corpus of African American song. It fascinated the negrophile collectors as a distinctly American form of the ballad that was both archaic (the genuine folk song of a primitive community) and new (an amalgamation of European and African song traditions to produce an innovative aesthetic form). John Wesley Work quotes Carl Holliday, 'instructor in English literature in the

---

[1] Edward Tylor, *Primitive Culture*, 3rd American from 2nd English ed. (New York: Henry Holt, 1889), 1:16.
[2] Édouard Glissant, *Caribbean Discourse: Selected Essays*, trans. J. Michael Dash (Charlottesville: University Press of Virginia, 1992), p. 175; cited in Neil Roberts, *Freedom as Marronage* (University of Chicago Press, 2015), p. 43.

University of Virginia', who argued that 'of all the builders of the nation the Negro alone has created a species of lyric verse that all the world may recognise as a distinctly American production'.[3] That America's distinctive lyric was a Black creation was profoundly disturbing to some white critics. Carl Engels, the editor of *Musical Quarterly*, complained in 1935 that the Lomaxes gave the unpleasant impression that 'the Spirit of America, when it blossoms forth – as that of other nations' flowers in the treasures of epic and lyric folk-poetry – necessarily finds its truest and most telling expression in the songs of Black "boys" who have exchanged their identity for a number and go by such picaresque nicknames as Iron Head, Clear Rock, Chin Shooter, Lead Belly'.[4] This exchange of a name for a number or a nickname is not a willing adoption of a poetic persona, but a consequence of the disciplinary regimes of the prison and chain gang. Much of this chapter will concern how the poetics of impersonality, decontextualisation and opposition to affect promulgated through American academic criticism in the mid-twentieth century seems to respond negatively to this corpus. By looking at those ideas of lyric that New Criticism and turn-of-the-century folklore shared, I hope to demonstrate how a version of American formalism was in fact shaped by those songs of bondage it attempted to repress or exclude from the academy and from the hierarchies of critical value created there.

Radicals and Naturalists

I'll begin this story with two articles published in the *Atlantic Monthly* in the late 1860s. The first is by Charlotte Forten (Grimké), an African American abolitionist and educator who journeyed to the Sea Islands in Georgia in 1862 to teach its Black children. The second is by Thomas Wentworth Higginson, a white abolitionist whom we have already encountered. Higginson commanded a regiment of African American soldiers, the First South Carolina Volunteers, during the Civil War. Forten's essay was published during the war, in 1864; Higginson's appeared in 1867, after it had ended. That date is important. Higginson said that the songs' 'minor-keyed pathos used to seem to me almost too sad to dwell upon, while slavery seemed destined to last for generations; but now that

---

[3] John Wesley Work, *Folk Song of the American Negro* (New York: Negro Universities Press, 1915), p. 33.
[4] Carl Engels, 'Views and Reviews,' *Musical Quarterly* (1935), p. 108, cited in Jerrold Hirsch, 'Modernity, Nostalgia, and Southern Folklore Studies: The Case of John Lomax,' *The Journal of American Folklore* 105.416 (Spring 1992), pp. 183–207 (191–2).

their patience has had its perfect work, history cannot afford to lose this portion of its record'.[5] Like other white folklorists, he feared that Emancipation would lead to the withering of these traditions. But he also suggests that during slavery, the work of collecting them was too painful to countenance.

Forten similarly anticipates that these traditions are 'destined to pass away': her record will be an important attempt to document a disappearing history. But she grounds the songs in the recent depravities of slavery. For example, she depicts a 'shout' she attends one evening in the Praise House, led by 'the figure of the old blind man, whose excitement could hardly be controlled, and whose attitude and gestures while singing were very fine'. Although there is an exoticism in Forten's account of the 'wild, whirling dance', the 'old blind man' is not a romanticised Homer: his blindness 'was caused by a blow on the head from a loaded whip' by his master.

Forten's account of life on St Helena, both in the article and her *Journal*, is infused from beginning to end by song: boatmen sing; her party sings 'John Brown' to cheer themselves; congregations sing hymns at baptisms; holidays are commemorated in song; the article finishes: 'My heart sings a song of thanksgiving, at the thought that even I am permitted to do something for a long-abused race.' Her pupils perform for her:

> In the evenings, the children frequently came in to sing and shout for us. These 'shouts' are very strange, – in truth, almost indescribable. It is necessary to hear and see in order to have any clear idea of them. The children form a ring, and move around in a kind of shuffling dance, singing all the time. Four or five stand apart, and sing very energetically, clapping their hands, stamping their feet, and rocking their bodies to and fro. These are the musicians, to whose performance the shouters keep perfect time. The grown people on this plantation did not shout, but they do on some of the other plantations. ... We cannot determine whether it has a religious character or not. ... It is probable that they are the barbarous expression of religion, handed down to them from their African ancestors, and destined to pass away under the influence of Christian teachings.[6]

Like the folklorists discussed in the previous chapter, Forten says the songs are 'indescribable' – they need to be heard and experienced rather than

---

[5] Thomas Wentworth Higginson, 'Negro Spirituals', *Atlantic Monthly* 19 (June 1867), pp. 684–94 (694); reprinted in Thomas Wentworth Higginson, *Army Life in a Black Regiment (1870)* (East Lansing: Michigan State University Press, 1960), pp. 148–73 (173).

[6] Charlotte Forten, 'Life on the Sea Islands', *The Atlantic* (May 1864): www.theatlantic.com/magazine/archive/1864/05/life-on-the-sea-islands/308758/ (accessed 4 May 2021).

read – before she describes them. She also notices the syncretism of the songs, which combine Christian and African influences. As a teacher, she is attentive to the ways that these traditions are passed on between generations: the pedagogy of the song. But Forten's class position creates a gap between the authorial voice and her informants, similar to the one established in Talley's anthology, or Douglass's account of the people going to Great House Farm. 'We', the written authority, cannot determine the character of the song; 'some of the people' tell us what they think it is, but we know that it is a 'barbarous' survival of 'their' African ancestors.

These distancing strategies persist throughout Forten's journals. When she attends an African American wedding: 'comical as the costumes were, we were not disposed to laugh at them. We were too glad to see the poor creatures trying to lead right and virtuous lives.' This paternalism is also apparent in an anecdote about how she attempts to expand the children's musical repertoire by soliciting 'a beautiful Christmas Hymn from Whittier, written by request, especially for our children'. According to her *Journal*, Forten had written to John Greenleaf Whittier to request the hymn in late November.[7] Her response to their own seemingly improvised song shows the power of the more organic lyrics: 'It is one of the strangest, most mournful things I ever heard. It is impossible to give any idea of the deep pathos of the refrain, – "Sing, O graveyard!" In this, and many other hymns, the words seem to have but little meaning; but the tones, – a whole lifetime of despairing sadness is concentrated in them.' This is another example of paralepsis – the impossibility of conveying the 'tone', the words that simultaneously have 'but little meaning' (an echo of Douglass) and concentrate 'a whole lifetime of despairing sadness'. In that 'lifetime' is implied not the children's own brief lives, but a kind of ancestral lifetime or experience, whose wisdom and duration are concentrated in the short form of the song, and the short memories of the children.

In the Sea Islands, Forten became acquainted with Higginson, and was present at the New Year's festivals he led. Higginson's own article records his recollections of the songs he heard performed by his regiment and mixes Romantic racialism with naturalist ideas. Through direct contact with the men of his regiment, he was able to 'gather on their own soil these strange plants which I had before seen as in museums alone':

> Writing down in the darkness, as I best could, – perhaps with my hand in the safe covert of my pocket, – the words of the song, I have afterwards

---

[7] Charlotte Forten, *The Journal of Charlotte L. Forten: A Free Negro in the Slave Era*, ed. Ray Allen Billington (New York: W. W. Norton, 1981), p. 152.

carried it to my tent, like some captured bird or insect, and then, after examination, put it by. Or, summoning one of the men at some period of leisure, – Corporal Robert Sutton, for instance, whose iron memory held all the details of a song as if it were a ford or a forest, – I have completed the new specimen by supplying the absent parts.[8]

Like Dickinson scribbling her poems on any scrap of paper that she can find during her working day, Higginson improvises, hiding his note-taking. But where he strove to observe Dickinson without trapping her, Higginson is keen to 'capture' African American song like birds or insects. He must reassemble skeletal remains, patching up the specimen with his own conjecture or the 'iron memory' of others for whom it resembles a geography. Higginson observes, transcribes and classifies, adding the songs to his museum of natural history. Again, this white author has constructed an image of the Black person at the point of indistinguishability between human and animal life.

Strolling the camp like Henry V before the Battle of Agincourt, Higginson overhears his soldiers performing a ring shout:

> This hut is now crammed with men, singing at the top of their voices, in one of their quaint, monotonous, endless, negro-Methodist chants, with obscure syllables recurring constantly, and slight variations interwoven, all accompanied with a regular drumming of the feet and clapping of the hands, like castanets. Then the excitement spreads: inside and outside the enclosure men begin to quiver and dance, others join, a circle forms, winding monotonously round some one in the centre; some 'heel and toe' tumultuously, others merely tremble and stagger on, others stoop and rise, others whirl, others caper sideways, all keep steadily circling like dervishes; spectators applaud special strokes of skill; my approach only enlivens the scene; the circle enlarges, louder grows the singing, rousing shouts of encouragement come in, half bacchanalian, half devout, 'Wake 'em, brudder!,' 'Stan up to 'em, brudder!' – and still the ceaseless drumming and clapping, in perfect cadence, goes steadily on.[9]

Higginson emphasises the physicality of this performance, which builds in intensity through dance, stamping, clapping and whirling. Like Forten, he views this as a syncretic ritual, mixing religious and occult associations, Christian Methodism and a 'strange' residue of barbarism comparable to the Native American 'pow-wow': it is 'half bacchanalian, half devout'. He compares one spiritual to 'some Romaic song which I had formerly heard', adding: 'that association quite fell in with the Orientalism of the new tent-

---

[8] Higginson, *Army Life*, pp. 148–9.   [9] *Ibid.*, p. 13.

life'. The performers are marked in multiple ways as Others, half-civilised, half-savage, whose unthinking physicality is also the basis of their bravery as soldiers.

With such characterisations, Higginson represents the songs, and their singers, as placeless and timeless. He sees a resemblance to Scottish ballads, which cannot be attributed to any individual composer; 'no matter who made them, they were soon attributed to the minister of the parish whence they sprang'. Higginson wonders 'whether they had always a conscious and definite origin in some leading mind, or whether they grew by gradual accretion, in an almost unconscious way'. One day, he thinks he might get an answer: he meets an oarsman who told him that some spirituals 'are start jess out o' curiosity. I been a-raise a sing, myself, once.' As the oarsman begins to sing this song, 'the men, after listening a moment, joined in the chorus as if it were an old acquaintance, though they evidently had never heard it before'.[10] Whereas a Black scholar like John Wesley Work offered accounts of the origins of the songs in specific episodes reported to him by the descendants of enslaved ancestors, Higginson promotes an idealist notion that the songs are timeless and without origin.[11] To him it is as if, living outside of the liberal discourse of intellectual property or the tenets of philosophical universality, these performers are living outside of history, in an eternal, childlike present whose distant edges are the fading memory of African song traditions and the coming of Jubilee.

Higginson also reflects on how traditional songs become new through context or occasion – for example, at the regiment's New Year festivities. New Year was known as 'Heartbreak Day' among enslaved people, because of the custom of holding big slave auctions on that day.[12] But 1 January 1863 was different: it was the day that the Emancipation Proclamation came into effect. Higginson orders a feast for the regiment, and an assembly with song and sermons at which the Proclamation is read. Just as he is about to make his speech, 'a strong but rather cracked & elderly male voice, into which two women's voices immediately blended', began to sing 'My Country 'Tis of Thee': 'Irrepressibly the quavering voices sang on, verse after verse'; the white regimental leadership attempt to join in, but Higginson silences them.[13] 'I never saw anything so electric; it made all other words cheap; it seemed the choked voice of

---

[10] Higginson, *Army Life*, p. 170. [11] Work, *Folk Song*, pp. 76–88.
[12] Eileen Southern, *The Music of Black Americans: A History*, 2nd ed. (New York: W. W. Norton, 1983), p. 215.
[13] Thomas Wentworth Higginson, *The Complete Civil War Journal and Selected Letters*, ed. Christopher Looby (University of Chicago Press, 2000), pp. 76–7.

a race at last unloosed .... The life of the whole day was in those unknown people's song.'¹⁴ Their 'electric' song, a power that overflows and cannot be contained in written form or by the decorum of the moment, 'made all other words cheap': it diminishes his 'stupid' speech with its transcendent musicality. Again, it is 'unconscious', the spontaneous outpouring of spirit on 'the day of Jubilee', and collective, rather than the product of 'some leading mind'.

Higginson does not just mean New Year's Day, but the day of emancipation, predicted by Leviticus 25:9–10 to come every fifty years, when the faithful shall 'proclaim liberty throughout all the land unto all the inhabitants thereof: it shall be a jubilee unto you; and ye shall return every man unto his possession, and ye shall return every man unto his family.' Paul Gilroy argues that in the 'revolutionary eschatology' of Black thought, Jubilee 'possesses a utopian truth content that projects beyond the limits of the present'.¹⁵ In Gilroy's terms, the irrational, spiritual and violent irruption of Jubilee sounds like music. Music communicates the unspeakable regime of racial terror and its overcoming; music 'points directly to the formation of a community of needs and solidarity which is magically made audible in the music itself .... Words, even words stretched by melisma and supplemented and mutated by the screams which still index the conspicuous power of the slave sublime, will never be enough to communicate its unsayable claims to truth' (37). These 'unsayable claims' cannot be captured in language, but only in the embodied, collective and performed rhythms of Black music.

The Temporalities of the Sorrow Song

Forten's, Higginson's and Gilroy's essays, as different as they are, provide a route into the principle concerns of this chapter, which include the fantasies of historicity and ahistoricity, materiality and utopia that are projected on to African American song, and how that historicity is modelled through evolutionary theories of poetic development. Dividing the ages of Black music, Alain Locke cites the first moment before 1830 as an era of 'the plantation shout and "breakdown". Dominated by African Reminiscences and Survivals.' This was followed in 1830–50 by 'The Age of the Sorrow-Songs ... the Great Spirituals and the Folk Ballads.' Locke's 'ages' represent developmental stages in the evolution of African American

---

¹⁴ Higginson, *Army Life*, p. 31.
¹⁵ Paul Gilroy, *The Black Atlantic: Modernity and Double Consciousness* (London: Verso, 1993), p. 68.

music from African roots to the complexities of 'Classical Jazz'.[16] His version of this history is teleological. But much writing on Black music represents it as diachronic. For Frederick Douglass, the songs are presently being sung; they are a survival of the individual and racial past, held in memory; and they are demands for future emancipation. As we've seen, African American song was also represented in the scholarship of the twentieth century as a rapidly disappearing tradition, evidence of an enduring link to the African past, and a connection to the earliest and most primitive forms of human culture, which had to be preserved through the technologies of the future.

The songs inhabit what Édouard Glissant refers to as 'a prophetic vision of the past'. That vision, Glissant writes, is 'related neither to a schematic chronology nor a nostalgic lament. It leads to the identification of a painful notion of time and its full projection forward into the future.'[17] Glissant argues that Caribbean history 'emerges at the edge of what we can tolerate': 'the past, to which we were subjected, which has not yet emerged as history for us, is, however, obsessively present' (63). This dialectic of historical and ahistorical temporalities, subjugation and resistance, the lament for the past and the anticipation of Jubilee, can be found throughout the scholarship on African American song-making, starting perhaps with W. E. B. Du Bois. In *Black Reconstruction in America* (1938), Du Bois famously depicts the sorrow songs as 'America's one real gift to beauty':

> A great song arose, the loveliest thing born this side the seas. It was a new song. It did not come from Africa, though the dark throb and beat of that Ancient of Days was in it and through it. It did not come from white America – never from so pale and hard and thin a thing, however deep these vulgar and surrounding tones had driven. Not the Indies nor the hot South, the cold East or heavy West made that music. It was a new song and its deep and plaintive beauty, its great cadences and wild appeal wailed, throbbed and thundered on the world's ears with a message seldom voiced by man. It swelled and blossomed like incense, improvised and born anew out of an age long past, and weaving into its texture the old and new melodies in word and in thought.
>
> They sneered at it – those white Southerners who heard it and never understood. They raped and defiled it – those white Northerners who listened without ears. Yet it lived and grew; always it grew and swelled and lived, and it sits today at the right hand of God, as America's one real gift to beauty; as slavery's one redemption, distilled from the dross of its dung.[18]

---

[16] Locke, *The Negro and His Music*, p. 11.   [17] Glissant, *Caribbean Discourse*, p. 64.
[18] W. E. B. Du Bois, *Black Reconstruction in America* (1938); New York: Atheneum, [1938] 1977), pp. 124–5.

The song seems to come from nowhere (not from Africa, Asia, white America or the Indies, not from the North, South, East or West), and everywhere (it thundered on the world's ears). It is an intrinsically American art form, deeply embedded in the conditions of its production; and a transcendent music that escapes those constraints and ascends to 'the right hand of God'. It is a distillation or sublimation, a pure form; but it is also drastically female, in its message 'seldom voiced by man', its swelling and growing, and subjection to rape and defilement. It is diachronic, derived from the 'Ancient of Days' but a 'new song', 'born anew out of an age long past', weaving 'old and new' together.

As Simone White observes, 'Du Bois' turns of phrase occupy negative rhetorical space – not this, not that, "tones" nonetheless (humanly) heard, its "incense" drawn in, its "weave" sensed *intelligibly*, phonemonelogically, by *the world* – anticipating the groundwork of making the whole world Africa by way of explosive invention and dissemination of invention (of something from nothing) by way of the Music.'[19] This groundwork also establishes a pattern that can be found in numerous writers including Maud Cuney-Hare, Sterling Stuckley, Amiri Baraka, John Lovell and Gilroy, for whom the sorrow songs are evidence of a historical continuity between Africa and its diaspora. For many of these writers, it is rhythm that signifies the presence of the past and an opening on to the future that is both embodied and collective.

Writing in the early 1970s, John Lovell argues that 'the African is not bound to a temporal conception. His rhythm consists of a physical-sensual perception of accent impulses and their transformation into movement.'[20] This release through rhythm from 'temporal conception' into the 'physical-sensual' can seem uncomfortably close to the Hegelian characterisation of the African as living in an eternal present, unknown to universal history. But for scholars and poets such as Lovell, rhythm is both historical – a link to an ancestral past – and transcendent, an ahistorical element in Black culture. Derek Walcott referred to an 'ancestral, an ecstatic rhythm in the blood that cannot be subdued by slavery or indenture' in his Nobel lecture of 1992. Leopold Senghor's description of African rhythm is quoted in Frantz Fanon's *Black Skin, White Masks*: it is the 'thing that is most perceptible and least material', the 'archetype of the vital element', 'the first condition and the hallmark of Art, as breath is of life: ... This is rhythm in its primordial purity, this is rhythm in the masterpieces of

---

[19] Simone White, *Dear Angel of Death* (Brooklyn: Ugly Duckling Presse, 2018), p. 82.
[20] John Lovell, *Black Song: The Forge and the Flame* (New York: Macmillan, 1972), p. 44.

Negro art.'²¹ Lovell says Senghor told him that 'he was impressed by the so-called Negro Spirituals when he first heard them as a young man in France, partly because they reminded him of revered poems from his childhood in Senegal'.²² The spiritual provides a genealogy of the African cultural heritage in the United States, even when it is performed in concert settings in Europe.

What, in these remarks, does it mean to be 'African'? For Sterling Stuckey, 'slave music reflects the unity of West African culture through syncopation, antiphony, group singing, improvisation, and instruments used, and through its organic tie to dance'.²³ That unity is a consequence of the slave trade: 'the ring in which Africans danced and sang is the key to understanding the means by which they achieved oneness in America' (12). It was the slave ship that produced a syncretic African identity, Stuckey argues. But in an equally polemical argument, Kofi Agawu has challenged such 'unanimist constructions of Africa', demonstrating how they neglect massive variations across African musical traditions. Agawu provides examples from the eleventh through the twentieth century, to show that African music has frequently been characterised as possessing a rhythmic complexity that surpasses Euro-American notation or even comprehension. "African rhythm" is, he writes, 'an invention, a construction, a fiction, a myth, ultimately a lie'.²⁴ Nonetheless, many musicologists agree that along with instruments such as the banjo, the rhythms of African American song are evidence of the continuities of African musical cultures in the new world.²⁵

Rhythm, in these examples, serves to unify a disparate tradition and provides an index of both its historicity and its timelessness. Rhythm has served similar functions in the criticism of poetry. In his 1901 book *The Beginnings of Poetry*, Francis Barton Gummere defines poetry as 'rhythmic utterance, rhythmic speech, with mainly emotional origin.'²⁶ Gummere

---

[21] Frantz Fanon, *Black Skin, White Masks*, trans. Charles Lam Markmann (London: Pluto Press, 1986), p. 123.
[22] Lovell, *Black Song*, p. 46.
[23] Sterling Stuckey, *Slave Culture: Nationalist Theory and the Foundations of Black America* (Oxford University Press, 1987), p. 41.
[24] Kofi Agawu, 'Music Anthropologies and Music Histories: The Invention of "African Rhythm"', *Journal of the American Musicological Society* (Fall 1995), pp. 380–95 (387). For a critical review of Agawu's thesis, see Louise Meintjes, 'Representing African Music: Postcolonial Notes, Queries, Positions, by Kofi Agawu', *Journal of the American Musicological Society* (Fall 2006), pp. 769–77. I am grateful to Richard Wolf for this reference.
[25] See, for example, Gerhard Kubik, *Africa and the Blues* (Jackson: University of Mississippi Press, 1999), and Robert B. Winans (ed.), *Banjo Roots and Branches* (Urbana: University of Illinois Press, 2018).
[26] Francis Barton Gummere, *The Beginnings of Poetry* (New York: Macmillan, 1901), p. 30.

argued that the rhythms of poetry were based in primitive song, dance and labour: 'the main external source of rhythm ... is the habit of accompanying bodily movements with sounds of the voice, and these bodily movements were primarily movements in man's work' (109). Similarly, in his *Science of English Verse* (1880), Sidney Lanier's examples of rhythmic complexity include Mother Goose – 'the most complex rhythms of our language' – and the 'rudest music' of the South:

> I have heard a Southern plantation 'hand', in 'patting Juba' for a comrade to dance by, venture upon quite complex successions of rhythm, not hesitating to syncopate, to change the rhythmic accent for a moment, or to indulge in other highly-specialised variations of the current rhythmus. Here music, let it be carefully observed, is in its rudest form, consisting of rhythm alone: for the patting is done with hands and feet, and of course no change of pitch or of tone colour is possible.[27]

Lanier draws on his own observations of this '"patting" which the Southern negroes so delight in for a dance accompaniment', as well as the dynamics of 'a typical negro sermon' (276); he even gives a musical transcription of that speech. His suggestion that the greatest rhythmic complexity is a relic of the past is not unusual, and – as we will see – enables a critique of contemporary lyric as a genre whose gains in terms of the exploration of subjectivity entail losses, particularly of the relatedness of earlier communal forms. Like many of the negrophile collectors, Lanier's identification of African Americans as the pre-eminent technicians of rhythm was part of his attempt to uncover the primitive foundations of poetry.

Poetic Evolutions: from Ballad to Lyric

In *A Voice from the South* (1892), Anna Julia Cooper – a formerly enslaved woman who completed a doctorate at the Sorbonne, and who went on to work as an educator in Washington, D.C. – described the 'weird moanings' of African American labourers as 'truly poetic'.[28] The songs 'become, the more they are studied, at once the wonder and the despair of musical critics and imitators. ... There is material here, one might almost believe, as rich, as unhackneyed, as original and distinctive as ever inspired a Homer, or a Cædmon or other simple genius of a people's infancy and lisping childhood' (180). As in the ethnography of Talley, Work or Forten,

---

[27] Sidney Lanier, *The Science of English Verse* (New York: Scribner, 1880), pp. 186–7.
[28] Anna Julia Cooper, *A Voice from the South by a Black Woman of the South* (Xenia: Aldine, 1892), pp. 178–9.

Cooper's description alienates the authorial voice from this strange 'they', who are an heroic and original but misunderstood race that 'inspired almost the only distinctive American note which could chain the attention and charm the ear of the outside world' (224). This distinctive music inspires scholars, to whom it is both 'wonder and despair': a priceless object of study, but also an elusive one. Cooper's appeal is for the emergence of an African American scholar or poet who can do justice to this tradition, for a 'Black Chaucer' to memorialise it.

Cooper's comparison of African American song to the archaic poetry of Homer and Cædmon was echoed by many folklorists who, like Higginson, exhibited an intense excitement at being present at the formation of a folk tradition. John Lomax designated his informant Clear Rock a modern-day Homer, who 'seemed to have caught in his capacious memory the floating folk songs that had been current among the thousands of black convicts who had been his only companions for fifty years. He had a store equal in continuous length to the *Iliad*.'[29] Lomax also attempted to sanctify his materials by comparing them to the Modernist canon: 'When they are written out, these phrases often seem jumbled and disconnected, just as a page of *Ulysses* is at first confusing to an unprepared reader.'[30] Here again is the sorrow song as diachronic matter: both a relic of the deep past, and a blast from the literary future. That it resembles James Joyce's *Ulysses* is significant. Like the Modernists returning to an archaic and classical past, Lomax is drawing a connection between the modernity and ancientness of the songs.

The negrophile collectors heard the songs as the expression of sentiment or affect, unconstrained by reflection – qualities that the Romantics valued in so-called 'primitive' poetry. A key figure in this valorisation of folk song was Johann Gottfried von Herder. In his letters on Ossian from 1773, Herder expressed admiration for primitive song as the antidote to civilised alienation: 'the more wild and freely acting a people is ... the more wild, that is, the more lively, free, sensuous and lyrically acting its songs must be ... The farther from artificial, scientific ways of thought, speech and letters a people is, the less its songs are made for paper and for dead literate verses.'[31] Hugh Blair, whose own *Critical Dissertation on the Poems of Ossian*

---

[29] John A. Lomax, *Adventures of a Ballad Hunter* (Austin: University of Texas Press, 2017), p. 153. Lauri Ramey offers a contemporary example, comparing 'slave songs' to the poetry of Homer and Cædmon: *Slave Songs and the Birth of African American Poetry* (Basingstoke: Palgrave Macmillan, 2008), p. 40.

[30] John A. Lomax and Alan Lomax, *American Ballads and Folk Songs* (New York: Macmillan, 1934), p. xxxiv.

[31] Bendix, *In Search of Authenticity: The Formation of Folklore Studies* (Madison: University of Wisconsin Press, 1997), p. 38; on the search for authenticity in Black folk song see pp. 89–93.

(1763) influenced Wordsworth and Coleridge, also found in ancient or primitive poetry 'the language of passion, and no other'. The ancient bards 'sung indeed in wild and disorderly strains; but they were the native effusions of his heart'. Blair cites Native American song as a contemporary example of poetry in this 'savage state'. The passions of primitive people 'have nothing to restrain them: their imagination has nothing to check it'. This strong feeling and unconstrained imagination leads to picturesque, figurative speech. Blair's values informed Wordsworth's 1800 'Preface' to *Lyrical Ballads*, where he selects 'low and rustic life' because 'in that situation the essential passions of the heart … are less under restraint'.[32] Primitive poetry is associated with a lack of constraint, with the passionate outpouring of the experiences of the tribe. By contrast, lyric must be restrained: the spontaneous overflow of powerful feelings regulated by prosodic thought in tranquillity.

The efforts of Romantic European poets and scholars to revive the literary ballad influenced American collectors including Higginson.[33] He described himself as 'a faithful student of the Scottish ballads,' and had always:

> envied Sir Walter [Scott] the delight of tracing them out amid their own heather, and of writing them down piecemeal from the lips of aged crones. It was a strange enjoyment, therefore, to be suddenly brought into the midst of a kindred world of unwritten songs, as simple and indigenous as the Border Minstrelsy, more uniformly plaintive, almost always more quaint, and often as essentially poetic.[34]

Higginson hears echoes of border ballads and the Lyke Wake Dirge in these sorrow songs. Comparisons to Scottish and Irish ballads abound in his diary: 'I take great delight in writing down at leisure moments the songs & hymns of these people, often as graceful & beautiful as those of Scotland.'[35] Other collectors also recognised similarities between African American songs and 'the best English folk ballads'.[36] Antonín Dvořák, whose compositions were influenced by the African American songs that his student Harry T. Burleigh taught him, is often quoted comparing the 'unusual and subtle harmonies' of 'the so-called plantation melodies and slave songs' with the songs of Scotland and

---

[32] Hugh Blair, *Lectures on Rhetoric and Belles Lettres*, 2:314, 322–3; cited in Mary Jacobus, *Tradition and Experiment in Wordsworth's Lyrical Ballads* (Oxford: Clarendon, 1976), pp. 189–90.
[33] Derek Furr, 'Re-sounding Folk Voice, Remaking the Ballad: Alan Lomax, Margaret Walker, and the New Criticism', *Twentieth Century Literature* 59.2 (Summer 2013), pp. 232–59.
[34] Higginson, *Army Life*, p. 148.   [35] Higginson, *Complete Civil War Journal*, p. 78.
[36] Thomas Talley, *Negro Folk Rhymes: Wise and Otherwise* (New York: Macmillan, 1922), p. ix.

Ireland (in 1895).[37] Writing in 1937, the critic Sterling Brown notes: 'Although it strikes some collectors as odd to find a Negro singing "In London-town where I was born" the fact remains that the Negro folk, like other southern folk groups, have kept alive traditional English and Scotch ballads learned in early days' such as 'Barbara Allen'.[38]

The similarities often identified between African American and European song traditions are not merely thematic but also based on shared suffering and sympathy. In the revision of his autobiography, Douglass observes that 'I have never heard any songs like those anywhere since I left slavery, except when in Ireland. There I heard the same *wailing notes*' in the context of the Great Famine of 1845–6.[39] Other writers were more judgemental in discerning these musical genealogies. Drawing her own comparisons between the Irish, cleared Scots and enslaved African Americans, Frances Anne Kemble says that the song of the latter 'almost always has some resemblance to some tunes with which they must have become acquainted through the instrumentality of white men; their overseers or masters whistling Scotch or Irish airs'. She describes this as 'transparent plagiarism', invoking intellectual property models to disparage cross-cultural transmission.[40] Richard Wallaschek also says that the songs are 'imitations of European compositions' – an argument that John Wesley Work explicitly rejects: 'to assert that he has found any greater resemblance between the Negro's music and European music than would naturally result from the oneness of human nature, lays the writer open to the suspicion that he is uninformed, misinformed, superficial, unscientific, or all of these'. Recognising that some of the songs might incorporate 'the "long meters" of Dr Watts and other hymn writers', Work argues that their variations are so dazzling that the original is transformed into something unrecognisable.[41] 'Negro song', he suggests, is an expression of both universal humanity, and the unique character of the race. James Weldon Johnson also resists this notion in the preface to the first *Book of American*

---

[37] In *Century Magazine* (February 1895); see Lovell, *Black Song*, pp. 442–5.
[38] Sterling Brown, *Negro Poetry and Drama and the Negro in American Fiction* (New York: Athaneum, 1969), p. 23.
[39] Frederick Douglass, *Autobiographies* (New York: Literary Classics of the United States, 1994), p. 184. On Douglass's experiences in Ireland, see Peter O'Neill, 'Frederick Douglass and the Irish', *Foilsiú: An Interdisciplinary Journal of Irish Studies* 5.1 (2006), pp. 57–81; and Lee Jenkins, 'Beyond the Pale: Frederick Douglass in Cork', *The Irish Review* 24.1 (June 1999), pp. 80–95.
[40] Frances Anne Kemble, *Journal of a Residence on a Georgian Plantation in 1838–1839*, ed. John A. Scott (London: Jonathan Cape, 1961), p. 163; also pp. 129–30.
[41] Work, *Folk Song*, p. 29.

Negro Spirituals (1925): 'The statement that the Spirituals are imitations made by the Negro of other music that he heard is an absurdity.'[42]

For many of the folklorists, however, the resemblances between African American song and European balladry were not merely functional (in their relation to collective experiences) or thematic but also developmental. Hurston positions African American song within an evolution of human expressivity that includes the emergence of 'language and song', percussion and the song-arts used for storytelling that eventually became prose. 'The singing grew like this,' she says:

> First a singing word or syllable repeated over and over like frogs in a pond; then followed sung phrases and chanted sentences as more and more words were needed to portray the action of the battle, the chase, or the dance. Then a man began to sing of his feelings or moods, as well as his actions, and it was found that the simple lyre was adequate with the words expressing moods. The Negro blues songs ... belong in the lyric class; that is, feelings set to strings.[43]

The song evolves from senseless, almost animal sound, to the melody of the tribe in action (hunting or fighting), to the individual expression of feelings. These early lyrics then gave way to the ballad, with its capacity for narrative and 'objectivity' – a quality Hurston prized as more aesthetically advanced than subjective expression. Whereas Talley drew on chemical analogies, in her sketch of the evolutionary development of song forms Hurston uses metaphors from biology – 'the evolution of an organism is reviewed in embryo. In folk literature it is the same'; just as the child begins with nonsense words, 'the adult primitive does the same thing on his way to prose' (74).

Following a Hegelian and Social Darwinian logic, other critics also argued that the ballad was a compelling but uncomplicated early form, which expressed the collective consciousness through its embodied rhythms and emerged at the beginning of poetic evolution; but unlike in Hurston's schema, they regarded lyric as the consummation of the very written, artificial, subjective and individualised poetics of modernity. As Andrew Peart describes it, Child's *Ballads* contrasted 'the self-communion of an individual writing privately for an unforeseen public' with 'the cultural infancy of the ballad', as 'the anonymous expression of an entire

---

[42] Bernard Katz (ed.), *The Social Implications of Early Negro Music in the United States* (New York: Arno Press and the New York Times, 1969), p. xxxvi.

[43] Zora Neale Hurston, *Go Gator and Muddy the Water: Writings by Zora Neale Hurston from the Federal Writers' Project*, ed. Pamela Bordelon (New York: W. W. Norton, 1999), p. 71.

people having just reached a stage of intellectual and moral coherence'.[44] This view of ballad as more primitive than lyric is also apparent in the former's placement at the beginning of Cleanth Brooks and Robert Penn Warren's influential New Critical anthology *Understanding Poetry*.[45] But alongside this evolutionary model, critics imputed to the ballad a capacity to resist lyricisation and the alienation of the modern subject.

Francis Gummere and the Primitive Origins of Poetry

Francis Barton Gummere's 1901 book *The Beginnings of Poetry* offered a critical summary of the evolutionary theories of poetics, which sought to discover the origins of poetry in the song and verse of 'primitive' peoples and the babbling of infants – a nexus that preoccupied many social theorists in this period, including Sigmund Freud. Gummere, who had been a student of Francis James Child, traces the 'curve of evolution' from primitive poetries, which he argues 'spring from primitive song, dance, and labour, mainly under communal conditions', to the modern lyric.[46] He discusses the ballad at length as an example of a primitive oral poetry that is truly grounded in communal experience. The ballad, he writes, was the product of 'a homogeneous and unlettered community', such as existed in medieval Europe (164) – and arguably among the enslaved people of the South of the United States.

For Gummere, the communal conditions of primitive life produce 'consent': 'the primitive horde in festal dance and song, finding by increased ease of movement and economy of force, by keener sense of kind, by delight of repetition, the possibilities of that social consent which is born of rhythmic motion' (89). This makes poetry fundamentally 'a social act', which has evolved from communal origins, and not solitary utterance (Gummere scoffs at Mill, 52–3). Consent is also a name for the co-ordination of people through the rhythms of dance, ritual and work. Even in the era of industrial mass production, Gummere hears in the poem a legacy of the innate physicality and shared rhythms of communal labour. 'The poem now laboriously wrought at the desk goes back to the rhythm of work or play or dance in the life of primitive man'; rhythm was inalienable, 'the one tie that binds beginning and end' (63). Today's 'man of advanced

---

[44] Andrew Peart, '"The Abstract Pathos of Song": Carl Sandburg, John Lomax, and the Modernist Revival of Folksong', *New Literary History* 46.4 (2015), pp. 691–714 (696).
[45] Furr, 'Re-sounding Folk Voice', pp. 232–59.   [46] Gummere, *Beginnings of Poetry*, pp. 84, 80.

culture' works in isolation, but we can look across 'the spectacle of a long evolution':

> at one end of which, the uncertain, tentative beginnings of social life, we see human beings acting, alike in the tasks and in the pleasures of their time, with a minimum of thought and a maximum of rhythm; while at the hither end is a highly developed society, where the monotonous whir of machinery has thrust out the old cadence and rhythm of man's labour, where strenuous and solitary wanderings replace the communal dance, and where every brow is marked with the burden of incessant thought. (111–12)

Here are themes familiar from the ethnography of African American song: that the earliest songs are unreflective expressions of communal life; that they have been destroyed by the machine age. Rhythm is the index of all that has been lost in the civilising process. Industrialisation has alienated the 'advanced' (i.e. white) man from the rhythms of communal life. Nonetheless, Gummere urged a return to those rhythms as the antithesis of alienated labour:

> In rhythm, in sounds of the human voice, timed to movements of the human body, mankind first discovered that social consent which brought the great joys and the great pains of life into a common utterance ... The poet is still essentially emotional, and just so far as he is to utter the great joys and the great pains of life, just so far he must go back to communal emotions, to the sense of kind, to the social foundation. The mere fact of utterance is social; however solitary his thought, a poet's utterance must voice this consent of man with man, and his emotion must fall into rhythm, the one and eternal expression of consent. (114–15)

Rhythm is the 'sign and warrant of a social contract', and the expression of 'the sense and sympathy of kind' (115).

This notion of the 'kind', also the 'throng', is central to Gummere's evolutionary poetics. Virginia Jackson has written about the sociopolitical implications of the throng to Gummere. Gummere's emphasis on rhythm as 'the essential fact of poetry' is mixed, Jackson writes, with 'fantasies of racial identification'.[47] She argues that Gummere identifies 'communal forces' in rhythm that are both 'post-racial' and specifically Germanic/ English, providing a transition from race to culture in which whiteness is submerged in what he calls shared 'rhythmic and kindred instincts'.

---

[47] Virginia Jackson, 'The Cadence of Consent: Francis Barton Gummere, Lyric Rhythm, and White Poetics,' in *Critical Rhythm: The Poetics of a Literary Life Form*, ed. Ben Glaser and Jonathan Culler (New York: Fordham University Press, 2019), pp. 87–105 (89).

Although his focus is on European ethnic relations, Gummere also discusses Higginson's *Atlantic Monthly* article:

> The negro slaves of the South, finally, with their traditional dance and song, strangely influenced by one of the few elements of civilization which really came into their life, the religious element, offer another interesting bit of evidence to show how emotional speech, a rude poetry, is born of rhythm by consent of a throng. In those so-called 'spirituals' of the negro is the recitative or the chorus to be looked upon as original. Perhaps Colonel Higginson had as good a chance to study this communal song as any one could have; in an article written soon after the war he described the singing of the 'spirituals' by men of his regiment, now in camp, now on the march, now to the fall of the oars. He speaks of the trait so prominent in all primitive song, exact and inevitable rhythm, however harsh the voices and however uncouth the words. (97–8)

Gummere's ascription of rhythm to the 'negro slaves' is not unusual, but his notion of 'consent' is very difficult to absorb in the context of chattel slavery. Gummere is not interested in that context; rather, he praises Higginson's opportunity to 'study' the rhythms typical of the 'savage' and the 'primitive', for whom 'movement of body and rhythm of voice are the main consideration, while the words, on which civilized man imposes individual and syntactic correctness, are of very subordinate value' (99).

Gummere focused on the European ballad and was largely resistant to analogies between it and African American song. Nonetheless, his poetics had a powerful influence over folklorists and ethnographers in the early twentieth century. In a presentation on 'American Folk Songs in Music Education' in June 1939, Howard Odum quotes Gummere's definition of the ballad (from *The Popular Ballad*, 1907) as 'a conglomerate of choral, dramatic, lyric, and epic elements which are due now to some suggestive refrain, now to improvisation, now to memory, now to individual invention, and are forced into a more or less poetic unity by the pressure of tradition in long stretches of time'.[48] Odum then discusses the 'assumption' that 'the folk are the eternal source or spring of living cultures always basic to the building of new cultures when old cultures decline'. He also quotes Richard Wallaschek's 1893 book *Primitive Music*, which represents folk song as 'an organising power for the masses, the tie which enables the tribe to act as one body'.[49] While this tribal tie in the late 1930s represents

---

[48] Howard Washington Odum Papers, University of North Carolina at Chapel Hill Special Collections, 03167, folder 631 (Speeches, 1939).
[49] Richard Wallaschek, *Primitive Music* (London: Longmans, Green, 1893), pp. 294–5.

for Odum a potential danger ('the folk song and mass music routine make of a group of individuals under powerful totalitarian influence a literally irresistible power'), he argues that 'the educator and sociologist should seek from the folk those universal constant qualities which guarantee survival and normal evolutionary development'. The folk can also be a structure that binds the community together to resist fascist totalitarianism; 'consent' is the opposite of coercion, just as true folk culture is the opposite of the mass ornament.

African American song is Odum's example of folk song: though it is 'seemingly [an] unconscious motor-minded product', 'one may glimpse evidence of simple everyday experience, wishful thought, childlike faith, workaday stolidity, physical satisfaction, and subtle humor'. Odum finishes his speech by comparing Wordsworth's 'The light that never was on sea or land' to the song of a 'Negro worker', drawing out the Romantic heritage of the folklore methodologies in which he was trained. And, in a draft blurb for his book *Negro Songs* that reads like a sociologist's version of Allen Ginsberg's *Howl*, Odum repeatedly returns to African American song-makers as an undifferentiated mass, a 'throng' or 'horde':

> A VAST THRONG OF WORKADAY NEGROES SINGING, MIRRORS OF A RACE. WORKINGMEN IN THE SOUTHERN UNITED STATES FROM HIGHWAY, CONSTRUCTION CAMP, FROM RAILROAD AND FARM, FROM CITY AND COUNTRYSIDE, A MILLION STRONG. A HALF MILLION EMIGRANTS FROM THE SOUTH EASTWARD, NORTHWARD, WESTWARD AND SOME BACK AGAIN. NEGRO OFFENDERS IN THOUSAND FOLD IN LOCAL JAILS, COUNTY CHAIN GANGS, STATE AND FEDERAL PRISONS. A HORDE OF SOUTHERN CASUAL LABORERS AND WANDERERS DOWN THAT LONESOME ROAD.... A SWELLING CRESCENDO, A RACE VIBRATO INIMITABLE, DESCRIPTIVE SYMBOL OF GROUP CHARACTER, FOLK-URGE AND RACE POWER.[50]

As Jon Cruz notes, 'collective groups ... serviced the rise of a critical intelligentsia and the latter's capacity to bring modernity and its relentless transformations into some kind of understandable focus'.[51] For Odum, these collectivities were the emblems of a thriving, masculine American *demos* that could oppose the fascists.

---

[50] Odum papers, folder 663.
[51] Jon Cruz, *Culture on the Margins: The Black Spiritual and the Rise of American Cultural Interpretation* (Princeton University Press, 1999), p. 186.

From the Agrarians to the New Critics

The language of the throng also appears in the preface to Talley's *Negro Folk Rhymes* (1922). There, Walter Clyde Curry writes:

> The spectacle ... of a homogeneous throng of partly civilized people dancing to the music of crude instruments and evolving out of dance-rhythm a lyrical or narrative utterance in poetic form is sufficiently rare in the nineteenth century to challenge immediate attention.[52]

The book brings to light 'the musical and poetic life-records of a people', a *throng* that is only homogeneous in the constructed unanimist sense of Africanness that is created by diaspora. Nonetheless, Curry argues, the 'spectacle' of such a primitive people deserves attention, because it brings to life the origin stories of European culture:

> Here we have again, in the nineteenth century, the record of a singing, dancing people creating by a process approximating communal authorship a mass of verse embodying tribal memories, ancestral superstitions, and racial wisdom handed down from generation to generation through oral tradition. These are genuine folk-songs – lyrics, ballads, rhymes – in which are crystallized the thought and feeling, the universally shared lore of a folk. Recent theorizers on poetic origins who would insist upon individual as opposed to community authorship of certain types of song-narrative might do well to consider Professor Talley's characteristic study. (x–xi)

African Americans are 'a folk' whose cultural activities provide experimental data to furnish theorists contemplating 'poetic origins' of a more European type. Curry's contemporaries agreed that this *volk* was produced in the crucible of slavery: 'Nowhere save on the plantations of the South could the emotional life which is essential to the development of true folksong be developed,' Henry Krehbiel wrote in 1914.[53] It was not the Northern factory or the pioneer farm but the plantation that provided 'the romantic and emotional elements', combined with the 'ingenuous, native musical capacity' of enslaved African-Americans, to produce a real American folk song.

Curry was a medievalist at Vanderbilt University in Tennessee, where he taught Cleanth Brooks, one of the originators of New Criticism – a movement named after John Crowe Ransom's 1941 book. Vanderbilt was the hub for a circle whose members called themselves the Southern Agrarians and several of whom also contributed to the development of

---

[52] Talley, *Negro Folk Rhymes*, p. v.
[53] Henry Edward Krehbiel, *Afro-American Folksongs: A Study in Racial and National Music* (New York: G. Schirmer, 1914), p. 22.

New Criticism: Ransom, Allen Tate and Robert Penn Warren.[54] The Agrarian group-formation began in a magazine called (ironically, given their racial politics), *The Fugitive* (1922–25), in which Curry was also published. The Agrarian manifesto *I'll Take My Stand: The South and the Agrarian Tradition* was published in 1930, five years after Odum and Johnson's *The Negro and His Songs*. It included essays by Donald Davidson, John Gould Fletcher, Frank Owsley and John Wade.

The Agrarians regarded 'their chief antagonists to be a group of sociologists and regional planners at the University of North Carolina, led by Odum, Rupert Bance, and W. T. Couch'.[55] Odum is frequently named as an opponent by the Southern Agrarians, though he did not respond publicly to *I'll Take My Stand* in 1930.[56] In a letter found in Odum's papers, Davidson said that he was in favour of anything that gives integrity and independence to southern institutions: 'I am thoroughly tired of being servile and merely imitative. I am worn-out and sick of seeing the South made an experimental ground for any idea, no matter how half-baked and untested, that happens to originate in a New York or Chicago study' – governmental organisations and charitable foundations like the Rockefeller that sponsored Odum's research. He told Wade he also feared 'all the literary boys and girls are turning to the Left, to the New Masses, to Saint Lenin – that lard their talk with proletarian phrases and toast the coming revolution. Perhaps you and I are a little more conscious of these people than Odum is, or perhaps they get on our nerves more.' If communism were allowed to penetrate the teaching of literature, he feared:

> Will you be content, John Wade, to see your plantation divided up between the relations and friends of Richard, the yard boy, and Tom, the field hand? And will you be charmed to teach the milder English classics (those not too-too colored with 'bourgeois' sentiment) and the greater Russian classics to a class where kinky heads and blonde tresses mix in critical appraisal, and do not ever nod politely – and all this for a pittance . . . ?[57]

---

[54] Karen O'Kane, 'Before the New Criticism: Modernism and the Nashville Group', *The Mississippi Quarterly* 51.4 (Fall 1998), pp. 683–97 (683); Edward Pickering, 'The Roots of New Criticism', *The Southern Literary Journal* 40.1 (Fall 2008), pp. 93–108.
[55] Idus Newby, 'The Southern Agrarians: A View After Thirty Years', *Agricultural History* 37.3 (July 1963), pp. 143–55 (152).
[56] Donald Davidson, 'A Sociologist in Eden', in *The Southern Agrarians and the New Deal: Essays after 'I'll Take My Stand'*, ed. Emily S. Bingham and Thomas A. Underwood (Charlottesville: University of Virginia Press, 2001), pp. 104–23 (107–8); Alexander Karanikas, *Tillers of a Myth: Southern Agrarians as Social and Literary Critics* (Madison and Milwaukee: University of Wisconsin Press, 1966), pp. 106–8.
[57] Odum papers, letter from Donald Davidson to John Wade (Marshallville, Georgia), 3 March 1934, folder 343.

Here is a typical example of the Agrarian desire to police the teaching of literature in the academy through a racialised image of miscegenation.

Between the 1910s and the 1930s, Odum softened his allegiances to what Clyde Woods has called 'the planter thesis of African barbarism and Black inferiority'. He came to believe that 'the social sciences should identify the causes of racial, social, and economic differences and then propose governmental interventions to alleviate them.'[58] As chair of the North Carolina Commission on Interracial Co-operation, Odum sought to enhance opportunities for African American participation in education and politics, and to advance vocational training, culture and criminal justice in the South. He regarded the 'Nashville Group' at Vanderbilt as dangerous proponents of a revived sectionalism (rather than the federalist regionalism in which he was invested, and which he administered as part of several New Deal projects). Nonetheless, Odum entered into a cordial exchange with Davidson, and invited him to participate in a roundtable on Southern planning at the University of Chattanooga in 1934.[59] In a letter to Wade responding to Davidson's arguments, Odum wrote that:

> Whatever one may say about the Old South, there was in the upper brackets a culture of a very rich and to some extent mature sort. In the present South, my impression is that the upper group is neither rich nor mature ... there has been no mature development of culture at the top which would make an abiding contribution.[60]

Odum's argument in this letter that culture is a product of the elite is aligned, as we will see, with those of the Southern Agrarians, but is also personally contradictory, given his own work to collect folk song and stories from the poor white and Black tenant farmers of North Carolina.

During the Chattanooga conference, the discussion turned to 'the Negro population'.[61] The speakers (it is not recorded if these were Odum and Davidson) expressed an anxiety that Southern African Americans were being educated by Northern missionaries to have ideas inappropriate to 'the life which they must live'. (That this life *must* be lived is a good example of what Karen E. Fields and Barbara J. Fields describe as 'racecraft'.[62]) Moreover, 'the Negroes' were no longer satisfied 'to develop as dependents'; they were disillusioned and organising as an independent class. But despite these dangers,

---

[58] Clyde Woods, *Development Arrested: The Blues and Plantation Power in the Mississippi Delta* (London: Verso, 2017), pp. 100, 134.
[59] Odum papers, letter to Will Alexander, Commission on Interracial Cooperation, 7 May 1934, folder 348.
[60] Odum papers, letter to John Wade, 16 March 1934, folder 344.   [61] Odum papers, folder 348.
[62] Karen E. Fields and Barbara J. Fields, *Racecraft: The Soul of Inequality in American Life* (London: Verso, 2014).

which make the Black Belt population susceptible to the temptations of communism, 'The South presents an opportunity to study not only the Negro as a special type of individual, but here and there in the area there are small communities that have lived for a time isolated lives and are, therefore, especially available as subjects of social investigation.' This is an argument, as we have seen, that drove Guy Johnson's and the Lomaxes' collecting.

The Southern Agrarians lamented the passing of traditional Southern and Confederate lifeways and kinship structures under the pressure of economic modernisation and the threat of outside agitators. They were not alone in this; Odum, in a 1938 speech, observed that 'The swift-moving technicways are transcending the old, slow-moving folkways and supplanting almost entirely the mores and morals, thereby changing the entire rate of cultural evolution and accelerating the social and moral world as well as the physical and material world.'[63] Even Du Bois had worried about the 'rising Mammonism of the re-born South'. If 're-inforced by the budding Mammonism of its half-awakened black minions', industrialisation and the cash nexus would destroy the truth, goodness and beauty of the South, Du Bois argued, as well as the freedom of its African American citizens.[64] The Agrarians were likewise anxious that industrialisation and technological progress were ruining the South's unique culture – a culture that was both quintessentially local, they said, and a remnant of the best of Europe, particularly eighteenth-century England. Donald Davidson argues that 'this [Southern] consciousness, too often misdescribed as merely romantic and gallant, really signifies a close connection with the eighteenth-century European America that is elsewhere forgotten'.[65] For Ransom, their interest in 'formal and reactionary' aesthetics bespoke 'our need to make a return to the amenities which the European communities laboured to evolve, and defined perhaps as "civilisation"'.[66] Those cultural goods helped to 'humanise' natural man, just as Orpheus tamed the savage beasts. References to the evolution of specifically 'European' cultural amenities were racist dog whistles used by almost all of the Agrarians.

Ignoring the most distinctive contribution of the South to world culture – the African American musical tradition – the Agrarians argued that the South's

---

[63] Odum papers, folder 629.
[64] W. E. B. DuBois, *The Souls of Black Folk* (New York: Signet, [1903] 2012), p. 73.
[65] *I'll Take My Stand: The South and the Agrarian Tradition*, by Twelve Southerners (New York: Harper & Brothers, 1930), pp. 53, also 21, 171; on the Agrarians and industrialisation, see Lindon Barrett, *Blackness and Value: Seeing Double* (Cambridge University Press, 1999), pp. 164–82.
[66] John Crowe Ransom, 'A Poem Nearly Anonymous', *American Review* 1 (September 1933), pp. 444–67 (456).

culture had instead been produced by its white elites in their enjoyment of leisure. In a revived South, cultural and intellectual life would remain the province of that elite. Their banal pastoralism (none of the Agrarians actually lived on a farm) erased not just the culture but also the labour of enslaved people. They eulogised the Southern plantation as an 'Eden' before the fall, where the only snakes were Northern provocateurs and everything was sweetness and light, 'manners, the table, the hunt, politics, oratory, the pulpit . . . The South took life easy.'[67] Owsley, in an infamous paper on 'Scottsboro, the Third Crusade' delivered at the American Historical Association in 1933, contrasted the 'generous' treatment of the Negro on the plantation with the exploitation of labourers by Northern industrialists, and argued that constraints on African Americans in the South post-1860 were entirely the fault of abolitionist provocation.[68] He insisted in his contribution to *I'll Take My Stand* that 'The [Northern, progressive] white man was re-enslaving the Negro, cruelly using him, committing even greater wrongs against him than in the days of slavery' (184). Owsley believed that enslaved people were 'well treated as a rule', and regarded 'as a member of the family': consequently the 'separation of families was much less frequent under slavery than under the capitalistic industrial system of today'.[69] Where they did acknowledge the 'Negro problem', the Agrarians adopted an attitude of paternalism that seemed not to have advanced on William Grayson's poem 'The Hireling and the Slave' (1856). Davidson writes that if 'something like the old master-slave relation hangs on' in the South, it is 'merely because both races are used to it and like it'.[70] Ransom argues that the plantation's economic as well and social and cultural relations were distinct from the capitalist system: while the capitalist's relation with wage labourers was organised through the cash nexus, the slave system involved paternalistic care for enslaved people, protecting children and the elderly from the exploitation they would face in a Northern factory.

The Agrarian's anti-modernist pastoralism is not far, as we have seen, from the argument shared by many foklorists about the corrosive effects of modernity on Black song traditions. It was also not dissimilar to the way that Southern slaveowners represented their plantations in the 1840s and 1850s as places of 'tranquillity and quietude, punctuated with a healthy

---

[67] Ransom in *I'll Take My Stand*, p. 12; see also p. 32.
[68] Frank Lawrence Owsley, 'Scottsboro, The Third Crusade', in *The Southern Agrarians and the New Deal*, pp. 175–98 (182).
[69] Idus Newby, 'The Southern Agrarians: A View After Thirty Years', *Agricultural History* 37.3 (July 1963), pp. 143–55 (150).
[70] Donald Davidson, 'A Sociologist in Eden', in *The Southern Agrarians and the New Deal*, pp. 104–23 (117).

dose of humming industriousness and the melodies of singing slaves – and contrasted them with what they believed was the destructiveness of northern modernity'.[71] In these pastoral fantasies (of which Dunbar's poem 'A Corn Song' is an ambivalent example), the melodious singing of African American labourers is the antithesis of the horrendous whirring of factory machinery. 'Even the regime of production becomes naturalized as "the rhythms of work,"' Saidiya Hartman observes, 'as if slave labour were merely another extension of blacks' capacity for song and dance.'[72] The literary genre of pastoral played an important part in the ideological construction of these scenes of pleasure and *otium*. In the pastoral model, slavery is depicted as a totalising, 'organic relationship', locking master and slave into relations of paternalistic dependency and reciprocity that erase domination. This was exactly the strategy of the Agrarians, who argued that the South's pastoral tranquillity was the last defence against modern industrialism.

Strains of virulent racism repeatedly surface in this pastoral dreamscape. Ransom claimed that 'the darkey is one of the bonds that make a South out of all the Southern regions': the contribution of African Americans to Southern culture is its consolidation as white supremacy.[73] There is anger, too, in the odious essay 'The Irrepressible Conflict' by Owsley, which accuses the 'half-savage blacks' of humiliating and punishing the South during reconstruction (62–3), among myriad lies about Southern history (e.g. 'without slavery the economic and social life of the South would have not been radically different', 76; 'let the blood of slavery rest upon the heads of those who had forced it upon the South', 78, etc.). These arguments belie the gentility of the Southern Agrarian fantasy. So, too, does Allen Tate's answer to the question 'How may the Southerner take hold of his Tradition?': 'by violence' (174).

Although he did later undergo a conversion of sorts, Tate's execrable racism in the 1930s has been well documented, and does not bear repeating here.[74] Suffice to say that the famous anecdote about Tate's efforts to prevent Langston Hughes and James Weldon Johnson from attending a faculty party at Vanderbilt in 1932 by depicting that potential encounter

---

[71] Mark M. Smith, *Listening to Nineteenth-Century America* (Chapel Hill: University of North Carolina Press, 2001), p. 5.
[72] Saidiya V. Hartman, *Scenes of Subjection: Terror, Slavery, and Self-Making in Nineteenth-Century America* (Oxford University Press, 1997), p. 52.
[73] 'The Aesthetic of Regionalism,' *American Review* (Jan. 1934); cited in Karanikas, *Tillers*, p. 115.
[74] Thomas A. Underwood, *Allen Tate: Orphan of the South* (Princeton University Press, 2000), esp. pp. 149–52 and 290–6.

as miscegenation is an emblem of the way the Agrarians attempted to police or exclude Black arts from the academy.[75] Robert Penn Warren also came to regret his defence of segregation, blaming it on an idealisation of the South from a position of exile. In his later book of interviews and reflections on race, voter registration, education and leadership among African American communities in the South, *Who Speaks for the Negro?*, Warren notes that he wrote his contribution to *I'll Take My Stand* in 1929–30 while living in England. He had imagined the South where he grew up as 'an image of the unchangeable human condition, beautiful, sad, tragic'. Over the course of the 1930s, when he returned to the South and Jim Crow began to be challenged, he realised 'I could never again write the essay.'[76]

Not all the Agrarians experienced changes of heart in the way Warren, or to a lesser extent Tate, did. But what I want to draw attention to are the continuities between the positions they took in *I'll Take My Stand* and New Critical poetics. Influenced by English and German Romanticism, the Agrarians believed that good art was rooted in an organic relation to nature and the soil – a doctrine that was later reflected in the New Critical idea of the poem as an 'organic system of relationships', like a plant.[77] The logic is similar to Wordsworth's in the 'Preface' to *Lyrical Ballads* (1800):

> Low and rustic life was generally chosen because in that situation the essential passions of the heart find a better soil in which they can attain their maturity, are less under restraint, and speak a plainer and more emphatic language; because in that situation our elementary feelings exist in a state of greater simplicity and consequently may be more accurately contemplated and more forcibly communicated; because the manners of rural life germinate from those elementary feelings; and from the necessary character of rural occupations are more easily comprehended; and are more durable.[78]

In similar terms, Donald Davidson described the special blessing of the provincial Southern artist, for whom 'nature is an eternal balancing factor in his art, a presence neither wholly benign nor wholly hostile' (*Stand* 57–8). For Ransom, the Southern farmer tills the soil 'not too hurriedly and not too mechanically to observe in it the contingency and

---

[75] Michael Bibby, 'New Negro Renaissance Poetry and the Racial Formation of Modernist Studies', *Modernism/modernity* 20.3 (September 2013), pp. 485–501 (485).
[76] Robert Penn Warren, *Who Speaks for the Negro?* (New York: Random House, 1965), p. 12.
[77] Cleanth Brooks and Robert Penn Warren, *Understanding Poetry: An Anthology for College Students*, rev. ed. (New York: Henry Holt, 1938, 1950), p. xv.
[78] William Wordsworth, *Lyrical Ballads, and Other Poems, 1797–1800*, ed. James Butler and Karen Green (Ithaca, NY: Cornell University Press, 1992), ll. 67–75, p. 743.

the infinitude of nature; and so his life acquires its philosophical and even its cosmic consciousness' (*Stand* 20). This leisurely, nonmechanical contemplation of nature is not dissimilar to the leisurely, aesthetic contemplation of the poem that New Criticism proposed.

Emily Dickinson's poetry appealed to the Agrarians, particularly Tate, because he believed it was 'a deep mind writing from a deep culture' – the Puritan theocracy of New England – though her silence on slavery was also convenient.[79] The problem with modern writers in the Northern metropolis, as far as the Southern Agrarians were concerned, was their rootlessness. Tate argued that the modern writer is 'emancipated from the demands of social conformity' but not really free, because he is alienated from his community; at least the 'old Southern writer' existed in a 'defined', if narrow, place.[80] Although they might fetishise personal freedom, the writers of Northern industrialised modernity are unfree, because they are no longer grounded in the totality of relations; modernist literature has become as fragmented as modern society.[81] While there are echoes of Georg Lukàcs's *Theory of the Novel* (1916) in this argument, and the Agrarians' perception of the relationship between the economic base and the literary superstructure was not entirely dissimilar from Marxist aesthetics, Tate's idealisation of the plantation and Southern life were specifically marshalled *against* communism. Tate and Warren originally wanted to title *I'll Take My Stand* 'A Tract Against Communism', and many Agrarians articles were published in *American Review*, an explicitly fascist journal.

For the Agrarians, the organic totality of the artwork was achieved, and continued to be symbolised, by the organic economies of the plantation system.[82] The plantation was imagined as a self-sufficient polis in which everyone knew and kept to their place, and which protected its enslaved workers from the interference of Northern abolitionist and communist organisers. Similarly, the poem was a self-sufficient whole that organised relationships between its internal elements but rebuffed the interference of context or external referents in its production of meaning. Moreover, both the unit of the plantation and the unit of the poem are organised and

---

[79] Allen Tate, 'Emily Dickinson', in *Essays of Four Decades* (Oxford University Press, 1970), pp. 281–98 (296–7).
[80] Allen Tate, *The Poetry Reviews of Allen Tate*, ed. Ashley Brown and Frances Neel Cheney (Baton Rouge, LA: Louisiana State University Press, 1983), p. 143; cited in Mark Jancovich, *The Cultural Politics of the New Criticism* (Cambridge University Press, 1993), p. 49.
[81] Davidson, 'A Mirror for Artists', *I'll Take My Stand*, p. 50. I'm grateful to William Andrews for helping me rethink my argument in this paragraph.
[82] Pickering, 'The Roots of New Criticism', pp. 93–108.

guarded by constraint. Writing in 1933, Ransom distinguished between 'forms' of work and play. 'Tradition is the thing handed down by society, and the thing handed down is just a formula, a form.'[83] These forms can be economic or aesthetic. Art 'restrains' what Ransom calls the 'natural man', whose interests in an object are 'predatory and acquisitive' (453). Though his distinction between play and work forms draws on Schiller's notion of the play drive, Ransom's aesthetics are explicitly linked to his critique of Northern industrialism in contrast to Southern agrarian economies. Mark Jancovich notes that: 'Just as the Southern paternalists had seen the plantation as a check on the exploitation of labour, so Ransom argues that "aesthetic forms are a technique of restraint, not of efficiency".'[84] For Ransom the poem's formal constraints are the boundaries of an aesthetic object within which freedom can be enjoyed if the particularities of context or authorship are blocked out; similarly, the plantation is a utopian microcosm that blocks out the predations of capital and instrumental reason.

The Agrarians' arguments about organic wholes and idealised relations to nature are admittedly not far from Odum and Johnson's contention that 'without a knowledge of the Negro's nature and environment, one would scarcely realise the fullest appreciation of his folk songs'.[85] However, for the Agrarians, the 'Negro' lacked what Odum and Johnson praise as 'creative ability and esthetic sense'. Lindon Barrett has analysed the reluctance of the Agrarians or New Critics to recognise that African Americans can be involved in 'productions of sense and import'.[86] He argues that New Criticism and Agrarianism share a social vision, and 'a self-conflicted relationship' to science and industrial capitalism. 'The "spirit of life" of the Old South remains the rallying cry of an openly partisan Agrarian attempt to reclaim a lost patrimony, while the discrete text, in its shared antipathy to the industrial street, stands as a (re)transfiguration of that patrimony and as a symbol of a rigorous, objective disciplinary investigation' (180–1). For these reasons, I would go further than Joseph North's characterisation of New Criticism as a 'thoroughly idealist practice, based in a neo-Kantian aesthetics of disinterest and transcendent value, directed toward religious cultural conservatism'.[87] The New Critical valorisation of 'the autonomy of the work itself' is undoubtedly influenced by Immanuel Kant.[88] But the Agrarians also eulogised autonomy as the lost

---

[83] Ransom, 'A Poem Nearly Anonymous', p. 444.
[84] Jancovich, *The Cultural Politics of the New Criticism*, p. 37.
[85] Odum and Johnson, *The Negro and His Songs*, p. 29. [86] Barrett, *Blackness and Value*, p. 164.
[87] Joseph North, *Literary Criticism: A Concise Political History* (Cambridge, MA: Harvard University Press, 2017), p. 27.
[88] John Crowe Ransom, 'Criticism, Inc.', *Virginia Quarterly Review* 13 (Autumn 1937), pp. 586–602.

privilege of the eighteenth-century plantation owner, whose government of his property and law-making power over his chattel could be seen as the apotheosis of the autonomous individual depicted in Kant's 1784 essay 'What is Enlightenment?'

Although African American music presented the Agrarians with an excellent example of a distinctively Southern cultural form that had evolved from a close relationship to the soil, none (other than Curry) showed any interest in it. And yet they lamented the loss of poetry as an oral tradition. As Donald Davidson wrote in his essay 'Poetry': 'Today there are hardly any poets of merit who can or will write a literary ballad or would even consider composing a song lyric.' All that is left is poems in textbooks, which is 'a kind of death-in-life, to exist only on the printed page, not on the lips of men, not to be carried by their voices and therefore almost never carried in their memories, rarely in their hearts ... There is no place for poetry to go next unless it reasserts its old independence of the book and finds a way to restore some of its formal character.' He concluded glumly: 'That is what we mean when we say our culture is falling apart.'[89]

The Southern Agrarians could be considered a brackish backwater of twentieth-century regionalism, but for the influence they came to have, as New Critics, over the pedagogy of English literature. While in some critical accounts the ideas of the Agrarians are subordinated to New Criticism, with Agrarianism as the precursor or anticipation of the full maturity of New Critical thought, John Fekete has argued that New Criticism was in fact the outcome of the political 'failure' of the Southern Agrarians, who renounced 'all possibilities of reshaping the exterior world' and then retreated into academia where they 'could define their position as representatives of metaphysical and aesthetic value' amidst the 'rejection of all socio-historical dimensions' of the aesthetic object.[90] If New Criticism is the legacy of the defeat of the Agrarian programme (and this argument has been debated), this might force us to look differently at the models of poetic pedagogy it provided to twentieth-century universities.[91]

---

[89] Donald Davidson, *Still Rebels, Still Yankees and Other Essays* (Baton Rouge: Louisiana State University Press, 1957), pp. 19–22.

[90] John Fekete, *The Critical Twilight: Explorations in the Ideology of Anglo-American Literary Theory from Eliot to McLuhan* (London: Routledge & Kegan Paul, 1977), pp. 45–7. Pickering traces the shift from Agrarianism to New Criticism to 1937, when Ransom left Vanderbilt and set up the *Kenyon Review* ('The Roots of New Criticism', pp. 93–108).

[91] Karen O'Kane has provided an illuminating history of collaboration between the 'Nashville Group' and the New York Intellectuals in 'Before the New Criticism', pp. 683–97.

New Criticism emphasised textual ambiguity and 'impersonality' over readings that looked for textual origins in the biography of the writer. To be sure, this impersonality had its roots in different places, including Anglo-American high modernism, which had its own problematic identifications with African song and the 'primitive'.[92] 'Poetry begins, I dare say, with a savage beating a drum in a jungle, and it retains that essential of percussion and rhythm,' T. S. Eliot writes at the end of *The Use of Poetry and the Use of Criticism*.[93] Impersonality also reframed the lyric as a closet drama, divorced from its historical contexts and allowing the interplay of fictional subjectivities. As W. K. Wimsatt and Cleanth Brooks wrote in their influential textbook *Literary Criticism*: 'Once we have dissociated the speaker of the lyric from the personality of the poet, even the tiniest lyric reveals itself as drama.'[94] The ballad was cited in Brooks's and Robert Penn Warren's textbook *Understanding Poetry* (1938) as a pre-eminently dramatic poetic form. As Derek Furr notes, however, for Brooks and Warren 'folk voice is an idea, rather than a sound, and it receives its fullest expression in literary ballads, which raise the naive form to a higher level'.[95] It can remain an idea because the actual sound is either unrepresentable, or something they refuse to hear in the contemporary music of the South.

Jonathan Culler has written about the 'modern theoretical model' that has developed out of the New Critical doctrine of impersonality. It regards lyric poems as 'a fictional representation of a personal utterance': 'It is as if every poem began, "For example, I or someone might say . . .".'[96] Examples of this point of view include Robert Langbaum's *The Poetry of Experience: The Dramatic Monologue in Modern Literary Tradition* (1957), and Barbara Herrnstein Smith's *On the Margins of Discourse* (1978), which regarded 'all poetry' as 'mimetic or fictive discourse'.[97] It was New Criticism that taught us to read the speaker of the poem as a fictionalised persona. Herbert Tucker observes that until around 1940, criticism emphasised the expression of feeling as the essential characteristic of lyric; thereafter, the New

---

[92] On the vexed relation between Eliot and New Criticism in the United States, see Kenneth Asher, 'T. S. Eliot and the New Criticism,' *Essays in Literature* 20.2 (September 1993), pp. 292–309.
[93] T. S. Eliot, *The Use of Poetry and the Use of Criticism: Studies in the Relation of Criticism to Poetry in England* (London: Faber and Faber, 1944), p. 155.
[94] W. K. Wimsatt and Cleanth Brooks, *Literary Criticism: A Short History* (London: Routledge, 1957), p. 675.
[95] Furr, 'Re-sounding Folk Voice,' pp. 232–59.
[96] Jonathan Culler, 'Lyric, History, and Genre', *New Literary History* 40.4 (Autumn 2009), pp. 879–99 (891).
[97] Barbara Herrnstein Smith, *On the Margins of Discourse: The Relation of Literature to Language* (University of Chicago Press, 1978), pp. 25, 28.

Critics began to read lyric as a form of dramatic monologue, a term coined by Samuel Silas Curry to describe Browning's poems in 1908.[98] For John Crowe Ransom, the dramatic situation is 'almost the first head under which it is advisable to approach a poem for understanding'. Eventually, in 1965 Robert W. Boynton and Maynard Mack's *Introduction to the Poem* returned full cycle to Mill: 'in some instances this imagined speaker is in no way definite or distinctive; he is simply a voice'.[99] As we've seen, collectors including the Lomaxes believed the voice of the caged bird – or the Black prisoner – could also be transmuted into 'pure voice' through the apparatus of the recording.

Numerous anthologies, including the ones emerging from the University of North Carolina in the 1930s at the high tide of Agrarian activism, celebrated Black song as the direct and unmediated effusion of an oppressed subject. Did these contribute to the Agrarian, and thus New Critical, desire to bracket out the author? Good poetry, according to the New Critics, could be subjective, but the subject must be sublimated. Ransom argued, in his famous essay 'Criticism, Inc.' of 1937, that 'the first law to be prescribed to criticism, if we may assume such authority, is that it shall be objective, shall cite the nature of the object rather than its effects upon the subject ... We must regard as uncritical the use of an extensive vocabulary which ascribes to the object properties really discovered in the subject, as: moving, exciting, entertaining, pitiful.' Psychology must be excluded from the judgement of the literary work.[100] By contrast, drawing on what was originally a Romantic idea of the lyric, the negrophile collectors represented African American music as the spontaneous overflow of powerful feeling; a direct and unmediated expression of the lives and feelings of the singers. To them it was a primitive tradition that resisted reproduction and could only be represented – from Douglass through Odum – through its emotional effects on the hearer. If the New Critic was impersonal and detached, what the negrophile collectors repeatedly fell back on, given the insufficiency of their technologies of transcription, was the emotional impression of those works upon themselves. Meanwhile, the New Critics' emphasis on poetry as dramatic monologue, and the desire to resurrect

---

[98] S. S. Curry, *Browning and the Dramatic Monologue* (Boston: Expression, 1908). I am grateful to Ewan Jones for this information, and for his critical reading of this chapter as a whole.

[99] Cited in Herbert F. Tucker, 'Dramatic Monologue and the Overhearing of Lyric', in *Lyric Poetry: Beyond New Criticism*, ed. Chaviva Hošek and Patricia Parker (Ithaca, NY: Cornell University Press, 1985), pp. 226–43.

[100] Ransom, 'Criticism, Inc.', pp. 586–602. On the 'objectivity of form', see Allen Tate, 'Miss Emily and the Bibliographer', *The American Scholar* 9.4 (Autumn 1940), pp. 449–60, and Robert Langbaum, *The Poetry of Experience: The Dramatic Monologue in Modern Literary Tradition* (New York: Random House, 1957), pp. 28–30.

a populist oral poetry that could influence the progress of civilisation, is also a kind of return of the repressed: it acknowledges that poetry is rooted in song, one of the most wildly popular versions of which Allen Tate could hear if he simply turned on the radio.

Opening the Window

I want to conclude these two chapters by making a space in which African American song-making can reflect back at the critics I've discussed, and myself. I'll do this with a song recorded in Talley's *Negro Folk Rhymes* (1922), where it is called 'Song to a Runaway Slave':

> Go 'way from dat window, "My Honey, My Love!"
> Go 'way from dat window! I say.
> De baby's in de bed, an' his mammy's lyin' by,
> But you cain't git yō' lodgin' here.
>
> Go 'way from dat window, "My Honey, My Love!"
> Go 'way from dat window! I say;
> Fer ole Mosser's got 'is gun, an' to Miss'ip' youse been sōl';
> So you cain't git yō' lodgin' here.
>
> Go 'way from dat window, "My Honey, My Love!"
> Go 'way from dat window! I say.
> De baby keeps a-cryin'; but you'd better un'erstan'
> Dat you cain't git yō' lodgin' here.
>
> Go 'way from dat window, "My Honey, My Love!"
> Go 'way from dat window! I say;
> Fer de Devil's in dat man, an' you'd better un'erstan'
> Dat you cain't git yō' lodgin' here.[101]

This song uses the alternating four beat / three beat line known as common or hymn metre. As I noted in the discussion of Dickinson's use of hymn metre, the short three-beat lines are actually experienced as including a final unspoken beat, a pause or silence.[102] In the context of this poem, that pause conveys a moment of listening or of absence, a drawing of breath.

This is actually an ancient English song, one of the earliest print reproductions of which can be found in Francis Beaumont and John Fletcher's *The Knight of the Burning Pestle* (1611), although there is evidence for even earlier

---

[101] Talley, *Negro Folk Rhymes*, pp. 88–9.
[102] This 'virtual beat' is observed by Derek Attridge, *Poetic Rhythm: Art Introduction* (Cambridge University Press, 1995), p. 59.

witnesses.[103] As such, it exemplifies the continuities between European and African American balladry, and more broadly, of the provisionality and recurrence – *figura* – of lyric subjects across historical periods. What is particularly interesting, however, is the adaptation of the English source to a new context. The poem's diction is simple, and consists of anaphoric repetition of the first two lines, with each stanza providing a reason why you should 'Go 'way from dat window'. In most sixteenth-century versions of the song, the (female) singer urges her lover to go away because the weather is poor and his ship will soon sail away, or because her husband is at home. In this version, very different reasons are given: the baby is asleep, or crying; the Master has a gun and has sold you to a new owner, and the devil is in him. These explanations are rounded out in an accompanying note:

> The story went among Negroes that a runaway slave husband returned every night, and knocked on the window of his wife's cabin to get food. Other slaves having betrayed the secret that he was still in the vicinity, he was sold in the woods to a slave trader at reduced price. This trader was to come next day with bloodhounds to hunt him down. On the night after the sale, when the runaway slave husband knocked, the slave wife pinched their baby to make it cry. Then she sang the above song (as if singing to the baby), so that he might, if possible, effect his escape.

While its historicity and conventionality – the mother's croon, the listener at the window are stock figures from many ballad traditions – give it an element of deniability, the song is also specific: the husband has been sold into Mississippi. This is a song of, and about, fugitivity.

It also has a complex layering of audiences. There is the escaped husband; the other enslaved people who betrayed him; the enslaver; the trader and his dogs; the baby; the public; the reader, you, and me. The song must manage these competing audiences, providing information for some and not others. The singer performs for her baby, but also for the husband she addresses through their child; she conveys an intimate scene – mother and child lying in bed together – and produces the lodging, the domestic space, while also excluding the husband from it. The song is a lullaby and a warning. It soothes and it frightens. It is a denatured relic of history, and a new, improvised intervention in the present. It is traditional and innovative. Overhearing, as in Dunbar's poem 'A Corn Song', is conventional in plantation writing, and this song is certainly an overheard lament; but the fact that it is overheard

---

[103] 3.5.32–36 ('Go from my window, love go'). *The Traditional Ballad Index*, ed. Robert B. Waltz and David G. Engle: www.fresnostate.edu/folklore/ballads/ChWI146.html (accessed 4 May 2021). John Wilkinson set me off in pursuit of these earlier witnesses.

makes it eloquent, in Mill's sense, an utterance intended to persuade or produce an action in the listener: to make him flee. The voice in this poem feels utterly labile, but its lability is also a marker of the historic fungibility of Black bodies, of surveillance and watchfulness and performance not really as a redemptive mode of personal expression but as a means of surviving. It is a song of natality, and of natal alienation. It speaks to me, and not at all to me. It is the lyric I wanted, but once I become its reader it has already gotten away.

The story I have attempted to tell in these two chapters is not really about African American lyric, but about its critical reception. Black song-making presented enormous, sometimes apparently insoluble, problems for white collectors. Those problems were both technical and ideological, and exposed the limits of the white critical imagination and its vocabularies. Collection not only profited from but also *created* conditions for the performance and circulation of African American song that were oppressive and limiting. For many white critics in the late nineteenth and early twentieth centuries, the fantasy of a primitive, dramatic, balladic, oral tradition also provided the foundation for a theory of literary *and* social evolution for which the actuality of such a tradition was inconvenient.

The ascription of primitivism helped white critics and collectors to hold African American song at bay, transforming it into an object of study (like a specimen or artefact) whose meanings could be easily understood because it was simply the spontaneous effusions of the singer's lived experience. This was an exercise in containment, which refused to acknowledge how the songs' apparent unrepresentability challenged the methodologies of the collectors, or their meanings challenged the emergent structures of academic professionalisation. Rather, folklore was a 'key social-intellectual mechanism that blended the older strains of romantic disenchantment and nostalgia with the promise of science's ultimate capacity to adjudicate the anxieties that were produced by modern market society', as Jon Cruz asserts.[104]

Like these songs, lyric can look like the enactment of an authentic experience or condition; but it too is a re-enactment, performed for the audience whose perception of it as lyric depends on its authenticity and apparent lack of mediation. The white supremacist folklorists perceived Black song as spontaneous and incapable of reflection; when it sang out a common condition, they demeaned it as simple affect rather than philosophical inquiry. John Lomax wrote that 'a negro singing the folk-songs of his race might be termed a negro thinking aloud'.[105] The song of the race that is really the thought of an

---

[104] Cruz, *Culture on the Margins*, p. 177.
[105] John A. Lomax, 'Self-Pity in Negro Folk-Songs', *The Nation* 105 (1917), pp. 141–5 (141).

individual spoken aloud comes very close to collapsing one naïve vision of folklore into the liberal lyric as defined by Mill (lyric as the etiolated voice of the confined individual), or the spontaneous overflow of powerful feeling recollected in tranquillity (perhaps the supposed tranquillity of Emancipation, the period in which white collectors assumed these songs of suffering would pass away). Bryan Wagner shows that collectors like Lomax sought out 'manual labourers, loafers, and near-criminals', in the belief that they were the soulful and authentic custodians of the Black song tradition because 'they are the only ones who can be so easily mistaken for the perspective within their songs and sayings'.[106] This mistake is a lyric mistake, a violation which – under the influence of the New Critics – university lecturers like me continue to police: the confusion of the speaker of the poem with the author.

And yet in a parody of the New Critical valorisation of impersonality, the collectors erased the singers' identities: the singer disappears into the collective anonymity of a primitive origin, while the lyric poet is exquisitely identifiable as 'some leading mind'. This dichotomy enacts what Wagner refers to as a 'tension between individuality and typicality' in the songs (36). Typicality here could also be profitably read as collectivity. I've tried to put this dichotomy under pressure in the implicit contrast between the two works that end these chapters: Jess's ventriloquisation of the anonymised singers of the early twentieth century, which 'returns' a subjectivity to them which is the projection of an early-twenty-first century belief that feeling and empathy are the grounds of lyric, and that lyric could therefore be the testamentary grounds of a shared humanity; and the unindividuated ballad by an unnamed singer, which translates an ancient English song into a record of the very particular conditions of chattel slavery and fugitivity. The songster, in Wagner's formulation, is a machine for the reproduction of the song, a mere vessel whose typicality can't help but communicate a general condition – the memory of the race, etc.; the lyric poet, by contrast, is engaged in a synthesis of the particular that elevates it to the condition of the universal. Overcoming these ruptures may not depend on the reproduction by contemporary voices of the historical voices banished from the archive, or hidden there behind the smoothness of academic representation. It may mean changing the definition of lyric.

---

[106] Bryan Wagner, *Disturbing the Peace: Black Culture and the Police Power after Slavery* (Cambridge, MA: Harvard University Press, 2009), p. 34.

PART III
Pleasures and Ornaments

CHAPTER 9

A New Made Wound
Sadomasochistic Triumphs and Missing Feet in Ovid's Elegies

"'Romans' – *(Ovid) smiled* – *'will mock your slavish rhyme,*
the slaves your love of Roman structures'
                                                            – Derek Walcott

It is now time for a bone-shaking turn, from bondage and immiseration to the pleasures of constraint. In fact, we've dallied with the pleasures of bondage already; they were close to Wyatt's painful servitude and imagery of sexual enslavement, Halpern's provocative conflation of incarceration and sadomasochistic pleasure and Dickinson's aroused imagining of schoolchildren being flogged. Fantasies of submission are also evident in a series of enigmatic letters Dickinson wrote to a 'Master'.[1] In them, the speaker (Daisy) obeys the master and 'never flinched' so that 'he should not see the / wound' he causes. Her only wish is that the Master 'punish – dont banish / her – shut her in prison'. I'll return to the wounds of love, as masochistic injury and castration, throughout this chapter.

Sadistic pleasure is also made available to privileged white viewers or readers through what Hortense Spillers calls the 'pornotroping' of Black suffering: 'the captive body becomes the source of an irresistible, destructive sensuality'.[2] Saidiya Hartman seeks to avoid becoming complicit in this destructive sensuality by not reproducing an infamous scene involving the whipping of Aunt Hester in Frederick Douglass's autobiography.[3] But Austin Reed provokes it with his description of Strongman's 'milk white skin' dripping with blood. Reed experiences both horror and fascination,

---

[1] Emily Dickinson, *The Master Letters*, ed. R. W. Franklin (Amherst College Press, 1986), p. 22 (L2, early 1862).
[2] Hortense J. Spillers, *Black, White, and in Color: Essays on American Literature and Culture* (University of Chicago Press, 2003), p. 206.
[3] Saidiya V. Hartman, *Scenes of Subjection: Terror, Slavery, and Self-Making in Nineteenth-Century America* (Oxford University Press, 1997), pp. 3–4. On the sadism of that scene, see also Christina Sharpe, *Monstrous Intimacies: Making Post-Slavery Subjects* (Durham: Duke University Press, 2010), pp. 4–13.

repulsion and fetishisation, towards the tortured body of his friend. As I'll argue in the next chapter, many participants in sadomasochism think of it not as the reproduction of historical pornotropes but an opportunity for healing psychic wounds. These arguments recall Dionne Brand's description, too, of the Door of No Return as a concealed, compelling opening: 'It is the site of pain which will turn into the site of pleasure. Transform us into full being through its immutable knowledge. Transform us into being.'[4]

Even in Wordsworth's contentions that 'There is a pleasure in poetic pains / Which only poets know,' or that for the young 'Poetry is, like love, a passion,' but for older readers 'a necessity soon arises of breaking the pleasing bondage',[5] there is an element of sadism. Wordsworth argues that it is the role of poetry to conjure up and then temper 'painful feeling', and that 'whenever we sympathize with pain it will be found that the sympathy is produced and carried on by subtle combinations with pleasure'.[6] Expanding on the 'complex feeling of delight' that mingles with 'painful feeling' in metrical verse, Wordsworth compares the pleasure of discovering similitudes to 'the direction of the sexual appetite', and suggests that metre can also 'afford much pleasure' through similar operations.[7] Metre functions to 'restrain' passions and powerful sentiments, including images and feelings that 'have an undue proportion of pain connected with them', and so threaten to 'be carried beyond its proper bounds'.[8] This assertion anticipates Freud's argument in *Beyond the Pleasure Principle* that only once excitation is bound can it be 'resolvable' as pleasure (that is, can be discharged).[9]

The association of metre with sexual passion and bondage will be one of the central focuses of this chapter, which examines the performance of soft masculinity in Ovid's sequence of elegies, the *Amores*, in a translation by Christopher Marlowe from the early 1580s.[10] Ovid was a principle

---

[4] Dionne Brand, *A Map to the Door of No Return: Notes to Belonging* (Toronto: Vintage Canada, 2001), p. 93.
[5] William Wordsworth, 'Essay, Supplementary to the Preface', *Shorter Poems, 1807–1820*, ed. Carl H. Ketcham (Ithaca, NY: Cornell University Press, 1989), p. 643; see Rowan Boyson, *Wordsworth and the Enlightenment Idea of Pleasure* (Cambridge University Press, 2012), pp. 109–16.
[6] William Wordsworth, lines added to the 'Preface' in 1802, *Lyrical Ballads, and Other Poems, 1797–1800*, ed. James Butler and Karen Green (Ithaca, NY: Cornell University Press, 1992), ll. 360–2, p. 752.
[7] Wordsworth, 'Preface' (1800) to *Lyrical Ballads*, ll. 528–34, p. 756.
[8] Wordsworth, 'Preface' (1800) to *Lyrical Ballads*, ll. 500–3, p. 755.
[9] Sigmund Freud, *The Standard Edition*, vol. XVIII: *Beyond the Pleasure Principle, Group Psychology and Other Works*, ed. James Strachey (London: Vintage / Hogarth Press, [1955] 1991), p. 8.
[10] Throughout, I will use the following editions: J. C. McKeown, *Ovid: Amores. Text, Prolegomena and Commentary*, 4 vols. (Liverpool: Francis Cairns, 1987); Christopher Marlowe, *The Complete Works*, ed. Roma Gill, 4 vols. (Oxford: Clarendon, 1987), vol. 1: The Translations.

influence on Marlowe. He probably produced the translation during his student years in Cambridge, and it is often considered juvenilia, full of mistakes and metrical inconsistencies.[11] Algernon Swinburne harrumphed several centuries later that 'had every copy of Marlowe's boyish version or perversion of Ovid's Elegies deservedly perished in the flames to which it was judicially condemned by the sentence of a brace of prelates, it is possible that an occasional bookworm, it is certain that no poetical student, would have deplored its destruction'.[12] However, Harry Levin argues that translation taught Marlowe to master the form that 'would become the standard meter of English drama': blank verse.[13] Marlowe's translation is far from the musical and polished Latin that made Ovid one of the most important *auctores* in the Renaissance classroom, but also far from Marlowe's 'mighty line', which Ben Jonson would commend. Nonetheless, it is important as the first complete translation of Ovid's love elegies into any vernacular European language.

Swinburne alludes to the censoring of Marlowe's translation by what was called the 'Bishop's Ban'. It circulated in six surreptitiously printed editions in the 1580s and 1590s, including a volume of *Epigrammes and Elegies by I. D. and C. M.*, published surreptitiously in 1592.[14] That book contained ten of Marlowe's translations; the rest were published in *All Ovids Elegies: 3. Bookes by C. M. Epigrams by J. D.* (after 1602), with other editions in c. 1630 and c. 1640. Marlowe died in 1593. In 1596, John Whitgift, Archbishop of Canterbury, had attempted to regulate printed pamphlets, 'some conteyning matter of Ribaldrie, some of superstition and some of flat heresie. By means whereof the simpler and least advised sorts of her majesties subjects are either allured to wantonness, corrupted in doctrine or in danger to be seduced from that dutifull obedience which they owe to her highness.'[15] *Epigrammes and Elegies* was called in for burning under the Bishop's Ban in 1599.

The Bishop's Ban associated sexual licentiousness with sedition and atheism. Marlowe himself had been accused of being a spy, a Catholic

---

[11] Syrithe Pugh, 'Marlowe and Classical Literature', in *Christopher Marlowe in Context*, ed. Emily C. Bartels and Emma Smith (Cambridge University Press, 2013), pp. 80–9 (82).
[12] Algernon Swinburne, *The Age of Shakespeare* (New York and London: Harper, 1908), p. 12.
[13] Harry Levin, *The Overreacher: A Study of Christopher Marlowe* (Cambridge, MA: Harvard University Press, 1952), p. 10.
[14] On the publication history, see Charles Nicholls, '"At Middleborough": Some Reflections on Marlowe's Visit to the Low Countries in 1592', in *Christopher Marlowe and English Renaissance Culture*, ed. Darryll Grantley and Peter Roberts (Aldershot: Scolar, 1996), pp. 38–50.
[15] Ian Frederick Moulton, *Before Pornography: Erotic Writing in Early Modern England* (Oxford University Press, 2000), p. 103.

and a 'sodomite.' But this is not the only sense in which the translations are subversive. Marlowe's translation was part of an 'alternative' or 'counter discourse' to the courtly fashion for Petrarchan sonnets at the end of the sixteenth century.[16] Syrith Pugh argues that Marlowe's version of the *Amores* constituted 'an assault' on English Petrarchanism, 'the chastity of the unyielding Petrarchan mistress, and on the stance considered appropriate to the young man seeking advancement'.[17] Petrarch was deeply familiar with Ovid; he himself declared that 'there is no poet who can equal Ovid'.[18] Many of Ovid's conceits from the *Amores* can be traced in Petrarch's *Canzoniere* and *Trionfi* (the title draws on the Roman ritual of the triumph). But Petrarch strips Ovid of his carnality and converts his poetry to Platonic ends; Petrarch's Laura is very different from Ovid's Corinna.[19]

Ovid was also at the centre of early modern school curricula. But the scandalous *Amores* was less often recommended than Ovid's other works, particularly the *Metamorphoses, Fasti, Tristia* and *Heroides*, which were standard schoolroom texts in England in the sixteenth century.[20] Ovid's sexually explicit verse made him a potentially dangerous figure for the work of imitation that was meant to teach both rhetorical and ethical skills to the young, and even his well-known myths were 'poor illustrations of *Constantia, patientia,* and *pietas*, the Roman virtues that Elizabethan culture admired most'.[21] The subversive pleasures enjoyed by the elegiac lover are also reflected in the poems' meter: elegiac distich, a couplet consisting of one line of hexameter and a second line of pentameter. The hexameter line is affiliated with epic; the missing foot in the pentameter line signals the failure or incompletion of civic duty and epic ambitions in favour of a more subjective, private mood.[22] If the hexameter 'marks

---

[16] Gordon Braden, 'Love Poems in Sequence: The *Amores* from Petrarch to Goethe', in *A Handbook to the Reception of Ovid*, ed. John F. Miller and Carole E. Newlands (Oxford and Malden: Wiley Blackwell, 2014), pp. 262–76 (270); Jim Ellis, 'Imagining Heterosexuality in the Epyllia', in *Ovid and the Renaissance Body* ed. Goran V. Stanivukovic (University of Toronto Press, 2001), pp. 38–58 (38).
[17] Pugh, 'Marlowe and Classical Literature', pp. 80–9 (81).
[18] *Rerum memorandum liber* 2.20; cited in Braden, 'Love Poems in Sequence', p. 265.
[19] Warren Ginsberg, 'Dante's Ovids', in *Ovid in the Middle Ages*, ed. James G. Clark, Frank T. Coulson, and Kathryn L. McKinley (Cambridge University Press, 2011), pp. 143–59 (146).
[20] Ann Moss, *Ovid in Renaissance France*, Warburg Institute Surveys 8 (London: Warburg Institute, 1982), p. 3; T. W. Baldwin, *William Shakespeare's Small Latine & Lesse Greeke*, 2 vols. (Urbana: University of Illinois Press, 1944), 1:155-60, 2:417–55.
[21] Sean Keilen, 'Shakespeare and Ovid', in *A Handbook to the Reception of Ovid*, ed. Miller and Newlands, pp. 232–45 (237).
[22] Alastair Fowler, *Kinds of Literature: An Introduction to the Theory of Genres and Modes* (Oxford: Clarendon, 1982), p. 136.

a movement away from the singer', the pentameter 'indicates a return to the self'.[23] The distich is mimetic of the elegy's inward turn, away from public life and towards the vitiating pleasures of the bedroom.

In this chapter, I'll argue that the missing foot is not only the sign of desire as lack, but also resembles a kind of 'wound', inflicted by the lover's submission to the female mistress or *domina*. In Ovid's *Amores*, the fear of castration provokes a violent counter-reaction, inflicted on the bodies of women and slaves. As a form of bondage to which the lover/poet voluntarily submits, elegiac distich follows the pattern that has been discerned across this book: of the production of a gap or blank that disturbs the wholeness of the poem. That blank is both the missing foot in the pentameter line, and the voices of the slaves and women to whom the lover submits himself poetically, while retaining the power associated with his status as a free male citizen.

Soldiers and Slaves

Roman love elegy is a strikingly uniform and condensed genre, which is perhaps best known for its tropes of erotic servitude, the *servitium amoris* (love as slavery), and the *militia amoris* (love as military service). In performing these roles, the elegies repudiate the quintessential Roman values of *virtus*, *gloria*, *gravitas* and *dignitas*, along with the responsibilities of public office, government and law.[24] As Maria Wyke puts it, 'in a society that depended on a slave mode of production and in which citizenship carried the obligation of military service, these two metaphors define the elegiac male as socially irresponsible. As a slave to love he is precluded from participating in the customary occupations of male citizens. As a soldier of love he is not available to fight military campaigns.'[25] The elegists' retreat into the privacy of erotic life constitutes 'a subversion of the very ideological foundations of Roman life'.[26]

For the elegiac poets Callimachus, Propertius, Tibullus and Ovid, *militat omnis amans*: all lovers are soldiers. In his sixth elegy, Propertius rejects an invitation from Tullus, nephew of proconsul of Asia, to

---

[23] Georg Luck, *The Latin Love Elegy* (London: Methuen & Co, 1959 [1979]), p. 30.
[24] Orlando Patterson, *Freedom*, vol. I: *Freedom in the Making of Western Culture* (New York: Basic Books, 1991), p. 221.
[25] Maria Wyke, 'Mistress and Metaphor in Augustan Elegy', in *Latin Erotic Elegy: An Anthology and Reader* ed. Paul Allen Miller (London: Routledge, 2002), pp. 386–409 (403).
[26] Paul Allen Miller, *Lyric Texts and Lyric Consciousness: The Birth of a Genre from Archaic Greece to Augustan Rome* (London: Routledge, 1994), p. 135.

accompany him as member of his uncle's staff: 'Allow me, whom fortune has always made idle, / to deliver my spirit to extreme wantonness'; 'I wasn't born to praise or fighting: / the Fates forced me to my own kind of military' (i.e. love).²⁷ Propertius offers to fight 'hard battles' (*proelia dura*) with his mistress instead (3.5.1–2).²⁸ Tibullus similarly rejects the honour and wealth that accompany military service, though he did actually participate in Messalla's Aquitanian campaign. Instead, he depicts himself as a debased prisoner of love: 'It befits you, Messalla, to make war by land and sea / so that your house may display spoils taken from the enemy. / But the bonds of a lovely girl hold me, a prisoner . . .' (1.1.53–5).²⁹ The elegist Gallus was one of Augustus' most successful generals and served as governor in the new province of Egypt.³⁰

Ovid did no military service. But he constantly invokes the *bella Veneris* (wars of love). In *Amores* 1.2, the conventional assault by Cupid on the speaker is represented as a fight: 'Yielding or struggling doe we give him might' (l. 9, p. 14). In 1.9, seduction involves attacks, uprising and other military innuendos. The speaker in 2.9 pleads for clemency with Cupid, who continues to wound the speaker even though he has already been captured by love, and draws on imagery of war and hunting. Cupid is even said to demonstrate the art of war to Mars: 'Cupid, by thee Mars in great doubt doth trample, / And thy stepfather fights by thy example.' Elegy 2.14 situates abortion and pregnancy within the Roman war economy's need for workers and soldiers. 'What helps it Woman to be free from warre? / Nor being arm'd fierce troupes to follow farre?' (ll. 1–2, p. 52), the poet asks, if they will be killed by self-wrought wounds of reproduction. In 2.10, the lover contrasts the little death of orgasm with the honourable death of the soldier, or the merchant whose ships are lost at sea. He in 'loves mutuall skirmish slayes' (l. 29), and hopes that 'when I dye, would I might droupe with doing' (l. 35, p. 49). This desire to die from fucking, and for his eternal *fama* to be related to his sexual performance, is the epitome of a sexual devotion that turns its back on honourable occupations.

Roman elegy also frequently depicts the lover as a slave. He is debased, unable to act according to his own will, the property of the married *domina*. For Propertius, love is 'usual bondage' (*assueto . . . servitio*, 1.4.4); others will learn 'how heavy is her bondage' (*tum grave servitium nostrae cogere puellae / discrere*, 1.5.19–20). He declares: 'I am a slave not so much to genius as to suffering . . . / This is what I want my poetry known for' (*nec tantum ingenio*

---

²⁷ Sextus Propertius, *The Complete Elegies*, trans. Vincent Katz (Princeton University Press, 2004), 1.6.25–6, pp. 29–30.
²⁸ R. O. A. M. Lyne, 'The Life of Love', in *Latin Erotic Elegy*, ed. Miller, pp. 348–65 (358).
²⁹ Lyne, 'Life of Love', pp. 352, 355.   ³⁰ McKeown, *Ovid: Amores*, 1:29.

quantum servire dolori ... / *hinc cupio nomen carminis ire mei*, 1.7.7, 10); Cynthia makes me 'a slave at her command', and 'I am unable to break my chains, even when the yoke is fractured' (*sub sua iura viram* ... *quod nequeam fracto rumpere vincla iugo*, 3.11.2, 4); 'I was bound, my hands behind my back' (*vinctus eram versas in mea terga manus*, 3.24.14). The lover submits voluntarily (or, under Cupid's compulsion) to the fetters of erotic desire.

Similarly, Tibullus offers himself up to his mistress as a slave: 'Take me away; I will plough the fields at a mistress's command. / From chains and stripes my body shall not shrink' (*ducite: ad imperium dominae sulcabimus agros; / non ego me vinclis verberibusque nego*, 2.3.79–80).[31] His submission to demeaning manual labour also involves a masochistic acceptance of the 'chains and stripes' of whipping by which that labour was extracted. He invites his mistress to punish him: 'Brand me for my wildness, rack me lest it please me to speak anything / grandiloquent again. Tame my rough words' (1.5.5–6). The enslaved lover is reduced to a state of impotence, passion and weakness by female *eros*. Roman elegies do refer regularly to actual slaves (maids, hairdressers, go-betweens, guards and porters who police the boundary between inside and outside and frustrate the lover's attempts to see his mistress), but in those interactions the speaker tends to dominate, and there is no expression of solidarity around their supposedly shared status.[32]

A New-Made Wound

The elegiac tropes of the soldier and slave of love are dramatised in Marlowe's plays of outrageous imperialism: *Tamburlaine Part 1* and *Part 2*. Tamburlaine is a powerful warrior, the personification of Mars; but he goes further than the god, and rejects the enticements of desire. Confronted by a group of pleading virgins, he responds:

> I will not spare these proud Egyptians
> Nor change my Martiall observations,
> For all the wealth of *Gehons* golden waves.
> Or for the love of Venus, would she leave
> The angrie God of Armes, and lie with me.
> (*1 Tamburlaine* 5.1.121–5, *Complete Works* 5:65 65)

---

[31] *Catullus. Tibullus. Pervigilium Veneris*, trans. F. W. Cornish, 2nd rev. ed. G. P. Goold (Cambridge, MA: Harvard University Press, 1989), pp. 266–7.
[32] Laurel Fulkerson, '*Seruitium amoris*: The Interplay of Dominance, Gender and Poetry', in *The Cambridge Companion to Latin Love Elegy*, ed. Thea S. Thorsen (Cambridge University Press, 2013), pp. 180–93 (189).

He then immediately sees Zenocrate, and woos her in extravagant terms, before asserting 'how unseemly is it for my Sex, / My discipline of armes and Chivalrie, / My nature and the terror of my name, / To harbour thoughts effeminate and faint' (5.1.174–7, p. 67). Once he seduces her, Tamburlaine's sadism rubs off on Zenocrate: she begins as his prisoner, and ends up masochistically devoted to her husband and acting like a tyrant (Zenocrate addresses the captive queen Zabina as her slave, and even Zenocrate's handmaid Anippe threatens to have Zabina 'whipp'd stark nak'd').[33]

Both the *Amores* and *Tamburlaine* explore the tension between militarism and erotic love. But there is another connection between them, which is the matter of lameness. The name 'Tamburlaine' derives from the historical figure known as 'Timur the Lame', who was disabled as a child when he was shot by an arrow (by a shepherd, not by Cupid). This lameness relates to the distich, which in the early modern period was often known as a 'hobbled' metre. (Another poet whose physical disability was compared to his 'hobbling verses' was Byron: Matthew Bevis follows that story.)[34] To hobble in this period means 'to walk with an unsteady rising and falling gait,' to limp – that unsteady rising and falling is also a description of elegiac distich. Only in the nineteenth century would hobbling come to mean the act of making an animal limp to prevent it from kicking or straying – a meaning reminiscent of the elegist's depiction of himself as a bridled horse, or Wyatt's clogged heel.

Marlowe's translations of Ovid's *Amores* were central in establishing rhymed iambic pentameter as an English approximation of the Greek and Latin distich. His heroic couplets suit Ovid's poem, in which the period rarely stretches beyond the couplet;[35] the couplet might also have seemed like the closest approximation of the distich, though as Roma Gill notes, it was not widely used in the 1580s.[36] As a form of close coupling, yoking together like sounds and identical measures, the couplets resonate with the elegies' sexual themes, and their linking of form to sexual rebellion. In that sense, Marlowe's couplets can be read as queering Ovid's heteronormative distich by filling in the missing foot and de-feminising the verse form.

---

[33] *Tamburlaine* Part 1, 4.2.74 (*Complete Works* 5:53). See also Lisa S. Starks, '"Won with thy words and conquered with thy looks": Sadism, Masochism, and the Masochistic Gaze in *1 Tamburlaine*,' in *Marlowe, History, and Sexuality: New Critical Essays*, ed. Paul Whitfield White (New York: AMS, 1998), pp. 179–193 (186).

[34] Matthew Bevis, 'Byron's Feet', *Meter Matters: Verse Cultures of the Long Nineteenth Century*, ed. Jason David Hall (Athens, OH: Ohio University Press, 2011), pp. 78–104.

[35] McKeown, *Ovid: Amores*, p. 108.   [36] Marlowe, *Complete Works*, 1:3.

Whatever Marlowe's reasons for choosing this form, however, the failure to reproduce Ovid's metre leads to a paradoxical sequence of poems in which castration is described but not reproduced. It is particularly striking because Ovid repeatedly refers to the missing foot.

The foot in the *Amores* signals loss, conquest or intimacy: the erotically imagined bare feet of the beloved contrast with the 'stumpe-foot' of Vulcan in 2.17 (l. 20, p. 57), just as the hobbled feet of elegiac metre combines elegance and lameness. The speaker in 1.6 describes how love 'guides my feete least stumbling falles they catch' (l. 8, p. 19). In 2.19, Corinna wins the speaker's affections with her 'slowe feete' (l. 12, p. 59); in 3.3, 'her foote was small: her footes forme is most fit' (l. 7, p. 65); in 3.13, she is urged to 'use all tricks, and tread shame under feete' (l. 18, p. 83). As Havelock Ellis observes in his discussion of foot fetishism, Ovid 'is never weary of dwelling on the sexual charm of the feminine foot. He represents the chaste matron as wearing a weighted *stola* which always fell so as to cover her feet; it was only the courtesan, or the nymph who is taking part in an erotic festival, who appears with raised robes, revealing her feet.'[37] The dalliances of these feet, covering and uncovering, hiding and revealing, are fetishised in several of Ovid's elegies.

In elegy 1.4, the speaker pleads with the beloved not to forget him when she is with her husband: 'Lie with him gently, when his limbes he spread, / Upon the bed, but on my foote first tread' (ll. 15–16). The poem's 'feet' – its lines, which can be read – are part of their ardent and secret embodied communication: 'Take, and receive each secret amorous glaunce. / Words without voyce shall on my eye browes sit . . .'). It must proceed by duplicity and secrecy, while the husband can spread out his limbs on his own bed. Allowing himself to further imagine the scene, the speaker begs;

> Mingle not thighes, nor to his legge joyne thine,
> Nor thy soft foote with his hard foote combine.
> I have beene wanton, therefore am perplext,
> And with mistrust of the like measure vext.
>
> (ll. 43–6)

The husband's 'hard foot' could be compared to the hexameter, while the mistress's 'soft' one is the pentameter. But, while he is discouraging their coupling, the speaker also distrusts 'like measures', which would join hard with hard – as in epic metre, or male homosexual sex.

---

[37] Havelock Ellis, *Studies in the Psychology of Sex*, vol. 3: *Erotic Symbolism, the Mechanism of Detumescence, the Psychic State in Pregnancy* (New York: Random House, 1936), p. 24.

The mixing of the erotic and prosodic meanings of the foot continues in 3.1. The poem describes a vision of 'Elegia' who came to the speaker 'with haires perfumed sweete, / And one, I think, was longer, of her feete' (ll. 7–8, p. 61). The feet are the focus of this poem's struggle between Tragedy and Elegy:

> By her footes blemish greater grace she took.
> Then with huge steps came violent *Tragedie* . . .
>
> (ll. 10–11, p. 61)

Tragedy criticises and mocks Elegia's 'wanton spirit', and the speaker's waste of his youth in erotic dalliances, to which Elegy replies:

> Why treadst me downe? art thou aye gravely plaied?
> Thou deignst unequall lines should thee rehearse,
> Thou fightst against me using mine owne verse.
> Thy lofty stile with mine I not compare,
> Small doores unfitting for large houses are.
> . . . By me *Corinna* learnes, cousening her guard,
> To get the dore with little noise unbard.
> And slipt from bed cloth'd in a loose night-gowne,
> To move her feete unheard in setting downe . . .
>
> (ll. 36–40, 49–52, p. 62)

Here, several elegiac topoi are repeated: the 'unequal' verse, light style or content, locked doors, loose garments and bare feet. Tragedy threatens and cajoles the poet, urging him to grander ambitions; but she is ineffective. The elegiac muse has stronger enticements, as her winsomely unequal feet make way for Corinna's silent tread, and Elegia's 'thinne robe' (l. 9) becomes Corinna's 'loose night-gowne'. 'Palla-clad *Tragoedia* presents herself as a *matrona*, while *Elegia*, with her *vestis tenuissima* ("very scanty garment") suggests the appearance and demeanour of the *meretrix*.'[38] Elegy's 'lightness' and 'softness' may not be able to compete with Tragedy's gravity; but unlike Tragedy, she can pick a lock.

Amores 1.1 initiates the focus on the missing foot. It describes the consequence of the speaker's abandonment of the epic theme of arms and the man, and of epic metre in favour of the 'hobbled' distich:

> With Muse upreard I meant to sing of Armes,
> Choosing a subject fit for feirce alarmes.
> Both verses were a like till love (men say)
> Began to smile and tooke one foote away.

---

[38] Hunter H. Gardner, *Gendering Time in Augustan Love Elegy* (Oxford University Press, 2013), p. 129.

> [...] When in this workes first verse I trode aloft,
> Love slackt my Muse, and made my numbers soft.
> I have no mistris, nor no favorit,
> Being fittest matter for a wanton wit.
> Thus I complaind, but Love unlockt his quiver,
> Tooke out the shaft ordaind my hart to shiver:
> And bent his sinewie bow upon his knee,
> Saying Poet heere's a worke beseeming thee.
> Oh woe is me, hee never shootes but hits,
> I burne, love in my idle bosome sits.
> Let my first verse be sixe, my last five feete,
> Fare-well sterne warre, for blunter Poets meete.
>
> (1.1.5–8, 21–32, pp. 13–14)

Love took the foot away; I 'trod aloft' before being pulled back to earth. The opening line – 'I meant to sing of arms' – echoes the famous beginning of Virgil's *Aeneid*. Ovid writes: *Arma gravi numero violentaque bella parabam / edere, materia conveniente modis*: 'Arms and the violent deeds of men fighting in battle ... Those are the noble subjects I would address.' But this epic ambition is thwarted by Cupid's theft of one foot from the distich, and the only battles we witness thereafter are amorous ones. As Patrick Cheney has noted, Ovid thus reverses the Virgilian 'career progression', rejecting epic and tragedy to write in the lower form of amatory poetry.[39]

The poem's opening word, *arma*, was also a colloquial term for the penis. Further sexual innuendos and colloquial references to erections are seeded throughout the poem: '*nervus*' can mean sinew, muscle, strength, or literary vigour; while *attenuare* is used for the slackening after orgasm. *Opus* 'can mean a literary work', sexual intercourse or the penis.[40] Many of the elegies delight in the decline from epic weapons to sexual struggles.[41] Ovid compares the distich to a wave: *sex mihi surgat opus numeris, in quinque residat* ('in six numbers let my work rise, and sink again in five'). Coleridge, translating Schiller, compares the meter to a fountain: 'In the Hexameter rises the Fountain's silvery Column / In the Pentameter still falling melo-

---

[39] Patrick Cheney, 'Career Rivalry and the Writing of Counter-Nationhood: Ovid, Spenser, and Philomela in Marlowe's "The Passionate Shepherd to His Love"', *ELH* 65.3 (Fall 1998), pp. 523–55; Patrick Cheney, *Marlowe's Counterfeit Profession: Ovid, Spenser, Counter-Nationhood* (University of Toronto Press, 1997), p. 10.
[40] Duncan Kennedy, *The Arts of Love: Five Studies in the Discourse of Roman Elegy* (Cambridge University Press, 1993), pp. 58–9.
[41] J. N. Adams, *The Latin Sexual Vocabulary* (Baltimore: Johns Hopkins University Press, 1990), p. 21.

dious down.'[42] But Ovid plays up the erotic overtones of this rising and falling, surging and sinking. In Marlowe's punning translation, the Muse 'upreard' quickly slackens and softens after its upright phallic, but also anal, beginning.

In this opening poem, the elegist declares his intentions, only to immediately undercut them. The poem's form and content are determined not merely by a lack, but by a loss – something 'taken away'. This wound or castration applies to the male and the female speakers in different ways. Elegy 1.5 depicts a scene of love 'In Summers heate, and mid-time of the day'. Marlowe's translation again echoes Wyatt's poem 'They flee from me' ('She took me in her arms long and small, / Therewithall sweetly did me kiss . . .'):

> I snatcht her gowne: being thin, the harme was small,
> Yet striv'd she to be covered therewithal.
> And striving thus as one that would be cast,
> Betrayde her selfe, and yeelded at the last.
>
> (ll. 13–16, p. 19)

Her 'thin' gown translates *tunica . . . recincta*, ungirded tunic, and recalls Wyatt's 'thin array'. But where Wyatt's speaker is unable to capture his prey, Marlowe's poem represents an erotic consummation as violent conquest ('yeelded at the last' – *victa est*). And where Wyatt's beloveds are dainty animals pricking barefoot in his chamber like stalked deer or birds, the Ovidian beloved resembles Semiramis, powerful legendary queen of Babylon known for her sexual prowess.

The beloved is named here for the first time as Corinna, just as her body is blazoned in terms that dismember and fragment it.[43] The poem explores Corinna's arms, breast, stomach and thigh, but stops when it comes to her genitals:

> To leave the rest all lik'd me passing well,
> I cling'd her naked body, downe she fell,
> Judge you the rest, being tirde she bad me kisse;
> *Jove* send me more such after-noones as this.
>
> (ll. 23–6)

She falls, then she is 'tired' out by sexual exertion, and 'attired' only by the covering of a man. Both the centre of the poem's desire and its sexual climax are missing: '*cetera quis nescit*' (who doesn't know the rest)?

---

[42] Samuel Taylor Coleridge, 'The Ovidian Elegiac Metre Described and Exemplified, from Schiller', *Poetical Works*, vol. 1, in *The Collected Works*, 16 vols., ed. J. C. C. Mays (Princeton University Press, 2001), p. 532.

[43] Ellen Greene, *The Erotics of Domination: Male Desire and the Mistress in Latin Love Poetry* (Baltimore: Johns Hopkins University Press, 1998), p. 77.

A New Made Wound

In ancient erotic poetry, the woman's body is repeatedly imagined in its particularity as a site of fantasy, but also erased. As Amy Richlin argues, 'the parts of her body that evoke desire in the poet form a sort of circle around the genitalia: from the usually visible neck, shoulders, and arms, which need to be graceful, to the usually hidden breasts, to the belly ... It is as if there were a blank space in the middle of the woman.'[44] An example is *Amores* 3.2.35–6, where Ovid hints at Corinna's genitals: *suspicor ex istis et cetera posse placere, / quae bene sub tenui condita veste latent*; 'I suspect from those [legs] of yours that the rest, too, is nice, / that lies well hidden under your thin clothing' (46).

The figure of the unspeakability of the woman's genitals was also common in Renaissance verse: the 'fair thought which lies between maidens' legs' that Hamlet refers to as 'nothing' is perhaps the most famous example, but there is also the moment in Edmund Spenser's *Faerie Queene* in which Belphoebe is described:

> So faire, and thousand thousand times more faire
> She seemd, when she presented was to sight,
> And was yclad, for heat of scorching aire,
> All in a silken Camus lylly whight,
> Purfled vpon with many a folded plight,
> Which all aboue besprinckled was throughout,
> With golden aygulets, that glistred bright,
> Like twinkling starres, and all the skirt about
> Was hem'd with golden fringe[45]

This unusual hemistich in line 9 represents a moment of conspicuous self-censorship. The next stanza begins 'Below her ham her weed did somewhat traine,' and focuses on 'a rich Jewell' in which the golden bands are fastened in knots whose ends 'none might see' and 'fouldings close enwrapped.' Remembering that Belphoebe is a figure for Elizabeth I, Louis Montrose argues that the hemistich calls attention to what the poem cannot reveal: the queen's genitals.[46]

The gap in elegiac verse is a manifestation of the wound of heteroerotic desire. By submitting to his female lover, the male elegist becomes wounded himself, unable to perform sexually or poetically. The pentameter line is simultaneously the castrated remnant of the heroic masculinity

---

[44] Amy Richlin, *The Garden of Priapus: Sexuality and Aggression in Roman Humour*, rev. ed. (Oxford University Press, 1992), p. 47.
[45] Edmund Spenser, *The Faerie Qveene*, ed. A. C. Hamilton (London: Longman, 2001), 2.3.26, p. 184.
[46] Louis Montrose, 'Spenser and the Elizabethan Political Imaginary', *ELH* 69.4 (Winter 2002), pp. 907–46 (918–19).

associated with the hexameter, and the sign of the castrated female body. In Freudian terms, the verse materialises the fear of the male speaker at the sight of the female body as an apparently castrated version of his own; in Lacanian terms, it is the sign under which the subject is initiated into the Symbolic as a castrated object, driven by desire for the *objet a*, the lack which constitutes him. We may wish to argue that the dynamics of castration and the production of gender theorised by Freud and Lacan apply specifically to modern subjects. But castration, mythic and real, was more intensely present in Roman culture than it is in modernity. Hesiod represents Aphrodite as a creature born from the foam (*aphros*) where Ouranos' severed genitals were thrown into the sea. Myths of castration also articulated tensions around the transition from the *puer* to the *vir*. Marilyn Skinner describes the self-mutilation of Attis as his response to 'the painful struggle for psychosexual autonomy required to effect his transformation into a fully functioning adult male': stuck forever as a *puer* (boy), passive, receptive, Attis is an extreme form of what the elegiac lover desires and fears becoming, arrested in his progression towards adulthood.[47] Rome was also full of the *galli*, actually castrated men who 'were luxury items in elite households'.[48]

Ovid's elegies are thus an important early precursor of what Roland Barthes calls the 'pornogram': 'not merely the written trace of an erotic practice, nor even the product of a cutting up of that practice, treated as a grammar of sites and operations', but a 'fusion (as under high temperature) of discourse and body'. In this description of the Marquis de Sade's textual and sexual practices, Barthes imagines 'the erotic as a grammarian and . . . language as a pornographer'.[49] The grammar of parts of speech and parts of bodies, the interchangeability of body and text, of the pleasurable wounds of flesh and of prosody, will guide our thinking about poetic rhythm in the next chapter.

These features of the pornogram can also be found in a parody of the Ovidian tropes of sexual conquest and failure by 'Ignoto', who contributed three epigrams to the banned edition of *Epigrammes and Elegies* in which Marlowe's elegies appeared. The poems have been attributed to John

---

[47] Marilyn Skinner, '*Ego mulier*: The Construction of Male Sexuality in Catullus', in *Roman Sexualities*, ed. Judith P. Hallett and Marilyn B. Skinner (Princeton University Press, 1997), pp. 129–50 (137).
[48] Ellen Oliensis, *Freud's Rome: Psychoanalysis and Latin Poetry* (Cambridge University Press, 2009), p. 112.
[49] Roland Barthes, *Sade – Fourier – Loyola*, trans. Richard Miller (Berkeley and Los Angeles: University of California Press, 1989), pp. 158–9.

Davies. Against imagery of an enfeebled lover – either the akratic Petrarchan protagonist, or the impotent Ovidian one – Ignoto asserts his virility:

> Faith (wench) I cannot court thy sprightly eyes,
> with the base Viall plac'd betweene my thyghs,
> I cannot lispe nor to some fidell sing,
> Nor runne vpon a high strecht manikin,
> I cannot whine in puling Elegies,
> Intombing Cupid with sad obsequies,
> I am not fashioned for these amorous times,
> To court thy beawtie with lasciuious rimes:
> I cannot dally, caper, daunce, and sing,
> Oyling my saint with supple sonneting,
> I cannot crosse my armes or sigh ay me,
> Ay me forlorne? egregious foppery,
> I cannot busse thy fill, play with thy haire,
> Swearing by Ioue thou art most debonaire:
> not I by God, but shal I tell thee roundly,
> Harke in thine eare, Zoundes I can ( ) thee soundly.[50]

As in the first elegy from the *Amores*, this poem's elaborate *recusatio* sets up the speaker as someone who fails: who cannot do the things that courtly poets are required to do – write, sing, dance. He cannot take the feminised position of the viol-player, with someone else's instrument between his legs; he can't run his fingers along a 'minkin', a 'thin strand of catgut used for the treble strings of a lute or viol' (according to the Oxford English Dictionary) – but also a word used for a girl (cf. *mignon*) or a high-pitched voice. But there is something he *can* do. For obvious reasons, the poem's climactic verb – 'fuck' – cannot be written, and is instead suggestively rendered as a space between two curving brackets. This hole makes sex the thing that cannot be spoken but only done. And, while the poem is addressed to a 'wench', there is nothing here that specifies that the hole the poem creates is specifically feminine.

Soft Masculinity

Another epigram by Ignoto echoes the casual references to the whipping of slaves in Ovid:

> When Francus comes to solace with his whore
> He sends for rods and strips himselfe starke naked,

---

[50] *Epigrammes and Elegies by I.D. and C.M.* (At Middleborugh: [n.d., c. 1599]), sig. D4^{r-v}.

> For his lust sleepes and will not rise before
> By whipping of the wench it be awaked:
> I enuie him not, but wish I had the power,
> To make my selfe his wench but one halfe howre.[51]

The queerness of this poem is related to the uncertainty of its syntax: is Francus whipping his wench, or being whipped by her? The speaker's wish 'to make myself his wench' is simultaneously an assumption of the female identity of the *domina*, in order to punish the deviant Francus, and a desire to become Francus's effeminised erotic object, potentially to be whipped. Like the elegies, this epigram undermines normative masculinity and heterosexuality but allows itself the 'plausible deniability' that it is actually affirming them.

The instability of the speaker in terms both of gender and sexual positioning in this epigram by Ignoto reflects the characteristics of erotic desire in the ancient world. *Amor* tended to be categorised 'not by the gender but by the social class of the subject as well as the object of desire, and the adult Roman male citizen was always supposed to play the active role'.[52] Activity and passivity reflected not absolute gender positions, but who had the phallus and did the penetrating and who was penetrated. A man who was sexually penetrated by another man was described as *muliebria pati*, 'having [or suffering] a woman's experience': it was construed as effeminising and not pleasurable.[53] A woman could also take the role of the *puer* in anal sex. Jonathan Walters draws out the association between these sexualised roles and the violence of the slave economy: the powerless are vulnerable to the invasion of the boundaries of their bodies; 'the inability to defend one's body is a slavelike mark of powerlessness', and it is in this context that the active/passive polarity should be understood. The soldier, on the other hand, could be honourably penetrated – by a weapon.[54]

As Foucault has argued, sexual morality was also characterised in Graeco-Roman culture by an intense regime of self-rule or *ascesis*: as a boy passed through adolescent passivity or objectification to maturity and masculinity and became the *dominus* [master], he was required to negotiate carefully the process of 'remaining in one's role or abandoning it,

---

[51] *Epigrammes and Elegies*, sig. C3^r.

[52] Marilynn Desmond, 'Gender and Desire in Medieval French Translations of Ovid's Amatory Works', in *Ovid in the Middle Ages*, ed. James G. Clark, Frank T. Coulson and Kathryn L. McKinley (Cambridge University Press, 2011), pp. 108–22 (111).

[53] Holt N. Parker, 'The Teratogenic Grid', pp. 47–65 (48, 50); Jonathan Walters, 'Invading the Roman Body', pp. 29–43 (30); Marilyn B. Skinner, 'Introduction', pp. 3–25 (3), all in *Roman Sexualities*, ed. Hallett and Skinner.

[54] Walters, 'Invading', p. 40.

being the subject of the activity or its object'.[55] Boyhood represented an ambivalent stage, in which the boy's inferior status and expected sexual passivity triggered the desire of older, higher status men; but the boy's attractions and (limited) ability to resist seduction also gave him some power. When he reached marriageable age, he would occupy one of the more elevated positions in his household. But as a boy, he had to navigate the complex and agonistic structure of courtship: he wielded power as the object of pursuit, eventually becoming a passive recipient of the older man's sexual favours. That he would eventually have to transform into an adult male with potential to be a leader of the city is described by Foucault as 'the antimony of the boy' (221).

This cultural context shapes Ovid's *Ars Amatoria*, a didactic poem in which the *praeceptor* ('instructor') teaches young men how to seduce and pleasure young women. The need to teach these skills suggests they are not perceived to be widely diffused. In similar terms, Thomas Habinek argues that Ovid's *Amores* invented 'the category of the heterosexual male' for ancient Rome – a category that would need to be reinvented repeatedly.[56] Although the opening poem of the *Amores* suggests either a boy or a girl would be the right 'materia' for Ovid's love poems (*aut puer aut longas compta puella comas* – 'either a boy or a girl with long hair', 1.1.20; 'I have no mistress, nor no favorit, / Being fittest matter for a wanton wit,' is Marlowe's translation, ll. 23–4, p. 13), the sequence as a whole – like most Roman elegies – focuses on heterosexual desire.

Ovid also uses the elegiac form to explore the performativity of gender, and to mimic the inverted hierarchies of master/mistress and slave. *Amores* 2.17 compares the metre to the erotic relations of Calypso and Ulysses, Thetis and Peleus, Egeria and Numa, Venus and Mars. Ovid places the women on top, in the hexameter line, and their male lovers underneath in the pentameter.[57] The distich inverts conventional heterosexual position-taking, aligning the male with the hole of the missing foot, 'queering' both the verse and the social relations it represents. Such flamboyant heteroeroticism in Roman contexts was an inversion of normative relation of desire between an older man and a boy or *puer*. In that sense, Ovid's elegies

---

[55] Michel Foucault, *The Use of Pleasure: The History of Sexuality*, vol. 2, trans. Robert Hurley (London: Penguin, 1985), p. 47.
[56] Thomas Habinek, 'The Invention of Sexuality in the World-City of Rome', in *The Roman Cultural Revolution*, ed. Thomas Habinek and A. Schiesaro (Cambridge University Press, 1977), pp. 23–43 (31).
[57] Heather James, 'The Poet's Toys: Christopher Marlowe and the Liberties of Erotic Elegy', *MLQ* 67 (2006), pp. 103–27 (113).

explore 'the queer status of heterosexual desire in the context of ancient Roman culture'.[58]

Roman sexual *virtu* is imbricated in social and gender roles and performance. To be a *vir*, an adult male, was distinct from being a *hominis* (usually used for male slaves and lower-class men) or a *puer*: *vir* 'refers specifically to those adult males who are freeborn Roman citizens in good standing', and thus connotes not biological sex but gender as social status.[59] The opposite of *vir* is *femina*, but as a sexual object – and often in the elegies – she is denoted as a *puella* (girl).[60] The word *domina*, first used in Catullus 68.68, is nearly synonymous with *matrona*, but it originally signified a woman who owns slaves. Unlike the *puella*, the elegiac *domina* is sexually unrestrained and powerful. But her subjugation of the male lover does not allow her to occupy 'the position of social responsibility that has been taken from the male'.[61] She violates the decorum of Roman matronal femininity by betraying her husband and her domestic duties to indulge, like the male lover, in sensual pleasure. She also forces her lover to submit and obey her, confining him in private spaces – in other words, she imposes upon him the role and behaviour expected of women rather than the active, public civility that befits a man. For the male and the female lover, abandoning duty for pleasure undermines not just the status of the individual, but the *socius* to which they belong.

These connections between sexual life and the values and reproduction of the *socius* are made explicit in the *lex Iulia de adulteriis coercendis* (c. 18 BCE), which forbade married women from having sexual relations with men who were not their husbands. It divided women into two categories: 'prostitutes (and procuresses) on the one hand, and, on the other, all remaining women, who either were or should aspire to be *matronae*'.[62] Later, Augustus withdrew the law in response to widespread criticism.[63] But it may have played a part in Ovid's exile to Tomis. In the *Tristia*, Ovid famously says it was for 'a poem and a mistake' (*carmen et error*, 2.207). Augustus' granddaughter Julia was exiled for adultery in the same year, but Ovid's personal crime is not known. One reason often proposed is that he had either antagonised the emperor Augustus or violated this law.

Augustus' legislation was intended to reinforce the power of the familial patriarch and to affirm the *princeps* (prince) as the guardian of traditional

---

[58] Desmond, 'Gender and Desire', p. 122. [59] Walters, 'Invading', pp. 31–2.
[60] Parker, 'The Teratogenic Grid', p. 49. [61] Wyke, 'Mistress and Metaphor', p. 403.
[62] Roy K. Gibson, 'The *Ars Amatoria*', in *A Companion to Ovid*, ed. Peter Knox (Oxford and Malden: Wiley-Blackwell, 2009), pp. 90–103 (99).
[63] James, 'The Poet's Toys', p. 114.

civic and personal morality, including political service and a commitment to public life instead of the indulgence of private pleasure. The law asserted a regulatory power over sexuality that had previously been monopolised by the family.[64] It was a response to a crisis in the late republic and early Roman empire that manifested as anxiety about sexual and personal conduct. Women had previously been sold into marriage; their legal condition of *coemptio* was modelled on that of children and slaves. By Augustus' period, they had gained freedom and power: the husband's capacity to alienate his wife's property was constrained; the dowry reverted to the wife in the event of a divorce; women practised birth control and abortion, formed freely chosen amorous bonds, lived outside matrimony and enjoyed previously unthinkable sexual freedom.[65] The upper classes were apparently in decline: aristocratic men were increasingly perceived as effeminate, families were failing to reproduce sufficiently and social inequality was on the rise.[66] There was a fear that retreat from public honour into the domestic and sexual life of the individual would sap the state of its strength.

The speaker in Roman elegy is an image of that dissipated man Augustus tried to legislate out of existence. He is soft and akratic; he rejects militarism and public honour in order to enjoy the deliriums of sexual pleasure. *Mollitia* or softness, of the phallus and the verse, was a central characteristic of Roman elegy, and of the heterosexual masculinity it instituted. Propertius, who asserts that 'gentle Love looks for soft poems' (1.9.11–12), describes how a lover wishes in vain to compose soft verse (*mollem ... versum*, 1.7.19), a soft book (*mollis ... liber*, 2.1.2), and wear a soft wreath (*mollia ... corona* 3.1.19–20). This quality of softness is effeminising: a pseudo-etymology derived *mollitia* from *mulier* (woman).[67] Duncan Kennedy says that the adjectives *durus* (hard) and *mollis* 'were so gender-specific' that 'the noun *mollitia*, "softness", could be used without more ado to describe derogatively male behaviour that was thought to contain characteristics essentially female'; he cites the description by Velleius Paterculus of Maecenas, who 'would dissolve into an idleness and acts of softness almost beyond what one would expect of a woman' (*otio ac mollitiis paene ultra feminam fluens*, 2.88.2).[68] Softness also reveals the enervating effect of

---

[64] Habinek, 'The Invention of Sexuality', pp. 23–43 (29).
[65] Patterson, *Freedom*, 1:249–250, citing Cantarella, *Pandora's Daughters* (Baltimore: Johns Hopkins University Press, 1987), pp. 140–1.
[66] Paul Allen Miller, *Subjecting Verses: Latin Love Elegy and the Emergence of the Real* (Princeton University Press, 2004), p. 23.
[67] Maria Wyke, *The Roman Mistress: Ancient and Modern Representations* (Oxford University Press, 2002), pp. 168–9.
[68] Kennedy, *Arts of Love*, p. 31.

heterosexual desire on the male lover, particularly in relation to a hard (*dura*) and therefore masculine *domina*. Plutarch's 'Dialogue on Love' from the *Moralia*, for example, criticises that 'lax and housebound love, that spends its time in the bosoms and beds of women, ever pursuing a soft life, enervated amid pleasure devoid of manliness and friendship and inspiration – it should be proscribed, as in fact Solon did proscribe it'.[69] Unlike heroic poets who portray Achilles in 'tragick verse', the elegists 'sit in *Venus* slothfull shade', luxuriating in love and shame (2.18.1–3, p. 57).

Several of Ovid's elegies perform the softening or 'slackening' that follows both orgasmic expenditure and poetic enfeeblement. In the first poem, he complains: 'When in this workes first verse I trod aloft, / Love slackt my Muse, and made my numbers soft.' These lines are how Marlowe translates *cum bene surrexit veru nova pagina primo,* / *attenuat nervos proximus ille meos* ('when a new page has sprung up, with a good opening line, then the next line takes away my power', 1.1.21–2). The most explicitly sexual example of this loss of power is 3.6, Ovid's elegy on impotence. The poetic scenario is well known from John Wilmot, second Earl of Rochester's version. The speaker complains he cannot 'cast anckor'; despite all of Corinna's best efforts to revive him, he still lies 'Like a dull Cipher, or rude block' (ll. 6, 15, p. 71). He blames her – she is unattractive, or not trying her hardest; 'she kist not as she should', or used her 'cunning' as she ought (l. 55, p. 72). Eventually Corinna gives up: 'With that, her loose gowne on, from me she cast her, / In skipping out her naked feet much grac'd her' (ll. 81–2, p. 73). These lines recall the 'naked foot' of the beloved who stalks Wyatt's speaker in his chamber. Here, the naked, silent foot that signals sexual intimacy is related to the missing foot in elegiac metre, whose collapse from epic fullness is a sign of its inadequacy.

As in 2.10, whose speaker 'droupe[s] with doing' (l. 35, p. 49) or softens after sex, this elegy describes the speaker's soft penis in explicit terms. Though she attempts to stimulate him, it 'droupt downe, regarding not her hand' (3.6.76): 'like one dead it lay, / Drouping more than a rose puld yester-day' (ll. 65–6, p. 73). The speaker then laments that now, when he is trying to write, it has suddenly revived:

> Now, when he should not jette, he bolts upright,
> And craves his taske, and seekes to be at fight. (ll. 67–8, p. 73)

Potent, erect masculinity is signified as a desire to 'fight', a caricature of military valour from an elegist who refuses to go to war. But if elegiac

---

[69] Plutarch, 'The Dialogue on Love', *Plutarch's Moralia in Fifteen Volumes*, vol. IX, trans. Edwin L. Minar, F. H. Sandbach and W. C. Helmbold (London: Heinemann, 1961), pp. 750–1.

composition is a matter of 'numbers soft', erection interferes with that work. Heterosexual desire is represented as unruly and counterproductive, with slackness countering satisfaction and unintended hardness countering the production of verse.

The next elegy opens with a question: 'What man will now take liberall arts in hand, / Or thinke soft verse in any stead to stand' (3.7.1–2, p. 73)? The writing of verse and the practice of liberal arts are related to the impotence of and in the previous poem. The relation between writing and masturbation anticipates Halpern's description of transcribing the autopsy report, and the fantasy of fisting the detainee. In Ovid's poem, the verse is soft, the art cannot be taken in hand, the mistress is not moved by his poems; instead, she transfers her affections to a knight (*eques*) who wears 'a sharpe sword' (l. 14). The lover cannot force her to be repulsed by the body of his rival, scarred by war, whose right hand (writing hand) is 'bloud sprinckled' (l. 16). He can only stand by idly and offer his mistress an education in the ways of the world, which he explains is pillaged for political and economic gain, and enriches soldiers with blood: 'See a rich chuffe whose wounds great wealth inferr'd, / For bloodshed knighted, before me preferr'd' (*ecce recens dives parto per vulnera censu / praefertur nobis sanguine pastus eques*, ll. 9–10). Her preference for an actual soldier confirms that the speaker's impotence as a man is not overcome by his 'upreard' Muse or his powers of persuasion: poetic performance is no compensation for sexual failure. The inadequacy of the poet's powers of persuasion signal that outside the world of the elegy, the values of militarism are not so easily overcome.

Tamings and Triumphs

Although submission to love's enslavement is conventional in Roman elegy, the lover in the *Amores* cannot abide it for very long. He is at best an angry or recalcitrant slave. In 1.4, Ovid's speaker threatens to seize the kisses his mistress gives to her husband (*dicam "mea sunt" iniciamque manum* – 'I shall say "those are mine" and seize them') by 'putting a hand on you', which is the formula that can be traced back to the Twelve Tables as an assertion of legal ownership by which the rightful owner can reclaim his property, including his slaves.[70] Elegy 1.2 shows the tormented lover aspiring to be like the old oxen who get fewer beatings because they are used to drawing the plough, and not like the 'rough jades' whose mouths 'with stuborne bits are torne' (l. 15). Similar imagery can be found in Propertius: 'just as the bull at

---

[70] Miller, *Subjecting Verses*, pp. 178–81.

first rejects the plow, / but afterwards, becoming used to the yoke, comes mildly to the fields, so insolent youths are jumpy at first in love, / but, once dominated, endure just and unjust treatment' (2.3.47–50).[71]

Woman had been described by Cato the Elder in 195 BCE as an 'untamed animal of violent nature' (*impotenti naturae et indomito animali*) that must be reined in by men.[72] Chapter 1 gave some examples from Wyatt's poetry of animal training as an ambivalent metaphor for heterosexual relations, and of the fear that these animals could revert to their wild nature. In Ovid's elegies, the lover's humiliatingly bovine or equine submission soon becomes an image of domination *of* the woman. In 3.4, the mistress is herself compared to a horse who dashes 'against the bitte stiffe-neckt', and only 'stayde' when the reins are slackened (ll. 13–16, p. 67). In 2.2 the poet addresses domineering husbands 'whose care doth thy mistress bridle', assuring them that the wives are able to escape detection in their adulteries:

> On tell-tales neckes thou seest the linke-knitt chaines,
> The filthy prison faithlesse breasts restraines.
> ... I sawe ones legges with fetters blacke and blewe,
> By whom the husband his wives incest knewe.
> More he deserv'd, to both great harme he fram'd
> The man did grieve, the woman was defam'd.
>
> (2.2.41–2, pp. 47–50)

This depicts a much more literal bondage of a Roman woman, fettered to ensure her fidelity. The fear that women would subvert these controls was part of the heterosexual obsessions of the elegy. Elegy 3.4 claims that it is absurd to keep women in bondage, comparing the beloved to a stallion better handled with softness than a hard rein:

> I saw a horse against the bitte stiffe-neckt,
> Like lightning go, his strugling mouth being checkt.
> When he perceivd the reines let slacke, he stayde,
> And on his loose mane the loose bridle laide.
>
> (3.4.13–16, p. 67)

The image subverts the Platonic conceit of the horses of appetite restrained by reason by applying it to heterosexual domination.

But it is not just animals that symbolise domination in the *Amores*. In Marlowe's rendering the elegy continues, 'A free-borne wench no right 'tis

---

[71] Propertius, *Complete Elegies*, pp. 90–1.
[72] Judith Hallett, 'Women as *Same* and *Other* in Classical Roman Elite', *Helios* 16.1 (1989), pp. 59–78 (61).

up to locke: / So use we women of strange nations stock' (ll. 33–4). The control of women is likened to imperial conquest and sexual slavery. In 3.10, the jilted lover promises to foreswear his mistress:

> Now have I freed my selfe, and fled the chaine,
> And what I have borne, shame to beare againe.
> We vanquish, and tread tam'd love under feete,
> Victorious wreathes at length my Temples greete.
>
> (ll. 3–6, p. 78)

Yet the expression of emancipation is short-lived. Having caught his mistress in a tryst with another man, he is now wise to her betrayals, but unable to stop loving her. 'Bulles hate the yoake, yet what they hate have still' (3.10.35, p. 79).

In such moments, Ovid's lover refuses to occupy the position of the soft, enfeebled slave of love any longer. His desire to 'vanquish' and 'tame' what once dominated him, to turn the tables and win 'wreathes' of victory by reclaiming his masculine status through domination, leads to fantasies of sadistic violence. The speaker in 2.5 imagines attacking the mistress for her infidelity: though she seems 'comely', the speaker imagines 'kembed as they were, her lockes to rend, / And scratch her faire soft cheeks I did intend' (ll. 45–6, p. 42). In 1.7 the speaker invites his friends (or the reader) to 'Binde fast my hands, they have deserved chaines' for having struck his mistress (l. 1, p. 21): 'Slaughter and mischiefs instruments, no better, / Deserved chaines these cursed hands shall fetter' (ll. 27–8, p. 22). It lingers over her scratched cheeks, and imagines that her lips and shoulders a red from being 'bitten'.

Masculine authority is also reclaimed through violence against other members of the household.[73] In 1.8 the lover imagines taking revenge on the lady's maid for counselling her against their affair: 'her bleare eyes, balde scalpes thin hoary flieces / And riveld cheeks I would have puld a pieces' (ll. 111–12, p. 26). The lover is also sexually intimate with Corinna's slaves, perhaps as a form of revenge, or a way of reasserting the authority he has lost in his subjection to her. In 2.7, Cypassis, a female servant who was 'wont to dress thy head', is accused by Corinna of violating her mistress's bed (ll. 17–18, p. 45). (The following elegy confirms the charge.) The speaker assures Corinna that he hasn't slept with her slave, 'a base wench of despised condition' (*sordida contemptae sortis amica*, l. 20): 'With *Venus* game who will a servant grace? / Or any back made rough

---

[73] David Frederick, 'Reading Broken Skin: Violence in Roman Elegy', in *Roman Sexualities*, ed. Hallett and Skinner, pp. 172–93.

with stripes imbrace?' (*quis Veneris famulae conubia liber inire / tergaque conplecti verbere secta velit?*, ll. 21–2). The sadism of the slave economy is made visible in the scars of whipping that mark this woman's back.

Ovid's elegies also reclaim masculine domination through the ritualised spectacle of the triumph. In these pageants, defeated enemy soldiers and other booty would be paraded before the chariot of a conquering general to the Temple of Jupiter on the Capitoline Hill, where the general would make sacrifices and some prisoners might be executed. Mary Beard describes the procession: 'the spoils carried on wagons or shoulder-high on portable stretchers (*fercula*); the paintings and models of conquered territory and battles fought; the golden crowns send by allies or conquered peoples to the victorious general; the animals that were to be sacrificed, trumpeters and dancers; plus the captives in chains, the most important of them directly in front of the general's chariot'. The chariot was decorated with a *phallos* (to avert the evil eye); the hero's face was painted red, and he wore a laurel crown, holding an ivory sceptre in one hand, a branch of laurel in the other. Behind him stood a slave, who held a gold crown over his head, whispering 'Look behind you. Remember you are a man.' Behind the chariot were leading officers and Roman citizens who had been freed from slavery by the victory, wearing 'caps of liberty'. Finally came victorious soldiers, chanting the ritual cry *io triumphe*.[74] Sometimes prisoners were forced to perform as part of the spectacle. The triumph 're-presented and re-enacted the victory. It brought the margins of the Empire to its centre, and in so doing celebrated the new geopolitics that victory had brought about.'[75]

Elegy drew on the triumph, sometimes in deviant ways, to stage its own rituals of erotic power. Across a series of elegies that reference Rome's foreign wars and domestic struggles, and which (like Ovid's) fantasise about sadistic violence against the mistress as well as his rivals, Propertius imagines that Cynthia 'will be a victory dearer to me than conquered Parthians, / she will be my spoils, kings, and chariots,' and he will raise a memorial column to her name (*haec mihi devictis potior victoria Parthis, / haec spolia, haec reges, haec mihi currus erunt*, 2.14.23–5). His first elegy opens with the admission that Love 'pressed on my head with his feet' (*caput impositis pressit Amor pedibus*, 1.1.4).[76] This is the historic gesture of triumph, which was performed by the Byzantine emperor at the Circus in Constantinople. (It is notably also the gesture that

---

[74] Mary Beard, *The Roman Triumph* (Cambridge, MA: Belknap Press of Harvard University Press, 2007), pp. 81–2.
[75] *Ibid.*, p. 32.   [76] Propertius, *Complete Elegies*, p. 3.

Marlowe's Tamburlaine uses, turning the Ottoman emperor into his literal footstool.)

The language of the triumph also permeates the *Amores*. The lover is sometimes a conqueror, sometimes a captured and defeated slave, in a scene that places him at the heart of a Roman ritual of military and political power. The opening poem, dedicated to Cupid, proclaims the god's imperial power: 'Great are thy kingdoms, over strong and large, / Ambitious impe, why seekst thou further charge?' (ll. 17–18, p. 13) – the winged 'impe' has graduated to an *imperator*. Similarly, elegy 2.9 acknowledges that Cupid's empire is so vast, 'with great laude thou maiest a triumph move' (l. 16, p. 47). Cupid's geopolitical reach is mirrored by the Roman imperial economy, in which the lovers partake in trading in people and things: '*Germany* shall captive hair-tyers send thee, / And vanquisht people curious dressings lend thee' (1.14.45–6, p. 34). In 2.12 Ovid compares seduction favourably to the sacking of Troy; the speaker managed to conquer his mistress who was defended by 'her husband, guard, and gate' 'without bloud-shed' – presumably because her hymen had already been broken (ll. 3, 6, p. 51). Repeatedly drawing on the *militia amoris* trope ('I guide and souldiour wunne the field and weare her,' l. 13), the poem compares the conquest of Corinna to the battles with the Sabine women.

Cupid's expansive imperial ambitions are also commemorated in 1.2, the last poem in the volume of *Epigrammes and Elegies*. Cupid is prepared to 'burne' full many, 'and give wounds infinite at every turne' in love's battles (ll. 43–4, p. 15), until he enters Rome as a conqueror:

> Unwilling Lovers, love doth more torment,
> Then such as in their bondage feele content.
> Loe I confesse, I am thy captive I,
> And hold my conquered hands for thee to tie.
> What needes thou warre, I sue to thee for grace,
> With armes to conquer armlesse men is base,
> Yoke *Venus* Doves, put Mirtle on thy haire,
> *Vulcan* will give thee chariots rich and faire.
> The people thee applauding thou shalt stand,
> Guiding the harmelesse Pigeons with thy hand.
> Yong men, and women shalt thou lead as thrall,
> So will thy triumph seeme magnificall.
> I lately caught, will have a new made wound,
> And captive like be manacled and bound.
> Good meaning, shame, and such as seeke loves wracke,
> Shall follow thee their hands tyed at their backe.

> Thee all shall feare and worship as a King,
> *Io*, triumphing shall thy people sing.
>
> (1.2.17–34, pp. 14–15)

The lover seeks to avoid suffering through submission to the god of love, imagined as the most abject form of political subjection: he is a conquered slave, manacled, driven before the chariot of the conquering general, a spectacle for crowds of onlookers. This slave has been 'caught' and wounded (a wound I've associated with castration), but notably not by his mistress. Rather, his conqueror is Cupid: 'Beholde thy kinsmans *Caesars* prosperous bandes. / Who guards the conquered with his conquering hands' (ll. 51–2). Ovid refers to Cupid as *triumphator*, because the Julian family derived its descent from Jupiter via Venus and Aeneas; Caesar Augustus would thus technically be a 'kinsman' (*cognatus*) to Cupid. As Miller notes, the triumph at the time of Ovid had become 'the exclusive property of the imperial household': it is only because he is Caesar's cousin that *Amor* can be granted a triumph.[77] Cupid wears not the laurel that signifies both the triumphant conqueror and the poet, but a wreath of myrtle, used in the 'lesser' ceremony of *ovatio* and a plant sacred to Venus.[78]

In 1.7, the speaker urges the 'Conqueror' to raise 'glorious triumphs' to Jove, 'engirt thy hayres with baies, / And let the troupes which shall thy Chariot follow, / *Io* a strong man conquerd this Wench, hollow' (ll. 35–8, p. 22). But the identity of the conqueror is ambivalent: the mistress is both victor and victim. The elegy depicts the beloved as triumphant because she has been beaten by her lover and shamed him; but she is also the victim, led like a 'sad captive' before the chariot, displaying her 'hurt cheekes' rather than any amorous marks on her lips and neck. Moreover, he is spared from participating in the triumph itself; though he imagines his infamy being proclaimed publicly, his prostration before his injured mistress happens later, in private. As Ellen Greene notes, the scene has none of the sympathy for the victim of sexual assault that Ovid reveals in his depiction of the rape of the Sabine women in the *Ars Amatoria*, or in the assaults on virgin women in the *Metamorphoses*.[79] When the assaulted mistress walks before the chariot, like a prisoner, the emblems of her suffering undermine the masculine lover's triumph, but the poem seems to blame her for his public shame.

Roman accounts of the triumph represent prisoners being whipped, insulted and abused; their hands bound behind their backs, their eyes

---

[77] Miller, *Subjecting Verses*, p. 164. [78] Beard, *Roman Triumph*, p. 113.
[79] Greene, *Erotics of Domination*, p. 94.

downcast or full of tears. Ovid described several such sadistic scenes, including one in the *Tristia*:

> So all the populace can watch the triumph,
> Read names of generals and captured towns
> See captive kings with necks in chains and marching
> Before the horses in gay laurel crowns
> And note some faces fallen like their fortunes
> And others fierce forgetting how they fare.[80]

The desire to humiliate prisoners was balanced by the need to represent the conquest as against worthy opponents; defeating elite and noble enemies was more glorious than subjecting abject ones. Nonetheless, there were dangers that these elite enemies might also provoke pity or admiration. Beard cites the pity provoked by displays of the children of King Perseus at the triumph of Aemilius Paullus, or the Egyptian princess Arsinoe at Julius Caesar's triumph in 46 BCE (136). The authorities could not always control the audience's attention and sympathies. In the *Amores*, being beaten by a feeble girl is shameful; suffering does not ennoble the lover so much as spur him to imagine his revenge and reclaim his status as a free man. The speaker may be wreathed in laurel, but can only expect ironic commendations from the crowd: '*Io* a strong man conquerd this Wench' (l. 38).

Love is War

So why read Ovid, particularly in a juvenile sixteenth-century translation, in this moment of modern historical crisis? Because Marlowe's poems clarify an important fact about the canon of Western erotic poetry: over two millennia, love has been represented not just as a private space of refuge from militarisation and oppression, but also its continuation. Against some ideal of love as a relation of equality and mutual recognition, there exists a historical praxis in which the abjection of the lover – usually male – can be turned poetically into violence or fame, and the unspeakability of sex made into the creative reproductivity of verse.

Ovid's poetry, and Marlowe's translations, intermingle militarism and eroticism, masculine heroism and effeminate *otium*, paradoxically challenging the authority of Augustan and Tudor sexual norms through failure. This argument takes up the akratic nature of the erotic subject which we

---

[80] Ovid, *Sorrows of an Exile: Tristia*, trans. A. D. Melville and Edward J. Kenney (Oxford University Press, 1992), 4.2.19–24, pp. 27–8.

examined in relation to Wyatt and Halpern; but the elegistic subject does not remain in the abject, masochistic position in which he is abandoned to the whims of the sovereign. Instead, elegy couples the shame of effeminacy, impotence and failure with the reassertion of phallic domination, and shows off the ability to enact violence on the body of the female beloved, if not on the battlefield. The lover's erotic submission is figured not *against* but *within* the language and symbolism of militarised political life. The lover may claim to have shunned the *negotium* of law, politics and warfare, but love is repeatedly described as itself a kind of war.

The tension between impotence and the 'Muse upreard', heterosexual domination and queer defiance, plays out at the level of the metre, where writing is part of the performance of failure, and what is not written makes space for the subversion of heroic masculinity by feminised, passive bodies. By voluntarily locking themselves into the constrained form of the elegiac distich, with all its pleasures and dishonours, the elegists contribute to the idealisation of lyric constraint that I have explored throughout this book: they imitate slavery, draw on it figuratively and symbolically. At the same time, they fuck and whip actual slaves.

I've argued that Wyatt, who is often discussed as the first 'modern' English lyric poet, can tell us something about what we think the modern lyric is. So, too, with the Latin elegy, which has been identified – in both its metrical turn away from the public values expressed in the hexameter towards the 'personal' inwardness of the pentameter, and its thematic turn away from politics towards love – as an essentially *lyric* mode. Paul Allen Miller argues that Latin elegy is subversive, because while it is written in (and relies on) a slave economy, it presents a 'utopian vision of unfettered subjectivity', appearing to be free of those 'social processes and productive relations'.[81] But the multiple references to both the domestic and national economies, the symbolic apparatus of the triumph and imperial war in elegies mean that these poems do not in the least appear 'free' of the social processes by which gender, sexuality or status (free or enslaved) are reproduced. The elegists subject themselves to the *domina*, willingly becoming effeminised and weakened objects, while erasing parts of the female body whose reproductive labour sustains the *imperium*. For these reasons, elegy seems less utopian than emblematic of the way that poets appropriate the labour of others, and conjure fantasies of freedom and bondage by ceremonially inverting the actuality of enslavement.

---

[81] Miller, *Lyric Texts*, pp. 127–8.

CHAPTER 10

The Ecstatic Lash of the Poetic Line
Swinburne, Hopkins and the Pleasures of Bondage

> *my passion,*
> *first and last,*
> *is for the ecstatic lash*
> *of the poetic line*
> *and no visible recompense*
>
> — Fanny Howe

The previous chapter showed how in Ovid's elegies, the desire for mastery or submission is manifested prosodically, and invokes the civic and sexual mores and rituals of the Roman empire. But it is no more accurate to call the elegies or their characters sadomasochistic than it is to call them heterosexual, because these categories did not exist in imperial Rome. As Michel Foucault has taught us, it was not until the epistemological projects of the nineteenth century that sexual identities came to be defined based on specific practices. Sadism and masochism were framed as distinct perversions in 1886 by Richard von Krafft-Ebing in *Psychopathia Sexualis*, the monumental and popular sexological study that he expanded into twelve editions before his death in 1902. In the fifth edition, Krafft-Ebing refers to 'sadism', which had been coined by the French lexicographer Pierre Boiste (1765–1824) to describe the practices of Donatien Alphonse François, the Marquis de Sade.[1] Krafft-Ebing named masochism after Leopold von Sacher-Masoch, whose literary works like Sade's explored sexuality and domination alongside revolutionary politics and the histories of oppression and emancipation. These coinages have endured, and are commonly understood to refer to erotic dispositions to enjoy pain. However, even in the earliest diagnoses, sadism and masochism were understood primarily as the eroticisation of power, with pain as a secondary aim. For

---

[1] Jens De Vleminck, 'Sadism and Masochism on the Procrustean Bed of Hysteria: From *Psychopathia Sexualis* to *Three Essays on the Theory of Sexuality*', *Psychoanalysis and History* 19.3 (2017), pp. 379–406 (380).

Krafft-Ebing, the masochist 'is controlled by the idea of being completely and unconditionally subject to the will of a person of the opposite sex; of being treated by this person as by a master'.[2] This definition de-centres pain; 'the symbolism of subjection is the most important factor' (95). Krafft-Ebing's intuition that sadism and masochism were primarily relations of power rather than pain has been upheld in much contemporary theory and psychoanalysis. John Noyes defines masochism as a 'complex set of strategies for transforming submissiveness, pain, and unpleasure into sexual pleasure'.[3] Gaylyn Studlar also argues that masochism is not the pursuit of pain but a 'search for submission'.[4]

In this chapter, I'll refer to BDSM, an acronym that gathers a range of sexual behaviours: bondage/discipline, dominance/submission and sadism/masochism. Dominance and submission are related, but distinct, forms of kink that are also primarily oriented towards power exchange. Technically, the bottom, slave or 'sub' (submissive) cedes power to the top, master/mistress or 'dom'/'domme' (dominatrix, dominant) as part of an eroticised, though not always sexual, encounter. The focus in dominance scenes on fulfilling the bottom's desires allows him or her to make extensive (explicit and implicit) demands on the top. This paradox of submission as control is referred to as 'topping from the bottom'.[5] BDSM is also an elaborately discursive practice, in which participants negotiate limits and desires in advance of encounters that are surrounded by, and sometimes largely conducted through, talk.

In the Introduction, I quoted Terrance Hayes's comparison of the sonnet to a 'panic room'. The image of the poem as a prison cell has also recurred throughout this book. But for many poets, a BDSM dungeon is possibly a more accurate analogy for poetic constraint: a space within which the participants can voluntarily lock themselves, submitting to the constraints they elect for a certain duration, in the interest of pleasure, therapy or emancipation. This chapter will put further pressure on the voluntarism of poetic constraint, by thinking again about how pleasurable submission draws on and effaces the real conditions of historical domination.

---

[2] Richard von Krafft-Ebing, *Psychopathia Sexualis*, 7th ed., trans. Charles Gilbert Chaddock (Philadelphia: F. A. Davis, 1893), p. 89.
[3] John Noyes, *The Mastery of Submission: Inventions of Masochism* (Ithaca, NY: Cornell University Press, 1997), p. 11.
[4] Gaylyn Studlar, *In the Realm of Pleasure: Von Sternberg, Dietrich, and the Masochistic Aesthetic* (New York: Columbia University Press, 1988), p. 15.
[5] Danielle Lindemann, *Dominatrix: Gender, Eroticism, and Control in the Dungeon* (University of Chicago Press, 2012), p. 25.

I will test that position again, with close readings of poems by two very different white men writing during the birth of sexology: Algernon Charles Swinburne and Gerard Manley Hopkins. Both poets show how prosody and its pedagogies function as disciplinary instruments. Swinburne could be called a 'switch'; the fluidity of his poetic identifications with sadistic and masochistic positions is akin to the complex instabilities of gender in his poems.[6] Hopkins generally expresses a masochistic outlook, though it is sometimes masochism projected on to another – and thus involves a kind of scopophilic sadism. This chapter is balanced towards masochism, in part because it is relatively understudied, and in part because the voluntary submission to constraint that this book has theorised is closer to a masochistic than a sadistic position. I'll also argue that in these poetries, and in two classic prose texts of masochism (Leopold Von Sacher-Masoch's *Venus in Furs*, 1870, and *Histoire d'O*, 1954, by Pauline Réage), slavery or capitalist exploitation is repackaged as fantasy, a sign of the sexual liberty of the writing subject. But these fantasies are reliant on actual histories of domination that sadomasochistic practice must somehow disavow. That reliance destabilises some of the claims made by contemporary practitioners about the emancipatory potential of BDSM. My question in this chapter is whether it does the same for lyric poetry.

Beating Rhythms

In a letter to Robert Bridges, Hopkins attempts to explain his new theory of sprung rhythm with an example from his poem 'The Wreck of the Deutschland': 'Why, if it is forcible in prose to say "lashed: rod", am I obliged to weaken this in verse, which ought to be stronger, not weaker, into "lashed birch-ród" or something?'[7] Hopkins's example draws on a long historical association between discipline and prosody, going back to Aytoun's suggestion that the critic's 'paternal hand' should loosen the deviant poet's pantaloons and lay on his force 'till the blood comes'.

A more recent example of this association can be found in Eve Kosofsky Sedgwick's richly provocative 1987 essay, 'A Poem is Being Written'. In the essay, whose title riffs on Freud's 1919 essay 'A Child is Being Beaten', Sedgwick recalls childhood experiences of being spanked: 'When I was a little child the two most rhythmic things that happened to me were

---

[6] John Vincent, 'Flogging is Fundamental: Birch in Swinburne's *Lesbia Brandon*', in *Novel Gazing: Queer Readings in Fiction*, ed. Eve Kosofsky Sedgwick (Durham: Duke University Press, 1997), p. 284.
[7] Gerard Manley Hopkins, *The Letters to Robert Bridges*, ed. Claude Colleer Abbott (Oxford University Press, 1935), p. 46; hereafter cited as *LI*.

spanking and poetry.'[8] She memorialises the scene as a 'breath-holding space, a small temporary visible and glamorizing theatre around the immobilized and involuntarily displayed lower body of a child' (182–3). This space resembles 'the cropped immobilized space of the lyric and the dilated space around it of narrative poetry'. Sedgwick assimilates lyric to 'both the spanked body, my own body or another one like it for me to watch or punish, and at the same time the very spanking, the rhythmic hand whether hard or subtle of authority itself' (184). Lyric is not an expression of a privileged subjective interiority, but a contained instance of power exchange that releases the ambivalent pleasures of voyeurism and pain.

Numerous contemporary critics suggest that there is a speculative relationship between the rhythmicity of pleasure and pain and the rhythms of poetry. In a recent essay on poetic 'rhythm as coping', Alex Freer quotes Henri Lefebvre's *Rhythmanalysis*, which explores the recurrence of pleasure and pain: 'Pleasure and joy demand a re-commencement. They await it; yet it escapes. Pain returns. It repeats itself, since the repetition of pleasure gives rise to pain(s).'[9] These intervals of pleasure and pain are, for Freer, concentrated in the 'fort-da' game, which Sigmund Freud interprets in *Beyond the Pleasure Principle* as his grandson's attempt to cope with the painful absence of his mother through re-enactment, or play.[10] Freer admires this interpretation's foregrounding of the poetics of rhythm: 'by situating healthy affective life between impossible pleasure and unbearable pain, Freud sets the scene for the whole psychoanalytic economy of pleasure to be understood in rhythmical terms' (554). The oscillation between pleasure and pain, whose extremities are explored in sadomasochistic sex, could be the basis of a different understanding of poetic rhythm, one which is not grounded in simplistic biological metaphors (iambs as heartbeats, etc.; or, as in Chapter 7, racialised traits), but in hedonic temporalities. Theodor Reik argues that the masochist's knowledge of the inevitability of suffering is used to manipulate subjective temporality: he vacillates 'between pleasurable and anxious situations ...

---

[8] Eve Kosofsky Sedgwick, 'A Poem is Being Written,' *Tendencies* (London: Routledge, 1994), pp. 177–214 (182).

[9] Henri Lefebvre, *Rhythmanalysis: Space, Time, and Everyday Life*, trans. Stuart Elden and Gerald Moore (London: Bloomsbury, 2013), p. 22; cited in Alex Freer, 'Rhythm as Coping', *New Literary History* 46.3 (Summer 2015), pp. 549–68 (555).

[10] Sigmund Freud, *The Standard Edition of the Complete Psychological Works*, vol. XVIII: *Beyond the Pleasure Principle, Group Psychology and Other Works*, ed. James Strachey (London: Vintage / Hogarth Press, [1955] 1991), pp. 14–15.

[in] the attempt to attain pleasure and yet avoid pain'.[11] Rhythm, Freer similarly claims, 'ensures a level of tension we can endure'; the experience of pain comes with the knowledge that pleasure will follow.[12] Poetic rhythm is by analogy an experience of the pleasurable comings and goings of pain; it is embodied, and resembles life.

Behind these theorisations lies a long history in which the rhythms of poetry were inculcated by the rhythms of the birch. Punitive flagellation was common in schools from ancient times through the early twentieth century, but the high point of debates about its practice was the nineteenth century – when it aroused Dickinson's fantasies of punishing her brother's Irish pupils. Anthony Trollope complained of being beaten in the late 1820s at public school, where in twelve years 'no attempt had been made to teach me anything but Latin and Greek': 'I feel convinced in my mind that I have been flogged oftener than any human being alive. It was just possible to obtain five scourgings in one day at Winchester, and I have often boasted that I obtained them all.'[13] Charles Lamb, Samuel Taylor Coleridge, Thomas De Quincey and Robert Southey all refer to being beaten at school; Southey was even 'thrown out of Westminster School in 1792 for penning an attack on corporal punishment in a schoolboys' journal called *The Flagellant*'.[14]

William Shenstone's 'The School Mistress' (1737; rev. 1742, 1748), a parodic poem in Spenserian stanzas, describes a tyrannical country schoolteacher who intends 'unruly Brats with Birch to tame'. Adela Pinch argues that 'what the schoolmistress herself and her rod of birch may have had to teach in particular was a certain kind of beat: the Spenserian stanza'.[15] This poem was anthologised in a volume of *Elegant Extracts* by Vicesimus Knox, who 'was among the defenders of whipping – the "party of the Thwackums"'.[16] Knox was headmaster at Tonbridge School. He wrote in 1778 that 'exercising boys in the composition of Latin poetry' would instil 'manly behaviour' and 'virtue'.[17] Masculinity, prosody and leadership were all acquired by the same disciplinary instruments.

---

[11] Theodor Reik, *Masochism in Modern Man*, trans. Margaret H. Beigel and Gertrud M. Kurth (New York: Farrar & Rinehart, 1941), p. 71.
[12] Freer, 'Rhythm as Coping', p. 564.
[13] Anthony Trollope, *An Autobiography*, ed. Michael Sadleir and Frederick Page (Oxford University Press, 1980 [2008]), pp. 17–18.
[14] Adela Pinch, 'Learning What Hurts: Romanticism, Pedagogy, Violence,' in *Lessons of Romanticism: A Critical Companion*, ed. Thomas Pfau and Robert F. Gleckner (Durham: Duke University Press, 1998), pp. 413–28 (420).
[15] *Ibid.*, p. 418.   [16] *Ibid.*, p. 421.
[17] Vicesimus Knox, *Essays, Moral and Literary*, 3 vols. (London: J. Richardson, 1821), 1:15, 16; quoted in Jason David Hall, 'A Great Multiplication of Meters', *Meter Matters: Verse Cultures of the Long Nineteenth Century*, ed. Jason David Hall (Athens, OH: Ohio University Press, 2011), p. 8.

Although flogging and brutality were rife in nearly all types of school in the late eighteenth through the mid-nineteenth century, pedagogical flagellation was largely associated in the British imagination with public (exclusive, fee-paying, private) schools. This gave this form of sadomasochism strong class inflections. *The Rodiad,* a flagellation poem attributed to Swinburne's friend Richard Monckton Milnes, 1st Baron Houghton, attests: 'Nothing a gentleman's demeanor teaches / More than a graceful downfall of the breeches.'[18] He goes on to complain that while 'At Winchester, aristocratic prigs / Are twinged without reserve by apple twigs' (45), among the middling sort or tradesmen the birch is foregone. 'Time was – before the philanthropic trash – / When jails resounded with the hearty lash,' and criminals were whipped in public by the hangman; but no more: 'now, to turn a crank or tread a wheel / Is all the pain our criminals must feel' (49–50). For the lower classes corporal punishment has been replaced by the 'painless' treadmill.

This was, as we've seen, not the case. But Milnes exaggerates in order to distinguish between the punitive corporeal regime of the upper classes, which inculcates class and gender norms, and the debasing violence that afflicts common prisoners. In his commonplace book, Milnes notes in 1862 that one of Swinburne's Eton tutors told him 'he had no pleasure in flogging boys who were not gentlemen: the better the family the more he enjoyed it'.[19] The editors of a periodical, *The Graphic*, noted in 1888 that:

> it is remarkable how the parents of those days [earlier in the century, when whipping was ubiquitous] – many of them persons of high rank – accepted the flogging-block and the cane as necessary … However, among a lower class of people, we find a great difference. The parents themselves have rarely been subjected to stern yet kindly discipline; and they have less confidence in the judgment and forbearance of their children's instructors.[20]

These class associations may also have contributed to the popularity of flagellation scenes in theatre and literature. These scenes staged carnivalesque inversions of class and gender hierarchies, revealing aristocrats who paid to be whipped by sex workers, and women beating men.[21]

---

[18] George Coleman (pseud.), *The Rodiad* (London: Cadell & Murray, 1810 [actually published by J. C. Hotten, *c.* 1870]), pp. 23–4.
[19] Quoted in Ian Gibson, *The English Vice: Beating, Sex and Shame in Victorian England and After* (London: Duckworth, 1978), p. 125.
[20] 'Corporal Punishment of Boys,' *The Graphic* 37.960 (21 April 1888), pp. 418–19 (419).
[21] Peter Anderson, 'The Sterile Star of Venus: Swinburne's Dream of Flight', *Victorian Newsletter* 84 (Fall 1993), pp. 18–24 (21); see also Steven Marcus, *The Other Victorians: A Study of Sexuality and Pornography in Mid-Nineteenth-Century England* (New York: Basic Books, 1964 [1966]), p. 253.

Efforts to banish corporal punishment of children focused on the potential of schoolroom sadism to provoke potentially harmful feelings of excitation in everyone involved – the pupil, servant, master and any witnesses – which could persist as adult sexual perversions.[22] Krafft-Ebing, many of his patients and Freud cite Rousseau's *Confessions* (1782) as evidence that educationalists knew 'that painful stimulation of the skin of buttocks is one of the erotogenic roots of the *passive* instinct of cruelty (masochism)'.[23] Krafft-Ebing observes that many cases of sadomasochism originate in witnessing how 'lustful teachers whipped their pupils on the naked nates without cause' (82); 'boys are immediately excited sexually at the sight of punishment of their companions, and are thus determined in their later *vita sexualis*'. His patients acknowledge the sadism of the classroom as a source of their adult perversions:

> At the age of eight, while at school, he saw how the teacher punished the boys by taking their heads between his thighs and spanking them with a ferule. This sight caused the patient lustful excitement ... From that time [he] often masturbated, during which he always called up the memory-picture of a boy being punished.[24]

> According to his statements, he became sexually excited when he saw his father whip the children, and, later, when he saw the teacher whip his companions. When a spectator of such scenes, he always experienced lustful feelings ... He began to imagine how others were punished. This excited his lust, and he would then masturbate. Whenever he could, he managed to see others punished at school.[25]

The erotic interest in flagellation, which came to be known as '*le vice anglais*', was often attributed to its use in schools. In Thomas Shadwell's *The Virtuoso* (1676), the libertine Snarl comes to a young sex worker to be flogged, explaining: 'I was so us'd to't at Westminster School I cou'd never leave it off since.'[26]

The Rodiad magnifies the sexual excitement available to both master and pupils in scenes of whipping: advocating the use of a 'living horse' (a boy on whose back the victim leans) rather than a flogging block or 'wooden horse' that 'holds / The fast bound victim in its leathery folds' (12), the author

---

[22] Gibson, *The English Vice*, pp. 29 and 43–4.
[23] Sigmund Freud, *The Standard Edition of the Complete Psychological Works*, vol. VII: *A Case of Hysteria, Three Essays on Sexuality and Other Works*, ed. James Strachey (London: Vintage/Hogarth Press, [1953], 2001), p. 193.
[24] Krafft-Ebing, *Psychopathia Sexualis*, p. 83, Case 37.
[25] Krafft-Ebing, *Psychopathia Sexualis*, p. 83, Case 38.
[26] Noyes, *The Mastery of Submission*, p. 89.

imagines how 'The brute's excitement will increase your own: / Coarse birch, broad shoulders, and a rattling bum' (13). Referring also to the pleasure of whipping 'a virgin', a boy who 'shall lose his schoolboy maidenhead' (16), or how a boy might be tied up 'for hours with naked bum' so that other boy scan 'Shoot with their steel pens at him for a mark; / Aim their sharp pea-guns at his rosy hole; / Lick him, and kick him with the thickest sole,' until the master will finish him off 'And work the rod on his obdurate skin' (20–1), the poem is forthright about the homoerotic arousal that flagellation produces in participants, or seeks to provoke in the reader.

The Perversity of Swinburne

The poet whose practice is most readily identified with this conjunction of flagellation and sadomasochism, and who directly attributes his prosodic expertise to the floggings he received at school, is Algernon Swinburne. Swinburne has become the literary poster boy for the pleasures of bondage. As he writes in *The Flogging Block*, a series of twelve mock eclogues set in an Etonian pastoral setting, 'Flagellation and Algernon (Swish!) must appear / Synonymous terms.'[27] The poem dilates on a scenario of corporal discipline at a public school, restaged on page after page, with the blows ('swish!') embedded in loquacious exchanges between schoolmaster, students and bystanders. In these scenes, the sadistic masters and students relish the torture of other boys, elaborating it through endless repetitive chatter, while the beaten boy begs volubly for mercy, or lapses into orgasmic cries of pain: 'Oh! Oh! Oh!' In one version of 'Algernon's Flogging', the master's promise 'I'll whip you' is the beginning of sixteen consecutive lines, followed by a similarly anaphoric 'I'll flog you' for thirty-seven.[28]

Whipping is an important component, or even the central focus, in a number of Swinburne's works, including his unfinished novel *Lesbia Brandon* (begun in 1863); the pseudonymously published *Love's Cross-Currents* (written 1862, published 1877); and *The Whippingham Papers* (published in the late 1880s).[29] While at Eton in the early 1850s, he also wrote a play about the swishings inflicted there, 'First Fault for the Hundreth Time', in which a boy complains as he is being beaten: 'I can't

---

[27] BL MS Ashley 5256, fol. 53ʳ.   [28] BL MS Ashley A4395*, fol. 13ᵛ.
[29] On the sadomasochistic style of the former, see Patricia Pulham, 'Epistolary Sadomasochism in A. C. Swinburne's *Love's Cross-Currents*: A Year's Letters', *Mosaic: An Interdisciplinary Critical Journal* 50.3 (Sept. 2017), pp. 141–57. On Swinburne's Eton swishings, see Rikky Rooksby, *A. C. Swinburne: A Poet's Life* (Aldershot: Scolar Press, 1997), pp. 34–41.

see what the fellows behind me can read as a text / Written broad in red ink on my skin …'[30] As we've already scene in relation to Austin Reed's memoirs, the association of whipping with writing was not uncommon in the late nineteenth century.[31] In another tale, an Etonian named Arthur Clifford is flogged with a birch that 'left some fresh red letters there [on his bottom] to read':

> Weeks passed before the part inscribed forgot 'em,
> The fleshy tablets, where the master's creed
> Is written on boy's skin with birchen pen,
> At each re-issue copied fair again.[32]

Swinburne is perversely citing 2 Corinthians 3:2–3: 'Ye are our epistle written in our hearts, known and read of all men: Forasmuch as ye are manifestly declared to be the epistle of Christ ministered by us, written not with ink, but with the Spirit of the living God; not in tables of stone, but in fleshy tables of the heart.' But the fleshy tables of the heart have become the fleshy tables of the schoolboy's bottom. Reed fetishised the white skin made dark with bloody stripes; Swinburne extends this spectacle of desire into a bum-as-page, cuts-as-ink conceit, and depicts 'the fair full page of white and warm young flesh' (l. 129), 'the smooth seamy paper, white and pink' (l. 127), elaborating a scenario of the body as book, blood as ink and cuts as illustrations (woodcuts), in which the white paper 'Was crossed and scored and blotted with red ink' (l. 128). These examples reflect the eroticisation of the skin that Freud argues is typical of masochism; but the skin in Swinburne's flagellatory work is constantly imagined as a writing surface.[33]

Like Ovid's parody of Virgil in the opening lines of his *Amores*, *The Flogging Block* opens with a parodic prologue that recalls the elegiac demurral of 'heroic' epic: 'I sing the Flogging-block.'[34] Swinburne echoes both the *Aeneid* and Cowper's bathetic 'I sing the Sofa' in *The Task*; this parodic instinct is sharpened in the pedantic 'Notes to "The Flogging Block"' that follow the prologue, explaining why the Muse should be called

---

[30] Peter Leggatt, 'Swinburne and Swishing', *TLS* (8 January 2014).
[31] Lucy Bending, *The Representation of Bodily Pain in Late Nineteenth-Century English Culture* (Oxford: Clarendon, 2000), pp. 252–3; quote from *The Whippingham Papers* (privately printed, 1888), pp. 10–11.
[32] Algernon Charles Swinburne, from 'Arthur's Flogging', *Major Poems and Selected Prose*, ed. Jerome McGann and Charles L. Sligh (New Haven: Yale University Press, 2004), ll. 116–20, p. 421.
[33] For another extreme example of skin writing, see Michel de M'Uzan, 'A Case of Masochistic Perversion and an Outline of a Theory', *International Journal of Psychoanalysis* 54 (1973), pp. 455–67 (456).
[34] BL MS Ashley 5256, fol. 2ʳ.

'Red-cheek'd' and so forth. Swinburne then presents a scene of what Yopie Prins describes as metrical initiation:

> And most the Nurslings of the Muse require
> The Lash that sets their lyrick Blood on Fire,
> The Lash that ever when they cry keeps Time,
> When Stroke to Stroke responds in glowing Rhyme.
> And still the humbled Bottom hails the Rod sublime,
> Till Heart & Head the rhythmic Lesson learn
> From Wounds that redden & from Stripes that burn,
> As Twig by Twig imprints the Crimson sign in turn.[35]

The rhythms of the lash impart poetic measure; the twig 'imprints' its authoritarian signature on the pupils' bottoms, a correctional writing that instils the 'rhythmic Lesson' as bodily knowledge. Swinburne also specifies that young poets are picked out as the special victims of the flogging muse: 'For chief the Stripling Songster's Breech invites / The full Performance of thy frequent Rites' (fol. 3ʳ). In the Notes, the birch is said 'to clasp or entwine the Bum of the flagellated Youth (as Wreaths of Bay or Laurel the Head of a Conqueror or Poet)' (fol. 7ʳ).

Prins, Ian Gibson, Catherine Maxwell and others have drawn out the extensive associations between whipping and prosody in Swinburne's poetics.[36] In the *Flogging Block* eclogues, the beatings are inflicted with relish by a male master, who is the embodiment of the law, the institution and paternal discipline, and a sadist who enjoys his sexualised tyranny over a minor. Swinburne dilates on Algernon's multiple beatings, on his birthdays, by his father (fol. 18ʳ); the master asks insistently after the father as he beats the son: "Twould pleasure your father, wouldn't it, to see / His golden-haired boy's bottom soundly whipped? / How often does he flog you?'; 'How often last vacation did your father / Take down your breeches & apply the rod?'; 'How many cuts does he give usually?'[37] The father is not a protector, but complicit in the son's abuse. The master is his proxy, inculcating the son into a pattern of masculinity formed through what is

---

[35] Yopie Prins, 'Metrical Discipline: Algernon Swinburne on "The Flogging-Block"', in *Algernon Charles Swinburne: Unofficial Laureate*, ed. Catherine Maxwell and Stefano Evangelista (Manchester University Press, 2013), pp. 95–124 (106); citing BL MS Ashley 5256, fol. 3ʳ.

[36] Prins, 'Metrical Discipline'; Gibson, *The English Vice*, pp. 99–142; Jean Overton Fuller, *Swinburne: A Critical Biography* (London: Chatto & Windus, 1968), pp. 25–7, 67–8, 132–3, 144–7, 178–9, 270–1; Catherine Maxwell, *Swinburne* (Tavistock: Northcote House, 2006), pp. 21–4, 53, 90, 99; Catherine Maxwell, *The Female Sublime from Milton to Swinburne: Bearing Blindness* (Manchester University Press, 2001), chapter 5; and Niklaus Largier, *In Praise of the Whip: A Cultural History of Arousal* (New York: Zone Books, 2007), pp. 351–8.

[37] BL MS Ashley A4395*.

repeatedly specified as intergenerational suffering on the block: the son is being beaten in the same place that the father once was.

Gilles Deleuze suggests that what is beaten and humiliated in the masochist is the image and likeness of the father, forestalling the possibility of his aggressive return.[38] The masochist attempts to repudiate the father, making a pact with the mother to erase the father's dominance. In that sense, the hierarchies and institutional sanctions at play in Swinburne's whipping scenarios interact with fluid sexual and gender identifications that recall the instability of sexual position-taking along the axis of activity and passivity in Roman elegy. At the same time, they are part of an economy of punishment and violence that nourishes the homosocial institutions in which the British ruling class was invested with the qualities of masculinity and domination that would serve the empire.

Kaja Silverman argues that the male masochist constitutes 'a feminine yet heterosexual male subject' who wreaks havoc with sexual difference.[39] Masochism is also another way of naming what Leo Bersani and Ulysse Du Toit call the 'no-man's-land' of fetishism, which leaves the fetishist 'in the gender-land of neither the heterosexual nor the homosexual man', neither fully desiring the castrated woman, nor fully able to identify with the father and embrace homosexual desire.[40] This sexual and gender indeterminacy can be found in much of Swinburne's verse. In *The Flogging Block*, the master wields the birch; but the phallic instrument is also personified as female: 'Algernon's bottom and Birkenshaw's rod – / A'n't they a couple of lovers, by God!'; 'Rosy young Bottom & randy Miss Birch / Kiss like lovers outside the church' (fol. 17ʳ). The defenceless child, subjected to a hyperbolic disciplinary father, is inducted simultaneously into homo- and hetero-sexuality. Though his written fantasies focused on homoerotic whipping scenes, as an adult Swinburne reportedly visited female sex workers who specialised in whipping and rumours abounded that he was whipped by select male friends.[41] He was also an avid reader of the Marquis de Sade, who was central to his self-fashioning and to the formation of a select coterie – what he refers to in a letter to George Powell as a 'band of Sadique enthusiasts'. Only these men can enjoy the 'healthy pleasure and

---

[38] Gilles Deleuze, 'Coldness and Cruelty,' and Leopold von Sacher-Masoch, 'Venus in Furs', in *Masochism* (New York: Zone Books, 1991), p. 66.
[39] Kaja Silverman, *Male Subjectivity at the Margins* (New York: Routledge, 1992), p. 212.
[40] Leo Bersani and Ulysse Du Toit, *The Forms of Violence: Narrative in Assyrian Art and Modern Culture* (New York: Shocken Books, 1985), pp. 68–7, 72.
[41] Fuller, *Swinburne*, pp. 144–6; Philip Henderson, *Swinburne: The Portrait of a Poet* (London: Routledge & Kegan Paul, 1974), pp. 127–31; Rooksby, *A. C. Swinburne*, pp. 69, 118, 164–5, 181.

pure joys unknown to the base vulgar', which Swinburne imagines as 'Pain and Pleasure, twin sisters, [who] might dance hand in hand round the bloody red and rose altar of Love.'

The birch and the arse that kiss in *The Flogging Block* exemplify the orality and anality of Swinburne's sadomasochistic poetics. Throughout 'Laus Veneris', sadomasochistic desire is expressed as oral fixation. This long poem in quatrains is spoken by Tannhäuser, the medieval German poet who found the residence of Venus and spent a year worshipping her.[42] After a battle Tannhäuser loses his way, and comes upon the goddess wandering naked 'between the blossom and the grass'.[43] He devotes himself to her, recapitulating the liaison of Venus and Mars (or the classical elegiac lover and his mistress). But the poem's heterodox veneration of erotic love is tensed and despairing. The knight eventually abandons Venus to seek salvation in Rome, but is told he will not be forgiven until the Pope's staff blooms with life again. He returns to Venus and abandons himself to his barren desire. Tannhäuser explains how he was trapped by his own desire:

> Ah, with blind lips I felt for you, and found
> About my neck your hands and hair enwound,
> The hands that stifle and the hair that stings,
> I felt them fasten sharply without sound.
>
> (ll. 317–20, p. 19)

He is captured and bound in a soundless embrace initiated by his 'blind lips', held just as Adonis had been: 'With flesh and blood she chains him for a chain'; 'her lips divide him vein by vein' (ll. 134, 136, p. 13). In the opening stanzas, the lover's 'lips shut sucking on the place' on her neck, like a vampire (l. 5, p. 9). Venus' beauty inspires a heretical challenge to Christ: she once enticed 'All lips that now grow sad with kissing Christ,' but 'her mouth is lovelier' (ll. 14, 20, p. 10). The poem contains at least twenty-three references to lips, including lips that 'caught and clove' or are left 'charred' by the molten heat of lust (ll. 167, 170, p. 14). Venus' 'marvellous mouth' is the instrument 'whereby there fell / Cities and people whom the gods loved well' (ll. 193–4, p. 15). They resemble the 'large pale lips' of Semiramis, and are 'Curled like a tiger's that curl back to feed; / Red only where the last kiss made them bleed' (ll. 200–2, p. 15). The speaker sings of 'Lips that cling hard till the kissed face has grown / Of one same fire and colour with their

---

[42] Clyde K. Hyder, 'Swinburne's "Laus Veneris" and the Tannhäuser Legend,' *PMLA* 45.4 (Dec. 1930), pp. 1202–13.
[43] Swinburne, *Poems and Ballads*, l. 309, p. 19.

own.' The kiss is both injury and salve: 'Where his lips wounded, there his lips atone' (ll. 289–90, 292, p. 18).

Reflecting on an equally intense kiss in Shelley's *Epipsychidion*, Elisabeth Gitter summarises two traditions: one of which 'arose from the ancient belief that the *animus* is transmitted on the breath and which evolved into the commonplace medieval and Renaissance conceit of the soul-in-the-kiss', and another that represented the 'kiss as nourishment': the mouth of the beloved is represented as a flower, or honeycomb, or overflowing with milk or wine.[44] But what Swinburne's lovers consume is not nourishment, but the other, in a cannibalistic embrace that threatens to annihilate the beloved by internalising her. Freud describes the oral phase as sadistic: 'it seems, the external world, objects, and what is hated are identical. If later on an object turns out to be a source of pleasure, it is loved, but it is also incorporated into the ego.'[45] The mouth is the infant's primary erotogenic zone. Melanie Klein argues that the infant tries to relieve himself of his persecutory anxiety by projecting his anger and violence, his bad feeling, back into the mother. The infant craves the breast and attacks it, biting or refusing to feed. This is the origin of the sadistic tendency: 'From the beginning the destructive impulse is turned against the object and is first expressed in phantasised oral-sadistic attacks on the mother's breast, which soon develop into onslaughts on her body by all sadistic means.'[46]

This paradigm frames some aspects of Swinburne's poetry. The poems do not represent the other as a whole person; rather they dwell with the violence of the paranoid-schizoid position on fragmented bodies and devouring mouths. Sex in Swinburne's poems often entails autoeroticism (the incorporation of the other into the self facilitates self-pleasuring), and seems pre-genital; the absence of the phallus means that the lover can relate to his or her beloved object through mouths or wounds (or wounds as mouths) rather than through the regimens of gender. Another frequently cited passage from *Lesbia Brandon* describes a dream in which the protagonist Herbert sees 'the star of Venus, white and flower-like as he had always seen it, turn into a white rose and come down out of heaven, with a reddening centre that grew as it descended liker and liker a living mouth; but instead of desire he felt horror and sickness at the sight of it, and averted his lips.'[47] John Vincent reads this

---

[44] Elisabeth G. Gitter, 'The Victorian Literary Kiss', *Victorian Literature and Culture* 13 (Spring 1985), pp. 165–80 (165–6).
[45] Sigmund Freud, *The Standard Edition of the Complete Psychological Works*, vol. XIV: *On the History of the Psycho-Analytic Movement, Papers on Metapsychology, and Other Works*, trans. James Strachey (London: Vintage / Hogarth Press, 2001), p. 136.
[46] Melanie Klein, 'Notes on Some Schizoid Mechanisms' (1946), in *Envy and Gratitude and Other Works 1946–1963* (London: Vintage, 1997), p. 2.
[47] Swinburne, *Lesbia Brandon*, p. 281.

horrifying mouth surrounded by 'starry or flowery beams and petals' as an anus, and the white and red do resemble a passage in 'Arthur's Flogging' that compares the decoration of Arthur's bum to the York and Lancastrian roses. But I'm not sure the genitality of this dream-passage is entirely determinable; the petals could just as easily be labia, or the white flower with the red centre an image of the breast that is both wanted and rejected.[48] This image reflects not adult sexual desire and repression, but a mouth that is too close – out of proportion; in its movement and scale it is also like the nipple that appears to the baby, and can be the object of desire and anger.

Swinburne's poems represent subjects who desire like infants to incorporate the desired object into themselves through the mouth, in a kind of feeding conceptualised as parasitical grafting or gestational entombment. Venus' mouth 'Clove unto mine as soul to body doth' (l. 394, p. 21); the lovers 'cleave' to each other 'Till the ending of the days and ways of earth' (ll. 138–9, p. 13). Cleaving denotes both binding – 'Therefore shall a man leave his father and his mother, and shall cleave unto his wife: and they shall be one flesh' (Genesis 2:24) – and division: 'her lips divide him vein by vein'. It brings together imagery of the wholeness of the lovers in Aristophanes' fable from Plato's *Symposium*, and an infantile fantasy of merging with the body of the mother, with the splitting of the mother's breast into good and bad internal objects. It articulates a desire for a return to an oral phase before genital differentiation, when the other could be incorporated into the self through the mouth: auto-eroticism as a rejection of difference. Venus lays hold of the lover, and he forgets everything:

> Feeling her face with all her eager hair
> Cleave to me, clinging as a fire that clings
>
> To the body and to the raiment, burning them;
> As after death I know that such-like flame
> Shall cleave to me for ever; yea, what care,
> Albeit I burn then, having felt the same?
>
> (ll. 403–8, p. 22)

Like the tunic of Hercules, the fires of hell shall 'cleave' to his body with the same lascivious intensity as her impassioned body clings to him now. And like Aristophanes' lovers, the union threatens the lovers with perpetual hunger: mouths turned towards each other in devouring kisses feed off each other, obliviating other forms of sustenance.

In Swinburne's poem 'Anactoria', the lyric 'I' is the poet Sappho. Sappho is like Tannhäuser bound and blinded, burned and divided by

---

[48] Vincent, 'Flogging is Fundamental', p. 288.

desire. But unlike him, her suffering empowers her, transforming her from masochist to sadist. The poem begins with Sappho in a state of melancholic lovesickness, desperate for Anactoria whose eyes:

> Blind me, thy tresses burn me, thy sharp sighs
> Divide my flesh and spirit with soft sound,
> And my blood strengthens, and my veins abound.
>
> (ll. 2–4, p. 47)

The poem explores intervals of fission and fusion – the flesh divided, the sea 'severed the bones that bleach, the flesh that cleaves' (l. 9, p. 47). The sameness of the two female bodies stimulates a fantasy of painful merging that leaves marks: bruises, stings, crushing, burning:

> I feel thy blood against my blood: my pain
> Pains thee, and lips bruise lips, and vein stings vein.
> Let fruit be crushed on fruit, let flower on flower,
> Breast kindle breast, and either burn one hour.
>
> (ll. 11–14, p. 47)

The desire for their cleaving leads finally to an imagined annihilation of Anactoria: 'that from face to feet / Thy body were abolished and consumed, / And in my flesh thy very flesh entombed!' (ll. 112–14, p. 50). Sappho becomes the monument to her beloved, with Anactoria interred in Sappho's body like a crushed foetus.

As Prins has noted, the anatomised body of Anactoria emblematises the fragmented Sapphic poetic corpus. The text is a body, the body is a text; Swinburne's poem 'turns Sappho into a *figure for* the figure of abuse, a double catachresis that makes her both cause and effect of a rhetorical violence that forcefully scatters the body'.[49] Although her own body will serve as Anactoria's monument, Sappho threatens her beloved with oblivion: 'Yea, thou shalt be forgotten like spilt wine, / Except these kisses of my lips on thine / Brand them with immortality' (ll. 201–3, p. 52). The kiss is a 'brand' that leaves its smouldering mark of possession on the beloved. These labial fantasies culminate in a series of wishes that are often read as a description of cunnilingus:

> Ah that my lips were tuneless lips, but pressed
> To the bruised blossom of thy scourged white breast!
> Ah that my mouth for Muses' milk were fed
> On the sweet blood thy sweet small wounds had bled!
> That with my tongue I felt them, and could taste
> The faint flakes from thy bosom to the waist!
>
> (ll. 105–10, p. 50)

---

[49] Yopie Prins, *Victorian Sappho* (Princeton University Press, 1999), p. 116.

Sappho's perverse veneration of the tortured body echoes Richard Crashaw poring over Christ's 'wakeful wounds', which might be either mouths or eyes ('Each bleeding part some one supplies'). Using the vocabulary of 'scourge', 'thorns', 'blood', 'break', Swinburne manufactures a 'shocking equivalence between God the Father in Christ's Passion and role of sadistic partner, Sappho, in Anactoria's masochistic pleasures', Thaïs Morgan argues.[50] The lover's cannibalistic urge to consume and incorporate the other mimics the consumption of the Eucharist, transformed into a perverse sexual act. Swinburne's blazon moves over Anactoria's body, itemising each part for consumption: blood drunk as wine, in a parody of the sacrament; the mouth that feeds not on the milk of the Muses but the blood of the lover, in a parody of infantile suckling on the mother's breast.

John Noyes argues that the masochist eroticises the instruments of punishment and controlling mechanisms designed to punish the deviant body; 'the masochistic move is to seize upon the machinery of domination and pervert its usage' (11). The sacrilege in 'Anactoria' is one example of that perverse appropriation, but what exactly is the machine, the device Swinburne's poetry perverts? I would argue that it is not Christianity, but sound: the breath coming in intervals, resisting and relapsing; the 'shuddering semitones' and (musical or theatrical) interludes, the 'strain' that denotes both stress and melody. Read in this way, the labial fantasies in Swinburne's poetry are not (only) the expression of a psyche stalled in infantile orality, but the fetishisation of the organ of song.

Throughout Swinburne's poetry, the lips can also be instruments of pain and pleasure – 'stinging lips wherein the hot sweet brine / That Love was born of burns and foams like wine' (ll. 49–50, p. 48). They are a point of intensely intimate contact, and the zone in which feeding and carnality can be exchanged for the sublimity of poetic song or the howl of pain. They are also, repeatedly, 'tuneless'. Sappho's lips wish to be free of their miraculous song, not singing but stinging, made only for this sadistic kiss. This is a fantasy of desublimation: a return from aesthetics back to the pain-pleasure economies of the body. It is Anactoria's breath that 'divides' Sappho's flesh from her spirit 'with soft sound' (l. 3, p. 47), cleaving her into a musical interval. Eventually, Sappho promises, 'my songs once heard in a strange place' will 'Cleave to men's lives', in the same way the lovers cleave to each other (ll. 278–9, p. 54). Poetic memory operates through the same lustful, sadomasochistic grafting or incorporation that installs Anactoria in her

---

[50] Thaïs Morgan, 'Swinburne's Dramatic Monologues: Sex and Ideology', *Victorian Poetry* (Summer 1984), pp. 175–9.

lover's body; the song cleaves to its hearers (or readers), penetrates and fills them until they can no longer distinguish between themselves and it.

This thematisation of sound also surfaces in the sadomasochism of 'Laus Veneris'. Venus' hands and hair wind around her lover like a chain: 'I felt them fasten sharply without sound' (l. 320, p. 19); and when he escapes, he sees 'White cursed hills' that are 'Like a jagged shell's lips, harsh, untunable, // Blown in between by devils' wrangling breath' (ll. 344–5, p. 20). The demonic perversity of this setting is signified by its untunable breath, just as Venus' sadistic, bloody mouth and body enforce a soundless captivity. But the Hörsel is also constructed from sound:

> Her beds are full of perfume and sad sound,
> Her doors are made with music, and barred round
> With sighing and with laughter and with tears,
> With tears whereby strong souls of men are bound.
>
> (ll. 129–132, p. 13)

Sound and music are the insubstantial fabric of this erotic captivity, and also of this poem. When Tannhäuser finally abandons himself to despair, he invites God to search him, body and soul: 'There is not one sound thing in all thereof' (l. 382, p. 21) This soundless, unsound body disintegrates before our eyes into poetry's pure sound, which is finally the pleasure and property not of the dumb cis-hetero knight Tannhäuser, but of the lesbian poet Swinburne wanted to become.

Bound in Verse

Gerard Manley Hopkins's writings also reflect an intimate familiarity with both physical and psychic pain, and the desire for submission as pain's remedy. He suffered from various ailments including diarrhoea, vomiting, eczema, earaches, a broken ligament in his right arm and gout in the eyes; 'my old complaint' (haemorrhoids), which caused him to 'lose so much blood that I hardly saw how I was to recover' and for which he underwent surgery in 1872; and penile ulcerations that required adult circumcision in 1877.[51] He also frequently complained of being in a 'desolate frame of mind'.[52] Hopkins struggled with what he called melancholy or anxiety

---

[51] Gerard Manley Hopkins, *Diaries, Journals, and Notebooks*, ed. Lesley Higgins, *The Collected Works of Gerard Manley Hopkins*, vol. 3 (Oxford University Press, 2015), pp. 542, 546, 613, hereafter cited as *Diaries*; Julia F. Saville, *A Queer Chivalry: The Homoerotic Asceticism of Gerard Manley Hopkins* (Charlottesville: University of Virginia Press, 2000), p. 10.

[52] Gerard Manley Hopkins, *The Sermons and Devotional Writings*, ed. Christopher Devlin (Oxford University Press, 1959), p. 254. Hereafter cited as *Sermons*.

(*L1* 225): 'I think that my fits of sadness, though they do not affect my judgment, resemble madness' (*L1* 216). He was low-spirited during his residences in Manchester, Liverpool, Glasgow and London in the 1880s ('you cannot tell what a slavery of mind or heart it is to live life in a great town', he wrote to Bridges in 1881, *L1* 136), and fell into a 'deep fit of nervous prostration ... I did not know but I was dying' on arrival in Dublin in 1884, where he lived and taught classics until his death in 1889. There, he wrote the 'terrible' sonnets, which 'confront us with human forms that are impotent, disease-wracked, sweating, tortured – profoundly "comfortless"'.[53] These poems, Lesley Higgins argues, 'represent the culmination of Hopkins's commitment (as poet and priest) to an "aesthetics of pain".'[54]

Although there is little in his writings to suggest an erotic enjoyment of all this suffering, Hopkins could be characterised in Freud's taxonomy as a moral masochist; but Julia Saville's argument that his poetry constantly encodes a religious *ascesis* is also persuasive.[55] Hopkins practiced several forms of *ascesis*. While at Oxford he followed the advice of E. B. Pusey to wear 'round our loins a girdle of flannel or other material as a token of self-restraint'.[56] He used a scourge to flagellate himself during Lent in 1865, wore hairshirts ('the ever-fretting shirt of punishment'), and was given to practices of fasting and mortification throughout his life.[57] As he writes in 'Easter Communion', 'You striped in secret with breath-taking whips, / Those crookèd rough-scored chequers may be pieced / To crosses meant for Jesu's ... .'[58] Jesuit discipline as practised at Manresa House, where Hopkins began his initiation, included scourges made of knotted cords (used twice a week during Lent) and the wearing of 'a neat contraption of wire, horse-shoe links with points turning inwards, which you strapped around your thigh next your skin.'[59] Novices had to try hard not to limp when wearing it. Another Jesuit novice at Stonyhurst College described the use of the 'discipline' (the whip) and the 'chain':

---

[53] Lesley Higgins, '"Bone-house" and "lovescape": Writing the Body in Hopkins's Canon', in *Rereading Hopkins: Selected New Essays*, ed. Francis L. Fennell (University of Victoria, 1996), pp. 11–35 (26–7).
[54] Lesley Higgins, '"Bone-house"', p. 27.   [55] Saville, *A Queer Chivalry*, esp. pp. 29–31.
[56] Frederick Meyrick, *Memories of Life at Oxford* (New York, 1905), p. 173, quoted in Robert Bernard Martin, *Gerard Manley Hopkins: A Very Private Life* (London: Flamingo, 1992), pp. 57–8.
[57] Martin, *Gerard Manley Hopkins*, pp. 44, 94.
[58] Gerard Manley Hopkins, *The Poetical Works*, ed. Norman H. MacKenzie (Oxford University Press, 1990), ll. 3–5, p. 70.
[59] 'T' [Joseph Peter Thorp], *Friends and Adventures* (1931), p. 3, cited in Martin, *Gerard Manley Hopkins*, p. 196. See also Paddy Kitchen, *Gerard Manley Hopkins* (London: Hamish Hamilton, 1978), p. 125.

> as the preservatives of chastity among the novices: the former is made of whip-cord, and is a kind of cat-o'-nine-tails, with knots at the ends of each tail. The chain is made of steel-wire about the thickness of a whip-cord. The wire is bent into horse-shoe shaped links, and at every link the superfluous wire projects half an inch, not rounded off or pointed, but just as it has been cut or filed. These 'helps to holy living' are not in constant operation among the novices, but only at stated times, such as during Lent ... . Twice a week the porter goes round the cells and gives the order for 'mortification'. At this the novices – each sitting in his bed – uncover their shoulders and seize the whip.[60]

In their 'cells', spaces of painful delectation that recall both the prison cell and the BDSM dungeon, the novices are restricted to applying twelve rapid blows. 'In the excitement [...], very similar to a shower-bath, we could not help tossing the whip into the desk; and then, diving into the sheets, felt very comfortable indeed!' Apparently mortification by these devices also led to some pleasure. They also enforce the association between desire, pain, sin and shame that recurs frequently in Hopkins's darkest hours.

In Jean Laplanche's formulation, pain is 'the effraction of [a] boundary', 'an influx of "unbound" energy'.[61] Hopkins often speaks of pain as breaking through the boundaries of the self. Like Dickinson, he conceived of the self as strictly circumscribed; he drew this idea of determinate being as a bounded figure from Parmenides.[62] In an 1880 essay, Hopkins argues that the self consists of everything 'within a certain bounding line' (*Sermons* 127); it consists 'of a centre *and* a surrounding area or circumference' (127). For Walter Ong, Hopkins's work demonstrates that the 'self has a positive content limited by a border' that separates the 'not-I' from the 'I'; 'weakening of this border signals no less than total psychological collapse'.[63] This is the opposite of Swinburne's fascination with cleaving and incorporation of the beloved into the self. For Hopkins, the body is always at risk of flying apart. He repeatedly describes the self as a broken, fragmenting object that needs to be bound up. Arriving back in England from Ireland during a period of depression, Hopkins found that 'nature in all her parcels and faculties gaped and fell apart, *fatiscebat*, like a clod cleaving and holding only by strings of root. But this must often be' (*Diaries* 557). We've

---

[60] Quoted in William M. Cooper, *A History of the Rod in All Countries: From the Earliest Period to the Present Time* (London: William Reeves, 1908; London: Kegan Paul, 2002), pp. 100–1.
[61] Jean Laplanche, 'La position originaire du masochisme dans le champ de la pulsion sexuelle,' in *La révolution Copernicienne inachevée: Travaux 1967–1992* (Paris: Aubier, 1992), p. 38.
[62] Daniel Brown, *Hopkins' Idealism: Philosophy, Physics, Poetry* (Oxford: Clarendon Press, 1997), pp. 169–71.
[63] Walter J. Ong, *Hopkins, the Self, and God* (University of Toronto Press, 1986), p. 29.

encountered other selves at the point of falling to pieces, from Wyatt turned and torn by love, to writers such as Baca and Abbott fragmenting in solitary confinement.

Leo Bersani, as I noted, sees human sexuality as 'constituted as a kind of psychic shattering, as a threat to the stability and integrity of the self – a threat which perhaps only the masochistic nature of sexual pleasure allows us to survive'.[64] The infant is besieged by the world before he is able to tolerate it, and manages that excess of sensation by transforming it into masochism: a self-shattering in which 'the ego renounces its power over the world'.[65] Hopkins articulates the terrors of self-shattering, and translates them into masochism as ascesis. This is both a sexual and a theological position. Jessica Benjamin identifies the sadist as the partner who maintains the boundaries of the self, the masochist as the partner who allows those boundaries to be broken.[66] Hopkins desires the power of divine grace to break through the boundary of his self, just as John Donne did when he wrote in his *Holy Sonnets*: 'burne me O Lord, with a fiery zeale'; 'breake, blowe, burn and make me new'.

Hopkins's anxiety about maintaining the bounds of the self, its integrity and its compression, has an analogue in his poetics. He coined new terms for the force that maintained the internal cohesion of the self or of any object. 'Instress' is that force or energy that binds together the 'inscape' – the pattern or organisation of any object, its law, wholeness, essential structure or nature.[67] One could 'inscape' a flower, by patiently or passionately observing it until its true nature is discerned. 'Instress' is 'the action that takes place when the inscape of a given being fuses itself in a given human consciousness'; it brings 'the human self, this particularised human being, into the dynamics of the otherwise "objective" inscape'.[68] Instress is clearly related to stress – which Hopkins described as 'the making of a thing more, or making it markedly, what it already is; it is the bringing out of its nature'.[69] In a state of grace, inscape reveals itself to perception as a sign of God's incarnation; but for the damned, 'all that

---

[64] Leo Bersani, *The Freudian Body: Psychoanalysis and Art* (New York: Columbia University Press, 1986), p. 60.
[65] Leo Bersani, *Homos* (Cambridge, MA: Harvard University Press, 1995), pp. 94–5.
[66] Jessica Benjamin, *The Bonds of Love: Psychoanalysis, Feminism and the Problem of Domination* (New York: Pantheon, 1988), p. 64.
[67] R. K. R. Thornton, *Gerard Manley Hopkins: The Poems* (London: Edward Arnold, 1973), pp. 18–20.
[68] Ong, *Hopkins, the Self*, p. 17.
[69] *The Correspondence of Gerard Manley Hopkins and Richard Watson Dixon*, ed. Claude Colleer Abbott (Oxford University Press, 1955), p. 179. Hereafter identified as *L2*.

energy or instress with which the soul animates and otherwise acts in the body is by death thrown back upon the soul itself ... This throwing back of confinement of their energy is a dreadful constraint or imprisonment' (*Sermons* 137).

An example of how instress plays a role in the stability of inscape, of psychic or bodily containment, can be found in Hopkins's account of waking to find himself in a state of sleep paralysis in 1873. He feels as if something is sitting on his chest. I 'thought something or someone leapt onto me and held me quite fast' – a perception of domination, or even rape, which alludes to Gothic images of the nightmare as a succubus. At first he can only whisper, having lost 'all muscular stress':

> The feeling is terrible: the body no longer swayed as a piece by the nervous and muscular instress seems to fall in and hang like a dead weight on the chest. I cried on the holy name and by degrees recovered myself as I thought to do. It made me think that this was how the souls in hell wd. be imprisoned in their bodies as in prisons and of what St. Theresa says of the 'little press in the wall' where she felt herself to be in her vision (*Diaries* 562)[70]

This experience of constraint feels like torture, or imprisonment, with the body as a repressive container for the spirit. It is reminiscent of St Teresa's vision of hell as a 'long close alley, or rather like a low, dark, and narrow cavity, and the ground appeared to be like mire, exceedingly filthy ... At the end of it there was a certain hollow place, as if it had been a kind of little press in the wall, into which I found myself thrust, and closely pent up.'[71] Lacan has already provided a psychoanalytic reading of Teresa's visions, so we can simply notice how the anality of this image leads to a cul-de-sac of bondage. Hopkins turned to Teresa's beatific visions in another meditation, which describes hell as 'a place of imprisonment, a prison' where the damned serve Satan: 'they are his slaves and he has them in prison, his own prison' (*Sermons* 241, 243). 'Against these acts of its own the lost spirit dashes itself like a caged bear and is in prison, violently instresses them and burns, stares into them and is the deeper darkened' ('Fifth Meditation on Hell', 1881, *Sermons* 138). This hellish scene is the product of motionlessness, and seems like instress driven to the point of torture – which Hopkins can only express as a form of incarceration.

---

[70] This passage is discussed in Summer J. Star, '"For the Inscape's Sake": Sounding the Self in the Meters of Gerard Manley Hopkins', in *Meter Matters: Verse Cultures of the Long Nineteenth Century*, ed. Jason David Hall (Athens, OH: Ohio University Press, 2011), pp. 154–77 (173).

[71] *Diaries* p. 563; quoting *The Life of Saint Teresa, of the Order of Our Lady of Carmel*, ed. Henry Edward Manning (London: Hurst and Blackett, 1865), p. 77.

Hopkins's experiences of physical and psychic pain, or of a desire for sanctification through submission, or his reflexive metaphors of bondage and constraint to describe ontological unities and poetic rhythms, do not make him a masochist. But the intensities of his ascetic, self-critical psyche do take undeniably sexual pathways, and make use of sexualised vocabularies. He describes himself in terms of castration on multiple occasions.[72] While on retreat in Ireland in 1888, he acknowledged that 'all my undertakings miscarry: I am like a straining eunuch.' He wrote to Bridges in 1885 of his despair that 'anything of mine will ever see the light – of publicity nor even of day'; 'if I could but get on, if I could but produce work I should not mind its being buried, silenced, and going no further; but it kills me to be time's eunuch and never to beget' (*L1* 222). As in Ovid's elegy, a lack of poetic productivity is associated with sexual impotence. He is mortified, barren of poetry or desire. As he wrote in 1865, 'Trees by their yield / Are known; but I – / My sap is sealed, / My root is dry' (*Poetical Works* ll. 1–4, p. 83). His complaint about his 'fruit'less, loveless life suggests not only his decision to dedicate himself to priestly celibacy, but a sexless aridity that he applies to his poetic production.

Hopkins began to be read as a queer poet in the 1970s and 1980s.[73] His undergraduate journals provide extensive evidence of his attraction to men: he longs for the young Digby Dolben, a barefoot eccentric and cousin of Robert Bridges who drowned (or possibly committed suicide) as a teenager.[74] He enumerates many 'Unclean habits', including 'looking at a cartboy fr. Sanden's shopdoor'. He records numerous instances of the impulse to masturbate ('O. H.' or 'old habits'). He repeatedly considers whether he was culpable for having an orgasm in the night: 'I fear mortal sin, *effluxmina nulla adhibita mora* [night emissions to which no restraint was applied].'[75] In his discussions of sexual temptation he uses terms like 'evil thoughts', 'impurities of thought' and 'dangerous talking'.[76] He admitted

---

[72] Simon Humphries, 'A Eunuch for God: Gerard Manley Hopkins, SJ, Catullus and Castration,' *TLS* (22 & 29 December 2006), pp. 18–19.

[73] See, for example, Michael Lynch, 'Recovering Hopkins, Recovering Ourselves', *The Hopkins Quarterly* 6 (1979), pp. 107–17; Dennis Sobolev, 'Hopkins's "bellbright bodies": The Dialectics of Desire in His Writings', *Texas Studies in Literature and Language* 45.1 (Spring 2003), pp. 114–40.

[74] On his relationship with Dolben, see Norman White, *Hopkins: A Literary Biography* (Oxford: Clarendon Press, 1992), pp. 110–21, and Martin, *Gerard Manley Hopkins*, pp. 80–115.

[75] Norman H. MacKenzie, *The Early Poetic Manuscripts and Note-books of Gerard Manley Hopkins in Facsimile* (New York: Garland, 1989), p. 195.

[76] MacKenzie, *The Early Poetic Manuscripts*, pp. 157–203. See also Richard Dellamora, *Masculine Desire: The Sexual Politics of Victorian Aestheticism* (Chapel Hill: University of North Carolina Press, 1998), pp. 42–4; Martin, *Gerard Manley Hopkins*, p. 101.

to being erotically stimulated not only by his male companions, but by drawing a crucified arm,[77] and by a crucifix of his Aunt Kate's.[78]

Looking is central to Hopkins's sexuality. 'Temptation in thinking over boy I saw. Another about drawing Phillimore';[79] 'Looking at a man who tempted me in Port Meadow' (168); 'Looking at a face in the theatre' (169); 'Looking at boys, several instances' (173); 'Looking at tempting pictures' (183); 'Imprudent looking at organ-boy and other boys ... Looking at temptations, esp. at E. Geldart naked' (174). Hopkins's passionate looking finds a sanctioned outlet in his admiration of paintings of male labouring bodies, including 'a pretty medieval ploughing scene by Pinwell'[80] and Hamo Thornycroft's sculpture *The Sower*, and he also praised Frederick Walker's 'divine work' *The Plough*, and Walker's *Harbour of Refuge*, which he saw in 1873. In that painting:

> the young man mowing was a great stroke, a figure quite made up of dew and grace and strong fire: the sweep of the scythe and swing and sway of the whole body even to the rising of the one foot on tiptoe while the other was flung forward as if such a thing had never been painted before, so fresh and so very strong (*Diaries* 565).

In these visual works, it was the masculine agricultural labourer, making use only of his strength and simple machinery in the uncorrupted landscape of the countryside, that drew Hopkins's admiration.

Hopkins's interest in the aestheticised, constrained body of the labouring man can be seen in one of his last and most erotic poems, written at Dromore in County Down in September 1887. Hopkins describes 'Harry Ploughman' as 'a direct picture of a ploughman, without afterthought' (*L1* 262). The poem inscapes the straining figure of the workman, and revels in the strength and fluidity of bodily form:

> Hard as hurdle arms, with a broth of goldish flue
> Breathed round; the rack of ribs; the scooped flank; lank
> Rope-over thigh; knee-nave; and barrelled shank —
>   Head and foot, shoulder and shank —
> By a grey eye's heed steered well, one crew, fall to;   5
> Stand at stress. Each limb's barrowy brawn, his thew
> That onewhere curded, onewhere sucked or sank —
>   Soared or sank —,
> Though as a beechbole firm, finds his, as at a roll-call, rank

---

[77] MacKenzie, *Early Poetic Manuscripts*, p. 167.
[78] White, *Hopkins: A Literary Biography*, p. 114. [79] MacKenzie, *Early Poetic Manuscripts*, p. 181.
[80] Martin, *Gerard Manley Hopkins*, pp. 230–1.

>   And features, in flesh, what deed he each must do —   10
>   His sinew-service where do.
>   He leans to it, Harry bends, look. Back, elbow, and liquid waist
>   In him, all quail to the wallowing o' the plough: 's cheek crimsons; curls
>   Wag or crossbridle, in a wind lifted, windlaced —
>   See his wind-lilylocks-laced;   15
>   Churlsgrace, too, child of Amansstrength, how it hangs or hurls
>   Them — broad in bluff hide his frowning feet lashed! raced
>   With, along them, cragiron under and cold furls —
>   With-a-fountain's shining-shot furls.

This is a modified sonnet, which makes use of 'burden lines', shorter lines, as if for a chorus to recite (lines 4, 8, 11, 15, 19). It lacks, Hopkins said, an 'afterthought'; there is no volta, no change between the octave and the sestet. Catherine Phillips shows how Hopkins seeks to present 'the actions of the ploughman as he responds to the erratic movements of the plough': his foot 'hangs', 'to counterbalance the tipping plough as it catches on a tough clod (a movement that Walker captures in *The Plough*)'. For Phillips, the metrical markings and burden lines create a precarious balance 'between meaning and a flow of sound conveying movement'.[81] But what strikes me about the poem is its quality not of movement but of stasis; it resembles a frozen image, a photograph of a man in a condition of stress. That frozen quality, of the text, of the sculptural figure in the text, is also imitative of the stasis of the fetish — a frozen, arrested image that memorialises the last moment when the subject was able to believe in the female phallus, before being inducted into the trauma of castration.[82]

Masochism involves a state of (literal or psychic) suspension, in which expectation is preferable to fulfilment. Many theorists suggest that the defining quality of masochistic desire is not pleasure taken in discomfort, but 'pleasure in *expectation* of discomfort'.[83] Pleasure is stalled, constrained and contained, prevented from overflowing into orgasm. Even the experience of pain is a way of postponing the gratification of pleasure.[84] Gilles Deleuze argues that the masochist experiences 'waiting in its pure form'. Hopkins was keen on waiting; he wrote in his *Journals* that a delaying tactic of insight he called 'stalling' could sometimes sharpen the inscape of an object. In 1871, a

---

[81] Catherine Phillips, *Gerard Manley Hopkins and the Victorian Visual World* (Oxford University Press, 2007), p. 243.
[82] Deleuze, 'Coldness and Cruelty', p. 31.   [83] Reik, *Masochism in Modern Man*, p. 67.
[84] Jessica Benjamin, *Like Subjects, Love Objects: Essays on Recognition and Sexual Difference* (New Haven: Yale University Press, 1995), pp. 70–2.

year of rapturous inscaping of buds and clouds, Hopkins imagines that 'if the whole "behaviour" [of the flag flower] were gathered up and so stalled it wd. have a beauty of all the higher degree' (*Diaries* 513). Similarly in this poem, Hopkins freezes Harry in a sculptural image of labouring motion.

The freezing of Harry Ploughman in a state of tension bears comparison to Swinburne's fantasies about capturing the moment of flagellation. Swinburne rejoiced when his friend George Powell provided him with a photograph of the block, but laments that the 'scene is imperfect, a stage without actors, a hearth without fire ... I would give anything for a good photograph taken at the right minute – say the tenth cut or so – and doing justice to *all sides* of the question.' The absence of the victim, shown from all angles, leaves the fantasy unfulfilled; and Swinburne imagines 'If I were but a painter – ! I would do dozens of different fellows diversely suffering.'[85] His desire to freeze the fetishised scene in a situation of pictorial stillness draws out the masochistic pleasure in suspension and delay.

Swinburne's perversity may seem far from Hopkins's scrupulous self-restraint. But in 'Harry Ploughman', the labourer is also the object of a desiring, aestheticising and controlling gaze. Hopkins tells the reader to 'Look' at the 'Churlsgrace'. This looking configures this poetic scene like Ford Madox Brown's painting *Work* (1852–65), where Thomas Carlyle and Frederick Denison Maurice watch the labouring navvies from the shade in the margins.[86] Hopkins copied Brown's sonnet that accompanied this painting, and which celebrates the tanned flesh of 'lusty manhood', into his own commonplace book.[87] He also lists among his 'sins', from April 1865: 'Madox Brown's pictures ... Looking at navvies in Swiss Cottage Fields. Waste of time going to bed. Impurities.' Like the navvies, Harry is a thing to be looked at; the probing gaze is a substitute for touch.[88] But Hopkins's slippage from looking at a picture to looking at a person, from admiration for a worthy object (a painting) to sexual admiration, from the pleasures of aesthetic contemplation to the pleasures of masturbation, is also significant to our understanding of the ethical as well as aesthetic risks he takes in 'Harry Ploughman'.

---

[85] Lang, *Swinburne Letters* 1.265, letter to George Powell, 5 October 1867.
[86] Joseph Bristow, '"Churlsgrace": Gerard Manley Hopkins and the Working-Class Male Body', *ELH* 59.3 (Fall 1992), pp. 693–711 (696).
[87] W. H. Gardner, *Gerard Manley Hopkins, 1844–1889: A Study of Poetic Idiosyncrasy in Relation to Poetic Tradition*, 2 vols. (London: Secker and Warburg, 1949), 2:12.
[88] MacKenzie, *Early Poetic Manuscripts*, p. 158.

Hopkins said of the poem, 'I want Harry Ploughman to be a vivid figure before the mind's eye; if he is not that the sonnet fails' (*L1* 265). The poem exemplifies Hopkins's intensely visual imagination, which was undoubtedly honed by his practice of the Ignatian *Exercises*, with their emphasis on forming 'a certain imaginary vision' of Christ, or to 'set before the eyes of the imagination the length, breadth, and depth of hell'.[89] Hopkins's visual attentiveness to the natural world and to the artifices of painting is attested throughout his poems and letters. That Hopkins feared this attentiveness could sharpen into scopophilia is suggested by his undertaking of 'custody of the eyes', an ascetic practice recommended to him by Dr Pusey. In 'custody', the eyes were constrained, kept cast down, looking at neither people or things.[90] While Hopkins was a novice, Father Peter Gallwey gave an Exhortation to Novices that advised: 'One necessary effect of chastity is a positive hatred of all the pleasures of the senses – a loathing of all that gratifies the body. Custody of the eyes is actually custody of the mind.'[91] The temptation to look must be guarded against. As Hopkins writes in another poem, 'To what serves mortal beauty?', 'What good means – where a glance / Master more may than gaze' (*Poetical Works* ll. 4–5, p. 183). That poem declares that the beauty of 'wet-fresh windfall' lads must be 'met', the master can ogle the gorgeous slave; but then 'leave, let that alone' (*Poetical Works* ll. 6, 12–13, p. 183). Admiration of the male form can be sublimated into praise of the goodness of God's creations, but their wetness must remain an image, not a tactile sensation: look, but don't touch.

Undoubtedly, Hopkins's portrait of Harry is intended to convey a wholesome and 'sexless' admiration for the spiritual meanings of male physical beauty. And yet, a repressed homoerotic charge electrifies Hopkins's delight in Harry's form. Harry's 'cheek crimsons' with his labours, but the colour carries also the blushing heat of desire or shame (there are many crimson cheeks in *The Flogging Block*). Alongside Harry's hard muscularity there are also multiple reference to his fluidity: 'liquid waist', 'broth of goldish flue' to describe his body hair (flue is an obsolete, dialect word for soft down, fur or hair),[92] 'fountain's shining shot' or 'wet sheen shot'. This liquidity and jetting wetness recalls the 'wet-fresh windfall' lads, and the 'limber liquid youth, that to all I teach / Yields ténder as a púshed péach' in Hopkins's poem 'The Bugler's First Communion'

---

[89] Kitchen, *Gerard Manley Hopkins*, pp. 118–19. [90] Martin, *Gerard Manley Hopkins*, p. 196.
[91] Peter Gallwey's Exhortations to Novices, Farm Street; quoted in Phillips, *GMH and the Victorian Visual World*, p. vi.
[92] Norman H. MacKenzie, *A Reader's Guide to Gerard Manley Hopkins* (Ithaca, NY: Cornell University Press, 1981), p. 193.

(*Poetical Works*, ll. 22–3, p. 162). Hopkins often associates the 'motions of life' with liquidity.[93] However, wet shots, goldish flu(id)s, liquid waists and pushed peaches all appear to the modern reader as the insignia of queer desire. Reading the poem that way brings out the anatomical liquidity in the lines 'Back, elbow, and liquid waist / In him', and the 'wallowing' of the plough in the muddy gash that follows hard behind.

As the poetic gaze slides over Harry's body, that body is transformed into an ensemble of fetishised pieces that attract eroticised modifiers: 'hard as hurdle arms', 'sucked or sank', 'beechbole firm', 'sinew-service'. Hopkins attempts to 'inscape' Harry's physical beauty by anatomising his body, pushing it through the same poetic grinder in which Corinna was desiringly dismembered by Ovid – the blazon. Or, as Joseph Bristow puts it, Harry is butchered: chopped into a 'rack of ribs', a 'flank', 'shoulder and shank'.[94] This is not unlike the unintegrated, fragmented corpus of Sappho and other bodies in Swinburne's poetics. But Hopkins's poetic consumption of the body of Harry Ploughman as a system of strained and straining parts is very different from his own feeling of being fragmented by sleep paralysis. While Hopkins experienced as 'terrible' his body's discomposition ('the body no longer swayed as a piece by the nervous and muscular instress'), Harry's piecemeal anatomy seems suited both to the viewer's aesthetic consumption and his own labour as an extension of the equipment of plough and team. It is the sexualised idealisation of the division of labour, the worker as a series of moving parts.

Harry is depicted in a state of intense strain: the flank 'scooped', the shank 'barrelled', each part acted upon by intensely active verbs. The tension in Harry's body is a result of his holding, or being tied, in the reins; the language of the lash, rack and hurdle connote instruments of torture. Paul Mariani hears the crossbridle as a bridling, or reining in, by the cross: 'the wind which can "crossbridle the ploughman" ... is the Holy Spirit'.[95] But surely it is a horse that wears a 'crossbridle'. Harry is 'windlaced' as his hair blows like lily locks in the wind; his 'frowning feet' are 'lashed'. I've discussed the imagery of chains and bridles that associated the taming of a wife with the taming of an enslaved person or a wild beast. Harry is another of the figures that have recurred throughout this book, whose

---

[93] Brown, *Hopkins' Idealism*, p. 171. [94] Bristow, '"Churlsgrace"', p. 705.
[95] Paul Mariani, *A Commentary on the Complete Poems of Gerard Manley Hopkins* (Ithaca, NY: Cornell University Press, 1970), p. 272.

objectification by (erotic) lyric transforms him into a point of indeterminacy, halfway between the human and animal.

This is one way of thinking about the collapse between Harry and his team; but there is a more contemporary reference that also applies. Krafft-Ebing records a number of cases in which the masochist desired to be bound or 'harnessed ... before a carriage' by a mistress who 'made me take her for a drive' (105, case 150); one patient wishes to be:

> a proud, fiery steed, ridden by a beautiful lady. He felt her weight, the bit he had to obey, the pressure of the thighs on his flanks; he heard her beautiful, joyous voice. The exertion threw him into a perspiration; the touch of the spurs did the rest, and always induced pollution with great lustful pleasure. At other times he dreamed that he was a small, weak horse. Then a large, heavy woman came and mounted the horse, and set off on a long journey in the mountains. Recklessly, and without mercy, she allowed the poor animal to feel her weight; she made herself comfortable on his back; while he threatened to give out under her, she had the greatest enjoyment, and with calm mind enjoyed the beautiful scenery.[96]

As in this case, Hopkins's poem accentuates the difference between the physically strained bottom, and the top's disinterested contemplation. Harry is made into the perspiring, exerting mount, while the poetic voice – the top – can remain 'comfortable' and enjoy the scenery. This sense that Harry is being topped by the poetic observer is intensified by Hopkins's constrained and fragmentary syntax, which makes the horse and ploughman almost indistinguishable. The opening lines present a series of disjointed parts, without a declared subject to whom they can be tied; Hopkins works hard to erase even the 'his' in 'S' cheek crimsons'. 'Head and foot, shoulder and shank / By grey eye steered well': whose head and shank are these? Does the team or the ploughman or some composite of the two 'stand at stress'? Rather than simply personifying the harmony of a simple, labouring man with nature, his animals and tools, the poem presents a flickering image of Harry as a thing to be ridden.

As he holds and is held by the reins, Harry is also bound in the traces of Hopkins's verse (fig. 10.1). That 'verse' remembers the turning at the end of a ploughed furrow is significant for all the references to yoked figures throughout this book, and the regularity and irregularities of their lines. Hopkins experimented with stretching and contracting the foot through an elastic stress-based prosody. Those experiments can also be seen in the

---

[96] Krafft-Ebing, *Psychopathia Sexualis*, p. 112, case 51.

(a) 169   Harry Ploughman

Hard as hurdle arms, with a broth of goldish flue
Breathed round; the rack of ribs; the scooped flank; lank
                  { knee-nave;
Rope-over thigh; { kneebank; and barrelled shank—
        Head and foot, shoulder and shank—
By a grey eye's heed steered well, one crew, fall to;   5
                     { barrowy brawn, his thew
Stand at stress. Each limb's { barrowy-brawnèd thew
That onewhere curded, onewhere sucked or sank—
                Soared ór sánk—,
Though as a beechbole firm, finds his, as at a rollcall, rank
And features, in flesh, whát deed he each must do—   10
             His sinew-service whére dó.
He leans to it, Harry bends, look. Back, elbow, and liquid waist
In him, all quail to the wallowing o' the plough. 'S cheek crimsons; curls

(b)   { in a wind liftéd, windláced—
   Wag or crossbridle, { windloft or windlaced—
                  { Wind-lilylocks-laced;
                  { See his wínd-lílylócks-láced—;   15
Churlsgrace too, child of Amansstrength, how it hangs or hurls
{ Them
{ These—broad in bluff hide his frówning féet lashed! ráced
                          { cold furls—
With, along them, cragiron under and { flame-furls—
                      { With-a-fountain's shining-shot furls.
                      { With-a-wét-shéen-shót fúrls.

Fig 10.1 (a) and Fig. 10.1 (b) Gerard Manley Hopkins, 'Harry Ploughman', *The Poetical Works*, ed. Norman H. MacKenzie (Oxford University Press, 1990), pp. 169–70.

way Harry's 'frówning féet lashed' (in wrinkled leather boots) are described in the poem's uneven gait – the trochee and spondee refuse to settle into the typical pattern of Hopkins's dipodic verse; the ploughman 'stands at stress', halted by the poem's heavy beats. The traces of the plough and the verse are signalled very concretely by the busy brackets and ties that present multiple possibilities – like the variants in Dickinson's poetry, but here serving the function of stalling the resolution of the fantasy into one final outcome – lashed to the main body of the sonnet. Hopkins also makes use of what he called 'outrides', extra-metrical slack syllables, after which 'a slight pause follows as if the voice were silently making its way back to the highroad of the verse' (*L1* 262). This tensing, flexing and slackening of the verse is all under the strict control of the poet, who marks the poem's rhythm copiously in order to direct the reader's recitation; as Pamela Coren perceives them, 'the high number of pauses of different weight, dashes, the hyphenated words and run-on lines are an attempt at total control of the reader'.[97] These controls are also imposed in recognition of the gap between the voiced and printed poem, a theme much discussed in Victorian studies, which also recalls the discussion of the irreproducibility of African American speech in Chapter 7.[98] But they subject the reader to a controlling, if not to say sadistic, bondage that mirrors Harry's bondage by the plough.

That Hopkins associates verse with straining and muscular masculinity is clear from his admiration for Dryden's verse: 'he is the most masculine of our poets; his style and his rhythms lay the strongest stress of all our literature on the naked thew and sinew of the English language' (*L1* 267–8). Language or nature itself could be naked and straining – as in 'That Nature is a Heraclitan Fire', written around the same time as 'Harry Ploughman', which describes a fallen earth besmirched by 'throngs' of labourers:

> Squandering ooze to squeezed | dough, crúst, dust; stánches, stárches
> Squadroned masks and manmarks | treadmire toil there
> Fóotfretted in it. Million-fuelèd, | nature's bonfire burns on.
> (*Poetical Works*, ll. 6–8, p. 198)

The 'footfretted' earth, with its 'manmarks' of 'treadmire toil' (echo of the treadmill – the instrument of penal discipline), is scarred and trampled by human feet. The diction of this late poem reprises 'God's Grandeur':

> Génerátions have trod, have trod, have trod;
> And all is seared with trade; bleared, smeared with toil;
> And wears man's smudge and shares man's smell: the soil
> Is bare now, nor can foot feel, being shod.
> (*Poetical Works*, ll. 5–8, p. 139)

---

[97] Pamela Coren, 'Gerard Manley Hopkins, Plainsong and the Performance of Poetry,' *The Review of English Studies* n.s. 60.244 (April 2009), pp. 271–94 (288).
[98] Eric Griffiths, *The Printed Voice of Victorian Poetry*, 2nd ed. (Oxford University Press, 2018), esp. pp. 262–3, 332–3, 344.

Richard Dellamora has argued that these lines express a sexual repugnance – the smudge and smell as an orgasmic effusion that blears the good earth – while the 'dearest freshness' that lives deep down in unspent natural things is an image of 'unexpended seminal fluid', retained by the ideally celibate priest.[99] This sexualised language is used to critique industrial and agricultural labour, Hopkins's diction mimicking 'a slither into pollution, some travestying effluence of manufactured abundance which coats everything in reach', as Eric Griffiths puts it.[100] These fluids have a different tint than Harry's 'liquid waist' and 'broth of goldish flue'. But alongside their fluidity, Hopkins focuses on the unfeeling 'shod' feet of the workmen that stamp the soil, unlike the delicate aesthete Dolben, who wandered England's green and pleasant land barefoot.

Foot fetishism is associated by Freud with castration and scopophilia. The (male) child, looking for the mother's penis, is confronted with absence; the foot is the last thing the child sees before this traumatic recognition, and so is frozen as a fetish in his sexual imagination.[101] As Laura Mulvey explains it, the fetish object is a 'phallic replacement so that a shoe, for instance, could become the object on which the scandalised denial of female castration was fixated'. The male unconscious 'has two avenues of escape from this castration anxiety: preoccupation with the re-enactment of the original trauma (investigating the woman, demystifying her mystery) counterbalanced by the devaluation, punishment, or saving of the guilty object, ... or else complete disavowal of castration by the substitution of a fetish object or turning the represented figure itself into a fetish so that it becomes reassuring rather than dangerous'.[102] The former route – sadistic punishment of the mistress – is taken by the Ovidian lover, while we could argue that Swinburne combines the two, fetishistic scopophilia combined with the imagining of the annihilation of the other.

While a metapsychological reading of Hopkins as a foot fetishist would be hard to sustain, elements of scopophilia, castration and the return to the (metrical or labouring) foot can be found across his work. But this imagery combines sex and political economy. Again and again, Hopkins describes the relation of the labourer to the country's natural resources as one of violent extraction at the site of

---

[99] Dellamora, *Masculine Desire*, p. 53.   [100] Griffiths, *The Printed Voice*, pp. 283–4.
[101] Freud, 'Three Essays', p. 155.
[102] Laura Mulvey, *Visual and Other Pleasures* (Bloomington: Indiana University Press, 1989), pp. 11, 21.

the foot: the workers obliterate inscape, piercing the land with their hobnail boots. In 'Tom's Garland', which he wrote at the same time as 'Harry Ploughman', a labourer's 'fallowbootfellow pı̆les pı̆ck / By him and rips out rockfire homeforth' (*Poetical Works* ll. 2–3, p. 195). Later the country is described as 'mother-grŏund / That mammocks, mighty foot' (ll. 11–12).

'Tom's Garland' is subtitled 'on the unemployed', who are 'by Despair, bred Hangdog dull; by Rage, / Manwolf, worse; and their packs infest the age' (*Poetical Works* ll. 19–20, p. 195). The degradation of working people to the status of dogs and wolves is consistent with the racialised language of animality we've encountered throughout this book. In a gloss of the poem, Hopkins elaborates the traditional conceit of the body politic. The head is the sovereign,

> the foot is the daylabourer, and this is armed with hobnail boots, because it has to wear and be worn by the ground; which again is symbolical; for it is navvies or daylabourers who, on the great scale or in gangs of millions, mainly trench, tunnel, blast, and in other ways disfigure, 'mammock' the earth and, on a small scale, singly, and superficially stamp it with their footprints. And the 'garlands' of nails they wear are therefore the visible badge of the place they fill, the lowest in the commonwealth.[103]

Mariani hears 'mama' in mammocks, drawing out the sustenance from the mother-ground – though Hopkins may have found this dialect word in *Coriolanus*, where it is also used in the context of natural destruction and maternity (3.1.60–5).[104]

Hopkins's explanation of 'Tom's Garland' echoes Dickinson's comment on encountering a Black man that 'when the Head of the Nation shies, it confuses the Foot –' (L721, August 1881). But Hopkins keeps his head, and the feet of the British body politic keep their place. In a youthful 'red letter' to Bridges written in 1871, the year of the Paris Commune, Hopkins had declared that 'in a manner I am a Communist'; but later, his ministry induced feelings of shame and disgust toward the British working class. He complained of the 'filthy' drunks he encountered (1880; *L1* 110) and was convinced by his Liverpool and Glasgow experiences 'of the misery of town life to the poor and more than to the poor, of the misery of the poor in general, of the degradation even of our race, of the hollowness of this century's civilisation' (1881, *L2* 97). His association of poverty with the decline

---

[103] *L1* 273–4. See also Meredith Martin, 'Gerard Manley Hopkins and Sacred Language', *Religion & Literature* 45.2 (Summer 2013), pp. 166–174 (168).
[104] Mariani, *Commentary*, p. 277.

of the British empire is also apparent when he 'remarked for the thousandth time with sorrow and loathing the base and besotted figures and features of the Liverpool crowd. When I see the fine and manly Norwegians that flock hither to embark for America walk our streets and look about them it fills me with shame and wretchedness' (*LI* 127–8). This observation about the comparative 'baseness' of the (northern, working class) English alongside the 'fine and manly Norwegians' is immediately followed by remarks on shameful recent defeats of the British by the Boers in the Transvaal; 'at Majuba it was simply that our troops funked and ran' (*LI* 128).

Harry Ploughman appeals to Hopkins as a specimen of rough trade. It is helpful to Hopkins's fantasy that Harry is an agricultural and not an industrial worker; but his admiration of the individual worker's beauty is not only in tension with, but dependent upon, his animosity to Harry's class. Looking and dissecting the figure with his gaze, Hopkins tops Harry and freezes him as a fetish. 'Harry Ploughman' is paradigmatic of the tension in BDSM practices between the fantastic pleasures of dominance and submission and their historical actuality – or as I have argued throughout this book, between the metaphor of bondage and its reality. Across numerous sadomasochistic texts and poems, there are uneasy recognitions of how the sexualisation of historical oppression depends on tightly constrained acts of mimesis. Playing at masters and slaves, or at humans and animals, draws on a superstructure of signs whose basis in actual enslavement or exploitative class relations cannot be consciously acknowledged; but that basis is also essential to the economies of sadomasochistic pleasure.

Fantastic Slavery

In the late nineteenth century, Krafft-Ebing identified only a handful of cases of female masochism. One of the few was a woman who wished to commit herself voluntarily to a mental asylum so she could be beaten and mistreated like a patient: 'I fell upon this idea while reading how the director of an insane asylum pulled a lady by the hair from her bed and beat her with a cane and a riding-whip. I longed to be treated in a similar manner ... I liked ... to think of brutal, uneducated female warders beating me mercilessly.'[105] She fantasises that the torture of the asylum can be

---

[105] Richard von Krafft-Ebing, *Psychopathia Sexualis*, 12th ed., trans. F. J. Rebman (New York: Pioneer, 1939), p. 198.

experienced as pleasurable because she has consented to submit to it. Her fantasy is a correlative of the voluntary submission to poetic constraint that I've been tracing throughout this book.

But that fantasy is not of surrender in any given form. She wishes to be a slave to her male lover: 'but, mind you, not his female slave! For instance, I have imagined that he was Robinson and I the savage that served him.' Her desire is for a categorically different form of humiliation to what she normally experiences as a woman: 'after all, every woman can be the slave of her husband' (199). She wants to be oppressed like a 'savage' in the story of *Robinson Crusoe*, not like an ordinary wife under patriarchy. Most of Krafft-Ebing's male masochistic patients agree that the 'erotic ideal' was not to submit to 'women who wish to rule in the household and exercise petticoat sovereignty' (95), but a carefully staged scene that could not be assimilated to the conventional tyranny of the patriarchal household.

Given the sadism of the plantation, colony, school and prison, it should not be surprising to find that real slaves and prisoners so often pop up in masochistic fantasies. Several of Krafft-Ebing's patients anchor their desires in histories of actual enslavement. One masochist plans his encounters by 'reading about punishment, e.g., about the abuse of Roman slaves'.[106] For another, the thought 'that one man could possess, sell, or whip another, caused me intense excitement; and in reading "Uncle Tom's Cabin" (which I read at about the beginning of puberty), I had erections. Particularly exciting for me was the thought of a man's being hitched up before a wagon in which another man sat with a whip, driving and whipping him.'[107] (*Uncle Tom's Cabin* is also mentioned by Freud in his description of the progression from watching pedagogical abuse to auto-erotic pleasure in 'A Child is Being Beaten'.)

Another fantasises about a mistress 'who harnessed me before a carriage, and made me take her for a drive; whom I must follow like a dog; at whose feet I must lie naked, and be punished – i.e., whipped – by her'. Insisting that 'my masochistic tendencies have nothing feminine or effeminate about them', that what he is proposing is not just an inversion of patriarchal relationships, he declares that 'the general relation desired with her is not that in which a woman stands to a man, but that of the slave to the master, the domestic animal to its owner': ideally, like a dog or a horse.

---

[106] Krafft-Ebing, *Psychopathia Sexualis*, 7th ed., p. 76.   [107] *Ibid.*, p. 105, case 50.

Both 'are owned by masters, and punished by them; and the masters are responsible to no one. Just this unlimited power of life and death, as exercised over slaves and domestic animals, is the end and aim of all masochistic ideas' (109). Actual slavery and the domination of animals supply the grounds for masochistic fantasy. They work as fantasy because they can be held at a distance from the liberal subject's milder tyrannies, such as his domination of a wife. He wishes to perform the abjection of Blackness or animality, not to re-enact the familiar submissions of the bourgeois household.

Enslaved people appear throughout Sacher-Masoch's novel *Venus in Furs*. The hero, Severin, is a wealthy landowner who is reduced to a slave by his desire for Wanda. One of Wanda's earliest investments in Severin's masochistic desires is to buy a whip, 'like those they use in Russia on disobedient slaves'.[108] When Severin asks why their plan to enslave him seems unfeasible, Wanda insists it's 'because slavery does not exist any longer', to which Severin replies: 'Then let us go to a country where it does, to the Orient or Turkey' (194). Wanda then begins to enjoy her power, and the way it distinguishes her: 'What is the point in having a slave in a country where slavery is common practice? I want to be the only one to own a slave' (197). They go to Italy, where they sign a contract that surrenders his life to her will, thus 'giving a new application to the idea of the jurists of antiquity that slavery itself is based on a contract'.[109] At this moment, three 'Negresses' magically appear who bind Severin so that Wanda can whip him as they laugh (222–4). Shortly after this, Wanda asserts that 'You are whatever I want you to be, a man, a thing, an animal,' and the Negresses fasten a yoke on him, forcing him to plough a field as they goad him (232). The yoked figure of the lover directly imitates Tibullus (2.3.79–80), Propertius (2.3.47–50) and Ovid (1.2, 2.2, and 3.4), and recalls Harry Ploughman's identity with his team. Severin is reduced to a beast of burden by the Negresses, who impose on him conditions that resemble those endured by enslaved Africans in the Americas.

Slavery is also part of the apparatus of sadistic and masochistic domination in Pauline Réage's novel *Story of O*. The entirely obnoxious preface to that book, 'Happiness in Slavery' by 'Jean Paulhan of

---

[108] Leopold von Sacher-Masoch, 'Venus in Furs', in *Masochism* (New York: Zone Books, 1991), p. 183.
[109] Deleuze, 'Coldness and Cruelty', p. 75.

l'Académie Française', starts with an invented anecdote about a 'strange and bloody revolt' in Barbados in 1838. Paulhan – who is possibly the lover for whom Réage/Aury wrote the story, and who was a defender of French colonialism in Algeria[110] – tells the story of an enslaver called 'Glenelg' who emancipates the two hundred enslaved people he owns. They beg him 'to take them back into bondage'.[111] When he refuses, they massacre him and his family, and return to 'their cabins, their palavers, their labours, and customary rituals' (xxii). Paulhan imagines a notebook in which their grievances are recorded, which no doubt constituted an 'apologia for slavery' and 'today ... would be considered a dangerous book' (xxiii). The truth of that book, he concludes, is that 'Glenelg's slaves were in love with their master, that they could not bear to be without him' (xxxvi): if Réage's book suggests that love is like slavery, Paulhan feels sure that slavery is like love.

In the novel, the figure of the racialised servant also recurs as witness to the white woman's abasement. Sir Stephen, the aristocratic Englishman who becomes O's master, employs an 'elderly mulatto servant' (88) called Norah who sometimes whips O on his command (172). In one scene, Norah enters the room while O is being fucked by Sir Stephen. Norah's 'black, beady eyes fastened on her own – and it was impossible for O to tell whether they bespoke indifference or not – those eyes set in a deeply furrowed, impassive face so bothered O that she made a movement to try and get away from Sir Stephen' (136). O is forced to dress in front of her; 'as she followed her, O could not take her eyes off the twin points of her Madras kerchief and, every time she opened a door, off her thin, swarthy hand on the porcelain handle, a hand that seemed as hard as wood' (134). The Black woman's kerchief, eyes and hand are her only features that appear visible to the white female gaze, and are racially marked in contrast to the smooth, cold whiteness of the porcelain. Though Norah, like O, seems to be performing her obedience to a command to practice custody of the eyes and not to speak, the two form no solidarity. O regards her as a 'dangerous and formidable' enemy, not human but a mute weapon: 'hard as wood'. Later, O becomes a willing slave. Sir Stephen inscribes his claim on O by piercing her labia with a ring from which is suspended chains stamped with Sir Stephen's monogram and O's name, and branding his

---

[110] Sabine Broeck, *Gender and the Abjection of Blackness* (Albany: SUNY Press, 2018), p. 128.
[111] Pauline Réage, *Story of O: A Novel*, trans. Sabine d'Estrée (New York: Ballantine Books, 2013), p. xxi.

initials on her ass. These marks of ownership degrade O to the status of livestock, or an enslaved person.

Venus in Furs and *Story of O* are examples of how the voluntary, wilful submission of the subject to sexual constraint enacts a phantastic ritual of bondage, incarceration or enslavement, in which the *actual* conditions of enslaved and imprisoned people or dominated animals are conjured up – imagined in detail, used as a fantastic repertoire – but must simultaneously be disavowed. Contemporary BDSM practices get tangled up in these dynamics as well. Margot Weiss describes a BDSM 'slave auction' in the Bay Area. Everything is going along happily, until an African American woman is advertised for sale by her 'master'; everyone seems uncomfortable and responses are extremely subdued.[112] Similarly, Geoff Mains draws on the imagery of the primitive, animalistic, 'aboriginal soul' in his cult classic *Urban Aboriginals: A Celebration of Leathersexuality* (1984), which begins: 'This book is a journey into the aboriginal soul. It is not a voyage into forests that reverberate with drums, but into an abyss upon which, precariously, western civilisation balances … . These are men not apart but of the very blood of that civilisation. Urbane and savage in the same breath, they are animal and human in the same stroke.'[113] Identifying BDSM practitioners with the 'aboriginal soul', Mains takes the reader on a racialised journey through modern anthropology, Darwin and Victorian morality backwards into the roots of a 'tribal culture' based on 'the animal reality of the human condition' (10). Mains eulogises BDSM as natural, authentic, and a rejection of the veneer of civility by drawing on fantasies of primitivism and Romantic racialism that we've already encountered in the work of the negrophile collectors and T. S. Eliot.

The sadomasochism of settler colonialism is beyond the scope of this chapter. But I'll end with one final example. Swinburne's oral sadism and fascination with the cannibalistic kiss found an imperial context through his membership of the 'Cannibal Club', the nickname for a clique of the London Anthropological Society that was founded in January 1863 (Swinburne was elected Fellow in April 1865).[114] Stuffed with members of the Victorian elite, the Cannibals shared sadomasochistic lingo, pornography, pseudo-scientific sexual and racial research, and an interest in British imperial ventures.

---

[112] Margot Weiss, *Techniques of Pleasure: BDSM and the Circuits of Sexuality* (Durham: Duke University Press, 2011), p. 4.
[113] Geoff Mains, *Urban Aboriginals: A Celebration of Leathersexuality* (San Francisco: Gay Sunshine Press, 1984), p. 9.
[114] Rooksby, *A. C. Swinburne*, p. 116.

Several had been colonial officials overseas.[115] They used a gavel shaped like a 'Negro's head'.[116] One of the sources of their pornographic materials was Frederick Hankey. Swinburne described Hankey's collection of erotica as 'unrivalled upon earth – unequalled, I should imagine, in heaven … . There is every edition of every work of our dear and honoured Marquis.'[117]

In their *Journals*, Edmond and Jules de Goncourt tell a sensational story about Hankey, who had convinced the famous Parisian bookbinder Bauzonnet to make bindings for his collection embossed with crossed whips and bleeding bottoms. Hankey told his visitors that:

> I'm waiting for a skin … For a binding. The skin of a young girl. One of my friends is supposed to get it for me … They tan it, you know … It takes six months to tan it … Really you need two, from two women … I have a friend, Dr Barth, you know … He travels in Africa. He's promised to get me a real skin, during one of the massacres … Something really fine …[118]

The book Hankey wanted, and could not have, was to be derived, materially and metaphorically, from the murder of African women. Richard Burton, who was given this appalling commission, was not able to satisfy his friend. On a mission to the Kingdom of Dahomey in 1863, Burton wrote to Monckton Milnes that 'I have been here for 3 days … Not a man killed, nor a fellow tortured. The canoe floating in blood is a myth of myths. Poor Hankey must still wait for his *peau de femme*.'[119] The anecdote draws on the sadomasochism of colonial violence, which was inscribed in the literary imagination, in fact and on the actual bodies of people of colour, desired here as the literal site of sadomasochistic writing: as a binding.

Many writers dwell on the theatricality of sadomasochism, which troubles the line between the fantastic and the real. This line is nonetheless central to the preservation of fantasy. Some men and women wish to play at being slaves and animals without becoming real ones. The symbolism of bondage is useful in the production of intimate and private fantasies, in

---

[115] Lisa Z. Sigel, *Governing Pleasures: Pornography and Social Change in England, 1815–1914* (New Brunswick: Rutgers University Press, 2002), pp. 57–8.
[116] *Ibid.*, p. 53.
[117] Jann Marson, 'Bibliography Behaving Badly: The Secret Life of the Portrait fantaisiste du Marquis de Sade,' *Book History* 16 (2013), pp. 89–131 (122).
[118] G. Legman, *The Horn Book: Studies in Erotic Folklore and Bibliography* (New Hyde Park: University Books, 1964); see James Pope-Hennessey, *Monckton Milnes: The Flight of Youth, 1851–1885* (London, 1951), pp. 17–20.
[119] Sigel, *Governing Pleasures*, p. 50.

which the thrill and power of inflicting or receiving pain depends on the resemblance of the scene, *up to a certain point*, to actual violence. The poem is also a space in which consenting adults agree to suspend normal relations in order to pursue the intensities of fantasy, within certain rules and limits. For Roland Barthes, the text is an 'anagram of the erotic body' and 'fetish object'.[120] He has described the text's '*will to bliss*: just where it exceeds demand, transcends prattle, and whereby it attempts to overflow, to break through the constraint of adjectives' (13). This overflowing of constraint or containment is similar to the psychic and theological transgression of boundaries that I discussed in relation to Hopkins, and to Dickinson's 'Bound a Trouble'. As Wordsworth also intimated, the text can only overflow if it is confined, 'constrained' by vocabulary or forms as binds against which the pleasure of the text strains for release.

Sadomasochistic violence also attempts 'a simulation of boundlessness' through boundedness; its ecstasies of pure embodiment can only be preserved through legalistic logics of contracts and safewords, which draw ecstatic lines between the permissible and the forbidden. As with poetry, which gains its power from the common knowledge that it is a lie, BDSM is based on a principle of ambivalent mimesis: it is desirable so long as it is like, but not too like, the reality it seeks to transform.

---

[120] Roland Barthes, *The Pleasure of the Text*, trans. Richard Miller (New York: Farrar, Straus and Giroux, 1975), pp. 17, 27.

CHAPTER 11

Soft Architecture
Lisa Robertson and Bondage as Ornament

> *Now here, now there, the roving Fancy flies,*
> *Till some lov'd object strikes her wand'ring eyes,*
> *Whose silken fetters all the senses bind,*
> *And soft captivity involves the mind.*
>
> – Phillis Wheatley

It is April in North Carolina and time, with Phillis Wheatley and Lisa Robertson, 'to return to the sex of my thinking'. One afternoon I leave my office to find the forest cloudy with pollen; the cars in the parking lot are buried under piles of cadmium yellow swarf, and I walk through the sexual effusions of pine and oak. Footprints trace wanderings in potentiality. It looks like a message: of the poem as beginning, of adornment, of the text of bliss and an erotics of rampant pastoral. Of excess. It reminds me of Robertson's poems: the hormone that becomes toxin, and vice versa; the human body as a host. The vestigial. And I read it, too, as the plumes of Wheatley's Fancy, sweeping upwards into the sky, the audacious outburst that makes something floral and living out of these violated grounds.

In the closing chapters of this book, which I began writing in the closing weeks of my fellowship in 2019, I am thinking about fellowship, excess and bondage as ornament in the work of these two very different poets. Phillis Wheatley established herself with incredible precocity as a voice of emergent American liberty, forming elegiac solidarities within her local Boston community and a transatlantic one, reaching back to her African kin while negotiating complex relations to the Bostonian and British elite. Robertson seeks out feminised solidarities across history as she re-centres the female body in a critique of subjectivity and speculative reason. In terms that could also apply to Wheatley, she writes: 'I feel it is my calling to annotate the sheathed cadence of life beside power.'¹ This 'life beside power' is the place where Hegel found women, the 'internal enemy' of the community who linger eternally in its ironic sidelines;² but to 'annotate' that life is not to surrender to minority. Rather it is a way of unlocking a feminist genealogy that might 'destruct the phantom body' of a history of writing from which women (particularly women of colour) have often been erased.

These two chapters conclude my study of the ways that poets invoke bondage as metaphor while effacing the actuality of bondage, by thinking with two poets who use genre, imitation and form to challenge the constraints known as gender and race. The *Endnotes* collective has analysed sex and gender as analogous to the duality of the commodity as both a use-value and an exchange-value. Biological sex, they argue, is 'the naturalisation of gender's dual projection upon bodies, aggregating biological differences into discrete naturalised semblances'. In the conditions of contemporary austerity that reveal the situation of reproduction to be one of abjection, they argue, gender has become increasingly denaturalised; but that denaturalisation might also lead to the abolition of this 'powerful constraint'.³ Robertson's work explores both the abjection of gender in late capitalism, and the potential for its abolition, through an ironic re-investment in masculinist poetic traditions – an irony that involves softening and ornamenting them; and through the radical temporalities of the female body, particularly the post-menopausal body of the 'she-dandy' as one that has abandoned its reproductive use-value. As she writes in her novel *The Baudelaire Fractal*, 'I needed to write in order to make a site for my body. There would be no other way to uncover my unwieldy desire':

> I would build new, ornate knowledge on the basis of a lived proposition. I mean that my shy, gawky, lusting body was constrained to undertake the ancient representation, to groom and flirt and refract as every contemporary girl seemed so constrained, to signify bounty and frailty, passivity and fate, but also at this time there was the fact that I loosely accepted the constraint. It taught me something about discipline and a lot about a history of form . . . I want to claim this word *free* for myself and I intend to use it wrongly very often.⁴

---

¹ Lisa Robertson, *XEclogue* (Vancouver: New Star, [1993] 2006), Eclogue Three, Liberty. Neither *XEclogue* nor *Debbie: An Epic* have page numbers, so I will provide the title of the poem in references to the former book, and line numbers in reference to the latter.
² G. W. F. Hegel, *The Phenomenology of Spirit*, trans. A. V. Miller (Oxford University Press, 1976), p. 288, §475.
³ Endnotes, 'The Logic of Gender', *Endnotes* 3 (2013), p. 79.
⁴ Lisa Robertson, *The Baudelaire Fractal* (Toronto: Coach House Books, 2020), pp. 42, 46–7.

But the notions of freedom from tradition, and gender as constraint, have a very different significance in the context of Wheatley's neoclassical poetics, the North American slave trade and its 'theft of the body'. What Hortense Spillers analyses as the 'ungendering' of the African female subject is distant from white feminist gender abolition.[5] These chapters will elaborate those distinctions as they follow a pathway from the enfleshed poetics of a contemporary Canadian white woman in Europe, back to the revolutionary claims and melancholy sublimations of a Black African woman in colonial America. Reversing the chronological order that has thus far structured the book, I begin with Robertson and conclude with Wheatley. This reversal is intended to subvert the suggestion that contemporary poets have some weak messianic power to fulfil the claims and potentialities of earlier ones, or that they are constrained only to imitate earlier innovations. But I also want Wheatley to have the last word.

The Figure of Irony

In a prose poem on 'The Collective', Lisa Robertson imagines a 'school' of self-organised, trans-temporal collectors, whose autodidacticism aligns them with a variety of historical sodalities, including Black Mountain:

> the beer-fuelled living-room readings attended by loggers, architects, camp cooks, lefty lawyers and students; the communal meeting halls of 1871 Paris in the month of March, where radical shoemakers, seamstresses and pre-school teachers lectured on citizenship; the experimental chemistry clubs of 17th-century revolutionary London; the romantic meteorologists of Cambridgeshire; Fourier's passionate associations and phalansteries; the peripatetic conversants of the Epicurean garden, where women and men shared the lively and living pursuit of philosophy, in contradiction to the discourses of the state.[6]

This is praise of an aesthetics and politics of gathering, that emerges not from the individual author, but through the shared labour of the collective. 'The feeling of having an inner life, animated by a cold-hot point of identification called "I," is a linguistic collaboration. We speak only through others' mouths,' she writes elsewhere.[7]

---

[5] Hortense J. Spillers, *Black, White, and in Color: Essays on American Literature and Culture* (University of Chicago Press, 2003), pp. 206–7. The Endnotes essay is significantly flawed by its failure to explicitly consider the racialisation of gender, and the way that 'antiblackness constitutes and disrupts sex/gender constructs'. Zakiyyah Iman Jackson, *Becoming Human: Matter and Meaning in an Antiblack World* (New York University Press, 2020), p. 9.
[6] Lisa Robertson, 'The Collective', *Canadian Art* (Spring 2017), p. 67.   [7] Robertson, *Baudelaire*, p. 160.

Robertson's own intellectual formation is also catalogued here. From the autonomous working-class intellectuals of the Commune, the utopians, Romantics and natural philosophers, and from her own experiences, she gathers methods of contradiction. Robertson was born in Toronto in 1961, and joined Katimavik, a 'collectivist youth work programme', in 1978. She lived and worked in tree-planting camps and free cabins in western Canada before settling in Vancouver, where she was a member of the Kootenay School of Writing, a bookseller and a participant in the visual arts scene.[8] The Kootenay collective is described, with much love, in another essay.[9] Much of her writing celebrates the sidelines and margins, the colonial outcrop and urban ruin, as spaces where people might 'walk beside the wresting and burning of commodities'.[10]

The aim of her imaginary Collective, Robertson explains, is 'to help the collapse of time as metrics, and encourage its transformation into a luxuriously distributed lubricant, an enticingly shimmering and moving fabric, a shared yet contested décor'.[11] This is typical of her aesthetics, and the transformation of the bondage of time into a softening textile or ornament. Through such fictions Robertson imagines time as lived, not quantified; as the apparel of being, engine of delight and collaboration, rather than a constraint within which we must be absolutely drained of our labour power.

Robertson's thinking about time has been influenced by Eric Auerbach's essay on the figure. She cites it in her own essay, 'Time in the Codex', where she writes of the figure's ability to change through its enfolding and unfolding over time:

> an object or an image figures when it receives more of our imaginative projection than its social or mythic function would require. This margin of excess (an excess of potential intepretability inherent to a shapeliness) can be differently inflected through time. Conceptual and historical fluctuations exceed the bounded or perceptible limits of a thing .... The opacity, the inconspicuousness of its [the figure's] folds permits the interpretive differential.[12]

---

[8] Ryan Fitzpatrick and Susan Rudy, '"If Everything Is Moving Where Is Here?" Lisa Robertson's Occasional Work on Cities, Space and Impermanence', *British Journal of Canadian Studies* 26.2 (2013), pp. 173–89 (174–5).
[9] Lisa Robertson, 'The Collective', *Poetry Foundation* blog (2017): www.poetryfoundation.org /harriet/2017/04/the-collective (accessed 4 May 2021).
[10] Lisa Robertson, *Cinema of the Present* (Toronto: Coach House Books, 2014), p. 57.
[11] Robertson, 'The Collective', *Canadian Art*, p. 67.
[12] Lisa Robertson, *Nilling: Prose Essays on Noise, Pornography, the Codex, Melancholy, Lucretius, Folds, Cities and Related Aporias* (Toronto: Bookthug, 2012), p. 11.

Robertson's conceptualisation of time as plastic, contingent and embodied is important for understanding the role of imitation in her poetics, which I discuss below. Time is the medium in which the figure's boundedness or bondage can be loosened and turned to new uses. The figure's 'plasticity – this propensity of the figure to actively fold within itself an agency, an inflection that modulates perception – is the trait that permits the ongoing activity of the figure in time'.[13] It is here that the poet sets to work, loosening the bondage of thing, its limitations in time and opening it up to the flourish of the ornamental.

The plasticity of the figure is one way of understanding Robertson's relation to the past. Her handling of poetic time, of a lyric tradition associated with male desire and empire-building, draws its power not from refusal or rejection, but from imitation, which takes the form of an over-investment in the bodily hexes and gendered, classed and raced subjectivities that are the objects of desire within that tradition. Robertson's poetic career can be tracked everywhere in Lucretius' and Virgil's snow. Virgil wrote his *Eclogues* and *Georgics* before attempting his epic; Ovid subverted this *cursus* by reclining from the epic singing of *arma virumque* into the pleasures of sexual love. Robertson takes her own swerving feminist course from *XEclogue* (1993), a book of pseudo-Enlightenment pastoral featuring the 'roaring boys', Nancy the shepherdess, and Lady M (Lady Mary Wortley Montagu), to *Debbie: An Epic* (1997). These ironic feminist revisions persist in her georgic poems *The Weather* (2001), in which 'everything is lifted', copied from eighteenth- and nineteenth-century works of natural history. Later works tangle with other poetic forefathers: *The Men* (2006) with Petrarch and the Renaissance love lyric, *R's Boat* (2010) with Rousseau. It is both the male authors and the genres they dominate that operate as constraints. In *The Baudelaire Fractal* (2020), the speaker – Hazel Brown – awakens to discover that she is the dandiacal author of all Baudelaire's works. Thinking of him, of Ted Hughes, Ezra Pound, George Baker and Proust, Robertson doesn't forget all the 'she-poets' who 'perished beneath the burden of beauty and scorn': 'Who was I then, what was I, when I, a girl, was their reader, the reader of the beautiful representations? Who was I if I became the describer?' 'With all of her predecessors erased, how can she recognise her tradition? To begin was an internal attack on the feminine constraint.'[14] Starting as the passive, even masochistic reader, she becomes the author, laying claim to an ironic subjectivity that displaces the male voices of a largely erotic poetic

---

[13] Robertson, *Nilling*, p. 12.   [14] Robertson, *Baudelaire*, pp. 83, 108.

tradition. By voluntarily submitting to and détourning this patriarchal corpus, Robertson seeks to turn the bondage of history into a feminist ornament: 'I was a girl. I entered literature like an assassin, leaking, fucking, wanting, drinking' (107).

This girl enters literature ironically. Robertson approaches classical literature through an engagement with the ironies of the eighteenth century, with Alexander Pope (and Edith Sitwell's remarkable biography of Pope, 'which taught me to attend to syllabic texture'), and with Lady Mary Wortley Montagu; *XEclogue* reverberates with the ironic charge of the city eclogue or the mock epic.[15] But her own ironic poetics is also a manifestation of gender. She writes: 'Some of my organs were outside history, which gave me an advantage.'[16] Lauren Berlant has argued that, because woman's castration is given, women can have ironic relation to their erotic repetitions: they can admit to them without disavowing or doing violence to them.[17] Irony is a feminised way of standing back from the wound of castration. I've argued that contact with the female body in Ovid's elegies is signified by a missing foot, and that body is itself represented as a blank. But the injury of castration that instantiates femininity is met, in Robertson's poetics, with a plenitude of speech and ironic laughter. While

> Good citizens reproduce the traumas
> Of memory and transgression, thus
> Guaranteeing a futurity for
> Rome's citation. I myself walk towards
> The fantasy of the Imperium.[18]

Walking *towards* the fantasy of the Imperium to subvert it, Robertson's feminist poetics engage in deeply ironic ways with the institutions of patriarchal history.

Chief among those institutions is Rome. Palimpsest of historical sovereignties and ruins, the 'eternal city' is a key site for Robertson's contestation and enjoyment of the legacies of the past. Rome is a historical fact, a monumental inscription, a textual corpus, an architecture, and – in Auerbach's terms – a figure, whose provisionality continues to shape and be shaped by our ideas about empire, the law, freedom and slavery. Repeatedly in Robertson's verse, the 'free and unfree went walking / To

---

[15] Kai Fierle-Hedrick, 'Lifted: An Interview with Lisa Robertson', *Chicago Review* 51/52 (Spring 2006), pp. 38–54 (50).
[16] Lisa Robertson, *Lisa Robertson's Magenta Soul Whip* (Toronto: Coach House Books, 2009), p. 51.
[17] Lauren Berlant, *Desire/Love* (Brooklyn: Punctum, 2012), p. 41. [18] Robertson, *Magenta*, p. 87.

the unseen city of antiquity'.[19] References to 'Latinity' as a figure for domination recur throughout her poems. In *XEclogue*, 'a tiny flapping boy ... bullies the dust' 'In the Empire of no tense'; 'So what about his consummate Latinity?' Shortly thereafter, Venus is invited to 'get dressed in a better Latinity. Wear that salted harness beyond the need for abnegation.'[20] 'In young women enamoured of their own intensities the Latin element wells up and knits from lust the pelt on the wall' – anticipating the soft architecture we'll encounter later.[21] A dog 'swims in toxic Latin / Licks his Latin paws'.[22] Tweaking Lacan's assertion that the unconscious is structured like a language, Robertson's subject rebels against the 'Latin' of the unconscious (*'As for the unconscious, she is breathing in its Latin'*), the philosophy which 'comes from her having difficulty', from her paradoxical 'experience of scale'.[23] Latin provides the linguistic scale, and Rome the architectural one, for the burdens of history that a feminist poet manages ironically, or wears like a salted harness.

Like Wheatley, Robertson regrets that she cannot raise a Latin song: 'I "have" no Latin. I sound through it. Most of the *Aeneid*, when I was writing *Debbie*, during *The Weather* the *Georgics*, and now Lucretius. All these gorgeous syllables, nothing to do but bask in them. Definitely it's connected to rhythm, and most specifically to metre.'[24] Nonetheless, her poems draw on Latin as a sonic texture and a set of imperial coordinates. *XEclogue*'s feminised protagonists

> took the immeasurable risk of piercing his description: we wedged Virgil's evening as demotic ghosts who refused to reproduce 'freedom'. On the blurred selvage we tucked Liberty in our cheek like a tongued and rotten dictation.[25]

A 'selvage' can be the edge of a cloth, which has been finished so that it does not fray; or a margin of igneous rock along a fault line. The words salvage, savage and self-edge are compacted in it. But there is something much darker about this image of 'a tongued and rotten dictation' than the basking in 'gorgeous syllables' Robertson describes in her interview. The poems ask: if it is not Latin, but Liberty itself, whose beginnings are encoded in Virgil's descriptions, how can an excluded feminised subject participate in the making of political freedom or its poetics, except through violence? How can she unbind herself from this history, and its inscription of and in her body?

---

[19] Lisa Robertson, *R's Boat* (Berkeley: University of California Press, 2010), p. 72.
[20] Robertson, *XEclogue* 8: Romance.   [21] Robertson, *Magenta*, p. 90.
[22] Robertson, *R's Boat*, p. 32.   [23] Robertson, *Magenta*, p. 45.   [24] Fierle-Hedrick, 'Lifted', p. 50.
[25] Robertson, *XEclogue* 10: Utopia.

Lingering in the edges and margins, Robertson's feminised subjects haunt Virgilian pastoral and epic, refusing either to be exiled or dormant and calling up 'desire and stupidity' as ways of inhabiting the bondage of history without surrendering to a fantasy of false emancipation. In *Debbie*, some women assert

> this fact: we were half made when the empire
> died in orgy. Because we are not free
> my work shall be obscure
> as Love! unlinguistic! I
> bludgeon the poem with desire and
> stupidity in the wonderful autumn
> season[26]

The 'arrogance' of this gesture, a speaking back to the epic forefathers, cannot outface the absence of women from the writing of empire – Sulpicia, alone amongst the elegists. 'We were half made when the empire / died.' Working in the new imperia of North America, still 'not free', Robertson's female characters dwell in the liberties of the city, revel in the queer indeterminacy of their half-made state and embrace 'desire and / stupidity' as they catch a ride in Venus's 'rosy car'.

Robertson's poems are populated by fugitive feminised figures who dwell in the edges, backstreets, shacks, porches, vestibular and derelict sites where the flow of capital ebbs. Debbie and her emancipatory pleasures are to be found not in the arena, but behind it:

> I am going behind the arena
> to get some pleasure – and all the civic
> ornaments of my clever flesh: Borrowed
> from rivals. Roman I, I father my
> subservience the sententious
> thrill the organ public
> in magnificence I will have borrowed
> what animal and dire rumour outwore
>
> (ll. 532–538)

Corinna was driven before the triumphal chariot in a spectacular display of her abuse by a male lover. Going 'behind the arena', which is the place of rivalry and blood sport, the symbol of Rome's grandeur, Debbie is determined to 'get some pleasure' not as a repudiation of the *civis*, but a displacement of it with the 'civic / ornaments of my clever flesh': the body reclaimed for the feminised subject herself, pleasurably ironising public rhetoric and symbolism until these fetters can be softened into garlands.

---

[26] Lisa Robertson, *Debbie: An Epic* (Vancouver: New Star, 1997 [2003]), ll. 428–39.

Throughout her epic, Debbie reworks the devices of her 'father' Virgil, throwing off the constraining 'heavy / crown of filial debt' and softening the hardness of militarism and its poetries with her sexual delight.[27] She heckles the 'Fathers of liberty's bastard / antiquities', asking 'are we Virgil's bastard daughters' (l. 705)? Debbie's position is dictated by her citizenship and her place in the patriarchal family: 'Roman I, father my / subservience' (ll. 534–5). But the phallic father can be resisted with softness:

> AS IF BECAUSE OF FATHER I WENT DOWN TO
> the soft forced notions of boats
> went as wax before repleteness
> in summer's heat and animate
> skirmish incomparably breasting slick
> uncertainty or the sexual if
> I have loved history's premonitions
> urgencies these parts lovingly I speak
> in the dialect of servility
>
> (ll. 223–4)

The poem re-ironises the already ironic 'dialect of servility' in which the Roman elegists spoke, by translating the performance of the enslaved and effeminised lover into the speech of a female protagonist who loves softness and a history replete with examples of her violation. Here is a different meaning of softness: not soft architecture, but elegiac *mollitia*, the softness of verse that in the hands of a masculine poet connotes impotence and disappointment. Robertson attributes this softness to the 'forced notions' of the boats and all they stand for in poetic history: rape, war, slaughter, loss and wandering. The presumptive subject of 'went as wax' is I, who melts under summer's heat. Wax is the binding agent for Icarus's botched escape attempt. But it is also a word for growth, and a reusable writing surface; *cera* appears throughout Ovid's elegies as the coating for the *tabellae*, wooden tablets by which the lovers communicate, and an eroticised substance that can be made pliant by heat. While I speak in the dialect of the *servitium amoris*, I can grow into 'these parts': taking on different characters, speaking from degraded body parts, my words 'breasting slick / uncertainty' in the midst of masculinity's serial skirmishes. Debbie asks to be excused 'if I throw myself / absolutely outside of my sex'. But to be 'outside of my sex' is not to be sexless, in either the sense of androgyny or of celibacy; rather, it is to expand the sex of thinking and 'my sense of my body' to include 'both dog

---

[27] Robertson, *Debbie*, intertext at l. 611.

and owning state's daft / glamour': the bestial and the imperial, the unadorned animal and Debbie's glamorous poetics of resistance.

Dissolving Subjects

Robertson's indeterminate pronouns, her indulgence of the indexical, her unowned 'you', the grammar that ranges from brightly adorned to crisply declarative pronouncements, create a surface that deflects biographical probing or the sense of lyric as a well of deeply feeling interiority. 'Whatever pronoun a work is organised around, you have to trouble it,' she said in an interview.[28] 'I', the speech of the feminised subject whose 'silken rupture spills into history'; 'you'; 'her, this word that explodes', as Anne Carson writes in *The Beauty of the Husband*: Robertson detonates them all.[29] In *Cinema of the Present*, she writes: 'Yours is the prosody of being misapprehended. It has been called shame and has a conventional pronoun' (29). That pronoun is presumably the feminine one, which 'leaks thus' (44), like the leaky vessel of the female body; and like that vessel, '*What is a pronoun but a metaphor?*' (62). This points to Robertson's concurrence 'with a lineage of feminist thinkers (such as Butler and Wittig) who demonstrate that there is no such thing as a "woman", only constructions of femininity and their enforcements, codifications and institutionalizations.'[30] Nonetheless, as this book has shown, being able to take a category as metaphor – whether it is gender, race or bondage itself – is often an outcome of particular forms of privilege.

This desire to dissolve the constraint of gender extends to her dealings with the subject in general, especially the one that is bound in the lyric 'I'. Adorned with time stamps and geographical locations and other details, her poems seduce the reader into a false sense of the specificity of that subject:

> *In Vancouver as the dark winter tapered into spring*
> *I undertook to sing*
> *My life my body these words*
> *The men from a perspective.*[31]

---

[28] Fierle-Hedrick, 'Lifted', p. 43.
[29] Anne Carson, *The Beauty of the Husband* (London: Jonathan Cape, 2001), p. 34.
[30] Lisa Robertson and Steve McCaffery, 'Philly Talks 17' (3 Oct 2000), p. 22.
[31] Lisa Robertson, *The Men* (Toronto: Bookthug, 2006), p. 69.

The poet is specifically located: in Vancouver, at the end of winter, repeatedly in the Dantean 'middle of my life'.[32] But this specificity is not necessarily reliable. Robertson has revealed that the time stamps in *R's Boat* were drawn from novels she had on her shelves.[33] What seems like a carefully localised reference to the speaker in time and space is actually generic, a framing convention from a secondary source. As we'll see again in Wheatley's poems, the 'I' is not an expression of the authentic and particular subjectivity associated with post-Romantic lyric, but an impersonal node, a site of enunciation. Though full of subjects, her poems abide by an anti-subjective aesthetics: 'I use the word subjectivity in a resolutely collective, un-private, and non-possessive sense, considering that it is the historical energy that travels between voices,' she writes.[34]

Robertson flaunts the dissolution of the one into the trans-subjective, varied and anonymous positions of feminised citizens. This dissolution occurs through compositional processes such as the use of found text and chance procedures; but it is also a product of reading. In her essay on the codex, Robertson celebrates reading as enabling a 'dallying and surge among a cluster of minute identifications', where I find an 'infinite and inconspicuous surface complexity which is not my own'.[35] She explores kinds of reading that privilege surfaces rather than depths. The reader ought not to 'identify with' characters or find herself in the book; through the book I become 'foreign and unknowable to myself'. The self's unknowability is liberating. Reading 'shows the wrongness of the habitual reification of "the social" and "the personal" in a binary system of values. It submits this binary to a ruinous founding. And so, an erotics' (12–13). In this 'founding', I hear a foundation, a finding, a foundling and a foundering. These words, which connote construction and loss, structure and wavering, imply that the erotics of reading preserve a space to practise building and breaking down the antagonisms of the individual and the collective. Reading creates the conditions for an impersonal intimacy, as 'I' move 'among a multiple and open series, where memory is impersonal' (14).

Robertson's pleasurable suspension of self-consciousness in 'the vertigo of another's language' (26) recollects the impersonal sociality that Leo Bersani discovers in *jouissance*. She invokes 'Bersani's notion of self-shattering, subjective and erotic dispersal, as pleasurable and potentially transformational. Arcadia could be the erotic agency of shattering, the

---

[32] Robertson, *The Men*, p. 51, 64; *R's Boat* p. 32   [33] Fierle-Hedrick, 'Lifted', p. 52.
[34] Robertson, 'The Collective', *Poetry Foundation* blog.   [35] Robertson, *Nilling*, p. 13.

asideness of the dispersal of the centre. And when I say erotic I mean political.'[36] A case of such shattering, and a text whose erotics of reading reveals not the rejection of hyperbolic masculine control but an overdetermined submission to it, is Pauline Réage's novel *Histoire d'O*. For Robertson the novel poses 'the pleasure of its own representational proliferation and shattering'.[37] This pleasure is not just the result of a sadistic readerly delight in the destruction of O's personhood and her reduction to a surface on which the desires of men are inscribed. Pleasure is also a complex effect of that shattering on the feminised reader, whose instinct to identify with O as a bound and effaced subject (and reading as identification is, as I've just noted, not what Robertson recommends) might lead to a discovery of the emptiness of her own subject position:

> If I identify with O, I seal myself textually within the pact of self-annihilation. To witness one's own complicity in such an effacement is untenable. And I do identify, in part because I can't resist her sentences, which are groomed as O's own over-described and perfumed body. (31-2)

Aligning rhetoric and the erotic, Robertson takes the novel as a paradigm for the text's ambivalent seductions of the reader. Réage overcomes the reader's resistance, her 'repeated need to stop and build a moral defense against her own identificatory immersion in the textual imaginary, her own identification with punitive sadism', through style. The text's 'restrained', 'balanced', 'modest' style undermines the reader's ability to resist the urge to identify with the masochistic object as she passes into obliteration. Réage's grooming elicits the reader's desire to lose herself in the character of O, and so lose herself; O, meanwhile, is being effaced through the sadistic operations of other characters as emptily formulaic as herself. The masochism *of* the text duplicates the masochism *in* the text. The reader collaborates in the emptying of O, and identifies with her effacement; the text becomes a bind, in which the masochistic reader is trapped. As Robertson puts it, 'when I read O, I feel myself caught, as if in a venal snare, in a complete transgression of the proprieties of identity' (31–3).

This argument about the text as a trap unveils a masochistic element that Robertson shares with the poets discussed in the previous two chapters. In *XEclogue*, Robertson addresses a 'Superlative mistress who hurts! My grief is no accident. I am hovering between plunder and awe. I am howling through the thick accretions of liberty, not

---

[36] Robertson and McCaffery, 'Philly Talks 17', p. 21.   [37] Robertson, *Nilling*, p. 33.

harmonious, not patterned, but inconceivably voluptuous as thick rope.'[38] The sub address Lady Liberty, represented as a domme who hurts (herself, or others; it's not clear whether the verb is transitive), from a position of 'awe' (idealisation) and 'howling' (pain). Later 'Lady M' enters the scene, 'sinuously flanked by Roaring Boys who pan her stance with flicks of birch' (her name, short for Lady Mary Wortley Montagu, could also be that of a dominatrix).[39] Whether the boys flagellate her as erotic or intellectual discipline, Lady M escapes them; towards the end of the book, the companions have 'shifted our cathexis. We shatter into all the boring beauties, the smug voluptuaries, all the masochisms of the intellect. In parked cars we shame their ubiquitous pleasure.'

Freud and the sexologists of the late nineteenth and early twentieth century doubted whether women could be masochistic in a perverse way, given that femininity was in a sense already perverse: passive, submissive, masochistic by nature. Robertson does not so much deny such typologies, as ironise them through an excessively zealous performance – not unlike O. Overinvestment in a social script can undermine that script. This is a strategy of subversion performed by the girl, the drag queen, Chaplin's tramp, the dandy. In *The Men*, Robertson coerces straight men into a similar position, by lading them with a zealously heavy admiration of their powers. Arriving 'at the end of nine centuries of rhyme',[40] Robertson wonders whether 'I could, like a poet of some previous epoque, praise them / In some sparse rhyme / And with humble touches.'[41] Punning on Petrarch's *Rime sparse* (scattered rhymes), the book speculates on what the world would have been if 'Laura never died', if Petrarch had not found cause in the idealised woman's mortality to break off the 'reticence of intimacy' and write into a space that was neither reticent nor intimate. Arriving at the end of nine centuries of rhyming male fantasies of reticent Platonic mistresses, the feminist poet confronts a set of deep structures that she can either demolish or inhabit. Inhabitation of these structures means not dwelling as bourgeois possession, but a precarious, transient camping on the margins and porches of the imperial city and its literatures. It also requires her to find ways to make those sites nourishing: to translate the bondage of tradition into ornament.

---

[38] Robertson, *XEclogue* 3: Liberty. [39] *Ibid.*, Eclogue 6: Nostalgia.
[40] Lisa Robertson, *3 Summers* (Toronto: Coach House Books, 2016), p. 98.
[41] Robertson, *The Men*, p. 63.

Sex of My Thinking

So how does a feminist poet think, especially when thinking is too often (as it seems to be in *The Men*) an abstracted and disembodied activity associated with the dry heave of the concept? By returning to her body:

> 4:16 in the afternoon in the summer of my 52nd year
> I'm lying on the bed in the heat wondering about geometry
> as the deafening, uninterrupted volume of desire
> bellows, roars mournfully, laments
> like a starling that has flown into glass.
> These are two things that I want to remember permanently:
> the dog straining diagonally after the hare at dusk last night
> and the glittering disco sky.
> I am no longer afraid of being misunderstood when I state
> the old men's docile gadgetry –
> I don't buy it.
> What suits me better is to stargaze or to lie in stylish baths.
> Now it's time to return to the sex of my thinking.
> How long do I get?
> A fly moves across the pages of an open book
> (the pages are quivering)
> I want stimulants, relaxants, hallucinogens
> – I'm not good at order.
>
> The men who tremble a little bit
> while speaking about passivity –
> they're all right. I could compare them
> to a song[42]

This section of the opening poem of *3 Summers* gives us a luxuriant speaker, at ease, loafing. Queer, determined and indeterminate, halfway on life's journey, she relishes 'the insurrection of my unplaced body' (77). Now she is no longer afraid of the old men, she can use their poems as she pleases ('If you can never be mine / I'll get some Swinburne': 'Using Ovid maybe / You'd lay your tongue across my art'). She has surrendered her claim on an intimate 'you'; 'I am alone, transcribing.' While 'Some are masters of desire, all deferral / and expletives, using the word triumphant / while they lounge in their marriages' (13), she is in the bath, thinking with her companion animal, and her reflections are abstract and geometrical, as well as particular – the dog, the sky. She rejects the couple form and the

---

[42] Robertson, *3 Summers*, p. 10.

triumph of sexual conquest. The poem's position – ready to start, not yet starting, and making that its start – allows it to circle the immediacy of a sexed body, thinking, not resolving ('I have no idea what song means'). This is a sex and a poetics of the increment, which resists the closure or instrumentality signified by reproductivity. Remembering, wondering about the future, she is a figure: an enfolding of imaginative excess in the overly determined, and indeterminate, site of the female body.

Obsolete but durable, emancipated from the bondage of femininity and engaged in the transvaluation of feminised leisure, the speaker in *3 Summers* enjoys her body and its ornamentality. Her poetics prowls the whole of the body as an erotogenic zone. The sex of her thinking has been liberated from its reproductive functionality, while her liver, spleen and cell pulse with sexual charge. The hard-won privilege of this position is examined in more detail in Robertson's *Proverbs of a She-Dandy* (2018). In the preface, she recoils from the Situationists' description in *The Poverty of Student Life* of the university as 'the menopause of the mind'. Instead, she writes:

> menopause turns females into dandies. Some of our organs become purely self-referential. They have no further potential for family or spectacle or state: they're outside every economy. So now their meaning is confected in relation to convivial and autonomous pleasure only . . . . The hormones the ovaries used to make are now made by all the parts of the body, so that every tissue, every limb and fold continuously invents its own mode of transformation. The entire body becomes a fungible thinking whose purpose it is only to express its own communicability, for the pleasure, the intensity, the integrity of it.[43]

The she-dandy is both the product and ironic reflection of the capitalist city; 'THAT SHE EXISTS AND MOVES IN THE CITY IS AN AFFRONT TO THE WILL OF CAPITAL' (15). Like the dandy, who 'pertained to the spiritual aestheticization of limits' and in this sense engaged in 'a constraint-based practice of the self' (3), the menopausal dandy 'embodies the aesthetic law of constraint' (16). Performing her ruination on the theatre of the street, the menopausal dandy 'IS THE MASTERPIECE OF THE ANCIENT SUPERIORITY OF THE IMPRODUCTIVE. SHE NEITHER BEGETS NOR WORKS, BUT DRIFTS' (19).

Menopause names a resistant, feminised temporality, another way to 'help the collapse of time as metrics, and encourage its transformation into a luxuriously distributed lubricant', a contradiction of the discourse of

---

[43] Lisa Robertson, 'To the Reader', *Proverbs of a She-Dandy* (Paris and Vancouver: Morris and Helen Belkin Art Gallery / Libraires-Editeurs, 2018), p. 2.

the state: for 'THE STATE HAS NO MENOPAUSE, ONLY PRODUCTIVITY AND LOSS' (9):

> If in the bourgeois ideology the female body was constrained to represent reproductive value, indeed, functioning as a kind of money (that other value in flux), once freed of this significatory role as she entered *l'âge critique*, ... her ruinous social presence problematized the very necessity of productivity. (4)

The menopausal dandy is in this sense 'perverse', because she 'puts the body and the world of objects to uses that have nothing whatever to do with any kind of "immanent" design or purpose'.[44] Her sex is liberated from use value and becomes an ornament. Living past the constraints of gender and nature, the she-dandy is able 'to choose the dystopia of the obsolete' and overcome the mania for productivity. 'When capital marks women as the abject and monstrous ciphers of both reproduction and consumption, our choice can only be to choke out the project of renovation. We must become history's dystopic ghosts, inserting our inconsistencies, demands, misinterpretations and weedy appetites into the old bolstering narratives: We shall refuse to be useful.' Robertson's utopian premise in this portrait of the *She-Dandy* is that this refusal of use, enforced leisure and transvaluation of what is called ruination can become the sources of pleasure and riches: 'SHE WILL DECIDE WHAT TO DO WITH HER INNER WEALTH, WHICH IS ENTIRELY AUTONOMOUS' (22). This is another example of the phenomenon that we've discovered throughout this book: what looks like constraint is really a mechanism of autonomy.

Refusing use is also a refusal of the rhythms and temporalities ascribed to female bodies doing the work of reproduction. It is another form of 'nilling', which Robertson defines – drawing on Hannah Arendt – as 'a charged refusal. That is to say that in reading, I undo a text, as I resist my own autonomy. This undoing animates passivity, all that negates and resists rather than insists. It is a slightly unpleasant thought, and it pertains to the ambivalent discomfort of pornography.'[45] Through her nillings, choking the project of renovation, the poet uncovers a temporality founded in the rhythms of the body rather than the units of productive time into which labour power is transformed: 'the temporal unit is sprung on the refusal of the regularisation of time, which must remain situated in the body, *as* the body's specificity, its revolt' (61). 'I am interested in whatever mobilizes and rescues the body', she writes, including hormones, menopause and the erotic and resistant capacities of skin,

---

[44] Kaja Silverman, *Male Subjectivity at the Margins* (New York: Routledge, 1992), p. 187.
[45] Robertson, *Nilling*, p. 27.

organ, fold and fashion.⁴⁶ For her, the body is not a reductive trope but a mystery that has the potential to exceed the constraints imposed on it by capitalism: 'Now you know that all along it's been the body that you don't understand ... / *The question for you becomes what are we doing with our bodies?*'; 'You always describe potential with your body.'⁴⁷

This temporal, potential body becomes what Henri Lefebvre calls a 'Rhythmanalyst', a subject who attends to the polyrhythmia of their surroundings:⁴⁸

> The body consists of a bundle of rhythms, different but in tune . . . . It is not only in music that one produces perfect harmonies. The body produces a garland of rhythms, one could say a bouquet . . . 'The eurhythmic body, composed of diverse rhythms – each organ, each function, having its own – keeps them in metastable equilibrium . . . . But the surrounding of bodies, be they in nature or a social setting, are also *bundles, bouquets, garlands* of rhythms, to which it is necessary to listen in order to grasp the natural or produced ensembles. The rhythmanalyst will not be obliged to *jump* from the inside to the outside of observed *bodies*; he should come to listen to them *as a whole* and unify them by taking his own rhythms as a reference: by integrating the outside with the inside and vice versa. (30)

Lefebvre describes the rhythmic modes in which the divisions between the inside and outside, of bodies or of buildings, are softened, as a 'garland' – we'll come across garlands of blackberries and textiles later. Robertson's poetry is sympathetic to Lefebvre's argument for a rhythmicity that connects the individual subject to the 'bouquets' of urban rhythm, of living and inanimate matter.

Against Lefebvre's account of rhythm, however, is a humanist theory proposed by Émile Benveniste, in an essay that is very important to Robertson. Benveniste's philology unpicks the claim that *rhuthmos* is etymologically linked to the play of the waves and flowing tides; instead, he associates rhythm with sociality – the slow and rapid gestures of the dancing body, of 'a song, of a speech, of work', and all the human movements 'organised in time'.⁴⁹ Form is 'not a limit' but 'a gestural passage that we can witness upon a garment in movement, a face in living expression, or in the mobile marks of a written character as it is traced by the pen', as Robertson summarises his argument. She cites Benveniste also as another way of apprehending gender:

---

⁴⁶ Robertson, *R's Boat*, p. 12.   ⁴⁷ Robertson, *Cinema*, pp. 51, 57.
⁴⁸ Henri Lefebvre, *Rhythmanalysis: Space, Time, and Everyday Life*, trans. Stuart Elden and Gerald Moore (London: Bloomsbury, 2013), p. 26.
⁴⁹ Émile Benveniste, 'The Notion of "Rhythm" in its Linguistic Expression', *Problems in General Linguistics* (University of Miami Press, 1971), pp. 281–9 (278).

rhythm for Benveniste is 'not a measure, not a temporal phenomena of Nature, but "the form in the instant that is assumed by what is moving, mobile and fluid, the form of what does not have organic consistency." A girl has no organic consistency.'[50]

Robertson develops these theories about the crises and garlands of embodied rhythm, the integration of inside and outside, and their relation to temporality through a language of hormones and toxins. 'The poem is a hormone';[51] 'I've been the transparent instrument of / certain chemicals':

> The word will be called the linguistics of the hormone.
> As for the completely human and dandiacal gland,
>   trans-corporeal and trans-historical
> it became literature
> and the body is impersonal, in contradiction
> which is form. (64)

Part of returning to the sex of thinking is to create a form by unweaving the body's discrete unity into a complex heterogeneity where the inside and the outside fashion each other as rhythm does. While hormones are commonly associated with reproduction and gender expression, Robertson focuses on how they entangle the body with its environment; they are a chemical expression of the indeterminacy of the subject. Like a hormone, a poem is 'a pierced cell unwinding to the sound of tearing mousseline'; by it, 'Feminism enters the poem, death enters the poem, rhetoric enters the poem'.[52] The hormone can become a toxin, a different kind of excess whose potential is associated not with nourishment but with death; and a toxin can become a hormone, incorporating artificial chemical disruptions into the body's own internal processes. The hormone, like the poem, shows the porousness of boundaries:

> When we stumble against limits we blush. Disproportion and fragility are shameful and funny. This is ornament. Colour, like a hormone, acts across, embarrasses, seduces. It stimulates the juicy interval in which emotion and sentiment twist. We groom in that pharmakon. This is architecture, an applied art.[53]

The poem, like the hormone or the toxin, uses a body to express itself. Hormone comes from the Greek for 'to set in motion'; it is a message that is transmitted over distances within the body. As such it is also correlate for

---

[50] Robertson, *Baudelaire*, pp. 184, 93. [51] Robertson, *3 Summers*, p. 10.
[52] Robertson, *R's Boat*, p. 20.
[53] Lisa Robertson, 'How to Colour', *Occasional Work and Seven Walks from the Office for Soft Architecture* (Astoria, OR: Clear Cut Press, 2003), p. 149.

what we will consider further in the following chapter as poetic Fancy – mobile, active, unconstrained.

Surface and Ornament

The ornamental is a central trope in Robertson's feminist poetics. The ornamental and the superficial are often synonymous with the meretricious: with tricks and with women. Women are derided *as* ornaments, their beauty adorning men's activities. Superficiality is derided as bad style. Meanwhile, the plain, unadorned and unornamented have been taken as models for virtuous femininity, and for honest discourse (I'm thinking, for example, of Montaigne's adoption of the voice of his servant to tell the story of the cannibals, or the assumption that the imprisoned writer addresses us in 'plain speech').[54] The ornament shows an excessive concern with surfaces; surfaces are deceitful, allegories of moral and intellectual shallowness. The ornament is not useful. It papers over deep structure with a sense of transience, adornment and pleasure. Surface effects are cheap; structure is deep.

Robertson argues otherwise, celebrating 'the ornamental grammar of the surface' as the site of figuration – where 'corporal historicity and change' are communicated. In the essay on 'How to Colour' from which I took the quotation that concludes the previous section, she keys architectural surface to 'a historical rhetoric of use'. On the surface we can trace the labour and the contingencies of the bodies of anonymised makers: 'Application is a persuasive and pleasurable folding; the surface is comprised of bodily traces and fixations – rubbing, flecking, scrubbing, weaving, stroking are tactile instrumentations in time. They address both substance and the future of bodies. Hence the surface poses a rhetorical index even while temporal contingency renders it partly unaccountable. We wish to face the unaccountable.'[55] The surface is tensed as the 'future conditional' – a site of possibility, of what might occur, rather than what has already been made; like the figure, it disturbs linear temporalities and the anaclitic relation of present to past. As she writes elsewhere, 'If architecture is entombed structure or *Thanatos*, ornament is the frontier of the surface. It is at the surface where lively variability takes place .... The chaos of surfaces compels us towards new states of happiness.'[56]

---

[54] Michel de Montaigne, 'Of Cannibals', *Essays*, trans. John Florio (1603), (London: Everyman, 1965).
[55] Robertson, *Occasional*, pp. 148–9.   [56] *Ibid.*, pp. 127–8.

Ornaments can be botanical, architectural, sartorial or rhetorical. In a garment they can displace functional features, or disguise wear and tear or sites where a seam is reinforced. Although a dress could be made to conceal the body or protect it, parts may become so ornamental that they draw attention to themselves. Often, ornaments are made from natural motifs, such as abstracted flowers; they are built from repetition of an idiosyncratically reduced unit into a grammar. This repetition imparts an artificial unity to the body, garment or building, making bodies seem more 'architectural', even as the unity is fabricated from the repetition of a part.[57] In a poetic essay on the Canadian artist Lucy Hogg, Robertson observes her 'expression / of a unique and persistent melancholy / become ornament'. Hogg's awkwardness, her 'fondness for acts of disproportion / and spatial / discomfort', reveals the awkwardness in the social: the 'joints left undisguised' (unornamented), 'the rehearsed / spontaneities of genius, ambition / and anguish'.[58] By not ornamenting these surfaces, we are left 'free blithe and social' to play with the surface. But ornament is also another name for recurrence, which translates traumatic repetition into an ironic or recuperative engagement. 'The girl within the Baudelairean body of work will undo it by repeating it within herself, as indeed she repeats girlhood, misshapen.'[59] As such, ornament is linked to Robertson's revisions of patriarchal genres. In all these cases, the work is done on the surface: 'Instead of seeking the cause of the men, the cool plunging into them, the labour of the men like foam, I supply the surface with men. By this procedure men gain.'[60]

One example of the liveliness of surface ornamentation that draws Robertson's admiration is the blackberry. This plant thrives in the midst of 'decay, blanketing and smothering, shedding, dissolution and penetration, and pendulous swagging and draping, as well as proliferative growth, all in contexts of environmental disturbance and contingency rather than fantasized balance'.[61] It is not cultivated, but grows in the contingent spaces left by urban development and neglect. It is chains become flowers, a garland of living rhythm that attaches itself to construction. It has a 'bracingly peri-modern tendency to garnish and swag and garland any built surface it encounters' (127). It is 'an exemplary political decoration, [and] a nutritious ornament that clandestinely modifies infrastructural morphology' (130). The blackberry is a figure of the relationship between surface, rhetoric and an erotic corporeality – an allegory of precarity and

---

[57] Michael Snodin and Maurice Howard, *Ornament: A Social History Since 1450* (New Haven: Yale University Press, 1996), pp. 112–15.
[58] Robertson, *R's Boat*, p. 81.   [59] Robertson, *Baudelaire*, p. 136.   [60] Robertson, *The Men*, p. 55.
[61] Robertson, *Occasional*, p. 130.

nourishment. Similarly, for the city's precarious citizens, life happens not in a utopian state of balance, but in the selvages, behind the arenas; like the blackberry, they ornament any space left to them. Wild, profuse, spontaneously emergent within the detritus that marks the places where the commons once were, the blackberry resembles sociality, but also the poem. It is commodious. It binds structures together and ornaments them. It evades private ownership and turns the constraining structures it encounters into opportunities for a civic flourishing in which everyone can partake. Everyone can harvest its fruit for their pies. This is how the nourishing, erotic poem and the impersonal and trans-subjective come together, across the seams between the personal and the social: as ornaments.

In Robertson's aesthetics of the surface, ornament is a key figure for the uselessness of art, its seductive undulation between concealment and revelation, the softening of form and the abandonment of the hard aridities of the concept. In *R's Boat*, the ornament is a hinge between temporality and prosody: 'I write this ornament, yet I had not thought of time' (5) becomes: '*I write this ornament, yet I had not thought of rhyme*' (11). Rhyme is an ornamentation of time, adorning the passage between instants of reading with its repeating sound. The ornament is 'written', and can 'articulate transitions';[62] but it is also visual. In *Nilling*, she argues that 'The lens is a social ornament .... Often what pleases in vision is contingency held within a frame or screen. I use the word ornament in this way' (51). The contingency of the blackberry, of fashion, against their backgrounds of bodies and cities, allows us to focus that lens on the processes of biological life or structures of capitalism that they adorn. Ornament is normally considered the object of the gaze; but Robertson offers a Lacanian caveat: 'From its vulnerable perch at the cusp of the polis, ornament perceives' (54). The things we look at, looked at us first.[63]

The ornamental and the superficial are also ways of describing a literary style. Robertson crafts her poems as surfaces across which subjects can move playfully:

> On this very beautiful surface
> Where I want to live
> I play with my friends

---

[62] Robertson, *Magenta*, p. 64.
[63] Jacques Lacan, 'What is a Picture?', *The Four Fundamental Concepts of Psycho-Analysis*, ed. Jacques-Alain Miller, trans. Alan Sheridan (London: Penguin, 1977), p. 109.

> Like they do down there.
> I don't understand what I adore.
> ... I believe my critique of devastation
> Began with delight. Now what surprises me
> Are the folds in political desire....[64]

Living and playing with friends on the 'beautiful surface' allows the subject to dwell with delight and surprise, rather than drilling down in an attempt to 'understand what I adore'. Here the fold appears 'in political desire', delight and devastation, binding utopia and critique as part of the same structure of a 'beautiful surface / Where I want to live': the surface of the existing and the imagined, a feminised utopia. When she allows herself to enjoy the beautiful surface, the poetic subject is able at last to make what she calls 'my first true speech':

> And this with a decorous amplitude
> And this in the middle of my life, the
> Streets silent and the night all covered in questions
> And this desire which discerns
> Is my desire
> And this ornament
> Is my ornament.[65]

Soft Architecture

Key to understanding Robertson's poetic worlding is the language, the real and imaginary spaces, prepared by her readings of Rem Koolhaas, Gottfried Semper and Aby Warburg. These writers underpin Robertson's preference for surface over depth, ornament over structure, which she translates into a copious poetic style. Robertson has said that 'Architectural thought has been feeding me means for considering subjectivity as a flow across systems, an access and escape agency that absorbs, mimes, enfolds, rejects, becomes, severs and transforms spaces and forms of the whole urban complex. I started to read architectural theory before any exposure to contemporary avantgarde poetics.'[66] She underlined this passage from *S, M, L, XL,* a book by Rem Koolhaas and Bruce Mau (writing as the Office for Metropolitan Architecture or O. M. A.):

---

[64] Robertson, *Magenta*, p. 19. [65] Robertson, *The Men*, pp. 64–5.
[66] Robertson and McCaffery, 'Philly Talks 17', p. 22.

The seeming failure of the urban offers an exceptional opportunity, a pretext for Nietzschean frivolity. We have to imagine 1,001 other concepts of the city; we have to take insane risks; we have to dare to be utterly uncritical; we have to swallow deeply and bestow forgiveness left and right. The certainty of failure has to be our laughing gas/oxygen; modernization our most potent drug.[67]

In *S, M, L, XL* one of the projects of 'Nietzschean frivolity' proposed by the O. M. A. is 'an architectural oasis' for the city of London. This utopian polis would establish a zone of 'collective facilities that fully accommodate individual desires' in baths, parks, institutes and allotments dedicated to hedonistic exploration. The inhabitants would be 'Voluntary Prisoners', who abandon the historical city to be incarcerated in conditions of 'luxury and well-being' (3–19). The proposal recasts constraint and incarceration as voluntary, desirable conditions, under which distinctions between public and private can be massaged and individuals can explore moods of 'exhilaration, depression, serenity and receptivity' (11) through new intensities of the body discovered in sex, aggression, swimming or construction. As such, this imagined project is an analogue to the dialectic of (voluntary) constraint and emancipation that this book has argued is central to fantasies of lyric subjection.

The frivolity of decorous amplitude, the bliss of the ornamental and the fashion for soft architecture in Robertson's work also reflect the influence of the nineteenth-century art historian Gottfried Semper, whose *Style in the Technical and Tectonic Arts; or, Practical Aesthetics* (1870–3) she cites in several essays. Semper claimed that architecture is centred on a *Bekleidungsprinzip* (principle of dress). Structures are 'dressed' in ornamental surfaces, and 'the beginning of building coincides with the beginning of textiles'.[68] Robertson paraphrases his argument:

> The flesh of the building, its cladding, for Semper referred to the archaic textile and ceramic arts that had provided the materials and techniques that divided and defined space. For Semper, architectural ornamentation should quote the tactile history of these applied decorative arts. Building structure served only as the framework for socially performative enclosure, rather than as an expression of authenticity and permanence.[69]

---

[67] Rem Koolhaas and Bruce Mau, *S, M, L, XL*, ed. Jennifer Sigler, photography by Hans Werlemann (New York: Monacelli Press, 1995), p. 971.
[68] Gottfried Semper, *Style in the Technical and Tectonic Arts; or, Practical Aesthetics*, trans. Harry Francis Mallgrave and Michael Robinson (Los Angeles: Getty Publications, 2004), p. 247.
[69] Robertson, 'How to Colour', *Occasional*, pp. 147–8.

For Semper, solid structures are merely 'inner and unseen support for the true and legitimate representation of the spatial idea – which is the more or less artfully woven and knitted textile wall'. He believed that the pen or fence, a partition constructed of interwoven branches, was the earliest architectural construction. 'Next came the invention of *weaving*; with weaving, and partitions, humans began 'dividing the "home", the *inner* life from the *outer* life, as a formal construct of the spatial idea.'[70] As Rebecca Houze summarises, the decoration of the dividers that marked the inner and the outer world were for Semper 'the manifestation of a primal artistic urge, a fundamental human need for play that relied upon symbolic representation'.[71]

For Semper, design elements are not merely symbolic; they provide the grounds for a materialist theory of the subject and the collective. For example: in a discussion of string as the oldest form of textile, he claims 'the unity to which the string refers contrasts . . . with the plurality through which the authority and homogeneity of the subject are emphasised and enhanced'.[72] Binding is a principle of 'almost primeval validity', which is prelinguistic and (in the form of the knot, labyrinth and loop) gains a 'mystical and religious significance' in the oldest civilisations (155). We've already encountered several such knots, including Petrarch's *caro nodo* and Halpern's ligature. Semper also says that bands and seams are not only practical; by connecting that which was once separate, they emphasise 'both the unified nature of the parts and their relation to the whole', while tassels and fluttering bands function as 'symbols of *unrestraint*' (118). This contrasts with the cover or spatial enclosure: 'everything closed, protected, enclosed, enveloped, and covered presents itself as unified, as a collective; whereas everything bound reveals itself as articulated, as a plurality' (123). In each case, Semper draws from architecture allegories of the relation between the individual and the collective, constraint and freedom, the wild and the cultivated. His aesthetics are profoundly aligned with Robertson's poetics, whether in his focus on dressing, surface, personhood as masking, the hardness of structure and the softness of fabric, performance and the ornamentation of the body, or the division of the inner and the outer life that can be both hidden and marked by a decorative seam. As Robertson's speakers walk the city mollified like cloth, all 'she-dandies in incredibly voluptuous jackets ribboning back from our waist, totally lined in pure

---

[70] Semper, *Style*, p. 248.
[71] Rebecca Houze, 'The Textile as Structural Framework: Gottfried Semper's *Bekleidungsprinzip* and the Case of Vienna 1900', *Textile* 4.3 (2006), pp. 292–311.
[72] Semper, *Style*, p. 113.

silk, also in pure humming',[73] gauze is everywhere; 'our manners are software. We feel sartorial joy.'

Semper's theories also offer a different way of thinking about whiteness as enclosure that I introduced at the start of this book. As the *domus* is separated from the *civis*, the private from the public, the sphere of reproductive labour from the sphere of wage labour, the divisions or boundaries between these domains is decorated and softened by feminised aesthetic activities such as weaving. Textiles are a constant signifier of both feminisation and freedom in Robertson's poetics. They materialise the historic relationships between weaving, female creativity and speech that goes back to ancient Greek thought. Ann Bergren describes weaving as the 'metaphorical speech' of feminised subjects who are not citizens, and who themselves circulate as signs in the reproductive economies of the *oikos*, weaving families together socially and genetically.[74] Citing Semper and theorising gender as an architecture, Bergren describes Penelope's weaving, twisting and knotting, manipulating 'the circular reciprocity between what is bound and what is binding', as a material *tropos* (216). As such, Penelope was the first female textual artist, and her poetics was an art of making and unmaking a surface to dramatise the trap of marriage: turning her bondage into ornament.

As Bergren explains, men appropriated weaving as a metaphor for speech, poetry, prophecy and political philosophy, 'modes of creativity from which women in Greece are largely barred and thus might be thought to envy' (224). The proximity of speech to dress is a commonplace of rhetoric, and made evident by such sartorially derived terms as bombast, fustian or 'embroidering' the truth. Emerson Marks offers copious examples from the Renaissance through Modernism of writers who regarded 'the characteristics of verse as raiment adorning the "body" of a poet's thought'.[75] This trope – which is also traditional in the medieval courtly lyric of love, and is explicitly taught by the *artes poeticae* – highlights the ambiguity of function that clothing shares with poetic eloquence: A. C. Spearing contends that 'in civilised societies [sic] garments are designed not only to conceal but to reveal partially and indirectly'.[76] Rhetoric, like clothes, conceals and reveals. Sometimes the garment calls

---

[73] Robertson, *Magenta*, p. 8.
[74] Ann Bergren, *Weaving Truth: Essays on Language and the Female in Greek Thought* (Cambridge, MA: Harvard University Press, 2008), pp. 16, 250, 220.
[75] Emerson R. Marks, *Taming the Chaos: English Poetic Diction Theory since the Renaissance* (Detroit: Wayne State University Press, 1998), p. 55.
[76] A. C. Spearing, *Readings in Medieval Poetry* (Cambridge University Press, 1987), p. 97.

attention to its own magnificent surface, using ornament to distract attention from what it covers; sometimes it draws the gaze or the imagination to the form beneath.

This takes us back to Roland Barthes, who traces the familiar etymology of text to textile:

> *Text* means *Tissue*; but whereas hitherto we have always taken this tissue as a product, a ready-made veil, behind which lies, more or less hidden, meaning (truth), we are now emphasizing, in the tissue, the generative ideas that the text is made, is worked out in a perpetual interweaving: lost in this tissue – this texture – the subject unmakes himself, like a spider dissolving in the constructive secretions of its web.[77]

Barthes locates the pleasure of the text in the surface's gaping and concealment, in its dynamics of disclosure and secrecy. These are the dynamics of allegory, and for Barthes they resemble both folds in a garment, and wounds in the skin: the readerly 'abrasions I impose upon the fine surface' and the 'deep laceration the text of bliss inflicts upon language itself'.

Robertson comes across such a laceration. During some research on Lucretius, she comes across a page of vellum with a cut in it that another reader has decorated: 'it was a flaw inherent in the structure of the vellum; the trace of an animal's wound perhaps'. That wound becomes an ornament and an aperture; through it, 'I fall into the lace of the text, the vellum; caught there, I contemplate my masters. From the point of view of the world, the site of my capture remains invisible.'[78] The vellum – porous skin of the animal – becomes the 'lace' of the text, a woven textile made of substance and absence, like Barthes's web. From this site of indeterminacy and constraint, of making and unmaking, 'I contemplate my masters': my own captivity and harvesting by the text. This writing on the skin offers a way of softening the trauma of epidermal marking through an emphasis on the ornamental. Text and textile are material signifiers of generation and loss.

The Fold

In Robertson's poetry, the fold is where the surface and its ornaments, the sex of thinking and the trans-temporal dissolution of subjectivity, the real and the possible cluster. A fold is an aperture and a blockage, a space of

---

[77] Roland Barthes, *The Pleasure of the Text*, trans. Richard Miller (New York: Farrar, Straus and Giroux, 1975), p. 64.
[78] Robertson, *Nilling*, p. 22.

holding and of transit, a structure that conceals and reveals, a doubling of substance; a curve, an entanglement of inside and outside, a textile and architectural softness. The vagina is a fold. Skin folds. The enfolding of something holds it within the reticence of intimacy; the unfolding of something is a revelation of truth. If femininity and authorship are forms of 'augmentation', 'the augmenter is the one who inserts extra folds into the woven substance of language'.[79] Language is folded, the body is folded, enfolded by lust 'like a voluminous shawl or scarf' (157), and folds of fabric give the self a mobile, fluid form, which is to say a rhythm:

> And if I become unintelligible to myself
> Because of having refused to believe
> I transcribe a substitution
> Like the accidental folds of a scarf.
> From these folds I make persons
> Perfect marriage of accident and need.[80]

The 'substitution' of a transcription – a written mark – for the unintelligible self is 'like' the folds of a scarf, in that it is a soft architecture that appears as if by design, when it is really an accident; it is an adornment that serves a function; and it is something worn outwardly, which has an inwardness to it (within the fold). It is a form that moves, like 'a robe which one arranges at one's will ... improvised, momentary, changeable'.[81] In that sense, it is – following Benveniste – a kind of rhythm.

The fold is the epitome of soft architectures, and a reminder to notice the surface. Robertson has argued that, through artifice, 'the potent surface leans into dissolution and disrupts volition – it's not a secluding membrane or limit. To experience change, we submit ourselves to the affective potential of the surface. This is the *pharmakon*: an indiscrete threshold where our bodies exchange information with an environment.'[82] This notion of the surface not as a 'secluding membrane' but a 'threshold', a space between inner and outer dimensions that can be crossed, fuses architecture and embodiment. Poems as hormones cross between the body of the self and the materiality of the collective; skin is a threshold, and a writing surface, a protective barrier, a container, and an erotic sensory organ. The psychoanalyst Didier Anzieu characterises the skin as a 'sac which contains and retains inside it the goodness and fullness accumulating there', an interface or 'barrier which

---

[79] Robertson, *Baudelaire*, pp. 142, 140. [80] Robertson, *R's Boat*, p. 81.
[81] Benveniste, 'The Notion of "Rhythm"', p. 278. [82] Robertson, *Occasional*, p. 143.

protects against penetration by the aggression and greed emanating from others' and a 'site and a primary means of communicating with others, of establishing signifying relations ... an "inscribing surface" for the marks left by those others' – literally so, in some of the texts we've encountered in this book.[83]

Anzieu proposes the idea of a 'skin-ego', a psychic formation that emphasises not depth but the interface of inner and outer that manifests as and in the fold. The ectoderm forms both the brain and the skin of the embryo; the skin has a double surface, 'and this complex structure of surfaces, rather than the old image of thought penetrating through into a truth-core, can help us understand the physical, psychical and intellectual worlds in a different way'. Through this doubling of surfaces (a fold), Anzieu displaces depth psychology models and articulates a creatural ambivalence about what is inside and what is outside. In the embryo, 'the brain, a sensate surface protected by the cranium, is in permanent contact with that skin .... The brain and the skin are both surface entities' (9). Similarly, Robertson writes: 'Say the mind is not a point of origin, but a skin carrying sensation into the midst of objects. / Now it branches and forks and coalesces.'[84] If the inside and outside of the building were demarcated by the soft architecture of (female-produced) textiles, the skin is the (female-produced) soft organ that marks a similarly porous division between self and world. Her feminist poetics could be understood as an enfolding of the internal and external, a sensory and cognitive encounter between bodies and surfaces whose branching, forking and coalescing materialise the subject's entwining with the world.

But the fold is also an important art-historical decoration, and as such becomes a way of thinking through the figural temporalities that nourish Robertson's poetics. She envisions the figure of Venus, modelled from 'folded paper' with 'the exigent season called Spring': ' 'Venus emerges / her sea-scarf's swirling.'[85] Robertson refers to the many representations of Venus emerging from the ocean, from the foam where Cronos' genitals were thrown. While the birth of Venus Anadyomene as the product of castration links her to my earlier discussions of BDSM, Robertson's reference to Spring suggests she's thinking of Botticelli's *Birth of Venus*, in which the goddess – aloft on a crenelated shell, her hair streaming in the wind and covering her genitals – is about to be enfolded in rich drapery by her attendant, the Hora of the Spring.

---

[83] Didier Anzieu, *The Skin Ego*, trans. Chris Turner (New Haven: Yale University Press, 1989), p. 40.
[84] Robertson, *R's Boat*, p. 67.   [85] Robertson, *3 Summers*, p. 41.

Aby Warburg focuses on the folds and undulations of the cloth in this image and its repertoire of sources in his 1893 essay on 'Sandro Boticelli's *Birth of Venus* and *Spring*'. He argues that the 'antique' directed the Renaissance artist's attention 'to the most difficult problem in all art, which is that of capturing images of life in motion', epitomised by the fluttering garment.[86] Robertson refers to Warburg's description of 'the representation of swirling folds of cloth and blowing strands of hair – "the surface mobility of inanimate accessory forms," in his terms – in Botticelli's *Venus* that brought a vitalistic, pagan engram forward into the Florentine mind, not as an abstract or formal proposition, but as an active energetic charge.' Robertson designates the 'characteristic Greco-Roman undulating line' the 'nymphae', from Warburg's association of it with the 'nymphs' who appeared in a Paduan procession in 1466, and were the basis of a portrait of the 'nymph' Simonetta in Poliziano's *Giostra*. This line, as Robertson paraphrases it, '*embodied* – as opposed to *represented* – time; it directly transmitted the haptic time of uncertain historical corporality, "passionate agitation," by an engrammatic transmission.'[87] This resonates with the idea of the collapse of time as metrics, and its transformation into 'an enticingly shimmering and moving fabric, a shared yet contested décor.' The fold in time brings the past of antiquity, present of Renaissance pictorial art and the future of Warburg's scholarship into an active figural relationship, each conditioning the other.

The representations of Venus can also be linked to the iconology of Truth, daughter of Time. In Cesare Ripa's *Iconologia* (1593), Truth is represented as a naked woman, whose nudity indicates 'that truth is a natural state and, like a nude person, exists without need for any artificial embellishment'. But Truth's genitals are modestly covered with a bit of drapery, like the *Venus Pudica* with whom Truth is commonly linked.[88] The female body is the bearer of truth in her desirable nakedness, her lack of protection or ornamentation or the distractions and fabrications of dress and cosmetics; but her truthfulness also depends on the suppression of her full delight, the cloaking of the folds of her sex in a fold of fabric.

---

[86] Aby Warburg, *The Renewal of Pagan Antiquity* (Los Angeles: Getty Research Institute, 1999), pp. 89–156 (esp. 125–6, 140–1).

[87] Lisa Robertson, *Thinking Space* (Brooklyn: Organism for Poetic Research Editions, 2013), pp. 8–10; citing Aby Warburg, 'Italian Art and International Astrology in the Palazzo Schifanoia,' in *Renewal*, p. 586; and Warburg, 'Sandro Boticelli's Birth of Venus and Spring,' in *Renewal*, p. 141.

[88] Christopher Braider, *Baroque Self-Invention and Historical Truth: Hercules at the Crossroads* (Aldershot: Ashgate, 2004), p. 48.

I'll end with a letter that Robertson wrote to the poet Steve McCaffrey, while flying – not like Wheatley through the empyrean, but from San Francisco to Vancouver:

> I don't know whether what 'I' experience is 'myself' but to some extent, in order to be useful, I have to suspend disbelief .... In terms of subjectivity, if I consider the surface of the body as a representational limit that mediates the contexts it moves among, as it is mediated by them ... 'I' mediates.[89]

The skin is a surface, and a limit, which encloses the fiction of the 'I' in which I must 'suspend disbelief'. The limits imposed by the representational marker of the skin will come into play in a different way in the next chapter, and it is notable here that – while she contends that the poet must attend to the way that 'the potential engagements of bodies with spaces are differently shaped and constrained' – Robertson's concern is with gendered and classed constraints rather than racialised ones. She instructs McCaffrey to look at how the ancient Greek woman was constrained, 'coded female by its enclosure in the oikos'. Or as we might now say, the enclosure of the oikos, however prettified with soft hangings, reproduces gender, and is aligned with the reproduction of private property by whiteness as enclosure. However, once in a while, Robertson adds, 'Athenian women's sacral-spatial festival took place over architecture – on rooftops only, not in structures, or as a flow among them, in the polis.' And so:

> I'd like to propose an architecture of arson, of rooftops, clouds, much more than I want to repeat the word woman, the word subject. I too want an architecture, a poetry, that is both delusional and critical, a ludic zone, precisely because I cannot conceive of a site as innocent. Every site is a form of governance, command. I don't believe there is an outside, I don't believe grammar has an exit. For myself I can only misuse it, cast it in the wrong scale, because I have no conception of how I could ever bracket what extends frontierless into every perception and mode of sociality. Every suspension of this totalizing structure is delusion. Therefore the necessity to shape or describe delusional space.

This conflation of architecture and poetry recalls Koolhaas and Mau's voluntary prison: a delusional space, a parody, a social critique and a radical revision of the sensory possibilities triggered by the built environment. If no site is innocent, that includes Robertson's own poems. The dissolution of subjectivity that we have seen is one result, intentional or

---

[89] Robertson, 'Philly Talks 17'.

otherwise, of carceral isolation has been translated here into a 'ludic zone' without exit, which cannot be suspended. But for Robertson, the body can still move through this zone, plying its surfaces, building shacks, dressing itself and its environment, and harvesting blackberries: garlanding the totalising structure with provisions. These 'tiny, flickering inflections are the only agency I believe':

> More and more poetry is becoming for me the urgent description of complicity and delusional space. The description squats within a grammar because there is no other site. Therefore the need for the urgent and incommensurate hopes of accomplices.

Finding the spaces for poetry to squat amongst the weapons, Robertson's poems enact not so much a raid on patriarchal authority as a softening of its architecture. This softening envelops the subject, the fictive 'I' rooted deep in the structures of neoliberalism, its poetries and moneys. For it to work, it needs accomplices, collectives, not the fiction of the solitary self.

So, too, did Phillis Wheatley. Casting the Black lyric self in the wrong scale, Wheatley's poems – like Robertson's – aim to make an inhospitable literary tradition into what Robertson calls 'a precariously inhabitable social sculpture'.[90] They also use a language of softness and ornamentation. But this softness, and her subversive impersonation of a white male poetic tradition, have been almost constantly misread. Derided as derivative, Wheatley's poetics of imitation occupied the sites and forms of governance and command – poetic and political sites marked by and for white use – until they could secure for her a more than merely aesthetic liberation.

---

[90] Robertson, 'The Collective'.

CHAPTER 12

Silken Fetters
Phillis Wheatley and Ornament as Bondage

The I-speaker on your silken rupture spills into history.

— Lisa Robertson

Lisa Robertson has called the poem 'the speech of citizenship'. Thinking I suspect of Hannah Arendt and Jacques Rancière, she speculates:

> If, in the Greek *polis* and in the Roman city, citizenship was limited to male speakers of the master-language, in a pointed elimination of women, beasts and barbarous speakers from a linguistically bordered polity, her *domus*, her *civis*, the commodious, illustrious and exilic vernacular, will shelter her for the rhythmic duration of a refusal.[1]

That is: in order to hear the speech of the woman, the beast, and the barbarian in imperial histories of linguistic and political domination, we must search the home, which is also the city. There we find Phillis Wheatley, affirming her sentimental attachments to the white family who had purchased her, polishing her exilic vernacular, expanding the idea of citizenship that was vigorously contested during the struggles of the American colonies against the British imperium. Not only that. Wheatley's eloquence enabled her carefully to manage emergent racialised hierarchies of language and being. In 1774, after her manumission, she replied with a strong no to a suggestion that she return to Africa as a missionary: 'Upon my arrival, how like a Barbarian Should I look to the Natives; I can promise that my tongue shall be quiet for a strong reason indeed being an utter stranger to the language.'[2] Implying that as far as Africans were concerned, it was the English she now spoke which was the 'barbarian' language,

---

[1] Lisa Robertson, *Nilling: Prose Essays on Noise, Pornography, the Codex, Melancholy, Lucretius, Folds, Cities and Related Aporias* (Toronto: Bookthug, 2012), pp. 84, 87.
[2] Letter to John Thornton, 30 October 1774, in Phillis Wheatley, *Complete Writings*, ed. Vincent Carretta (New York: Penguin, 2001), p. 159. All further references to Wheatley's poems will be to this edition.

Wheatley refuses to give up her power of speech, even if she was bereft of her mother tongue.

Wheatley's authorship of her poems was attested by 'the most respectable Characters in Boston', who reported to the readers of her *Poems on Various Subjects, Religious and Moral* (1773) that the poems had indeed been written 'by PHILLIS, a young Negro Girl, who was but a few Years since, brought an uncultivated Barbarian from *Africa*, and has ever since been, and now is, under the Disadvantage of serving as a Slave in a Family in this Town. She has been examined by some of the best Judges, and is thought qualified to write them' (8). Henry Louis Gates Jr imagines her 'trial' – which literalises the metaphoric relationship between critic and judge (though there is no evidence that any such examination actually took place) – as 'the primal scene of African-American letters'.

The white men's affidavits declared that Wheatley was an honest woman and a good poet; but at stake was the more fundamental question of whether she was fully human. Gates wonders if this precocious young writer knew that she was 'auditioning for the humanity of the entire African people'.[3] White supremacist critics of the period habitually compared Black writers to animals, such as Robert Nickol's malignant remark in 1788: 'I have not heard that an ourang outang has composed an ode.'[4] The use of animals like parrots to condemn African people as naturally imitative can be found across Enlightenment thinkers (including David Hume and Immanuel Kant); we've also encountered it in the caged birds who sang out in the Lomax recordings. Wheatley, on the other hand, was proof that Africans were human. Joseph Woods writes that 'it cannot be expected that, in their low state of civilisation, the Africans can have arrived at any great attainment in the arts; but the letters of Ignatius Sancho, and the Poems of Phillis Wheatley, sufficiently prove that they are neither deficient in the feelings of humanity, nor the powers of the understanding'.[5] Wheatley's credentialled verse provided abolitionists with textual proof of the capacity of Black people for thought and suffering; for Gates she was 'an exemplary African with whom to refute the claims of racists and proponents of slavery that the African was "by nature" fit to be nothing but a slave'.[6]

---

[3] Henry Louis Gates Jr, *The Trials of Phillis Wheatley: America's First Black Poet and Her Encounter with the Founding Fathers* (New York: Basic Books, 2003), pp. 26–7.

[4] Vincent Carretta, *Phillis Wheatley: Biography of a Genius in Bondage* (Athens, GA: University of Georgia Press, 2011), p. 199.

[5] Joseph Woods, *Thoughts on the Slavery of the Negroes* (London: James Phillips, 1784), p. 14.

[6] Henry Louis Gates Jr, 'From Wheatley to Douglass: The Politics of Displacement', in *Frederick Douglass: New Literary and Historical Essays*, ed. Eric J. Sundquist (Cambridge University Press, 1990), pp. 47–65 (52).

This is one of the more extreme examples of a claim that has resurfaced throughout this book – that lyric attests to the inalienable humanity of oppressed people. As June Jordan writes in 'The Difficult Miracle of Black Poetry in America':

> A poet writes in her own language. A poet writes of her own people, her own history, her own vision, her own room, her own house where she sits at her own table quietly placing one word after another word until she builds a line and a movement and an image and a meaning that somersaults all of these into the singing, the absolutely individual voice of the poet: at liberty. A poet is somebody free. A poet is someone at home.
>
> How should there be Black poets in America?[7]

Jordan's painful question follows a set of self-evident propositions: that to write poetry is to be at home in place and language, in the private room where we found Emily Dickinson, in freedom. That Wheatley could not be at home or at liberty is also self-evident. Her transformation into a poet, 'the first' poet, is a testament to her brilliance and fortitude. She 'assimilated' the 'white man's literature', Jordan says, but 'it was she who created herself a poet', in an act of autonomous self-fashioning.

Wheatley feels like the right ancestral poet to conclude this book's discussion of constraint, because she has been forced so often to stand in the crossroads between what Lindon Barrett calls *singing* and *signing*,[8] a lost history of song and a supposedly conformist manner of written lyric; because she was so viciously constrained, and brilliantly unconstrained, by her status as an enslaved girl and woman; and because she found a way to translate those constraints into ornament. The politics of the surface, of softness, are as central to her poetics as they are to Robertson's. Wheatley's poetry regularly imagines soaring away from the body, into the sublimation of the skies where emancipated subjects can devote themselves for eternity to the worship of God. But this fantasy entails an almost obsessive delineation of the earthly body as chained, disciplined and precarious matter.

Alexander Weheliye uses the topos of *habeas viscus* – 'you shall have the flesh' – to signal 'how violent political domination activates a fleshly surplus that simultaneously sustains and disfigures ... brutality, and, on the other hand, to reclaim the atrocity of flesh as a pivotal arena for the politics emanating from different traditions of the oppressed'.[9] Resisting

---

[7] June Jordan, *Some of Us Did Not Die: New and Selected Essays* (Perseus Books, 2002).
[8] Lindon Barrett, *Blackness and Value: Seeing Double* (Cambridge University Press, 1999).
[9] Alexander G. Weheliye, *Habeas Viscus: Racializing Assemblages, Biopolitics, and Black Feminist Theories of the Human* (Durham: Duke University Press, 2014), p. 2.

a biopolitics elaborated by Giorgio Agamben and Michel Foucault that aspires to transcend racialisation by recourse to a notional human being as absolute biological matter, Weheliye rejects a universalising ontology of the human. He returns instead through Black feminist thought to the 'fleshly surplus' of Blackness upon which sovereignty works in specific, irreducible ways.

I am also returning through Wheatley's poetry to the irreducible site of chattel slavery. My discussion of Robertson's poetics showed how she breaks open the 'I' of a privileged white feminised subject to find a set of accomplices, who work together to find pleasure behind the arena, in the shacks and derelictions of the neoliberal city or patriarchal tradition. But Wheatley's verse is a reminder also of the painful costs of trying to achieve that 'I' in the first place. Her battle for survival was very different from that of many of the poets discussed in this book, and while she found accomplices who helped her be published and secure her freedom, she was also beset by enemies who read her attempt to establish solidarity through imitation and mourning as the marks of a servile imagination.

This chapter concludes my discussion of the ways that poets invoke bondage as metaphor while effacing the actuality of bondage, by thinking with a revolutionary poet who imagined a way to translate her literal iron chains into the 'silken fetters' of verse. Wheatley's work is often dismissed as merely imitative, not just of other poets, but of the values of whiteness more generally. I will argue that her skilful repetition with variations of particular tropes – silk, ocean, chain, wing – reveal the traces of Wheatley's specific life experiences. In this sense, she also left behind proof that ornament is sometimes bondage.

Only a Sickly Little Black Girl

Given that Wheatley's aesthetics aimed at an etherealisation of the body, it is striking how often her critics zero in on her body. In her essay 'In Search of Our Mothers' Gardens', Alice Walker scorns Wheatley as a 'sickly, frail black girl', whose 'loyalties were completely divided, as was, without question, her mind'.[10] Referring to Wheatley's personification of Liberty as a goddess who 'moves divinely fair, / Olive and laurel binds her golden hair' (ll. 9–10, p. 89), Walker says: 'so torn by "contrary instincts" was black, kidnapped, enslaved Phillis that her description of "the Goddess" – as she

---

[10] Alice Walker, *In Search of Our Mothers' Gardens* (New York: Harcourt Brace Jovanovich, 1983), pp. 231–43.

poetically called the Liberty she did not have – is ironically, cruelly humorous. And, in fact, has held Phillis up to ridicule for more than a century. It is usually read prior to hanging Phillis's memory as that of a fool' (405). Walker arrives at a kind of toleration of Wheatley in the end:

> But at last, Phillis, we understand. No more snickering when your stiff, struggling, ambivalent lines are forced on us. We know now that you were not an idiot or a traitor; only a sickly little black girl, snatched from your home and country and made a slave; a woman who still struggled to sing the song that was your gift, although in a land of barbarians who praised you for your bewildered tongue. It is not so much what you sang, as that you kept alive, in so many of our ancestors, *the notion of song*. (405)

It is not Wheatley's actual poetry that Walker can admire, but the vestiges in that poetry of a *notion* of song, her *mother's* song: 'perhaps Phillis Wheatley's mother was also an artist. Perhaps in more than Phillis Wheatley's biological life is her mother's signature made clear.' The written texts Wheatley herself left behind are, for Walker, only the faltering echo of that vigorous African song that even Wheatley herself seems to have forgotten.

According to Margaretta Matilda Odell, the great-grandniece of her mistress Susanna Wheatley, Phillis had no memory of her homeland or her parents, 'excepting the simple circumstance that her mother poured out water before the sun at his rising'. It is sometimes argued that Wheatley's 'Hymn to the Morning' recollects these libations.[11] Antonio T. Bly associates the diacritical markings in her manuscripts with the African scriptive practice of *nsibidi*, her watery elegies to Senegambian beliefs that the dead were separated from the living by bodies of water, and her authorial voice to a west African 'sass'.[12] But we have little concrete evidence of what she remembered from her childhood in Africa. We are back where we started, with the melancholy of lost songs – unless we take the path of memory that M. NourbeSe Philip's work points to. As Philip writes: 'memory has a poetics that history lacks, appearing to reside in our bodies and not solely in the mind'.[13] As we'll see, memory is central to Wheatley's poetics; perhaps the 'bodymemory' of place and language lingers in Wheatley's sensation of flight, not just her sickness.[14]

---

[11] Antonio T. Bly, 'Wheatley's "On the Death of a Young Lady of Five Years of Age,"' *Explicator* 58.1 (1999), pp. 10–13 (10).

[12] Antonio T. Bly, '"By her unveil'd each horrid crime appears": Authorship, Text, and Subtext in Phillis Wheatley's Variants Poems,' *Textual Cultures* 9.1 (Winter 2014), pp. 112–41.

[13] M. NourbeSe Philip, *Bla_k: Essays & Interviews* (Toronto: Bookthug, 2017), pp. 66–7.

[14] Katherine McKittrick, *Demonic Grounds: Black Women and the Cartographies of Struggle* (Minneapolis: University of Minnesota Press, 2006), pp. 48, 52.

Wheatley may not have been the 'Black Prometheus' or heroic figure of African emancipation that Jared Hickman has tracked.[15] But neither was she 'only a sickly little black girl'. The name Phillis connotes an ironic pastoralism; as Hortense Spillers observes, 'the loss of the indigenous name/land marks a metaphor of displacement for other human and cultural features and relations'.[16] Phillis was not her Indigenous name. It was the name of the ship on which Wheatley arrived in Boston on 11 July 1761, as 'a slender frail, female child, supposed to have been about seven years old, at this time, from the circumstances of shedding her front teeth'.[17] She was bought by John and Susanna Wheatley 'for a trifle, as the captain had fears of her dropping off his hands, without emolument, by death'. O'Dell says she was 'naked', covered only by 'a quantity of dirty carpet about her like a filibeg' (a kilt) – though Wheatley's biographer Vincent Carretta suggests she was probably completely naked.[18] Her nakedness implies a state of nature, stripped of the culture and protection afforded by clothes. Her frailty, her 'trifling' body, made her a kind of impulse buy for the Wheatleys; she was purchased for amusement, or as a substitute for a recently dead child, not to perform hard labour.

At home, the Wheatleys allowed Phillis to mingle with their guests; according to Carretta, 'some white Bostonians were startled to discover they were expected to share tea table with her'. Including Phillis in their social life was the Wheatleys' way of displaying their status, piety, charity and commitment to evangelical Christianity, and to advertise that they could afford to spare her drudgery.[19] One of the Wheatleys' children, Mary, began to teach Phillis to read. Within sixteen months Wheatley could read 'the most difficult Parts of the Sacred Writings'.[20] By 1765, she had also written her first poem. She had been speaking English for only four years.

Several of these poems arose from acquaintances she made in the drawing room. In 1767, when she was in her early teens, Wheatley published her first poem, 'On Messrs. Hussey and Coffin', in the *Newport Mercury*. Her elegy 'On the Death of the Rev Mr George Whitefield. 1770' reached an even wider circulation, being published in Boston, Newport,

---

[15] Jared Hickman, *Black Prometheus: Race and Radicalism in the Age of Atlantic Slavery* (Oxford University Press, 2016).
[16] Hortense J. Spillers, *Black, White, and in Color: Essays on American Literature and Culture* (University of Chicago Press, 2003), p. 217.
[17] On Phillis's naming, see Christina Sharpe, *In the Wake: On Blackness and Being* (Durham: Duke University Press, 2016), pp. 41–53.
[18] Carretta, *Phillis Wheatley*, p. 14.   [19] *Ibid.*, p. 23.   [20] Wheatley, *Complete Works*, p. 7.

New York, Philadelphia and London. The poem included an address to Whitefield's patron Selina Hastings, Countess of Huntingdon, who would play a pivotal role in Wheatley's London publication. The idea that Wheatley should publish a collection was first floated in advertisements in the Boston *Censor* in spring 1772, which invited subscriptions to a planned volume. But the proposal was unsuccessful. Drawing on Susanna Wheatley's evangelical networks, Wheatley then pursued publication in London. *Poems on Various Subjects, Religious and Moral* appeared there in 1773. The Countess of Huntingdon agreed to being the volume's dedicatee, and insisted that an engraving of Wheatley be included as the frontispiece. That famous image, probably created by Scipio Morehead, depicts Wheatley in profile, a simple string collar (an advertisement in plainness of her virtue, or a trace – like Wyatt's collar, or the detainee's ligature – that she was someone's property) around her neck.[21] She sits at a desk, with pen, inkwell, paper and book, in a moment of contemplation in the midst of composition. But the image is framed by an inscription that makes clear that she is the 'Negro servant' to Mr John Wheatley; and that it is his generosity that allows her to work on her poems instead of labouring in the household (fig. 12.1).

An early nineteenth century editor of Washington's works judged that Wheatley was 'a whig in politics after the American way of thinking; and it might be curious to see in what manner she would eulogise liberty and the rights of man, while herself, nominally at least, in bondage'.[22] Several of her poems do exploit the comparison often drawn in Whig rhetoric between colonial status and political slavery, rhetoric that featured in many of the sermons Wheatley heard.[23] In an elegy, she imagines the revolutionary war general David Wooster ask as he lays dying:

> But how, presumptuous shall we hope to find
> Divine acceptance with th' Almighty mind?
> While yet (O deed Ungenerous!) they disgrace
> And hold in bondage Afric's blameless race?
> Let Virtue reign? And thou accord our prayers
> Be victory our's, and generous freedom theirs. (ll. 27–32, p. 93)

---

[21] On the portrait's iconography, see Astrid Franke, 'Phillis Wheatley, Melancholy Muse', *The New England Quarterly* 77.2 (June 2004), pp. 224–51.
[22] William H. Robinson, *Critical Essays on Phillis Wheatley* (Boston: G. K. Hall, 1982), p. 52.
[23] James A. Levernier, 'Phillis Wheatley and the New England Clergy', *Early American Literature* 26.1 (1991), pp. 21–38 (27–9); Peter Dorsey, 'To "Corroborate Our Claims": Public Positioning and the Slavery Metaphor in Revolutionary America', *American Quarterly* 55.3 (2003), pp. 353–86; Eric Slauter, 'Neoclassical Culture in a Society with Slaves: Race and Rights in the Age of Wheatley', *Early American Studies* 2.1 (Spring 2004), pp. 81–122.

Fig. 12.1 'Phillis Wheatley, Negro servant to Mr John Wheatley, of Boston', by Scipio Moorhead; in *Poems on Various Subjects, Religious and Moral* (London: Archibald Bell, 1773).

If 'Virtue' is to reign in the new nation, then Africa's 'blameless race' surely merits its share in the freedom for which Americans were fighting. 'We' all risk our salvation so long as 'they' keep people in captivity: Wheatley's prophetic tendency to speak in the first person plural for the collective has its limits; she cannot bring herself to say 'we hold in bondage Afric's blameless race'.

Wheatley was eventually able to claim her rights to personal freedom and the profits of her poetry. Where the 1772 proposal identified her as 'at present a Slave', by 1773 she was 'A Negro Servant to Mr Wheatley of *Boston.*' Her change of status may have been part of a bargain for her return from London to Boston. Given that the Somerset case in 1772 had resolved that 'No master ever was allowed here to take a slave by force to be sold abroad because he deserted from his service, or for any other reason whatever', her visit presented an opportunity to stay in England and be free; but she sailed for Boston on 26 July 1773, two months before the book appeared.[24] She had secured manumission papers, copies of which she sent

---

[24] On the 'temptation' to remain, see Wheatley, *Complete Writings*, pp. xxv–xxxi.

to her London agent. She writes in 1773 that 'Since my return to America my Master, has at the desire of my friends in England given me my freedom. The Instrument is drawn, so as to secure me and my property from the hands of the Exectutrs. [sic], administrators, & c. of my master, & secure whatsoever Should be given me as my Own.'²⁵ The powerful accomplices she had impressed in London had helped her to negotiate her freedom. But she was still vulnerable: 'I am not upon my own footing and whatever I get by this [sale of her books] is entirely mine, & it is the Chief I have to depend upon.' The end of Wheatley's life was a time of intense precarity. Following the deaths of Susanna, John and Mary Wheatley, she married John Peters in 1778. Peters was imprisoned for debt, and their three children all died in infancy. Her poetic profile was in decline; a proposed second volume came to nothing. Wheatley died in 1784.

Snatching Laurels

In his *Notes on the State of Virginia* (1787), Thomas Jefferson makes a famous, scathing criticism of Wheatley: 'Misery is often the parent of the most affecting touches in poetry. Among the blacks is misery enough, God knows, but not poetry. Love is the peculiar oestrum of the poet. Their love is ardent, but it kindles the senses only, not the imagination. Religion, indeed, has produced a Phillis Whatley [*sic*]; but it could not produce a poet. The compositions published under her name are below the dignity of criticism. The heroes of the Dunciad are to her, as Hercules to the author of that poem.'²⁶

There's much that can be said about this vile commentary, but I want to focus on how Jefferson attacks Wheatley for her indebtedness to Alexander Pope. He was not the last critic to do so. William J. Long wrote in 1913,

> Here is no Zulu, but drawing-room English; not the wild, barbaric strain of march and camp and singing fire that stirs a man's instincts, but pious platitudes, colorless imitations of Pope, and some murmurs of a terrible theology.... It is too bad. This poor child has been made over into a wax puppet; she sings like a canary in a cage, a bird that forgets its native melody and imitates only what it hears.²⁷

---

²⁵ Letter, 18 October 1773, in Wheatley, *Complete Writings*, p. 147.
²⁶ Thomas Jefferson, *Notes on the State of Virginia* (1784), Query 14, in *Writings*, ed. Merrill D. Peterson (New York: Library of America, 1984), pp. 266–7.
²⁷ William J. Long, *American Literature* (Boston, MA: Ginn, 1913), pp. 145–6, in Robinson, *Critical Essays*, p. 59.

The caged bird is a familiar figure to us; Katherine Lee Bates uses it to describe Wheatley in 1898 as 'the rare song-bird of Africa [who] was thoroughly tamed in her Boston cage'.[28] But here again is the image of Wheatley as feeble, a 'poor child' and producer not of 'Zulu' marching songs but 'colorless' imitations (which efface her own colour). She can only 'imitate' the white poetic tradition, not contribute to it; her 'native melody', as Walker also put it, is irrevocably lost.

Although recent critical attention has revealed Wheatley's agency within anti-slavery and revolutionary politics, and in the production and promotion of her printed works, since the time of her first publication she has been continuously faulted for being merely imitative of the idioms of Milton and Pope. In his inventory of Wheatley's reception, Gates quotes Wallace Thurman, who in 1928 said she was a 'third-rate imitation' of Pope;[29] Amiri Baraka, who said her 'pleasant imitations of eighteenth-century English poetry are far and, finally, ludicrous departures from the huge black voices that splintered southern nights with their *hollers, chants, arwhoolies,* and *ballits*' – closer to the Agrarians' ideal of Southern poetics than to revolutionary Blackness (76); Nathan Higgins, who in 1971 described her voice as that of 'a feeble Alexander Pope rather than that of an African prince' (77); and June Jordan, who attributed her verse to 'regular kinds of iniquitous nonsense found in white literature, the literature that Phillis Wheatley assimilated, with no choice in the matter' (80). Terence Collins finds in her poems 'what has come to be called the slave mentality – or self-hate by blacks based on introjection of the dominant culture's estimate of their worth'. He argues that because she was 'sickly and weak', she was 'exempted from the usual lot of slaves and was encouraged toward refinement and cultivation' – her poetry is a product of her illness and her privilege, and it shows.[30] Keith Leonard quotes other readers who referred to Wheatley as 'lobotomized'.[31] These critics find Wheatley to be feeble, ludicrous, her poor health another way in which she resembles Pope.

In effect, these critiques of Wheatley's imitations repeat a trope that can be found as far back as Quintilian: that grappling with another author, in a contest of strength (*vis*) and wit (*ingenium*), will allow the poet to

---

[28] Katherine Lee Bates, *American Literature* (New York, NY: Macmillan, 1898), pp. 78–9, in Robinson, *Critical Essays,* p. 58.
[29] Gates, *The Trials,* p. 75.
[30] Terence Collins, 'Phillis Wheatley; The Dark Side of the Poetry', *Phylon* 36.1 (1975), pp. 78–88 (78, 79).
[31] Keith D. Leonard, *Fettered Genius: The African American Bardic Poet from Slavery to Civil Rights* (Charlottesville: University of Virginia Press, 2006), p. 22.

distinguish him or herself. As Colin Burrow summarises, 'An imitation *should* be a thriving exercised body, capable of conquering and controlling, which is rich in fertility, which has absorbed the excellences of others into its body and which consequently strengthens and enriches its own *vis* and *ingenium*.'[32] But alongside ableist characterisations of Wheatley as a sickly little black girl is the suggestion that the most significant constraint on Wheatley's poetry is whiteness. Whiteness imposes its form on her; whiteness is the practical, political and aesthetic bondage from which she is not finally able to free herself.

Imitation in Wheatley's time was also described in terms of ingestion: the incorporation and transformation of another writer's idiom rather than simple reproduction.[33] It allowed the writer to demonstrate their mastery of a tradition and readiness to undertake rhetorical performances within new contexts. Wheatley's imitations of Milton, Pope and other poets include significant revisions of their diction or emphasis.[34] By resituating their idioms within her own social contexts, she enacts subtle shifts in meaning that allow her to perform her obedience to white cultural norms while showing how those norms exclude Black subjects. Moreover, as Burrow has shown, imitation in the late eighteenth century was bound up in questions of property and propriety: not just copyright, but philosophical considerations of language as an unenclosed commons. Depending on your perspective, language was either a *terra nullius* to be cultivated by authors and therefore claimed as their own, or must be held in trust for the whole of humanity as a common good. Burrow draws on John Locke's labour theory of property and the example Locke gives of the appropriation of land from native peoples in America as a basis for claims to intellectual property.[35] These arguments, which draw on colonial jurisprudence, have a special force in relation to an author who was herself identified as property.

Eric Slauter situates Wheatley's publication at the beginning of a Romantic backlash against 'slavish' neoclassical imitativeness, where submission of the creative intellect to the precedence of another is allegorised as a form of bondage. He quotes Edward Young (1759): 'Modern writers have a Choice to make. They may soar in the Regions of Liberty, or

---

[32] Colin Burrow, *Imitating Authors: Plato to Futurity* (Oxford University Press, 2019), p. 100.
[33] G. W. Pigman III, 'Versions of Imitation in the Renaissance', *Renaissance Quarterly* 33.1 (Spring 1980), pp. 1–32.
[34] Marsha Watson offers compelling close readings of Wheatley's revisions of Pope as not 'blind adherence' but 'a licence for innovation': 'A Classic Case: Phillis Wheatley and Her Poetry', *Early America Literature* 31.2 (1996), pp. 103–32 (120).
[35] Burrow, *Imitating Authors*, p. 339.

move in the soft Fetters of easy Imitation!'[36] Soaring or lingering in soft fetters are key tropes in Wheatley's work, as we'll see. But Wheatley's contemporaries regarded her imitations not as an act of cultural assimilation, or an attempt to win sympathy and respect by conforming to prevalent poetic norms, but as a racialised instinct. James Parton, writing about her in 1878, concurred that 'a fatal facility of imitation stands in the way of this interesting race .... To the present hour the negro has contributed nothing to the intellectual resources of man. If he turns "negro minstrel," he still imitates the white creations of that black art.'[37] These remarks recall the racist assertions by John Lomax that the 'Negro' is 'naturally imitative'. Rather than showing her mastery of conventional poetic idiom, Wheatley's imitations are reduced to mimicry. Even to perform Blackness in this context would be to 'turn minstrel': to imitate a white imitation.

Another review from 1774 argued that 'the poems written by this young negro bear no endemial marks of solar fire or spirit. They are merely imitative; and indeed, most of these people have a turn for imitation, though they have little or none for invention.'[38] The fire that should be marked on her skin (the heat of the sun) has left nothing in the poems. She can, like her 'people', only imitate. Ironically, this is a position satirised by Pope himself in *An Essay on Criticism*, where he observes that critics attribute wit 'To *one small* sect, and All are *damn'd beside*':

> Meanly they seek the Blessing to confine,
> And force *that Sun* but on a *Part* to Shine;
> Which not alone the *Southern Wit* sublimes,
> But ripens Spirits in cold *Northern Climes*[.][39]

I'll return to the importance of Pope's poem to Wheatley in a moment.

Wheatley began reading Milton and Pope in Boston, but her interest in their poetries was encouraged during her trip to London to oversee the publication of her works. She records that William Legge, 2nd Earl of Dartmouth – who is the subject of an important poem by Wheatley, discussed below – 'made me a Compliment of 5 guineas, and desird me

---

[36] Slauter, 'Neoclassical Culture', p. 107.
[37] James Parton, 'Antipathy to the Negro', *North American Review* 127 (Nov–Dec. 1878), pp. 487–8; in Robinson, *Critical Essays*, p. 55.
[38] Review of Wheatley's *Poems on Various Subjects* in *London Monthly Review* 49 (October 1447); in Robinson, *Critical Essays*, p. 30.
[39] Alexander Pope, 'An Essay on Criticism', *The Poems: A One Volume Edition of the Twickenham Pope*, ed. John Butt (London: Methuen, [1963] 1984), ll. 397–401, p. 156. All quotations of Pope's works will be from this edition.

to get the whole of Mr Pope's Works, as the best he could recommend to my perusal'; she was also presented 'with a Folio Edition of Milton's *Paradise Lost*, printed on a Silver Type'. On the same trip, the abolitionist Granville Sharp gave her a copy of his *Remarks on Several Very Important Prophecies* (1768), and 'attended me to the Tower & Show'd the Lions, Panthers, Tigers, & c.'[40] We can only speculate on their conversation as they gazed at these caged animals.[41]

Miltonic cadences can be heard throughout Wheatley's poems. Her paraphrase of Isaiah 63:1–8 begins, 'SAY, heav'nly muse ... ', an obvious echo of Milton's 'Sing Heav'nly Muse' from the invocation to book I of *Paradise Lost* (l. 6). Similarly, her reluctance to try to depict the joys of the blessed in heaven – 'But of celestial joys I sing in vain: / Attempt not, muse, the too advent'rous strain'[42] – quotes Milton's famous attempt at an 'adventrous Song',

> That with no middle flight intends to soar
> Above th' Aonian Mount, while it pursues
> Things unattempted yet in Prose or Rhime.
> (*Paradise Lost*, 1.13–16)

The soaring of Milton's muse inspires Wheatley to her own imaginary flights, while the conventional description of the epic written text as a song points to a history (in which Walker's critique could be included) of poetry aspiring to the condition of music: a lost, transcendent music of which the written text can only be an impoverished echo.

Wheatley had probably read Milton in Thomas Newton's 1752 edition, which was owned by her neighbour, Mather Byles. As a young man, Byles had corresponded with Pope and Isaac Watts.[43] Byles was a poet as well; his *Poems on Several Occasions* (1744) include lines 'Written in Milton's *Paradise Lost*'. Byles's verses were praised by his contemporaries for their ability to imitate Milton's 'Airy rapid flights, / And mount with ardour to his godlike heights'.[44] In her poem 'To Maecenas', Wheatley imitated Byles imitating Milton (and Pope).[45] While Byles writes 'Thus with ambitious Hand, I'd boldly snatch / A spreading Branch from his immortal

---

[40] Letter, 18 October 1773, in *Complete Writings*, p. 146; Carretta, *Phillis Wheatley*, p. 118.
[41] See David Waldstreicher, 'The Wheatleyan Moment', *Early American Studies* 9.3 (2011), pp. 522–51 (532–8).
[42] 'To a Lady and her Children, on the Death of her Son and their Brother', ll. 21–2, p. 44.
[43] Gates, *The Trials*, p. 9.
[44] John Adams, 'To a Gentleman [Byles] on the Sight of Some of his Poems', *A Collection of Poems, By Several Hands* (Boston, 1744), p. 6; quoted in Leon Howard, 'The Influence of Milton on Colonial American Poetry', *The Huntington Library Bulletin* 9 (April 1936), pp. 63–89 (65).
[45] Franke, 'Melancholy Muse', p. 241.

Laurels,' echoing Pope's *Essay on Criticism* ('to *snatch* a *Grace* beyond the Reach of Art', l. 155, p. 149), Wheatley asserts:

> While blooming wreaths around thy temples spread,
> I'll snatch a laurel from thine honour'd head,
> While you indulgent smile upon deed.[46]

But the verb 'snatch' is the same one she uses in her poem to Dartmouth, where she complains that she 'Was snatch'd from *Afric's* fancy'd happy seat'. The repetition aligns Wheatley's invasion of the laureate's benign retirement with the slave traders' invasion of the pastoral bounty of her childhood.

John Wheatley had said that Phillis 'has a great Inclination to learn the Latin Tongue, and has made some Progress in it'. On the evidence of 'A Conversation between a New York Gentleman & Phillis', she had only read Pope's translations of Homer's *Iliad* and *Odyssey*, and other works of classical literature in translation.[47] Like Robertson, she came to the classics through Pope, and like Robertson she also sought to reproduce and disrupt a classical Latinity that excluded her. Her *Poems* opens with an address 'To Maecenas', Horace's and Virgil's patron. There she asks: 'What felt those poets but you feel the same?' (l. 3, p. 9). The question poses the commonality of feeling shared by patron and poet, across boundaries of wealth, status, hierarchy and time: the poet's 'noble strains your *equal* genius shares' (l. 5, my emphasis). She also goes on to wish:

> O could I rival thine and *Virgil's* page,
> Or claim the *Muses* with the *Mantuan* Sage;
> Soon the tame beauties should my mind adorn,
> And the same ardors in my soul should burn:
> Then should my song in bolder notes arise,
> And all my numbers pleasingly surprise;
> But here I sit, and mourn a grov'ling mind
> That fain would mount, and ride upon the wind.
>
> (ll. 23–30, pp. 9–10)

This imagery of riding and taming is very different from the one of gendered violence we've found in Ovid, Wyatt's trained hawks or the fetishistic horseplay of Victorian sexology. But as in those contexts, constraint is translated into pleasure: Wheatley makes the transcendence of her song, its ability to 'ride upon the wind', dependent on submission – on the

---

[46] Wheatley, *Complete Writings*, ll. 45–7, p. 10; on her snatching, see John C. Shields, 'Phillis Wheatley's Subversive Pastoral', *Eighteenth Century Studies* 27.4 (1994), pp. 631–47 (637–9).
[47] Carretta, *Phillis Wheatley*, p. 51.

Muses being tamed by her. Given the gendering of animal taming I've discussed, this is a forceful assertion of her desire for the kinds of power that were in her society the privilege of men.

'To Maecenas' has many debts to Pope. 'When gentler strains demand thy graceful song, / The length'ning line moves languishing along' (ll. 15–16) is an echo of the most famous passage in his *Essay on Criticism* (ll. 370–3, p. 155), while those final lines echo his *Essay on Man*:

> Reason the card, but Passion is the gale;
> Nor God alone in the calm storm we find,
> He mounts the storm and walks upon the wind.
> (Epistle II, ll. 108–110, p. 519)[48]

Perhaps Wheatley's admiration for that poem was also sparked by Pope's sympathy for the 'poor Indian, whose untutor'd mind / Sees God in clouds', and who wishes to find 'Some happier island in the watry waste, / Where slaves once more their native land behold, / No fiends torment, no Christians thirst for gold!' (Epistle I, ll. 99–100, 106–8; p. 508).[49]

But the first epistle of Pope's *Essay on Man* is also concerned with the Great Chain of Being, a hierarchy of creatures that extends from plants through animals, humans and angelic natures to the divine, in which each has a providentially assigned place. This 'scale of sensual, mental pow'rs ascends' until it arrives at 'Man's imperial race' (ll. 208–9, p. 512). Pope says that brute sensuality is divided from the rational thought that is man's special province by 'thin partitions' (l. 226, p. 513), but any attempt to break through would lead to disaster, the upsetting of the whole cosmic order. He therefore commands the reader to 'submit': 'Whatever IS, is RIGHT' (l. 294, p. 515). Wheatley, exercising her reason in the composition of her poems, lays claim to a position on the human side of the partition. But Zakiyyah Iman Jackson, commenting on the use of the Chain of Being in abolitionist rhetoric, argues that the continuity of the scale imperilled the claims of Black people to humanity: 'if Black people were human but represented the lowest human rung of the ladder, and thus, embodied the specter of "the animal" within the human, then the extension of human recognition dissimulated rather than simply abated race's animalizing discourse' – a discourse that was applied with cruel specificity, as we've

---

[48] G. J. Barker-Benfield, *Phillis Wheatley Chooses Freedom: History, Poetry, and the Ideals of the American Revolution* (New York University Press, 2018), p. 106.

[49] On this passage and Pope's sympathies and use of slavery as a metaphor, see Howard Erskine-Hill, 'Pope and Slavery', *Proceedings of the British Academy* 91 (1998), pp. 27–53.

seen, to Wheatley's attempts to 'imitate' not only the poetics of white authors, but their humanity.[50]

Treading the Line

Wheatley's 'To Maecenas' can be read as a paradoxical assertion of modesty, in which her ambitions (to rival Virgil, through her reliance on Pope; to ride upon the wind) are acknowledged and foresworn. Although she is imitating Pope, she is taking on his poetics at their most authoritative: confidently giving the rule to other poets, and moderating his philosophy through her own situation. This imitation swivels on a performance of modesty that is sharpened by Wheatley's particular condition: 'But I less happy, cannot raise the song, / The fault'ring music dies upon my tongue.' She is less happy, less fortunate, not merely because she (humbly) lacks Pope's music, but because she is enslaved. And yet, the poem's polished heroic couplets give the lie to this confession that her music is 'fault'ring' and sickly.

Wheatley's poetry treads this difficult line between freedom and bondage, the universal doctrine of rights and the catastrophe of chattel slavery, white literary culture and her African heritage.[51] On the one hand, her origin story helped to distinguish her among her poetic contemporaries, to market her books and to make her accomplishments a symbol of the humanity of enslaved people. On the other hand, she had to appear to transcend that origin through an enlightenment that was the gift of white Christians. As the publisher's announcement of her *Poems* attested, hers was 'one of the greatest instances of a pure, unassisted genius, that the world ever produced', cultivated through 'the happiness of a liberal education'.[52] Wheatley affected some of this *ingenium* or 'native genius', describing herself as 'A muse untutor'd, and unknown to fame'.[53] But the fact that she could imitate white poetries was also taken as proof that Black people could be taught. As Slauter argues, the publication of her poems 'coincided with a British vogue for uneducated poets and "natural geniuses." It also appeared at a moment when abolitionists wished to demonstrate both the innate mental equality of Africans as well as their educability.'[54]

---

[50] Zakiyyah Iman Jackson, *Becoming Human: Matter and Meaning in an Antiblack World* (New York University Press, 2020), p. 49.
[51] Further discussion of Wheatley's equivocations can be found in Paula Bennett, 'Phillis Wheatley's Vocation and the Paradox of the "Afric Muse,"' *PMLA* 113.1 (1998), pp. 64–76.
[52] Wheatley, *Complete Writings*, p. xviii.
[53] 'Philis's [sic] Reply to the Answer in our last by the Gentleman in the Navy', l. 10, p. 87.
[54] Slauter, 'Neoclassical Culture', p. 105.

These tensions reach an uneasy settlement in her poem 'On Being Brought from Africa to America' (1768), which Gates calls 'the most reviled poem in African-American literature'.[55] Here it is in its entirety:

> 'Twas mercy brought me from my *Pagan* land,
> Taught my benighted soul to understand
> That there's a God, that there's a *Saviour* too:
> Once I redemption neither sought nor knew.
> Some view our sable race with scornful eye,
> 'Their colour is a diabolic die.'
> Remember, *Christians*, *Negros*, black as *Cain*,
> May be refin'd, and join th' angelic train.
>
> (ll. 1–8, p. 13)

Wheatley claims that her transportation into bondage was a deliverance from the 'night' of the soul; it saved her from the worse fate of ignorance of the Christian God. Wheatley's description of her 'benighted soul' also draws a parallel between her dark skin and 'the state of all those living in sin'.[56] She subscribes to the myth, which David Brion Davis discovers amongst European writers from the beginning of the seventeenth century, that the mysterious 'mark' that God imprinted on Cain was blackened skin.[57] Wheatley reminds her readers that 'Negros, black as Cain' can be 'refin'd' in spirit, as she was; but they would still bear that mark. The paratactic concision of her phrase 'Remember, Christians, Negros' brings these categories into a tense proximity: Negroes can be Christians, and scornful Christians are perhaps worse than the outwardly 'dyed' and stigmatised Negroes they wish to exclude from salvation. Calling attention to the suffering of 'our sable race', the poem's first-person plural is both a signal that Wheatley's readers might be members of her own race, or imply that white readers, benighted and condemned to mortality by sin as she is, are also its 'dyed' members.

The delicate balance Wheatley strikes between references to her own enslavement, and celebrations of the liberties afforded by Christian salvation, is also apparent in her 1767 address to students at Harvard, 'To the University of Cambridge in New England', composed at the age of fifteen. Despite her age, race, gender and status, Wheatley's tone of admonishment is hardly humble. Her faith allows her to speak with prophetic authority to these 'blooming plants of human race divine'. Wheatley contrasts her own

---

[55] Gates, *The Trials*, p. 71.
[56] Mary McAleer Balkun, 'Phillis Wheatley's Construction of Otherness and the Rhetoric of Performed Ideology', *African American Review* 36.1 (Spring 2002), pp. 121–35(129).
[57] David Brion Davis, *Inhuman Bondage: The Rise and Fall of Slavery in the New World* (Oxford University Press, 2006), p. 69.

ignorance with the Harvard students' learning. She reminds them that her race and origins are opposite to theirs:

> While an intrinsic ardour prompts to write,
> The muses promise to assist my pen;
> Twas not long since I left my native shore
> The land of errors, and *Egyptian* gloom:
> Father of mercy, 'twas thy gracious hand
> Brought me in safety from those dark abodes.
>
> (ll. 1–6, p. 11)

She is motivated by an 'intrinsic ardour', an untaught and instinctive impulse to write; that ardour is 'assisted' by the muses, who promise only to help her 'while' she is under the influence of that naïve, innocent impulse. She comes from the 'land of errors' (l. 4), a land she says she 'left', rather than one from which she was violently kidnapped, suggesting that she herself actively pursued the enlightenment available beyond her native shores, as the students must also do in their studies.

But while Wheatley was shipped in a densely packed hold, the students can soar under their own agency:

> Students, to you 'tis giv'n to scan the heights
> Above, to traverse the ethereal space,
> And mark the systems of revolving worlds.
>
> (ll. 7–9, pp. 11–12)

In these lines, Wheatley's debt to Pope is apparent not only in her prosody and diction, but in her argument. In his *Essay on Man* (epistle II), Pope insists that 'The proper study of Mankind is Man' (l. 1). He instructs:

> Go, wond'rous creature! mount where Science guides,
> Go, measure earth, weigh air, and state the tides;
> Instruct the planets in what orbs to run,
> Correct old Time, and regulate the Sun;
> Go, soar with Plato to th' empyreal sphere . . .
> Then drop into thyself, and be a fool!
>
> (ll. 19–23, 30)

Similarly, Wheatley warns the students not to get confused by their intellectual voyages, but to 'improve your privileges' and shun sin:

> An *Ethiop* tells you 'tis your greatest foe;
> Its transient sweetness turns to endless pain,
> And in immense perdition sinks the soul.
>
> (ll. 28–30, p. 12)

The bathos of the soul 'sinking' in the immensity of perdition also recollects the voyage that the 'Ethiop' had to survive in order to become acquainted with the everlasting sweetness of Christ.

In 'America' (1768), the 'Ethiop' poet's ability to offer moral lessons is a miraculous proof of the benefits of Christianity: 'Thy Power, O Liberty, makes strong the weak / And (wond'rous instinct) Ethiopians speak' (ll. 5–6, p. 125). However, Wheatley secures her foundation myth on the annihilation of the New World's living creatures, its animals, and implicitly its Indigenous people:

> New England first a wilderness was found
> Till for a continent 'twas destin'd round
> From field to field the savage monsters run
> E'r yet Brittania had her work begun
>
> (ll. 1–4, p. 125)

The 'savage monsters' expelled or destroyed, Britannia – styled here as a loving but stern mother – can attempt to control her son, 'the Best of Infants' (l. 16). With the 'scourges' of taxes Britannia attempts to suppress 'New English force' (l. 30). But she 'fear'st his Tyranny', while America 'weeps afresh to feel this Iron chain' (ll. 30–1). The poem shows Wheatley identifying with the subject position of the white colonists, challenging British imperial authority through a conventional image of political maternity and slavery. Its sentimental 'Simile' also speaks to her own loss of her mother, and its ambivalence – the mother who weeps with pity, while chaining up her own son – of Susanna Wheatley's substitute maternity.

The closest Wheatley ever comes to addressing the devastating loss of her own family is in the congratulatory epideictic 'To the Right Honourable William, Earl of Dartmouth', on his promotion to Secretary of State for the Colonies in 1772. The poem, which was composed on demand, celebrates the appointment of an apparent friend of the colonies who had helped secure the repeal of the Stamp Act:[58]

> No more, *America*, in mournful strain
> Of wrongs, and grievance unredress'd complain,
> No longer shalt thou dread the iron chain,
> Which wanton *Tyranny* with lawless hand
> Had made, and with it meant t' enslave the land.
>
> (ll. 15–19, p. 40)

---

[58] Waldstreicher, 'The Wheatleyan Moment', pp. 524–5.

A letter with a copy of the poem that she sends to Dartmouth apologises with some irony for 'this freedom from an African, who with the (now) happy America, exults with equal transport' in Dartmouth's appointment.[59] She was transported, not in conditions of equality, to an America where she is now transported with happiness; she must apologise for her rhetorical freedom, being (as an African) unfree, but (as a Christian in America) emancipated from sin and ignorance. The terms of the letter are politely generic; but in the poem Wheatley personalises her portrait of freedom, through an explicit reference to her own political formation:

> Should you, my lord, while you peruse my song,
> Wonder from whence my love of *Freedom* sprung,
> Whence flow these wishes for the common good,
> By feeling hearts alone best understood,
> I, young in life, by seeming cruel fate
> Was snatch'd from *Afric's* fancy'd happy seat:
> What pangs excruciating must molest,
> What sorrows labour in my parent's breast?
> Steel'd was that soul and by no misery mov'd
> That from a father seiz'd his babe belov'd:
> Such, such my case. And can I then but pray
> Others may never feel tyrannic sway?
>
> (ll. 20–31, p. 40)

Her experience of being 'snatch'd' from her father's arms is emblematic of the intense grief of those denied their liberty. She personifies in her individual life the suffering of the collective. But her capture and transport from Africa to America is part of an arc from ignorance to enlightenment, which might also lead Dartmouth from his governance to a heavenly apotheosis. She ends the poem by hoping that 'on the wings of fleeting *Fame*' – fleeting meaning both quick, and temporary – Dartmouth will be elevated: 'May fiery coursers sweep th' ethereal plain, / And bear thee upwards' to heaven (l. 42, p. 40).

Flights of Fancy

Wheatley uses the licence of the prophet, the naïve girl or 'Ethiop' to create a space for her own expression within the constraints imposed by imitation. Under the smoothness of her neoclassical style, Wheatley manages an almost impossible situation of enslavement. Rafia Zafar has described her 'willed, forced dissemblance' of dispassion in the face of enslavement as an example

---

[59] Wheatley, *Complete Writings*, p. 143.

of the 'necessity of literary masking' that characterises much early African American writing.[60] But there are some moments when traces of Wheatley's personal history break through. In addition to her poem 'Ocean', a mythical account of her voyage from Boston to London, Wheatley wrote several poems about sea voyages undertaken by others. Her first published poem celebrated the escape of Messrs Hussey and Coffin from a wreck on Cape Cod; the poem presents a series of questions to the sailors, who had been guests of the Wheatleys: 'Did Fear and Danger so perplex your Mind, / As made you fearful of the Whistling Wind?' (ll. 1–2, p. 74). Although the poem settles into Christian consolation – never fear, God will protect you – it dwells compassionately on the panic one might feel in stormy seas. 'To a Gentleman on his Voyage to *Great-Britain* for the Recovery of his Health' remarks that 'I to R— would paint the *British* shore, / And vast *Atlantic*, not untry'd before' (ll. 11–12, p. 47). The Atlantic was 'not untried' by her; she had endured it as a child. She knew first-hand how few people 'without dying gain'd th' immortal coast'.[61] Only death, she insisted, could 'still the tumult of life's tossing seas'.[62] Now, she wishes for it to be calm, to carry this gentleman, or her mistress Susanna, or a lady escaping a hurricane to land in North Carolina, or another lady leaving the diseased heart of slavery in Jamaica, to health and restoration.[63]

That this oceanic imagery might be the return of a repressed memory of her own experience of the Middle Passage seems more likely when we consider the numerous references to bondage, chains and shackles in her poems. Addressing 'a Lady on the Death of Her Husband', Wheatley affirms (in terms that recall Dickinson's dead housewife): 'Clos'd are his eyes, and heavy fetters keep / His senses bound in never-waking sleep' (ll. 13–14, p. 18). Another elegy 'On the Death of a young Lady of Five Years of Age' warmly invites the parents not to 'deplore' her loss, for 'She feels the iron hand of pain no more' (l. 6, p. 16). In another, a creepy infant is relieved that it died 'E'er yet the lash for horrid crimes I felt'.[64] Another 'strove the tyrant [Death] to withstand, / And the dread terrors of his iron hand'.[65] The deceased Rev Dr Sewell benefited from grace 'which rescues

---

[60] Rafia Zafar, *We Wear the Mask: African Americans Write American Literature, 1760–1870* (New York: Columbia University Press, 1997), p. 16.
[61] 'To His Honour the Lieutenant-Governor, on the Death of his Lady. *March* 24, 1773', l. 12, p. 61.
[62] 'On the Death of a Young Gentleman', l. 14, p. 18.
[63] 'Ode to Neptune. On Mrs. W — 's Voyage to England', p. 41; 'To a Lady on her coming to North-America with her Son, for the Recovery of her Health', pp. 41–2; 'To a Lady on her remarkable Preservation in a Hurricane in North-Carolina', p. 43.
[64] 'A Funeral Poem on the Death of C. E. [Charles Eliot], an Infant of Twelve Months', l. 19, p. 38.
[65] 'To Mr and Mrs —, on the Death of their Infant Son', ll. 13–14, p. 94.

sinners from the chains of guilt' (ll. 40–1, p. 14). And when Susanna died in 1774, Wheatley wrote of her mistress's desires 'to be freed from the cumbrous Shackles of a mortal Body, which had so many Times retarded her desires when Soaring upward'.[66]

This conventional imagery of earthly life as bondage revisits Wheatley's own past, transfiguring oceans and chains into symbols of spiritual redemption. Her poems show a deep need for the Platonic and Christian promise that the spirit might fly away from the chains of the body. Repeatedly, death is figured as a release from bondage and a voyage (through air, or even 'seas' of air) into an ideal, abstracted place 'beyond the skies' (l. 34, p. 46). An elegy on a five-year-old declares 'Th' enraptur'd innocent has wing'd her flight' into 'fair etherial light' (ll. 1–2, p. 16). A beloved son 'upon pinions swifter than the wind, / Has left mortality's sad scenes behind';[67] a toddler named Avis (bird) is 'enlarg'd' 'to waft triumphant through the seas of air'.[68] A mother asks 'Where flies my *James?* . . . . Some angel tell me where / He wings his passage thro' the yielding air?'[69] A daughter 'unreluctant flies to see no more / Her dear-lov'd parents on earth's dusky shore'; instead, 'She with swift progress cuts the azure plain.'[70] The soul of a brother ascends: 'Awful he moves, and wide his wings are spread . . . / From bondage freed, the exulting spirit flies / Beyond *Olympus*, and these starry skies.'[71] So, too, does a twelve-month-old infant: 'through airy roads he wings his instant flight / To purer regions of celestial light'.[72] 'On the Death of the Rev Dr Sewell' imagines this 'saint ascending to his native skies; / From hence the prophet wing'd his rapt'rous way', and exhorts us all to 'with the same vigour rise' (ll. 6-7, 11-12, p. 13). The elegy for Whitefield beholds this second 'prophet in his tow'ring flight! / He leaves the earth for heav'n's unmeasur'd height,' and 'wings with rapid course his way, / And sails to *Zion* through the vast seas of day' (ll. 11–14, p. 15). The bereaved are also exhorted to reject their grief:

> O come away, her longing spirit cries,
> And share with me the raptures of the skies; . . .
> Let grief no longer dam devotion's fire,
> But rise sublime, to equal bliss aspire.[73]

---

[66] Letter to John Thornton, 29 March 1774, *Complete Writings*, pp. 154–5.
[67] 'To a Lady and her Children, on the Death of her Son and their Brother', ll. 15–16, p. 44.
[68] 'To a Gentleman and Lady on the Death of the Lady's Brother and Sister, and a Child of the Name *Avis*, aged one year', ll. 26–7, p. 45.
[69] 'On the Death of J. C. an Infant', ll. 19–21, p. 49.
[70] 'To the Honourable T. H. Esq; on the Death of his Daughter', ll. 15–18, p. 52.
[71] 'To a Lady on the Death of Three Relations', ll. 9–12, p. 30.
[72] 'A Funeral Poem on the Death of C. E. an Infant of Twelve Months', ll. 1–2, p. 37.
[73] 'To a Clergyman on the Death of his Lady', ll. 17–18, 34–5, p. 31.

These images of the dead soaring to a celestial heaven are conventional in Christian poetry, and their appeal to poets writing in actual bondage is evident; another enslaved poet, George Moses Horton, would also insistently turn to motifs of flight.[74] In Wheatley's poems, death entails transportation to an unknown shore. Her Christian beliefs encouraged her to believe that destination will be a welcome improvement over this life. But her poems suggest she was also struggling with the ideology that asserted she had already undertaken a version of such an improving journey.

Wheatley's elegies obsessively repeat motifs of flight. Either she is just a redundant poet, or poetry was for her a form of sanctioned fugitivity: an escape from constraint, through constraint. Death, faith and the imagination offer a release from earth's carceral frame. Her poem attacking Deism asks for inspiration: 'Arise the pinions of Persuasions here' (l. 17, p. 71). Another proclaims that at the sight of true merit would 'dawning genius rise / And stretch her pinions to her native skies'.[75] A poem to the painter Scipio Morehead hopes that immortal fame will 'High to the blissful wonders of the skies / Elate thy soul', and that by looking at his paintings we, too, can be moved on 'seraphic pinions' to 'view the landscapes in the realms above'.[76] God instructs his Son to descend to earth, and 'act in bounties unconfin'd / Enlarge the close contracted mind, / And fill it with thy fire' ('An Hymn to Humanity', ll. 16–18, p. 51). The human mind is 'close contracted', oppressively narrow and can be inflated by divine 'fire' to enjoy an 'unconfin'd' heavenly enlightenment. She grovels, but she would like to burn.

Wheatley's 'Thoughts on the WORKS of PROVIDENCE' begin with the command: 'Arise, my soul, on wings enraptur'd, rise / To praise the monarch of the earth and skies'; its Miltonic invocation continues: 'Celestial muse, my arduous flight sustain, / And raise my mind to a seraphic strain!' (ll. 1–2, 9–10, p. 26). Through these contemplations, 'my soul in rapture soars' (l. 45, p. 27). A twelve-month-old soul in flight from the earth 'Beneath him sees the universal whole':

> Planets on planets run their destin'd round,
> And circling wonders fill the vast profound.
> Th' ethereal now, and now th' empyreal skies
> With growing splendors strike his wond'ring eyes
>
> (ll. 4–7, p. 38)

---

[74] John L. Cobbs, 'George Moses Horton's "Hope of Liberty": Thematic Unity in Early American Black Poetry', *CLA Journal* 24.4 (June 1981), pp. 441–50 (446–50).
[75] 'To a Gentleman of the Navy', ll. 5–8, p. 83.
[76] 'To S. M. a Young *African* Painter, on seeing his Works', ll. 112–12, 25–6, p. 60.

The Harvard students also scan the heavens' heights and 'traverse the ethereal space', attaining through knowledge a perspective on the universe that is usually granted only to the dead. Poems create a space where the possibility of soaring, beyond our limitations, is temporarily enacted – like those dreams in which flight is possible only in exhilarating short bursts of lightness, when the dreamer pushes herself forcefully from the ground.

The power of imaginative flight to release the soul from captivity is a common image in the poetry of bondage and Neoplatonic thought, which I've discussed since the Introduction under the sign of Boethius. Pope satirises it as prideful ambition in *An Essay on Man*; 'Go, soar with Plato to th' empyreal sphere, / To the first good, first perfect, and first fair ... / Then drop into thyself, and be a fool!' (Epistle II, ll. 23–4, 30, p. 517). But Wheatley's soaring imagination can also be understood as the manifestation of the powers of Fancy. Fancy is an archaic, frilly word, tinged with the erotic, but undergirded by a serious anti-hegemonic theory of creative practice; as such, it feels appropriate for Robertson's ornamental poetics and theory of rhythm as social movement as well as Wheatley's fugitive imagination. In an important discussion of Fancy in the eighteenth century, Julie Ellison observes that it 'represents subjectivity that is at once ungrounded – liberated from or deprived of territory – and mobile, committed to ambitious itineraries through international space and historical time. As a motion of escape and mastery, Fancy lends itself to complex ambitions for public-minded poets of both sexes and of different races. As such, it plays a crucial role in the fundamental reorientation of sensibility to the needs of global culture.'[77] This imaginative mobility is for Wheatley a reparative notion. It temporarily emancipates her from constraints on her physical and social movement. By the operation of her Fancy, she also achieves an actual mobility, and is permitted to travel to England, the metropolitan centre.

Fancy, according to Ellison, is a literary form of the prospect – offering cosmic perspectives on empires and world history, 'the big pictures of civilisation's ebb and flow'. But these pictures 'bring into fancy's view vignettes of the national or racial other. And with the appearance of a stereotypical sufferer, fancy modulates into sensibility directed toward the alienated figure of the slave, the Indian, the oriental, the poor, the homeless, and – persistently combined with all these other identities – the

---

[77] Julie Ellison, *Cato's Tears and the Making of Anglo-American Emotion* (University of Chicago Press, 1999), p. 100.

female.'⁷⁸ An example is Wheatley's imagination of 'pleasing Gambia', in her 'Reply' to a poem praising her by Samuel Graves, Vice Admiral of the Royal Navy. Graves had served along the Gold Coast of Africa, and described that 'happy land' to Wheatley. Through his 'fair description' and charming 'painting', Wheatley says her 'soul returns' to her native land, which she represents as a series of pastoral clichés. That this is a poetic transportation rather than a reawakening of her own memories is suggested later in the poem, where she praises 'Europa's bard, who the great depth explor'd, / Of nature, and thro' boundless systems soar'd' (163), the prospect-taking Fancy that surveys continents from its 'soaring' perspective. She invokes Milton and Newton as the geniuses of this exploration, which makes explicit the connections between imperialism and the poetic imagination.

To Wheatley herself has been attributed the discovery or invention of a pre-Romantic Fancy; but what is important to this chapter is the way Fancy's flight ironises and subverts Wheatley's captivity.⁷⁹ According to Jeffrey Robinson, Romantic Fancy synthesises new materials from the associative activities of the mind. It nurtures the mind's 'flights', its motion outwards through a mental domain of images, words, sounds.⁸⁰ Rather than unity, containment or closed forms, Fancy is dispersive, 'bent on proliferation'; it blurs distinctions between subjects and objects; it is 'linked to forms of the unregulated and transgressive mind', and ready to accept a limitless world. Fancy is whimsical, physical, sexual, popular; 'winged', 'sportive' and difficult to 'fetter'. Rather than work and usefulness, it emphasises play. In the poetics of Fancy, poetic form 'reveals a mind-in-motion and makes concrete the un-fettering of the mind … Instead of burrowing into the "self", the poetry of the Fancy locates the speaker, often through parataxis, in the "cosmos" of the world elements' (13–14). This location of the lyric subject not within a stable interiority, but 'at the point of encounter with the world', also produced a 'cheerfulness', a poetics of 'abundance' and 'pleasure in the sheer athleticism of mental activity' (15). These hedonic, dispersive and ludic attributes apply to Robertson's poems as well as Wheatley's. But Robinson's analysis brings home the emancipatory qualities of Fancy: it is a device of fugitivity and lightness, unfettered from the existent world. Fancy's emphasis on

---

[78] Ellison, *Cato's Tears*, pp. 101–2.
[79] John C. Shields, *Phillis Wheatley and the Romantics* (Knoxville: University of Tennessee Press, 2010), pp. 68, 74, 101.
[80] Jeffrey C. Robinson, *Unfettering Poetry: Fancy in British Romanticism* (Basingstoke: Palgrave Macmillan, 2006), pp. 3–15.

mobility rather than subjectivity also makes it a useful tool for a Black poet whose subjecthood was always at issue.

'Fancy' is a word Wheatley herself repeatedly uses to explain the operations of the poetic imagination. Fancy appears in her Miltonic ode, 'On Recollection' (1772). The poem's composition was prompted by a visitor. Wheatley was 'in company with some young ladies of family, when one of them said she did not remember, among all the poetical pieces she had seen, ever to have met with a poem upon RECOLLECTION. The *African* (so let me call her, for so in fact she is) took the hint, went home to her master's, and soon sent what follows.'[81] The resulting poem begins with an address to its muse, Mneme (Mnemosyne):

> MNEME begin. Inspire, ye sacred nine,
> Your vent'rous *Afric* in her great design.
> *Mneme*, immortal pow'r, I trace thy spring:
> Assist my strains, while I thy glories sing:
> The acts of long departed years, by thee
> Recover'd, in due order rang'd we see:
> Thy pow'r the long-forgotten calls from night,
> That sweetly plays before the *fancy's* sight.
>
> (ll. 1–8, p. 34)

Taking up the identification that was ascribed to her by the headnote, Wheatley seeks the Muses' inspiration as a 'vent'rous *Afric*', pursuing her Miltonic 'great design'; in another version, hers is a 'deep design' (l. 2, p. 121). Her poetic ambitions are hazardous, like a sea voyage. That hazard is not just the attempt to write a philosophical poem on an abstract topic like the function of memory, but also to allude to the 'long departed years' and 'long-forgotten calls' of her own African childhood. In the poem at least, those calls will not be recovered. Wheatley displaces her own personal memories with generalised reflections that situate her own mental processes within the universal operations of a human faculty.

Mneme first visits the receiver in the shape of 'nocturnal visions' (l. 9) and dreams; she soars 'swift from above' on wings in 'silent flight / Through *Phœbe*'s realms' (ll. 11–12, p. 35). She gives aid to 'the high-raptur'd poet', and diffuses her celestial light 'through the unbounded regions of the mind' (ll. 14–15, p. 35) – or, in another version, 'the lab'ring mind' (l. 17, p. 122). Memory is like Fancy, soaring above the constrained body, able to see the whole of the world, and 'ev'ry tribe beneath the rolling sun' (l. 18). And yet, elsewhere, Wheatley writes that one of the prospects

---

[81] Carretta, *Phillis Wheatley*, p. 84.

presented to her Fancy is universal death: 'On *Death's* domain intent I fix my eyes, / Where human nature in vast ruin lies.' Her Fancy can take in pleasant prospects, but it can also 'search' the abode of death, revealing 6,000 years' worth of Death's 'offspring'; 'endless numbers', 'Whole kingdoms' and 'nations mix with their primeval dust'. Wheatley's own elegies participate in the census-taking of this charnel landscape. Mneme's vision reminds us that 'the big picture of civilisation's ebb and flow' is not necessarily a space of pleasant reflection on the eternal verities, but for Wheatley at least, offered a glimpse of the mass production of Black death.

As in 'On Recollection', Wheatley's poem 'Providence' first discovers the operation of Fancy in dreams:

> When action ceases, and ideas range
> Licentious and unbounded o'er the plains,
> Where *Fancy's* queen in giddy triumph reigns.
>
> (ll. 86–8, p. 28)

God's providential intervention then restores reason's power. But Wheatley suggests that by giving humans the power to dream (or imagine), the merciful God allows us to forget our 'wants and woes' (ll. 100–4, p. 28). In another elegy, that is the comfort Fancy offers to the parents of a dead infant. They dream he is still alive: 'Illusive fancy paints the phantom o'er; / Fain would we clasp him, but he wings his flight: / Deceives our arms, and mixes with the night.'[82] Fancy is a means of forgetting trauma. But the work of the poet – as a poem like 'Recollection' advertises – is remembrance. 'Can *Afric's* muse forgetful prove?,' she asks in her 'Hymn to Humanity' (l. 31, p. 51). The answer is no; the poem is the necessary outcome of her inability to forget. And yet, as we've seen, Wheatley's ability to remember her own childhood is hardly attested in her poetry, apart from a generalised comment on her father's loss of her. The poem makes us remember; Fancy helps us to forget.

Silken Fetters

Fancy is also personified in 'On Imagination', which praises the inalienable liberty of the imagination as a form of mobility:

> Now here, now there, the roving *Fancy* flies,
> Till some lov'd object strikes her wand'ring eyes,
> Whose silken fetters all the senses bind,
> And soft captivity involves the mind.

---

[82] 'To Mr and Mrs—, on the Death of their Infant Son', ll. 30–2, p. 95.

> *Imagination!* who can sing thy force?
> Or who describe the swiftness of thy course?
> Soaring through air to find the bright abode,
> Th' empyreal palace of the thund'ring God,
> We on thy pinions can surpass the wind,
> And leave the rolling universe behind:
> From star to star the mental optics rove,
> Measure the skies, and range the realms above.
> There in one view we grasp the mighty whole,
> Or with new worlds amaze th' unbounded soul.
>
> (ll. 9–22, p. 36)

Like Recollection, Imagination frees the body, allowing it to soar to vantages that reveal the cosmos, to range freely in the zodiac of its own wit. These perspectives reveal 'new worlds' to 'th' unbounded soul'. This ranging is the idealised alternative to the enforced transport that exposed Wheatley's bounded soul to a new world in the Americas. Wheatley argues that the sensory faculties are bound in 'silken fetters' and 'soft captivity': imagination releases the mind from non-productive limits by replacing them with generative ones; compulsory constraints become soft and ornamental through the operation of Fancy.[83]

Imagination is the faculty that acts as sovereign and judge. In terms that recall the conflation of poet and judge in Wordsworth's 'Sonnets upon the Punishment of Death', Wheatley argues that Imagination holds her 'sceptre o'er the realms of thought':

> Before thy throne the subject-passions bow,
> Of subject-passions sov'reign ruler thou;
> At thy command joy rushes on the heart,
> And through the glowing veins the spirits dart.
>
> (ll. 37–40, p. 37)

In 'Recollection', memory plays a similarly judicial role: 'enthron'd within the human breast', she 'Has vice condemn'd, and ev'ry virtue blest' (ll. 19–20, p. 35). While her music is sweeter than Virgil's poetry to the just, to 'the race / Who scorn her warnings, and despise her grace' (ll. 25–6) memory is dreaded, exposing crimes and misspent lives. A similar weaponisation of memory was at the heart of Enlightenment prison reforms. These poems are often read as indications of Wheatley's own Puritanical self-scrutiny; and yet, as the virtuoso of memory and imagination, the poet is here setting

---

[83] She borrows the phrase 'silken fetters' from Mark Akenside's *The Pleasures of Imagination* (1744), 2.562 ('The silken fetters of delicious ease'). Shields, *Wheatley and the Romantics*, p. 4.

herself up as either judge or first minister to poetic sovereignty. We can think of the poem as a reversal of the so-called trial of Wheatley's authenticity by her readers: she can bless and condemn them instead.

In 'Imagination', Wheatley proposes that even in the cold of a New England winter, Fancy might produce scenes of vernal liberation:

> Though *Winter* frowns to *Fancy's* raptur'd eyes
> The fields may flourish, and gay scenes arise;
> The frozen deeps may break their iron bands,
> And bid their waters murmur o'er the sands.
>
> (ll. 23–26, p. 36)

The imagery of shackled water derives from Horace's *Odes* 1.9, or at least Dryden's translation of it: 'Again behold the winter's weight / Oppress the labouring woods below; / And streams, with icy fetters bound, / Benumbed and crampt to solid ground.'[84] But in Wheatley's poem the frozen waters *may* break their fetters, and a scene of benevolent pastoral *might* reassert an ordered sovereignty. This provisionality speaks to what Auerbach described as the concealed eventuality, future conditional as a space of possibility. But the poem's subjunctives could also be interpreted as foregrounding the non-transformative qualities of Fancy. Poetic imagination can soar away from the world's frigid verities, but we can't truly 'leave the rolling universe behind'; our escapes are temporary, until we die. The modest ending of 'Imagination' again undermines Fancy's powers:

> *Fancy* might now her silken pinions try
> To rise from earth, and sweep th' expanse on high:
> From *Tithon's* bed now might *Aurora* rise,
> Her cheeks all glowing with celestial dies,
> While a pure stream of light o'erflows the skies.
> The monarch of the day I might behold,
> And all the mountains tipt with radiant gold,
> But I reluctant leave the pleasing views,
> Which *Fancy* dresses to delight the *Muse*;
> *Winter* austere forbids me to aspire,
> And northern tempests damp the rising fire;
> They chill the tides of *Fancy's* flowing sea,
> Cease then, my song, cease the unequal lay.
>
> (ll. 41–53, p. 37)

The subject's inability to submit to Imagination's absolute sovereignty leaves her chilled, stuck with winter who 'forbids me to aspire'. Winter's resistance

---

[84] John Dryden, *Selected Poems*, ed. Paul Hammond (London: Pearson/Longman, 2007), p. 341.

undermines Imagination's rule, and keeps Fancy pinned to earth; though she '*might*' attempt to rise, and 'the monarch of the day I *might* behold', her power is tempered by a reality that includes Wheatley's own status as an enslaved person. While 'Imagination's freewheeling potency is a manifestation of her perfect self-government' and sovereignty over the 'subject-passions', Wheatley's admission that hers is an 'unequal lay' signals the gap between her desire for poetic flight and her enslaved situation.[85]

The limited sovereignty of Fancy is also apparent in her poem to the Earl of Dartmouth. Wheatley again uses the image of soft constraint that connects her to Robertson's poetics:

> HAIL, happy day, when smiling like the morn,
> Fair *Freedom* rose *New-England* to adorn:
> The northern clime beneath her genial ray,
> *Dartmouth*, congratulates thy blissful sway:
> Elate with hope her race no longer mourns,
> Each soul expands, each grateful bosom burns,
> While in thine hands with pleasure we behold
> The silken reins, and *Freedom's* charms unfold.
>
> (ll. 1–8, p. 39)

In this wintery climate Fancy's operations might have stalled; but they are warmed by freedom. A more intense ardour 'burns' in the bosoms of its subjects, Wheatley and other Americans gathered together in that non-discriminatory 'we'. We look gratefully at the 'silken reins' in Dartmouth's hands that restrain our movement without cruelty or force. And yet, like Wheatley herself, we burn while we seem to grovel.

Wheatley represents Fancy as a force that can elevate the mind, allowing it to soar to cosmic vantages where it can take in 'ev'ry tribe beneath the rolling sun', new worlds of the living and the legions of the dead. Fancy offers an enlightenment comparable to the visions of the spirit after death. It allows one to forget actuality and dwell in the sweeter imagery of memory. All of this is commensurate with a good, submissive subject. But the taste of freedom offered by the imagination may be harder to control.

Fancy can also be chilled by something as simple as winter. Its 'giddy' sovereignty is not absolute. Reality has a power to ground the fanciful subject and force her to contemplate her surroundings. Fancy, as Wheatley's own reception shows, cannot overcome enslavement; it can only ameliorate it. But it is also the means by which the 'long-forgotten' claims of the past can be heard again. The expanding, burning souls held in

---

[85] Paula Loscocco, *Phillis Wheatley's Miltonic Poetics* (Basingstoke: Palgrave Macmillan, 2014), p. 121.

the 'silken reins' might consent for the time being to submit; but if even the iron chains that fetter the body can be broken, then it will be a moment's work to break those elegant constraints. Wheatley's soaring muse is trying to imagine how to do it.

Chains and Roses

Robertson and Wheatley are poets who engage with histories of patriarchal literature and ideology, not by refuting those traditions, but by walking *towards* them: through imitation, repetition and recollection. Their poems produce a non-linear temporality of the imagination; time is plastic and elliptical, the figures of the past (like Maecenas or his poets Virgil and Horace) available for deformation. Both are bastard daughters of a Latinity they do not entirely possess. When Robertson's heroines say, 'on the blurred selvage we tucked Liberty in our cheek like a tongued and rotten dictation', they tongue the rot that also fills the golden-haired goddess of American liberty in Wheatley's poems. Both poets are charmed by ornament and surface. Both use the imagery of softness – silken reins and fetters, soft architecture – to circumvent constraint and to mitigate gender.

But more significant, perhaps, are the many conditions they do not share. Where Robertson is at leisure to abandon the fiction of the lyric 'I', for Wheatley that is still the pronoun that explodes: a claim on a subject position in poetry that she cannot easily make in person. Robertson imagines skin as a porous threshold that renders obsolete the fictions of inner and outer worlds; for Wheatley, it is a racialised marker of difference that condemns her to slavery and loss. The solidarities across time that Robertson constructs with a female community of writers are fashioned by Wheatley across place, as she tries to create kinships in faith and grief with people who do not need her. In a Robertson poem, 'you' define 'city' as '*a peopled-through sensing*', a situation of collective affect.[86] That is close to the poetic cities constructed in Wheatley's elegies. While such affect is typical of what has been called American Puritan elegy in this period, in Wheatley's case it is a ghostly reminder of all the unmourned, unmournable loss that cannot be accounted for, the memories of the Middle Passage, of the shipped. If Wheatley, the enslaved African girl, mourns with a white mother for the loss of her infant, turning that mourning into the ruinous founding of the separation between the personal and the social, then why can't the white mother be induced to mourn for the Black girl who lost her

[86] Lisa Robertson, *Cinema of the Present* (Toronto: Coach House Books, 2014), p. 76.

own mother and everything else? Could sharing that mourning lead to a shattering of categories of identity and, more importantly, the brutal practice of slavery? Wheatley's reception history answers: hardly at all. She was manumitted but still died in poverty, and her work was read through the lens of her racialised deficiencies. The problem, as Wheatley saw, is that no matter how much delightful spectacle Fancy offers, the cold blast of winter is enough to make one sink.

In 1747, William Mason wrote 'Musaeus', a poem in which Chaucer, Spenser and Milton attend Alexander Pope in a grotto, and shower him with praise.[87] Mason ventriloquises Milton, forcing him to praise Pope's 'harmonious, manly, clear, sublime' verse, which would 'soar seraphic heights'. Milton attempts to 'soothe' Pope 'in these irksome hours of pain' with praise for having subdued rhyme, 'the minstrel rude / Of Chaos, Anarch old' (15):

> Her the fiend
> Opprest; forcing to utter uncouth dirge,
> Runic, or Leonine; and with dire chains
> Fetter'd her scarce-fledg'd pinion. I such bonds
> Aim'd to destroy, mistaking: bonds like these
> 'Twere greater art t'ennoble, and refine.
> For this superiour part MUSAEUS came:
> Thou cam'st, and at thy magic touch the chains
> Off dropt, and (passing strange!) soft-wreathed bands
> Of flow'rs their place supply'd: which well the Muse
> Might wear for choice, not force; obstruction none,
> But lov'liest ornament.
>
> (ll. 152–69)

This is the language of fettered pinions and soft-wreathed bands Wheatley discovered when she set to work. And if you want an example of bad imitation, this is it: Mason's cod-Miltonics show how lightly Wheatley rises above the charge that she produced nothing but ludicrous, third-rate, sickly versions.

Milton in Mason's poem has come to realise that he told the wrong story of the fiend. It was the chaining of poetry in Gothic rhymes that was the real drama. And while he did his best to destroy those 'bonds', his figural revolution could only be fulfilled by another. Pope would see the necessity of those bonds and make the iron chains of rhyme into the silken reins and

---

[87] William Mason, *Musæus: A Monody to the Memory of Mr Pope, in Imitation of Milton's Lycidas* (London, 1747); see my essay 'From Grief to Leisure: Lycidas in the Eighteenth Century', *Modern Language Quarterly* 77.1 (2016), pp. 41–63.

floral garlands of the heroic couplet. Higginson advised poets like Dickinson to 'wreathe the chain with roses'.[88] If English must be chained up in rhymes, if the Muse cannot be free, Keats hoped she could at least be 'bound with garlands of her own'. Bondage might become ornament. But soft-wreathed bands of flowers are still bondage, unless they are worn 'by choice, not force'.

How did Wheatley wear hers? It is hard to say. Musaeus decided not to cast off the chains of tradition, but to ennoble and refine them. Wheatley attempted to translate force into choice, but many of her readers refused to believe her. She was bound with garlands, they said, but they didn't belong to her. Milton chose another way: revolution. Rhyme, as he said in the note on the verse of *Paradise Lost*, is not a 'necessary Adjunct or true Ornament of Poem or good Verse'. It is the 'Invention of a barbarous Age, to set off wretched matter and lame Meter'.[89] We recall that white people declared Wheatley's African language barbarous, a word the Greeks invented to describe humans who sounded like they were making animal noises when they spoke; and images of the lameness of metre, shackled by prosody, have been with us since the opening pages of this book.

For Milton, blank verse was 'an example set, the first in English, of ancient liberty recovered to heroic poem from the troublesome and modern bondage of rhyming'. This remark has echoed in my head for many years. Its mystery led me to write this book. Milton wanted to recover 'ancient liberty' through blank verse, and through the overthrow of the monarchy. Ornamented bondage is still bondage, and nothing but revolution – not poetry alone – will cast it off. This is a truth that Phillis Wheatley, wearer of chains and survivor of the sea, Black girl on trial who secured her freedom and died in poverty with her three babies at the age of thirty-one, fugitive on the wings of the Imagination, poet of the revolution, understood very well.

---

[88] Thomas Wentworth Higginson, *The Magnificent Activist: The Writings of Thomas Wentworth Higginson (1823–1911)*, ed. Howard N. Meyer (New York: Da Capo, 2000), p. 536.
[89] John Milton, *Paradise Lost*, ed. Alastair Fowler, rev. 2nd ed. (Harlow: Pearson, 2007), pp. 54–5.

Index

Abbott, Jack Henry, 139–40
Abu Ghraib, 61, 64
Adorno, Theodor, 183, 242
Adshead, Joseph, 90
Agamben, Giorgio, 384
Agawu, Kofi, 255
Aguila, Pancho, 125
akrasia, 33, 67, 77, 79, 81
Alexander, M. Jacqui, 191
Allen, William, 213
Allewaert, Monique, 82
animals, 6, 23, 24, 31, 32–6, 41, 42, 47, 50, 52, 53, 55, 59, 60, 62, 69, 92, 95, 96, 102, 103, 128, 132, 165, 167, 175–6, 181, 204, 236–7, 250, 260, 276, 290, 338, 342, 343, 344, 345, 347, 357, 359, 363, 375, 382, 395
   hunting, 31, 32, 33, 35, 41, 42, 52, 53, 55, 56, 57, 60, 98, 151, 154, 164–7, 250
   taming, 53–8, 303–4, 337, 395
   wild, 12, 16, 32, 33, 35, 52, 53, 54, 55, 57, 58, 59, 60, 79, 95, 96, 99, 164, 220, 304
anthologies, 15, 22, 37, 72, 113, 127, 261, 276
Anzieu, Didier, 376–7
apostrophe, 20, 72
archive, 21, 182, 183, 212, 241, 242, 243, 244, 245, 280
Arendt, Hannah, 57, 381
Aristotle, 35, 36, 55, 64, 67, 95, 140
Armstrong, Tim, 244
Ashker, Todd Lewis, 144
Auerbach, Eric, 25, 26, 60, 207, 278, 353, 355, 409
Augustine, 57
Aytoun, William Edmonstoune, 156, 313

Baca, Jimmy Santiago, 116, 134–6, 140, 330
Bacon, Francis, 95, 110
ballad, 215, 246, 251, 252, 257–63, 265, 275, 279, 280
Baraka, Amiri, 15, 20, 254, 390
Barrett, Lindon, 273, 383
Barthes, Roland, 235, 296, 349, 375

Bates, Catherine, 54
Bates, Katherine Lee, 390
Baucom, Ian, 195
Baxter, Carolyn, 129–30, 232
BDSM, 296–8, 311–49
   masochism, 25, 32, 42, 68, 70, 310, 354, 360–2
   pleasure and pain, 60
   sadism, 32, 51, 71, 156–9, 287, 303–9, 310
   sadomasochism, 24, 25, 170, 283–4, 287–91
Beard, Mary, 306, 309
Beaumont, Francis, 277
Beaumont, Gustave de, 11, 86, 87, 89, 94, 144
Beccaria, Cesare, 84, 107
Bender, John, 93
Bentham, Jeremy, 11, 83, 84, 89, 105, 107
Benveniste, Émile, 366–7
Bergren, Ann, 374
Berlant, Lauren, 355
Bersani, Leo, 68, 70, 321, 330, 360
Best, Stephen, 21
Betts, Reginald Dwayne, 128
Bevis, Matthew, 5, 20, 290
Bhabha, Homi K., 239
Bingham, Millicent Todd, 152
Binny, John, 86, 90, 96
Blair, Hugh, 257–8
Blake, William, 3, 13–14, 26
blank verse, 13, 14
Boas, Franz, 216
Boethius, 17–19, 25, 31, 43, 54, 55, 118, 136, 148, 152, 404
bondage
   as metaphor, 2–4, 14, 22, 23, 38, 42, 60, 63, 75, 76, 83, 92, 116, 118, 119, 146, 154, 188, 200, 287, 332, 343, 348, 351, 359, 384
   bridles, 18, 32, 42, 47, 48, 78
   cages, 54, 58, 112
   chains, 18, 19, 103, 104, 154, 304, 401
   collars, 48, 77–9, 387

Index

fetters, 2–4, 5, 7, 12, 13, 14, 16, 17, 18, 19, 38, 39, 43, 44, 84, 98, 103, 104, 105, 154, 159, 289, 304, 350, 357, 384, 392, 401, 407, 408, 409, 411
  iron gag, 89
  knots, 48, 77, 373
  lockstep, 89
  traps, 32, 38, 48, 50, 53, 70
  whipping, 91, 92, 156, 157, 158, 297–8, 313–22
Bonner, Edmund, 43
boundaries, 38, 41, 42, 57, 58, 60, 69, 71, 106, 135, 146, 156, 273, 289, 298, 329, 330, 349, 367, 374
Bowles, Samuel, 169, 170
Boynton, Robert W., 276
Brand, Dionne, 284
Brathwaite, Edward Kamau, 196–7
Bridges, Robert, 313, 328, 332
Bristow, Joseph, 337
Brooks, Cleanth, 261, 275
brown, adrienne maree, 147
Brown, Drea, 188–9
Brown, Fahamisha Patricia, 231
Brown, Ford Madox, 335
Brown, John Mason, 213, 226
Brown, Michelle, 113
Brown, Sterling, 259
Browning, Robert, 173
Bryan, Francis, 38, 44
Bugg, John, 93, 101
Burkett, Steve John Sr., 125
Burleigh, Harry T., 258
Burney, Charles, 103
Burrow, Colin, 391
Burton, Richard, 348
Butler, Judith, 61, 64, 80, 359
Byles, Mather, 393
Byron, George Gordon Lord, 3, 5, 97–9, 160, 290

Callimachus, 287
Campion, Thomas, 20
Cannibal Club, 347
Cantine, Holley, 144
Carnochan, W. B., 118, 119
Carretta, Vincent, 386
Carson, Anne, 58, 359
Caruth, Cathy, 177
castration, 283, 287, 291, 294, 295–6, 308, 332, 334, 341, 355, 377
Catullus, 300
Certeau, Michel de, 17
Chamayou, Gregoire, 62
Charles d'Orléans, 56
Chaucer, Geoffrey, 18, 36, 43, 257, 412
Chevigny, Bell, 116

Child, Francis James, 215, 260, 261
Childs, Dennis, 120, 225, 226
Christina, Diana, 139
civil death, 62, 105, 130
Clark, Judy, 131
Clay, John, 93
Cleaver, Eldridge, 123
Coleridge, Samuel Taylor, 5, 85, 97, 148, 211, 237, 258, 293, 315
Collins, Terence, 390
Connor, Steven, 36, 91, 92
constraint, x, 1, 2, 4, 5, 17, 18, 25, 31, 41, 54, 66, 78, 100, 131, 143, 154, 155, 159, 162, 164, 166, 175, 177, 181, 183, 190, 258, 273, 283, 310, 312, 313, 331, 332, 344, 349, 351, 352, 353, 354, 359, 364, 365, 372, 373, 375, 379, 383, 391, 394, 403, 410, 411
Cooper, Anna Julia, 256–7
Crashaw, Richard, 326
Crawford, William, 88, 91
Crewe, Jonathan, 34
Cromwell, Thomas, 42, 44, 45, 53
Cruz, Jon, 264, 279
Culler, Jonathan, 21, 72, 146, 147, 275
Cummings, Brian, 37
Cuney-Hare, Maud, 220, 254
Curry, Samuel Silas, 276
Curry, Walter Clyde, 265, 274

Dabydeen, David, 181
D'Aguiar, Fred, 181
Dandurand, Karen, 172
Darrell, Elizabeth, 42
Darwish, Mahmoud, 148
Davidson, Donald, 266–7, 268, 269, 271, 274
Davies, Ioan, 118
Davies, John (Ignoto), 296–8
Davis, Angela, 88, 145
Davis, David Brion, 397
Dayan, Colin, 59, 134, 143, 194
de Quincey, Thomas, 315
Deleuze, Gilles, 321, 334
Dellamora, Richard, 341
Derrida, Jacques, 191
DeWeaver, Emile, 147
Dickens, Charles, 99–100, 105, 108, 137, 156, 158, 169
Dickinson, Austin, 157, 158, 167, 168, 171
Dickinson, Edward, 169, 170–1
Dickinson, Emily, 22, 25, 98, 112, 135, 151–79, 180, 182, 193, 196, 202, 215, 221, 232, 237, 243, 250, 272, 277, 315, 329, 340, 342, 383, 401, 413
  and boundaries, 152, 156, 158, 159, 178–9
  and chattel slavery, 153–4, 167–71, 173–7

Dickinson, Emily (cont.)
    and enclosures, 159–64
    and fugitivity, 163–5
    and hunted animals, 164–7
    and prisons, 158, 159–63, 283
    and sadomasochism, 156–9, 283
    and the Civil War, 172–3
    and whiteness, 167
Dickinson, Susan Huntingdon, 159, 167
Dickson, William, 221–4
Dinerstein, Joel, 226
Dolben, Digby, 332, 341
Dolven, Jeff, 51
Donne, John, 165
Dost, Shaikh Abdurraheem Muslim, 19
Douglass, Frederick, 82, 171, 177, 193, 209–12, 225, 249, 253, 259, 283
Dryden, John, 3, 156, 340, 409
Du Bois, W. E. B., 217, 220, 232, 253–4, 268
Du Toit, Ulysse, 321
Dunbar, Paul Laurence, 218, 230–4, 237, 270, 278
Dvořák, Antonín, 258

elegy (funeral), 385, 387, 403, 407, 411
elegy (Roman erotic), 57, 284–310, 311, 355, 358
    and militarism, 306–10
    and softness, 293, 303, 310, 358
Eliot, T. S., 3, 17, 275
Ellis, Havelock, 8, 291
Ellison, Julie, 404–5
Emerson, Ralph Waldo, 3, 151, 175, 237
enclosure, 23, 27, 28, 38, 51, 109, 122, 146, 176, 372, 373, 374, 379
Engels, Carl, 247
Equiano, Olaudah, 180
Erasmus, Desiderius, 52
Erkkila, Betsy, 167

Fanon, Frantz, 254
feet, 5–8, 35, 56, 57, 80, 140, 156, 164, 168, 290–3, 341
Fekete, John, 274
Fenner, Thomas, 213
Ferry, Anne, 37
fetish, 8, 34, 82, 91, 284, 335, 341, 343, 349, *See also* feet
Fields, Karen E. and Barbara J., 267
figura. See Auerbach, Eric
Fleetwood, Nicole, 114, 116, 123
Fletcher, John, 277
Fletcher, John Gould, 266
flight, 19, 163, 383, 393, 402–4
folklore studies, 215–16, 230
Folsom, Ed, 175
Forten, Charlotte (Grimké), 237, 247–9, 256

Foucault, Michel, 11, 83, 94, 108, 298, 299, 311, 384
fragmentation. *See* shattering
Fredrickson, George, 212, 220
free verse, 3, 14–15, 16, 17, 135
freedom, x, 2, 3, 4, 9, 12, 13, 14, 15, 16, 17, 18, 19, 22, 23, 27, 32, 33, 35, 37, 39, 41, 48, 53, 57, 58, 77, 100, 102, 112, 114, 123, 128, 130, 134, 136, 140, 145, 148, 161, 163, 166, 167, 172, 175, 182, 207, 208, 210, 211, 230, 240, 241, 246, 252, 268, 272, 273, 301, 306, 310, 313, 350, 352, 355, 356, 358, 361, 362, 373, 374, 383, 384, 387, 388, 396, 400, 407, 410, 411, 413
Freer, Alex, 314–15
Fretwell, Erica, 175
Freud, Sigmund, 50, 77, 261, 284, 296, 313, 314, 317, 319, 323, 328, 341, 344, 362
Friedlander, Benjamin, 153
Frost, Robert, 17
fugitivity, 52, 69, 91, 129, 152, 154, 168, 176, 177, 231, 234, 235, 246, 278, 279, 280, 357, 403, 404, 405, 413
Fugitive Slave Law, 167
Furr, Derek, 275
Fuss, Diane, 164
Fussell, Paul, 12, 13

Gates, Henry Louis Jr, 382, 390, 397
Genet, Jean, 117
Gibson, Ian, 320
Gilmore, Ruth Wilson, 114, 115
Gilroy, Paul, 200, 252, 254
Ginsberg, Allen, 264
Gitter, Elisabeth, 323
Glissant, Edouard, 3, 185, 206, 221, 246, 253
Godwin, William, 103, 107
Goffman, Erving, 132
Goncourt, Edmond and Jules de, 348
Gordon, Avery, 119
Grass, Sean, 99
Grayson, William, 269
Greenblatt, Stephen, 41
Greene, Ellen, 308
Greene, Roland, 35
Greene, Thomas, 56
Griffiths, Eric, 341
Grossman, Allen, 11
Guantánamo Bay detention camp, 19, 25, 60–83, 148
Guenther, Lisa, 132
Gumbs, Alexis Pauline, 147
Gummere, Francis, 244, 255, 261–4

Habinek, Thomas, 299
Haiti, 22, 25, 101, 174, 175, 176
Hall, Raymond Umar, 130, 138

Index 417

Halpern, Rob, 25, 31, 60–82, 83, 93, 106, 113, 181, 221, 283, 303, 310, 373
  blockages, 70
  patiency, 68, 70–1, 74, 77
  rhetoric, 65
Haney, Craig, 137
Hankey, Frederick, 348
Hanway, Jonas, 87–8
Haraway, Donna, 53
Harris, Cheryl, 23
Harrison, Gary, 106
Hartman, Saidiya, 207, 225, 242, 270, 283
Hastings, Selina Countess of Huntingdon, 387
Hayes, Terrance, 1–2, 17, 241, 312
Hazlitt, William, 3, 5
Hegel, Georg Wilhelm Friedrich, 11, 22, 48, 148, 200, 220, 260, 351
Henderson-Uloho, Maryam, 138
Henry VIII, 33, 39
Henry, Paget, 199
Herder, Johann Gottfried von, 257
Hesse, Barnor, 183
Hickman, Jared, 386
Higgins, Nathan, 390
Higginson, Thomas Wentworth, 151–2, 155, 156, 157, 164, 173–5, 179, 215, 237, 247–8, 249–52, 257, 258, 263, 413
Hogg, Lucy, 369
Holmes, Oliver Wendell, 3, 154
Homer, 3, 248, 256, 257, 394
Hopkins, Gerard Manley, 19, 25, 313, 327–43
  and queer desire, 332–7
  asceticism, 327–9
  instress, 330
  poems
    'Harry Ploughman', 333–43, 345
    'God's Grandeur', 340
    'That Nature is a Heraclitan Fire', 340
    'The Bugler's First Communion', 336
    'The Wreck of the Deutschland', 313
    'To what serves mortal beauty?', 336
    'Tom's Garland', 342
  scopophilia, 332–3, 336
Horton, George Moses, 403
Houze, Rebecca, 373
Howard, John, 84, 85, 103, 107
Howe, Fanny, 311
Howe, Susan, 4, 166–7, 169
Hughes, Langston, 217, 270
Hunt, Erica, 21, 25, 182
Hurston, Zora Neale, 216–18, 260

imagination, 4, 5, 10, 15, 16, 23, 34, 40, 44, 70, 74, 88, 99, 100, 105, 110, 111, 132, 133, 147–8, 152, 161, 163, 175, 178, 219, 232, 239, 258, 279, 336, 348, 384, 389, 403, 404, 405, 406, 407–10, 411, 413
imitation, 239, 259–60, 266, 286, 380, 389–96

Jackson, George, 117, 120
Jackson, Virginia, 20, 21, 152, 262–3
Jackson, Zakiyyah Iman, 24, 54, 176, 395
Janowitz, Anne, 10
Janson, Derek, 112
Jefferson, Thomas, 15, 389
Jeffreys, Mark, 23
Jess, Tyehimba, 239–45, 280
Johnson, Guy, 213, 216, 220, 227, 237, 266, 268, 273
Johnson, James Weldon, 214, 232, 259, 270
Johnson, W. R., 20
Jones, Paul Christian, 109
Jonson, Ben, 285
Joplin, Scott, 242
Jordan, June, 383, 390
Jubilee Singers, 211, 239, 240
Judy, Ronald, 216

Kaba, Mariame, 113
Kant, Immanuel, 273, 382
Kaufman, Bob, 141–3
Keats, George, 8
Keats, John, 7–9, 237, 413
Kemble, Frances Anne, 225, 259
Kennedy, Duncan, 301
Kerrigan, John, 49
Kittredge, George Lyman, 214, 215
Klein, Melanie, 323
Knight, Etheridge, 2
Knoll, Michael, 132–3
Knox, Vicesimus, 315
Koolhaas, Rem, 371–2, 379
Krafft-Ebing, Richard von, 311–12, 317, 338, 343–5
Krehbiel, Henry, 236, 265

Lacan, Jacques, 44, 76, 296, 331, 356, 370
Langbaum, Robert, 275
Lanier, Sidney, 236, 256
Laplanche, Jean, 329
Leadbelly, 229, 241, 245, 247
Lébron, Lolita, 130
Lefebvre, Henri, 314, 366
Leonard, Keith, 390
Lerer, Seth, 45
Levin, Harry, 285
liberalism, 9–12, 14, 24, 130
literary criticism, 5, 22, 27, 114, 115, 116, 118, 156, 185, 213, 242, 245, 247, 255, 274–7, 279, 280, 382
Liu, Alan, 106

418 Index

Locke, Alain, 216, 252
Locke, John, 391
Lomax, John and Alan, 118, 215, 216, 217, 219, 226, 227, 228–30, 234, 237, 238, 242, 244, 247, 257, 268, 276
Long, William J., 389
Lord, Otis, 158
Lott, Eric, 224
Lovelace, Richard, 19
Lovell, John, 254, 255
Lowell, James Russell, 109
Lucretius, 353, 354, 356, 375
Lukàcs, Georg, 272
Luxemburg, Rosa, 148
lyric, 20–4, 31
   and absence, 33, 60, 62, 63, 73, 75, 76, 78, 81, 211, 212, 215, 233, 241, 277, 294, 335, 357, 375
   and address, 10, 12, 20, 72, 73, 109, 114, 116, 117, 126, 130, 131, 135, 152, 193, 362, 387, 394, 397, 406
   and authenticity, 19, 66, 73, 83, 117, 118, 214, 218, 224, 234, 238, 243, 244, 245, 279, 409
   and autonomy, 4, 31, 34, 40, 41, 49, 50, 64, 71, 112, 123, 131, 141, 182, 183, 198, 199, 200, 273, 364, 365, 383
   and erasure, 50, 60, 81, 119, 130, 179, 182, 208, 212, 221, 233, 239, 245
   and feeling, 9, 22, 212, 219, 233, 243, 258, 260, 279
   and humanness, 21, 24, 27, 61, 113, 195, 259, 280
   and individuality, 9–12, 22, 51, 83, 123, 130, 145, 146, 205, 262, 280, 343
   and intimacy, 57, 58, 60, 62, 63, 68, 69, 76, 77, 218, 291, 302, 360, 362, 363, 376
   and inwardness, 37, 51, 59, 60, 131
   and orality, 142, 211
   and whiteness, 5, 22–5, 32, 34, 49, 60, 145, 154, 383
   collectives, 12, 20, 22, 53, 58, 71, 74, 83, 123, 144, 145, 148, 182, 183, 190, 199–205, 207, 209, 213, 224, 226, 244, 252, 254, 260, 264, 280, 343, 352–3, 360, 372, 373, 376, 388, 400, 411
   evolutionary theories of, 213, 246, 252, 256–64, 279
   lyricisation, 21, 23, 261
   rhythm, 6, 147, 197, 223, 225–6, 234–6, 254–6, 261–3, 313–15, 320, 332, 340, 356, 365–7, 381

Mack, Maynard, 276
Mains, Geoff, 347
Mallarmé, Stéphane, 140, 141
Mansfield, William Murray Lord, 180
Mariani, Paul, 337, 342
Marlowe, Christopher, 22, 25, 42, 284–310

Tamburlaine, 289–90
Martin, John Sella, 225
Marvell, Andrew, 156, 162
Marx, Karl, 14, 82
Mason, William, 412, 413
Mau, Bruce, 371–2
Maultsby, Portia, 197
Mauss, Marcel, 46
Maxwell, Catherine, 320
Mayhew, Henry, 86, 90, 96
McCaffrey, Steve, 379
McCanles, Michael, 37
McKittrick, Katherine, 192
McKoy, Mille and Christine, 241
Medley, Mark, 132
melancholy, 6, 20, 21, 77, 129, 207, 225, 227, 233, 327, 352, 369, 385
Menocal, Maria, 50
Mill, John Stuart, 9–12, 19, 63, 66, 83, 130, 153, 219, 227, 238, 261, 276, 279, 280
Miller, Paul Allen, 21, 308, 310
Milnes, Richard Monckton, first Baron Houghton, 316, 317–18
Milton, John, 3, 13, 26, 100, 232, 390, 392–3, 405, 413
   poems
      Paradise Lost, 13, 15, 156, 393, 413
      Samson Agonistes, 13
mimesis, 190, 205, 241, 244, 343, 349
Mirpuri, Anoop, 115, 118
Mitchell, Domhnall, 153
Mohamed, Binyam, 71
Montagu, Lady Mary Wortley, 354, 355, 362
Montaigne, Michel de, 368
Montrose, Louis, 295
More, Thomas, 39, 45, 118
Morehead, Scipio, 387
Morrison, Toni, 23
Moten, Fred, 4, 20, 82, 191, 201, 207
mourning, 61, 64, 76, 77, 202, 203, 206, 208, 242, 384, 411
Mowitt, John, 204
Muir, Kenneth, 56
Mullen, Harryette, 190
Mulvey, Laura, 341
Murray, Aïfe, 167

Nagy, Gregory, 205
Nelson, Brian, 132, 138
New Criticism, 11, 243, 244, 246, 247, 265, 271, 272, 273–7
New Narrative, 60
Ngai, Sianne, 76
North, Joseph, 27, 273
Noyes, John, 312, 326

Index

O'Hara, Frank, 6
O'Sullivan, John, 109
Odell, Margaretta Matilda, 385
Odum, Howard, 213, 216, 220, 227, 264, 266–8, 273, 276
Olson, Charles, 189
Ong, Walter, 329
Oppen, George, 68
orality, 197–8, 261, 265, 274, 279, 322
Orpheus, 32, 51, 52, 268
Ovid, 8, 18, 22, 25, 42, 57, 79, 284–310, 311, 319, 332, 337, 341, 345, 354, 355, 358, 363, 394
  poems
    Amores, 284–310
    Ars Amatoria, 299, 308
    Heroides, 286
    Tristia, 286, 300, 309
Oviedo (Gonzalo Fernández de Oviedo y Valdés), 35
Owsley, Frank, 266, 269, 270

Parton, James, 392
pastoral, 232, 269–70, 318, 350, 354, 357, 386, 394, 405, 409
Patterson, Orlando, 35, 129
Paulhan, Jean, 345
Peabody, Charles, 228
Peart, Andrew, 260
Petrarch (Francesco Petrarca), 7, 31, 34, 35, 39, 48, 49, 60, 63, 67, 73, 77, 286, 297, 354, 362, 373
Philip, M. NourbeSe, 25, 151, 177, 180–208, 221, 241, 242
  and collectivity, 199–205
  and haunting, 190–4, 204, 207
  and i-mages, 198–200
  and law, 180–1, 194–6, 207
  and mimesis, 186–9, 198, 205
  and orality, 197–8
  and performance, 200–5
  and ritual, 193, 194, 205, 244
Philips, Catherine, 334
Phillips, Rowan Ricardo, 211
Pinch, Adela, 315
Plato, 18, 33, 67, 132, 324, 398, 404
pleasure and pain. *See* BDSM
Plutarch, 52, 302
Pope, Alexander, 3, 389–90, 392–6, 412–13
  poems
    Essay on Criticism, 392, 394, 395
    Essay on Man, 395, 398, 404
Porter, David, 155
Posmentier, Sonya, 201, 217
Powell, George, 321, 335
Price, Kenneth, 175

Prins, Yopie, 21, 320, 325
prisons, 1–2, 4, 6, 11, 13, 17–19, 27, 31, 37, 38, 39, 41, 56, 58, 59, 65, 156, 157, 158, 170, 221, 237, 238, 247, 312, 329, 331, 344, 372, 379, 408
  abolition, 107, 109, 115, 119, 146, 147, 148
  and class, 88, 96
  and contagion, 84, 86, 144
  and labour, 88
  and race, 88, 119, 126, 130
  and song, 226–7, 238–9
  and temporality, 128–30, 138
  Auburn State Penitentiary, 85, 89, 95, 105
  chaplain, 93–4
  Coldbath Fields, 90
  Eastern State Penitentiary, 11, 85, 90, 99, 105, 137
  Folsom Prison Creative Writers' Workshop, 123–5
  Millbank, 95
  Nashville State Penitentiary, 227
  nineteenth century, 83–111, 131, 136
  Norfolk Prison Brothers, 120, 127
  Parchman Farm, 230
  Pelican Bay State Prison, 136, 137, 144
  Pentonville, 11, 86, 95, 96
  rehabilitation model, 120, 126, 127
  Secure Housing Unit syndrome, 135–43
  silent system, 89–91, 131
  strikes, 125, 126
  The Tombs, 162
  Tower of London, 37, 38, 40, 43, 83, 393
  twentieth century, 112–48
Propertius, 287, 288, 301, 303, 306, 345
prosody, 4, 5, 6, 12, 14, 15, 17, 31, 36, 69, 128, 155, 156, 198, 233, 236, 258, 277, 284, 290–3, 296, 299, 310, 313–15, 318, 320, 334, 338, 341, 359, 370, 398, 413
Pugh, Christina, 155
Pugh, Syrithe, 286
Pusey, E. B., 328, 336

Quintilian, 390

Radano, Ronald, 218
Rainer, Dachine, 144
Rambsy, Howard, 243, 244
Rancière, Jacques, 381
Ransom, John Crowe, 265, 268, 269, 270, 273, 276
Réage, Pauline, 313, 345–7, 361
Reed, Anthony, 187
Reed, Austin, 89, 91, 92, 94, 169, 283, 319

Reik, Theodor, 314
Rhodes, Lorna, 119
Richardson, Ruth, 65
Richlin, Amy, 295
Ripa, Cesare, 378
Robertson, Lisa, 25, 350–80, 381, 383, 384, 394, 404, 405, 410, 411
  and masochism, 360–2
  and rhythm, 365–7, 376
  and textiles, 353, 372–6, 377
  irony, 351, 355, 358
Robinson, Jeffrey, 405–6
Rodríguez, Dylan, 114, 115, 120
Rosenberg, Susan, 145
Rothenberg, Jerome, 15
Rousseau, Jean-Jacques, 317, 354
Rush, Benjamin, 85, 89, 105
Ruskin, John, 6, 236
Rustbelt Abolition Radio, 147
Ruzas, Jackie, 19

Sacher-Masoch, Leopold von, 311, 313, 345
Sacks, Peter, 37
Sade, Donatien Alphonse François, Marquis, 118, 184, 296, 311, 321
San Quentin Days, 121, 123, 126
Sánchez-Eppler, Karen, 168
Sartre, Jean Paul, 57
Saville, Julia, 328
Sawday, Jonathan, 64
Scarborough, Dorothy, 214
Scott, Walter, 258
Sedgwick, Eve Kosofsky, 313–14
Semper, Gottfried, 371, 372–4
Senghor, Leopold, 254–5
servus amoris, 32, 42, 46, 48, 49, 287, 288–9, 358
Sexton, Jared, 68, 128, 193, 195
Shadwell, Thomas, 317
Shakespeare, William, 14, 76, 107
shame, 9, 66–7, 69, 70, 74, 75, 77, 87, 91, 106, 153, 165, 170, 172, 213, 238, 291, 302, 305, 307, 308, 309, 310, 329, 336, 342, 343, 359, 362, 367
Sharp, Granville, 180, 221–4, 393
Sharpe, Christina, 27, 207
shattering, 68, 141, 186, 203, 206, 329, 330, 337, 360, 412
Shelley, Percy Bysshe, 98, 230, 323
Shenstone, William, 315
Shoptaw, John, 174
Sidney, Philip, 4, 196
Silverman, Kaja, 321
Simon, John Oliver, 125
Sitwell, Edith, 355
Skinner, Marilyn, 296

Skinner, Quentin, 35
Slauter, Eric, 391, 396
slavery, 4, 5, 12, 13, 22, 23, 26, 31, 32–6, 39, 45, 46, 50, 58, 59, 60, 67, 79, 82, 84, 91, 100, 120, 128, 219, 253, 254, 259, 287, 290, 298, 299, 303, 305, 306, 310, 336, 337, 346, 352, 358, 410
  abolition, 153, 174, 189
  as fantasy, 313
  chattel slavery in the Caribbean, 221–4
  chattel slavery in the United States, 8–9, 167–71, 173–7, 179, 209–15, 220, 224–6, 239–42, 246, 247–52, 268–70, 277–9, 413
  classical slavery, 35–6, 42, 55, 68, 289, 305–7, 308, 355
  fantasies of, 343–9
  slave narratives, 183
  slave trade, 180–208
Smith, Barbara Herrnstein, 275
Smith, Caleb, 27
solidarity, 33, 62, 111, 113, 119, 125, 127, 136, 143, 144, 145, 252, 289, 346, 384
solitary confinement, 11, 19, 22, 31, 37, 66, 83, 91, 93, 94, 95–100, 102, 103, 112, 113, 119, 131, 132, 136–44, 148, 153, 238, 239, 330
  in the nineteenth century, 85–8
solitude, 9, 10, 11, 70, 83, 84, 85, 95, 100, 112, 118, 139, 140, 142, 143, 207, 215, 261, 380
sonnet, 1–2, 4, 7–9, 32, 35, 79, 98, 107, 108, 109, 110, 128, 240, 241, 312, 328, 330, 334, 336, 340
Southern Agrarians, 265–77
Southern, Eileen, 224
Southey, Robert, 103, 315
sparagmos. *See* shattering
Spearing, A. C., 374
Spenser, Edmund, 295, 412
Spillers, Hortense, 169, 209, 283, 352, 386
Spivak, Gayatri, 192
St. John, Paul, 125–6
Stewart, Susan, 145
Stowe, Harriet Beecher, 176, 344
Streier, Richard, 77
Stuckey, Sterling, 254, 255
Studlar, Gaylyn, 312
Sulpicia, 357
Swinburne, Algernon Charles, 25, 285, 313, 316, 318–27, 329, 335, 337, 341, 348, 363
  and orality, 322–7, 347
  and sound, 327

poems
   'Anactoria', 324–7
   'Laus Veneris', 322–3, 324, 327
   'The Flogging Block', 318–22

Talley, Thomas, 6–7, 218, 219, 249, 256, 260, 265, 277
Tate, Allen, 266, 270, 271, 272, 277
Taylor, Samuel Coleridge, 231
Thomson, Patricia, 46
Thornycroft, Hamo, 333
Thorpe, Thomas Bangs, 165
Thurman, Wallace, 390
Tibullus, 8, 287, 289, 345
Tocqueville, Alexis de, 11, 16, 86, 87, 89, 94, 144, 176
Todd, Mabel Loomis, 152, 154
Tottel, Richard, 45
Trollope, Anthony, 315
Truth, Sojourner, 171
Tucker, Herbert, 275
Turner, J. M. W., 181
Tylor, Edward, 246

Valéry, Paul, 3, 6
Varro, Marcus Terentius, 36
Vazquez, Judith, 138
Villa, C. F., 138
Vincent, John, 323
Virgil, 293, 319, 354, 356, 358, 394, 396, 408, 411

Wade, John, 266, 267
Wagner, Bryan, 212, 280
Walcott, Derek, 254, 283
Walker, Alice, 384, 390
Walker, Frederick, 333
Wallaschek, Richard, 259, 263
Walters, Jonathan, 298
Wang, Jackie, 147–8
Warburg, Aby, 371, 378
Warren, Robert Penn, 261, 271, 272, 275
Watts, Isaac, 259, 393
Weheliye, Alexander, 24, 383, 384
Weiss, Margot, 347
Western, Charles, 87
Wheatley, John, 386, 387, 394
Wheatley, Phillis, 19, 25, 188, 221, 350–1, 352, 356, 360, 379, 380, 413
   and Africa, 381, 385, 387, 394, 396, 397–400
   and flight, 402–4
   Fancy, 404–11
   health, 384–6, 390

   imitation, 384, 389–96, 398
   poems
      'On Imagination', 407–10
      'Thoughts on the Works of Providence', 407
      'America', 399
      'On Being Brought from Africa to America', 397
      'On Recollection', 406–7
      'To Maecenas', 393–6
      'To the Right Honourable William, Earl of Dartmouth', 399–400, 410
      'To the University of Cambridge in New England', 397–9
Wheatley, Susanna, 385, 386
White, Newman Ivey, 214, 220
White, Simone, 254
whiteness, 27, 60, 65, 91, 146, 153, 167, 170, 177, 212, 219, 221, 227, 245, 262, 270, 279, 346, 374, 379, 380, 384, 391, 396
Whitman, Walt, 3, 16, 26, 135, 140
Whittier, John Greenleaf, 19, 211, 232
Wieners, John, 143
Wiggins, 'Blind' Tom, 239, 244–5
Wilde, Oscar, 26, 83, 118
Wilderson, Frank B. III, 24, 168, 206, 207
Williams, William Carlos, 16–17
Wimsatt, W. K., 275
Woods, Joseph, 382
Wordsworth, Dorothy, 5
Wordsworth, William, 5, 9, 10, 100–11, 134, 195, 220, 238, 258, 264, 271, 284, 349, 408
   Lyrical Ballads, 101, 103, 107, 109, 258, 271
   poems
      'Sonnets upon the Punishment of Death', 107–11
      'The Convict', 103–6
      'The Old Cumberland Beggar', 101–2
Work, John Wesley, 214, 218, 246, 251, 256, 259
wounds, 13, 27, 51, 52, 53, 62, 63, 66, 75, 76, 154, 166, 176–7, 178, 193–4, 283, 287, 288, 294, 295, 304, 307, 308, 326, 355, 375
   scars, 36, 44, 92, 93, 154, 169, 177, 201, 303, 306
Wyatt, Thomas, 8, 22, 25, 31–59, 60, 62, 69, 70, 78, 79, 81, 83, 92, 93, 96, 97, 106, 118, 133, 134, 153, 164, 165, 166, 176, 193, 221, 231, 283, 290, 294, 302, 304, 310, 330, 387, 394
   ambassadorial role, 42, 45, 50
   imprisonment, 32, 41, 42–5

Wyatt, Thomas (cont.)
  manuscript transmission of poems, 37
  poems
    'Luckes [Lux], my faire falcon', 53
    'Myne owne John Poynz', 41
    'The knott that furst my hart dyd strayn', 48
    'They fle from me that sometyme did me seke', 55–9
    'Who so list to hounte', 32–6, 46, 68, 79
  rustication to Kent, 41
  service, 42–9, 50
Wyke, Maria, 287

Xenophon, 55

Young, Edward, 391

Zafar, Rafia, 400
Zim, Rivkah, 118

For EU product safety concerns, contact us at Calle de José Abascal, 56–1°, 28003 Madrid, Spain or eugpsr@cambridge.org.

www.ingramcontent.com/pod-product-compliance
Ingram Content Group UK Ltd.
Pitfield, Milton Keynes, MK11 3LW, UK
UKHW041842121025
463898UK00001B/1